The Cinema and Cinema-going in Scotland, 1896–1950

Trevor Griffiths

EDINBURGH
University Press

First published in hardback in 2012 by
Edinburgh University Press Ltd
22 George Square, Edinburgh EH8 9LF
www.euppublishing.com

This paperback edition 2013

Typeset in 10/12pt Goudy Old Style by
Servis Filmsetting Ltd, Stockport, Cheshire, and
printed and bound in Great Britain by
CPI Group (UK) Ltd, Croydon CR0 4YY

A CIP record for this book is available from the British Library

ISBN 978 0 7486 3828 4 (hardback)
ISBN 978 0 7486 8521 9 (paperback)
ISBN 978 0 7486 6804 5 (webready PDF)
ISBN 978 0 7486 6805 2 (epub)

Contents

Acknowledgements

In the period covered by this book, the practice was for credits to be screened at the start of the feature. In following this tradition, I am pleased to acknowledge the support of my studio bosses at EUP and the consistent help and enduring patience of the commissioning editors of Scottish History, particularly Esmé Watson and John Watson, who must at times have feared they had taken on a project likely to rival, in terms of completion dates, the Edinburgh tram.

Star billing, with names above the main title, must go to the archivists of collections listed in the bibliography whose efforts have ensured that the ensuing discussion remains grounded in a rich and diverse documentary detail. Particular thanks go to Ronald Grant and the staff at the Cinema Museum in Lambeth, who tolerated my presence while I read through the excellent collection on cinema in Aberdeen, in the process acquiring familiarity with the daytime schedule of Radio 4, from *Woman's Hour* to *PM*. At the Scottish Screen Archive, I have benefited immeasurably from the help of Kay Foubister and, most notably, Janet McBain, whose work in building up the archive and in encouraging its widest possible use deserves to be recognised in full. It is to be hope that this work will stimulate more projects which exploit the Archive's rich resources.

Key supporting roles were taken by Rita Connelly, who generously allowed me access to her mother's diaries, the Carnegie Trust for the Universities of Scotland, which funded an extended stay in London, allowing me to make full use of the Cinema Museum's collections, Ernest Mackie for the extended loan of the 1948 edition of the *Kinematograph Year Book*, and Messrs Dickson Middleton of Stirling for permission to cite material from the Steel Maitland family papers.

Edinburgh, I am pleased to report, continues to provide a setting conducive to the pursuit of original research. In the period in which I worked on this book, successive heads of Economic and Social History, namely David Greasley, Stana Nenadic, and Martin Chick, provided exactly the right balance of encouragement and support. All colleagues in ESH, current and former, and many across the School of History, Classics and Archaeology have responded with patience and understanding to my attempts to give a cinematic twist to any topic of conversation. To them and to audiences at seminars and conferences in Edinburgh, Glasgow, Dundee, Reading, London, and Bo'ness who responded with interest to earlier versions of the material presented herein, I extend my thanks.

Providing the kind of vital but often unacknowledged technical support that keeps a production such as this on track over the years, thanks go to Malcolm Cook, Fife's own 'King of the Quota Quickies', David Jarman, Jane George, Julia Wilding, Gus McLean, Jane Goldman, Annette Davison, maker I can honestly write of the finest courgette soup I have tasted, Iris Bosa, Lucie Green, and John Burnett. Away from Edinburgh, a comparable role has been fulfilled by Graeme, Angela, Sam, and Evie Morton, Robert Cook, Ian and Eleanor Mackie, Jan Martin, John and Barbara Howarth, and Sylvia Marsden, who can recall taking a (much) younger me to see *The Wizard of Oz* at the Odeon in Burnley and the terror induced by the sight of the flying monkeys, as a result of which I continue live in fear of sharp-faced women with greenish complexions.

The most fundamental debt of gratitude remains to immediate family members, to my mother, an inveterate cinema-goer herself in the 1940s, whose judgement on films of the period is often more critical than my own, and to Janet and Kelvin Lawton, and it is to all three that this book is dedicated with the deepest love.

Introduction

By the mid point of the twentieth century, the cinema and film more gener-ally had put down deep and extensive roots across Scotland. With over 600 fixed sites in use for the commercial screening of motion pictures, there were more cinemas and cinema seats per head of population north of the border than across Britain as a whole.[1] Although unevenly distributed, the picture house was a fixture in all towns and cities of any note and boxed the compass, from Kirkwall (Orkney) and Stornoway (Lewis) in the north to Stranraer (Wigtownshire) and Coldstream (Berwickshire) in the south. The *Kinematograph Year Book* for 1948 revealed that the cinema was present in some 261 centres of population and that, while 30 per cent of houses were located in the four major cities of Glasgow, Aberdeen, Dundee, and Edinburgh, over a quarter operated in towns or villages each with popula-tions of 5,000 and below.[2] Cinema-going was a pursuit that encompassed small-town- and city-dweller alike, and was practised on a scale and with a frequency that eclipsed all other commercial leisure forms. Returns from the collection of entertainments tax offer powerful evidence of cinema's then dominant place in the world of popular entertainment. Across Britain, it accounted for almost 83 per cent of all admissions to taxable entertainments in 1950. As a point of contrast, football, often seen as the leading passion of the average working-class Scottish male, accounted for a mere 5 per cent of the total. Tightening the focus to Scotland reinforces the importance of the movie-going habit. Cinema seats were not only more abundant north of the border, they were also filled more frequently than was the case elsewhere. So, at a time, in 1950–1, when the British were the most inveterate cinema-goers in the world, visiting picture houses on average twenty-eight times a year, the average Scot went thirty-six times. Even this figure masked significant varia-tions, so that Glaswegians and those living in towns of between 50,000 and 100,000 each saw the insides of cinemas an average of fifty-one times a year.[3] Whatever measure is taken, the cinema was confirmed as a significant pres-ence in the everyday lives of many, perhaps most, Scots.

Yet its appeal was not comprehended by commercial screenings alone. In areas to the north and west of the central belt, where a dispersed popula-tion rendered the operation of shows from fixed sites problematic, exhibi-tors toured in a manner reminiscent of the early days of moving pictures.

From the later 1940s, the efforts of private exhibitors were augmented by units operated by the Highlands and Islands Film Guild. Funded in part by the Carnegie UK Trust and the Scottish Education Department, the Guild mounted shows on a non-profit-making basis through circuits active from Argyll to Shetland. In the last nine months of 1950, over 2,000 shows were staged across this area. Each attracted an average audience of sixty-five, indicating that, by the mid twentieth century, access to film extended to the smallest and most remote of communities.[4] For some, engagement with the medium went further and was sustained by an increasingly dense network of film societies. Active across Scotland, from Dumfries to Shetland, societies promoted a film culture that often offered an alternative to the mainstream offerings of commercial cinema. By 1950, they extended from metropolitan Glasgow to small-town Keith in Banffshire, encompassing in the process a wide social range, taking in privately educated pupils at George Watson's College in Edinburgh and members of the Connoisseur Circle in the industrial town of Wishaw in the west-central belt.[5]

At one level, then, this book is concerned to trace the emergence and development of a recreational form of peculiar importance to Scotland and the Scots in the decades from the late nineteenth to the mid twentieth century. It may also be seen to contribute to a growing historiography concerned to construct a more rounded and more truly 'national' history of British cinema. Early works in this field were, understandably enough, preoccupied with charting the variable fortunes of British film production, adopting in the process a perspective substantially centred on London and the south-east of England.[6] Yet subsequent investigations have indicated that the view from Wardour Street was never all-encompassing. The endeavours of early provincial film pioneers along the south coast, as well as in West Yorkshire and South Wales, have been noted, while, more recently, the contribution of the Lancashire firm of Mitchell and Kenyon to film output across the north of England and beyond has come to more general notice, with the discovery of a substantial cache of their films in the mid 1990s.[7] The subsequent development of distinctive structures of film exhibition, distribution, and, on occasion, production has been charted in Wales and Northern Ireland.[8] Although aspects of Scottish film and the cinema-going experience north of the border have been captured by the existing literature,[9] we are still some way short of the kind of overarching view required to locate Scotland fully within the complex constellation of forces that went to make up the British cinematic experience.

Yet the lens through which we view the emergence and development of this key recreational form must also be sensitive to the wider forces at work. Many recent studies in cinema history have been concerned to look beyond film texts, taking us beyond the confines of the auditoria within which people gathered to view movies to consider the broader social, economic, and cultural forces that brought them there and so shaped the manner in which texts were comprehended and consumed. One such approach relates cinema's emergence to a sequence of change comprehended by the term 'modernity'. Drawing on the writings of social theorists, such as Benjamin and Simmel, such work depicts cinema as 'the fullest expression and combination of modernity's attributes'.[10] It is thus seen as a substantially urban phenomenon, flourishing most obviously in the rapidly expanding cities of late nineteenth-century Europe and the United States. These increasingly large concentrations of population called forth new modes of production and consumption, based upon standardisation and achieved through the widening application of machine technologies. In the case of the cinema, it was, as Tom Gunning has observed, the machinery itself rather than the films being projected which often constituted the medium's primary attraction.[11] The application of mechanical techniques rendered images infinitely reproducible, allowing access to audiences regardless of physical distance or cultural difference, in the process placing cinema at the heart of a social order based around the idea of the 'mass'. For some commentators, its influence went further. With working lives in office and factory increasingly subject to the repetitive rhythms of the machine, city dwellers at the turn of the century sought release in their leisure time through sensory stimulation. The pace and complexity of urban living was seen to generate a preference for immediate gratification, as, between home and work, the individual encountered a world of movement in which incidents unfolded in seemingly random and disconnected fashion.[12] The early cinema programme, which offered its audiences sequences of short subjects juxtaposing sober actuality with fictional forms that, at times, tended towards the surreal, appeared to capture the dynamics of city life with unusual fidelity.

Although originally formulated in the context of late nineteenth-century Paris and inter-war Berlin, the notion of modernity set out here may also be applied to Britain in general and Scotland in particular in the decades which witnessed cinema's rise to prominence. In both, the urban population expanded at an unprecedented rate from the third quarter of the nineteenth century, a product of an accelerating exodus from rural areas. A nation that mid century censuses had found to be largely urban, with over half its population so disposed by 1851, had by the start of the next century come to be dominated by cities and large towns, so that 60 per cent of those living in England and Wales and almost half of all Scots now lived in centres of population of 20,000 or more.[13] For contemporary observers, the change in location had wrought a qualitative change within the population. The 1911 Census of England, in which it was found that some 80 per cent of children born over the previous decade had been raised in a wholly urban environment, remarked on the emergence of a new 'urban type' within the nation.[14] The presence of the 'type' was felt at various points in the first decade of the new century. In the Boer War, it was evident in the enfeebled condition of many of those volunteering for military service overseas and in what were seen as irrational outbursts of jingoistic excess, such as accompanied news of the relief of Mafeking in 1900.[15] More generally, it was reflected in concerns expressed over the state of the nation's youth. Often lacking the close control of family and workmates, and obliged to spend large portions of their time both at work and play on the streets, where they were exposed to the constant tumult of urban society, the young were especially prone to the 'restlessness' that was seen to mark modern living.[16] This manifested itself most clearly in their use of free time, which valued immediate excitement over more improving, reflective pursuits. As the young made up one of early cinema's most reliable constituencies, the link between film and one of the key 'problems' of contemporary urban society appeared clear. Yet, if the modernity thesis helps to clarify many of the concerns that came to coalesce around the cinema and other popular leisure forms in the early years of the twentieth century, its ability fully to account for the appeal of the moving image and to explain its social and cultural importance over the first five decades of that century remains open to doubt.

Film scholars in the United States have recently turned to question the association of the cinema with modernity. They point to the widespread popularity of moving picture shows in a country in which, by official definitions, over 60 per cent of the population lived in areas designated as 'rural'. Cinema thus flourished in settings far removed from the metropolitan centres most obviously associated with 'modern' modes of living.[17] Similar observations may be offered, despite higher levels of urbanisation than in the United States, about Britain in general and Scotland in particular, around the turn of the century. From the first, itinerant exhibitors took film to remote, thinly populated districts and the first wave of fixed-site cinema development towards the end of the first decade of the twentieth century confirmed this pattern of dispersal. *Kinematograph Year Books* published during the early years of the First World War listed over fifty settlements across Scotland each with populations of 5,000 or below with venues at which shows were regularly mounted.[18] If this suggests the inability of a single cultural theory to encapsulate cinema's appeal, the objections can be taken further, to extend into the very settings in which 'modernity' may have been expected to develop most fully. The importance which attaches to the dislocation of 'modern' urban living, in which the individual felt him- or herself to be subsumed within a seething anonymous mass, seems, in the light of writings on urban communities both by historians and by those born and raised in these districts, to be misplaced. If outward appearances suggested a dulling uniformity, the lived experience of towns and cities in the early twentieth century was more akin to a series of 'urban villages', often comprising little more than a few streets. Within this narrow and restricted span, everyday life was conducted and strong personal attachments often developed.[19] An abiding sense of locality, more often associated with pre-industrial, pre-modern societies, continued to flourish in outwardly modern, urban settings. The extent to which cinema-going served to reconfigure or to confirm existing patterns of everyday living thus constitutes a key theme in the work that follows.

Theories of modernity are also open to the charge that they fail adequately to explore the nature of the cinema audience. While cultural critics often viewed cinema-goers as an undifferentiated mass, responding in a uniform, mostly uninformed manner to what was shown on the screen,[20] picture house proprietors were made aware, through constant fluctuations in the balance sheet, of the varied and unpredictable nature of audience taste. Throughout the period, they remained concerned to chart in unequalled detail changes in audience behaviour, relating them to a range of variables, extending from the quality of the films shown, to the availability of alternative attractions, and the state of the weather. The result of their efforts provides this book with a substantial portion of its raw material. Literature directed at cinema managers reiterated the need to pay constant attention to audience preferences through regular measures of behaviour and crucially emphasised the need to disaggregate cinema-goers, identifying sections within them to which particular films or programmes would appeal. One work, published in 1927, advised managers that 'the same appeal is not equally effective for all prospective patrons because they vary in age, in sex, in racial characteristics, in education, in reading habits, in their environment, in buying power, in experience and even in language limitations'.[21] As the listing suggests, the intended recipients of this advice were managers in the United States. However, it is known that the book was acquired for use across the Green circuit in west-central Scotland, suggesting that the observations it offered had, in outline at least, a broader relevance.

Recognition of the film audience's varied character serves further to question any straightforward relationship between the cinema and 'modernity'. Theories which relate the quest for instant gratification in leisure time to a stultifying and repetitive work experience emphasise the lot of the adult male worker, increasingly subject to the insistent demands of the machine.[22] Yet cinema's principal constituency for much of its early career lay elsewhere, among children, youths, and women, whose exposure to new production technologies was, at best, limited. Most women, separated from the world of formal paid work beyond the home after marriage, experienced a work regime that lacked a fixed duration and which varied in intensity, activity being most marked at particular points in the day associated with the needs of other family members. 'Free' time was thus available intermittently and was not experienced as part of a fixed and unvarying block of time. What is more, 'leisure' time was rarely distinctly separable from work time, often being consumed with tasks essential for the welfare of the household.[23] If the cinema appeared to offer a more definite break in routine for most women, its role in this regard was not always straightforward. For women at one London cinema in the 1920s, the hazy distinction between work and leisure was, if anything, maintained, as they sat watching the films while peeling potatoes.[24] A visit to the picture house could thus fulfil a variety of needs, as indicated by the experience of one elderly woman from Brechin, recounted in the trade paper *Scottish Cinema* in 1919: the 2d admission charge to the local cinema represented, for her, a saving on the cost of heat, light, and, in her words, 'a wee tickie in the bottle', which would have been incurred by an evening spent at home.[25] Rather than providing a source of spectacle and excitement, for this picture-goer, the cinema represented a space for rest and repose, for on taking her seat she wrapped herself in her shawl and promptly fell asleep. Much of the analysis that follows proceeds on the assumption that most members of the audience remained awake for the duration of the programme, but however unusual such behaviour may have been, in Brechin or elsewhere, it does indicate the often varied role that cinema could play in lives that, in the absence of a closely regulated work routine and in their intensely local focus, often appeared the very antithesis of 'modernity'.

If all this encourages some scepticism as to the ability of a single overarching cultural theory to explain cinema's emergence and rise to popularity in the half century to 1950, it does not mean that the idea of the 'modern' should be entirely disregarded. Nevertheless, its utility is conditional on it being rooted in a precise chronological and geographical context. So, Scotland, like Britain as a whole in the early twentieth century, was subject to a variety of social, economic, and cultural forces, within which cinema can be located. Yet, however similar such forces may have been across the country, the response to them in Scotland was, in many respects, distinct. Two, of particular significance, may be identified. The first manifestation of the 'modern' that might be noted was the growing impact of national and international forces at an everyday level. In many respects, the first half of the twentieth century witnessed the high-water mark of 'Britishness'. Heightened by periods of national emergency, such as wartime, when administrative priorities required that local differences be overridden, the trend across the period was for a growing range of organisations to be structured and to function on a British canvas. So, between the wars, broadcasting acquired a self-consciously 'British' character through the BBC, although this was a 'Britishness' inflected through the stern Presbyterianism of the Corporation's first Director-General, John Reith.[26] The growth of 'British' influence was also apparent on the cinema screen. By the 1940s, the production of films, and to some degree their distribution and exhibition, was increasingly centred on London, a trend viewed with disquiet by many Scots, who saw the loss of control over the sponsorship of film production (in abeyance since the outbreak of war in 1939) and cinema ownership as evidence of Scotland's increasing effacement as a nation.[27] The threat did not emanate from London only. The bulk of films screened across Scotland in the period were American in origin, projecting what some came to see as an alternative morality, based on material acquisition and the pursuit of personal gratification. For many in Britain, Hollywood's dominance of the industry presaged broader cultural, economic, and ultimately political hegemony by the United States, justifying moves to shore up a native production capacity through legislative action in the later 1920s.[28] Similar concerns circulated in Scotland, and were compounded by the perception that the cinema, whether originating from London or Los Angeles, was also an agent of secularisation. The decline of formal religious observance and the concomitant rise of secular modes of thought appeared further evidence of the modernising forces at work in society in the decades from 1900.[29] That the cinema was a catalyst for change was made manifest by the recurring controversy surrounding the opening of picture houses on Sundays, so that the industry came to be viewed as an instrument for the dissemination of metropolitan modes of thought and behaviour. To that extent, the cinema appeared to challenge the very basis of what, for some, it was to be Scottish.

In charting the nation's growing engagement with film, this book is not only concerned to chronicle the emergence and elaboration of a popular leisure form, it also seeks to explore aspects of Scotland's engagement with the modern. Existing work on Scottish cinema has already, in part, addressed this question and concluded that the relationship was far from straightforward. In contrast with this book, which is primarily concerned with the exhibition and reception of film regardless of origin, such research has centred on an area in which Scotland has often been perceived, in cinematic terms at least, to have punched considerably below its weight: production. Representations of the nation on screen are thus seen to have been almost wilfully backward-looking, drawing on the mythic symbolism of tartanry and the comforting domestic tropes of the kailyard. Harnessing the elemental forces of nature and romance, the Scotland of the silver screen is often seen to embody the anti-modern 'other', which, when confronted by the values and expectations of the contemporary world, operates to challenge and subvert them.[30] This view has not, however, gone unchallenged. Treatments of Scottish subject matter rarely originated within Scotland, more often than not reflecting interpretations imposed from outside. Their reception within Scotland, both among critics and the mass of local picture-goers, has rarely been considered. Equally, the privileging of such themes offers, it has been argued, a selective and distorted picture of film production in and about Scotland.[31] When viewed in the round, the admittedly modest output of Scottish-produced film in the years to 1950 appears more diverse in nature with a strong emphasis on documenting 'reality'. Originating in the local topical, actuality shots of everyday events, which did so much to cement cinema's early appeal, these developed into the more formalised productions of the 1930s. Often seen as the most distinctively 'British' of cinematic forms, the documentary, like the BBC, carried a strong Scottish imprint, in this case through the forceful personality of John Grierson, the guiding force behind the group that coalesced around first the Empire

Marketing Board and then the General Post Office. Grierson's belief in the interpretive potential of actuality, although it drew heavily on nineteenth-century Idealism, was also informed by a modern visual aesthetic influenced by Eisenstein.[32] A rounded picture of Scottish film output thus suggests the inadequacy of seeing this solely or even predominantly in terms of a confirmation of well-worn cultural models.

Indeed, a readiness to engage with the 'modern' can also be seen in the emergence of societies anxious to promote an awareness and appreciation of a cinema that originated beyond the dream factories of Hollywood and which, by the 1940s, had taken root well beyond Scotland's largest urban centres. What is more, key institutions of Scottish life through the period, embracing education and the Church, were increasingly active in promoting the use of film to further their designs among an audience increasingly attuned to the idioms of visual forms of communication. At all levels, Scots' engagement with film was deep and complex, necessitating its investigation from a variety of perspectives.

In the chapters that follow, two distinct but complementary approaches are taken. Running through the book are chapters that, while chronologically arranged, also seek to address particular phases in cinema history. The first traces early developments in the presentation and consumption of moving pictures, from their origins as fairground novelties and occasional 'chasers' on variety theatre and music hall bills, to their emergence as the centrepiece of a more distinct entertainment form, staged in discrete and increasingly elaborate venues. Here, it is the speed of cinema's growth that commands attention, and the degree to which this can be understood as being founded on the appeal of novelty and 'modernity' inherent in a new technology, or on the medium's continued attachment to more established recreational forms. An examination of the backgrounds of the early film exhibitors and producers active across Scotland assists in clarifying the forces at work in cinema's rise. A key question centres on the emergence, in the years immediately before the outbreak of the First World War, of an increasing number of shows based on fixed and dedicated sites and whether this is to be interpreted as marking the transition to a new mode of exhibition, a further stage in the evolution towards a more organised, capital-intensive industry, or as an alternative method of presentation, existing alongside established, more 'traditional' entertainment forms.

Such questions carry over into the next sub-period, running from the outbreak of war in 1914 to the end of the silent era in the late 1920s. This mature phase of 'silent' cinema remains one of the most thinly researched in the industry's history in Britain. Much of the existing literature centres on the mounting problems faced by British film production, confronted by the growing international dominance of Hollywood from the war years onwards.[33] By contrast, the fortunes of film exhibition during the Great War remains unclear, although a case has been made for a wartime spike in attendance as alternative outlets for recreational spending were closed off.[34] Yet the industry also faced a series of external challenges in this period, through escalating costs and the imposition of taxation, both of which challenged its standing as a cheap, mass recreational form, as well as calls for tighter regulation and censorship. How the cinema and cinema-goers fared in the war years and in the volatile economic conditions that followed the Armistice repays close examination. In Scotland, the later silent years culminated in the construction of larger and more luxuriously appointed picture houses, the first true picture palaces, among which was what was thought to be the then largest cinema in Europe, Green's Playhouse on Renfield Street in Glasgow, capable of holding 4,200 at one sitting.[35] The increasing density of documentation available for the later silent era enables us to identify the forces behind the emergence of these early picture palaces and to locate them more firmly within the cinema-going culture of the time.

The first decade of sound cinema in Britain has, by contrast, excited research that is both extensive in coverage and varied in approach. This is a phase of cinema history dominated by deliberate attempts to bolster film production across Britain by legislative means, in particular the Cinematograph Films or Quota Act of 1927. Much of the literature on the succeeding decade is concerned to evaluate the impact of this measure. In aesthetic terms, the verdict has more often than not been negative. In her official history of the British film, Rachael Low laments the proliferation of cheaply made product whose every outing merely served to undermine further the reputation of the British industry.[36] Of late, however, more positive views have emerged. John Sedgwick has pointed to the more than respectable box-office performance of large-budget British pictures, particularly later in the decade, while Steve Chibnall has detected in the mass of low-budget films the making of a truly indigenous popular cinema of appeal to largely provincial, non-metropolitan audiences.[37] The cinema audience, so long seen en masse, is now being broken down into its constituent elements, reflecting various points of difference, based around age, class, gender, and geography. Scotland's place in this increasingly diverse mix is significant, given what was perceived to be a rooted distaste for British films north of the border. The validity of this view is tested here by utilising box-office data from cinemas across the country. These enable us to reconstruct film preferences among a variety of what Sue Harper has termed 'taste communities'.[38] In the process, the degree to which the Scots may be said to have constituted a coherent and distinct cinema-going community, as opposed to one fractured along lines of social and geographic difference, may be assessed.

In the 1940s, cinema-going attained new heights of importance, both statistically and culturally. The absence of alternative recreational outlets during the Second World War and in the years of austerity that followed enhanced further cinema's place in the leisure experience of the bulk of the population. At the same time, however, access to British films was rendered more difficult as the demands of the wartime economy dictated that production be cut back.[39] The debate over the comparative popularity of domestically produced as opposed to Hollywood films thus carried over into the war years and beyond, although in terms rather different from those which informed the pre-war period. The 1940s represents a point at which British film production attained a degree of critical respectability, a result in part, it has been argued, of a greater drive for quality over quantity in output.[40] The degree to which audiences in Scotland were more receptive to British films, at a time when ideas of 'Britishness' may have been expected to resonate culturally and politically, remains a central issue.

Interwoven into this narrative strand are a series of more thematically centred chapters, concerned to explore some of the wider implications of the rise of cinema and cinema-going through the period. Two examine the regulatory context within which moving picture shows were obliged to operate from the 1890s. Initially at least, the cinema operated within a local framework of controls shaped by nineteenth-century Police Acts. Over time, new, more national structures emerged, particularly with regard to the regulation of film content. If the adjudications of the British Board of Film Censors gained increasing acceptance across Scotland, influence continued to be exerted by local opinion, as expressed through more explicitly 'Scottish' agencies, such as the Church. A particular point of contention throughout was the comparative accessibility of film shows to children across Scotland. Here, as elsewhere, the position north of the border was often compared, unfavourably, with that in England, with the result that repeated calls for closer regulation were made. All, however, would encounter opposition informed by economic self-interest and alternative ideas as to cinema's function within the wider life of the community.

A further recurrent controversy, and one of particular resonance for many Scots, centred on the question of permitting cinemas to open on Sundays. Observance of the Sabbath was, for large sections of Scottish society, central to Scotland's Presbyterian character and was at the heart of what it was that made her a distinctive nation.[41] At various points through the period, under prompting from forces both within and beyond Scotland, that practice, at least as it related to the cinema, came under challenge. The pressure for change was not consistent, nor did it always tend in the same direction. So, on occasion, the controls on Sunday opening became more, rather than less restrictive. The debates around this issue do not support a narrative based around the relentless secularisation of society in the first half of the twentieth century. Rather, the story is one of fitful and uneven change. So, even though the range of activities deemed permissible on the Sabbath had widened by 1950 to include cinema-going, opening remained highly localised and continued to be subject to close regulation.

Films had long been available on the Sabbath in settings distinct from cinema's commercial mainstream. From the 1930s, a diverse assortment of film societies offered Sunday screenings to their members, their shows often comprising productions that questioned the prevailing moral and political consensus. This alternative, more openly intellectual film culture formed part of the broader civic function conceived for moving pictures through the period. By 1939, film was increasingly being employed by educational and Church bodies as a new and more effective means of disseminating information and ideas. Beyond urban Scotland, this approach was taken up from the late 1940s by the Highlands and Islands Film Guild. Conceived initially as a way of discouraging widespread abandonment of more remote communities, particularly by the young, the Guild increasingly saw its role as being to generate and sustain in rural districts the kind of participatory civic culture upon which urban Scotland had long been seen to thrive.

A final chapter traverses more familiar ground, in exploring Scotland's career as a centre of film production. An inclusive overview of Scottish output would take in actuality subjects, in the production of which Scotland is seen to have played a full and constructive role, and fictional representations, where the record is seen to be markedly more variable. The factors privileging the one form over the other merit consideration here, along with the obstacles which prevented the development of an infrastructure capable of sustaining output at a more consistent level. Attention is also given to the exhibition and reception of Scottish films, to assess how far opportunities for viewing locally produced footage existed, and also the degree to which the subjects selected for treatment were likely to resonate with native audiences. In this respect, the analysis of Scottish production further informs an appreciation of the 'taste communities' among cinema-goers in the first half of the twentieth century.

For very good reasons, discussion of Scotland within this period has often centred on the travails of heavy industry and the social problems that flowed from them.[42] The pages that follow offer some insight into the ways in which Scots sought to manage the stresses of economic depression, poor housing, and wartime dislocation. Yet they also suggest that this perspective is, in many ways, seriously incomplete. If the cinema is often seen, in rather straightforward terms, to have offered an escape from the realities of everyday living, it is a view that fails to capture the range of factors drawing people to engage with the moving image or the varied manner in which they did so. The cinema-going experience was diverse, reflecting in full the complexities of the society that encouraged and sustained it.

NOTES

1. In 1951, there were 8.6 Scots for every cinema seat, while in England the number was 12.2, H. E. Browning and A. A. Sorrell, 'Cinemas and Cinema-Going in Great Britain', *Journal of the Royal Statistical Society*, Series A (General), 117(2) (1954), p. 137.

2. *Kinematograph Year Book 1948*, Thirty-Fifth Year (London, 1948), pp. 417–44.

3. Browning and Sorrell, 'Cinemas and Cinema-Going', pp. 135–6, 138–40.

4. National Archives of Scotland (hereafter NAS), ED 30/2, Highlands and Islands Film Guild, Minutes of Meetings, Report of Discussion of Conference in Inverness, 30 May 1946; Report of Secretary for period April to December 1950.

5. Scottish Screen Archive, National Library of Scotland (hereafter SSA), 2/1/2, Federation of Scottish Film Societies, Minutes of Council, Meetings at Central Hotel, Glasgow, 1 Oct. 1949; 21 May 1950.

6. See, for example, the five volumes in which Rachael Low set out to provide an 'authentic history' of the British film from 1896 to 1939: R. Low and R. Manvell, *The History of the British Film, 1896–1906* (London, 1948); R. Low, *The History of the British Film, 1906–1914* (London, 1949); id., *The History of the British Film, 1914–1918* (London, 1950); id., *The History of the British Film, 1918–1929* (London, 1971); id., *The History of the British Film, 1929–1939: Film Making in 1930s Britain* (London, 1985); R. Armes, *A Critical History of British Cinema* (New York, 1978); J. Curran and V. Porter (eds), *British Cinema History* (Totowa, NJ, 1983); R. Murphy, 'Under the Shadow of Hollywood' and J. Petley, 'The Lost Continent', in C. Barr (ed.), *All Our Yesterdays: 90 Years of British Cinema* (London, 1986), pp. 47–71, 98–119.

7. F. Gray (ed.), *Hove Pioneers and the Arrival of Cinema* (Brighton, 1996); D. Berry, *Wales and Cinema: The First Hundred Years* (Cardiff, 1994); P. Yorke, *William Haggar (1851–1925): Fairground Film-maker* (Bedlinog, 2007); J. Barnes, *The Beginnings of the Cinema in England, 1894–1901. Volume Four: 1899* (Exeter, 1996), pp. 64–8; on Mitchell and Kenyon, see V. Toulmin, S. Popple, and P. Russell (eds), *The Lost World of Mitchell and Kenyon* (London, 2004); V. Toulmin, *Electric Edwardians: The Story of the Mitchell & Kenyon Collection* (London, 2006).

8. Berry, *Wales and Cinema*; P. Miskell, *A Social History of the Cinema in Wales, 1918–1951: Pulpits, Coal Pits and Fleapits* (Cardiff, 2006); J. Hill, *Cinema and Northern Ireland: Film, Culture and Politics* (London, 2006).

9. Useful works here include D. Cloy and J. McBain, *Scotland in Silent Cinema: A Commemorative Catalogue to Accompany the Scottish Reels Programme at the Pordenone Silent Film Festival, Italy, 1998* (Glasgow, 1998); J. McBain, *Pictures Past: Scottish Cinemas Remembered* (Edinburgh, 1985); D. Bruce, *Scotland the Movie* (Edinburgh, 1996); A. Martin, *Going to the Pictures: Scottish Memories of Cinema* (Edinburgh, 2000).

10. L. Charney and V. R. Schwartz, 'Introduction', in id., *Cinema and the Invention of Modern Life* (Berkeley, Los Angeles, and London, 1995), p. 1.

11. T. Gunning, 'The Cinema of Attractions: Early Film, its Spectators and the Avant-Garde', in T. Elsaesser and A. Barker (eds), *Early Cinema: Space, Frame, Narrative* (London, 1990), pp. 56–62.

12. B. Singer, 'Modernity, Hyperstimulus [*sic*], and the Rise of Popular Sensationalism', in Charney and Schwartz, *Cinema and the Invention of Modern Life*, pp. 72–99.

13. R. J. Morris, 'Urbanisation and Scotland', in W. Hamish Fraser and R. J. Morris

(eds), *People and Society in Scotland. Volume II: 1830–1914* (Edinburgh, 1990), p. 74; M. Anderson, 'The Social Implications of Demographic Change', in F. M. L. Thompson (ed.), *The Cambridge Social History of Britain, 1750–1950. Volume 2: People and their Environment* (Cambridge, 1990), pp. 4–6; J. Harris, *Private Lives, Public Spirit: Britain, 1870–1914* (Harmondsworth, 1994), pp. 41–5.

14. Harris, *Private Lives*, p. 45.

15. G. R. Searle, *A New England? Peace and War, 1886–1918* (Oxford, 2004), pp. 284–7, 375.

16. S. Humphries, *Hooligans or Rebels? An Oral History of Working-class Childhood and Youth, 1889–1939* (Oxford, 1981), ch. 1; G. Pearson, *Hooligan. A History of Respectable Fears* (London, 1983).

17. K. H. Fuller-Seeley (ed.), *Hollywood in the Neighborhood: Historical Case Studies of Local Moviegoing* (Berkeley, 2008); K. H. Fuller, *At the Picture Show: Small-Town Audiences and the Creation of Movie Fan Culture* (Washington, DC and London, 1996); R. C. Allen, 'Race, Region, and Rusticity. Relocating U.S. Film History', in R. Maltby, M. Stokes, and R. C. Allen (eds), *Going to the Movies. Hollywood and the Social Experience of Cinema* (Exeter, 2007), pp. 25–44; G. A. Waller, *Main Street Amusements. Movies and Commercial Entertainment in a Southern City, 1896–1930* (Washington, DC and London, 1995).

18. *Kinematograph Year Book, Diary and Directory* (London, 1915 and 1916).

19. R. Hoggart, *The Uses of Literacy: Aspects of Working-class Life with Special Reference to Publications and Entertainments* (London, 1957); id., *A Local Habitation. Life and Times: 1918–1940* (Oxford, 1989); R. Roberts, *The Classic Slum. Salford Life in the First Quarter of the Century* (Manchester, 1971); R. McKibbin, *Classes and Cultures. England, 1918–1951* (Oxford, 1998), ch. V; P. Johnson, 'Conspicuous Consumption and Working-class Culture in late-Victorian and Edwardian Britain', *Transactions of the Royal Historical Society*, 5th ser., 38 (London, 1988), pp. 27–42; A. Davies, 'Leisure in the "Classic Slum", 1900–1939', in A. Davies and S. Fielding (eds), *Workers' Worlds. Culture and Communities in Manchester and Salford, 1880–1939* (Manchester, 1992), pp. 102–32.

20. D. Strinati, *An Introduction to Theories of Popular Culture* (London, 1995), chs 1 and 2; W. Benjamin, 'The Work of Art in the Age of Mechanical Reproduction', reprinted in G. Mast and M. Cohen (eds), *Film Theory and Criticism* (New York and Oxford, 1979), pp. 848–70.

21. J. F. Barry and E. W. Sargent, *Building Theatre Patronage. Management and Merchandising* (New York, 1927), p. 94.

22. E. J. Hobsbawm, 'The Formation of British Working-class Culture' and 'The Making of the Working Class, 1870–1914', in id., *Worlds of Labour* (London, 1984), pp. 176–213.

23. C. Langhamer, *Women's Leisure in England, 1920–60* (Manchester, 2000), part 1; H. Clark and E. Carnegie, *She Was Aye Workin'. Memories of Tenement Women in Edinburgh and Glasgow* (Oxford, 2003); further contemporary insight into the time budgets of working-class women can be found in M. Pember Reeves, *Round About a Pound a Week* (London, 1913), pp. 160–7.

24. L. McKernan, '"Only the Screen was Silent . . .": Memories of Children's

Cinema-going in London before the First World War', *Film Studies*, 10 (Spring 2007), 10.

25. *Scottish Cinema*, 27 Oct. 1919, p. 30.

26. J. Curran and J. Seaton, *Power Without Responsibility: The Press and Broadcasting in Britain* (London, 1985), ch. 8; A. Briggs, *The History of Broadcasting in the United Kingdom. Volume II: The Golden Age of Wireless* (London, 1965), parts II and III; W. H. McDowell, *The History of BBC Broadcasting in Scotland, 1923–1983* (Edinburgh, 1992), chs 2 and 3; *The BBC Year-Book 1934* (London, 1934).

27. An early expression of such concerns may be found in A. Dewar Gibb, *Scotland in Eclipse* (London, 1930); in the next decade, they gave rise to ambitious projects to develop a sizeable production base north of the border, SSA, 4/4/1, Scottish National Film Studios, Ltd., booklet 'Scotland on the Screen'.

28. S. Street, *British National Cinema* (London, 1997), ch. 1; M. Dickinson and S. Street, *Cinema and State: The Film Industry and the British Government, 1927–84* (London, 1985), chs 1–3; S. Chibnall, *Quota Quickies: The Birth of the British 'B' Film* (London, 2007), ch. 1.

29. J. Obelkevich, 'Religion', in F. M. L. Thompson (ed.), *The Cambridge Social History of Britain, 1750–1950. Volume 3: Social Agencies and Institutions* (Cambridge, 1990), pp. 348–56; C. G. Brown, *Religion and Society in Scotland since 1707* (Edinburgh, 1997), chs 6 and 7; id., *The Death of Christian Britain. Understanding Secularisation, 1800–2000* (London, 2001), esp. ch. 7.

30. C. McArthur, 'Scotland and Cinema: The Iniquity of the Fathers', in id. (ed.), *Scotch Reels: Scotland in Cinema and Television* (London, 1982), pp. 40–69; J. Richards, *Films and British National Identity. From Dickens to Dad's Army* (Manchester, 1997), ch. 7.

31. J. Caughie, 'Representing Scotland: New Questions for Scottish Cinema', in E. Dick (ed.), *From Limelight to Satellite: A Scottish Film Book* (London, 1990), pp. 13–30; F. Hardy, *Scotland in Film* (Edinburgh, 1990), chs 1–5.

32. On local topicals, see J. McBain, 'Mitchell and Kenyon's Legacy in Scotland – The Inspiration for a Forgotten Film-making Genre', in Toulmin, Popple, and Russell (eds), *The Lost World of Mitchell and Kenyon*, pp. 113–21; A. Higson, '"Britain's Outstanding Contribution to the Film": The Documentary-Realist Tradition', in Barr, *All Our Yesterdays*, pp. 72–97; I. Aitken, *Films and Reform: John Grierson and the Documentary Film Movement* (London, 1990), chs 2–5; id. (ed.), *The Documentary Film Movement: An Anthology* (Edinburgh, 1998), chs 1 and 2; P. Swann, *The British Documentary Film Movement, 1926–1946* (Cambridge, 1989), chs 1–3; F. Hardy, *John Grierson: A Documentary Biography* (London, 1979), ch. 3; id. (ed.), *Grierson on Documentary* (London, 1946), part 2.

33. See, for example, K. Bamford, *Distorted Images: British National Identity and Film in the 1920s* (London, 1999); G. Bakker, 'The Decline and Fall of the European Film Industry: Sunk Costs, Market Size and Market Structure, 1890–1927', *The London School of Economics and Political Science, Working Papers in Economic History*, 70/03 (Feb. 2003).

34. N. Hiley, 'Let's Go to the Pictures: the British Cinema Audience in the 1920s and 1930s', *Journal of Popular British Cinema*, 2 (1999), pp. 39–53.

35. SSA, 5/8/13, George Green, Ltd., cutting from *Kinematograph Weekly* [hereafter *KW*], 22 Sept. 1927.

36. Low, *Film Making in 1930s Britain*, pp. 115–16.

37. J. Sedgwick, 'Cinema-going Preferences in Britain in the 1930s', in J. Richards (ed.), *The Unknown 1930s: An Alternative History of the British Cinema, 1929–39* (London, 1998), pp. 1–35; id., *Popular Filmgoing in 1930s Britain: A Choice of Pleasures* (Exeter, 2000); Chibnall, *Quota Quickies*, pp. 249–56.

38. S. Harper, 'A Lower Middle-Class Taste-Community in the 1930s: Admissions Figures at the Regent Cinema, Portsmouth, UK', *Historical Journal of Film, Radio and Television*, 24 (2004), pp. 565–87.

39. Dickinson and Street, *Cinema and State*, pp. 103–49; R. Murphy, *British Cinema and the Second World War* (London and New York, 2000).

40. R. Murphy, *Realism and Tinsel: Cinema and Society in Britain, 1939–49* (London, 1989); C. Drazin, *The Finest Years: British Cinema of the 1940s* (London, 2007).

41. Brown, *Religion and Society in Scotland*, pp. 177–87.

42. T. M. Devine, C. H. Lee, and G. C. Peden (eds), *The Transformation of Scotland: The Economy since 1700* (Edinburgh, 2005), esp. chs 8 and 9; C. H. Lee, 'Scotland, 1860–1939: Growth and Poverty', in R. Floud and P. Johnson (eds), *The Cambridge Economic History of Modern Britain. Volume II: Economic Maturity, 1860–1939* (Cambridge, 2004), pp. 428–55.

1

From Variety Hall to Picture House: The Emergence
of Scottish Cinema to 1914

I

At the outbreak of the First World War, less than two decades after the first public exhibition of moving pictures, the cinema had come to occupy a central place in Scotland's popular recreational culture. With shows taking place in almost 600 venues dispersed widely across the country, Scots' engagement with the moving image was frequent and profound. If cinema flourished most obviously in metropolitan settings such as Glasgow, where, in 1913, eighty-five buildings were licensed for shows under the Cinematograph Act of 1909, it was also a presence in small communities, such as the Highland village of Beauly, north of Inverness, with a population of 882.[1] Although statistics on attendance were not, as yet, centrally gathered, contemporary estimates placed the average weekly audience across Britain at between seven and eight million.[2] Assuming that cinema-goers in Scotland at least conformed to the behaviour indicated by the average, then the equivalent of between 17 and 18 per cent of the total population was drawn to local picture houses each week. Given subsequent evidence at mid-century of Scots' unequalled enthusiasm for the movies, this figure is likely, if anything, to understate levels of attendance. Whatever credence is given to such estimates, and they are, it must be admitted, highly conjectural, they convey something of cinema's breadth of appeal and go some way towards validating the observation offered in the first issue of the Glasgow paper *The Entertainer* in October 1913, that 'The popularity of the cinema knows no bounds.'[3]

The function of this chapter is to explore the factors underlying that growth and to account for both its rapidity and extent. Within the existing literature, conflicting perspectives are offered on this question. Some point to the cinema's associations with novelty and modernity, as reflected in the moving images themselves, as well as the mechanisms by which they were recorded and projected. In the absence of compelling narratives, it was the juxtaposition of varied images, subject to recurrent changes, which constituted the cinema's main attraction for many.[4] Others, however, place the cinema within a longer, evolving history of visual representations, the moving picture show of the 1890s emerging organically from magic lantern displays and their variants.[5] From this perspective, cinema's early success is traceable to the fact that it emerged embedded within an established visual entertainment culture. The degree to which cinema marked, for Scots, a point of departure, a source of continuity, or elements of both is considered here in relation to a number of themes: the figures responsible for the staging of early moving picture shows, their backgrounds, and the ways in which these may have coloured their approach to film exhibition; the nature of the shows they mounted, reflected both in the content of programmes and the manner in which they were presented; the settings in which film was presented also demand attention, particularly in the period prior to the emergence of dedicated picture houses, and what this may have to tell us about the nature of the audience, more especially with regard to its class background, as well as its gender and age balance.

All aspects of the industry were subject to significant change in the period to 1914. Perhaps the most dramatic concerns the emergence of the fixed site as the preponderant setting for film exhibition in the years from 1910. The rise of the picture house was the outcome of a wave of investment in cinema building that also heralded a major shift in the commercial organisation of the exhibition business.[6] Dominated in its first decade by shows with strong links to a wider entertainment culture, the prevailing mode of organisation from 1910 became the limited company, in which the everyday running of the business was left to professional managers answerable to boards of directors and shareholders. From this, it has been argued, a new approach to exhibition resulted. Whereas the moving image had initially prospered in what are seen as solidly working-class milieux, such as the fairground and the music hall, the quest for dividends among picture house companies required that businesses broaden their social appeal, emphasising cinema's respectable character. In seeking a more middle-class audience, the development of more complex film narratives, which demanded a deeper engagement from the audience and which were shown in more elaborate buildings subject to more stringent regulation, was crucial.[7] It is thus possible to construct an overarching narrative, in which technical and aesthetic developments are closely informed by the broader social, cultural, and political context. Nevertheless, this framework has not been accepted without question. Jon Burrows' work on early cinema in Edwardian London has pointed up the existence of cheap shows located in, among other places, shop fronts, a popular form of urban entertainment which, far from being expunged by the changes around 1910, continued to thrive at least until the outbreak of the First World War. Burrows' work does much to challenge the notion of a transition from a largely proletarian pursuit, rooted in traditions of popular showmanship, to a more commercially sophisticated industry openly seeking bourgeois patronage.[8] Later sections of this chapter are concerned to establish the degree to which the Scottish experience confirms or contradicts this view.

II

From the first, the varied appeal of the moving image was evident. At its debut in Scotland, at H. E. Moss' Empire Palace Theatre on Nicolson Street, Edinburgh, on 13 April 1896, the Cinématographe was hailed as 'The Latest Scientific Triumph', offering pictures 'Endowed with Life'.[9] The first show in Glasgow, at the newly opened Real Ice Skating Palace on Sauchiehall Street, while emphasising the entertainment's fashionable appeal as 'The Rage of the Season', also made much of its capacity to capture reality through 'Scenes of Actual Life'.[10] By September, animated photography had spread to Aberdeen, although here the medium was first encountered courtesy of R. W. Paul's 'cinematoscope', supplied by arrangement with David Devant of the Egyptian Hall in London's Piccadilly. A few days prior to its first public outing at the Music Hall in Union Street, a private exhibition had been mounted in the drawing room of Glenmuick House, at which a select gathering including Lord and Lady Glenesk, 'Her Serene Highness Princess Victor of Hohenlohe', and the Russian Ambassador, M. de Staal, witnessed pictures which reproduced 'all the actual movements of real life'.[11] At the very outset of its public career, then, the moving image constituted an entertainment that combined amusement and instruction. In this, it followed a well-established pattern. For much of the nineteenth century, agencies of social and moral improvement, from missionary to temperance societies, had utilised the techniques of popular entertainment to promote their aims.[12] For audiences in 1896, the distinctions between the polite, encompassing ideas of rationality founded upon intellectual improvement, and the popular in terms of leisure and recreation were less than clear cut. The ability of new forms of entertainment, such as the cinema, effectively to straddle the two would prove a potent force in shaping their early and continued success.

This is reflected, in large degree, in the backgrounds of those who sought to exploit the initial impact of Paul's and the Lumières' machines across Scotland. A key group, possessing both specialist engineering knowledge and some familiarity with the chemical processes involved in developing film, were those active in the optical instrument trade. As early as January 1897, the firm of J. Lizars, with branches across the country, was advertising the sale or hire of magic lanterns and cinematographs. As the latter could vary in price between twelve guineas and £40, prospective buyers were likely to be few.[13] However, Lizars were not content to trade in equipment only. They also dealt in film, offering some 280 subjects for hire by September 1897.[14] By the following year, they had diversified further into production and exhibition. In cooperation with the Musselburgh pharmacist James Forster, they are known to have filmed the first leg of the challenge match between the two leading Scottish golf professionals, Willie Park Jr and Willie Fernie over the local links. Park also featured in another match, filmed in 1899, against Harry Vardon and exhibited via Lizars' Bioscope at Edinburgh's Empire

Palace Theatre.[15] From 1898, the company organised shows at venues across Scotland, appearing at Glasgow's Empire Theatre in August 1901, while around Aberdeen exhibitions were mounted for diverse audiences, from the inmates of the West Poorhouse, to members of Bucksburn YMCA, and the scholars of Mannofield Parish Church Sunday School, whose annual soirée was enhanced by scenes of the school picnic 'with an unmistakable likeness of the popular pastor in the immediate foreground'.[16] Unlike many of the cinema pioneers drawn from the optical instrument trade, Lizars remained in the exhibition business until at least the end of the first decade of the twentieth century. In 1909, the company's Bioscope operators played a prominent part in Saturday concerts at Edinburgh's Methodist Central Hall and halls run by Glasgow Corporation.[17]

In Edinburgh, Lizars' example was followed by others active in the optical instrument trade. By late 1897, James Buncle was taking bookings for exhibitions of animated pictures via his 'New Cinematograph'. Advertised as 'The Novelty of the Season for Sabbath Schools and Entertainments', Buncle's apparatus was a highlight of the New Year demonstration of the Carrubber's Close Mission Gospel Temperance Association in January 1898, the programme including film of the Diamond Jubilee procession in London.[18] Buncle remained active into the new century, his 'Celebrated Cinematograph' appearing for an extended season at Edinburgh's Livingstone Hall, with footage of the recent Coronation of Edward VII.[19] Another Edinburgh firm of opticians, Fraser and Elrick, was by December 1898 advertising the cinematograph and a large selection of films 'combined with the Finest Dissolving Views for Christmas Parties and Entertainments'.[20] In the early years of the following century, bolstered by a royal seal of approval secured in the wake of a private show at Balmoral, they moved more fully into film exhibition, with seasons organised at halls across Edinburgh and accompanied by an appropriate sense of showmanship. So, in November 1902, at Queen Street Hall, the programme was preceded by a performance of selected national airs by the Royal Roumanian Orchestra, complete with 'Picturesque Roumanian Costume'.[21] By 1904, the firm was sufficiently confident of the returns from this part of the business to form a limited company, one of whose declared objects was 'To give and conduct cinematograph, phonographic, electrical, and lime-light view and variety entertainments.'[22] However, within a few weeks of the end of its 1905–6 season at Methodist Central Hall, mounting liabilities forced the company into liquidation.[23]

If anything, the link between the manufacture and retail of optical equipment and the moving picture business was even closer elsewhere. For example, in Dundee, Peter Feathers, who had traded as an optician and photographic dealer since the early 1890s, moved towards the end of the decade to film local scenes for public exhibition. This marked the beginning of a more wholesale transition into the cinema business, as Feathers came to offer shows from his own Electric Theatre, becoming one of the first exhibitors in the city to take out a licence under the Cinematograph Act of 1909 for the Stobswell Cinema.[24] If such examples serve to point up the links between cinema and technological modernity, reflected in a combination of precision engineering alongside advanced chemistry, they also illustrate how that relationship was shaped by the cultural expectations of the time, whereby science could also be applied for entertainment purposes.

So, when the Modern Marvel Co., Ltd, was established, with offices at Shandwick Place in Edinburgh, in March 1897, although its first declared object was 'To give scientific demonstrations', this was coupled with the aims 'To provide and promote entertainment in public and in private' and 'To exploit scientific instruments and apparatus appropriate to the purpose of popular entertainment or technical education.'[25] In its subsequent career, built in part around annual visits at Christmas and New Year to Edinburgh's Queen Street Hall, the company offered programmes that aspired to be both educative and amusing. For example, in 1904–5, the films comprised travelogues with scenes of Palestine and Italy, along with 'a fantastic series of pictures' depicting a trip to the Sun. In addition, audiences were offered a practical demonstration of the properties of liquid air courtesy of the 'magic kettle', which, among other things, rendered India rubber 'as brittle as Glass' and turned grapes into hailstones. The owner of the kettle was, however, 'careful to explain that there was no trickery or conjuring about his exhibition; it was simply a scientific demonstration'.[26] Cinema's ready acceptance within polite society relied in part therefore on its adherence to an established performing tradition in which enlightenment and amusement were both seamlessly combined and mutually reinforcing. For William Walker of Aberdeen, there appeared a natural progression from dealing in books with an educative purpose to organising and mounting magic-lantern displays, through which information was conveyed visually, to the exhibition and production of films from the latter months of 1896.[27] Initially, Walker's activities centred on Aberdeen and the surrounding area. By the end of 1896, exhibitions had been mounted in Stonehaven, Banchory-Devenick, and Aboyne, in addition to Aberdeen itself.[28] Shortly thereafter, emboldened by the royal imprimatur, gained following a private show at Balmoral in October 1898, Walker was exhibiting across Scotland, including several appearances at Glasgow's City Hall. That of March 1904, as the grandiloquently styled 'Royal Cinematograph and Electro-Drama', was accompanied by advertisements heralding the use of Walker's own 'Flickerless Steadfast Machine'.[29] By that point, the Walker Company had become part of a growing network of itinerant exhibitors, which was to play a central role in first cementing and then furthering the popularity of cinema across Scotland.

As Deac Rossell points out, the travelling show of the early twentieth century assumed a variety of forms. The most significant for cinema's long-term development have been identified as fairground entertainments, to which moving pictures were added from the later 1890s, and those mounted by exhibitors in venues rented for short seasons of a few weeks at most.[30] Both figure prominently in the development of the early moving picture business across Scotland. For example, the Green family, which by the outbreak of the First World War ran one of the largest cinema circuits north of the border, comprising twelve houses from Ayr in the west to Leven in Fife in the east, was active in the 1890s in mounting shows at fairs across Scotland and the north of England. Its interest in moving pictures commenced as early as 1896, when George Green, seeking a novelty to offer at the family's newly opened 'Carnival' site at the Old Barracks in Glasgow, encountered R. W. Paul's Theatrograph in London. Installed at the Carnival for the Christmas season that same year, moving pictures proved such a success that they became a central element in Greens' touring shows from 1898 and were offered at fairs extending from industrial Lancashire to southern and central Scotland.[31] On occasion, management was leased out to other showmen. So, Peter Swallow is known to have overseen Greens' amusements that appeared at Ayr and Kilmarnock, along with carnivals in Greenock and Edinburgh. Significantly for the longer term, Swallow went on to become one of the first showmen to take out a cinematograph licence in Glasgow, for shows under his own auspices.[32]

Other travelling showmen are also known to have made the transition into permanent cinema exhibition from fixed sites. 'President' George Kemp began his working life as a solicitor's clerk before turning to the more exotic setting of the fairground. Moving pictures had been incorporated into his shows by the turn of the century, by which point they were prominent attractions at fairs in Nottingham and Hull, as well as south-west Scotland. Kemp maintained a close interest in film over the following decade, investing in 1907 in a machine to allow the showing of subjects with synchronised sound featuring Harry Lauder.[33] Soon after, the travelling shows were sold to fund the building first of the Pavilion Theatre in Johnstone and, two years later, of the La Scala in the coastal resort of Saltcoats, at whose fairs Kemp's shows had been an annual fixture for several years.[34] Others who opted to cease travelling at about the same time included Alfred Palmer, who established the first permanent cinema in the Lanarkshire village of Lesmahagow, members of the Biddall family, who turned to manage houses in Annan, Dumfries, and Dumbarton, and Arthur Henderson, Yorkshire by birth, who, after working for a travelling show around Dundee, had established two cinemas in the town by late 1910.[35]

Alongside the regular cycle of fairs which punctuated the recreational calendar and sustained the efforts of large numbers of showpeople was another circuit of concert parties and entertainment troupes which appeared at a series of fixed venues across the country. For some, the inception of moving pictures offered the opportunity to develop further an existing interest in the provision of visual entertainment. The Poole family had exhibited their variant of the travelling panorama, the 'Myriorama', so called for its ability

to vary the view being offered so as to incorporate some element of anima-
tion into the picture, since the 1830s. Among the seven shows operated by
the family at the turn of the century were those at the Royal Italian Circus in
Glasgow and Cook's Circus in Edinburgh.[36] At this point, the Pooles were
still anxious to differentiate their entertainment from the upstart cinema.
Indeed, as late as 1907, an advertisement for the Myriorama was forthright
in declaring 'This is NOT a Cinematograph Entertainment, but an Artistic
Display of Mechanical Works of Art, intermixed with Refined Specialities
by Poole's.'[37] By this point, moving pictures had insinuated themselves into
the bill of fare, albeit initially fulfilling a subsidiary role. As early as 1901,
the supporting programme to the Myriorama included the 'Edison-Poole
Eventograph', and if, by the start of the following decade, the cast of supporting players remained, they had come to cede ground to the exhibition of
'The Very Latest and Best Pictures on the Bioscope'.[38] By the latter date, the
Myriorama had become a fixed point in Edinburgh's recreational calendar,
appearing each New Year at the city's Synod Hall, a position it would continue to occupy until the end of the 1920s.[39]

Continuity with earlier forms of visual entertainment was also provided
by the magic-lanternist Robert Calder, who, after assisting at one of Lizars'
early shows in Aberdeen in December 1896, mounted his own cinematograph
exhibition in Inverurie Town Hall. As with William Walker, Calder developed a local circuit of shows in and around Aberdeen, before widening his
coverage. By the early years of the following century, his 'cinematograph and
pictorial concert party' had become a regular feature of Glasgow's entertainment calendar.[40] Other troupes came to see the inclusion of moving pictures
as essential to their success. For example, 'Prince' Bendon headed a party that
performed around Glasgow and the west of Scotland, with Bendon himself
providing a ventriloquial turn. By 1905, the company's annual appearance
in Kirkintilloch was billed as 'Bendon's Animated Pictures and Grand
Ventriloquial Entertainment', an indication of Bendon's move around this
time into film rental and distribution.[41] Other groups regularly encountered
in and around Glasgow at the turn of the century included Madame Lloyd's
Musical Scenic Co., J. M. Hamilton's Grand Concert, and the Ormonde
family, grandiloquently billed in 1899 as 'The World Renowned "Mahatmas
of the West" and Rosicrucian Psychognomists'. By 1903, their programme
at Kirkintilloch's Temperance Hall included, in addition to Mlle Ormonde's
hypnotic trance visions, the Vivo-Tableaux, offering 'The World's History
day by day'.[42] Another to make the transition from concert party entertainment to motion picture exhibitor was Dove Paterson of Aberdeen. For much
of cinema's first decade, Paterson continued his career as an elocutionist,
offering public recitations of the works of popular authors, most notably
Burns and Kipling. On occasion, as with his appearance at the city's Music
Hall in May 1899, moving pictures also figured on the bill, giving point to his
lecture entitled 'The Funnygraph'. Over time, however, Paterson acquired a

more direct interest in cinematography, following a brief flirtation with still images and their use in magic-lantern exhibitions. By the outbreak of the war, Paterson operated three cinemas locally, confirming his status as 'The Man Who "Made" Pictures in Aberdeen'.[43]

The evident popularity of the moving picture show encouraged many speculative ventures into cinema exhibition. In the late summer of 1903, Alexander Mathieson, one of a family of musicians from Aberdeen, sought to gather an ad hoc concert party for a tour, lasting some three weeks, of towns across West Lothian and Lanarkshire. The programme was to include vocal and instrumental music, provided in part by Mathieson's sister Agnes, who travelled down from Aberdeen for the tour. However, the centrepiece of each evening's entertainment was to be the cinematograph, for which Mathieson hired the apparatus, the operator or projectionist, and the film itself from the Glasgow entertainment agent J. F. Calverto.[44] The opening night of the tour in the Public Hall, Broxburn, did not proceed according to plan. Although the opening numbers, combining music and dancing, were reported to have been well received, the operation of the cinematograph gave rise to problems when it was found that the film did not fit the gate in the projector. After several unsuccessful attempts to begin the exhibition, Mathieson took the decision to abandon the evening, along with all subsequent engagements, so that he saw little return on an outlay estimated at £65 13s 6½d.[45]

Alongside the troupes managed by individual showmen were increasingly sophisticated organisations, capable of mounting exhibitions at several venues, the running of which devolved to managers. Among the companies appearing in Glasgow in the early years of the century was the Royal Canadian Animated Photo Co., which in 1903 presented '10,000 Animated Pictures, 10,000 Depicting Life in Canada and the Events of the World', the Great USA Animated Picture Co., which opened at the Waterloo Rooms at New Year in 1907 with a programme that included *Aladdin and his Wonderful Lamp,* and most notably New Century Pictures, which first appeared at the Queen's Variety Theatre in December 1901, but which by the middle of the decade was offering extended seasons at the city's St Andrew's Hall. That of 1906 lasted over two months and boasted footage of the San Francisco earthquake.[46] The company was also prominent in the development of cinema exhibition further east. In 1901, as Edison's Animated Pictures, it commenced an extended lease at the Operetta House in Edinburgh's Chambers Street. Two years later, and after a season extending over forty-eight weeks, the cinematograph appeared set to become 'a permanent institution' at the theatre.[47] Among the managers employed by the New Century north of the border was J. J. Bennell. A native of Colchester, he gained his first experience of Glasgow as business manager of Professor André's Swiss Alpine Choir. After a period running shows for Sydney Carter of New Century Pictures, Bennell was invited to take over the management of the Wellington Palace in the Gorbals district of Glasgow, previously used for concerts by the Good Templars Harmonic Association.[48] The hall became the first centre for BB Pictures, said to have been named after Bennell's wife Blanche, but also standing for 'Bright and Beautiful', a name expressive of the temperance ideals that had recommended Bennell to the management of the Good Templars. By 1914, the business operated several cinemas across the central belt, from Greenock to Perth and Kirkcaldy, while Bennell cemented his standing as 'father of the Scottish cinema trade' by playing a leading part in the development of an organisation for exhibitors in Glasgow and the west of Scotland.[49] It is significant, then, that through the second decade of the century, a crucial phase in the industry's development, rental and exhibition interests across Scotland were headed by Bendon and Bennell, two figures who had gained their initial experience of the moving picture business through their links with itinerant showmanship.

As this suggests, the impact of the travelling shows on the later cinema trade was long, varied, and profound. Their role in boosting the popularity of moving pictures extended, as Vanessa Toulmin has noted, to the production and commissioning of films depicting events of local interest, thus ensuring that programmes were tailored to the particular tastes of each audience.[50] So, the New Century's shows at St Andrew's Hall, Glasgow in 1906, while dominated to a degree by scenes of the aftermath of the San Francisco earthquake, trumpeted as 'The Sight of a Lifetime', were also punctuated by subjects of more parochial interest, including a Boys' Brigade inspection at Yorkhill and shipping on the Clyde.[51] Itinerant entertainers were also crucial in extending cinema's reach across the nation. The network of fairs serviced by the Greens, Swallow, and their like embraced rural areas not otherwise well served by commercial forms of entertainment. Travelling concert parties also worked to bring moving pictures to smaller population centres. At the conclusion of its New Year season in Edinburgh, the Modern Marvel Company regularly took its shows on tour. That in the spring of 1903 took in villages across East Lothian and into eastern areas of Fife. This ensured that places at some remove from centres of metropolitan activity were not strangers to the moving image. One of Kirkintilloch's earliest encounters with film was via a concert and exhibition organised by a Monsieur Léotard from Glasgow. Thereafter, the town would form part of an annual itinerary for the Bendon and Ormonde troupes and be the venue for one-off visits by parties such as Hector Logan's Grand American Bioscope, whose films were supplemented by the appearance of Professor Fred Howard, 'the great Ventriloquist, Musical Expert and World's Greatest Bone Soloist'.[52] Further east, at Uphall, in the oil-shale producing area of West Lothian, exposure to the moving image was confined to short visits by such as Bendon's company and Scot's Cinematograph.[53] Itinerant shows thus did much to ensure the pervasive presence that cinema had become across Scotland by 1914.

The legacy of the travelling entertainer may also be seen in the extent to which the practice of showmanship became embedded in early cinema exhibition. The need to identify and respond to variations in audience preferences had long been recognised by providers of earlier forms of visual entertainment. The Pooles, for example, had found that Myriorama subjects did not always travel well. In Ireland, the depiction of Rorke's Drift evoked enthusiasm but not of the kind anticipated, as audiences responded with cries of 'Up the Zulus' and 'Come on the Zulus'. Equally problematic was a presentation of a British Army parade in the presence of royalty in Aggra. As Jim Poole recalled,

> So bad were the scenes and the riots, with the guide bespattered with tomatoes and other forms of projectiles that my father's comment apparently was, well, for tomorrow and for the rest of the Irish tour they were going to black out the faces of Queen Victoria and the Prince of Wales and this was going to be an entry of an Indian rajah into Aggra.[54]

The need to 'sell' film, rather than rely on the habitual behaviour of potential picture-goers, was deeply ingrained from the start, and was reflected in the elaborate language used to describe the machinery by which images were projected and the pictures themselves. Where necessary, the thesaurus was systematically plundered to convey an appropriate sense of occasion. One notice for Edison's New Animated Pictures at Edinburgh's Operetta House in December 1901 employed the adjective 'wonderful' on four occasions, alongside such terms as 'gorgeous', 'costly', and 'spectacular', culminating in an encomium to the 'Most Wonderful, Curious, Amazing, Mystifying, Humorous, and Interesting Animated Pictures ever presented'.[55]

Enthusiastic advocates of 'showmanship' could also be found among the final group of cinema promoters to demand our attention, the managers and proprietors of local theatres and music halls. Arthur Hubner quickly came to appreciate the commercial potential of the cinematograph when manager of the Real Ice Skating Palace, the house at which moving pictures made their Glasgow debut. He was thus keen to ensure that it figured prominently in the entertainments at the various houses under his charge, including the Britannia Music Hall in the Trongate and the Hippodrome on Sauchiehall Street, the successor to the Ice Skating Palace. Here, from 1903, Hubner staged one of the earliest attempts to make film the principal attraction at an evening's entertainment at a Glasgow theatre.[56] The arts of showmanship reached new heights with the man who took over management of the Britannia from Hubner in 1906, A. E. Pickard. In addition to the Britannia, renamed the Panopticon, this self-styled 'King of Clydebank', 'Cardinal of Cowcaddens', 'Archbishop of Anderston', and 'Raja of Rothesay', among others, also ran the nearby Museum and Waxworks, making up 'The Cheapest Amusement resort on Earth'. Here, the diversions ranged from the mummified body of a cat to life-like reproductions of such luminaries as the Prime Minister, Sir Henry Campbell-Bannerman, and Dr Crippen, alongside such curiosities as Tom Thumb – 'The Most Diminutive Prodigy in Existence', The Bear Woman – 'The Most Curious Freak on Earth', and The Original Half-Lady. By 1914, Pickard ran five cinemas in and around Glasgow.[57]

The films which Pickard, Hubner, and their like endeavoured to 'exploit' varied markedly, ranging from sober actuality to surreal fantasy. Even in cinema's earliest days, longer films were not unknown. For example, footage of Queen Victoria's Diamond Jubilee procession in 1897 was edited together to form a presentation lasting some twenty minutes.[58] However, most subjects produced during cinema's first decade were brief, a product of technical limitations in the recording and editing of pictures, as well as perceptions of audience preferences. A key element in early programmes was the presentation of local scenes. The attraction such footage held for early cinema-goers has been examined by Vanessa Toulmin and Martin Loiperdinger, who note the appeal of the immediate and the familiar, sometimes extending to a recognition of individuals or, at its most immediate, the self on the screen.[59] From the first, Scottish exhibitors recognised and sought to exploit the attractions of the local in their programmes. In their earliest advertisements, William Walker and Co. made much of the cinematograph's ability to capture 'Scenes from Everyday Life' showing 'Actual Movements of Real Life'. Local scenes thus figured prominently in its programmes at the end of the nineteenth century. These encompassed material that had resonance beyond the immediate area, such as footage of the Braemar Gathering in 1897 or the Gordon Highlanders leaving their barracks, a subject that could be revived whenever patriotic emotions required stirring.[60] Yet the local could also be highly specific, as on Walker's visit to Huntly in 1899, when the films included scenes of a military inspection at Inverurie 'in which Huntly men were easily discerned'. Equally, the programme for a concert in aid of the benevolent fund for the local branch of the National Union of Dock Labourers included scenes of the Hospital Saturday procession, in which union members had featured. Advertising copy exploited the appeal of the familiar by stressing the possibility of seeing yourself as others saw you. For a concert at Aberdeen's Music Hall in October 1898, Walker's publicised the showing of local pictures, posing the question, oft repeated subsequently, 'Have You Been Cinematographed?'[61] The following year, footage of the cycle parade of employees at McKinnon's engineering works was seen to arouse considerable interest as 'it was quite evident that some of the actual participants in the parade were amongst the audience, and had the unique experience of "seeing themselves as others saw them"'. Nor was identification left to chance. A show at Banchory Town Hall in April 1900 included footage of the local Gordon Volunteers, their names being read out as they appeared on the screen.[62]

If the commissioning and production of local films was an obvious marketing strategy for exhibitors whose sphere of operations, initially at least, was confined to a particular geographical area, it was also undertaken by concerns whose activities were more national in scope. Firms renting halls for any length of time found that the inclusion of local material was important if they were to attract the necessary level of support. During its stay at Edinburgh's Empire Theatre in 1899, the American Biograph included film of a military review in the city's Inverleith Park. Similarly, New Century Pictures sought to maximise interest by including scenes that appealed for their immediacy and topicality. So, at Edinburgh's Operetta House, where until 1903 the company operated as Edison's Animated Pictures, programmes depicted local citizenry at work and play. On one bill, they were to be seen leaving work, attending a cup tie between Hibernian and Dundee at Easter Road, walking along Princes Street, and enduring 'Waverley Steps on a Windy Day'.[63] By such means was the seemingly humdrum character of everyday life transformed into matter for general interest and amusement.

Exploitation of the local continued into cinema's second decade. In June 1908, audiences at Clydebank's Gaiety Theatre were invited to 'Come and See Yourself on the Filmograph', while the hall's proprietor, the redoubtable A. E. Pickard, worked to encourage a close identification with the wider community by giving prominence on several programmes to 'factory-gate' films. In November of the same year, a leading attraction was 'John Brown and Co.'s Employees Leaving the Clydebank Shipyard'.[64] With the spread of dedicated picture houses from 1910, the importance of the local was, if anything, confirmed. Even circuits based outside Scotland, such as Provincial Cinematograph Theatres, which opened houses in central Glasgow and Edinburgh in the years to 1914, recognised the need to supply audiences with familiar images. At the opening of the combine's Picture House on Sauchiehall Street in December 1910, it was noted that 'A special feature will be made of current local events', while local topicals were also produced for patrons of the New Picture House on Edinburgh's Princes Street from November 1913. All tended to confirm the view expressed by the Scottish correspondent of *The Bioscope* in March 1911 that 'The ideal show, I hold, ought always to embrace at least one up-to-date and specially taken local event.'[65]

Conversely, the absence of 'local' footage had the potential seriously to compromise a show's chances of success. Alexander Mathieson's difficulties at Broxburn did not begin with the failure of the cinematograph apparatus. Takings for the night were estimated at a mere £1, insufficient even to meet the cost of hiring the hall, put at £1 17s 6d, including 7s 6d for the hire of the piano. Although the programme provided by Calverto included Méliès' *Trip to the Moon*, this was by the autumn of 1903 a familiar and well-worn subject and it is difficult not to conclude that the lack of more distinctive footage may have worked against Mathieson.[66]

Not surprisingly, then, exhibitors were keen to employ showmanship to exploit a preference for the immediate and the familiar. Few were as inventive as Arthur Hubner, who, in January 1904, announced to audiences at the Sauchiehall Street Hippodrome the concealment of a cheque for £20, payable by the Commercial Bank of Scotland, at a location on the outskirts of the city. As an aid to its discovery and an inducement to people to attend performances at the Hippodrome, the programme through the week was to include 'Animated Pictures of the Treasure Ground and its surroundings'. After two weeks, a notice announced the discovery of the prize by a man from Thornliebank.[67] In addition to providing the subject for such occasional 'stunts', the local became a powerful tool for marketing film more generally. So, in common with houses elsewhere, local topicals were central to the programmes at Aberdeen's Gaiety Picture House from its opening in September 1908. Here, however, the proprietor Dove Paterson sought to add further local colour, exploiting his previous experience as an elocutionist by supplying his own bespoke 'soundtrack'. This was not performed alone but with the assistance of a female voice artiste, Miss Marie Pascoe, soon to become Mrs Paterson.[68] The use of male and female speakers suggests that the aim was to interpolate dialogue into each picture, offering an interpretation of plot that extended beyond the mere recitation of intertitles. So effective was this approach seen to be that *The Bioscope* observed that 'it is often hard to say which attracts the crowds, the elocutionary efforts of Mr and Mrs Paterson, or the pictures'.[69] Certainly, the idea enjoyed sufficient success to encourage another husband and wife team to emulate the Patersons. In early 1911, Bert Gates transformed the East End Mission in Aberdeen into the Star Picture House. Here, along with his wife Nellie, Gates 'spoke to' the pictures for the better part of two decades, spicing the dialogue with references to local personalities and events.[70] The value which attached to the elocutionist's art in rendering a variety of subjects into the Doric was reflected in relative rates of pay. The Aberdeen Picture Palaces, Ltd, which ran both the Star and the Globe cinemas by 1914, paid its female elocutionists 50 per cent more than its female pianists, a weekly rate of 30s for the former compared with 20s a week for the latter, in 1915.[71]

The importance of the elocutionists may have rested in part on their ability to manage the often abrupt transition between different items on the programme. A key point here is that the local was never seen in isolation. Early programmes often juxtaposed scenes of the immediate area with footage of events at some distance. On occasion, the two could dovetail neatly into a single overarching narrative, so that the images of Banchory's Gordon Volunteers, at which individuals were mentioned by name, formed part of a broad patriotic pageant staged by Walker and Co., in the early months of the Boer War, entitled 'The Fight for the Flag'. Here, the locality was placed within the wider imperial effort. At other times, the linkages were more implicit, so that the footage of Edinburgh at work and play exhibited at the Operetta House in February 1903 sat alongside images of the Delhi Durbar, comprising 'Miles and Miles of Jewelled Elephants', and of a journey across Canada. In this instance, the audience was navigated through the various subjects not only by the band of the 17th Lancers but by the explanations afforded by Mr Lester King, who also performed baritone song solos.[72] Lecturers were often key figures in early cinematograph shows, their significance reflected in the attention accorded them in publicity material. The success of the Modern Marvel Co.'s annual visits to Edinburgh around Christmas and New Year in the early years of the century owed much to the firm's 'raconteur and manager', T. J. West.[73] At times, lecturers received almost as much attention as the films they were employed to describe. So, in May 1910, West staged an exhibition of still and animated photographs marking the life of the recently deceased Edward VII. The person entrusted with commenting on the life and times of the late king was a former London County Councillor, Director of the Tropical Institute at Liverpool University, and Irish peer, William Geoffrey Bouchard de Montmorency, 6th Viscount Mountmorres. For Mountmorres, film lectureship represented but a brief phase in a varied public career: his expository skills would later be applied to an altogether higher purpose in the service of the Church. The following year, Mountmorres returned to Edinburgh, on this occasion it would appear operating on his own account, to present films of the recently crowned King George V. The show attracted an appreciative notice in *The Scotsman*, which remarked on how the lecturer did

> not allow the pictures to speak for themselves. He possess [*sic*] the gift of vivid description, and his running commentary on every depicted item in the lives of the King, the Queen, the Prince of Wales, and Princess Mary is not only happily phrased, but always interesting and instructive.[74]

At times, the nature of the cinema programme, with its juxtaposition of diverse subjects, made serious demands on the lecturer's art. For example, at the Operetta House in March 1901, footage of Queen Victoria's funeral procession was immediately followed by scenes from the Scottish Cup semi-final between Hibernian and Heart of Midlothian at Tynecastle, although the 1–1 scoreline may have assisted in maintaining a broadly neutral tone.[75]

The varied and frequently disconnected nature of early programmes raises questions about audience response. In this respect, it may be significant that picture-goers may already have become habituated to such a mode of presentation via the popular press. Mass-circulation magazines from the 1880s, such as *Tit-Bits* or *Answers to Correspondents*, offered their readers a diet of random snippets of information with little if any attempt to draw out any links between them. Their tendency to present narratives in highly specific and personal terms provided a further overlap with the world of moving pictures.[76] The 'language' of early cinema was thus familiar to members of the audience, enabling this new entertainment form to reach out to a wide and varied constituency.

The settings for film shows also provide powerful, if indirect, evidence of the extent of cinema's appeal in these early years. Advertisements stressed the capacity of the moving image to adapt to a variety of settings. Walker and Co. made much of their use at 'After-Dinner and Drawing-Room Parties, Bazaars or Fund-raising Exhibitions', while Lizars pointed to the cinematograph's popularity at 'Bazaars, Concerts, or Evening Parties'.[77] That moving pictures could be conceived as flourishing in both private and public settings reflected the varied ways in which they could be encountered. Historians of early cinema have rightly emphasised that there was nothing inevitable about the medium's emergence as an entertainment exhibited in public spaces to large numbers of people simultaneously. In the late 1890s, alternative modes of viewing were available, including the Mutoscope, a peep-show arrangement by which short subjects could be seen by individual spectators. In Scotland, the Mutoscope made its public debut during the Christmas season of 1897, when theatrical impresario H. E. Moss included a number of machines at his Carnival on Edinburgh's Waverley Market. Here, entertainment and science coalesced in a manner familiar to late-Victorian pleasure-seekers, so that the Mutoscope shared billing with the Cinématographe, a demonstration of Röntgen X-rays, the Indian Liliputians, each no more than 28 inches high, and 'The Imperial Baby Incubators, with Living Babies', the latter a development of wider interest in a period of stubbornly high levels of infant mortality.[78] The success of the Mutoscope, drawing an average of 31s a day per machine over the course of the Carnival, led to the flotation in February 1898 of the Scottish Mutoscope Co., Ltd, which aimed to rent out some 1,000 such machines at a charge of £20 each. By June, some sixty-two machines had been installed across Glasgow.[79] Yet for all its apparent early success, the Mutoscope quickly faded from the scene, re-emerging in less propitious circumstances at the opening ceremony of Glasgow's International Exhibition of 1901, when a restless horse caused one to fall on a member of a local Boys' Brigade troop. Within months, the Scottish Mutoscope Co., was wound up in a general restructuring of the business of the British Mutoscope and Biograph Co., of which it was a part.[80] How close the company came to meeting its target of 1,000 machines is not known, but if the Scottish experience reflected that of the British business as a whole, it would have fallen resoundingly short.

By 1900, more certain returns were promised by the exhibition of moving pictures to large collectivities, capitalising on broader trends in the market for commercial leisure: in particular, growing access to wider forms of recreation produced by improved living standards over the later decades of the nineteenth century and greater acceptance of leisure in the public sphere among groups which had previously evinced a deep suspicion of such pursuits due to their perceived associations with idleness and the non-productive use of time.

From its earliest days, the cinematograph and its equivalents fitted readily into this burgeoning recreational culture. In Aberdeen and district, operators mounted shows in a diversity of venues, taking in halls within and beyond the city, churches, schools, and, on occasion, private residences. As an example of the latter, in January 1898 Sir Allan and Lady Mackenzie organised an entertainment for the local tenantry at Brackly House that incorporated Walker and Co.'s cinematograph.[81] Moving pictures quickly came to form a central element in the gatherings of many organisations, from local bodies such as the Aberdeen Highland Association, to branches of national organisations, including the YMCA, the Oddfellows, and the Primrose League.[82] Their pervasive presence provides a clear indication of the cinematograph's social reach and its capacity to transcend established political, cultural, and economic points of difference. The suggestion is then that the early audience for moving pictures was socially diverse. It has, however, been argued that by the early years of the new century, cinema's following was more unambiguously working-class in character. Certainly, at times, the industry's reputation suffered as entrepreneurs with little experience of the trade offered entertainments on technically deficient equipment, often making use of elderly, exhausted film stock. Mathieson's misfortunes at Broxburn were thus seen by the local press to be symptomatic of wider problems within the industry, so that his show was seen to constitute 'Another Confidence Trick' perpetrated on the public.[83] Yet despite such setbacks, the broader picture, reflected in the venues used for cinema shows across the medium's first decade, suggests that its wide social appeal was substantially maintained.

The prominence of the fairground in early exhibitions of moving pictures has often been taken as evidence of cinema's ready integration within contemporary working-class culture. Yet the fair was part of an older but still vital leisure calendar based upon the seasons. Its precise function varied over place and time. Many had been occasions for the trading of local produce or the hiring of agricultural labour. Across much of rural Scotland, the hiring fair as a mechanism for the recruitment of farm labour retained its utility into the early twentieth century. On such occasions, workers, having received payment at the end of their contracts, usually extending over six months, had money to spend on a range of diversions, so that the fair came to represent a powerful confluence of business and pleasure. Elsewhere, it had come to fulfil a more purely recreational function, as was the case with the Marymass Fair at Irvine, where the event marked the commencement of the local holidays.[84] Whatever their precise function, fairs punctuated the year, expressing and promoting a close sense of attachment to the locality, which, temporarily at least, held in abeyance everyday points of difference based on economic status or cultural outlook. The fair was thus accessible to rich and poor, respectable and rough. Not all found the promiscuous diet of entertainments on offer equally congenial. The respectable mid Victorian artisan John Sturrock frequented Dundee's fairs in the 1850s, although rarely going so far as to venture within booths that promised diversions as varied as a revivalist preacher, a 'wonderfully large pig' capable of jumping through a hoop, and a man whose speciality was the skinning of live rats with his teeth.[85] By the end of the century, the cinematograph was one of a more decorous range of amusements still capable of drawing in a socially mixed audience.

Across urban Scotland, the spirit of the fairground lived on in the variety theatres and music halls that sprang up over the later decades of the nineteenth century. Here, the moving image, appearing in various guises, became a fixture from the later 1890s. In Glasgow, the Empire Palace, the Coliseum, the Palace, the Tivoli and Queen's Theatres, along with the Scottish Zoo and Hippodrome, and the Britannia Music Hall, all made regular mention of the Bioscope and its near relations on their bills. The prominence given to film varied over time. Depictions of public events of national or local significance received extensive publicity. Particular attention was paid to affairs of monarchy, as royal events from funerals to coronations and provincial tours received extensive coverage.[86] More often the moving image, conveyed via machines whose diversity was reflected in their varied nomenclature (Bioscope, Biograph, Bio-Motograph, Animatograph, Vivascope, Edisonograph, etc.), formed part of an exotic bill of fare. This comprised acts that varied from the musical (Sid Bendon, the Singing Goalkeeper; Maggie Walsh, the Original Lancashire Singing Mill Girl; The Musical Shipbuilders; and The Ten Loonies, a group of self-ascribed 'mad musicians'), to the acrobatic (The Bouncing Dillons; The Donatos, Marvellous One-Legged Acrobats; Zarmo the Quaint – the Upside Down Juggler), alongside animal acts (Professor Duncan's Dog Orchestra; Billy, the Horse with the Human Brain; Captain Woodward's Performing Seals and Sea Lions – 'They can do everything but talk'), and novelty acts, concerned to exploit new technologies (Lydia and Albino, Electrical Gymnasts; Dr Walford Bodie, MD's The Electrocuted Man). In addition were acts that recalled the world of the freak show. Testing the boards of many Glasgow theatres and demonstrating in the process the latent entertainment potential of morbid obesity were Johnny Trunley, the Fat Boy of Peckham, weighing in at 10 stone at the age of five, and his local counterpart, Charlie Dunbar, the Clydebank Fat Boy, 4 ft 3 inches in height and some 12 lb heavier than Master Trunley. Of greater significance for this book, Dunbar secured wider celebrity as part of Bostock and Wombwell's touring Menagerie. In May 1906, the Bioscope at the Scottish Zoo and Hippodrome, owned by Bostock, included footage of 'A Day in Cornwall with Bostock and Wombwell's Menagerie including a Special Picture of the Clydebank Fat Boy', raising the possibility of Charlie Dunbar being seen as Scotland's first cinema star.[87]

Available evidence does not allow a detailed reconstruction of the social composition of Variety Theatre audiences. However, its likely income range is suggested by prices, which, in most houses, varied between 6d and 3s. A useful point of comparison is provided by the Whitevale Theatre, located in

Glasgow's poorer east end and opened by the Green family in 1904. Here, seats were available for between 4d and 1s 6d.[88] Most houses, it would appear, attracted audiences among which there was a sizeable presence of the wealthier sort. For them, moving pictures provided an enduring attraction, to such a degree that most of Glasgow's variety theatres took out cinematograph licences from 1910.[89]

A further indication of early cinema's capacity to attract middle-class patronage is provided by developments in legitimate theatre. At Glasgow's Metropole, managed by Arthur Jefferson, an evening of live drama usually concluded with a series of moving pictures. Indeed, over time, the presentation of stage performances at the Metropole became imbued with a quest for realism that reflected an almost cinematic aesthetic. So, a production of *Man to Man* in September 1908 was advertised as including 'The Realistic Railway Smash!', while in the following March much was made of the authentic effects provided for the staging of *Driven from Home*, which included a 'Real Circular Saw'.[90] Elsewhere, cinema's impact was even more direct. In May 1908, Glasgow's Royalty Theatre announced a short season of moving pictures, with Gaumont's Chronomegaphone offering synchronised sound, while in August 1909, the Franco-British Picture Co. opened at the Lyceum in Govan. One year later, the Grand Theatre in Glasgow announced its reopening as a picture house.[91] The impact of these changes varied. Within two years, animated pictures at the Grand were confined to a period prior to the raising of the curtain, while from 1914 the Royalty was reconfigured as a theatre combining pictures and variety and renamed the Lyric.[92] The progressive infiltration of cinematic practices and images into the theatre indicates an audience receptive to and accepting of moving pictures. In Scotland at least, cinema's ability to draw on a respectable middle-class following pre-dated the coming of the picture palace.

Such findings take on additional significance, given the apparent absence of a sizeable sector of shop-front shows or 'penny gaffs' operating across urban Scotland in the first decade of the century. Conducted for the most part from small premises, and charging a nominal admission fee, so requiring a large number of shows to generate a return, such ventures have been identified as playing a key role in the development of film exhibition in the United States, and have been detected in areas of London, where they are seen to have constituted a submerged, popular form of cinema.[93] Although concerns were voiced in the Edwardian period over the impact of cheap picture shows, these do not appear to have been directed at anything that could justifiably be described as a 'nickelodeon' or 'penny gaff' operation. In 1913, the Glasgow Labour periodical *Forward* responded to what it perceived to be a campaign to restrict popular amusements across the city. Prominent in this movement was the local parish council, which some years before had undertaken an inquiry into the nature of moving picture shows, more especially in the east end. Much had been made of the make-up of the audience which 'in all cases is representative of the LOWER WORKING CLASS, and comprises all ages from the <u>unwashed infant</u> in its DIRTY MOTHER's arms to the elderly modeller'. (Emphases in original)[94] The date on which these original observations were made is unclear. Although *Forward* placed it five years earlier, in 1908, it was only in October 1910 that the parish council approached the city's magistrates on this question.[95] It is difficult to determine, therefore, how far the parish council's findings reflect conditions in the trade before rather than after the passage of the Cinematograph Act of 1909, which came into force on the first day of 1910 and which enforced stricter regulations on the conduct of film exhibitions. Even if the report is taken to pre-date the Act, the kind of operations being described seem somewhat removed from any that might be comprehended by the term 'penny gaff'. So, at one show, prices were noted to range between 1d and 6d, comparable to charges made at the Picture Palace opened by Ralph Pringle at Glasgow Cross in November 1907.[96] Although lower than the prices levied at local variety theatres, this was far from the uniform 1d charged for admission to cheap shows in London. What is more, most of the exhibitions surveyed by the parish council and discussed by the city magistrates operated on a two houses per night basis and so did not depend on the rapid turnover of patrons characteristic of the nickelodeon. Theatres operating in Glasgow's east end for which we have evidence had capacities considerably in excess of the 300 or so identified by Jon Burrows as typical of the London penny shows. Pringle's Picture Palace, for example, held over 1,000, while the nearby Whitevale Picturedrome, run by the Green family, could accommodate some 950.[97] While cheap theatres or 'geggies' flourished in many Scottish towns and cities from the nineteenth into the twentieth century, there is little evidence of a significant overlap with the world of the early picture show and certainly no indication that they provided the basis for an intermediate stage of development for the industry between the itinerant show and the fixed-site cinema house.[98]

If the absence of detailed documentation precludes any definitive statement as to the absence or otherwise of penny gaffs from the early history of Scottish cinema exhibition, their failure to endure into the more regulated phase of the industry's development under the 1909 Act, a period in which penny shows are seen to have flourished in London, is at least suggestive. Certainly, any attempt to exhibit films on nickelodeon lines seems to have been short-lived. In November 1908, the Glasgow magistrates gave permission for Norman Macleod Allan of Pollokshields to open a venue at 28 Argyle Street comprising coin-operated phonographs, animated picture machines, and stereoscopes fitted with peephole lenses.[99] Six years later, this became the site of the Vaudeville Picture House, which charged a standard admission fee of 3d for a programme lasting half an hour. Within a matter of weeks, however, the Vaudeville had adopted the two-hour programme typical of many other Glasgow houses.[100]

The penny gaff's absence north of the border may have owed something to the availability of other cheap sources of amusement. From the middle of the nineteenth century, the Abstainers' Union in Glasgow had supported regular Saturday concerts, and these were augmented from the 1870s by the series organised by the Good Templars Harmonic Association and, from the 1890s, by one run under the auspices of the City Corporation itself.[101] Although envisaged as vehicles for 'rational recreation', promoting improving alternatives to the debauched diversions offered by neighbouring public houses, these concerts often employed those itinerant troupes whose wider careers have already been noted. The Good Templars, at various times in the early years of the twentieth century, offered 'Prince' Bendon's concert party, as well as Arthur Hubner's Animatograph.[102] By 1910, cinematograph companies, including BB Pictures, Lizars' Imperial Bioscope, Hunter's Royal Bioscope, and the Royal Canadian Animated Picture Co., were installed at most corporation halls across the city, providing shows each Saturday at prices as low as 1d. In all, by the outbreak of the First World War, fifteen corporation-run halls were licensed for cinematograph shows. With an average capacity of 1,500, they did much both to stimulate and to satisfy local demand for cinema.[103] They may also be seen to have played a key role in influencing the nature of the audience for film in the first decade of the century.

As is the case with most mass leisure pursuits, descriptions of those in attendance remain few and far between. Nevertheless, the presence of large numbers of young men among the crowds at Edinburgh's Operetta House attracted the attention of the city's Licensing Committee in 1903. Here, the house's appeal lay less, it was thought, in the programmes of films on offer and more with its possession of a drinks licence, reflecting its former career as a variety theatre. The presence of women behind the bar was a further inducement to frequent the hall, so that the magistrates were drawn to conclude 'that there should be men employed in place of women, when there would be no temptation to young men to hang about the bars as they did at the present time'.[104] Beyond that, the insights afforded by available sources are frustratingly few. However, they do suggest that the concerts staged by town councils and societies advocating measures of moral reform tapped a new audience for popular entertainment. Many were held on Saturday afternoons, when working-class Scottish males indulged their passion for sport, and charging a nominal entrance fee, they appear to have generated a substantial and significant female following. The tendency for women to attend such concerts unaccompanied or, as contemporary wisdom had it 'unprotected', by their men-folk was noted in 1900 and confirmed by later reports such as that of the Glasgow Parish Council. In response to the charge that this left them open to demoralisation, one widowed mother of eight pointed to the change in her life brought about by access to cheap film shows: 'Prior to their advent, poverty kept me from getting any entertainment; now I can get to a picture show every week for twopence, my children for a penny.'[105] The latter observation was of particular significance, for it was cinema's ability to appeal to the young that so impressed contemporaries. Writing to Glasgow's *Evening Citizen* in 1908, 'East End' described shows which served up a regular diet of 'murder and other nervous subjects' as 'the Mecca of every youngster who can get a copper'.[106] The correspondents of Glasgow's Parish Council also made much of the presence at cheap shows of infants in the arms of older children, justifying the conclusion that 'the main portion of the gallery is composed of children'.[107] Calls to regulate children's attend-ance at film shows across Scotland, which were made forcefully in the years to 1914, provide further, albeit indirect evidence of the comparative youth of the moving picture audience.

For much of its first decade, the cinema's ability to exploit the emergent mass leisure market had been constrained by issues of price and related problems of film supply. Such obstacles were only overcome towards the end of the first decade of the twentieth century, so that the years from 1910 would witness what some have seen as a new phase in cinema's development, marked by the emergence and proliferation of the fixed-site picture house. It is to those changes and the factors underlying them that we now turn.

III

The surge in investment in film exhibition and distribution in the five years leading to the outbreak of the First World War was marked. Across Britain, Board of Trade returns, as reported in *The Bioscope*, reported only three picture theatre companies formed in 1908. The following year, this rose to 103 and, in 1910, to 295, before accelerating further to reach 464 in 1912.[108] Scotland appears to have participated fully in this growth. Of the eighty-five venues licensed for cinema shows across Glasgow in 1913, at least thirty-five had only commenced operations from 1910. Rates of company formation showed few signs of slowing in the final pre-war months and may even have reached new heights. Certainly, the valuation of cinemas approved by Glasgow's Dean of Guild Court, which oversaw all plans for new erections and alterations to existing structures, reached a new high of £57,523 in 1913–14.[109] The result of this investment was immediate and obvious, even if it did not meet with universal favour. One week in Glasgow sufficed to convince Peter Macaskill, a draper from Fort William, subject of a fictional sketch by Neil Munro, that 'There's nothing yonder to be seen but picture-palaces. I went to them even on, day after day, and I can tell you I was sick o' them!'[110]

In explaining the rise of the dedicated picture house, importance attaches, for some, to the first generation of itinerant and fairground exhibitors. In Scotland, the prominence of the Green, Kemp, and Poole families, to name but a few, among the leading cinema proprietors of the immediate pre-war period, suggests the importance of showmen to the industry's continued evolution.[111] Yet the evidence suggests that fairground exhibitors rarely took the lead in the development of fixed-site theatres and were more often to be found following an established trend. For example, the Green family's move into exhibition from a dedicated site was, by comparison with others, slow. In March 1904, they opened the Whitevale Theatre, offering the people of Glasgow's east end, 'at the smallest cost, and with the greatest comfort and safety, all the leading and best Plays now before the public'.[112] At between 4d and 1s 6d, seats at the Whitevale were cheaper than those available in houses further west, but above those that would apply later in the decade at most of the city's first cinemas. The difference reflected the Greens' use of the Whitevale for live performances. There is no evidence in its first year, and in contrast to practices at other houses such as the Metropole, that animated pictures formed a regular or even occasional feature of the bill. Towards the end of the first month, the entertainment was supplemented by 'snapshots' of the area around the theatre, and accompanied by the promise that 'anyone recognising his or her own photograph in the view [would be] handsomely rewarded'.[113] This exercise in what would appear to have been the use of still photography was not repeated. The Whitevale thus functioned as a distinct branch in the Greens' amusement business until at least 1908, at which point the hall was transformed into a moving picture and variety theatre.[114] By then, the potential profitability of such a venture had been demonstrated by Ralph Pringle's Picture Palace in nearby Watson Street and the opening of BB Pictures at the Wellington Palace. Thereafter, while the Greens came to develop interests in a variety of fixed sites, this process only commenced from late 1910, by which point the picture-house boom locally was well under way.[115] It should also be noted that the family's cinemas operated alongside rather than in place of its travelling shows. Green's cinematographs continued to feature on fairgrounds up to 1914, until the death of one of his sons persuaded George Green to place all the firm's travelling shows on the market.[116] If the Greens may be said to have followed rather than initiated the trend towards dedicated cinemas, the same is also true of 'President' Kemp, who funded the building of a picture theatre in Johnstone late in 1912, following two years in which he had tested the local appetite for moving pictures during his lease of the town hall.[117]

Whatever the importance of showmen in instilling the principles and practices of exploitation in the trade, their role in promoting organisational change is more open to doubt. It might be noted that itinerant exhibitors, who encountered different audiences on their travels, had less need than most of a regular change in programme to maintain interest in their offerings. The demand created for a greater volume of film production and a more developed distribution network to maintain a supply of subjects that would enable a regular change in programme originated primarily from firms operating from fixed sites. In the early years of the century, the capacity to sustain prolonged seasons was confined to concerns whose national scope permitted them access to a wide range of materials. At Edinburgh's Operetta House, shows were offered virtually all year round, first by The Thomas Edison Animated Photo Co. and then, following a successful legal challenge to the use of the Edison name, the National Pioneer Animated Photo Co.[118] As offshoots of New Century Pictures, both had access to a substantial body of films, a point regularly emphasised in advertising copy, which made reference to '10,000 Animated Pictures' and which stressed that 'Material changes are made in the programme nightly'.[119] The suggestion is that it was only with the spread of exhibition from fixed sites that a more elaborate network of film distribution would develop.

More direct insights into the factors promoting the acceleration in picture-house construction are afforded by surviving business records, which help to establish the sources of capital that went to fund such ventures. Here again, the contribution of those already active in the trade or indeed in the entertainment business more generally appears to have been slight. This is indicated by details on the directors and shareholders of some forty-six cinema companies established across Scotland between December 1909 and July 1914. While most were located in or close to the central belt, the sample also includes flotations from as far north as Invergordon on the Cromarty Firth.[120] Of the companies surveyed, only thirteen had board members who had an identifiable connection with the entertainment trade. If expressed in terms of board personnel, the presence is further diluted. Those with links to the amusements industry accounted for a mere 19 out of 154 company directors in the sample as a whole. Most were established cinema proprietors, such as J. J. Bennell of The BB Pictures, Ltd, and A. E. Pickard of Glasgow Electric Theatres, Ltd.[121] However, those responsible in some form for the provision of the entertainment were also present. So, the board of The Palace (Arbroath), Ltd, included a music hall artiste, while a pianist was among the directors of The Highland Cinematograph and Variety Co., Ltd, while an operator (projectionist) figured on the board of The Shettleston Premier Picture Theatre Co., Ltd, in Glasgow.[122] The pattern of share ownership conveys a similar impression. Rarely more than one or two individuals with interests in the entertainments sector figure in the lists returned to the Companies' Register. Exceptional clusters appear at The Highland Cinematograph and Variety Co., Ltd, which made three allotments to pianists, one of whom was female, and two to operators, and BB Pictures, Ltd, whose stock was taken up by several figures in the cinema trade, including T. J. West, formerly of the Modern Marvel Co., Ltd, an operator based in Glasgow, and a pianist/lecturer from Airdrie.[123] Despite all this, the evidence points ineluctably to the conclusion that the capital which funded the first wave of cinema building across Scotland came from outside the moving picture business itself.

In tracing the social background of investors in or directors of early cinema companies, a clear contrast with another popular leisure pursuit becomes apparent. Wray Vamplew has found that substantial minorities of both board members and shareholders of Scottish football league clubs were drawn from the local working class. Predominantly drawn from skilled or semi-skilled workers, they accounted for just under half of all share owners and held around a quarter of all shares.[124] They had no equivalent in the companies under review here. Although occupational designations provided in the Companies' Register are so sparse as to preclude precise ascription to a particular status group within the working class, most workers holding shares in local picture houses belonged to those supervisory grades which shaded, both materially and culturally, into the lower middle class. The job title most frequently encountered in the returns was 'warehouseman'. One foreman potter from Portobello held shares in two companies, The Kirkcaldy Picture House, Ltd, and The Palace (Edinburgh), Ltd.[125] Otherwise, the bulk of shareholders who might, on a generous definition, be designated 'working class' pursued careers in small-scale, independent trades as cabinet makers (four), plumbers (nine), tailors (one), and watch makers (five). Missing are the ranks of workers in heavy industry who figure prominently in most economic histories of Scotland for this period. That it is possible to discover two miners among the shareholders, one with a stake in The Armadale Picturedrome, Ltd, the other from Markinch in Fife, who acquired fifty shares in BB Pictures, Ltd, in 1910, merely serves to point up their broader absence.[126] Equally, the legion of domestics whose labours helped to sustain patterns of urban living across Scotland and who, in terms of age and gender, may be thought to have constituted an important source of support for local cinemas, were represented by one domestic servant who bought ten BB shares in the first allotment in 1910.[127] Their absence, along with that of other workers, may be variously explained. Most of the companies surveyed here were private, limiting the take-up of capital to relatives or close associates.[128] Yet even where opportunities were available, workers' propensity to invest in picture houses remained limited. So, BB Pictures offered its scrip for public sale and Bennell's enthusiasm for the cause of respectable and rational recreation, reflected in his advocacy of temperance and links with the ILP, may have been expected to generate support from like-minded elements within the working class. Certainly, it sufficed to induce Keir Hardie, along with his wife and son, to acquire 200 shares in the business late in 1910. Yet, more generally, worker involvement remained marginal. Those who could, on a broad definition, be ascribed working-class status accounted for just over 14 per cent of all allotments of shares, amounting in total to a mere 2.6 per cent of the firm's ordinary stock.[129] At all points, the contrast with the 'beautiful game' was marked. If the purchase of shares in a football club expressed deeper underlying loyalties often based on locality, investment in the cinema seems to have been driven by more openly commercial considerations, reflecting the rather different relationship that had developed between picture houses and their patrons. Allegiances were rather less fixed, so that a run of what were perceived to be poor programmes could induce audiences to seek their amusement elsewhere, whereas a succession of indifferent results on the football field may have excited exasperation, or worse, but rarely led to a wholesale shift in loyalties.

Beyond the importance of commercial calculations in decisions to invest in Scottish cinemas before 1914, other generalisations may be offered. So, it would appear that share capital was generated overwhelmingly from within national borders. Of 1,903 allotments made by 43 companies between 1909 and 1914, only 150 or 7.8 per cent were made to individuals beyond Scotland, the great majority of whom resided south of the border. Indeed, the only shareholder located beyond the British Isles was a Postal Commissioner in the Chinese Postal Service in Shanghai, who purchased 200 shares in the Central Picture House, Portobello, in 1914.[130] Within Scotland itself, local clusterings in share ownership were evident. So, sixty of the first ninety-four allotments made by the Aberdeen Picture Palaces, Ltd, were to people residing in the city. Equally, over half the allotments by the Dunfermline Cinema House, Ltd, were made locally.[131] Yet, in other instances, ownership was dispersed more widely across the country. Shares in both The Methil Picture Palace Co., Ltd, and The North of Scotland Cinematograph, Ltd, were held by individuals as far apart as Aberdeen and Stranraer. In each case, Glasgow figured prominently in the pattern of allotments, indicating a readiness to invest in businesses at some distance from the place of residence.[132] Surplus funds were thus being applied not just to boost recreational provision in the immediate locality, but in search of the best rate of return. The motives which induced a university lecturer from Glasgow to acquire shares in the Central Picture House in Portobello, or an assistant professor of mathematics from Liberton in Edinburgh to invest in The Methil Picture Palace Co., Ltd, must remain a matter for speculation, although some may be inclined to place confidence in the ability of the latter at least to calculate the relative rates of return generated by such holdings.[133] By contrast, the presence of women not in gainful employment beyond the home, and so presumably dependent on investment income, among the ranks of cinema shareholders appears altogether more suggestive. In all, 211 allotments or just over 11 per cent of the total were made to women designated as married, spinsters, or widows, making them perhaps the largest single group to hold stock in local picture houses in this period. Given the depressed state of the housing market in the years to 1914, it is plausible to suggest that the cinema represented one of the few forms of urban property that might be expected to yield adequate returns.[134] That may help to account for the fifty-three allotments made to women who had no occupational designation by The Scottish Electric Picture Palaces, Ltd, from June 1910. Twenty-four were to women resident outside Scotland, in places as diverse as Whitehaven and Twickenham, while those in Scotland were drawn from a wide area, covering Newton Stewart in the south-west to Dinnet in Aberdeenshire.[135]

Women were thus a significant presence in shareholders' lists dominated by a professional and commercial middle class attuned to the emergence of new investment opportunities. In all this, the solicitor was a key figure, crucial not only in expediting the formal business of company formation but also in advising clients of potentially profitable applications for their surplus funds. Solicitors figured on the boards of fifteen companies in the sample and held shares in thirty-three of the firms covered. Among the directors of The Scottish Electric Picture Palaces, Ltd on flotation were a solicitor, a jeweller, a theatrical manager, and a wholesale stationer. The prospectus of the company, inviting subscriptions from a wider public, clarifies the thinking driving its ambition. The firm proposed to construct eight halls across Scotland, claiming that there was 'an increasing demand for these entertainments, which can be provided to the public at admission charges well within the means of all'. Predictions of profitable business were based on the performance of the Ayr Picture Palace, acquired as a going concern, which had generated a sizeable surplus in its first twenty-two weeks of operation (£685 8s before tax). In setting out the prospects of planned houses, much was made of their intended situation and the rationale behind the choice of sites explained. All were to be close to major transport arteries, served by tram or train. Beyond the passing trade, the localities themselves displayed features which held out the prospect of success. As the company's architect explained, 'The inhabitants of these centres are composed mostly of the classes which, experience shows, will liberally patronise Cinematograph Theatres, and for which at present no such popular form of entertainment has been provided.' One site, at the corner of Glasgow's Cornwall and Park Streets, was deemed particularly favourable, located as it was 'in the centre of a densely populated working class district within a few yards and easily visible from Paisley Road tram car lines, the main route from Glasgow to Paisley and Govan'. Similarly, the projected hall in Port Glasgow was 'in the very centre of a large working class population where there are almost no recreations'.[136] Similar calculations applied elsewhere. In September 1913, the Tivoli on Edinburgh's Gorgie Road opened its doors with prices between 2d and 6d, geared explicitly to attracting a working-class clientele.[137] Overall, the audience for cinema remained socially diverse, so that picture houses could be found along the leading thoroughfares of Scotland's cities. The Palace, which opened in December 1913, thus became the fourth cinema along Edinburgh's Princes Street. In Aberdeen, the Electric Theatre in Union Street acquired new owners in September 1911. Here, in making their pitch for subscribers, the directors made much of the entertainment's attractions beyond the masses. It made, they argued, 'a forcible appeal to the pocket of the middle class public' by offering 'innocent entertainment of a high class and instructive character'.[138] The Scottish Electric Picture Palaces, Ltd also sought to accommodate this social mix, by varying its pricing according to the nature of the district in which its cinemas were located. So, as the company's prospectus explained, whereas prices in poorer areas could be as low as 2d, elsewhere they would be pitched higher at 6d to 1s.[139] The contrast with previous practice was marked. At the start of the decade, New Century Pictures had adopted a uniform pricing structure for its shows.[140] By 1910, however, the potential for cinema to reach out to a new mass audience was being recognised.

Economic conditions may be seen to have encouraged this shift in approach. If the later decades of the nineteenth century had witnessed consistent and marked improvements in living standards, the trend across the first years of the next century were rather less certain. Modest but sustained price inflation and short-lived but intense economic downturns threatened to reverse advances in material circumstances for many.[141] So, the heavy industries of the west of Scotland experienced a sharp contraction in activity from late 1907, which persisted through the following year. As late as 1910, the tonnage of shipping built on the Clyde remained considerably down on its pre-recession peak. Yet, as contemporaries were aware, the impact of the downturn was far from uniform. In August 1908, close to the trough of the cycle, *The Evening Times* in Glasgow published a cartoon in which a bemused Saint Mungo was confronted by notices offering different perspectives on the city's fortunes: so that 'Distress in the City', and 'Proposed Increase in Rates' were juxtaposed against 'Great Crowds at the Football Matches'.[142] Popular entertainments displayed a marked resilience in the downturn of 1908–9. Indeed, this was the point at which Ralph Pringle began to offer regular film shows at low prices at his Picture Palace and, from March 1908, his Bijou Picture Hall in Cowcaddens, and from which Bennell's Bright and Beautiful Pictures were launched from the Wellington Palace.[143] Not only this, we have noted earlier the tendency for legitimate theatres to offer moving pictures in place of more expensive live performances. The experience of cyclical depression in the Edwardian period may well have demonstrated to a public deprived of alternative investment openings the potential for profit inherent in the moving picture business, preparing the ground for the wave of investment which transformed the industry once recovery in the wider economy set in. So, the advent of the picture palace, which has been presented as part of a bid for respectable, often middle-class patronage, may perhaps be more plausibly presented as a move to exploit a mass audience, in which the working class and more especially women and children were prominent.[144]

Surviving business records suggest that the expectation of profit that motivated many to acquire shares in cinemas was, for the most part, realised. The balance sheets of publicly floated companies recorded comfortable profit margins in the years to 1914. In 1912, for example, the West of Scotland Electric Theatres, Ltd, declared a net profit of £3,368 13s 11d, enabling payment of an interim dividend of 20 per cent, a decision repeated the following year.[145] More detailed accounts exist for one cinema, part of the growing

chain owned by R. V. Singleton. The records do not allow precise identification of the hall, although there are indications that they relate to the Paragon
Electric Theatre in Tobago Street, Glasgow, opened in 1910. Covering the last
twelve months to the outbreak of war in August 1914, the returns record each
day's receipts via the box office and provide a breakdown of the main items of
expenditure on a weekly basis. Taken together, they indicate a business operating almost consistently in the black. Indeed, in the fifty-three weeks covered
by the accounts, losses were recorded in two only. In each case, the lapse into
deficit could be ascribed to particular circumstances: additional payments to
staff in Christmas week 1913 raised expenditure by a third, producing a loss
of £3 8s 8d, while reduced business in the first days of war meant that for the
first week of the conflict, the hall showed a deficit of £1 1s 3d. Otherwise, the
Paragon ran a regular surplus on an average weekly turnover of £32 6s.[146] The
success of such a moderately sized business owed much to limited running
costs, a point of which much was made in company prospectuses. That for
The Scottish Electric Picture Palaces, Ltd was not unusual in emphasising the
company's ability to generate profits while charging low admission prices.
The circle was squared by the removal of any need to pay the salary of live
performers, allowing significant savings to be made in overall costs.[147] A comparison with earlier itinerant shows captures the contrast. In 1903, Alexander
Mathieson had paid out an estimated £65 13s 6½d before commencing his
three-week tour of West Lothian and Lanarkshire. In this, the largest single
outlay was on the cost of hire of the halls (39.6 per cent of the total). For the
Paragon, rents and taxes absorbed 25 per cent of all expenditure. Mathieson's
need to publicise each show through dedicated bills also raised his advertising budget (16.2 per cent of all spending) above that of the fixed show of the
immediate pre-war period. Yet the key difference was, perhaps, the outlay of
£14 1s 3½d each week for the two entertainers on Mathieson's programme.
Had the tour proceeded, that cost would have risen to 37.7 per cent of the
whole, a figure further inflated if the £9 a week payable for the hire of film,
cinematograph apparatus, and operator is added. In that case, the total cost
of mounting quite a basic show would rise to 62 per cent of all expenditure.
For the Paragon, by contrast, the hire of film contributed a mere 16 per cent
to overall expenses.[148] To that degree, the economics of the industry had
been transformed, facilitating the provision of what the prospectus of The
Aberdeen Electric Theatre Co., Ltd characterised as 'elevating and inexpen-
sive entertainment'.[149]

Yet the degree to which the coming of the picture palace heralded a
fundamental departure in exhibition practices as a whole is more open
to question. Nicholas Hiley's work on the first wave of cinema building
indicates that established venues quickly gave way before the spread of the
dedicated picture house. Indeed, the suggestion is that by 1913 'purpose-
built cinemas' accounted for some 95 per cent of venues operating across
Britain.[150] The Scottish evidence, however, points to a more protracted and

piecemeal sequence of change. The continued presentation of films at variety and 'legitimate' theatres in the years preceding the outbreak of war has been noted. What is more, corporation concerts in Glasgow made increasing use of the cinematograph, as film's growing popularity was recognised. So, in contrast to the position found by Hiley in cities such as London and Leeds, where some 82 per cent and 88 per cent respectively of licences were held by purpose-built picture houses, the proportion in Glasgow in July 1913 was nearer 50 per cent.[151] The fortunes of the itinerant fairground shows were more varied. In July 1912, the absence of cinematograph booths from the annual Greenock Fair was linked to the opening of the local Picture Palace.[152] Elsewhere, the fairground show continued to thrive. The Green family's visit to Irvine's Marymass Fair in August 1911 proved to be their last, as the company opened the Picturedrome in the town the following year. Despite this, and the presence of a second house at the Empire Institute Hall, where pictures ran alongside such novelties as Mademoiselle Sarah's Marblesque Trio, offering the rather less than enticing 'Not Nude Statuary', Green's place on the fairground was filled by others. In 1912, it was reported, good business was done by cinematograph shows, including Biddall's Ghost Illusion, Manda's American Coliseum, and Paulo's Varieties, the latter of which incorporated cinema within a circus performance.[153] One year later, at what would prove to be the last pre-war Marymass Fair, Paulo's was joined by a new show, Dawson's Cinema De Luxe.[154] Far from marking a distinct and novel stage in the industry's development, the picture house represented a mode of film exhibition that worked alongside, supplementing and complementing, rather than supplanting existing practices. Such a perception guided firms in developing exhibition strategies. For example, the prospectus of The Scottish Electric Picture Palaces, Ltd, as well as outlining plans for the construction of eight halls, also declared the intention of providing 'touring entertainments in the less populous districts of the country, which experience shows to be highly remunerative'.[155]

IV

Up to 1914, then, the picture house represented but one of the ways in which Scots encountered moving pictures. By that date, the cinema's place in the national affections appeared secure. The notion that the movies would share the fate of more transitory popular pursuits, such as roller skating, was discounted over time, so that the question posed by *The Entertainer* in November 1913, 'has the picture theatre come to stay?', increasingly assumed a rhetorical tone.[156] Within two decades, the cinema had risen from the status of scientific curiosity to become an established part of the recreational calendar of large parts of the population. Its new position owed much to the manner in which it was able to embed itself within existing leisure forms. It was thus readily accommodated within an established pattern of living, a recreational round that in places had become part of everyday routine, but which elsewhere continued to be shaped by the changing seasons. The novelty, or modernity, it represented was thus tempered throughout by an appeal to the familiar. This was reinforced by the content of shows, in which the immediate was juxtaposed against wider national, imperial, and international perspectives. Enlarging on the social function of the picture house, *The Entertainer* made much of its role in altering perceptions:

> From the public-house and the billiard saloon, from the street corner, it is taking the people in to see the passing of those events that give a clearer outlook upon life and a larger horizon to those who, in former times, did not see beyond their own dim environment.[157]

Yet in exploring broader vistas, the cinema did not overlook the enduring appeal of the local, varying its focus where appropriate in a manner made familiar by the popular literature of the time. If the audience attracted by the moving picture was socially diverse, new sources of support were also tapped. The presence of large numbers of working-class women and children was widely noted and did much to justify the decision to calibrate the entertainment to the cheaper end of the market. The potential for profit offered by this new mass audience provided one of the principal stimulants to the surge in investment that resulted in the construction of large numbers of picture houses across Scotland from 1909. Much of this funding was speculative in character and was drawn from individuals with little experience or knowledge of the trade. To that extent, the industry's development was being shaped by forces beyond it.

Yet to privilege the influence of impersonal social and economic forces may also be to miss much. The cinema was integral to a recreational culture subject at all points to regulation through the working of the law. For film exhibitors, the legal framework within which they operated would determine the nature of the show, in particular the balance between film and live entertainment, the content of what was shown, the settings within which shows were mounted, and, to an increasing degree, the make-up of the audience at whom the programme was directed. It is to the development and impact of that regulatory regime that we next turn.

NOTES

1. National figures derived from *The Kinematograph Year Book Diary and Directory* (London, 1915 and 1916); Glasgow figures from Glasgow City Archives (hereafter GCA), D-OPW 61/5, List of Premises Licensed under the Cinematograph Act, 12 July 1913.
2. Low, *History of the British Film, 1906–1914*, p. 25.
3. *The Entertainer, Theatrical, Vaudeville, Musical, Social and Athletic*, 4 Oct. 1913, p. 13.

4. Elsaesser and Barker, *Early Cinema*, esp. ch. 1; Charney and Schwartz, *Cinema and the Invention of Modern Life*; Barnes, *Beginnings. 1894–1896*; for contemporary reactions, see C. Harding and S. Popple (eds), *In the Kingdom of Shadows: A Companion to Early Cinema* (London, 1996), esp. ch. 1.

5. M. Chanan, *The Dream That Kicks: The Prehistory and Early Years of Cinema in Britain*, 2nd edn (London, 1996); C. Musser, *The Emergence of Cinema: The American Screen to 1907* (Berkeley, Los Angeles, London, 1990), part one; V. Toulmin, '"Curios Things in Curios Places": Temporary Exhibition Venues in the Victorian and Edwardian Entertainment Environment', *Early Popular Visual Culture*, 4 (2006), pp. 113–37.

6. N. Hiley, '"Nothing More than a Craze": Cinema Building in Britain from 1909 to 1914', in A. Higson (ed.), *Young and Innocent? The Cinema in Britain, 1896–1930* (Exeter, 2002), pp. 111–27.

7. L. S. Sanders, '"Indecent Incentives to Vice": Regulating Films and Audience Behaviour from the 1890s to the 1910s', in Higson, *Young and Innocent?*, pp. 97–110; A. Shail, '"A Distinct Advance in Society": Early Cinema's "Proletarian Public Sphere" and Isolated Spectatorship in the UK, 1911–18', *Journal of British Cinema and Television*, 3 (2006), pp. 209–28; S. Hanson, *From Silent Screen to Multi-Screen: A History of Cinema Exhibition in Britain since 1896* (Manchester, 2007), pp. 25–9.

8. J. Burrows, 'Penny Pleasures: Film Exhibition in London during the Nickelodeon Era, 1906–1914' and 'Penny Pleasures II: Indecency, Anarchy and Junk Film in London's "Nickelodeons", 1906–1914', *Film History*, 16 (2004), pp. 60–91 and 172–97.

9. *Scotsman*, 13 April 1896, p. 1.

10. *The Bailie*, 13 May 1896, p. 5; *Scotsman*, 1 June, p. 1; 4 June 1896, p. 1.

11. *Aberdeen Journal* (hereafter *AJ*), 28 Sept., p. 5; 29 Sept. 1896, p. 5.

12. R. J. Morris, 'Leisure, Entertainment and the Associational Culture of British Towns, 1800–1900' (unpublished paper, delivered to the Third International Urban History Conference, Budapest, August 1996); id., 'Clubs, Societies and Associations', in Thompson, *Cambridge Social History of Britain. Volume 3*, pp. 395–443.

13. *Scotsman*, 14 Jan., p. 1; 28 Jan. 1897, p. 1; the price of early apparatus is indicated in Barnes, *Beginnings. 1897*, ch. 3.

14. *AJ*, 9 Sept. 1897, p. 1.

15. P. N. Lewis, 'Who Short Willie Park Jr? The Place of the Park v. Fernie Match in Early Scottish Film History', *Through the Green* (March 2008), pp. 40–50; *Scotsman*, 21 May 1898, p. 11; 31 July 1899, p. 1; 1 Aug. 1899, p. 5.

16. *Evening Times* (hereafter *ET*), 5 Aug. 1901, p. 8; *AJ*, 15 Jan., p. 6; 25 Jan., p. 7; 22 Jan. 1898, p. 6.

17. *Scotsman*, 6 Oct. 1909, p. 1; *ET*, 4 Oct. 1909, p. 8, noting Lizars' Imperial Bioscope at Springburn Hall.

18. *Scotsman*, 13 Oct. 1897, p. 1; 5 Jan. 1898, p. 6.

19. Ibid., 26 Sept. 1902, p. 1.

20. Ibid., 8 Dec. 1898, p. 1.

21. Ibid., 4 Nov. 1902, p. 1.
22. NAS, BT2/5562/3, Fraser and Elrick, Ltd, Memorandum of Association, p. 4.
23. Ibid., 13, Extraordinary General Meeting, 7 March 1906; *Scotsman*, 17 Oct. 1905, p. 1; 16 Jan. 1906, p. 1.
24. SSA, 5/7/382, cutting from *Courier and Advertiser*, 19 May 1943 (Feathers' obituary); D. M. Naulty, *Dundee Cinemas: A Personal Account* (Dundee, 2004), pp. 22–4; Dundee City Archives (hereafter DCA), Dundee Town Council Minutes, 3 Nov. 1909– 3 Nov. 1910, p. 1341, Magistrates' Committee, 27 Sept. 1910.
25. NAS, BT2/5449/1, Modern Marvel Co., Ltd, Memorandum of Association, 5 March 1897.
26. *Scotsman*, 3 Jan., p. 1; 10 Jan. 1905, p. 8.
27. B. H. Gates, 'Cinema in Aberdeen', in *Fifty Years of Scottish Cinema* (Educational Film Bulletin, No. 23, Sept. 1946), pp. 16–17; M. Thomson, *Silver Screen in the Silver City: A History of Cinemas in Aberdeen, 1896–1987* (Aberdeen, 1988), pp. 7–8.
28. *AJ*, 28 Nov., p. 4; 30 Nov., p. 5; 14 Dec. 1896, p. 1.
29. SSA, 5/3/1, Walker Family Collection, Programme of Cinematograph and Optical Lantern Exhibition at Balmoral Castle, Monday 24 October 1898; *ET*, 25 March 1904, p. 8.
30. D. Rossell, *Living Pictures: The Origins of the Movies* (Albany, 1998), ch. 7; Barnes, *Beginnings. Volume 3: The Rise of the Photoplay*, ch. 2; Toulmin, *Electric Edwardians*, pp. 101–6; id., '"Curios Things in Curios Places"'.
31. *Kinematograph Year Book* (London, 1915 and 1916); SSA, 5/8/42, Green Family Collection, Letter, Herbert Green to Henry Simpson, n.d.; 5/8/75, Cuttings on George Green, *Bioscope*, 25 Nov. 1915, p. 929; J. McBain, 'Green's of Glasgow: "We Want U In"', *Film Studies*, 10 (Spring 2007), pp. 54–7.
32. SSA, 5/8/26, Green Family Collection, Agreement between George Green and Peter Swallow, 14 Jan. 1892; 5/8/28, Correspondence, Peter Swallow to George Green, 20 April 1903; 17 Jan. 1905; 3 March 1905; GCA, Glasgow Corporation Minutes, April–Nov. 1910, Magistrates' Committee, 5 May 1910.
33. SSA, 5/18/1, George Kemp, Ltd, Showmen and Exhibitors, 'Puffer': A Look Around, 14 April 1961; 5/18/2, galley proofs of article by Harry Kemp, n.d.; 5/18/3, extracts from 'Merry Go Round', third extract, pp. 10–11; V. Toulmin, 'The Cinematograph at the Nottingham Goose Fair, 1896–1911', in A. Burton and L. Porter (eds), *The Showman, the Spectacle and the Two-Minute Silence* (Trowbridge, 2001), pp. 76–86.
34. SSA, 8/47, Interview with Mr George Kemp, 28 June 1983, transcript, pp. 4–6; *Bioscope*, 28 Nov. 1912, p. 670; 26 March 1914, p. 1421.
35. SSA, 5/7/345, Miscellaneous Film Material, Palmers of Lesmahagow, undated cutting; Notes on Palmer's Picture House; 5/7/257, Notes by Dr Ida Kimber on Arthur Henderson, Dundee cinema and theatre proprietor; *Kinematograph Year Book* (London, 1915 and 1916); DCA, Minutes of Meetings of the Town Council of Dundee and its Committees, Magistrates' Committee, 22 Feb. 1911.
36. SSA, 5/4/1, Poole Family, One Hundred Years of Showmanship: Poole's, 1837–1937; 5/4/44, Scottish Life and Letters, transcript of BBC transmission, 23

April 1967, Jim Poole on the Myriorama, pp. 12–14; *Scotsman*, 18 March 1901, p. 1; *ET*, 15 Jan. 1901, p. 6.

37. *Scotsman*, 1 Jan. 1907, p. 1.
38. Ibid., 19 Jan. 1901, p. 1; 2 Jan. 1911, p. 1; *ET*, 18 Jan. 1901, p. 8.
39. SSA, 5/4/8, Poole Family, advertisement from *The Scots Pictorial*, 1906; the Myriorama's final appearance, for three weeks at New Year 1927–8, is recorded in 5/4/15, Diary of Attendances at Synod Hall, 1924–32.
40. Gates, 'Cinema in Aberdeen', p. 17; *AJ*, 14 Dec., p. 6; 24 Dec. 1896, p. 6; *Aberdeen Weekly Journal* (hereafter *AWJ*), 21 April 1897, p. 7; *ET*, 2 Jan., p. 6; 4 Jan. 1900, p. 6; 5 March 1901, p. 6.
41. *ET*, 10 Feb., p. 8; 10 March 1902, p. 8; *The Kirkintilloch Gazette, Lenzie and Campsie Reporter* (hereafter *KG*), 8 Sept. 1905, p. 2, for this and for subsequent references to Kirkintilloch, I am grateful to Mr Malcolm Cook; *Scottish Cinema*, 29 Sept. 1919, p. 26, for a biographical sketch of Bendon.
42. *ET*, 29 Aug., p. 8; 5 Sept., p. 8; 16 Nov. 1900, p. 8; *The Kirkintilloch Herald and Lenzie, Kilsyth, Campsie and Cumbernauld Press* (hereafter *KH*), 6 Sept. 1899, p. 4; 14 Jan. 1903, p. 4.
43. *AJ*, 2 May 1899, p. 6; *Bioscope*, 2 Sept., p. 15; 7 Oct. 1909, p. 71; *Kinematograph Year Book, Diary and Directory* (1915 ed.).
44. NAS, CS 96/1483, Letter Book of Alexander Mathieson, n.d., Mathieson to Mr Calverto; 23 Aug. 1903, Mathieson to Miss Morgan; Mathieson to 'Agnes'.
45. NAS, CS 248/4062, Copy Correspondence, IC, Alexander Mathieson and J. F. Calverto, 26, 29 Aug. 1903, Calverto to Mathieson; First Division, 24 Nov. 1903, Closed Record in Causa Alexander Mathieson against J. F. Calverto, List of Expenses Incurred by Pursuer in Connection with his Tour.
46. *ET*, 8 April 1903, p. 6; 1 Jan. 1907, p. 6; 17 Dec. 1901, p. 6; 6 April 1906, p. 8.
47. *Scotsman*, 1 Jan. 1901, p. 6; 1 Sept. 1903, p. 6.
48. *Scottish Cinema*, 22 Sept. 1919, p. 20; *Bioscope*, 21 Dec. 1922, p. 50; *The Scottish Kinema Record* (hereafter *SKR*), 23 Dec. 1922, p. 1.
49. SSA, 5/7/135, *The Story of the B.B. Pictures*, n.d.; NAS, BT2/7670/8, The BB Pictures, Ltd, Prospectus; R. Brown, 'New Century Pictures: Regional Enterprise in Early British Film Exhibition', in Toulmin, Popple, and Russell (eds), *The Lost World of Mitchell and Kenyon*, pp. 72–3; *Kinematograph Year Book, Diary and Directory* (1915 ed.); *Bioscope*, 22 Feb. 1912, p. 515.
50. V. Toulmin, '"Local Films for Local People": Travelling Showmen and the Commissioning of Local Films in Great Britain, 1900–1902', *Film History*, 13 (2001), pp. 118–37.
51. *ET*, 2 May, p. 8; 23 May 1906, p. 8.
52. *Scotsman*, 5 March, p. 1 to 14 April 1903, p. 1, for details of the tour; *KH*, 29 Dec. 1897, p. 4; *KG*, 24 April 1903, p. 2.
53. West Lothian Local History Library, Blackburn, Uphall Public Hall and Cinema, Cash Book, 1889–1922, entries for 31 Aug., 30 Sept. 1909, 9 Feb., 18 Sept., 8 Nov. 1910.
54. SSA, 5/4/44, Poole family, *Scottish Life and Letters*, introduced by George Bruce, transcript of BBC transmission, 23 April 1967, p. 14.

55. *Scotsman*, 31 Dec. 1901, p. 1.

56. J. Bowers, *Stan Laurel and Other Stars of the Panopticon: The Story of the Britannia Music Hall* (Edinburgh, 2007), pp. 89–90; SSA, 5/9/23, ABC, Sauchiehall Street, Material for Exhibition on History, undated programme for The Hippodrome; *ET*, 26 Oct., p. 8; 17 Nov. 1903, p. 6.

57. Bowers, *Stan Laurel*, pp. 109–58; *ET*, 28 Jan., p. 8; 20 May, p. 8; 22 July, p. 8; 19 Aug. 1907, p. 8; 25 July 1910, p. 8; *Kinematograph Year Book, Diary and Directory* (1915 ed.).

58. Barnes, *Beginnings. 1897*, ch. 8; *Scotsman*, 1 Nov. 1897, p. 6.

59. V. Toulmin and M. Loiperdinger, 'Is It You?: Recognition, Representation and Response in Relation to the Local Film', *Film History*, 17 (2005), pp. 7–18.

60. *AJ*, 30 Oct. 1896, p. 4; *AWJ*, 13 Oct. 1897, p. 7; Barnes, *Beginnings. 1897*, p. 174.

61. *AJ*, 30 Sept., p. 6; 11 Nov. 1899, p. 7; 14 Oct. 1898, p. 1.

62. *AJ*, 2 Oct. 1899, p. 4; 30 April 1900, p. 6.

63. *Scotsman*, 18 April 1899, p. 5; 20 Feb. 1903, p. 1.

64. *ET*, 1 June, p. 8; 2 Nov. 1908, p. 8

65. *Bioscope*, 22 Dec. 1910, p. 53; 6 Nov. 1913, p. 533; 2 March 1911, p. 17.

66. NAS, CS 248/4062, First Division, 24 Nov. 1903, Closed Record in Causa Alexander Mathieson against J. F. Calverto, Summons, p. 6; Copy Correspondence between the Pursuer and Hallkeepers, 20 Aug. 1903, James Burt, Hallkeeper, Broxburn Public Hall to Mathieson.

67. *ET*, 30 Jan., p. 6; 16 Feb. 1904, p. 6.

68. *Bioscope*, 22 Sept., p. 15; 17 Nov. 1910, p. 57; 23 Feb. 1911, p. 57.

69. *Bioscope*, 10 Oct. 1912, p. 87; Thomson, *Silver Screen in the Silver City*, pp. 46–7.

70. Thomson, *Silver Screen in the Silver City*, pp. 52–5; on the decision to end the practice of speaking to pictures at the Star, see Cinema Museum, Lambeth (hereafter CM), Aberdeen Picture Palaces, Ltd, Minute Book 2: October 1922–October 1930, p. 101, Meeting of Directors, 18 Feb. 1926.

71. CM, Aberdeen Picture Palaces, Ltd, Minute Book 1, pp. 78, 80, Meetings of Directors, 14 April, 12 May 1915.

72. *AJ*, 30 April 1900, p. 6; *Scotsman*, 10 Feb., p. 5; 20 Feb. 1903, p. 1.

73. *Scotsman*, 11 Feb. 1902, p. 5; 1 Jan. 1907, p. 1, where West is described as 'The Original and Acknowledged Entrepreneur of Cinematography in Edinburgh'; NAS, BT2/3449/5, The Modern Marvel Co., Ltd, 21 Feb. 1898, Summary of Capital and Shares, for West's initial involvement in the concern.

74. *Scotsman*, 11 July 1911, p. 10; 27 May 1910, p. 1.

75. *Scotsman*, 11 March 1901, p. 1; A. Lugton, *Making of Hibernian* (Edinburgh, 1995), p. 235.

76. R. Hoggart, *The Uses of Literacy: Aspects of Working-class Life with Special Reference to Publications and Entertainments* (Harmondsworth, 1958), pp. 120–31; K. Williams, *Get Me a Murder a Day! A History of Mass Communication in Britain* (London, 1998), ch. 3.

77. *AJ*, 30 Oct. 1896, p. 4; *Scotsman*, 24 Nov. 1897, p. 1.

78. *Scotsman*, 18 Dec. 1897, p. 2; Musser, *Emergence of Cinema*, pp. 145–57; R. Altman, *Silent Film Sound* (New York and Chichester, 2004), ch. 2.

79. NAS, BT2/3758/1, The Scottish Mutoscope Co., Ltd, Memorandum of Association; *The Scotsman*, 18 Feb., pp. 1, 2; 8 June 1898, p. 6; R. Brown and B. Anthony, *A Victorian Film Enterprise: The History of the British Mutoscope and Biograph Company, 1897–1915* (Trowbridge, 1999), p. 86.

80. *Scotsman*, 3 May 1901, p. 6; 14 Feb. 1899, p. 1; NAS, BT2/3758/11, The Scottish Mutoscope Co., Ltd, Extraordinary General Meeting, 30 Jan. 1902; Brown and Anthony, *Victorian Film Enterprise*, ch. 6.

81. *AWJ*, 5 Jan., p. 6; see also 2 Feb. 1898, p. 7, for an exhibition at Skene Central School provided for the local tenantry.

82. *AJ*, 25 Jan., p. 7 (Buckhaven YMCA annual social meeting); 14 Nov. 1898, p. 1 (Aberdeen Highland Association); 13 Nov. 1899, p. 7 (Primrose League); *AWJ*, 14 Dec. 1898, p. 11 (Free Gardeners, and Oddfellows, Inverurie).

83. NAS, CS248/4062, Copy Correspondence IC Alexander Mathieson and J. F. Calverto, 7 Sept. 1903, Messrs Paterson and Salmon to Messrs Russell and Duncan; CS248/4066, First Division, Lord Kincarny Ordinary. Summons IC, Alexander Mathieson v. West Lothian Printing and Publishing Co., Ltd; T. A. Blake, 'The Cinematograph Comes to Scotland, 1896–1902', in *Fifty Years of Scottish Cinema* (Educational Film Bulletin, No. 23, Sept. 1946), pp. 13–14; Hanson, *From Silent Screen to Multi-Screen*, ch. 1.

84. F. Bruce, *Showfolk: An Oral History of a Fairground Dynasty* (Edinburgh, 2010), ch. 2; T. Griffiths, 'Work, Leisure and Time in the Nineteenth Century', in T. Griffiths and G. Morton (eds), *A History of Everyday Life in Scotland, 1800–1900* (Edinburgh, 2010), pp. 170–95; R. Anthony, *Herds and Hinds: Farm Labour in Lowland Scotland, 1900–1939* (East Linton, 1997), pp. 184–91; J. Burnett, *Riot, Revelry and Rout: Sport in Lowland Scotland before 1860* (East Linton, 2000), pp. 111–24.

85. C. A. Whatley (ed.), *The Diary of John Sturrock, Millwright, Dundee, 1864–65* (East Linton, 1998), p. 31; I. McGraw, *The Fairs of Dundee* (Abertay Historical Society No. 34, Dundee, 1994), pp. 55–7, 59.

86. *Scotsman*, 12 May, p. 6; 19 May 1903, p. 4; *ET*, 18 May 1903, p. 8, for films of the royal tour of that year.

87. *ET*, 7 May 1906, p. 8; Dunbar is also noted in the edition for 14 March 1906, p. 7. The other acts listed here feature in advertisements in the *Evening Times* in the early years of the century.

88. *ET*, 29 Feb., p. 8; 2 March 1904, p. 8; for prices at the Sauchiehall Street Hippodrome and the Tivoli, see 12 Jan., p. 8; 26 Jan. 1903, p. 8.

89. GCA, D-OPW 61/5, List of Premises Licensed under the Cinematograph Act, 12 July 1913.

90. *ET*, 28 Sept. 1908, p. 8; 8 March 1909, p. 8.

91. *ET*, 11 May, p. 8; 18 May 1908, p. 8; 9 Aug. 1909, p. 8; 1 Nov. 1910, p. 8; *Bioscope*, 12 Aug. 1909, p. 13; 23 Aug. 1910, p. 17.

92. *Bioscope*, 12 Sept. 1912, p. 799; 4 June 1914, p. 1029.

93. Musser, *Emergence of Cinema*, ch. 13; Burrows, 'Penny Pleasures' and 'Penny Pleasures II'.

94. *Forward*, 15 March 1913, p. 2.

95. GCA, Glasgow Corporation, Magistrates' Committee Minutes, April to November 1910, 27 Oct. 1910.

96. *Forward*, 15 March, 1913, p. 2; *ET*, 9 Nov., p. 6; 11 Nov. 1907, p. 8; the impact of the Cinematograph Act is discussed in more detail in the next chapter.

97. Burrows, 'Penny Pleasures', pp. 71–2; *Forward*, 15 March, 1913, p. 2; GCA, D-OPW 61/5, List of Premises Licensed under the Cinematograph Act, 12 July 1913.

98. A. Scullion, 'Geggies, Empires, Cinemas: The Scottish Experience of Early Film', *Picture House*, No. 21 (Summer 1996), pp. 13–19.

99. GCA, Minutes of the Corporation of Glasgow, Nov. 1908–April 1909, Magistrates' Committee, 19 Nov. 1908.

100. *Bioscope*, 16 July, p. 228; 1 Oct. 1914, p. 65.

101. E. King, 'Popular Culture in Glasgow', in R. A. Cage (ed.), *The Working Class in Glasgow, 1750–1914* (Beckenham, 1987), pp. 142–87; P. Maloney, *Scotland and the Music Hall, 1850–1914* (Manchester, 2003), p. 191; for similar developments elsewhere, see I. Maver, 'Leisure and Culture: The Nineteenth Century', in W. Hamish Fraser and C. Lee (eds), *Aberdeen, 1800–2000: a New History* (East Linton, 2000), pp. 402–3.

102. *ET*, 1 Nov. 1901, p. 6; 24 Jan., p. 8; 20 Oct. 1902, p. 8.

103. See for example *ET*, 11 Feb., p. 8; 18 Feb., p. 8; 4 Nov. 1910, p. 8; GCA, D-OPW 61/5, List of Premises Licensed under the Cinematograph Act, 12 July 1913.

104. *Scotsman*, 28 May 1903, p. 4.

105. *Forward*, 22 March 1913, p. 1; Maloney, *Scotland and the Music Hall*, pp. 192–3, citing the *North British Daily Mail* on the presence of members of the 'fair sex'.

106. *Evening Citizen*, 16 Nov. 1908, p. 8.

107. *Forward*, 15 March 1913, p. 2.

108. *Bioscope*, 27 March 1913, p. 941.

109. GCA, D-OPW 61/5, List of Premises Licensed under the Cinematograph Act, 12 July 1913; *Bioscope*, 8 Oct. 1914, p. 153.

110. N. Munro, 'From Fort William', reprinted in B. D. Osborne and R. Armstrong (eds), *Erchie & Jimmy Swan* (Edinburgh, 1993), p. 347.

111. Hanson, *From Silent Screen to Multi-Screen*, pp. 14–15; J. Kissell, 'Cinema in the By-ways', in *Fifty Years of Scottish Cinema*, pp. 22–7; McBain, 'Green's of Glasgow'; although see the cautionary note in Toulmin, *Electric Edwardians*, p. 74.

112. *ET*, 2 March 1904, p. 8.

113. Ibid., 29 March 1904, p. 6.

114. *Bioscope*, 15 July 1909, p. 13.

115. Ibid., 3 Nov., p. 37; 22 Dec. 1910, p. 21.

116. SSA, Green's Film Service File, unidentified cutting dated July 1914.

117. *Bioscope*, 19 Dec. 1912, p. 889.

118. *Scotsman*, 3 Feb., p. 5; 20 Feb., p. 8; 6 March, p. 9; 24 Nov. 1903, p. 7.

119. Brown, 'New Century Pictures'; *Scotsman*, 20 Feb. 1903, p. 1; 15 Nov. 1904, p. 6.

120. See Appendix 1.

121. NAS, BT2/7476/2, The Glasgow Electric Theatres, Ltd, Memorandum of Association, 21 March 1910; BT2/7670/6, The BB Pictures, Ltd, List of Directors, 3 Oct. 1910.

122. NAS, BT2/9201/10, The Palace (Arbroath), Ltd, Register of Directors, 21 Sept. 1914; BT2/7601/8, The Highland Cinematograph and Variety Co., Ltd, Copy of Register of Directors, n.d.; BT2/7695/5, The Shettleston Premier Picture Theatre Co., Ltd, Register of Directors, 16 Nov. 1910.

123. NAS, BT2/7601/9, 10, The Highland Cinematograph and Variety Co., Ltd, Returns of Allotments, 8 Aug., 29 Sept. 1910; BT2/7670/11, The BB Pictures, Ltd, Return of Allotments, 17 Oct. 1910.

124. W. Vamplew, *Pay Up and Play the Game: Professional Sport in Britain, 1875–1914* (Cambridge, 1988), pp. 155–9.

125. NAS, BT2/8428/12, The Kirkcaldy Picture House, Ltd, Return of Allotments, 7 Jan. 1913; BT2/8375/11, The Palace (Edinburgh), Ltd, Return of Allotments, 18 Nov. 1912.

126. NAS, BT2/8062/6, The Armadale Picturedrome, Ltd, Return of Allotments, 31 Dec. 1912; BT2/7670/11, The BB Pictures, Ltd, Return of Allotments, 17 Oct. 1910.

127. NAS, BT2/7670/11, The BB Pictures, Ltd, Return of Allotments, 17 Oct. 1910.

128. The point is noted more generally in J. Burrows and R. Brown, 'Financing the Edwardian Cinema Boom, 1909–1914', *Historical Journal of Film, Radio and Television*, 30 (2010), pp. 1–20.

129. Figures calculated from NAS, BT2/7670/11, 12, 16, 18, 22, 23, 24, 25, 27, Returns of Allotments, 17, 21 Oct., 23 Dec. 1910; 1 Feb., 25 Dec. 1911; 26 June, 27 Aug., 9 Sept., 12 Dec. 1912; on Bennell, see *Scottish Cinema*, 22 Sept. 1922, p. 20.

130. NAS, BT2/9030/7, Central Picture House, Portobello, Ltd, Return of Allotments, 11 May 1914. The reduced number of companies referred to here reflects the failure of some to proceed to allotment after the initial flotation.

131. CM, Aberdeen Picture Palaces, Ltd, Register of Members &c.; NAS, BT2/8516/11, 13, 14, 16, Returns of Allotments, 3 Feb. 1912; 5 May 1913; 19 March, 14 Dec. 1914.

132. NAS, BT2/8288/9, 10, 12, The Methil Picture Palace Co., Ltd, Returns of Allotments, 15 Aug., 28 Sept., 12 Nov. 1912; BT2/9204/11, 18, 19, 20, 21, 22, The North of Scotland Cinematograph, Ltd, Returns of Allotments, 26 Dec. 1914; 12 June, 25 July, 6 Sept., 28 Nov., 5 Dec. 1916.

133. NAS, BT2/9030/11, Central Picture House, Portobello, Ltd, Return of Allotments, 11 May 1914 (Robert G. Nisbet, Lecturer in Humanity at the University of Glasgow); BT2/8288/10, The Methil Picture Palace Co., Ltd, Return of Allotments, 28 Sept. 1911 (James Goodwillie, MA, BSc).

134. On the wider property market, see J. A. Yelling, 'Land, Property and Planning', in M. Daunton (ed.), *The Cambridge Urban History of Britain. Volume III: 1840–1950* (Cambridge, 2000), pp. 467–93; A. Offer, *Property and Politics, 1870–1914: Landownership, Law, Ideology and Urban Development in England* (Cambridge,

1981); R. Rodger, *Housing in Urban Britain, 1780–1914: Class, Capitalism and Construction* (Basingstoke, 1989), pp. 52–62.

135. NAS, BT2/7567/10, 16, 18, 19, Scottish Electric Picture Palaces, Ltd, Returns of Allotments, 18 June, 7 July, 27 July, 12 Oct. 1910.

136. SSA, 5/8/23, Green Family Collection, The Scottish Electric Picture Palaces, Ltd (1910), Prospectus.

137. *Bioscope*, 11 Sept. 1913, p. 841.

138. NAS, BT2/7981/8, The Aberdeen Electric Theatre Co., Ltd, Prospectus, 7 Sept. 1911; *Bioscope*, 1 Jan. 1914, p. 17.

139. SSA, 5/8/23, Green Family Collection, The Scottish Electric Picture Palaces, Ltd (1910), Prospectus.

140. Brown, 'New Century Pictures', p. 79.

141. M. MacKinnon, 'Living Standards, 1870–1914', in R. Floud and D. McCloskey (eds), *The Economic History of Britain since 1700. Second Edition. Volume 2: 1860–1939* (Cambridge, 1994), pp. 265–90; I. Gazeley, 'The Cost of Living of Urban Workers in late-Victorian and Edwardian Britain', *Economic History Review*, 2nd ser., XLI (1989), pp. 207–21; P. Wardley, 'Edwardian Britain: Empire, Income and Political Discontent', in P. Johnson (ed.), *Twentieth-Century Britain: Economic, Social and Cultural Change* (Harlow, 1994), pp. 61–6.

142. *ET*, 17 Aug. 1908, p. 4; 29 June 1910, p. 3.

143. On the opening of the Bijou in the former Alexandra Music Hall, see *ET*, 10 March, p. 8; 18 March 1908, p. 8.

144. Hanson, *From Silent Screen to Multi-Screen*, pp. 26–7; Low, *History of the British Film, 1906–1914*, p. 26.

145. NAS, BT2/7366/25, 27, West of Scotland Electric Theatres, Ltd, Balance Sheets at 31 Dec. 1912; 31 Dec. 1913.

146. SSA, 5/26/112, Singleton Collection, Notebook, Weekly Accounts, August 1913–August 1914.

147. SSA, Green Family Collection, The Scottish Electric Picture Palaces, Ltd (1910), Prospectus.

148. Mathieson's figures calculated from NAS, CS248/4062, First Division, 24 Nov. 1903, Closed Record in Causa Alexander Mathieson against J. F. Calverto, List of Payments Made by Pursuer in Connection with Tour; SSA, 5/26/112, Singleton Collection, Notebook, Weekly Accounts, August 1913–August 1914.

149. NAS, BT2/7981/8, The Aberdeen Electric Theatre Co., Ltd, Prospectus, 7 Sept. 1911.

150. Hiley, '"Nothing More than a Craze"', Table 2, p. 120.

151. Ibid., p. 120; GCA, D-OPW 61/5, List of Premises Licensed under the Cinematograph Act, 12 July 1913.

152. *Bioscope*, 18 July 1912, p. 171.

153. *Irvine Herald and Ayrshire Advertiser*, 16 Aug., p. 4; 30 Aug. 1912, p. 4; on the Irvine Picturedrome, see SSA, 5/8/75, Green Family Collection, Cuttings on George Green, cuttings from *The World's Fair*, n.d.; 6, 13 July 1912.

154. *Irvine Herald*, 29 Aug. 1913, p. 8.

155. SSA, 5/8/23, Green Family Collection, The Scottish Electric Picture Palaces, Ltd (1910), Prospectus.
156. *Entertainer*, 22 Nov. 1913, p. 16.
157. Ibid., 13 June 1914, p. 1.

2

Regulating Scottish Cinema: Censorship and the Child Audience

The recreational culture within which cinema made its bow in the 1890s was one already subject to close legal controls. Fixed places of popular amusement had operated under licence from the passage of the Disorderly Houses Act of 1751. In the case of the music hall, the progenitor of those variety theatres which provided an early setting for the projection of moving pictures, systems of regulation had become more pronounced as the nineteenth century proceeded, extending in later decades to the disposition of the audience within the building, separating the provision of amusements from the supply of predominantly alcoholic refreshments, to the content of the material being presented. The latter was controlled through systems of strict timetabling, which limited scope for the potentially subversive ad lib, and through house rules that prohibited reference to specified subjects. For some, therefore, the evolution of the music hall was shaped by the growing dominance of large concentrations of capital, so that the medium is seen to have operated within a broad 'culture of control'.[1]

As an emerging form of mass entertainment, the cinema was unlikely to escape the attentions of those concerned for the welfare, both physical and moral, of the audience. The earliest measure specifically concerned to regulate the conditions under which moving pictures were exhibited, the Cinematograph Act of 1909, was ostensibly intended to minimise the dangers posed to audiences attending exhibitions using highly flammable celluloid in an enclosed space. Yet it also provided the means by which local licensing authorities attempted to influence the nature of film content. The censorship debate that resulted has been extensively documented in a literature that places the control of film texts at the centre of the relationship between the cinema industry and the law.[2] Key stages in the development of that relationship can be clearly identified. By allowing licensing authorities latitude in determining the content of film shows, the 1909 Act created uncertainty for the production side of the industry, so that the need for a national body whose judgment would override local points of difference became paramount. The British Board of Film Censors, established in 1912, was a trade body which aimed, through a system of certification, to offer guidance to licensing authorities on the suitability of the films it reviewed. At first, the certificates merely distinguished between those subjects deemed suitable for all audiences, even those made up of children only at matinees ('U'), and those deemed appropriate for more 'public' exhibition, at which some adult presence could be presumed ('A').[3] Over the following decades, the criteria governing the Board's recommendations were amplified and clarified. By 1917, as the President of the Board T. P. O'Connor explained to the Commission of Enquiry set up by the National Council of Public Morals, some forty-three grounds for intervention had been identified, the great majority of which were concerned with issues of morality, taking in nudity and depictions of violence and cruelty. By contrast, seven addressed matters of current political controversy.[4] The Board's rules were further elaborated in the light of experience in subsequent years. Throughout, however, its judgments remained advisory. The final decision over what could and could not be shown rested at all times with local licensing authorities. To begin with, then, the variations in practice that the Board had been established to address persisted, as comparatively few authorities agreed to adhere to the Board's decisions. By the mid 1920s, under pressure from the Home Office, most had agreed to incorporate within their licences the stipulation that exhibition would, save where the authority decreed otherwise, be confined to subjects carrying a BBFC certificate. A growing number also came to accept conditions governing the showing of films granted an 'A' certificate as agreed by the London County Council in 1923, whereby those under sixteen years of age would only be admitted to programmes including such films if accompanied by a parent or responsible adult.[5]

The sequence suggests the gradual consolidation of a more uniform system of regulation. Yet the accuracy of such a perspective may be open to question. Annette Kuhn has shown how censorship practices developed through more than the imposition of one common set of standards. Rather, the BBFC and its decisions were part of a broader network of interests and power relations which together shaped approaches to the regulation of film content.[6] If this was true nationally, it applied with equal force to the areas within which the final decisions on censorship were taken. Here, licensing authorities were subject to a variety of influences, from the economic interests of exhibitors to the pressures exerted by various interest groups. The first part of this chapter examines the interplay of such forces and their impact on regulatory practices across Scotland. Here, the existence of a distinct legal system means that many familiar landmarks in the narrative of censorship policy assume a different significance. So, the importance often assigned the 1909 Act, acceptance of the BBFC's guidelines, and the interpretation of the 'A' certificate cannot be accepted without question. Scotland's way with censorship thus repays closer examination.

Throughout the period, the most active lobbyists for a more assertive approach to film censorship were to be found among religious, educational, and women's organisations. Their primary interests lay not so much in the moral impact of the cinema generally as in its impact on one particular section of the audience. In March 1920, as proposals to formalise censorship in Edinburgh and across Scotland more generally were under discussion, *The Scotsman* identified the key area of concern: 'The problem of the cinema censorship . . . is largely the problem of the children. The ready attractive-ness of the moving pictures and the low charge of admission makes this form of entertainment pre-eminently one sought after by the young.'[7] The impact of film on impressionable minds would be a recurrent point of concern across the first half of the twentieth century, so that the second part of this chapter is largely devoted to the issue of cinema and its perceived effects on children. The debates of the time extended beyond the content of film, to take in the times at which children attended, and the degree of supervision to which they were subject while in the auditorium.[8] This acts as a reminder that regulation was concerned not merely with the films themselves, but extended to the cinema-going experience as a whole. Censorship, for all its importance, is but one of the themes under examination here. The nature of early film shows was shaped by many forces, including systems of licensing which pre-dated more formal attempts at determining content.

II

Across urban Scotland, venues used for the exhibition of moving pic-tures were subject to close controls well before the passage of the 1909 Cinematograph Act. Here, all places of public entertainment were subject to licensing regulations as part of a well-established and highly localised system of urban governance. Until the 1890s, in most burghs, these were overseen by local Justices of the Peace. However, by the Burgh Police (Scotland) Act of 1892, licensing powers became vested in magistrates' committees, ena-bling them to attach conditions to the issuing of licences and to introduce by-laws to enforce the same. From 1903, this authority could be transferred to the town council itself.[9] By contrast, in larger burghs, namely Aberdeen, Dundee, Edinburgh, Glasgow, and Greenock, powers were defined by a series of separate local acts. In the capital, the key measure was the Edinburgh Municipal and Police Act of 1879, while in Glasgow, the magistrates assumed licensing responsibilities under the Further Powers Act of 1892.[10] In most cases, licences were awarded on an annual basis, and were subject to a prior inspection of premises to ensure that arrangements for audience safety and the maintenance of good order were adequate. In Edinburgh, the Burgh Engineer and the Firemaster made recommendations to the Magistrates' Committee, while in Glasgow, the requirement from September 1908, over a year before the Cinematograph Act came into operation was

> that before any cinematograph exhibition or such like show is allowed in any
> theatre, music hall, or any other hall in the city, a report on each application by

the Master of Works, the Chief Officer of the Fire Brigade, and the Electrical Engineer, be submitted.[11]

In Paisley, the requirement was added that all cinematograph equipment be operated from within a fire-proof box.[12] Licensing conditions were further reinforced by building regulations overseen by local Dean of Guild Courts, which reviewed and approved all new buildings and alterations to existing structures. From 1900, courts such as that in Edinburgh could prohibit the use of a building for purposes of popular entertainment unless satisfied that audiences were adequately protected from the threat of fire and that exits sufficed to enable audiences to be evacuated promptly in case of emergency.[13]

Indications are that regulations were vigorously enforced. In April 1908, following a report by the Master of Works, the Chief Officer of the Fire Brigade, and the Chief Constable of Glasgow, proposals to mount a moving picture show from a Pullman railway car situated in Jamaica Street were blocked. Later in the year, shows planned for local churches were also prohibited on grounds of public safety.[14] From this we may suggest that, rather as Jon Burrows discovered in London, a system of licensing and building regulation was in place across Scotland which effectively precluded the emergence of shows in small shop conversions, comprising short programmes at cheap prices.[15] The law thus contributed significantly to impeding the development of a nickelodeon sector in Scotland.

Existing arrangements also served to mitigate the impact of the 1909 Act north of the border. The need for legislation specific to cinematograph shows was justified by the threat of fire arising from the use of highly flammable celluloid. Outbreaks were not unknown in Scotland prior to 1909 but were, for the most part, minor. In November 1908, the Saturday night show at Hengler's Circus in Sauchiehall Street was brought to a premature end by an explosion in the Bioscope apparatus. Panic among the audience of 1,800 had ensued, following cries of 'Fire' from the gallery, but order was, according to most accounts, quickly restored, with restoratives provided to those who had fainted. The following year, when film in the cinematograph at Glasgow's Gaiety Theatre caught fire, the audience in the circle was promptly evacuated while those in the body of the hall remained in their seats, diverted by the live entertainments provided on stage.[16] The 1909 Act sought to allay any concerns arising from such incidents by establishing licensing arrangements specifically for cinematograph shows. Detailed provisions, to be included in all licences, were set out by the Secretary of State for Scotland, but could be amended by magistrates who retained the ultimate authority in determining the conditions under which shows could proceed. The requirements set out by the Secretary of State included the provision of adequate exits, indicated by illuminated signs, and set out the arrangements for the enclosure from which the cinematograph apparatus was to be operated. This should be situated outside the auditorium, but where this was not possible, a barrier of at least 2 ft was to separate the enclosure from the audience.[17]

The apparent stringency of the new regulations attracted particular comment. The *Edinburgh Evening News* was of the view that

> If the cinematograph was as dangerous as a mad dog, as deadly as a Maxim gun, as invidious as an escape of carbonic acid gas, they [the magistrates] could not have shown a more nervous solicitude for the public safety.[18]

The result of such concern would, it was anticipated, be the closure of some 90 per cent of all shows, with temporary exhibitors operating in church halls expected to be incapable of meeting the requirement for a separate fire-proof enclosure, while the insistence of the Edinburgh authorities that a fire officer be present even where non-flammable film was being used would add significantly to the costs of any performance, potentially rendering them uneconomic. The refusal, within days, of the optician James Buncle's application for permission to mount an exhibition of films in Dalkeith Parish Hall appeared to justify such pessimism and gave weight to the warning in the trade paper *The Bioscope* that 'Those intending to enter the bioscope exhibition world would do well to steer clear of Scotland.'[19] In the absence of complete information on the number of shows put on before and contemplated after the 1909 Act came into force, precise quantification of the measure's impact is impossible. Nevertheless, evidence elsewhere suggests that the outcome was altogether less apocalyptic than had been predicted. The annual entertainment at Burntisland's Erskine Church was able to proceed in 1910 on assurances that the projection apparatus would be physically separated from the audience.[20] More importantly, existing licensing arrangements, which already allowed for safety inspections, had long worked to check the growth of shows in temporary venues, and these remained in force after 1910. Indeed, in December 1912, the Edinburgh magistrates confirmed that applications for licences under the 1909 Act should be accompanied by a certificate signed by the Burgh Engineer, the Firemaster, and the Electrical Engineer.[21] In effect, the 1909 Act supplemented rather than supplanted existing regulations.

The point was confirmed in March 1910 by an action brought before Edinburgh's Burgh Court against John Stewart for operating a Bioscope entertainment on Sunday. This was held to be in contravention of the licence taken out by Stewart under the Edinburgh Municipal and Police Act of 1879. Stewart's defence was that the existing licence was effectively superseded by that required under the Cinematograph Act of 1909, which contained no conditions relating to Sunday opening. As defence counsel argued, it could hardly be intended 'that a licence granted in 1909 was to be granted on terms and conditions made by the Magistrates in 1879 and not altered since'.[22] In his judgment, however, the presiding bailie concluded otherwise and reiterated that, as a consequence of the new measure, 'an Act had been added to the 1879 Act for a specific purpose – to safeguard the public'.[23] Crucially, then, the Cinematograph Act was seen to be primarily a safety measure, a verdict not subsequently challenged in the Scottish courts, so that other aspects of the show continued to be governed by prior legislation. As a result, the discretion which a number of licensing authorities in England came to exercise over film content was denied their counterparts north of the border. The limitations which this imposed on magistrates' area of authority became clear later the same year, when concern was voiced over the likely appearance in Scotland of the film depicting the heavyweight title fight between Jack Johnson and Jim Jeffries. Within days of the contest in Reno, Nevada, in which the black Johnson defeated the white Jeffries, the possible exhibition of the film locally was being debated in Glasgow's Council Chamber. Reviewing the discretion available to the magistrates under the Further Powers Act of 1892, the town clerk advised that, once a licence had been issued, the authority had no right to intervene over the content of the show.[24] At this point, well in advance of the film's arrival in Scotland, the problems it posed remained hypothetical. In the weeks that followed, however, the controversy stoked up by the film allowed exhibitors full scope for the application of well-honed skills of showmanship and exploitation. In October, for example, placards announced the film's arrival in Greenock. Despite concern expressed by local church ministers, the exhibition proceeded, but was found to comprise a series of still lantern slides of the contest.[25] Two months previously, A. E. Pickard, proprietor of Glasgow's Panopticon Music Hall, long practised in the art of exploiting the popular relish for the sensational, advertised the showing of 'The Race War, Fight Picture, Black and White'. That the film in fact comprised footage of a fight from the previous year between Sam Langford and Iron Hague at London's National Sporting Club appears to have deterred few, as it was retained for a second week.[26] When the Johnson v. Jeffries film finally arrived in Glasgow in November, its first showing at the Scottish Zoo was blocked by legal action, although this centred on an alleged breach of an agreement with the film's renters, rather than any move to prohibit the exhibition on moral grounds.[27] With the inability of magistrates to intervene in matters of such controversy confirmed, the film finally made its legitimate debut in Glasgow early in December at the Paisley Road Electric Picture Palace, its appeal reflected in admission prices that started at 1s.[28]

The obstacles to the exercise of censorship powers were reiterated two years later by the debate sparked by the five-reel Kalem production *From the Manger to the Cross*. Banned by magistrates in Liverpool, the film played in Aberdeen and Edinburgh over the Christmas and New Year period in 1912–13.[29] In the first two weeks of January, it drew almost 50,000 to the Olympia in Edinburgh, a success which was a cause of much 'grief and pain' to the local Free Church Presbytery, which protested to the city's magistrates 'against a subject so sacred and indeed awful as the suffering and death of the

Divine Saviour, being made a source of entertainment and pecuniary profit'. With Liverpool's example before it, the Presbytery proceeded to express regret that 'our Scottish cities should have adopted a lower standard in a matter so sacred, than . . . has been maintained by some of the leading cities of England'. In their response, the Edinburgh magistrates restated the limits to their authority, making clear that this remained confined to the build-ing within which the show took place and did not extend to 'the pictures and representations presented therein nor were these submitted for their approval'.[30] The 1909 Act, then, had not led to the assumption of censorship powers by Scottish licensing authorities, which remained for the most part content to limit their attention to issues of safety.

In other respects, however, its impact was altogether more profound. With the exception of authorities such as Aberdeen, which required cinemas to take out music hall licences, the 1909 Act established separate conditions for entertainment forms which, in practice, shared many common features.[31] The Bioscope and its variants had long been and continued to be a fixture on variety theatre bills, while the early picture houses employed variety turns at key points of the programme. In December 1911, music hall proprietors across Glasgow petitioned the city magistrates to press the case that the simi-larities between the entertainments provided by variety halls and cinemas justified the introduction of a common system of licensing. As this would extend the requirements for fire prevention from the projection area to the remainder of the theatre building, picture house proprietors faced the pros-pect of a significant increase in their costs. In a deputation to the magistrates, exhibitors argued that variety turns were only employed to cover changes in film reels and were a preferred alternative to plunging the auditorium and audience into silence and darkness.[32] Fears over the moral outrages commit-ted in poorly lit public spaces had for a time fuelled criticism of the cinema.[33] Live artistes thus maintained continuity in entertainment and contributed to a higher moral tone overall. It was further emphasised that most of the artistes employed in picture houses were drawn from the immediate area. However, to limit the competition with neighbouring music halls, a proposal was tabled to limit the number of turns to two each night. Despite this, the magistrates voted to require all cinemas employing variety artistes to operate under music hall licences. The effect, in the words of one local newspaper was to render the cinema a 'voiceless entertainment', while it was estimated that some 250 performers would have their employment affected by the decision.[34] Proposals to circumvent the new conditions by placing artistes behind the screen were rejected, leading some to question whether other conventions, such as the employment of a lecturer to explain the scenes as they unfolded, or even the practice of managers addressing the audience, could be maintained without an additional licence. In the end, such ques-tions were never put to the test. In September, after it emerged that the new conditions effectively prohibited the staging of cheap Saturday concerts in corporation halls, the magistrates voted to rescind the requirement that music hall licences be taken out.[35] Variety artistes thus remained a central part of many cinema bills into the third decade of the century, until rendered redundant by the coming of synchronised sound. The debate over the law thus has much to tell us about the dynamics of early cinema shows, but also indicates how regulation was influenced, in some degree, by economic interests and, in this case, the differing and conflicting perspectives of areas of the entertainment business that were, in practice, far from discrete.

On occasion, a more lasting change in performance practice was effected. In May 1910, Airdrie magistrates ordered that picture houses no longer use 'touts' to shout for business along the town's streets.[36] This echo of fairground methods of procuring business, while suited to an occasional, often rural recreational form, was less acceptable in an urban setting, where the leisure calendar was more regular and where places of entertainment shared space with other business and residential users. Elsewhere, however, by-laws which threatened to impose a significant additional financial burden on cinemas were successfully challenged. In 1913, for example, Dundee exhibitors secured an exemption from the requirement to employ a member of the local fire brigade to attend each show at a minimum cost of 15s for a six-day week, including one matinee performance. Local magistrates agreed to amend the by-laws, so that exhibitors, whose shows were made up entirely of moving pictures, were only called upon to fund a series of regular inspections. Otherwise, fire-fighting equipment was to be maintained by a member of staff trained in its use.[37] Briefly, this decision threatened to create a separate tier of licensing, whereby entertainments that relied exclusively on film would be marked out from those in which variety artistes were employed. Within weeks, however, the by-laws requiring the attendance of a fire officer at the proprietor's expense were declared ultra vires, so that from March 1913 a uniform charge applied, covering the cost of regular safety inspections.[38]

Such passing problems aside, relations between the cinema trade and licensing authorities across Scotland in the first years after the passage of the 1909 Act remained broadly harmonious. In his chairman's address to the annual meeting of the Edinburgh and East of Scotland branch of the Cinematograph Exhibitors' Association in 1914, R. C. Buchanan praised the 'sympathetic and intelligent' view taken by local magistrates on matters affecting the industry.[39] In adopting a strict interpretation of their remit under the 1909 Act, licensing authorities across Scotland largely renounced any attempt to influence film content, although calls for the imposition of tighter censorship controls were made by a variety of interest groups, some national in character, such as the Scottish Christian Social Union, and others more local in their scope, including the Citizenship Committee in Kirkcaldy.[40] In practice, the arguments of bodies such as these, identified by some as 'local busy-bodies and kill-joys', barely intruded on official delib-

erations in the period prior to the outbreak of the First World War.[41] As
a result, the actions of Scottish licensing authorities appear to have played
little, if any part in encouraging moves within the industry to establish its
own regulatory body, the British Board of Film Censors, in 1912. This
may account for reactions to the board north of the border which, for the
most part, ranged from scepticism to indifference. In early 1914, the BBFC
circulated magistrates across the country, pressing that a clause be included
in cinematograph licences stipulating that only films passed by the Board
should be exhibited. Having reviewed the films on show locally, Edinburgh's
magistrates concluded that no action was required and so set the Board's
letter aside.[42] Of the Scottish licensing authorities, only Falkirk appears to
have voted to take up the BBFC's suggestion, becoming the first Scottish
authority to include in its licences the requirement that only subjects
carrying a Board certificate be shown locally.[43]

In their response to the Board, exhibitors were, more often than not,
equally unenthusiastic. At a meeting in Glasgow in January 1913, the month
the BBFC commenced operations, the expectation was voiced that, for the
Board to be effective, it would need Home Office backing. Significantly,
State intervention was a development many appeared to welcome. A. E.
Pickard, not always identifiable as a voice of respectability, was of the view
that only a censorship system based on involvement by central government
was likely to prove effective, while another exhibitor declared that 'it would
be a thousand times better to have a government official as censor'.[44] In
subsequent years, when the debate over approaches to censorship resumed,
this was the view that prevailed. At the height of the First World War, with
the BBFC's ability to act as an effective instrument of regulation in doubt, in
the face of the continued assertion of local autonomy, a move towards State
censorship was extensively discussed. In line with exhibitors elsewhere in
Britain, Scottish cinema proprietors broadly welcomed this development.
Interviewed for *The Bioscope* in September 1916, J. J. Bennell of BB Pictures,
the name justified by the drive to use film for moral uplift, reaffirmed the
need for a central form of censorship possessing the power to override local
interests.[45] The only doubts voiced over the Home Office's greater involvement centred on the degree of influence any centrally constituted body could
exercise, with local authorities reluctant to surrender completely the ability
to determine what could and what could not be shown, and the make-up of
the body that would adjudicate on censorship decisions, the cinema trade
claiming the right to at least a 50 per cent representation.[46] A change in
government at the end of 1916 would ensure that plans for an official censorship were set aside. Nevertheless, exhibitors continued to press the need for
greater centralisation. A variety of factors coloured their reasoning. First, it
would override what for some were increasingly meddlesome local interests,
such as the Kirkcaldy Citizenship Committee which, in 1915, pressed the
local Licensing Court to suspend the licence of a cinema that had distributed

what were deemed to be offensive handbills advertising the film *A Pair of Silk Stockings*, and some Glasgow magistrates who, it was claimed, were capable of finding moral offence in the display of an uncovered leg of mutton in a butcher's shop window.[47] A second consideration, unsurprisingly given prominence by Bennell, was the potential it offered to rid the exhibition sector of 'questionable' films and so enhance the industry's moral reputation. With this in mind, Bennell had long prohibited the showing of race or fight films by cinemas owned by BB Pictures, despite their evident popularity with audiences.[48] A third factor, related to this, and which assumed growing importance as the war progressed, was the problem of undue competition within the trade.

In part, this was linked to the rise, in the middle years of the war, of the super film. Distinguished from the standard cinematic fare of the time by size of budget and length of narrative, the first runs for such productions were, for the most part, in local theatres. Not only did this satisfy producers' desire to imbue their efforts with the respectability of legitimate drama, the large audiences capable of being accommodated in these venues also offered better prospects of a financial return on the limited number of showings which an extended running time made possible.[49] So, D. W. Griffith's epic of the Civil War and Reconstruction phases in American history, *The Birth of a Nation*, first played in Scotland at His Majesty's Theatre, Dundee, before proceeding to the Theatre Royal, Glasgow, and the Royal Lyceum in Edinburgh.[50] If trade papers such as *The Bioscope* were inclined to play down the threat posed by such exhibition strategies, arguing that the use of theatrical venues attracted a new audience to the cinema, the emergence of another film genre towards the war's end gave rise to rather deeper concerns.[51] These centred on so-called 'propaganda' features, films which, by means of fictional narratives, sought to address some of the leading social, political, and moral issues of the day. In general, the BBFC refused to pass such subjects for public exhibition, preferring to define cinema's central role as one of 'entertainment'.[52] Yet the subject matter of these 'propaganda' films justified their circulation among as wide an audience as possible. Most dealt with issues of sexual health, which acquired immediacy with the disruption of 'normal' gender relations as a result of the First World War. In 1919, therefore, the Lanarkshire County and Burgh Committee for the Combating of Venereal Diseases pressed for the exhibition of the Famous Players-Lasky production, *The End of the Road* at the Co-operative Hall, Cambuslang, expressing confidence in 'the unique qualities and all-round excellence of the film, and the material influence it must exercise in fighting this scourge'.[53] A year earlier, another American film, *Where Are My Children?*, which took birth control as its central theme, followed the exhibition route already charted by *The Birth of a Nation*.[54] The temporary hiring of buildings for use as cinemas, many of which did not and were not required to match the conditions set out in licences issued under the 1909 Cinematograph Act, constituted, for many, an important threat to

the industry's commercial viability.[55] Not only were such films held by some
to compromise the trade's bid for respectability, they also proved powerful
popular attractions. In 1920, the trade paper *Scottish Cinema* reported the
booking of a lecture hall in Nottingham to show propaganda subjects. One
film, initially booked for one week, had been retained for three in all and
resulted in queues for admission which stretched along three streets. The
paper was of the view that 'the word "propaganda" is becoming little more
than a camouflage for objectionable plays on sexual matters designed to
benefit financially a certain class of producer'.[56] Six months later, when *The
End of the Road* arrived at the Music Hall in Aberdeen, *The Scottish Kinema
Record* reported that 'so great was the rush that police had to be brought on
the scene to control the struggling mass of excited femininity', resulting in
the kind of incident which had not been witnessed in the Granite City since
'the days when Mrs Pankhurst and her followers were in their most aggres-
sive mood'.[57] Exhibitors raised particular objection against itinerant companies hawking potentially lucrative subjects around the country for short runs
which maximised audiences at the expense of permanent exhibitors who had
to manage with films which varied in popularity week to week.[58]

The latter were finally drawn to act early in 1920, with the arrival in
Edinburgh of a further treatment on the theme of venereal disease, the
G. B. Samuelson production of *Damaged Goods*.[59] In February, the film
opened at Synod Hall, a venue leased from the City Corporation and at
which another 'propaganda' subject denied a BBFC certificate, *Auction of
Souls*, had recently been shown. A private screening was later arranged at
the West End Cinema for local councillors and representatives of interested
parties, including the editor of the *Catholic Herald*.[60] A week later, the local
branch of the Exhibitors' Association approached the city magistrates to
press that only films bearing a certificate should be allowed to be screened
in licensed premises. The magistrates agreed, although reserving to themselves the right to permit the exhibition of 'uncensored' films under conditions which they would determine.[61] By May, the Glasgow magistrates had
agreed a similar line and the policy was being pressed on authorities across
Scotland.[62] Progress was, as Ritson Bennell reported to the Exhibitors'
Association's June meeting, uneven. A number of branches, such as those at
Greenock and Dundee, refused to adopt the new clause limiting exhibition
to films approved by the BBFC.[63] For the most part, however, the conditions
were accepted, with the result that *Damaged Goods*, having secured quite a
wide showing across Scotland, was denied screening in Peebles in August
1920 on the grounds that it lacked certification. While one local correspondent bemoaned the fact that cinema-goers in Peebles were denied access to a
film which could be seen in industrial centres south of the border, such as
Bradford, the editor of *The Scottish Kinema Record* rejected the implication
'that what is good enough for Bradford is good enough for Peebles or any
other town'.[64]

A framework for censorship practices across Scotland had been estab-lished, not as a result of intervention from magistrates or at the prompting of movements for moral reform, although these were active through the period, but as a result of the economic self-interests of exhibitors. It might be noted that the CEA nationally had been pressing the adoption of a similar policy from the start of 1920.[65] However, the speed of the response by Scottish exhibitors, quickened by local concerns over specific films, placed the industry north of the border ahead of that in England. Weight is often given, in discussion of the evolution of censorship practices, to the decision by the Middlesex County Council to include in all licences the requirement only to exhibit certificated films. Yet this decision came in August, some months after exhibitors in Edinburgh had pressed this approach on local magistrates and its adoption by the Scottish Association more generally.[66] In practical terms, the impact of the change was immediately evident. In June 1920, Edinburgh's magistrates refused to allow Synod Hall to be leased for a showing of the horror melodrama *Ghosts*, a subject which did not match any accepted notion of the term 'propaganda'.[67] Over the longer term, a frame-work had been established that would guide approaches to censorship over the succeeding decades. While it would be tedious and somewhat repeti-tive to examine its workings on a case-by-case basis, the broader principles shaping its application may be identified.

First, Scottish licensing authorities broadly accepted the guidance offered by BBFC certification and the definition of what did and what did not constitute a 'propaganda' vehicle which that implied. Sensitive political subjects rejected by the Board rarely received the backing of magistrates. For example, in May 1939, an application by the Edinburgh and District Committee for Spanish Relief to show the Soviet film *Professor Mamlock*, which offered a sustained critique of anti-Semitism in Nazi Germany, was refused by the city magistrates.[68] The changed political climate later that year, which rendered criticism of Nazi policies somewhat more acceptable, led to this feature, along with the American film *I Was a Captive of Nazi Germany*, being belatedly granted certification by the Board.[69] Licensing authorities promptly reconsidered their stand, with the result that *Professor Mamlock* played at Edinburgh's Playhouse cinema during the first winter of the war. The accompanying publicity made much of the initial controversy stirred by the film, while offering reassurance, in suitably restrained lower-case type, that it had gained the approval of the censors:

SEE NAZIDOM STAND CONDEMNED!
SEE PROFESSOR MAMLOCK
THE FILM THE CENSOR BANNED
(Now Awarded an 'A' Certificate).[70]

Only occasionally were the Board's judgments set aside. So, religious sub-jects, although excluded from certification by the BBFC's prohibition on films including 'The materialization of Christ and the Almighty', were more often than not deemed acceptable for public showing north of the border.[71] Cecil B. DeMille's 1927 epic *The King of Kings* was exhibited in both Glasgow and Edinburgh.[72] In the following decade, magistrates revisited the case of *From the Manger to the Cross*, re-released in 1938, complete with spoken commentary drawing on the Bible, and a music soundtrack. Having reviewed the new version, Edinburgh's magistrates substantially endorsed the view expressed by Robert Henderson-Bland, who played Christ, that 'The old film is restrained, reverent, and intensely moving', and allowed its screening locally.[73]

Political subjects excited greater controversy and were, at times, productive of differences between licensing authorities. In 1928, under prompting from the Foreign Secretary, Austen Chamberlain, the Board refused a certificate to the British and Dominions production *Dawn*, a dramatisation of the trial and execution for espionage of the British nurse Edith Cavell. Particular controversy centred on the execution scene, in which a German officer was seen to despatch Cavell after the firing squad had refused to shoot.[74] The Foreign Office's concern that such scenes risked offending the sensibilities of the democratic Weimar government were not, it would seem, shared by *Dawn*'s director and producer, Herbert Wilcox, who sought to override Board objections by inviting licensing authorities to evaluate the film directly. Most, including Glasgow's magistrates, sided with Wilcox, securing the film a wide distribution.[75] By early 1929, this extended to the village of Moray, where a show in aid of the local police fund for destitute children was only blocked on the order of the magistrates of nearby Grantown on Spey. In this case, the objection was not to the film itself, which had played locally for several days, but to plans to run the charity show on a Sunday.[76] In the end, only one Scottish licensing authority appears to have rebuffed Wilcox. In May 1928, after viewing the film at Synod Hall, Edinburgh's magistrates voted unanimously to prohibit its exhibition locally, a decision reaffirmed the following month after a further request by the film's distributors, W&F. Significantly, the magistrates based their decision not on the desirability of maintaining amicable relations with the Weimar regime, but on the need to sustain the authority of the BBFC. As a result, Edinburgh became the only authority in Britain outside the Chamberlain heartland of Birmingham to ban showings of the film.[77]

The example of *Dawn* suggests that access to politically controversial material was not universally denied. Greater concern in the later 1920s centred on the productions of Soviet cinema, whose mainstream exhibition was consistently prohibited.[78] A potential means of circumventing such restrictions was provided by private shows, often organised to encourage a broader appreciation of film as an artistic medium. Such initiatives enjoyed fitful success. In 1930, the London County Council refused the Masses Stage and Film Guild, a body with close links to the Labour Party, permission to mount an exhibition of Pudovkin's *Mother* in a licensed cinema. The Guild's attempts to put the show on in a theatre drew an equally discouraging response from the Lord Chamberlain.[79] That same year, however, the film was screened north of the border, at Pringle's Atmospheric Theatre on Elm Row, Edinburgh. The show was mounted by the recently formed Edinburgh Workers' Progressive Film Society. Here again, Edinburgh found itself anticipated by only one other licensing authority, although in this case the bedfellow was the rather more unlikely socialist hotbed of West Ham.[80] Crucially, the magistrates' decision was conditional on the show remaining strictly 'private'. The Masses Stage and Film Guild had been denied permission to exhibit the film in part because the low subscription charge, designed to maximise access, was also seen to render Guild shows public affairs. Similar problems surrounded the Edinburgh Society's activities. The police reported that guest tickets had been available for sale for as little as 1s 6d each, compromising the supposedly private nature of the show. In the light of police concerns, the Society was refused permission by local magistrates to show Pudovkin's later film *Storm over Asia*, although subsequent screenings were allowed at the Salon Picture House. On this occasion, the private character of the show was ensured by limiting the number of guests to one per member and the requirement that a membership list be available for inspection at any point during the performance.[81] It might be noted that comparable conditions were imposed on screenings by the Edinburgh Film Guild from its formation in 1930, suggesting that they were not designed primarily with the intention of restricting the activities of a left-leaning organisation.[82] Rather, the aim appears to have been to ensure that an effective distinction was maintained between private shows and those subject to BBFC conditions.

Discretion was also exercised over those films deemed by the Board to constitute 'propaganda'. For the most part, such subjects were granted public screenings by Scottish licensing authorities, although agreement was most likely where the film had the backing of agencies of moral reform and where the show was so managed as to minimise associations with 'entertainment'. So, while the application in May 1931 by United Artists to allow the exhibition of *Her Child* (possibly *Her Unborn Child*) was refused by Edinburgh magistrates, the more overtly propagandist production *The Dangers of Ignorance* secured screenings across central Scotland early in 1928.[83] The film's didactic purpose figured prominently in the publicity accompanying showings, such as that at Glasgow's St Andrew's Hall in April. Potential cinema-goers were assured that the subject had been passed by the Central Council for Health Education, while the city's Medical Officer of Health offered further endorsement, declaring that the film addressed 'a difficult subject in a suitable and convincing manner'. Details of the exhibition itself underlined the fact that this was far from a standard show. As was customary with 'propaganda' subjects, separate screenings were organised for men and women, while prices at 1s and 1s 6d were considerably above the norm for cinema shows, and reflected the fact that the exhibition was to be confined to adults only. Finally, the film's message was to be reinforced at each performance by a lecture from a member of the medical profession.[84] The absence of subsequent comment in the press suggests that the screenings in both Glasgow and Edinburgh (where shows at the city's Music Hall were agreed by magistrates in March 1928) proceeded without incident. How far this was a consequence of the explicitly didactic tone which accompanied each exhibition cannot be established with certainty. What is clear is that the emphasis placed on improvement and respectability did not always have the desired effect. When *The Dangers of Ignorance* reached Bradford in West Yorkshire, the female-only screening, timed, as in Glasgow, for 7 p.m., drew large crowds, which began to gather three hours before the doors were due to open. As 7 p.m. approached, a crowd estimated at some 5,000 had gathered around the cinema, creating an obstruction to the movement of local traffic. As a result, the police were called in, but met with a less than welcoming response from picture-goers, who proceeded to knock constables' helmets from their heads and rip open their tunics. Ultimately, this crowd, likened by the press to 'excited Amazons', was only quelled by the arrival of mounted reinforcements.[85] Reaction at male shows, while notable, assumed a rather different character: at a screening in Leeds Town Hall, it was reported that some thirty-seven men had been carried out in dead faints.[86] All the evidence is that the response of Scottish audiences was altogether more stoical.

Once local audiences had had demonstrated to them *The Dangers of Ignorance*, it would be some five years before a film grappling with the problems of sexually transmitted disease would again reach Scottish screens. In November 1933, the British Social Hygiene Council applied to Edinburgh's magistrates to have the film *Damaged Lives*, a US–Canadian production, publicly exhibited. Unlike previous screenings of 'propaganda' vehicles, it was proposed that shows be mounted at a mainstream commercial cinema, the Palace on Princes Street.[87] Agreement followed, once the film had been reviewed by magistrates and reports had been received from the local Medical Officer of Health and the Clinical Medical Officer. However, five conditions were attached to the film's exhibition: these included the requirement for separate screenings for men and women, and a prohibition on attendance below the age of sixteen. In addition, advertisements were to indicate clearly the nature of the picture, which would be emphasised by the stipulation that the supporting programme be confined to newsreels or films of a similar nature. Finally, each performance was to be followed by a brief address from a figure approved by the Medical Officer of Health.[88] As a result of lobbying by the British Social Hygiene Council, mixed-sex screenings, which had been the norm at previous showings of the film, were allowed, although the Council emphasised that advance publicity would play up the production's educative intent. Synopses, along with 'suitable posters', were to be distributed to 'all factories, clubs, etc., where people are employed or congregate in any numbers'.[89] Prospective patrons thus received assurance of the film's 'honesty and sincerity in addressing its subject with a delicacy to which no one could possibly take exception' and were advised that 'It is a film that should be seen by every youth about to set out along the difficult path of manhood and womanhood.'[90] Having agreed the change in screening arrangements, magistrates then ordered the deletion of five minutes from prints on the recommendations of the Clinical Medical Officer.[91]

Despite or perhaps because of such actions, the popular response to the film, marketed by the Palace as a 'Drama and medical lecture', was strong. An attendance of 17,733 in the first week represented the highest audience secured by the 800-seater cinema and was more than double the average April attendance at the Palace.[92] The success attending these screenings and the apparent absence of any wider controversy smoothed the way for the Social Hygiene Council's next subject, the remake of *Damaged Goods*, released as *Marriage Forbidden*, which played at the Palace during the first winter of the Second World War. On this occasion, the magistrates were satisfied with the requirement that admission be limited to those aged sixteen years and over.[93] Here again, the popularity of the subject was marked, with the film securing what was by some distance the largest weekly attendance of 1940 of 13,222, which compared with an average audience across the year of 6,084 and was comfortably ahead of the next highest attendance, 9,615 for the Deanna Durbin musical comedy *It's a Date*.[94] The comparative rarity of 'propaganda' features undoubtedly contributed to their wider impact and may also have served to mute objections to their screening by other exhibitors. They also confirm a desire, among female picture-goers especially, for something other than mere entertainment from the cinema: 'propaganda' films offered access to valuable and otherwise unattainable bodies of information.[95]

On occasion, the conditions attending exhibition could be tightened further. Later in 1940, for example, Edinburgh's magistrates sanctioned the showing of *The Birth of a Baby*, a drama produced by the American Committee on Maternal Welfare. As with *Damaged Lives*, there was concern that the film's educative function should not be compromised by juxtaposition with inappropriate subjects. In this case, the definition of 'adult' was further tightened to exclude all below the age of eighteen, perhaps on the grounds that issues surrounding childbirth only acquired real salience at that point.[96] The film enjoyed a revival after the war, when debate turned on the minimum age at which admission should be allowed. Although the city's Public Health and Education Committees raised no objection to its exhibition to those aged sixteen and over, the magistrates confirmed a higher minimum of eighteen.[97] By the late 1940s, restrictions by age had become the principal condition governing the public exhibition of 'propaganda' films. Three subjects, in which the issue of abortion figured prominently, *La Femme du Pendu*, *Street Corner*, and *We Want a Child*, were all granted screenings in Edinburgh to audiences aged sixteen and over.[98] A rather different approach, however, was taken with *Manon*, Henri-Georges Clouzot's realisation of Abbé Prévost's oft-adapted novel. Initially, Edinburgh's magistrates voted to prohibit any exhibition of the film, presumably being unconvinced that the treatment of prostitution fulfilled any 'propaganda' purpose. The doubts were such that the proposal to limit attendance to those aged sixteen and over was also defeated. An alternative restriction was suggested by the town clerk, who proposed that the film's exhibition be confined to one cinema, the Cameo.[99] Opened in 1949 by J. K. S. Poole, the Cameo was planned as a theatre specialising in the screening of European films in their original language, as well as British and US productions 'of unusual merit'. Poole had detected a taste for foreign-language features among British troops with whom he had served during the Italian campaign, when he acted as Film Officer for the Eighth Army. The theory was first put to the test in Edinburgh at the family's other cinema, Synod Hall, with the screening of *Les Enfants du Paradis*. The results were sufficiently encouraging to persuade the Pooles to launch the Cameo.[100] For the town clerk, the audience drawn to the new theatre differed markedly from those filling cinema seats elsewhere in the city. As he explained, 'the type of film shown at this cinema as a rule attracted adult audiences, [so that] the enforcement of the age condition could be more easily and conveniently secured'.[101]

Locally, then, censorship policy came to revolve around creating and maintaining a hard and fast distinction between adult and child audiences. If this could be achieved quite readily with 'propaganda' subjects, the controls available for limiting access to more mainstream cinematic entertainments were much less developed, particularly north of the border, where even the minimal filter offered by the 'A' certificate was not used to any degree. A review of the Scottish evidence suggests that established accounts, which centre on the Cinematograph Act of 1909 and the creation and operation of the British Board of Film Censors, miss much. In particular, they overlook the profound impact of earlier forms of regulation based on local systems of licensing, which did much to determine the nature of early cinema shows and the kinds of setting within which film was presented to the first generation of cinema-goers. The system of highly localised urban governance inherited from the nineteenth century would cast a long shadow across the first fifty years of the succeeding century. If the trend was towards greater uniformity in the regulation of cinema, that process was both slow and piecemeal and remained coloured throughout by highly local interests. That the BBFC's writ would eventually run widely across Scotland was due less to the imposition of common moral standards as a result of pressure from government or movements for moral reform and more to narrow calculations of economic self-interest among exhibitors, anxious to safeguard the trade's reputation for offering respectable entertainments and to squeeze out unwelcome competition from itinerant operators. The Scottish way with film regulation thus confirms Annette Kuhn's observation that the law should not be seen as an autonomous agent of control, imposed on an industry which was then obliged to operate within a closely defined regulatory framework.[102] Rather, it was itself shaped by diverse influences, political, cultural, and economic in nature, with the manner of its operations determined by whichever prevailed.

Throughout the period, recurrent expressions of concern were offered over what was seen as a failure effectively to regulate access to cinema among the young. It is to the nature of those concerns and their impact that we now turn.

III

The unusual attraction which cinema was thought to have for the young in general and children in particular was apparent from the industry's earliest years. Glasgow Parish Council's investigations into the cheap shows mounted in the city's east end late in the first decade of the century made much of the presence of large numbers of children in morally dubious surroundings. As one observer had it, 'the main portion of the gathering is composed of children', many of whom it was noted lacked parental or adult supervision. Girls thought to be aged eight to twelve years were thus to be found with infants in their arms.[103] The council's findings that children were among the most enthusiastic of picture-goers would be confirmed by subsequent surveys through the period, many of which attempted more precisely to quantify the habit. One of the earliest, undertaken by a Special Committee of Leith School Board, found that almost 40 per cent of local schoolchildren had entered a picture house at least once in the week commencing 19 February 1917.[104] Similar investigations in later decades would reveal a pursuit growing in extent and frequency. So, the Edinburgh Cinema Enquiry, concerned to investigate film's attraction for and importance to the young, conducted in 1932, reported that almost 70 per cent of schoolchildren across the city aged nine and over frequented the pictures at least once a week, while almost one in four were more frequent visitors.[105] Six years later, analysis of school pupils of a similar age across West Lothian found that, although overall the frequency of attendance was lower, over 60 per cent of a sample numbering 8,000 still went once a week or more, while as many as one in four patronised the cinema at least twice each week.[106] In the following decade, investigations at both local and regional levels confirmed the depth and tenacity of the cinema-going habit. In 1948, returns for Rothesay, on the Isle of Bute, a town with three cinemas, indicated that, among primary school pupils, the proportion which could be identified as frequent attenders (at least once a week) varied between 40 per cent at the fee-paying Rothesay Academy to 100 per cent at the Catholic Church-run St Andrew's School.[107] By far the most comprehensive survey of the period was that undertaken in 1945 by Dr R. M. McIntosh, Director of Education at Fife County Council. With the assistance of branches of the Scottish Educational Film Association, information was gathered on the behaviour of over 36,000 children across Ayrshire, Edinburgh, and Glasgow, in addition to Fife. Those undertaking visits to the cinema weekly or more frequently ranged from 72 per cent in Ayrshire to 90 per cent in Glasgow. As well as tracing its geographical extent, the survey also mapped cinema-going by age. So, while 84 per cent of secondary schoolchildren saw the inside of a picture house at least once a week, the same was true of a lower but still impressive 73 per cent of pupils in infant departments.[108]

The extent and persistence of cinema's appeal to the young proved a recurrent source of controversy across the first half of the twentieth century. Anxiety arose from two main sources: the growing perception of childhood as a distinct phase of life with its own values and characteristics that were to be nurtured and cherished, and the particular nature of the entertainments provided in picture houses. The notion of childhood as a period of develop-ment marked by innocence had gained ground over the later decades of the nineteenth century, as extended periods of compulsory education served increasingly to separate and inoculate children from the world of work. Alongside formal schooling, the propensity for play would be encouraged by access to regular exercise, backed by systematic medical inspections, while moral development would be secured through parenting which paid due regard to the psychological needs of each child.[109] The cinema chal-lenged all aspects of this ideal, transforming children before their time into consumers, insinuating base commercial values into this period of supposed innocence. Not only that, early film exhibitors made no attempt, other than through different charges for admission, to distinguish between the various sections of the audience, so that the same programme was available to all able and willing to pay for the privilege.[110] The potential for children becoming exposed to scenes that many deemed unsuitable was thus thought to be great. The danger was seen to be all the greater given the supposedly indiscriminate approach children had to cinema-going. Attendance figures uncovered in successive reports suggested that patronage carried the force of habit and was undertaken regardless of what was being shown. What is more, the characteristics with which childhood was supposed to be imbued also meant that the young were incapable of exercising the self-censorship practised by adult picture-goers. Investigations from the Edinburgh Enquiry through to McIntosh's survey of 1945 concluded that the propensity to attend took no account of the nature of the pictures being exhibited.[111] Their inherent natures enhanced the potential for harm, making children exemplars of the passive consumption of commercial entertainments thought to be charac-teristic of the new mass audience of the early twentieth century.[112] To moral was added the threat of physical damage, as film content worked to stimu-late nervous excitement at the same time that the brightness of projection in a darkened setting worked to weaken eyesight. To a society increasingly inclined to sanctify childhood, the cinema was seen as a dangerous and profane influence.

Specific aspects of the cinema experience gave added force to such concerns. So, Glasgow Parish Council made much of children attending second houses late into the evening, raising concerns over their ability to undertake schoolwork effectively the following day.[113] Evidence on the extent of the practice is mixed. The Edinburgh Enquiry on the whole discounted such anxieties, noting that fewer than 10 per cent of junior school pupils were likely to enter cinemas after 7 p.m.[114] However, figures from elsewhere suggest that late-night attendance was more common than such findings indicate. Accounts prepared by the Stranraer Picture House, Ltd for the year to April 1934 included details on admissions to each house, comprising two evening shows and the occasional matinee, distinguishing adult from juvenile (under sixteen years of age) picture-goers. In all, 36,128 half-price tickets were sold through the year, of which barely 11 per cent were at matinees. By contrast, second shows accounted for 44.1 per cent of juvenile admissions.[115] The degree to which the latter figure was inflated by the presence of young wage earners is uncertain. That said, the comparatively even spread across the two houses suggests that schoolchildren may have been prominent in both audiences. Whatever the position, this was but one of the objections raised by the parish council in Glasgow. The conditions in which films were viewed also gave rise to concern. Visitors to shows in Glasgow's east end around 1910 expressed alarm that so much of children's free time was spent in an atmosphere vitiated by a combination of smoke, variable personal hygiene, and 'vile' language, and in which moral constraints were loosened by the all-pervading darkness. The charge that, in and around the cinema, children were peculiarly vulnerable to acts of gross indecency was levelled on several occasions across the period, although when one Glasgow minister sought to raise the case of a girl said to have been seduced in the vicinity of a picture hall, one Labour councillor responded by pointing to two girls who were rumoured to have undergone a similar experience while attending the same minister's Bible class.[116] That the cinema was a setting replete with moral and physical dangers for children was a view frequently voiced through the period. Yet the principal source of unease throughout remained the nature of the entertainment provided and the presumed failure of censorship mechanisms put in place over the period to offer effective protection for young and impressionable minds.

Over the first fifty years of the century, then, a variety of concerns coalesced around the issue of children's cinema-going. At various points, particular issues would assume prominence and specific regulatory remedies were sought. The earliest legislation to acknowledge the problems occasioned by a sizeable juvenile presence in the cinema audience was the Children Act of 1908, which set out minimum requirements as to the number of attendants needed to supervise shows substantially attended by the young. In 1913, it was used by Edinburgh magistrates to stipulate that nine members of staff be employed to oversee Saturday matinees at the Operetta House.[117] The conditions attached to licences issued under the Cinematograph Act of 1909 applied without regard to the age composition of the audience. Nevertheless, in 1910, licensing authorities came under pressure to address concerns raised by children attending shows without parental accompaniment and their presence at late-night shows. In some areas, the response was to prohibit attendance beyond a specified hour. In Fraserburgh, Aberdeenshire, from 1912, children of school age were to be banned from entering picture houses after 9 p.m., regardless of whether they were accompanied or not.[118] More generally, admission was made conditional on the presence of an adult, given that, as many exhibitors argued, to prohibit children's attendance would effectively exclude their parents. Mothers, it was argued, would be deterred from cinema visits if, in order to do so, they were obliged to leave their children unaccompanied at home.[119] Such was the position adopted in Glasgow where, in 1912, the magistrates were pressed to take on the censoring of film content.[120] Although the limited nature of existing powers under local Police Acts, confirmed as has been seen by the provisions of the Cinematograph Act and the creation of the British Board of Film Censors, were thought to preclude any move to adopt local systems of censorship, the magistrates were prepared to act on the question of children's attendance. From March 1913, therefore, they recommended that new conditions be attached to cinema licences. These included the requirement that no child under fourteen years of age be allowed into licensed premises after 9.30 p.m., unless accompanied by a parent or guardian, and that at other times, unaccompanied children of school age be provided with separate seating accommodation.[121] Despite protests by George Green, in his capacity as chairman of the local Exhibitors' Association, that managers would be unable to determine the ages of children seeking admission or to establish whether the adult accompanying was, in truth, their parent or guardian, the by-laws were confirmed at a subsequent sitting of the Licensing Court.[122] The following year, the Glasgow regulations were cited by the Educational Institute of Scotland in its call for similar controls on children's attendance in Edinburgh. Here, in consultation with the local School Board, the magistrates agreed in May 1914 on a condition being added to cinematograph licences whereby 'a child under twelve years of age shall not be allowed to remain in such premises after nine o'clock pm unless accompanied by a parent or guardian'.[123] Exhibitors had pressed the case for a lower age on the grounds of practicability. Despite this, doubts persisted as to how far such regulations were enforceable, to the degree that magistrates felt bound to acknowledge that strict compliance with the conditions would not be expected. At the half-yearly meeting of the Edinburgh and East of Scotland branch of the Cinematograph Exhibitors' Association the following October, the executive reported a discussion with the local licensing authorities at which the assurance had been given 'that so long as exhibitors did their best to comply with the rule, its observance would not be rigidly enforced'.[124] Recognition at this early date of the essentially discretionary nature of such regulations suggests that their practical impact was limited. Indeed, the fact that in 1926 the United Free Church Presbytery of Glasgow could press for the introduction of similar restrictions, in this case barring unaccompanied children after 7.30 p.m., suggests that, by that date, the original by-law had become a dead letter.[125]

An alternative approach to the issue of children's cinema-going was attempted from early 1914, when a number of halls in central Glasgow introduced matinees of educational films. Synopses of the subjects to be shown were made available to children in advance, in order that the programmes could provide the basis for school lessons.[126] In the end, however, problems over the supply of such subjects as well as entrenched scepticism over the motives of proprietors in providing such shows, limited their development. For some critics, matinees, for all their supposed educational purpose, merely worked to inculcate and nurture a cinema-going habit that worked in the main to undermine the influence of the classroom. So, the proposal of Eastwood School Board in 1915 to reward children with unblemished attendance records with trips to educational film shows, received a less than encouraging response from HM Inspector of Schools.[127] Unqualified enthusiasm for the cinema, as at Kirkintilloch, where the local School Board considered allowing children whose attendance was considered exemplary free admission to the town's picture houses, remained wholly exceptional.[128]

Longstanding concerns over the wider impact of children's cinema-going acquired additional force in the altered circumstances of wartime. Even before 1914, a tendency to cite attendance as a factor contributing to problems of juvenile delinquency had been noted by exhibitors.[129] As rates of offending among the young appeared to escalate in the early months of the war, suspicions over the damage wrought by the cinema hardened, in many cases, into certainty. Figures compiled by the Edinburgh School Board on cases of theft involving the young showed a continuous rise from 1910–11, the rate of increase accelerating in the first year of the war. At that point, the number stood at almost three times the levels of four years before. In explaining the trend, much was made of a perceived weakening in parental controls, with many fathers absent in the forces, while mothers were often obliged to take on paid work outside the home, thereby compromising their domestic authority. Streets darkened by lighting restrictions and fuel shortages, along with police forces depleted by enlistments in the military, served to compound the problem of maintaining order. In addition to these, a prime factor seen to encourage criminal behaviour was the example provided by films on local release. Detailed evidence was cited in support of this view, including the case of three children, aged nine to eleven, who appeared before an English court, having broken into a safe 'by means of a flat-iron, a chisel, and nails' to steal £30 in gold, which was used to indulge several pleasures in the immediate vicinity, including, almost inevitably, a trip to the local picture house. 'The whole plan', it was observed, 'savours of the screen.'[130] In court, attendance at the cinema was occasionally advanced, in mitigation, as a factor inducing the young to offend. The agent for five boys who appeared before Edinburgh's Juvenile Court in March 1917, charged with the theft from a Roseburn tobacconist's of 135 cigars, 1,460 cigarettes, and 19s 6d in cash, thus sought to explain that 'their conduct was largely due to the harmful effect upon them through seeing crime pictures at the cinema houses'.[131] Alongside school bodies, the Church also pointed to the cinema's contribution to a growing social problem. The report of the Church of Scotland's Committee on Social Work to the 1916 meeting of the General Assembly used 'the evil influence on the youthful imagination of sensational and objectionable cinema films' to argue the case for a more rigorous film censorship.[132]

The case against the cinema did not go unanswered. J. J. Bennell was one of many in the trade to seek to deflect criticism by pointing to the broader impact of war and 'the prevalent glorification of violence'.[133] In a circular to patrons of Glasgow's Lorne Cinema, issued around the time of the Somme offensive, the manager A. B. King rather more mischievously made reference to the 'abnormal conditions' then prevailing, in which 'human life is held cheap, and Press and Pulpit are applauding the glories of war'.[134] If some sort of defence could be anticipated from the industry itself, it received telling support from the police. Early in 1917, the National Council of Public Morals, comprising educationists and representatives of child welfare organisations, approached licensing authorities as part of its drive to gather evidence for its inquiry into 'the physical, social, educational, and moral influences of the cinema, with special reference to young people'.[135] Chief constables north of the border largely rejected any notion of a direct link between the cinema and juvenile crime. In Dundee, the view was that, while theft was often motivated by a desire to gain access to places of entertainment, there was no evidence that picture houses were the sole or even a leading influence on behaviour. Gaming machines, placed in ice-cream parlours, appeared to many a more certain inducement to crime.[136] In his extended evidence to the National Council's Commission of Inquiry, the Chief Constable of Edinburgh, Roderick Ross, praised the cinema as a source of increased sobriety and saw wartime social dislocation as a more powerful influence on juvenile behaviour.[137] Most of Ross' colleagues broadly endorsed this view, although the Chief Constable of the Border town of Hawick dissented, reasserting the view that the desire to gain admission to local picture houses had drawn a number of youngsters into crime. The problem was such, in his opinion, as to necessitate the introduction of a local censorship to oversee films intended for children's matinees.[138] In general, the police view sufficed to block moves to tighten further the regulation of local cinemas. At the same time, however, it fell short of fully exonerating the industry. Ross was not alone in expressing concern over the cinema's potential to influence those of an impressionable age through material that was often suggestive of immoral conduct. For the Chief Constable of Stirling, that problem could only be addressed through the wholesale elimination of any such subject by means of 'the most strict censorship'.[139] In its report, the National Council would broadly endorse the police line, concluding that, while the cinema could not be seen directly to induce crime, it was still capable of exercising a more insidious influence on the young, encouraging imitation of actions witnessed on the screen. The door thus remained open to further calls for tighter controls of the industry. One Baptist minister in Hawick was unequivocal, declaring the cinema to be 'one of the Devil's most blatant instruments for the destruction of all that was pure and holy'.[140]

If the investigation of 1917 had revealed the need for some measures to protect young cinema-goers, action when it came was driven by other, more immediate concerns. The influenza outbreak in the last weeks of the Great War led to proposals to contain the spread of infection which, in Edinburgh at least, included closing local schools and prohibiting children below the age of fifteen from attending picture houses. The restrictions applied for some three weeks, from which point a partial lifting was agreed, so that children were allowed to attend cinemas where separate rather than continuous shows were the norm, provided an interval of at least 30 minutes between screenings was observed, to allow the auditorium to be ventilated. In the case of continuous shows, children were only to be allowed in before 5 p.m.[141] Not until mid December, some six weeks after the original regulations had been introduced, was the incidence of the disease considered sufficiently under control to justify a return to 'normal' conditions.[142] Subsequently, more localised outbreaks generated calls for comparable measures. In February 1922, Inverness Town Council ordered the closure of all schools and debated extending restrictions to local cinemas, although in the latter case action was stayed by doubts as to the extent of the council's authority.[143]

Local emergencies apart, the regulations governing children's cinema-going by the end of the war remained largely unchanged from those in force before 1914. Nevertheless, pressure for reform would intensify in the early post-war years, a consequence of heightened concern over what was perceived to be the undue financial independence of the young in a period of economic prosperity, along with lingering uncertainty as to the suitability of many of the films on release.[144] If the exhibitors' action in limiting screenings to those subjects approved by the BBFC helped to allay some fears, it did not eliminate them entirely. Across many parts of Scotland, then, licensing authorities moved further to tighten the regulations governing children's attendance. Late in 1920, Dumbarton magistrates pressed that no child under the age of five be allowed to attend picture houses.[145] Yet the

most concerted attempt to amend the cinema-going behaviour of the young
was attempted in the far north-east of the country. In September 1920, the
Director of Education for the County of Caithness voiced concern over the
effect that frequent visits to the cinema were having on the young, proposing
as a solution that only children accompanied by an adult be admitted.[146] In
addressing such problems, the authorities in Wick and Thurso went further,
barring children of school age and under from attending anything other than
Saturday matinees. The avowed intention behind the move was to ensure
that school attendance did not suffer through the unwelcome diversions
offered by local picture houses. Hall managers pressed for some relaxation
of the rule, arguing that allowing attendance only on Fridays and school holidays would be equally effective in meeting the councils' aims. The original
decision was, however, confirmed. The effect of what *The Scottish Kinema
Record* dubbed 'Wick Wisdom' was welcomed by some. One former bailie
reported approvingly that the absence of children had rendered screenings at
Wick's Pavilion 'as peaceful as a Wee Free prayer meeting', not an effect, it
may be thought, that many exhibitors actively strove to achieve.[147]

More generally, pressure for additional measures more effectively to
safeguard the moral welfare of young cinema-goers was maintained across
the first post-war decade. Concerns over the perceived links between regular
attendance and delinquent behaviour resurfaced in the early 1920s, following an inquiry in Edinburgh by the Scottish National Council of Juvenile
Organisations. While it was accepted that the cinema was often cited in
court as a means of exonerating criminal behaviour, cases such as that of a
boy aged ten, found guilty of arson and who was said to have been inspired
by witnessing similar actions in numerous western films, were seen to justify
the need for greater vigilance. The report was the occasion for an approach
to the city magistrates by the local Juvenile Organisations' Committee, pressing the prohibition of films judged by the BBFC to be suitable 'for adults
only'.[148] In Glasgow, a similar call for tighter civic censorship was made. This
involved barring children of school age or below from second houses and
eliminating from all shows they were allowed to attend all subjects considered 'sensational and nerve-wracking'. Here, the city's Education Authority
became the focus for a sustained campaign to introduce local censorship
through the 1920s. The most developed statement of this position was elaborated in 1925, when it was proposed, following a report by the Association
of Headmasters and Headmistresses, that a Joint Committee of the City
Corporation and the Education Authority act as a local censorship board.
In place of the BBFC's system of certification, a three-fold classification of
films was outlined: those considered suitable for both adults and children;
those fit for adult viewing only; and those unsuitable for either. To back this
up, more effective restrictions on the attendance of unaccompanied children
were set out. In general, the trade remained dismissive of the efforts of those
it designated as 'cranks', 'busybodies', and 'Holy Willies'.[149] Exhibitors

had long viewed local censorship as an obstacle to commercial effectiveness and this attitude was only likely to harden further as increasing numbers of cinemas developed shared booking arrangements so as to achieve savings on the cost of hiring films.[150] So, Thomas Ormiston, who, as chairman of the Glasgow branch of the CEA, headed repeated representations against the Education Authority's proposals, was responsible by the later 1920s for booking films for some eighteen halls across south and central Scotland, from Ayr in the west through to Lochgelly in Fife.[151] With each house potentially subject to different decisions over what could or could not be shown, the viability of the business would be seriously called into question. Little wonder, then, that exhibitors through the period favoured a more uniform and legally binding system of censorship that would eliminate scope for local variations.

Significantly, civic leaders were equally unenthusiastic about taking on additional responsibilities. In 1926, Glasgow's magistrates voted against the Education Authority's latest call for local censorship.[152] Their decision reflected the conviction that existing conditions attaching to cinematograph licences, in particular the requirement only to show films passed by the BBFC, offered sufficient safeguards for the audience. The ability of local authorities to assume further powers was also questioned by officials at the Scottish Office, which advised that as the guidelines drafted by the Secretary of State following the passage of the 1909 Act had been confined to questions of audience safety, that effectively defined the areas over which licensing authorities could claim competence. The law was seen to offer no leeway for the introduction of local censorship.[153] By the end of the 1920s, critics of existing arrangements began to adopt an alternative approach. Instead of a tightening of local regulations, a more uniform approach to censorship was envisaged, bringing Scotland into line with practices across England and Wales. Since 1913, the Home Office had been pressing local authorities to observe 'model conditions', including the requirement to display at entrances and on screens immediately prior to each show the classification of each film in the programme and, more importantly, to prohibit the admission of children below the age of sixteen to films considered unsuitable for universal exhibition unless accompanied by a parent or bona fide guardian. By early 1931, this definition of conditions attaching to the 'A' certificate, first devised by the London County Council, had been adopted by some thirty-four out of eighty-three English County Boroughs.[154] In Scotland, however, the narrower definition of licensing powers set out by the Secretary of State meant that no distinction in terms of admissions could be made between 'U' and 'A' films.[155] The only regulations in force remained those agreed by the exhibitors, limiting showings to films carrying BBFC certificates. At the same time that the Home Office intensified pressure to have the 'model conditions' accepted, reform groups came to press their adoption north of the border. In March 1932, the Standing Committee of the

Scottish branch of the National Council of Women, a body which had long concerned itself with the effectiveness of controls on children's film-going, approached the Edinburgh magistrates on just this question. In response, the town clerk noted that one of the Committee's demands, that screenings be limited to films approved by the BBFC, was already in place. On adopting other aspects of the 'model conditions' he was, however, more doubtful. If the principal concern was the effect of a film on the young, that, he argued, would hardly be altered by the presence or otherwise of an accompanying adult. Furthermore, effective enforcement of the 'A' rule was considered impossible, while the further proposal to designate 'A' films as suitable for adults only would be counterproductive, as 'to require a notice or an intimation to be published that a film is for adults only is to stimulate a desire on the part of youth to see the film'. Given such arguments, the magistrates declared a preference for a simplified system of certification whereby all films passed by the BBFC would be deemed suitable for universal exhibition.[156]

If this approach to the magistrates was promptly rebuffed, the issue of censorship was taken up again, this time with rather more effect, by the Edinburgh and District Juvenile Organisations' Committee. Having for some time concerned itself with the impact of the cinema on the young, in 1931 the Committee approached interested parties to contribute to an investigation of the subject.[157] Unlike similar inquiries launched at the same time south of the border, which were informed by an entrenched hostility towards the industry, the Edinburgh investigation adopted a more neutral, openly scientific approach. Questionnaires drafted by the Educational Institute of Scotland, under advice from the Director of the Research Council for Scotland, sought to reconstruct patterns of attendance and film preferences among local schoolchildren, while separate surveys gathered the opinions of parents and teachers.[158] While the returns did not offer a blanket condemnation of the industry, they did little to challenge the belief that children were poorly served both by the cinema trade and by the law. Whereas teachers appeared divided over the question of whether exposure to pictures stunted or nurtured children's creativity, over 90 per cent agreed that the average programme served up to young cinema-goers was unsuitable. This perception was reinforced by the reports of visitors to local picture houses, which found that, although the 'U' film predominated, almost 40 per cent of these were considered more fitting for adult audiences, given the prominence accorded sex as a theme, while over two-thirds encouraged an 'unhealthy excitement' among child viewers.[159] Despite the absence from the final report of anything resembling a 'moral panic', it provided the basis for a renewed call to the Secretary of State for an official inquiry into film censorship north of the border. The First World War apart, politicians had consistently shied away from any close involvement in the regulation of film content, preferring to leave such matters to the trade itself. In a similar vein and in an attempt to deflect calls for any more detailed investigation, the Secretary of State, Sir

Godfrey Collins, now urged Scottish exhibitors to adopt the Home Office's 'Model Conditions'. Here, progress was uneven. It was agreed that BBFC classifications for each film would be displayed outside cinemas, so that *The Scotsman* remarked in April 1934 on 'A' and 'U' certificates appearing 'like a rash . . . among the picture house advertisements'.[160] Beyond that, however, exhibitors proved reluctant to go, declining to take responsibility for excluding anyone on the grounds of age. Reformers reluctantly accepted this argument, on the understanding that the workings of the new agreement would be reviewed after twelve months. In the interim, the findings of unofficial inquiries offered little cause for comfort. The National Council of Women found 'convincing proof that children in very considerable numbers are frequently present during the exhibition of "A" films'.[161] The Scottish Office also sought to gather evidence on the certification of films and the presence of unaccompanied children at programmes where 'A' films were shown. The information gathered was not made public and appears not to have survived, save for isolated cases such as the burgh of Rutherglen, where it was found that while 'A' films made up only 40 per cent of films screened in local cinemas over the first eleven months of the agreement, they featured in almost two-thirds of all programmes. If this suggested that children, as regular attenders, were repeatedly exposed to what was deemed 'adult' material, the returns from Rutherglen also suggested that in the great majority of cases they were accompanied by a parent or bona fide guardian. Only at the Grand Central Picture House were unaccompanied children found to account for as much as 10 per cent of the audience.[162]

For all this, pressure to accept the 'Model Conditions' in full did not abate and was taken up two years later by a new Secretary of State, Walter Elliot. On this occasion, exhibitors responded by offering to review conditions for children-only shows. As has been seen, until the 1930s, shows specifically aimed at the young were confined to special screenings of material that was explicitly educational in content. In addition to the matinees already noted, in the 1920s, the manager of Edinburgh's Savoy cinema, Jimmy Nairn, oversaw programmes designed to inform children of the work of a variety of organisations, from the Scottish Society for the Prevention of Cruelty to Animals, to the League of Nations.[163] Similarly, early in 1931, schoolchildren from across the city were treated to special matinee screenings of the Wardour interest film *Cape to Cairo*.[164] At more mainstream, commercial exhibitions, the programmes rarely differed from the standard bill of fare offered through the rest of the week. In part, this reflected an unwillingness to bear the costs that would be incurred in hiring films for single screenings, and also the desire to limit potentially disruptive elements attending adult shows and so deterring other patrons from attending. The latter point was advanced by James Graham, proprietor of six houses across Glasgow and, more notoriously, the Glen Cinema in Paisley, scene of the worst disaster in British cinema history, when cries of 'Fire' during the matinee on Hogmanay in 1929 led to a panic culminating in seventy deaths, as children rushed for an exit that was found to be blocked.[165] At the trial of the Glen's manager on a charge of culpable homicide, further reflections on the motives behind such shows were offered:

> Q. – Were the matinees for children all more in the nature of a charitable thing than a business concern? A. – Well, I should say as far as during the week was concerned, it was a charitable thing. The drawings on this occasion on the 31st December were just a little over £3.[166]

In the case of the Glen, the limited takings appear to have provided the justification for the minimal level of staffing in place that afternoon. When the programme began, some 700 children were overseen by one male attendant, a former furnace-man, for whom poor health precluded regular employment, and a fifteen-year-old girl, whose main responsibility, when not selling chocolates, was to check the back entrance to ensure that children could not gain entry without paying – here, it would seem, the limits of charity had been reached. Although the manager was acquitted of the charge of culpable homicide, staffing arrangements were considered in breach of the terms of the Children Act of 1908.[167] In the wake of the disaster, therefore, licensing authorities moved to reaffirm the levels of supervision required at children's shows.[168]

This may have had the effect of reinforcing the need to minimise the costs incurred elsewhere in the hire of film, among other things. Certainly, the National Council of Women's investigation into the working of the voluntary agreement between exhibitors and the Secretary of State over adoption of the 'Model Conditions' revealed programmes in which 'inappropriate' subjects continued to preponderate. Visits to two Glasgow cinemas, at each of which children's matinees were held twice weekly, showed that, in one fifteen-week period, out of sixty films exhibited, fifty had carried 'A' certificates, while in another period in which note was taken of the content of programmes, this time covering seven weeks, 'A' films accounted for twenty out of twenty-eight items on programmes.[169] Elliot's approach to exhibitors was thus partly driven by the renewed criticism to which such findings gave rise. In response, rather than the wholesale adoption of the 'Model Conditions' that had been proposed, proprietors advanced a further voluntary agreement whereby only films granted a 'U' certificate would be shown at children's matinees. This suggestion drew in part on the success of matinee performances in both Edinburgh and Glasgow, organised by the Edinburgh Film Guild, the Scottish Educational Film Society, and the Scottish Educational Sight and Sound Association. Although the bulk of programmes comprised, as might be expected given this provenance, educational subjects, this was mitigated somewhat by the inclusion of one of Disney's growing output of cartoons.[170] Along with this, a more general shift in film production in favour of 'U' certificate subjects as the Production Code in the USA was more rigorously enforced, rendered the policy now advanced by exhibitors more practicable.[171] Nevertheless, it proved to be not without difficulties of its own. Shortly after the new policy on matinees had been agreed, Disney released its first feature-length cartoon, *Snow White and the Seven Dwarfs*. Whether because of its less than sympathetic presentation of step-parenthood or the unorthodox cohabitation arrangements depicted therein, the film was awarded an 'A' certificate by the BBFC, prompting exhibitors to go back to Elliot to seek a relaxation of their self-denying ordinance.[172]

With the intervention of another war, it would be the late 1940s before attention turned in concerted fashion once more to the issue of children's cinema-going. Interest centred on the work of the growing number of Cinema Clubs active across Britain. Originating in the 1930s and most closely associated with the Odeon, ABC, and Granada chains of theatres, the notion of organised matinees with programmes designed specifically with children in mind was taken up and developed further by J. Arthur Rank, who, by the latter years of the war, controlled both the Odeon and Gaumont-British chains.[173] Offering 'uplift with a smile', the clubs endeavoured to encourage an active approach to leisure among the young, so that, along with cinema-going, children could be involved in sports, dramatic presentations, and club outings. Publications, from magazines to annuals, stressed cinema's place as a collective focus for identification. Here, members' activities were extensively documented, while a sense of belonging was encouraged further through club songs and mottoes.[174] Furthermore, as the chairman of the club at Edinburgh's New Victoria Cinema emphasised, by involving children in the running of such organisations, they also assisted in developing a sense of civic responsibility among the young.[175] Some questioned Rank's altruism, arguing that clubs were primarily intended to instil a taste for cinema-going at an early age. An investigation by the Edinburgh Education Committee in 1948 found, however, that club members were drawn disproportionately from children with higher than average academic attainments and who were already active in a range of other organisations. By contrast, 'the "tough" element', comprising those prone to 'truancy and delinquency' rarely figured on club rolls. Doubts also continued to be expressed about club programmes, which were not always thought to match Rank's vision of moral uplift.[176] The Parliamentary Secretary to the Board of Trade offered a neat summation of the division of opinion over the clubs: 'Fifty per cent. of the people I meet seem to be in favour of them, and the other 50 per cent. regard them as the work of the devil in the person of Mr Rank.'[177]

For the Committee, a point of significance was that attendance at Saturday matinees was, for most members, additional to rather than in place of visits to standard cinema shows. Unease over the cinema's capacity to colour young minds thus endured and was given renewed impetus by complaints voiced by the Association of County Councils in England over the working of the censorship system.[178] In response to such criticisms, the Committee on Children and the Cinema was established, allowing some Scots once more to lament the absence of statutory powers to regulate children's attendance. The cinema continued to be credited with exercising a damaging influence over the development of the young, encouraging, in the view of the Bute Education Committee, 'either precocious cynicism or distorted appreciation of the purpose of living', and contributing significantly to 'the present very low standard of manners and speech'. In addressing such problems, councillors proposed a wholesale revision of cinematic provision for the young, calling for a prohibition on admissions to picture houses below the age of ten, the limit to be raised in successive years until the ban extended to all under fifteen years of age. In place of ordinary commercial shows, separate performances for children would be mounted at which all films would be previewed and approved by a board on which educational interests would be fully represented.[179] The need to construct alternative forms of cinema exhibition was also pressed by the Association of County Councils in Scotland, in its submission to the Committee on Children and the Cinema (the Wheare Committee) in September 1948. Attention focused on the role of Cinema Clubs in offering programmes of an appropriately educational character. Their ability to do so would be enhanced, it was argued, through developing close links with local education authorities. Furthermore, by encouraging connections with other youth leisure organisations, Clubs would contribute to a more rounded approach to the use of free time. The picture house would thus form one aspect of a more varied recreational routine, removing the worst excesses of contemporary patterns of cinema-going.[180] In its final submission, the Association was somewhat less ambitious, contenting itself with an expression of hope that Cinema Clubs would work to encourage a demand for more 'appropriate' films. To assist in this, an additional subsidiary classification of films within the 'U' category was proposed, identifying subjects suitable for children. The principal concern, however, remained that the regulations governing children's attendance south of the border should also apply in Scotland.[181] Yet after their only meeting north of the border, members of the Committee expressed doubts over the likely impact of any such change, arguing that the 'Model Conditions', particularly as they applied to admitting under-sixteens to the exhibition of 'A' films, were less than effective.[182] In its final report, published in 1950, the Committee proposed no change in the conditions attaching to 'U' and 'A' certificates, although it did recommend the creation of the 'X' certificate (an elaboration of the 'H' certificate introduced in the later 1930s), to identify films suitable for exhibition to audiences aged eighteen and over. Additional regulations covering the admission of younger children were also proposed, including a minimum age of seven for unaccompanied children at mainstream film shows, a prohibition on children below the age of five attending any exhibition, even if intended for child audiences, and, in a distant echo of controls attempted before 1914, the exclusion of children below the age of twelve from shows scheduled to start after 8 p.m., unless accompanied by an adult.[183]

IV

Implementation and the wider impact of the Wheare Committee's recommendations lie beyond the scope of the present investigation. However, the deliberations that informed its report were indicative of the persistence of concerns surrounding the regulations governing the cinema and their ability adequately to protect young picture-goers in particular. The terms of the debate appear barely to have altered over four decades. The findings of the inquiry undertaken by the National Council of Public Morals in 1917 that, while no direct link with delinquent behaviour could be established, the influence of the cinema on the minds and outlook of its patrons remained real, informed most of the criticisms voiced by subsequent investigations.[184] That such sustained pressure for reform, from educationists, Church representatives, and women's groups proved incapable of effecting significant change points to the existence of powerful countervailing forces. Throughout, the attitude of local politicians and the police, fortified by energetic lobbying on the part of representatives of the cinema trade itself, sufficed to deflect calls for a radical overhaul of censorship practices. The history of the cinema's first half century in Scotland thus confirms Annette Kuhn's contention that regulatory frameworks were the outcome of the interplay of competing interests.[185] A variety of forces, operating at both national and local levels, came together to determine the decisions of individual licensing authorities. In Scotland, a further influence may be identified in a distinctive pattern of local governance, so that the system of local licensing created in the Victorian period would continue through the early decades of the following century. Legislative changes, such as the Cinematograph Act of 1909, supplemented existing regulations concerned with audience safety, but left existing licensing arrangements substantially intact. The creation of the British Board of Film Censors also evoked a muted response in its early years. While greater uniformity in terms of censorship practices was achieved in later decades, this was not the result of the campaigns of moral reformers, but a consequence of economic self-interest among exhibitors, for whom adoption of BBFC guidelines offered the most effective means of marginalising the competitive threat emanating from itinerant shows. Once that challenge had been removed, calls for the adoption of further rules on certification were stoutly resisted. To exhibitors' concerns over the practicability of distinguishing between different members of the audience by age were added the views expressed by 'Kinoman' in the *Evening Times* that, through such changes, Scots law was being overridden.[186] A 'British' system of regulation was to be resisted, with the result, which to many appeared paradoxical if not downright unnatural, that the regulations governing censorship north of the border remained more relaxed than those which applied to the south.

One point upon which both critics and champions of the cinema were agreed was the importance which this leisure form had come to assume in the everyday life of Scots. In its evidence to the Wheare Committee, the Association of County Councils in Scotland noted the particular allure of the picture house to those living in poor social conditions, so that 'The more comfortless the home, the more incentive is offered to the child to go to the cinema.'[187] What before 1914 had appeared a recreational novelty of uncertain lasting power had become by the middle decades of the century a central thread in the social fabric for many. To a large degree, that change was effected in the phase of cinema's development encompassing the years of the Great War and the economically and politically turbulent decade that followed it. It is to that decade and a half, marking the organisational and artistic maturation of silent cinema, that we now turn.

NOTES

1. Burrows, 'Penny Pleasures', p. 66; J. Earl, 'Building the Halls', in P. Bailey (ed.), *Music Hall: The Business of Pleasure* (Milton Keynes and Philadelphia, 1986), pp. 1–32; P. Bailey, 'Custom, Capital and Culture in the Victorian Music Hall', in R. D. Storch (ed.), *Popular Culture and Custom in Nineteenth-Century England* (Beckenham, 1982), pp. 180–208; id., *Leisure and Class in Victorian England: Rational Recreation and the Contest for Control, 1830–1885* (London, 1978), ch. 7; D. Russell, *Popular Music in England, 1840–1914: A Social History*, 2nd edn (Manchester, 1997), chs 5–7; P. Summerfield, 'The Effingham Arms and the Empire: Deliberate Selection in the Evolution of Music Hall in London', in E. and S. Yeo (eds), *Popular Culture and Class Conflict, 1590–1914: Explorations in the History of Labour and Leisure* (Brighton, 1981), pp. 209–40.
2. J. Richards and J. C. Robertson, 'British Film Censorship', in R. Murphy (ed.), *The British Cinema Book*, 3rd edn (London, 2008), pp. 67–77; Low, *History of the British Film, 1906–1914*, ch. 2; A. Aldgate and J. C. Robertson, *Censorship in Theatre and Cinema* (Edinburgh, 2005); T. D. Mathews, *Censored* (London, 1994), chs 1 and 2; D. R. Williams, 'The Cinematograph Act of 1909: An Introduction to the Impetus Behind the Legislation and Some Early Effects', *Film History*, 9 (1997), pp. 341–50.
3. A. Kuhn, *Cinema, Censorship and Sexuality, 1909–1925* (London, 1988), ch. 2; S. J. Smith, *Children, Cinema and Censorship: From Dracula to the Dead End Kids* (London, 2005), ch. 2; Low, *History of the British Film, 1906–1914*, pp. 87–9; N. Hiley, '"No Mixed Bathing": The Creation of the British Board of Film Censors in 1913', *Journal of Popular British Cinema*, 3 (2000), pp. 5–19.
4. Low, *History of the British Film, 1914–1918*, pp. 134–8; National Council of Public Morals, *The Cinema: Its Present Position and Future Possibilities, being the Report of and Chief Evidence Taken by the Cinema Commission of Inquiry instituted by the National Council of Public Morals* (New York, [1917] 1971), Minutes of Evidence, Mr T. P. O'Connor, MP, pp. 254–5.
5. Kuhn, *Cinema, Censorship and Sexuality*, pp. 25–7; Low, *History of the British Film, 1918–1929*, pp. 55–70; Smith, *Children, Cinema and Censorship*, pp. 32–3.
6. Kuhn, *Cinema, Censorship and Sexuality*, ch. 1.

7. *Scotsman*, 6 March 1920, p. 9; Smith, *Children, Cinema and Censorship*.

8. Burrows, 'Penny Pleasures II', p. 186; McKernan, '"Only the Screen was Silent . . ."', pp. 12–13.

9. GCA, RU4/2/15, Rutherglen, Cinematograph Act, 1909. Scottish Office to Town Clerk, County Clerk, and Clerk of the Peace, 19 June 1935.

10. J. Lindsay, Corporation of Glasgow, *Review of Municipal Government in Glasgow* (Glasgow and Edinburgh, n.d.), p. 29.

11. Edinburgh City Archives (hereafter ECA), SL119/2/6, Edinburgh Corporation, Magistrates Minutes, 1909–16, 22 Oct. 1909; GCA, Minutes of Corporation of Glasgow, Magistrates Committee, 14 Sept. 1908.

12. *Bioscope*, 23 Sept. 1909, p. 17.

13. R. Rodger, *The Transformation of Edinburgh: Land, Property and Trust in the Nineteenth Century* (Cambridge, 2001), pp. 485–6; Maloney, *Scotland and the Music Hall*, pp. 74–5.

14. GCA, Minutes of Corporation of Glasgow, Magistrates Committee, 2, 16 April; 17 Dec. 1908.

15. Burrows, 'Penny Pleasures', pp. 66–8.

16. *ET*, 9 Nov. 1908, p. 6; 18 Dec. 1909, p. 7.

17. Statutory Rules and Orders, 1910. No. 289 S. 9. *Cinematograph Scotland. Regulations, dated March 10, 1910, Made by the Secretary for Scotland under the Cinematograph Act, 1909 (9 Edw. 7, c. 30)*; ECA, SL 119/2/6, Magistrates Minutes, 1909–16, 9 Feb. 1910; GCA, MP41/106, Memorandum by Town Clerk on the Cinematograph Act, 1909, and Relative Regulations made by the Secretary of State for Scotland on 10 March 1910.

18. *Bioscope*, 17 Feb. 1910, p. 30.

19. Ibid., 17 Feb., pp. 5, 39; 24 Feb. 1910, p. 37.

20. Ibid., 17 Feb. 1910, p. 41.

21. ECA, SL 119/2/6, Magistrates Minutes, 1909–16, 4 Dec. 1912.

22. *Scotsman*, 29 March 1910, p. 9.

23. Ibid., 29 March 1910, p. 9; *Bioscope*, 7 April 1910, pp. 15, 17.

24. *ET*, 7 July 1910, p. 6; the fight took place on 4 July.

25. *Bioscope*, 13 Oct., p. 21; 20 Oct. 1910, p. 9.

26. *ET*, 1 Aug., p. 8; 8 Aug. 1910, p. 8.

27. Ibid., 14 Nov., p. 8; 15 Nov., p. 8; 18 Nov. 1910, p. 6; *Bioscope*, 17 Nov. 1910, p. 22.

28. *ET*, 29 Nov. 1910, p. 8.

29. *Bioscope*, 28 Nov., p. 625; 5 Dec., p. 711; 12 Dec., p. 779; 26 Dec. 1912, p. 957.

30. *Bioscope*, 9 Jan. 1913, p. 131; *ET*, 7 Jan., p. 5; 10 Jan. 1913, p. 1; ECA, SL 119/2/6, Magistrates Minutes, 1909–16, 31 Jan. 1913, for the exchange with the Presbytery.

31. *Bioscope*, 23 Sept. 1909, pp. 19–21, for Aberdeen's regulations.

32. *Bioscope*, 28 Dec. 1911, p. 909; 22 Feb., p. 517; 4 April 1912, p. 55.

33. McKernan, '"Only the Screen Was Silent"', pp. 12–14.

34. *Bioscope*, 18 April, p. 179; 16 May, p. 481; 23 May 1912, p. 557.

35. *Bioscope*, 6 June, p. 731; 26 Sept. 1912, p. 925.

36. *Bioscope*, 19 May 1910, p. 11.
37. DCA, Dundee Town Council Minutes, Magistrates Committee, 27 Nov. 1912; Police and Lighting Committee, 13, 20, 30 Dec. 1912; 7 Jan. 1913.
38. DCA, Dundee Town Council Minutes, Police and Lighting Committee, 25 March 1913.
39. *Bioscope*, 9 April 1914, p. 193.
40. *Bioscope*, 26 March, p. 1420, for the criticisms of the Scottish Christian Social Union; 21 May 1914, p. 861, for the activities of the Kirkcaldy Committee.
41. The phrase was employed during a later debate on censorship, *Bioscope*, 14 Sept. 1916, p. 1035; the *Kinematograph Year Book* also devoted a section to what it termed 'Busybodies, Meddlers and others', see 1918 edn (London, 1918), p. 424.
42. ECA, SL 119/2/6, Magistrates Minutes, 1909–16, 20 Feb. 1914.
43. *Bioscope*, 4 June 1914, p. 1027.
44. *Bioscope*, 30 Jan. 1913, p. 347.
45. *Bioscope*, 14 Sept. 1916, p. 1061.
46. Low, *History of the British Film, 1914–1918*, pp. 130–4; *Bioscope*, 13 July, p. 159; 14 Sept., p. 1035; 28 Sept., p. 1263; 12 Oct. 1916, p. 185; *Entertainer*, 11 Nov. 1916, p. 7; *Scotsman*, 1 Dec. 1916, p. 4.
47. *Bioscope*, 3 June 1915, p. 993; 14 Sept. 1916, p. 1035.
48. *Bioscope*, 14 Sept. 1916, p. 1061.
49. M. Hammond, *The Big Show: British Cinema Culture in the Great War, 1914–1918* (Exeter, 2006), pp. 154–6; Hanson, *From Silent Screen to Multi-Screen*, p. 42.
50. *Bioscope*, 13 July 1916, p. 161; *Scotsman*, 11 July 1916, p. 7; *Entertainer*, 15 July, p. 5; 22 July 1916, p. 7.
51. *Bioscope*, 13 July 1916, p. 161.
52. Kuhn, *Cinema, Censorship and Sexuality*, pp. 64–74.
53. *Scottish Cinema*, 10 Nov. 1919, pp. 9, 16.
54. *Entertainer*, 28 May 1918, p. 10 (Her Majesty's Theatre, Dundee); *Scotsman*, 28 May 1918, p. 1 (Lyceum Theatre, Edinburgh)
55. *Bioscope*, 18 May 1916, pp. 817–18, where it was noted that corporation halls were not under the same obligation to provide fixed seating.
56. *Scottish Cinema*, 2 Aug. 1920, p. 31.
57. *SKR*, 19 Feb. 1921, p. 17.
58. *Scottish Cinema*, 23 Feb. 1920, p. 9, on the problem of 'propaganda' features; SSA, 5/11/17, Cinematograph Exhibitors' Association, Edinburgh and East of Scotland Section, Minute Book, Meeting at Princes Cinema, 8 Aug. 1922, on the enduring threat posed by super films.
59. Kuhn, *Cinema, Censorship and Sexuality*, pp. 64–72; the evidence presented here suggests that the statement in Aldgate and Robertson, *Censorship in Theatre and Cinema*, p. 8 that '*Damaged Goods* has never been shown publicly anywhere in Britain' is in need of emendation.
60. *Scottish Cinema*, 2 Feb., p. 14; 9 Feb., p. 27; 1 March, p. 7; *SKR*, 28 Feb., p. 11; *Scotsman*, 27 Feb. 1920, p. 1.
61. SSA, 5/11/17, CEA, Edinburgh Section, Minute Book, Meetings at Princes

Cinema, 17 Feb., 13 May; *Scottish Cinema*, 8 March, p. 27; *SKR*, 6 March, p. 15; 24 April, p. 14; *Scotsman*, 27 Feb. 1920, p. 6; ECA, SL 119/1/2, Edinburgh Corporation, Magistrates Committee, Scroll Minute Book, Feb. 1910– July 1920, 26 Feb.; 16 April 1920.

62. *SKR*, 22 May, p. 11; *Scottish Cinema*, 24 May 1920, p. 8. By then *Damaged Goods* had secured its first showing in Glasgow, at Hengler's Circus, *Scottish Cinema*, 10 May 1920, pp. 3, 24.

63. *Scottish Cinema*, 21 June, p. 8; *SKR*, 19 June 1920, p. 6.

64. *SKR*, 28 Aug., p. 1; 4 Sept. 1920, p. 1.

65. *Scottish Cinema*, 26 Jan., p. 8; *SKR*, 24 Jan. 1920, p. 8.

66. Kuhn, *Cinema, Censorship and Sexuality*, p. 25; Low, *History of the British Film, 1918–1929*, p. 57.

67. *SKR*, 10 July 1920, p. 9; ECA, SL 119/1/2, Edinburgh Corporation, Magistrates Committee, Scroll Minute Book, Feb. 1910–July 1920, 28 June 1920.

68. *Scotsman*, 2 May 1939, p. 13; ECA, SL 119/3/9, Edinburgh Corporation Committee Minutes, Magistrates, Session 1938–9, 4 May 1939.

69. ECA, SL 119/3/9, EC Magistrates Minutes, 1938–9, 27 Sept. 1939; J. C. Robertson, *The British Board of Film Censors: Film Censorship in Britain, 1896–1950* (1985), pp. 99, 124.

70. NAS, GD289/2/4, Playhouse Cinema, Running Book, 11 Oct. 1940–30 Jan. 1943, 8–13 Jan. 1940; the film performed respectably, drawing 19,724 and garnering a profit of £106 14s 6d over six days, supported by the British musical *Discoveries*, with Carroll Levis and Issy Bonn, GD289/1/1, Playhouse Cinema, Profit and Loss Ledger, week ending 13 Jan. 1940.

71. Low, *History of the British Film, 1906–1914*, p. 89; J. C. Robertson, *The Hidden Cinema: British Film Censorship in Action, 1913–75* (1989), pp. 11–12; id., *British Board of Film Censors*, pp. 6–7.

72. *ET*, 6 April, p. 7; 16 April, p. 3; 20 April 1928, p. 3, reporting good business done at Green's Playhouse; ECA, SL 119/1/4, Edinburgh Corporation Magistrates' Committee, Scroll Minutes, 1926–9, 22 March 1928; the film also featured in the programme for Edinburgh's brief experiment with Cinema Sundays in 1931, *Scotsman*, 27 Jan. 1931, p. 9.

73. ECA, SL 119/3/8, EC Magistrates Minutes, Session 1937–8, 31 May; 26 Oct.; SL 119/3/9, Session 1938–9, 14 Nov. 1938; *Scotsman*, 1 June, p. 10; 27 Oct., p. 9; 2 Nov. 1938, p. 15.

74. Low, *History of the British Film, 1918–1929*, pp. 66–8; Mathews, *Censored*, pp. 99–100; *Scotsman*, 17 Feb., p. 11; 28 Feb. 1928, p. 9.

75. *ET*, 11 May, p. 3; 15 May, p. 2; 18 May 1928, p. 3, for discussion of the screening of *Dawn* at Green's Playhouse; *Scotsman*, 12 May 1928, p. 9, reporting the film's acceptance in various English boroughs.

76. *Scotsman*, 9 Jan. 1929, p. 7; see Chapter 4, p. 148, for further details.

77. ECA, SL 119/1/4, EC Magistrates' Committee, Scroll Minutes, 1926–9, 11 May, 6 June 1928; *Scotsman*, 12 May 1928, p. 9; 5 Jan. 1929, p. 12.

78. Mathews, *Censored*, pp. 40–5; Low, *History of the British Film, 1918–1929*, pp. 66–8; Robertson, *The Hidden Cinema*, pp. 27–31, 33–6.

79. S. G. Jones, *The British Labour Movement and Film, 1918–1939* (1987), p. 105; *Scotsman*, 25 Feb. 1930, p. 10.

80. *Scotsman*, 21 April 1930, p. 2; *Workers' Cinema: Official Organ of the Federation of Workers' Film Societies*, Nov. 1931, pp. 2, 4; Glasgow had to wait until November to see the film, when it was shown at the City Hall, *ET*, 3 Nov. 1930, p. 2; B. Hogenkamp, *Deadly Parallels: Film and the Left in Britain, 1929–39* (London, 1986), p. 41.

81. ECA, SL 119/3/1, EC Magistrates Minutes, Session 16 May 1930–16 Oct. 1931, 10 May; 17 June; 15 July; 18 Nov.; 28 Nov. 1930; 13 Jan. 1931; *Scotsman*, 15 Jan. 1931, p. 7.

82. *Scotsman*, 3 Oct. 1930, p. 12; ECA, SL 119/3/1, EC Magistrates Minutes, Session 1930–1, 16 Feb. 1931.

83. ECA, SL 119/3/1, EC Magistrates Minutes, Session 1930–1, 7 May; 22 May 1931; SL 119/1/4, Scroll Minutes, 1926–9, 13 March 1928; *ET*, 9 April, p. 7; 11 April 1928, p. 3.

84. *ET*, 11 April 1928, p. 7.

85. *ET*, 17 May 1928, p. 8; ECA, SL119/1/4, Edinburgh Corporation, Magistrates Committee, Scroll Minutes, 1926–9, 13 March 1928.

86. *Daily Herald*, 7 May 1928, p. 5.

87. ECA, SL 119/3/3, EC Magistrates Minutes, Session 1932–3, 1 Nov. 1933.

88. ECA, SL 119/3/4, EC Magistrates Minutes, Session 1933–4, 15 Nov. 1933.

89. Ibid., 6 Dec. 1933.

90. *The Evening Dispatch* (Edinburgh), 13 April 1934, p. 8.

91. ECA, SL 119/3/4, EC Magistrates Minutes, Session 1933–4, 6 Dec. 1933; 10 Jan. 1934.

92. NAS, GD289/2/15, Palace Cinema, Running Book, 2 Jan. 1933–4 April 1936, week ending 21 April 1934; GD289/1/3, Palace Cinema, Profit and Loss Ledger, weeks ending 21 April–5 May 1934. The film was retained for two subsequent weeks, securing audiences of 12,512 and 7,967. Audiences were maximised by running a show, additional to the four scheduled daily screenings, on Saturday morning at 11 a.m., *Evening Dispatch*, 17 April, p. 1; 19 April 1934, p. 1.

93. ECA, SL119/3/10, EC Magistrates Minutes, Session 1939–40, 3 April 1940.

94. NAS, GD289/1/3, Palace Cinema, Profit and Loss Ledger, weeks ending, 9 March, 16 March, 6 April, 9 Nov., 16 Nov. 1940. Retained for a second week, *Marriage Forbidden* still secured an above-average audience of 8,383. On each occasion, it played alongside the Gene Autry western, *Colorado Sunset*.

95. P. Thompson, *The Voice of the Past: Oral History*, 3rd edn (Oxford, 2000), pp. 297–8, for the importance of personal contacts in disseminating information on issues of birth control.

96. ECA, SL119/3/10, EC Magistrates Minutes, Session 1939–40, 3 July 1940; the film had already been shown in Glasgow, *Scotsman*, 27 March 1940, p. 7.

97. ECA, SL119/3/17, EC Magistrates Minutes, Session 1946–47, 2 July; 23 July 1947.

98. ECA, SL119/3/18, EC Magistrates Minutes, Session 1947–May 1949, 7 Oct.

1948; SL119/3/19, Session 1949–50, 1 March 1950; SL119/3/20, Session 1950–1, 16 June; 1 Nov.; 3 Dec. 1950; *We Want a Child* played at the Palace Cinema in the week commencing 18 Dec. 1950, with the Universal comedy *The Man Who Lost Himself* as support. It secured an audience of 8,055, NAS, GD289/1/3, Palace Cinema, Profit and Loss Ledger, 1925–55.

99. ECA, SL119/3/20, EC Magistrates Minutes, Session 1950–1, 7 Sept.; 23 Nov. 1950.

100. SSA, 5/4/17, Poole Family Collection, Folder and Album of Press Cuttings, cutting from *Edinburgh Pictorial*, 26 Feb. 1954; cutting from *Scotsman*, 7 March 1949; cutting from *Evening Dispatch*, 4 March 1949.

101. ECA, SL119/3/20, EC Magistrates Minutes, Session 1950–1, 23 Nov. 1950.

102. Kuhn, *Cinema, Censorship and Sexuality*, pp. 4–8.

103. *Forward*, 15 March 1913, p. 2.

104. *Scotsman*, 20 March 1917, p. 2.

105. J. Mackie (ed.), *The Edinburgh Cinema Enquiry Being an Investigation Conducted into the Influence of the Film on School Children and Adolescents in the City* (Edinburgh, 1933), pp. 11–12; *Scotsman*, 4 March 1933, p. 17.

106. NAS, CO1/4/200, Committee on Children and the Cinema, 1948, D. M. McIntosh, *Attendance of School Children at the Cinema* (Scottish Educational Film Association, Research Publication No. 1) (Glasgow, 1945), p. 3.

107. NAS, CO1/4/200, County Clerk, County Council of Bute to George Davie, Secretary, Association of County Councils, 6 April 1948.

108. NAS, CO1/4/200, McIntosh, *Attendance of School Children*, p. 6.

109. H. Hendrick, *Children, Childhood and English Society, 1880–1990* (Cambridge, 1997), ch. 2; H. Cunningham, *Children and Childhood in Western Society since 1500* (London, 1995), ch. 7; Humphries, *Hooligans or Rebels?*, ch. 1.

110. T. Staples, *All Pals Together: The Story of Children's Cinema* (Edinburgh, 1997), p. 22; R. Ford, *Children in the Cinema* (London, 1939), ch. 1.

111. Mackie, *Edinburgh Cinema Enquiry*, p. 11; NAS, CO 1/4/200, Memorandum of Evidence to Committee on Children and the Cinema, n.d.

112. Strinati, *Introduction to Theories of Popular Culture*, chs 1 and 2.

113. *Forward*, 15 March 1913, p. 2.

114. Mackie, *Edinburgh Cinema Enquiry*, p. 59.

115. SSA, 5/25/9, Stranraer Picture House, Ltd, Annual Accounts, Abstract of Admissions for year to 21 April 1934.

116. *Forward*, 15 March 1913, p. 2; McKernan,'"Only the Screen was Silent"', pp. 12–14.

117. ECA, SL119/2/6, Edinburgh Corporation, Magistrates Minutes, 1909–16, 6, 30 June 1913.

118. *Bioscope*, 13 June 1912, p. 777.

119. *Bioscope*, 10 April 1913, p. 117.

120. GCA, Minutes of Corporation of Glasgow, Magistrates, 24 Oct. 1912.

121. GCA, Glasgow Corporation Minutes, Magistrates, 20 Dec. 1912; 10 April 1913; *Bioscope*, 27 March 1913, p. 975.

122. *Bioscope*, 17 April, p. 195; 15 May 1913, p. 487.

123. ECA, SL119/2/6, Edinburgh Corporation, Magistrates Minutes, 1909–16, 19 Dec. 1913; 18 March; 25 May 1914; *Bioscope*, 1 Jan., p. 37; 9 April 1914, p. 193.

124. *Bioscope*, 15 Oct. 1914, p. 245.

125. *Scotsman*, 10 March 1926, p. 10.

126. *Bioscope*, 12 March, p. 1109 (Picture House); 26 March, p. 1420 (Theatre De Luxe); 2 April 1914, p. 55.

127. Low, *History of the British Film, 1906–1914*, pp. 35–41; *Bioscope*, 23 Sept. 1915, p. 1403.

128. *Bioscope*, 6 Feb. 1913, p. 411.

129. *Bioscope*, 15 May 1913, p. 491.

130. *Scotsman*, 11 Nov. 1916, p. 11; see also the report to the Presbytery of Glasgow, in which much was made of 'the influence of sensational pictures at the cinema houses', 30 March 1916, p. 8.

131. *Scotsman*, 5 March 1917, p. 4.

132. *Scotsman*, 31 May 1916, p. 10.

133. *Bioscope*, 14 Sept. 1916, p. 1061.

134. *Bioscope*, 6 July 1916, p. 64.

135. National Council of Public Morals, *The Cinema: Its Present Position*, Introduction, p. ix.

136. National Council of Public Morals, *The Cinema: Its Present Position*, Appendix III, pp. 333–72.

137. National Council of Public Morals, *The Cinema: Its Present Position*, statement of Mr Roderick Ross, MVO, pp. 176–7; *Entertainer*, 17 March 1917, p. 9; *Scotsman*, 13 March 1917, p. 7.

138. National Council of Public Morals, *The Cinema: Its Present Position*, David Thom, Chief Constable of Hawick, pp. 354–5.

139. National Council of Public Morals, *The Cinema: Its Present Position*, George Nicol, Chief Constable of Stirling, p. 368.

140. National Council of Public Morals, *The Cinema: Its Present Position*, The Report, pp. xlvi–xlvii; *Entertainer*, 20 Oct. 1917, p. 16; *Scotsman*, 10 Oct. 1917, p. 11.

141. *Scotsman*, 31 Oct., p. 4; 2 Nov., p. 4; 23 Nov. 1918, p. 6; *Entertainer*, 16 Nov. 1918, p. 8; SSA, 5/11/17, Cinematograph Exhibitors' Association, Edinburgh and East of Scotland Section, Minute Book, Emergency Meeting at Princes Cinema, 30 Oct.; Meeting at Princes Cinema, 5 Dec. 1918.

142. SSA, 5/11/17, CEA Minutes, Meeting at Princes Cinema, 20 Dec. 1918; *Scotsman*, 14 Dec. 1918, p. 6.

143. *SKR*, 18 Feb. 1922, p. 13.

144. T. Griffiths, *The Lancashire Working Classes, c.1880–1930* (Oxford, 2001), pp. 244–5; D. Fowler, *The First Teenagers: The Lifestyle of Young Wage-earners in Interwar Britain* (London, 1995), ch. 4, for the view that this level of affluence was sustained in the decades that followed.

145. *SKR*, 4 Dec. 1920, p. 13.

146. *SKR*, 25 Sept. 1920, p. 1.

147. *SKR*, 9 April, p. 1; 23 April, p. 1; 27 August, p. 1; 15 Oct. 1921, p. 1.

148. *Scotsman*, 12 Feb., p. 7; 10 April 1923, p. 5; ECA, SL119/1/3, Edinburgh Corporation, Magistrates Committee, Scroll Minutes, 1920–6, General Purposes Committee, 9 April 1923.

149. *Scotsman*, 14 Dec. 1923, p. 9; 16 May, p. 7; 1 July 1925, p. 11; 12 March 1927, p. 13.

150. See Chapter 3, pp. 122–3, for more on this.

151. *Scotsman*, 27 Jan. 1926, p. 11; *Kinematograph Year Book* (London, 1928).

152. *Scotsman*, 13 Jan., p. 7; 17 Feb. 1926, p. 11.

153. NAS, AB54/95, Lord Advocate's Dept, Opinion of the Law Officers of the Crown and the Scottish Law Officers.

154. Smith, *Children, Cinema and Censorship*, pp. 32–3; Low, *History of the British Film, 1929–1939*, p. 54.

155. Statutory Rules and Orders, 1923, No. 1147/S.62. *Cinematograph, Scotland. Regulations Dated September 22, 1923, made by the Secretary for Scotland under the Cinematograph Act, 1909 (9 Edw. 7, c. 30)*; *Scotsman*, 17 Oct. 1930, p. 5, reporting a meeting of the National Council of Women, at which it was observed that in Scotland 'there were no model rules and no safeguards in connection with cinemas'.

156. ECA, SL119/3/2, Edinburgh Corporation, Magistrates Minutes, Special Committee, 9 March 1932; *Scotsman*, 5 Feb. 1932, p. 6.

157. *Scotsman*, 11 March 1932, p. 7; Mackie, *Edinburgh Cinema Enquiry*, pp. 3–6.

158. Mackie, *Edinburgh Cinema Enquiry*, pp. 11–12, 30, 33, 40; Smith, *Children, Cinema and Censorship*, pp. 82–3; *Scotsman*, 7 May 1932, p. 17.

159. Mackie, *Edinburgh Cinema Enquiry*, pp. 41–50; *Scotsman*, 4 March 1933, pp. 14, 17. It was claimed by the Enquiry's chairman that the initial intention had been to promote a more official investigation into the workings of censorship.

160. *Scotsman*, 8 July, p. 14; 12 July 1933, p. 11; 6 Jan., p. 10; 17 April 1934, p. 6.

161. *Scotsman*, 31 Aug., p. 6; 5 Oct. 1934, p. 6; NAS, GD193/205/40, Steel-Maitland Papers, National Council of Women of Great Britain, Cinema Sectional Committee, meeting of 11 April 1935.

162. *Scotsman*, 29 March 1935, p. 8; 11 Feb. 1936, p. 9; GCA, RU 4/2/15, Rutherglen, Cinematograph Act, 1909, W. Olens Kerr, Inspector, Lanarkshire Constabulary to Town Clerk, Rutherglen, 1 April 1935.

163. SSA, 5/14/17, James S. Nairn Collection, Volume of Correspondence, John Cameron, hon. sec., Edinburgh branch of League of Nations Union to J. S. Nairn, 30 March 1926; 5/14/13, Volume of Press Cuttings, n.d. (c. 1928).

164. ECA, SL119/3/1, Edinburgh Corporation, Magistrates Committee, General Purposes Committee, 16 Feb. 1931.

165. *ET*, 1 Jan. 1930, pp. 1, 7; NAS, HH1/1981, Scottish Home Dept, Cinemas, Paisley Catastrophe, Report to the Rt. Hon. The Secretary of State for Scotland on the Circumstances Attending the Loss of Life at the Glen Cinema, Paisley, on the 31st December 1929 by Major T. H. Crozier, H.M. Chief Inspector of Explosives, Dated 5 May 1930, pp. 4–6; Extended Notes of Proceedings in Paisley Cinema Disaster. Trial of Charles Dorward, evidence of Alexander Rossie, pp. 97–108.

166. NAS, HH1/1981, Extended Notes, evidence of Charles Dorward, pp. 301–2.

167. NAS, HH1/1981, Report, pp. 4, 18; Extended Notes, evidence of James Glover, pp. 119–39; evidence of Isabella Campbell Muir, pp. 331–5; JC26/1930/54, Trial Papers, Trial of Charles Dorward, Manager of Glen Cinema, Paisley; *ET*, 29 April, p. 1; 30 April, p. 1; 1 May, p. 1; 2 May 1930, p. 1.

168. Smith, *Children, Cinema and Censorship*, pp. 160–2; proposals circulated within a week of the disaster, *ET*, 7 Jan., pp. 3, 5; 31 July 1930, p. 7.

169. *Scotsman*, 16 Jan. 1935, p. 11; NAS, GD193/205/36, National Council of Women of Great Britain, meeting at Murray House, Vandon St, SW1, 14 Feb. 1935.

170. *Scotsman*, 10 Feb., p. 15; 28 Nov., p. 7; 19 Dec. 1932, p. 7; 30 Jan., p. 7; 6 March 1933, p. 7; on the work of film societies, see Chapter 6, pp. 224–5, 233–4.

171. M. Bernstein (ed.), *Controlling Hollywood: Censorship and Regulation in the Studio Era* (2000); R. Maltby, 'The Production Code and the Hays Office', in T. Balio, *Grand Design: Hollywood as a Modern Business Enterprise, 1930–1939* (Berkeley and Los Angeles, 1993), pp. 37–72.

172. *ET*, 28 Oct. 1937, p. 2; 27 Jan. 1938, p. 9.

173. G. Macnab, *J. Arthur Rank and the British Film Industry* (London, 1993), chs 1 and 2; V. Porter, 'Methodism versus the Marketplace: The Rank Organisation and British Cinema', in Murphy, *The British Cinema Book*, pp. 267–75; Dickinson and Street, *Cinema and State*, pp. 100–2.

174. Ford, *Children in the Cinema*, ch. 6; Staples, *All Pals Together*, chs 4 and 6; see successive editions of *The Boys' and Girls' Cinema Clubs Annual* (n.d.); J. P. Mayer, *Sociology of Film: Studies and Documents* (London, 1946), chs 4–6; M. C. Parnaby and M. T. Woodhouse, *Children's Cinema Clubs: Report* (London, 1947).

175. *Scotsman*, 6 Jan. 1948, p. 4.

176. *Scotsman*, 30 Dec. 1947, p. 4; 25 May 1948, pp. 3, 4.

177. *Scotsman*, 22 Jan. 1948, p. 4.

178. *Scotsman*, 2 July 1947, p. 6; NAS, CO1/4/200, Committee on Children and Cinema, 21 Sept. 1948, Association of County Councils in Scotland, Meeting of Sub-committee appointed to give oral evidence before Committee on Children and the Cinema.

179. NAS, CO1/4/200, Committee on Children and the Cinema, 1948, County Clerk, County Council of Bute to George Davie, Secretary, Association of County Councils, 6 April 1948.

180. NAS, CO1/4/200, Association of County Councils in Scotland, Meeting of Sub-committee appointed to give oral evidence before Committee on Children and the Cinema, 21 Sept. 1948.

181. NAS, CO1/4/200, Memorandum of Evidence to Committee on Children and the Cinema, n.d., pp. 2–3.

182. NAS, CO1/4/200, Committee on Children and the Cinema, Ninth Meeting of Committee held in St Andrew's House, Edinburgh, 30 Sept.–1 Oct. 1948, pp. 1–3.

183. Smith, *Children, Cinema and Censorship*, pp. 70–3; *Scotsman*, 6 May, p. 7; 8 May 1950, p. 8.

184. National Council of Public Morals, *The Cinema: Its Present Position*, The Report, pp. xxxiv–xliv.
185. Kuhn, *Cinema, Censorship and Sexuality*, ch. 1.
186. *ET*, 28 Oct. 1937, p. 2.
187. NAS, CO1/4/200, Memorandum of Evidence to Committee on Children and the Cinema, n.d., p. 2.

3

Through War and Peace: The Changing Fortunes of Scottish Silent Cinema, 1914–29

I

The literature on the decade and a half of British cinema history from the outbreak of the First World War to the coming of the sound film in the late 1920s has centred, for the most part, on the travails of the production sector. Hollywood's growing dominance of international film markets, along with what some see as flawed production strategies at home, conspired to exclude native output from British screens. As a result, by the mid 1920s, barely 5 per cent of films released in Britain were produced there.[1] The problems encountered by native film-makers chimed in well with the protectionist instincts of the Baldwin government, in office through the middle to later years of the decade, resulting in the first deliberate attempt to encourage the creation of a viable production industry by guaranteeing a proportion of the home market to British producers.[2] If the fortunes of one sector prior to the passage of the Cinematograph Films Act of 1927 appear clear, those of exhibitors have failed to attract comparable attention. In part, this reflects the belief that the problems which so exercised producers were not experienced by other groups within the industry. In many respects, the interests of producers and exhibitors diverged sharply, so that the block booking of American films, which worked to limit the screen time available to native subjects, was welcomed by cinema managers, anxious to fill their schedules with marketable product.[3] Exhibitors were seen to profit from the consolidation of cinema-going as the main commercial leisure pursuit of the period, an activity increasingly embedded in the rhythms of everyday life, for a sizeable proportion of the population. In contrast to the production of films, the exhibition sector offered evidence of marked prosperity, reflected in waves of investment in cinema building, in the years immediately following the Great War and from the middle of the first post-war decade. The latter phase especially would see the construction of super cinemas, distinguished from their more modest predecessors by their large capacities and elaborate decor. The outward display of opulence and luxury was itself a demonstration of commercial confidence.[4] Both investment surges would leave their mark on the Scottish industry, so that by the end of the silent era, it could boast what was, at the time of its construction, the largest cinema in Britain,

Green's Playhouse on Renfield Street, Glasgow, capable of accommodating over 4,000 at each screening, while another super cinema, also the Playhouse, was in course of erection in Edinburgh.[5] In the absence of detailed box-office data, such as exists from the mid 1930s, the built record provides one of the most tangible measures of how the industry was faring.

Yet as recent work has sought to suggest, the evidence it provides is far from ambiguous. In one of the few studies to attempt a reconstruction of audience trends across the later silent period, Nicholas Hiley has argued that, rather than experiencing sustained prosperity, the exhibition sector was itself subject to marked fluctuations in fortunes over the two decades. Attendances, it is argued, rose markedly in wartime, reaching a peak in 1917 that would not be matched until the early 1940s, during another military conflict. In the intervening years, admissions are seen to have slumped, with the fall most pronounced in the immediate post-war period. In explaining this trend, Hiley makes much of changes in prices, discouraging attendance among the very people who, he argues, had been the mainstay of the pre-war audience. This trend is also seen as symptomatic of an industry in transition, seeking greater financial security by endeavouring to draw patrons from a wider social mix. The new generation of super cinemas offered congenial surroundings to this new respectable audience, which was further attracted by the screening of films with longer and therefore more involved and engaging narratives.[6] Hiley's argument merits extended consideration, as it provides a useful framework for understanding the period as a whole and, in the absence of further work in the area to date, seems set fair to become the new orthodoxy on the subject.[7]

Before it does so, however, it is important that it be fully evaluated in the light of the available evidence. For Scotland, records of individual businesses survive in greater volume in this period than for the years prior to 1914. Company documentation, comprising balance sheets and directors' minutes, used alongside the growing body of trade papers available for key parts of this period, helps to clarify the fortunes of the exhibition sector north of the border both in war and in peace. These, as will become clear, were subject to marked fluctuations across both phases, in a manner that suggests that Hiley's chronology and the conclusions derived from it are in need of some emendation. To clarify the point, the chapter that follows breaks the period down into three sub-periods, encompassing the war, the immediate post-war years, and the period from the early 1920s to the end of the silent era. These were years of marked economic, social, and political instability which the cinema, as the prime leisure attraction of the time, was bound to reflect.

II

Perceptions of a pronounced 'bubble' in attendances during the First World War derive substantially from one contemporary estimate. In 1917, as part of his submission to the inquiry undertaken by the National Council of Public Morals into cinema's wider social impact, F. R. Goodwin, chairman of the London branch of the Cinematograph Exhibitors' Association, suggested that the audience across Britain, excluding Sundays, amounted to an annual figure of 1,056,375,000.[8] This may be compared with pre-war estimates of between 364 and 411 million a year and the earliest figures based on entertainments tax returns which indicate admissions totalling 903 million in 1934, pointing up what would appear to have been a significant wartime surge followed by a slump in cinema-going between the wars.[9] Despite the interpretive weight it has been required to bear, the means by which Goodwin arrived at his figure was not made explicit in his evidence to the Commission. It appears to have been an extrapolation from an estimated average daily audience of 750 at each of Britain's 4,500 cinemas. Goodwin himself inclined to the view that this represented a distinctly conservative estimate of wartime numbers.[10] However, the Scottish evidence, although indirect, suggests that it may in fact substantially overstate matters. As has been seen, prior to the outbreak of war in 1914, a large proportion of the venues used for cinematograph shows comprised halls used only for occasional screenings. In Glasgow, the halls owned by the City Corporation, whose capacities were among the largest of any of the places used for film exhibitions, mounted screenings on a weekly basis and then only during the autumn and winter months.[11] By the early 1920s, although the number of venues offering shows across the week had grown, the overall frequency with which exhibitions were mounted, when set alongside estimates of total capacity, suggests an average attendance considerably below Goodwin's figure. Of 551 Scottish venues listed in the *Kinematograph Year Book* for 1921, details on the regularity of shows were available for 389. Of these, 115 (almost 30 per cent) offered only one show per night or even fewer. What is more, of 78 cinemas mounting two shows an evening, only one in three was capable of accommodating in excess of 1,000 at a single sitting.[12] It would thus require an unusually high level of utilisation for Scottish cinemas to match up to Goodwin's estimate. While this does not, of itself, dispose of the idea of a marked wartime peak, it does suggest that such a figure may reflect the distortions produced by a heavily metropolitan perspective.

An alternative view is provided by the trade press and surviving business records and although this does not enable us to propose alternative numbers to those offered by Goodwin, it does indicate that the impact of war was, initially at least, rather more variable than many have allowed, so that evidence of an audience spike of the magnitude suggested by subsequent commentators appears questionable. The immediate impact of the outbreak of war was markedly to depress box-office receipts, as recruiting stations proved powerful counter-attractions to the lure of the picture house. In the first three days of the conflict, takings at the Paragon, the one Glasgow cinema for which detailed pre-war records survive, were barely half those of the August average for Wednesday, Thursday, and Friday. For only the second time in the twelve-month period for which information exists, a loss was recorded on the week's business. However, by Saturday, the last day for which we have records, receipts once more approached the level of the equivalent month in 1913, suggesting that in this instance disruption may have proved short-lived.[13]

In the weeks that followed, the uncontrolled and uncoordinated rush to the colours threatened to create difficulties for the local cinema trade. In some areas, high rates of voluntary enlistment had the potential severely to deplete the number of potential picture-goers. By February 1915, some 28,413 Scottish coal miners, the equivalent of just over one in five of the pre-war workforce, had left for the forces. In particular districts, losses approached one in three.[14] The impact could be profound. Reviewing the first season of Kirkintilloch's Municipal Cinema in May 1915, Tom Johnston noted that the business, one of three picture houses in the burgh, had generated a profit despite the loss of some 1,300 men to war service.[15] Overall, however, the net effect of recruitment was, in the early months at least, modest, as many of those enlisting were simply displaced to other areas in Scotland to undergo training. So, *The Bioscope* was able to report that business continued to flourish where troops were stationed close by. In Dunfermline, to October 1914, the presence of 6,000 Territorials was considered to have more than maintained attendances, and similar observations were offered from Dundee, Kilmarnock, Troon, and Inverness.[16] The need to fill the leisure hours of men under arms created often close cooperation between the cinema trade and the military authorities. So, troops were encouraged to attend the Pavilion in Hawick, which was considered 'in bounds' for the local camp.[17] Where a military presence was sustained for the duration of the war, as at Edinburgh, where troops were maintained to defend the Forth estuary, the years from 1914 came to be seen, in retrospect, as a period of unrivalled prosperity for the industry. Such at least was the view of the local correspondent of the trade journal *Scottish Cinema*, in reviewing the fortunes of local houses in March 1920.[18] Financial returns relating to specific companies suggest that this generally optimistic picture was broadly warranted. In Dunfermline, the Cinema House, which was registered for business in 1913, recorded substantial profits in each of the first two years of the conflict.[19] The same was also true of the Kinema Palace in Kirkcaldy, another town to benefit from a sizeable troop presence in the early stages of the war.[20]

Economic conditions also worked to confirm local prosperity. The demand for the materials of war created unusually favourable conditions for the heavy industries on which Scottish fortunes had come to rely from the later decades of the nineteenth century. The fluctuations in activity to which industries such as coal, iron and steel, and shipbuilding had long been vulnerable were held temporarily in abeyance under conditions of war. Consistently full-time work was thus reported across west-central Scotland, from Coatbridge to Clydebank.[21] Although prices rose markedly in the early years of the war, as government struggled to control inflationary pressures, increases were offset by longer, more consistent hours of work, and the adoption of overtime in several key industries.[22] The effect was, at the very least, to sustain levels of demand for commercial recreations, including the cinema, more especially as the price of admission was not as yet subject to any upward revision. In real terms, then, the cost of a cinema seat was falling in the early months of the war. As *The Bioscope* noted, this produced changes not so much in the size of the audience as in its make-up and the overall pattern of attendance. So, by July 1915, a shift in favour of higher-priced seats was noted in areas where local industry prospered.[23] Perhaps of more lasting significance, working conditions posed increasing obstacles to the attendance of male wage earners who, although possessed of sufficient money, no longer had the same degree of choice over the times they could visit the cinema. A growing tendency was thus noted for men on shift work to attend first houses, early in the evening, while in many other cases their cinema-going came to centre, to an increasing degree, on Saturdays. For the remainder of the week, as *The Bioscope* had it, 'the audience was mostly composed of mere youths and young girls, while in the cheaper seats the majority of the audience was also female'. The conditions of war thus had the effect of consolidating further a previously perceived gender and age bias among picture-goers, amounting, it was claimed, in some areas to a three to one preponderance of females.[24] This development also drew comment from beyond the trade. In August 1915, the Scottish Football Association considered the propriety of staging professional competitions in wartime. While some pointed, in the game's defence, at the continuance of other leisure forms, including the cinema, not all were convinced that the suggested parallel had real validity. Major Quirk of Motherwell FC pointed up a key difference between the two activities:

> the people who frequented cinema houses were a different class of people from those who attended football. In the cinema houses they found old men and women, and children and young women, and a sprinkling of young men, who perhaps would be better in khaki than in the cinema house. But if they went to a football field they would find the manhood of the nation.[25]

The constituency that would provide the basis for the industry's subsequent prosperity had become more sharply defined in the peculiar conditions of wartime.

Economic conditions also worked to boost the cinema trade away from the central belt. By mid 1915, large attendances were being reported on a regular basis at Britain's most northerly dedicated picture house, the North Star Cinema in Lerwick. Here, although the war had disrupted the local fishing trade, the payment of separation allowances to those whose husbands or sons had volunteered for military service may have worked to ensure families more stable and predictable income flows than the sea had provided, from which it was possible to budget for regular visits to the cinema.[26] More generally, as the war progressed, other changes were seen to work in the industry's favour. Restrictions on alternative uses of free time became more pronounced from 1915 onwards and, although league football north of the border continued at the highest level for the duration of the conflict, albeit on a more limited basis geographically, controls on alcohol consumption served to limit the time and money devoted to drink.[27] Unsurprisingly, perhaps, *The Bioscope* was confident that the cinema was the prime beneficiary of reduced pub opening hours. The paper's Scottish correspondent felt justified in asserting, in August 1915, that the industry had never been in better shape.[28]

Yet even the trade press, whose prevailing tone was almost invariably optimistic, sustained by the printing of largely congratulatory copy, was bound to acknowledge occasional sources of difficulty. From the earliest days of the war, business in east-coast towns had been adversely affected, more generally by the disruption of trade with the near Continent, but more specifically in the case of cinema by the imposition of lighting restrictions.[29] Furthermore, while the redeployment of manpower as a result of recruitment worked to benefit some areas, it also had the effect of depleting potential audiences in others. Houses in rural and suburban areas were not thought to have shared in any initial surge in attendance.[30] Indeed, business records cast doubt on the extent of any expansion in audiences as a consequence of the war. In the West Lothian village of Uphall, the weekly rent on the Public Hall, leased on a continuous basis as a cinema from early in 1913, was reduced to a level that, in peacetime, applied in the summer months only. The summer rate of 30s a week, which applied from the end of May 1914, was thus maintained through the remainder of the year and into 1915, suggesting a consistently lower level of business through the early months of the war. Indeed, at a time when prices more generally were rising, the next change in rentals was a further reduction to 25s a week in October 1915.[31] Problems were not confined to small towns, however. In Aberdeen, the Queen's Cinema on Union Street had reported a profit of some £680 on a turnover of £3,060 in the last year before the outbreak of war. In the twelve months to July 1915, by contrast, receipts fell by over a quarter to £2,270, all but eliminating any trading profit. Over the following year, while takings remained steady at £2,223 10s, increased costs meant that the business recorded a net loss of over £200.[32] At the company's other hall in Stonehaven, profitability was sustained, but the box office still showed a fall of over 20 per cent in the first year of the war.[33] A similar story can be traced through the records of the Aberdeen Electric Theatre Co., Ltd. Here, where profit margins in the two years up to the outbreak of war had been robust (£1,036 in the year to September 1913 and £876 8s in the following twelve months), a marked slump in trading performance was evident in the year to September 1915 (£102 profit), before the business slipped into the red in the second full year of war.[34] Such trends were not confined to the north-east. At Glasgow's Cinema House, income from admissions and the sale of tobacco and confectionary, which amounted to £19,925 10s in 1912–13, had more than halved two years later to stand at £8,447 5s.[35] Here, it must be acknowledged, business may have been affected by an intensification in local competition. In the city centre, halls were opening at such a rate around 1914 that, as *The Bioscope*'s correspondent noted, Sauchiehall Street was coming to be known as 'Picture Avenue', reflecting the six halls operating along it by the March of that year.[36] If the Cinema House's fortunes cannot be held directly to reflect the impact of war, they do indicate that any upturn in business on the outbreak of hostilities was not of a magnitude sufficient to offset the effects of new building.

The evidence presented thus far suggests that wartime prosperity was patchy and more a product of local circumstances than of any broad and sustained upswing in cinema-going. For all the confidence communicated through the pages of the trade press, there is little indication of the kind of audience surge depicted by Goodwin's figures. A rather different impression is conveyed through the middle years of the war, a period in which even the normally sanguine trade publications would come to recognise that the industry was 'passing through the furnace'.[37]

The immediate occasion for this latter observation was growing criticism of the cinema, as described in the previous chapter, for its presumed propensity to undermine the morals of the young. Yet this was merely the latest entry in a mounting catalogue of difficulties that conspired to complicate the work of exhibitors in the middle years of the war. The intensified recruitment campaign, which would culminate in the introduction of conscription early in 1916, compounded problems caused by the loss of potential patrons while adding a further burden by the removal of often key members of staff. Few shared the misfortune experienced by Tom Gilbert, an exhibitor and distributor based in the Fife village of Crossgates, who found, in March 1916, that most of his staff had been called up, leaving him with the services of one twenty-one year old, rendered unfit for military service by virtue of being possessed of only one leg. That this did not preclude him undertaking a range of duties was acknowledged by Gilbert himself, who attested, in a subsequent employment reference, that 'he can go up a ladder with ease'.[38] In most cases, the loss of personnel was more gradual and perhaps, as a consequence, more difficult to resist. If some authorities were of the view, as expressed by the presiding officer of the Lanarkshire Appeal Tribunal in July 1917, that 'this cheap form of entertainment was a national necessity', there was also a belief that it could continue to function with the same or a lower level of staffing.[39] So, the appeal on behalf of the manager of Dalbeattie's one cinema for exemption from military service on the grounds that he was 'engaged on work which was of great national and educational importance', words which deliberately echoed George V's verdict on the official war film

The Battle of the Somme, was not entertained.[40] The Tribunal in Lanarkshire was equally unimpressed by the arguments advanced in support of the thirty-seven-year-old manager of Glasgow's Palace Theatre. The claim that men over fighting age were incapable of overseeing the running of picture houses led the presiding sheriff to inquire, 'You mean you need a man of fighting capacity to manage these theatres?', to which the manager's agent responded, 'This is a qualification.' In spite of this, exemption was refused.[41] The increasing problem of maintaining adequate staffing levels drew comment from the trade press. How far, if at all, it contributed to perceived shortcomings in the musical provision at many Scottish cinemas is difficult to determine. Nevertheless, *The Bioscope*'s musical correspondent J. Morton Hutcheson was scathing of the standard of accompaniment encountered in a number of leading houses in the summer of 1916. At the La Scala in Edinburgh, he found, no obvious attempt was made to synchronise the music with the image on screen, with the result that whole sequences passed in silence. One film which fell victim to this laxity was *The Fate of a Woman* (possibly *Fate and the Woman*), where

> the accompanists started after three or four scenes had been run through, finished the number they started, had a chat, tuned up and went off again without any regard to the scene or situation on the screen which they were *supposed* to be accompanying. (Emphasis in original)[42]

Given all this, the retention of experienced staff of proven competence assumed increasing importance for managers. Yet at the same time, the turnover among workers rendered this increasingly difficult. By the last year of the war, complaints were circulating of operators being induced to change their place of employment and then offering little or no notice. In one case, it was reported, a wage of £3 5s a week had proved insufficient to prevent one operator quitting his position.[43] In conditions of greater scarcity, labour was well placed to press for higher wages. In December 1914, the directors of the Queen's Cinema in Aberdeen agreed an increase in the manager's salary to dissuade him from accepting an offer of work from BB Pictures.[44]

Other, more general factors also exerted increased pressure on the wage bill, already the largest single item of expenditure incurred by most houses.[45] Before 1914, general price stability had worked to link wage demands to the trading performance of the relevant industries, so that rates of pay were related to levels of profitability. However, with the acceleration in price inflation consequent upon the outbreak of war, wage bargaining came to be driven more by general movements in the cost of living.[46] As a result, the cinema trade faced pressure for increases in pay at a time when, in many cases, takings and profit margins were depressed. So, the Amalgamated Musicians' Union sought a flat-rate increase of 5s a week for those playing to smaller halls from July 1916.[47] In Glasgow, demands for a greater advance were lodged late in 1917 and resulted in an agreed rise of 7s 6d a week from

March 1918.[48] That same month, Aberdeen exhibitors were faced with a demand from the National Association of Theatrical Employees for an adjustment in rates of some 50 per cent.[49]

Other costs were also subject to inflationary pressures at this time. Fuel charges rose from mid 1915, as Glasgow Corporation announced a 15 per cent increase in electricity prices.[50] While the impact of such a change was general, others were more specific to the cinema industry. In particular, the cost of film hire rose significantly over the second decade of the century. Not all of this could be attributed to the effects of war, as changes in the way in which films were marketed also operated to raise prices. In particular, the war years witnessed the rise of the exclusive, which involved exhibitors paying a premium to secure the sole rights to screen a picture in a specified area for a limited duration.[51] Whereas before 1914, cinemas had largely competed on the basis of attractions ancillary to the programme, now the films themselves and the stars appearing therein became the principal points of attraction for audiences. Some producers and distributors attempted to exploit the market power garnered through this change, in particular, the Essanay Company in the USA, fortunate to have on its books in 1915 the world's biggest box-office attraction, Charlie Chaplin. In September of that year, Essanay announced that in future all cinemas seeking to book a Chaplin subject would be obliged to book other films produced under its banner. Exhibitors in both Glasgow and Edinburgh, working through their respective Associations, organised a boycott of Essanay products, a prohibition which the organisation in Edinburgh sought to enforce by means of legal action against one company, the Lyric Picture House, that had concluded a separate agreement with the distributors. In December, a judgment in the Court of Session found against the Lyric on the grounds that it had been a signatory to the initial resolution to abstain from trading with Essanay. However, before the case could proceed further, Essanay agreed to allow Chaplin films to be booked on a separate contract, a decision that led the secretary of the Edinburgh branch of the CEA to assert that 'The battle of free-trade in films had been really decided in Scotland.'[52]

Yet if the ambitions of one producer had been contained, the trend more generally towards exclusive contracts and the block booking of a company's product continued substantially unchecked. By September 1916, the Cinema House in Glasgow was advertising itself as 'The Scottish House of Fox Films', having booked first runs locally for all that company's subjects for six months ahead.[53] Such arrangements had a powerful appeal, providing as they did a means of containing the escalating costs of booking on exclusive terms, a problem that, by the middle years of the war, exercised more than one board of directors. Having agreed contracts for fifty-nine films with six different distributors, the Aberdeen Picture Palaces, Ltd moved in November 1916 to limit its weekly expenditure on films to £10 for each of its halls.[54] At the same time, the Queen's Rooms Cinema Syndicate, Ltd, also based in

Aberdeen, proposed reducing the cost of film hire by pooling its booking arrangements with a neighbouring concern.[55] This approach to securing economies in what was, for most exhibitors, their second largest outlay, was extensively adopted during the war and in its immediate aftermath and provided the basis for the rise to prominence of figures such as Alex B. King, originally manager of Glasgow's Lorne Cinema, who, by early 1920, oversaw bookings for some nineteen halls across central Scotland, from Rothesay to Dundee.[56]

Increases in film costs were not solely a consequence of developments within the trade. Government policies concerned to boost tax revenues to finance the war effort worked towards the same end. In September 1915, celluloid was one of a number of commodities subject to a 33.33 per cent ad valorem duty, introduced by the Chancellor of the Exchequer, Reginald McKenna. An increase of 10 per cent in the price of film hire was anticipated as a consequence of the tax, although exhibitors remained, for the most part, confident that any adverse impact on the trade could be contained. Interviewed by *The Scotsman*, some were of the view that the effect was more likely to be to encourage greater purchases of home-produced films, while others pointed out that, as most imported films were shown from prints manufactured in Britain, any upward pressure on costs would be limited. More significant, it was argued, prices of admission would not require adjustment in the light of the McKenna duty, given that, as one Edinburgh exhibitor had it, 'the programme was not the biggest item of expenditure for a cinema house'.[57]

Despite this, a rise in the cost of attending the cinema was not long delayed. The imposition of a duty on imported film had encouraged calls to exploit what appeared to be an invariable popular appetite for entertainment by placing a tax on ticket sales. As outlined in McKenna's Budget of April 1916, duty was imposed on a sliding scale, varying according to seat prices. On tickets up to 2d, a charge of ½d was levied, rising to 2s on seats costing 7s 6d or more.[58] Criticism immediately centred on the tax's regressive nature, with the cheapest seating bearing the highest marginal charge. For exhibitors such as Arthur Henderson of Dundee, who described himself as an 'amusement caterer for the working classes of the city', the tax would inevitably result in reduced admissions as, particularly at a time of a general escalation in the cost of living, not all would be able to afford the higher prices.[59] Drawing on his experience of Aberdeen's east end, Bert Gates predicted a shift in favour of the cheaper seats, along with the wholesale exclusion of those previously unable to afford other than the lowest prices.[60] Although the Exhibitors' Association lobbied for a remission of the tax on the cheapest seats, the only concession granted was on children's matinees, which would remain free from tax, provided the price of admission was fixed at 1d.[61] Although proprietors sought to make a virtue of the levy, arguing that it rendered cinema-going an act of patriotism, so that 'Every visit to the

Picture Theatre is a smack in the eye for the Kaiser', the trade press reported an overall downturn in business in mid 1916.[62] Here, the effect of the tax was seen to be compounded by the introduction of daylight saving, which, by extending the period available for outdoor pursuits at the height of summer, further discouraged cinema attendance. In June, *The Bioscope* noted the plight of one exhibitor whose takings were said to be down by 50 per cent, although in this case the effect of daylight saving was thought to outweigh the impact of any price rise by a ratio of 60:40.[63] So, while the entertainments tax loomed large in exhibitors' complaints over poor trade, the industry's problems at this point of the war appeared attributable to a variety of factors. The Glasgow-based trade paper *The Entertainer* had hinted at a fall off in business before the introduction of the tax and while closures, rumoured by May 1917 to be running at 700 halls across Britain as a whole, were substantially attributed to the impact of price rises, other sources of difficulty were also noted, from increasing levels of recruitment, and the resultant shortage of essential manpower, to escalating wage costs.[64]

Aggregate indices of industrial performance in this period remain elusive. However, at company level, the trade's mounting difficulties can be charted with some certainty. At its most extreme, the outcome would be closure. On the east coast, The Portobello Picture Palace, Ltd opted for liquidation some months prior to the expiration of its lease on the local town hall and also, significantly, in advance of the imposition of entertainments tax.[65] Similarly, after several months operating consistently at a loss, the Queen's Rooms Cinema Syndicate placed its Aberdeen business on the market late in 1916.[66] At the neighbouring Aberdeen Electric Theatre Co., Ltd, the balance sheet slipped further into the red in 1917, resulting in an overall loss of £426, and although profitable trading was maintained at the Dunfermline Cinema House, BB Pictures, Ltd, and the Hillhead Picture House, both of the latter two in Glasgow, margins were seriously squeezed by the third year of the war.[67] At the Aberdeen Picture Palaces, Ltd, a fall of £750 17s 11d in takings over the six months to the end of October 1916, compared with the same period the year earlier, contributed to transforming an operating surplus of £1,641 2s 1½d in the year to April 1916 into an overall loss of £80 2s 8½d for the following twelve-month period.[68] Particular problems had been encountered at the firm's house in the east end of the city, the Star, where, as Bert Gates reflected, 'speaking to the Pictures had now ceased to be effective'. The adoption of variety entertainments at a neighbouring hall had, it was thought, rendered the practice of declaiming dialogue from behind the screen increasingly antiquated. Yet the move to engage turns, backed by an orchestra, involved the house in considerable additional expenditure, estimated by Gates at between £16 and £21 a week. Although drawings received a short-term boost, this did not suffice to compensate for the additional outlays and, within two months, the decision was taken to downsize the musical accompaniment from an orchestra to a single pianist. Even so, losses continued at the Star, so that the house's brief flirtation with variety was ended early in 1917 and the elocutionists were restored to their rightful place behind the screen.[69] Surveying a difficult trading year, the company's directors pointed to the particular circumstances that had led to the move into the red: 'the War, impact of Amusements Tax, and the experiment of variety shows, the latter having proved a disastrous failure financially'.[70]

So, rather than constituting a period in which cinema-going rose to new heights, the years of war to 1917 may be more accurately seen as a time of mounting challenges for the trade as it sought to operate in an often unfavourable economic and political climate. Yet as the war entered its fourth year, the difficulties facing the industry appeared, contrary to the trends suggested in other accounts, to abate. The report of the inquiry instigated by the National Council of Public Morals, while not finding the cinema entirely blameless over the question of delinquent behaviour, at least exonerated the trade from the more specific charge of inciting criminality.[71] What is more, company balance sheets, which had charted a deteriorating trading performance over the previous twelve months, increasingly took on an altogether healthier appearance. Significantly, this occurred despite a further increase in entertainments duty in 1917. Announced in the Budget of that year, its implementation was delayed, following lobbying by exhibitors, until early autumn, a point at which it was thought business tended to pick up after the summer lull.[72] Turnover, which in a number of cases had fallen markedly with the first imposition of tax in 1916, now showed greater resilience. The Aberdeen Picture Palaces, Ltd recorded consistent and growing profitability over the second half of 1917, culminating in record returns being reported at both its houses. Overall, the company, which had shown a loss in 1916–17, achieved a profit to February 1918 of close to £1,250, sufficient to justify payment of a 10 per cent dividend.[73] Returns elsewhere suggest that this trend was not exceptional. The Scottish Electric Picture Palaces, Ltd reported its highest level of profit to date in the year to June 1918, while over the same twelve-month period, takings at the Glasgow Cinema House rose by almost 30 per cent.[74] Such was the strength of this revival overall that an upward revision of prices, considered an essential response to the continued escalation in operating costs, was delayed early in 1918, on the grounds that greater admissions were, of themselves, generating higher levels of income.[75] When an increase in prices was finally agreed in July 1918, it did nothing to check the growth in picture-going. In Aberdeen, it was reported, business reached new heights in 1918, so that the industry anticipated the period after the war more in hope than in trepidation.[76] As early as October 1917, some thirty new cinemas were being planned for the Glasgow area alone.[77]

Renewed optimism was rooted in a more benign economic climate, in which wages gradually caught up with the surge in prices that had set in from 1914. Assisting this process, increases in the cost of living were moderated as price controls and rationing were applied to many essential foodstuffs.[78] By

1918, then, potential cinema patrons were judged better placed to bear the impact of a hike in entertainments tax and an advance in basic seat prices. Far from marking the beginning of a sustained and serious decline in attendance, as some of the literature would have it, the final year of the war heralded an intensive, if short-lived, period of prosperity for the industry.

III

Reflecting the central place it had come to occupy in the leisure culture of the time, the cinema benefited fully from the boom conditions that prevailed across the economy in the immediate aftermath of the Armistice. Over the previous twelve months, potential purchasing power had accumulated rapidly, as higher incomes, both in real and money terms, combined with limited spending opportunities to create a growing pent-up demand.[79] Once controls on spending were relaxed, the enthusiasm for moving pictures was in full spate, diverting money and other resources into the expansion of the business, particularly the exhibition sector. Reviewing progress in the trade across 1920, *The Kinematograph Year Book* was able to list some 142 Scottish cinemas that had opened or had been reopened after a period of closure.[80] This figure included coastal halls which operated seasonally and so whose revival in the summer months was in the normal run of things. Such exceptions apart, however, the listing provides powerful evidence of new or augmented facilities for film exhibition in the aftermath of war. For example, in December 1919, the Dennistoun Picture Houses, Ltd was registered with a view to acquiring the Palladium, one of two cinemas in this eastern district of Glasgow, and constructing a new picture house at a cost of £30,000, which included £1,871 14s for the purchase of the site. Once the hall was up and running, the company turned to plans to increase the Palladium's capacity of 1,200, to this end acquiring the neighbouring roller-skating rink.[81] Additions to seating levels were widely reported at this time. In 1919, both the Western Cinema in Partick and the Picturedrome on Edinburgh's Easter Road announced plans to double their respective capacities.[82] Green's also looked to replace their first generation of Picturedromes with more substantial auditoria, more suited it was thought to post-war conditions. At Ayr, plans on hold since 1915 to develop a hall capable of accommodating over 2,000 were brought forward towards the end of 1920.[83]

The belief was widespread that the state of demand fully justified these and other schemes for expansion. Anxieties expressed before 1914 at the potential redundancy of plant, as construction ran significantly in advance of any growth in the audience, surfaced only fitfully after 1918. In July 1919, *The Entertainer*'s Paisley correspondent reported discussions on the question of whether the town was being 'over-cinemad'.[84] For the most part, however, the conviction that growth would continue at a rapid rate remained deeply rooted. Twelve months after the Armistice, the trade journal *Scottish Cinema* argued that, although already possessed of over 100 venues licensed for cinematograph shows, Glasgow had room for 'at least' another hundred. In its view, 'The Trade was never in a more flourishing condition.'[85] Problems of overcrowding as managers sought to extend capacities in the short term by installing additional seating or allowing patrons to stand suggested that there was more to this claim than the usual journalistic excess. From late 1919, Dundee Council moved to reduce standing room in cinemas across the city, while the following year action was taken against two halls in Greenock for overcrowding. Here, full-time working in the local shipyards provided a particular basis for prosperity in the cinema trade.[86] Even in the first flush of post-war optimism, it must be admitted, the industries of the central belt were not free of difficulties. Yet, for the most part, these remained highly localised and short-lived. In April 1919, for example, Dundee's cinemas were said to be operating considerably below capacity, a fact attributed to short-time working in the local jute trade, while in September the following year, *Kinematograph Weekly* reported that the threat of a coal stoppage had encouraged families to cut back on their spending, reducing takings across the mining villages of Ayrshire.[87] Overall, the flourishing state of Scottish industry worked to swell box-office receipts, so that one prospective Dundee councillor could refer to cinemas in October 1920 as 'veritable Klondykes'.[88]

Across the country, company balance sheets recorded operating margins which suggested that such a parallel was not entirely fanciful. At both the Scottish Electric Picture Palaces, Ltd and BB Pictures, Ltd, profits in 1918–19 approached £10,000, considerably in excess of the best returns hitherto posted by either firm.[89] After lower than usual returns in the middle years of the war, the Dunfermline Cinema House, Ltd reported high and rising levels of profit in the three years from 1918, while the Aberdeen Electric Theatre Co., Ltd, after two years of losses, returned to the black, albeit in modest fashion, from September 1918.[90] The nearby Picture Palaces concern had consistently generated higher rates of return, but the level of profit recorded in the first two post-war years were without precedent. Dividends of 20 per cent per annum had been paid on the company's shares in the early years of the war, but then rose to 40 per cent in 1919 and then to 90 per cent in 1920, drawing from *The Entertainer and Scottish Kinema Record* the somewhat wistful comment, 'lucky shareholders'.[91]

As a further indication of the extent of trading success, it might be noted that these unparalleled levels of profitability were achieved at a time of sharply escalating costs. Pressure was felt on most major items of expenditure. A renewal in general price inflation and the trade's much vaunted prosperity in the immediate post-war years combined to encourage demands for wage increases from staff who were increasingly likely to be unionised. By late 1919, it was estimated that 75 per cent of operators across Glasgow and the south-west of Scotland belonged to the National Association of Theatrical Employees (NATE), while membership elsewhere was closer to 50 per cent.[92] In some cases, operators paid to an alternative union, the electricians'. Organisation extended to other staff also, so that by 1920, NATE was also negotiating on behalf of ticket checkers.[93] Managements were not always sympathetic to such developments. In explaining a significant jump in the wages bill at Donald's Aberdeen cinemas to the Inland Revenue, one manager pointed to the engagement of an operator at a higher than usual salary before observing that 'the other workers had joined some union or other, with the result that their wages had all to be increased'.[94] So, operators secured standard wages according to the grade of cinema in which they worked from November 1919, before proceeding in 1920 to seek agreement on a minimum wage level of £3 5s a week and the adoption of a standard 48-hour week.[95] At the same time, a flat rate of 15s a week was agreed for ticket checkers, which represented an increase of 1s a week for most.[96] Finally, in December 1919, a 10s rise in the weekly minimum wage paid to musicians was conceded, along with an increase in overtime rates of 6d an hour, while a standard working week of 24 hours was agreed at houses offering two shows a night, along with a 22-hour week where shows were continuous.[97] The following year, minimum rates were increased by a further 15 per cent and separate payments introduced for directors of instrumental combinations with more than three players each.[98] Growth in the wage bill, while marked was also, for the most part, readily accommodated by firms enjoying the bounty of buoyant receipts.

Indeed, despite increased costs, the tendency in many cinemas from 1919 was to increase further the complement of musicians being employed. In May that year, an orchestra of unspecified size replaced a pianist as the main form of accompaniment at the Coliseum in Edinburgh, while in September, the La Scala in Aberdeen opted to augment its existing orchestra.[99] By 1920, concerns were being voiced that further wage increases, if conceded, would discourage recruitment and could lead to orchestras being reduced in size.[100] In August of that year, at cinemas across west-central Scotland owned by the Green family, all bar the pianists at each house were dismissed, leading to the AMU calling for a boycott of Green's shows and organising a picket of the company's halls.[101] This little local difficulty apart, the trade remained strikingly free of the kind of labour disputes affecting much of British industry in these years. The secondary nature of much employment in local cinemas, often undertaken at night in addition to principal daytime jobs, may have worked to blunt the force of labour militancy, as such work was rarely a family's primary means of support.[102] What is more, the ability of many firms to absorb additional costs must also have worked to contain potential sources of friction.

Evidence of high and persistent demand for cinema-going, communicated on a daily basis through the box office, persuaded managers that the growth in expenditure could be funded. The readiness of exhibitors to discuss further increases in admission charges also reflected confidence that much of the burden of any growth in expenses would be borne by ordinary picture-goers. In Dundee, an agreement to raise prices was concluded in May 1919, while in the autumn of that year exhibitors in Aberdeen raised minimum prices, children's matinees apart, to 4d.[103] By the end of 1919, a further increase to 5d was under consideration, demand having proved resilient in the face of the previous hike.[104] Balance sheets which remained stubbornly in the black in these early post-war years, provided continued justification for upward revisions in prices.

Crucially then, an overall rise in running costs, estimated in March 1920 to amount to some 150 per cent above pre-war levels, failed seriously to weaken the industry's performance.[105] Alongside the growth in the wage bill, exhibitors faced increases in other areas of expenditure in this period. The cost of film hire gave rise to occasional expressions of concern. In March 1920, the prospect of renters fixing minimum prices for subjects alarmed proprietors in Highland areas, who predicted that the change would result in widespread closures.[106] Later that year, proposals to alter the charge for renting from a flat-rate fee to one based on a percentage of takings mobilised opposition in Edinburgh, where exhibitors claimed that margins would be severely reduced as a consequence.[107] A more immediate challenge facing businesses across Scotland from 1919 was the first revision of rating values since the outbreak of war. Increases in assessments of 25 per cent in Edinburgh and 40 per cent in Aberdeen the following year gave notice that officials intended that local government's coffers would also benefit from the profitable business context.[108] Indeed, in Edinburgh, there were calls for firms to make their balance sheets available so that assessment could be based on actual trading performance rather than, as previously, the potential earnings represented by the number of seats and the prices charged for each. A defence based on the need to maintain commercial confidentiality succeeded in blocking any alteration to the basis of assessment.[109] Yet even in the absence of such a change, most halls faced a significant increase in their rates bills. In October 1920, rises of between 23.3 per cent and 80.9 per cent were agreed for cinemas in Greenock.[110]

Beyond the seemingly inexorable increase in operating costs, two other challenges confronted managers in the years immediately after the First World War. Both were the results of the industry's success. First, cinema building became a matter for debate in several council chambers across Scotland from 1919. Before the war, picture-going had largely received the endorsement of Labour and socialist groups, who saw it as a means of weaning workers away from the less rational activities that often filled their leisure time. In the mining town of Cardenden in Fife, proceeds from the local Gothenburg public house were used to fund cinema provision at the Picturedrome, run by the Bowhill Public House Society, Ltd.[111] Similarly, further west in Dumfriesshire, wartime controls over liquor consumption had encouraged the development of more improving recreational facilities, such as Gracies Banking Cinema in Annan.[112] After the war, however, sections of the labour movement came to view the cinema in altogether less favourable terms, seeing it as a leading obstacle to schemes of post-war reconstruction. Complaints that resources, primarily men and materials, applied to the construction of a new generation of picture palaces, were being diverted from crucial house-building programmes first surfaced in Dundee in the autumn of 1919, when it became a key issue in that year's council elections. The candidate sponsored by the local stonemasons' union was clear that cinema building was proceeding at the expense of the corporation's housing schemes.[113] The complaint was taken up early the following year by the Glasgow Labour Party's Housing Association, which in January passed a resolution against further cinema building.[114] Similar views were expressed, at about the same time, in Greenock and Aberdeen.[115] Yet it was in Dundee that what came to be referred to as 'anti-cinemamania' appeared most deeply rooted. Here, through its representatives on the local Housing Committee, Labour sought to protest against plans for extending cinema provision. So, proposals advanced by the District Board of Control to install facilities for moving pictures in Westgreen Asylum were greeted less than sympathetically by one Labour councillor: 'it seemed that the public outside Westgreen had gone Cinema mad, and that there was no need to put a Cinema in a madhouse'.[116] Although an effort was made to argue that picture halls provided some alleviation of the housing problem by offering a refuge from the worst housing conditions, the prevailing view, expressed by bodies such as the Trades and Labour Council in Cambuslang, was that cinemas were luxury buildings for which there was no overriding social need.[117] This provided the justification for the order prohibiting further cinema building approved by Greenock Corporation in March 1920, a measure also adopted the following month in Glasgow. Here, the Director of Housing argued that work on cinemas locally had led to a shortage of labour, preventing progress on the construction of the 57,000 houses said to be needed across the city.[118] In both cases, Appeal Tribunals, meeting under the Housing (Additional Powers) Act of 1919, found against the prohibitions. The judgment was that neither council had established that cinema building had contributed significantly to any shortfall in men and materials.[119] If this did little to deflect criticism of the trade by Labour representatives elsewhere, it did ensure that the protests of 'anti-cinemamaniacs' failed to exert a decisive impact on building activity from that point.

The other post-war challenge confronting the trade, although assuming a rather different form, also emanated from local council chambers. Particularly from 1918, a growing number of authorities across Scotland sought to develop a direct involvement in film exhibition. The idea of municipal cinema was not entirely new and had first been floated before 1914 by English municipalities, such as Ilkley and Bridlington in Yorkshire.[120] North of the border, city corporations had for some time been active in

the provision of popular entertainments, and Glasgow's Corporation concerts on Saturdays had increasingly incorporated moving picture shows.
Corporation concerts were primarily intended to elevate to some degree the
recreational taste of local citizens, and calls to extend the range of municipal
enterprise to the cinema itself drew on similar ideas.[121] Those promoting the
first such venture in Scotland, in Kirkintilloch in 1914, were of the view that
'it seemed high time public authorities controlled the great method of the
education of the future', by offering an entertainment that would 'educate
and elevate'.[122] Complementing this sense of moral purpose were narrower
economic calculations. In a period in which the revenue base of most urban
authorities was failing to expand at a rate to match the growth in services
provided, the cinema's record for profitability offered hope of an additional
buoyant source of income.[123] So, advocates of municipal cinema made much
of its potential to reduce pressure on the rates, and this became a key selling
point both in Bridlington in late 1913 and in Kirkintilloch the year after. In
the latter case, enthusiasm for local authority enterprise was advanced by a
powerful and active ILP group on the council, resulting in a range of public
initiatives within the burgh, varying from the provision of communal kitch-
ens, baths, and bowling greens, along with the cultivation of cabbages and
the rearing and keeping of pigs and goats, holding out, as one sceptic saw it,
'Promise of plenty of goats' milk for the babies, to combat tuberculosis'.[124]
Launching their scheme early in 1914, on the crest of the first wave of cinema
building, the advocates of local enterprise envisaged continued success.
Moving the resolution that entertainments be provided in the town hall
and that the council bear the cost of installing the cinematograph apparatus
and electrical plant, one baillie remarked, 'As far as I can see it is impossible to have a loss.'[125] Nevertheless, on the advice of the town clerk that the
rates could not be used to make good any deficit, the management of the
cinema operating from the town hall was entrusted to a committee of local
councillors.[126]

   Opposition to the spread of municipal enterprise delayed the opening
of Kirkintilloch's cinema until November 1914. Although circumstances
appeared less favourable to profitable trading, in its first season, the business recorded a surplus of £448, which went towards a reduction in admission charges, as well as part of the cost of a gala day for local children, and
a donation of £162 to the burgh's Common Good Fund.[127] The success of
the Kirkintilloch house would, over time, attract wider interest. Reports
of a further sizeable contribution to the Common Good Fund at the end of
the 1916–17 season led *The Entertainer* to hope that this would not encourage the spread of socialised cinema: 'let the individualistic effort flourish in
the picture house'.[128] Economic uncertainty and the shortage of manpower
would ensure that Kirkintilloch's initiative would not be replicated elsewhere
for the duration of the conflict. In the more benign conditions that prevailed
towards the war's end, however, other authorities laid down plans to follow

Kirkintilloch's example. In August 1918, Clydebank announced plans to run shows from the town hall and, in the first year after the Armistice, the idea was taken up in Montrose and Johnstone.[129] Initial returns appeared fully to justify the hopes invested in such ventures. In its first six weeks after opening in September 1919, Montrose's Burgh Cinema reported profits of £293.[130] By then, similar schemes were under consideration in a number of larger centres, including Perth and Paisley, and were being openly discussed in Glasgow, with the backing of several prominent politicians, including Paddy Dolan.[131]

The spread of municipal shows aroused concern in the cinema trade itself, to the extent that its Parliamentary spokesman, former Labour and now National Democratic and Labour MP J. A. Seddon, spoke out against the trend in December 1919. At a time of growing competition from itinerant and temporary exhibitors, the prospect of a further challenge to profitability was unwelcome, particularly as the suspicion remained that municipal halls rarely faced the same level of regulation as commercial cinemas and often secured the premises from which they operated on favourable terms.[132] Such was the charge levelled against Kirkintilloch's municipal cinema by critics, who were convinced that the profit paid into the Common Good Fund had been generated at the expense of revenue from the lease of the town hall, for which the business paid a lower than usual rental. Any net gain to the burgh was thus called into question.[133]

Despite such expressions of opposition, the prospect of alleviating the rates burden continued to provide a powerful inducement in favour of the adoption of municipal enterprise. So, trading success in Montrose and Johnstone, where steps were taken to augment the hall's capacity from October 1920, encouraged more authorities to consider launching their own schemes.[134] In the months that followed, municipal cinemas were reported to be under consideration in, among other places, Renfrew, Huntly in Aberdeenshire, Dysart in Fife, and as far north as Stornoway on the Isle of Lewis. Here, it was argued, the public provision of moving pictures would help to fund the building of facilities for meetings and entertainments, at the same time ensuring that the films being exhibited would be subject to effective local regulation, to the extent that they would be less likely to offend Free Church sensibilities.[135] In few cases, however, did discussion produce practical results. In larger population centres, the presence of a sizeable commercial entertainment sector was often sufficient to discourage plans for municipal enterprises. Reviewing the limited success of a series of corporation concerts, Perth Council concluded that conditions locally were not conducive to further public initiatives.[136] What is more, existing businesses acted as a powerful lobby against the spread of municipal competition. So, early in 1921, plans by the council in the Argyllshire resort of Dunoon to acquire the Pavilion to run films during the summer season were challenged in the courts by the owners of the local Picture House. The judgment laid down by the Court of Session that, in providing cinematograph entertainments funded out of the rates, the local authority was exceeding the powers granted by the relevant Police Acts, emboldened opposition elsewhere.[137] In December 1921, proprietors of the Empire Picture House in Montrose commenced a legal action against the shows run in the local Burgh Hall.[138] If such challenges may have worked to check the momentum behind the spread of municipal cinema, they did not prove an insuperable obstacle to its adoption. As has been seen, Kirkintilloch had circumvented doubts as to the legality of conducting a business chargeable on the rates by devolving managerial responsibility on to a committee of local councillors.

More decisive in blunting enthusiasm for municipal provision was the onset of a serious recession in the trade from the early months of 1921. The downturn was such that, after two years of solid profitability, the municipal cinema in Montrose recorded a loss in the year to July 1922.[139] Business was also sharply down at Kirkintilloch. Far from reducing the rates burden, municipal cinema seemed set fair to add to it. After eighteen months of depressed takings, the shows at Kirkintilloch Town Hall reverted to private control, while a separately constituted business took on the lease of Montrose Burgh Hall from September 1923.[140] In a context of sharply fluctuating income levels, the certainty of regular rental payments had an obvious attraction in helping to eliminate the vagaries of the balance sheet. Similar calculations appear to have informed the decision of the Trustees of the Public Hall in Gartcosh, Lanarkshire, to end their involvement in the running of the cinematograph business centred on the hall from August 1924. Three years earlier, the promise of consistent profitability had persuaded the Trustees to take over management from the original lessees. As the business slipped into the red, a position only partly modified by profits on confectionary sales, the virtues of reverting to previous arrangements became clear.[141] So, with the passing of the industry's 'Klondyke' phase, the vogue for publicly run cinema lapsed.

Underscoring the commercial forces driving the trade's wider development in the immediate post-war years was the ready availability of private capital. Despite escalating costs of men and materials, which in some cases worked to check building programmes, the funding required to finance new concerns and to enable existing businesses to extend their capacities was readily forthcoming.[142] Information derived from the Register of Dissolved Companies relating to some twenty-one concerns engaged in film exhibition and floated between 1915 and 1923 suggests that, as in the first wave of building before 1914, the primary source of investment capital remained Scotland's commercial middle classes. Figures active in cinema exhibition and the entertainment business more generally assumed rather greater prominence in this more mature phase of the industry's history, but were still only present on half the company boards in the sample, accounting for seventeen of the ninety directors traced. In shareholders' lists, their presence was further diluted.[143] Significantly, few of those employed in the trade sought to acquire a direct financial interest in its performance. Although the Palace Kinema (Dunfermline), Ltd numbered among its shareholders a Bioscope operator, and a musical director and female pianist acquired ten and 100 shares respectively in the St Andrew Square Picture House, Ltd in Edinburgh, such interests remained for the most part exceptional.[144] It was, however, reflective of a broader reluctance among Scottish workers to commit money to the trade, even during its expansive 'Klondyke' period. As before 1914, working-class investors, where encountered, were more likely to be drawn from skilled, supervisory grades or to be employed in small-scale, individual crafts, as with the rabbit catcher twice allotted shares in the Playhouse, Galashiels (1920), Ltd.[145] The ranks of the semi-skilled, who sustained Scotland's staple industries, were largely absent, although textile workers were evident at the Dunfermline and Galashiels houses already mentioned, as well as the Kilmarnock Picture House, Ltd and the Stockbridge Picture House, Co., Ltd in Edinburgh.[146] The latter also made allotments to coal miners, as did the Palace in Dunfermline.[147] For all its importance to the war effort, the manufacture of armaments generated only one representative, a munitions worker from Dalmuir, allotted 150 shares in the Wellington Picture Palace, Ltd in 1918.[148] Overall, then, working-class Scots were no more likely to view the industry as a potential source of investment after 1918 than they had been before 1914. Popular involvement in local picture houses rarely extended beyond viewing the films themselves.

In certain respects, however, the shareholders' lists effectively capture changes brought about by the war. The increased feminisation of the audience, remarked upon during the conflict, seems to have been sustained after the Armistice. In the early weeks of the peace, *The Entertainer* noted a preponderance of women among picture-goers, to the extent that in places they were estimated to make up 70 per cent of the audience.[149] Given this, the need to tailor the programme to meet female tastes appeared clear. The following year, the Edinburgh correspondent of *Scottish Cinema* saw the success at The Palace Cinema of Ethel M. Dell's *The Keeper of the Rose* as evidence of picture-going's importance in the lives of women of all ages.[150] For some, it would appear, this commitment went further. Returns to the companies' register recorded a growing number of allotments to women in the years from 1918. At three concerns floated between 1919 and 1921 – the Dennistoun Picture House, Ltd and the Waverley Picture House (1920), Ltd, both in Glasgow, and the St Andrew Square Picture House, Ltd in Edinburgh – all of which advertised shares for public sale, between 28 per cent and 38 per cent of all allotments were made to women.[151] Yet, when viewed in greater detail, the degree of change was, perhaps, rather less than these figures would suggest. In each case, as in all companies making up the post-war sample, shares for the most part were taken up by women who would not appear to have been in gainful employment. In most cases, designations, where offered, related more to the individual's marital status than to her occupational background, suggesting that shareholders were not women who had sought to exploit new employment opportunities created by the war. Rather, they were, like their pre-war counterparts, seeking a profitable outlet for the investment of small capital sums. Even where allotments were made to women in paid employment outside the home, they were more often than not engaged in forms of work in which a strong female presence was well established. Nursing (eight), teaching (ten), and retail (seven) jobs were prominent among the seventy-three allocations made at the three firms mentioned earlier. By contrast, only one female machinist, who took out twelve shares in the Dennistoun Picture House, Ltd, could be found. Against that, clerical work, the one area in which the wartime spike in female employment endured into the subsequent peace, was well represented, accounting for eighteen allotments in all.[152] When placed in context, however, the young economically active female, the embodiment of the 'modern' in interwar society, was not representative of women's financial involvement in the cinema trade in the early post-war years. Rather, the second wave of expansion in the industry shared many common features with the first, from 1910. Although separated by a decade and a world war, both were fundamentally driven by the quest for a secure yet profitable outlet for small-scale middle-class savings.

Further evidence of continuity may be found in the geographical origin of investment capital, which, whether in the form of bank loans or share subscriptions, was raised locally. At this point in the industry's history, exhibitors rarely had cause to look south of the Tweed or the Solway for their finances. The Playhouse in Galashiels was unusual in attracting funds from across Northumberland. Yet, even in this case, 43 per cent of allotments were made to subscribers within Galashiels itself.[153] Here, as elsewhere, local sources of funding were supplemented by capital raised in west-central Scotland. Glasgow supplied much of the initial impetus behind cinemas as far apart as Dumfries, Dundee (the Britannia Cinema, Ltd), Dunfermline (Olympia Pictures, Ltd), and Edinburgh (The Stockbridge Picture House Co., Ltd and the St Andrew Square Picture House, Ltd).[154] The net result was an industry that at the end of this second wave of expansion remained structured around individual locally owned and managed businesses. Such circuits as did function at this date remained centred on particular localities, as with the five houses run by the Aberdeen Picture Palaces, Ltd, all active within the city boundaries, or the halls operating in villages across the eastern Borders and overseen by the Border Cinema Co. The largest and most extensive circuit remained that managed by George Green, Ltd in Glasgow, which by 1921 comprised eleven cinemas mostly located within the central belt.[155] Figures who would become key to the industry's future, including Thomas Ormiston, Alexander King, and most notably John Maxwell through his Scottish Cinemas and Variety Theatres, Ltd, were active in the early post-war years, but their importance would only become apparent over the following decade, during which the exhibition sector was obliged to respond to markedly more difficult trading conditions.[156]

IV

Problems were apparent by the later weeks of 1920 and if the Aberdeen correspondent of *The Scottish Kinema Record* remained confident that any downturn would be more than offset by the seasonal boost to trade provided by Christmas and the New Year, the view further south was altogether less reassuring; the paper's correspondent in Greenock was of the view that conditions heralded an end to cinema's period of growth.[157] Conditions during the following months, as the British economy entered its sharpest period of contraction of the twentieth century, appeared fully to justify such pessimism.[158] Production and employment indices were all markedly down over the first half of 1921 and Scotland, with its reliance on heavy industries geared substantially to export markets, experienced the downturn in full measure. Paisley's thread mills reported extensive short-time working early in 1921, while in the year's second quarter the effects of recession were compounded by a prolonged stoppage in the coal industry as miners struck against a threatened reduction in wages.[159] With spending power seriously depressed among precisely those groups to which the cinema had pitched its appeal over the previous decade, the implications of such trends for the moving picture business were likely to be profound. Reduced activity was reported across industrial areas, with inevitable consequences for picturehouse takings. Reviewing conditions across the financial year to July 1922, the directors of the Scottish Electric Picture Palaces, Ltd felt drawn to enlarge on the conditions facing the business:

> the Country is passing through a period of unprecedented depression which is having a serious effect upon the entertainment business generally. Port Glasgow has been very seriously affected by the depression, and consequently there has been a very large decrease in the House receipts as compared to the previous year.[160]

This went some way to explaining the loss recorded over the year of £486, which contrasted with a profit over the previous twelve-month period of £2,559 8s.[161] Elsewhere, company balance sheets recorded a similar tale of commercial difficulty. The West of Scotland Electric Theatres, Ltd, having posted a net profit of £3,348 for 1920, slipped into the red to the extent of £403 13s 6d over the following year.[162] Similarly, three years of unprecedented profitability for the Dunfermline Cinema House, Ltd came to an abrupt end from March 1921. The two subsequent profit and loss accounts reported deficits of £241 and £1,168 10s respectively.[163] Things were little different away from the central belt. Having achieved modest profits in the immediate post-war years, the lapse into serious and sustained loss by the

North of Scotland Cinematograph, Ltd, which operated houses along the Moray coast, was, in the context of the time, unsurprising.[164]

Taking stock of the industry's position at the end of 1922, the *Kinematograph Year Book* remarked on 'a decline in public patronage so serious as to give rise to suggestions of revolutionary changes in the methods of the exhibiting and distributing side of the industry alike'.[165] For some businesses, the implications were even more drastic. Several houses had been forced to suspend operations in the early summer of 1921 as the prolonged coal stoppage threatened essential fuel supplies.[166] If this was a temporary response to an immediate challenge, the effect of mounting losses was soon felt in permanent closures. In December 1921, the Aberchirder Picture House in Aberdeenshire ceased business due to poor trading conditions, while the following year the West of Scotland Electric Theatres, Ltd, launched in 1909 in the first flush of enthusiasm for cinema construction, went into voluntary liquidation.[167] If elsewhere such decisions could be delayed, they could rarely be wholly averted. The restrictions imposed on picture houses in Wick through the prohibition on schoolchildren's attendance, while seen by some to be productive of the kind of peaceful atmosphere conducive to the ordered contemplation of the moving image, was altogether less favourable to the maintenance of good business. At the Breadalbane Hall, takings which had reached £80 a week in 1920 and 1921 fell to an average of between £11 and £20 the following year. By early 1924, the Hall's trustees were obliged to sue for bankruptcy.[168] Other business models also found themselves undermined by the effects of the downturn. As has been noted, enthusiasm for municipal cinema waned as the period of easy profitability passed into history.[169]

More generally, various options were available to managements anxious to restore company finances. Some, recalling that cinema's early appeal had been founded on its ability to offer entertainment at low prices, moved to lower admission charges, to reflect the reduced circumstances of potential patrons. In December 1921, the Bonnybridge Picture Palace announced a reversion to pre-war prices, while at Greenock, special matinee rates were introduced for those unable to afford admission to evening shows.[170] Over the following two years, this example was taken up extensively, if fitfully, in areas as far apart as Kilmarnock in the west to Wick in the north.[171] It was an approach informed in part by the conviction, widely held by exhibitors, that the trade's difficulties owed much to the imposition of entertainments tax, which had compromised cinema's reputation for offering cheap amusements. In most diagnoses of the industry's ills in the early 1920s, some weight was given to the effect of the tax. Almost invariably, however, it was accorded a subordinate role when set alongside the impact of the economic downturn.[172] Similarly, most remained sceptical that a reduction in prices alone would restore the industry's fortunes. Not only was it unclear that trade had been significantly boosted by the lowering in admission charges, there remained the problem that costs were still substantially above pre-war levels. So, while many within the trade continued to campaign for some remission in the rate of entertainments tax, a concession being secured on the price of the cheapest seats in the Budget of 1924, more immediate relief was sought through reductions in expenditure.[173]

Initial attention centred, unsurprisingly, on the wage bill, the largest single item in most companies' balance sheets. Rates of pay for most cinema staff had increased markedly in the immediate post-war years. Now, from early 1922, pressure was to be exerted for widespread and substantial wage cuts. In March, the Scottish branch of the CEA proposed a reduction of 30 per cent in rates paid to members of the Amalgamated Musicians' Union. Negotiations limited the cut to around 10 per cent and, that same month, a reduction was also agreed with the main operators' organisation, the Electricians' Trade Union.[174] Beyond collective agreements, individual concerns also sought reductions from their staff. Assisted by the manager's agreement to take a cut of 5s a week in his salary, the hall at Stonehaven run by the Queen's Rooms Cinema Syndicate had effected an overall reduction of 22s 6d in the weekly wage bill by early 1923.[175]

As these examples indicate, the process of negotiation rendered wage adjustments a slow and often uncertain means of achieving the desired economies. A more immediate remedy was sought in hiring, or, often more accurately, firing policies. Particular attention focused on the provision of music, long used by managers to enhance the emotional impact of the moving image or to supplement the cinema-going experience by supplying live entertainment before or between the films.[176] For particular programmes, deemed to have popular appeal, additional provision would be made to ensure that the programme's potential earning power was fully exploited. So, a showing of the Gaumont-British production of *Rob Roy* at the Theatre De Luxe on Glasgow's Sauchiehall Street in 1922 was accompanied by the Caledonian Reel and Strathspey Band, along with the Victoria Male Voice Quartette, while during the film appropriate airs were played on the bagpipes. *The Scottish Kinema Record* anticipated that this would 'create the Highland atmosphere all right'.[177] Alongside the employment of additional musicians for special occasions, halls supplemented their basic provision when resources allowed and where trading conditions promised a return. Anticipating improved business in the second half of 1923, the directors of the Queen's Rooms Syndicate announced the hiring of an orchestra for one night each week and expressed their confidence that 'with additional attractions which are to be inaugurated in the shape of orchestral music etc. the current year will prove a satisfactory one'.[178] Many Scottish cinemas had augmented their musical provision as profit margins widened following the Armistice. The additional costs incurred were often substantial. At the Cinema House in Aberdeen, owned by James F. Donald (Cinemas), Ltd, five musicians, comprising a conductor, two violinists, an organist, and a drummer, absorbed almost half of the hall's wage bill of just over £2,000 per annum.[179] While such costs were easily borne at times of prosperity, they were altogether more difficult to sustain during a downturn. For managers in search of economies, therefore, musicians were obvious targets, as the Star Picture Palace in Aberdeen had found during its brief departure from the use of elocutionists in 1916.[180] At Stonehaven, the optimism which had greeted the hiring of the orchestra in August 1923 quickly dissipated. By the start of the following year, the decision had been taken to dispense with the band's services. In its place, two players were taken on to augment the regular performers for one night each week.[181] This flexible approach to hiring labour was also evident in city-centre houses. At the Glasgow Cinema House, orchestral provision was trimmed during the summer months in the mid 1920s, as a fall in business was anticipated with the advent of better weather. The importance of effective musical support was still recognised, so that orchestral players were rehired each September, although their contributions centred on times of the day when attendances were expected to be highest: between three and five each afternoon, and after seven in the evening. At other times, the films were supported by a solo piano.[182] By a policy of flexible hiring, the cost of supplying music was contained, while its aesthetic and commercial role was not compromised.

Attention was not confined to the wage bill. After labour costs, the largest single outlay for most cinemas centred on the hiring of films. At the five halls run by the Aberdeen Picture Palaces, Ltd, spending on films accounted for between 25.3 per cent and 43.9 per cent of all expenditure during the financial year to February 1925.[183] A relatively minor item on the balance sheet before 1914, film hire had become increasingly expensive with the greater length of subjects and the emergence of star talent capable of commanding large salaries. Unsurprisingly then, discussion of the problems facing the trade, as prosperity turned to slump, gave prominence to the burden of film hire.[184] Yet the remedy to this problem was far from straightforward. A reduction in charges, through the hire of cheaper, often older subjects was deemed a false economy. The success enjoyed by small distributors such as Tommy Gilbert in marketing early Chaplin Keystone comedies during the post-war boom was seen not to reflect well on the trade's wider reputation.[185] So, the continued circulation of outdated subjects via substandard prints was regarded as a further problem to be addressed.[186] While reductions in hiring costs were sought, therefore, it was clear that this should not be at the expense of programme quality. That particular circle was squared by pooling film booking arrangements, a move that would also serve to correct to some degree imbalances in bargaining power between distributors and individual cinemas. Groups of exhibitors would, it was hoped, be able to secure more favourable hiring terms. At the height of the First World War, shared bookings were seen as one of the solutions to the financial difficulties plaguing the Queen's Rooms Syndicate in Aberdeen.[187] Similarly, in 1924, problems of film quality persuaded management at the Syndicate's Stonehaven house to contemplate cooperative booking arrangements.[188] The following year, collaboration between cinemas across central areas of Glasgow was proposed as a means of addressing the problems caused by renters' charges that were considered excessive.[189] Although by no means all the schemes advanced at this time came to fruition, enough did to effect a significant change in the exhibition sector. By 1924, *The Bioscope* estimated that one-third of houses across Scotland belonged to circuits for booking purposes.[190] Such collusion became the means by which figures such as Thomas Ormiston and Alex B. King assumed greater prominence within the trade. By the end of the 1920s, each handled the bookings for eighteen cinemas across the central belt.[191] Nor was this all; in May 1929, King assumed responsibility for booking films for the Regent Cinema, formerly the Cinema House, in Glasgow. Conditions were attached to his terms of service, including that no programme should be shared simultaneously with another house and that the weekly cost of programmes should not exceed £75.[192]

For all the importance that cost cutting and price reductions assumed in managerial strategies, it was clear to many that the trade's fortunes rested on more than adjustments to the balance sheet. Reviewing the problems confronting exhibitors in the early 1920s, both *The Scottish Kinema Record* and the *Kinematograph Year Book* concluded that the key to success continued to lie in the effective application of showmanship.[193] Various measures were available to enhance the particular appeal of shows. Although it was noted that most cinemas built in the immediate post-war boom made no provision for live entertainment alongside the films, some responded to reduced takings by adding variety to the programme.[194] By the mid 1920s, houses owned by George Green, Ltd in Bathgate and Rutherglen had moved to devote whole evenings to live acts, while the Central Hall in Broxburn experimented with a season of legitimate dramas in place of moving pictures.[195] So bad was business at Lesmahagow that the Palmer family, established there since 1916, contemplated taking to the road once more as a touring show.[196] Changes to that extent were not widespread, as live entertainment represented no saving on the cost of screening films and experience showed that audiences were not always appreciative of live acts. In 1919, rowdy behaviour had been reported at several houses where variety entertainments were offered. This reached such a pitch that at the Hippodrome Music Hall in Greenock, performers left the stage in protest. Here, it was reported, chairs and fittings had been damaged by disgruntled picture-goers, while in Aberdeen disapproval was expressed in a manner that defied conventional stereotyping, as pennies were thrown on the stage when variety artistes appeared.[197]

Fortunately, both for exhibitors and for Aberdonian pockets, alternatives were available. Depictions of local events, long a staple of cinema programmes, continued to draw audiences in the 1920s. Footage of the laying of the foundation stone for the local war memorial played well at the Banff

Picture House in June 1921,[198] while even supposedly more sophisticated metropolitan film-goers were considered susceptible to the lure of seeing themselves as others saw them. So, when the Glasgow Cinema House reopened after refurbishment in 1925, thought was given to means by which business could be boosted. One proposal advanced by the manager was 'to have a film taken of the leading thoroughfares of the various districts and invite the public to come to see themselves on your screen'.[199] At Port Glasgow, audience involvement was taken further, as picture-goers were filmed acting out a scene on stage which was then screened at later houses.[200] In a similar vein, the Vale Empire, Alexandria, ran a 'Fresh Faces' competition late in 1921, holding out the enticing, if somewhat remote prospect, 'you may be a Charlie Chaplin or Mary Pickford'.[201] More cerebral attributes were tested by the Mystery Box Guessing Competition instituted at the Coatbridge Cinema in December 1921, in which patrons were offered a prize of £5 for correctly predicting the household article contained in the box. Fortunately for the hall's coffers, only three out of 3,000 entrants were able successfully to identify a piece of delft plate.[202] At Lesmahagow, Palmers, having decided against a return to itinerancy, drew audiences through a range of activities calibrated to local tastes. These included a treacle- and scone-eating contest, a competition to catch a greasy piglet while blindfolded, and a draw to win a steak pie at each second house on Saturdays.[203] Finally, those with a taste for the savoury were catered for by an onion-eating contest at the Picture House, Kilmaurs, near Kilmarnock, late in 1921.[204]

If it is difficult to establish with any certainty the impact such efforts had on the behaviour of picture-goers, it is possible to locate them within the overall pattern of trade strategies. This becomes clear if we consider the campaign launched by the manager of the Pavilion, Rothesay, in July 1919. This involved printing numbers on programmes, with a winning number to be drawn at the end of the week, the winner to receive a 'real live baby', along with a cheque to cover the cost of its education and upkeep. As was intended, the competition provoked profound interest through the week, the local police fielding several complaints over the raffling of humanity. On Saturday, with the hall predictably packed, the draw was held, the winner proving to be a local slater, who stepped up to collect his prize, a piglet in the dress of a newborn baby, and a cheque for £5, which he undertook to apply in raising his newly acquired progeny in the manner which was to be expected, a promise he gave 'with a smack of his lips'.[205] As well as providing compelling evidence of prevailing attitudes to the different levels of creation, the Rothesay piglet also has much to tell us about the calculations informing the decisions of cinema managers in the 1920s. Its fate was determined during Glasgow Fair, a point in the year at which the takings of cinemas along the west coast were often at their highest. Here, then, showmanship was being applied to boost further a week that already promised burgeoning attendances. So, rather than seeking to moderate fluctuations in takings, exploitation sought to accentuate them, maximising returns from potentially profitable weeks. Showmanship was thus of a piece with policies on the hire of labour that were designed to accommodate variations in audience behaviour.

This perspective facilitates an understanding of a further aspect of cinema's development in this period: the emergence of the picture palace, a large auditorium, distinguished by elaborate decor and an ostentatious association with comfort and luxury.[206] As has been noted, additions to capacity were widespread in the immediate post-war years. Yet expansion was not solely a response to buoyant demand. To some degree, the changing economics of the business obliged exhibitors to build big. To make a return on the screening of longer, more expensive films, larger audiences had to be accommodated. Although, hypothetically, the means to achieving this were many and varied, in practice, options were more limited. Time constraints limited the number of screenings that were possible, as an increase in the number of shows would extend business into parts of the day or week when trade was notoriously slow. At the company's annual general meeting in 1927, the board of the Glasgow Picture House Co., Ltd commented on 'the difficulty of inducing an afternoon trade in Renfield Street'.[207] The preferred course of action was to seek higher returns from the same number of show-ings by accommodating larger audiences at peak times. In a submission to Glasgow's Valuation Court in October 1924, the Provincial Cinematograph Theatres, Ltd sought remission for the rates payable on one of its properties in the city on the grounds that the hall was closed pending alterations to raise the existing capacity of 1,084. This was deemed 'insufficient to enable the proprietors to show profitably the type of film now required'.[208] Other halls had already reached a similar conclusion. The first generation of smaller, older Picturedromes run by Green's, including the Whitevale and the Bridgeton theatres, consistently showed losses by the 1920s, foreshadowing their closure.[209] In the face of similar pressures, shareholders of the Glasgow Picture House Co., Ltd had agreed in April 1924 to expenditure aimed at lifting the hall's capacity and improving the decorative layout, despite con-cerns expressed over 'the unsettled state of the country and the very bad state of trade in general'.[210] Even before the impact of any reduction in enter-tainments tax was felt, therefore, schemes of expansion were being floated. If anything, for many houses, the uncertainties of the 1920s often acted more as a stimulus than a deterrent to investment.

While increases in capacity were, to a large extent, driven by the need to respond to escalating costs, such decisions were also shaped by anticipated income flows. Where new cinemas were planned, the factors informing managerial thinking were rendered explicit. In 1931, for example, a new hall was planned for the Dumfriesshire town of Lockerbie, for which Green's in Glasgow handled the film bookings, as well as offering guidance on matters such as pricing and seating capacity. The latter was provided by the firm's architect, John Fairweather, responsible for the two largest cinemas in Scotland at the end of the silent era, the Playhouses in Glasgow and Edinburgh. Fairweather was clear that 'the seating capacity of the house must be sufficient to accomodate [sic] the Saturday night audience. The house may be half-empty during the week and we must look to the Saturday night audience to pay the dividend.'[211] Cinema size was thus determined by peak rather than average levels of attendance, an approach that allowed exhibitors fully to exploit the potential of their programmes. At Green's houses in Tollcross and Rutherglen, overall profitability depended crucially on the success of particular weeks during the year.[212] Similarly, at the Palace Cinema on Edinburgh's Princes Street, in 1926, almost half the hall's net profit for the year of £5,182 was made over thirteen weeks. Although the business returned a profit of £99 13s a week on average, this concealed marked variations in box-office performance. A loss of £74 on the Fox Film drama *The Gilded Butterfly*, with Alma Rubens, contrasted with a profit of £273 in early October on *The Sheik*, a reissue of the star vehicle for Rudolph Valentino, whose death had been announced two months before.[213] At several levels, then, exhibitors responded to a pattern of attendance capable of marked fluctuations over a short period.

The effectiveness of this approach was to be seen in a pronounced upturn in the trade's fortunes, assisted by a revival in the wider economy from the mid 1920s. Barely eighteen months after its manager had declared that business was not all it should be, the Regent Cinema in Glasgow reported record takings and a net profit in the year to 1927 of £1,517.[214] More generally, the final years of the silent era witnessed a reversion to consistent profitability. The balance sheet prepared by directors of the Dunfermline Cinema House, Ltd in March 1929 showed a surplus of £1,323 14s 6½d; it was the sixth consecutive year in which they had been able to report a profit.[215] Equally, the weekly returns at Edinburgh's Palace Cinema consistently showed a profit across the whole of 1928, the smallest margin being a surplus of £2 for the re-release of Cecil B. DeMille's 1923 production *The Ten Commandments*. In thirty-three of the fifty-two weeks that made up the year, income exceeded costs by more than £100.[216] Yet, for all the evidence of greater financial stability, broader market conditions in the late 1920s remained highly uncertain. First, there was the looming prospect of fundamental technological change with the advent of talking pictures, an innovation which the secretary of the Aberdeen Picture Palaces, Ltd believed would revolutionise the industry and, by imposing significant additional costs, would adversely affect the business.[217] In addition, from 1928, the trade operated within a context of protection, which while designed to boost the output of home-produced films, had rather different implications for the exhibition sector. The requirement to show a proportion of productions of British origin threatened to complicate previously comfortable booking arrangements with major American producers, which had enabled the Regent in Glasgow, for example, to subsist for long periods on Fox products.[218] Not only this, but patterns of ownership were altered by the encouragement which protection gave to higher levels of industrial concentration. In particular, the late 1920s witnessed the creation of vertically integrated concerns, with interests in the production, distribution, and exhibition of films: the Gaumont-British Picture Corporation and The Associated British Picture Corporation.[219] Both moved to add to their theatre holdings at the end of the 1920s, and Scotland's profitable picture houses inevitably attracted much interest. The impact of the major British circuits on the industry north of the border, while it would gather momentum over the following decade, was thus already evident as the silent era approached its end. By the late 1920s, Gaumont-British had acquired seven halls across Scotland, while the interests of Associated British Cinemas ran to twenty-two houses, most of which were purchased through John Maxwell's Scottish Cinema and Variety Theatres, Ltd, now an ABC subsidiary.[220]

V

As the period of silent film drew to its close, indications of cinema's development as a mature and discrete branch of the entertainment industry were abundant. It was visibly manifested in the opulence and ostentation of the large picture palaces which flourished in city and town centres across Scotland. Yet it also found expression in an increasingly distinctive mode of presentation, which saw cinema shed its associations with sites of live performance. Practices redolent of fairground and theatre were, over the course of two decades, marginalised and then discarded. So, the employment of elocutionists to 'speak to' pictures from behind the screen, offering bespoke dialogue for the film being shown, and which had been inaugurated by Dove Paterson around 1910, was dropped from houses in Aberdeen's more affluent west end towards the end of 1920. While unusual levels of prosperity may have encouraged the greater use of music as an accompaniment to images on the screen, there was also an increasing recognition that speech was increasingly outmoded. In the view of the city's correspondent for the *Scottish Kinema Record*, 'the audience that requires dialogue to a picture nowadays seems to me to be lacking in intelligence'.[221] It would be six years before cinema-goers to the east would be deemed sufficiently cognisant of the grammar of the silent film to do without the efforts of elocutionists.[222] Yet, for all the outward signs of assurance, the industry was obliged to respond to several challenges in the years from 1914. Some were politically inspired, centring on issues such as cinema's moral impact and the effects of expansion on the contemporary house-building programme. Although intense, most controversies of this kind proved transient and offered no sustained challenge to cinema's growth. Perhaps the most insistent difficulty facing the trade in the decade and a half from the outbreak of the First World War was economic in origin, a product of a serious escalation in operating costs, set alongside marked short-term fluctuations in demand. In part, this chapter has been concerned to trace these variations, establishing in the process that the consolidation of cinema in the everyday life of Scots was far from inevitable. Throughout, this was an industry that remained peculiarly susceptible to movements in the wider economy. Given the tendency to base the appeal of moving pictures on the lure of low prices, this is, at one level, unsurprising. Yet it also reflects a consequence of the increasing feminisation of the audience detected by many from the war years onwards. In contrast to the period before 1914, when demand for moving picture shows had proved remarkably resilient, the changes observed during and immediately after the war, as women filled a greater proportion of cinema seats, ensured that levels of attendance would move more in step with developments in the economy as a whole.[223]

In another respect, the link between cinema and the society within which it operated appeared to be undergoing a profound change by the end of the 1920s. An industry which had grown, for the most part, as a result of local interest, drawing on savings accumulated in and generating ownership structures that centred on Scotland, was now increasingly subject to wider forces originating from south of the border. The irruption of London capital into the exhibition sector in particular raised doubts as to Scotland's ability to control its own fortunes; its very integrity as a nation appeared, to some, to be called into question by increasing concentrations of ownership. In the years that followed, such concerns fused with another long-running controversy over cinema's place in Scottish life, that surrounding the operation of picture houses on Sundays.

NOTES

1. Low, *History of the British Film, 1918–1929*, pp. 87–96; C. Barr, 'Before Blackmail: Silent British Cinema', in Murphy, *British Cinema Book*, pp. 148–51; Bakker, 'Decline and Fall'; Bamford, *Distorted Images*.
2. Dickinson and Street, *Cinema and State*, ch. 1; *The Motion Picture News* (Dec. 1927), pp. 5, 21–6, in which the text of the then bill is printed in full, along with the opinion that it constituted 'one of the greatest pieces of legislation of recent years' and would prove 'good for producer, exhibitor and public'.
3. Hanson, *From Silent Screen to Multi-Screen*, p. 41.
4. D. Sharp, *The Picture Palace and Other Buildings for the Movies* (London, 1969), ch. 6.
5. B. Peter, *Scotland's Cinemas* (Ramsey, Isle of Man, 2011), pp. 65–7, 69; SSA, 5/8/13, George Green, Ltd, cutting from *KW*, 22 Sept. 1927.
6. Hiley, 'Let's Go to the Pictures', pp. 39–53.
7. The argument receives endorsement in Hanson, *From Silent Screen to Multi-Screen*, pp. 38–41.
8. National Council of Public Morals, *Cinema Commission*, statement of Mr F. R. Goodwin, p. 3.

9. Low, *History of the British Film, 1906–1914*, p. 25; Browning and Sorrell, 'Cinemas and Cinema-Going', p. 134.

10. National Council of Public Morals, *Cinema Commission*, statement of Goodwin, p. 3.

11. In the first decade of the century, concert seasons ran from September to March, *ET*, 22 March 1901, p. 8.

12. *Kinematograph Year Book* (London, 1921).

13. SSA, 5/26/112, Singleton Collection, Notebook, Weekly Accounts, Aug. 1913–Aug. 1914. The loss for the week 3–8 August 1914 was £1 1s 3d.

14. Parl. Papers 1915, XXVII (7939), Report of the Departmental Committee appointed to Inquire into the Conditions Prevailing in the Coal-Mining Industry due to the War. Part I – Report, p. 7.

15. *KH*, 19 May 1915, p. 7.

16. *Bioscope*, 8 Oct., p. 153; 5 Nov., p. 553; 3 Dec. 1914, p. 1017; 4 Feb. 1915, p. 433.

17. *Bioscope*, 6 May 1915, p. 562.

18. *Scottish Cinema*, 22 March 1920, p. 24.

19. NAS, BT2/8516/18, 20, The Dunfermline Cinema House, Ltd, Balance Sheets at 5 May 1915; 4 May 1916.

20. NAS, BT2/8423/22, 25, Kirkcaldy Kinema Palace, Ltd, Balance Sheets at 9 May 1915; 9 May 1916; *Bioscope*, 11 March 1915, p. 953.

21. *Bioscope*, 20 Aug., p. 762; 26 Nov. 1914, p. 905; 20 May 1915, p. 783; C. H. Lee, 'The Scottish Economy in the First World War', in C. M. M. Macdonald and E. W. McFarland (eds), *Scotland and the Great War* (East Linton, 1999), pp. 12–14.

22. S. Pollard, *The Development of the British Economy, Second Edition, 1914–1967* (London, 1969), pp. 67–9; P. Dewey, *War and Progress. Britain, 1914–1945* (Harlow, 1997), ch. 2.

23. *Bioscope*, 8 July 1915, p. 191.

24. *Bioscope*, 20 May, p. 783; 8 July 1915, pp. 189, 191.

25. *Scotsman*, 4 Aug. 1915, p. 11.

26. Lee, 'The Scottish Economy', pp. 17–19, for the position of Scottish fishing more generally; P. Thompson, T. Wailey, and T. Lummis, *Living the Fishing* (London, 1983), ch. 15; *Entertainer*, 12 June 1915, p. 4, which noted rumours

> to the effect that A BOMB was discovered in Harbour Street, and beg to inform the public that the only thing approaching the nature of a bomb discovered by them has been an
>
> Unprecedented Bo(o)m in their Business
>
> As is evidenced by the huge crowds that visit the NORTH STAR CINEMA Nightly. They regret if the terrific reports emanating from the building each evening should have caused nervous pedestrians any apprehension whatever; and would explain that these reports are consequent, in the highly charged state of the atmosphere, with
>
> Explosions of Laughter
>
> and Thunder of Applause
>
> a condition always prevailing on the showing of their inimitable Comedies and Dramas.

27. J. Burnett, *Liquid Pleasures: A Social History of Drinks in Modern Britain* (London, 1999), pp. 132–3; D. Ross, *The Roar of the Crowd: Following Scottish Football Down the Years* (Glendaruel, 2005), pp. 33–5.

28. *Bioscope*, 12 Aug., p. 725; 2 Sept. 1915, p. 1045.

29. *Bioscope*, 10 Sept., p. 962; 5 Nov., p. 551; 3 Dec. 1914, p. 1017; 18 Feb. 1915, p. 651.

30. *Bioscope*, 5 Nov. 1914, p. 551; 12 Aug. 1915, p. 841.

31. West Lothian History Library, Blackburn, Uphall Public Hall and Cinema, Cash Book, 1889–1922.

32. CM, The Queen's Rooms Cinema Syndicate, Ltd, Minute Book, Ordinary General Meeting, 31 Aug. 1914; Second Ordinary AGM, 16 Aug. 1915; Third Ordinary AGM, 13 Sept. 1916.

33. Ibid., Ordinary General Meeting, 31 Aug. 1914; Second Ordinary AGM, 16 Aug. 1915. Drawings fell from £1,541 18s 2d to £1,222 9s 1d.

34. NAS, BT2/7981/20–23, The Aberdeen Electric Theatre Co., Ltd, Balance Sheets at 30 Sept. 1913; 30 Sept. 1914; 30 Sept. 1915; 30 Sept. 1916.

35. SSA, 5/22/8, The Glasgow Picture House, Ltd, Balance Sheets and Profit and Loss Accounts, 28 May 1913; 29 May 1915.

36. *Bioscope*, 26 March 1914, p. 1420.

37. *Entertainer*, 11 Nov. 1916, p. 11.

38. *Bioscope*, 9 March 1916, p. 1083; NAS, SC36/79/18, Letter Book of Thomas Gilbert, 22 May 1917, Gilbert to London Fire Appliance Co., Gallowgate, Glasgow; 4 June 1917, Gilbert to Picture House, Tranent.

39. *Scotsman*, 26 July 1917, p. 7.

40. *Scotsman*, 12 Sept. 1916, p. 3.

41. *Scotsman*, 26 July 1917, p. 7.

42. *Bioscope*, 31 Aug. 1916, p. 817.

43. *Entertainer*, 25 May, p. 9; 28 Sept. 1918, p. 13; the problem extended to members of the orchestra also, 17 Aug. 1918, p. 9.

44. CM, Queen's Rooms Cinema Syndicate, Ltd, Minute Book, Meeting of Directors, 2 Dec. 1914.

45. SSA, 5/26/112, Singleton Collection, Notebook, Weekly Accounts, August 1913–August 1914, wages accounted for 37.2 per cent of total expenditure by the business over the year.

46. Griffiths, *Lancashire Working Classes*, ch. 3; Dewey, *War and Progress*, ch. 2; Pollard, *Development of the British Economy, Second Edition*, pp. 78–82.

47. *Bioscope*, 13 July 1916, p. 159; *Entertainer*, 8 July 1916, p. 5.

48. *Entertainer*, 17 Nov. 1917, p. 13; 16 March, p. 7; 23 March 1918, p. 11.

49. *Entertainer*, 2 March 1918, p. 12.

50. *Bioscope*, 5 Aug. 1915, p. 611.

51. *Bioscope*, 8 April 1915, p. 139.

52. *Scotsman*, 6 April 1918, p. 4; the progress of the Essanay controversy can be traced through *Scotsman*, 7 Oct., p. 6; 13 Oct., p. 8; 11 Dec., p. 7; 15 Dec. 1915, p. 5; 5 Feb. 1916, p. 9; *Bioscope*, 9 Sept., p. 1159; 23 Sept., p. 1403; 30 Sept.,

p. 1505; 2 Dec., p. 1071; 16 Dec., p. 1224; 30 Dec. 1915, p. 1492; 3 Feb., p. 499; 10 Feb. 1916, p. 635.

53. *Entertainer*, 16 Sept. 1916, p. 9.
54. CM, Aberdeen Picture Palaces, Ltd, Minute Book, Meeting of Directors, 16 Nov. 1916.
55. CM, Queen's Street Cinema Syndicate, Ltd, Minute Book, Meeting of Directors, 15 Nov. 1916.
56. See the profile in *Scottish Cinema*, 26 Jan. 1920, p. 10; SSA, 5/12/6, A. B. King Collection, Scrapbook, Notice of Opening of Lorne Cinema, 25 Jan. 1915; cutting from *Glasgow Observer*, 19 June 1915.
57. *Scotsman*, 22 Sept. 1915, pp. 8–9.
58. *Scotsman*, 7 April 1916, p. 3.
59. *Bioscope*, 13 April 1916, p. 137.
60. Ibid., p. 218; see also *Scotsman*, 6 April 1916, p. 6, for the reaction of the Edinburgh and East of Scotland branch of the CEA.
61. *Scotsman*, 11 April 1916, p. 7; *Bioscope*, 13 April 1916, p. 209, where the 1d ticket was referred to as the backbone of the business.
62. *Entertainer*, 8 April 1916, p. 7.
63. *Bioscope*, 25 May, p. 917; 1 June 1916, p. 1033.
64. *Entertainer*, 25 March 1916, p. 12; 12 May 1917, p. 8.
65. NAS, BT2/8515/14, The Portobello Picture Palace, Ltd, Notice of Liquidation, 4 April 1916.
66. CM, Queen's Rooms Cinema Syndicate, Ltd, Minutes, Meeting of Directors, 23 Oct. 1916.
67. NAS, BT2/7981/24, The Aberdeen Electric Theatre Co., Ltd, Balance Sheet at 30 Sept. 1917; BT2/8516/21, The Dunfermline Cinema House, Ltd, Balance Sheet at 4 May 1917; BT2/7670/37, The BB Pictures, Ltd, Balance Sheet at 29 Sept. 1917; BT2/8454/23, The Hillhead Picture House, Ltd, Balance Sheet at 2 March 1917.
68. CM, The Aberdeen Picture Palaces, Ltd, Minutes, Meetings of Directors, 14 Dec. 1916; 4 April 1917.
69. Ibid., Meetings of Directors, 12 July; 9 Aug.; 19 Sept.; 13 Oct. 1916; 14 Feb. 1917.
70. Ibid., Meeting of Directors, 4 April 1917.
71. See Chapter 2, p. 78.
72. *Entertainer*, 5 May, p. 9; 12 May 1917, p. 8, in which the rather cynical observation was offered 'by the time September comes along the public will have forgotten that the scale has been raised at all'; prices were revised from 1 October, 29 Sept. 1917, p. 6.
73. CM, The Aberdeen Picture Palaces, Ltd, Minutes, Meetings of Directors, 11 July; 16 Aug.; 19 Sept.; 17 Oct.; 21 Nov.; 12 Dec. 1917; 9 Jan.; 13 Feb.; 13 March 1918.
74. NAS, BT2/7567/29, The Scottish Electric Picture Palaces, Ltd, Balance Sheet at 30 June 1918; SSA, 5/22/8, Glasgow Picture House, Ltd, Balance Sheets and Profit and Loss Accounts, 1 June 1918, in which receipts of £14,251 15s 7d compared with £10,983 18s 9d for 1916–17.

75. *Entertainer*, 23 Feb. 1918, p. 13.
76. *Entertainer*, 3 Aug., p. 5, prices in Edinburgh rose by between ½d and 1d; 13 July 1918, p. 8; 26 April 1919, p. 10.
77. *Entertainer*, 27 Oct. 1917, p. 7.
78. Pollard, *Development of the British Economy, Second Edition*, pp. 46–7.
79. S. Broadberry, 'The Emergence of Mass Unemployment: Explaining Macroeconomic Trends in Britain during the Trans-World War I Period', *Economic History Review*, 2nd ser., XLIII (1990), pp. 271–82.
80. *Kinematograph Year Book* (London, 1921), pp. 17–38.
81. NAS, BT2/10864/4, Dennistoun Picture Houses, Ltd, Memorandum of Association; 9, Prospectus, 30 Dec. 1919.
82. *Entertainer*, 19 July, p. 3; 4 Oct. 1919, p. 7.
83. *SKR*, 18 Dec. 1920, p. 11.
84. *Entertainer*, 5 July 1919, p. 7.
85. *Scottish Cinema*, 6 Oct., p. 6; 24 Nov. 1919, p. 3.
86. *Entertainer and SKR*, 13 Dec. 1919, p. 12; *Scottish Cinema*, 22 Dec. 1919, p. 31; 31 May 1920, p. 28.
87. *Entertainer and SKR*, 19 April 1919, p. 11; SSA, 5/7/386, Miscellaneous Film Material, cutting from *KW*, 2 Sept. 1920.
88. *SKR*, 30 Oct. 1920, p. 13.
89. NAS, BT2/7567/31, The Scottish Electric Picture Palace, Ltd, Balance Sheet at 30 June 1919; BT2/7670/39, The BB Pictures, Ltd, Balance Sheet at 27 Sept. 1919.
90. NAS, BT2/8516/23–5, The Dunfermline Cinema House, Ltd, Balance Sheets at 21 March 1919; 21 March 1920; 21 March 1921; BT2/7981/27, The Aberdeen Electric Theatre Co., Ltd, Balance Sheet at 30 Sept. 1919.
91. *Entertainer and SKR*, 17 April 1920, p. 14.
92. *Entertainer and SKR*, 23 Nov. 1919, p. 7.
93. *Scottish Cinema*, 22 March 1920, p. 24; SSA, 5/11/17, Cinematograph Exhibitors' Association, Edinburgh and East of Scotland Branch Minutes, Meeting at Princes Cinema, 16 Dec. 1919; *Entertainer and SKR*, 6 March 1920, p. 15.
94. CM, James F. Donald (Cinemas), Ltd, Grand Central Picture House, letter to W. M. Duff, Inspector of Taxes, Aberdeen, 13 May 1921.
95. *Entertainer and SKR*, 22 Nov. 1919, p. 7; 7 Feb. 1920, p. 9; *Scottish Cinema*, 9 Feb. 1920, p. 8.
96. *Entertainer and SKR*, 6 March 1920, p. 15.
97. *Scottish Cinema*, 15 Dec. 1919, pp. 9–10.
98. *SKR*, 27 Nov., p. 8; 18 Dec. 1920, p. 8.
99. *Entertainer and SKR*, 3 May, p. 9; 6 Sept. 1919, p. 10.
100. *Scottish Cinema*, 21 July 1920, p. 19.
101. *SKR*, 7 Aug., p. 2; 21 Aug., p. 7; 4 Sept. 1920, p. 9.
102. At the Queen's Rooms Cinema Syndicate, Ltd's Stonehaven house, it was the frequent practice of the resident pianist to seek alternative employment on weekday evenings, providing an alternative accompanist in his place, CM, The

Queen's Rooms Cinema Syndicate, Ltd, Minutes, Meeting of Directors, 3 Sept. 1913.

103. *Entertainer and SKR*, 17 May, p. 11; the increase in Dundee was opposed by some exhibitors as business threatened to turn down during the early summer, 31 May, p. 11; 2 Aug. 1919, p. 7.

104. *Entertainer and SKR*, 8 Nov., p. 11; 20 Dec., p. 11; 27 Dec. 1919, p. 8.

105. *Entertainer and SKR*, 20 March 1920, p. 1.

106. *Scottish Cinema*, 22 March 1920, p. 8.

107. *SKR*, 23 Oct. 1920, p. 13; SSA, 5/11/17, CEA, Edinburgh and East of Scotland Branch, Minutes, Meeting at Princes Cinema, 23 Nov. 1920.

108. *Entertainer and SKR*, 6 Sept. 1919, p. 12; *SKR*, 11 Sept. 1920, p. 16; SSA, 5/11/17, Meeting at Princes Cinema, 23 Sept. 1919.

109. *Scottish Cinema*, 22 Sept. 1919, p. 24; NAS, GD283/6/301, Valuation Appeal of Palace Cinema, 1919, Precognition of Forrest Hay Lightbody, FFS, FSI.

110. *SKR*, 2 Oct. 1920, pp. 10–11.

111. *Kinematograph Year Book* (London, 1915); for the involvement of Keir Hardie in BB Pictures, Ltd, see Chapter 1, p. 39.

112. *Scotsman*, 10 Jan. 1916, p. 5; 21 April 1917, p. 10; *Kinematograph Year Book* (London, 1921), p. 507.

113. *Scottish Cinema*, 22 Sept., p. 26; 3 Nov. 1919, p. 12.

114. *Scottish Cinema*, 5 Jan. 1920, p. 27; *Entertainer and SKR*, 3 Jan. 1920, p. 5.

115. *Entertainer and SKR*, 31 Jan., p. 12; 10 April 1920, p. 11; *Scottish Cinema*, 1 March, p. 29; 15 March 1920, p. 35.

116. *Scottish Cinema*, 26 Jan., p. 28; 8 March 1920, p. 29.

117. *Scottish Cinema*, 8 March, p. 15; 28 June 1920, p. 28.

118. *Scottish Cinema*, 22 March, p. 9; 29 March, p. 30; 12 April, p. 11; 26 April 1920, p. 9; *Entertainer and SKR*, 20 March, p. 10; 24 April 1920, p. 1.

119. *SKR*, 22 May, p. 13; 12 June, pp. 6–7; 10 July, p. 8; 17 July 1920, p. 12; *Scottish Cinema*, 24 May, p. 13; 14 June, p. 14; 19 July 1920, p. 20.

120. *Bioscope*, 12 Sept. 1912, p. 773; 11 Dec. 1913, p. 1097.

121. See Chapter 1, p. 35.

122. *KG*, 17 April 1914, p. 6.

123. J. Davis, 'Central Government and the Towns', and Yelling, 'Land, Property and Planning', pp. 261–86, 467–93; Offer, *Property and Politics*, ch. 18.

124. *KH*, 16 May 1923, p. 8, letter from 'No More Muddles'; *Bioscope*, 11 Dec. 1913, p. 1097.

125. *KG*, 17 April 1914, p. 6.

126. *KG*, 15 May 1914, p. 6.

127. *Bioscope*, 24 June 1915, p. 1307; *KH*, 30 June 1915, p. 8.

128. *Entertainer*, 14 July 1917, p. 13; *Bioscope*, 19 July 1917, p. 313.

129. *Entertainer*, 17 Aug. 1918, p. 5; 22 March, p. 6; 17 May, p. 5; 27 Dec. 1919, p. 8.

130. *Scottish Cinema*, 27 Oct. 1919, p. 12.

131. *Scottish Cinema*, 1 Dec. 1919, p. 38; 19 April 1920, p. 30; *Entertainer and SKR*, 4 Oct. 1919, p. 1; 17 Jan. 1920, p. 1; *SKR*, 22 May 1920, p. 17.

132. *Scottish Cinema*, 15 Dec. 1919, p. 4.

133. *KH*, 7 Feb., p. 8; 7 March 1917, p. 8.

134. *Scottish Cinema*, 12 April 1920, p. 28; *Entertainer and SKR*, 24 April 1920, p. 5; *SKR*, 16 Oct., p. 13; 13 Nov. 1920, p. 14.

135. *SKR*, 21 Aug., p. 14; 18 Dec. 1920, p. 1; 29 Jan. 1921, p. 12; 1 April 1922, p. 1.

136. *SKR*, 22 May 1920, p. 14.

137. *SKR*, 15 Jan., p. 1; 19 March, p. 17; 2 April, p. 8; 16 July 1921, p. 1.

138. *SKR*, 24 Dec. 1921, p. 1.

139. *SKR*, 24 June 1922, p. 1.

140. *KH*, 23 May 1923, p. 5; NAS, BT2/12826/2, Montrose Burgh Cinema Co., Ltd, Memorandum of Association, 30 Aug. 1923.

141. North Lanarkshire Archives, U129/1/1, Gartcosh Public Hall, Minutes, 25 July 1921; 22 June 1923; 22 Aug. 1924.

142. On the blocking of plans for new cinemas in Lochee, Dundee, and Lockerbie, see *Scottish Cinema*, 3 Nov. 1919, p. 12; *SKR*, 24 July 1920, p. 1.

143. For details of the companies covered in the sample, see Appendix 2.

144. NAS, BT2/9429/8, The Palace Kinema (Dunfermline), Ltd, Return of Share Allotments, 13 July–11 Aug. 1915; BT2/11663/27, The St Andrew Square Picture House, Ltd, Return of Share Allotments, 3 May 1921.

145. NAS, BT2/11407/13, 20, The Playhouse, Galashiels (1920), Ltd, Returns of Share Allotments, 9 Sept.–1 Oct. 1920; 4 Nov. 1921.

146. NAS, BT2/9429/8, Return of Share Allotments, 13 July–11 Aug. 1915; BT2/11407/13, Return of Share Allotments, 9 Sept.–1 Oct. 1920; BT2/11121/12, Kilmarnock Picture House, Ltd, Return of Share Allotments, 11 June 1920; BT2/11228/11, The Stockbridge Picture House, Ltd, Return of Share Allotments, 12 Jan. 1921.

147. NAS, BT2/11228/9, Return of Share Allotments, 19 May 1920; BT2/9429/8, Return of Share Allotments, 13 July–11 Aug. 1915.

148. NAS, BT2/10134/8, The Wellington Picture Palace, Ltd, Return of Share Allotments, 8 Nov.–4 Dec. 1918.

149. *Entertainer and SKR*, 4 Jan. 1919, p. 10.

150. *Scottish Cinema*, 22 March 1920, p. 24.

151. NAS, BT2/10864/14, Dennistoun Picture Houses, Ltd, Return of Share Allotments, 1 Dec.–31 Dec. 1920; BT2/11290/11, 12, Waverley Picture House (1920), Ltd, Returns of Share Allotments, 22 June 1920; BT2/11663/27, 31, 33, 36, 39, 40, 41, 42, St Andrew Square Picture House, Ltd, Returns of Share Allotments, 3 May; 3 May–20 Sept. 1921; 1 Oct., 1921–31 Dec. 1922; 1 Jan.–14 March 1923; 23 Feb.–23 April 1923; 30 May–22 June 1923; 24 Sept.; 24 Dec. 1923.

152. G. Braybon, *Women Workers in the First World War* (London, 1989), chs 7 and 8.

153. NAS, BT2/11407/13, 14, 20, The Playhouse, Galashiels (1920), Ltd, Returns of Share Allotments, 9 Sept.–1 Oct.; 5 Nov.–10 Dec. 1920; 4 Nov. 1921.

154. NAS, BT2/9718/8, The Cinema (Dumfries), Ltd, Return of Share Allotments, 21 Dec. 1916; BT2/10845/8, The Britannia Cinema (Dundee), Ltd, Return of Share Allotments, 5 Jan. 1920; BT2/11875/7, Olympia Pictures (Dunfermline), Ltd, Return of Share Allotments, 18 Oct.–31 Oct. 1921; BT2/11228/9, 11, 12, 13, 14, Stockbridge Picture House, Ltd, Return of Share Allotments, 19 May

1920; 12 June; 23 March–20 April; 27 April; 11 Aug. 1921; BT2/11663/27, 31, 33, 36, 38, 39, 40, 41, 42, St Andrew Square Picture House, Ltd, 3 May; 3 May–30 Sept.; 1 Oct. 1921–31 Dec. 1922; 1 Jan.–14 March; 15 March; 23 Feb.–23 April; 30 May–22 June; 24 Sept.; 14 Dec. 1923.

155. *Kinematograph Year Book* (London, 1921).

156. NAS, BT2/9707/13, Scottish Cinemas and Variety Theatres, Ltd, Particulars re Directors, 6 Sept. 1917.

157. *SKR*, 6 Nov. 1920, pp. 12–13.

158. D. H. Aldcroft, *The British Economy between the Wars* (Oxford, 1983), p. 13; B. Eichengreen, 'The British Economy between the Wars', in Floud and Johnson, *Cambridge Economic History of Modern Britain. Volume II*, pp. 323–4.

159. *SKR*, 1 Jan. 1921, p. 9; C. L. Mowat, *Britain between the Wars, 1918–1940* (London, 1968), pp. 120–3; B. Supple, *The History of the British Coal Industry, Volume 4: 1913–1946: The Political Economy of Decline* (Oxford, 1987), pp. 158–61; A. Charlesworth, D. Gilbert, A. Randall, H. Southall, and C. Wrigley, *An Atlas of Industrial Protest in Britain, 1750–1990* (Basingstoke and London, 1996), pp. 126–36.

160. NAS, BT2/7563/36, Scottish Electric Picture Palaces, Ltd, Minutes of Twelfth Ordinary General Meeting, 1 Dec. 1922.

161. NAS, BT2/7563/33, Minutes of Eleventh Ordinary General Meeting, 7 Oct. 1921.

162. NAS, BT2/7366/36, 38, West of Scotland Electric Theatres, Ltd, Balance Sheets at 31 Dec. 1920; 31 Dec. 1921.

163. NAS, BT2/8516/26, 27, Dunfermline Cinema House, Ltd, Balance Sheets at 21 March 1922; 21 March 1923.

164. NAS, BT2/9204/31–4, The North of Scotland Cinematograph, Ltd, Balance Sheets at 28 Nov. 1921; 28 Nov. 1922; 28 Nov. 1923; 28 Nov. 1924.

165. *Kinematograph Year Book* (London, 1923), p. 3.

166. *SKR*, 14 May, p. 9; 28 May 1921, p. 10.

167. *SKR*, 11 Feb. 1922, p. 5; NAS, BT2/7366/39, West of Scotland Electric Theatres, Ltd, Extraordinary General Meeting, 20 June 1922.

168. See Chapter 2, p. 79; *Bioscope*, 10 Jan., p. 47; 31 Jan. 1924, p. 61.

169. See above, p. 116.

170. *SKR*, 10 Dec., p. 5; 17 Dec. 1921, p. 1.

171. *SKR*, 15 April, p. 1; 25 Nov. 1922, p. 7.

172. See for example the leader in *SKR*, 30 Sept. 1922, p. 1.

173. *Bioscope*, 11 June 1924, p. 36; *Kinematograph Year Book* (London, 1923), p. 4; ibid. (1925), p. 21.

174. *SKR*, 20 May, p. 3; 27 May 1922, p. 3; SSA, 5/11/17, CEA, Edinburgh and East of Scotland Branch, Minutes, Meeting at Princes Cinema, 14 March 1922.

175. CM, Queen's Rooms Cinema Syndicate, Ltd, Minutes, Meetings of Directors, 22 March; 10 May 1923.

176. Altman, *Silent Film Sound*, chs 6 and 10; T. Griffiths, 'Sounding Scottish: Sound Practices and Silent Cinema in Scotland', in J. Brown and A. C. Davison (eds), *The Sounds of the Silents in Britain* (Oxford, forthcoming).

177. SKR, 23 Dec. 1922, p. 12; an earlier, private show had been distinguished by the pipe band of the Royal Scots Fusiliers from Maryhill Barracks and the Mossbank Boys' Pipe Band marching to the theatre, prior to the performance, 21 Oct. 1922, p. 8.
178. CM, Queen's Rooms Cinema Syndicate, Ltd, Minutes, Meetings of Directors, 25 July; 29 Aug. 1923.
179. CM, James F. Donald (Cinemas), Ltd, Cinema House, Employers' Schedule E Return, 1927–8.
180. See above, pp. 107–8.
181. CM, Queen's Rooms Cinema Syndicate, Ltd, Minutes, Meeting of Directors, 30 Jan. 1924.
182. SSA, 5/22/4, Glasgow Picture House Co., Ltd, Minutes, Meetings of Directors, 12 April; 3 Sept. 1926.
183. CM, Aberdeen Picture Palaces, Ltd, Accounts, Profit and Loss Account, 7 Feb. 1925.
184. SKR, 30 Sept. 1922, p. 1.
185. NAS, SC36/79/18, Letter Book of Tom Gilbert, 16 April 1920, Gilbert to M. Dunlop, Lyric Theatre, Edinburgh; Gilbert to F. B. Greer, Electric Theatre, Moffat; 16 Jan. 1920, Confirmation of Chaplin Bookings.
186. SKR, 30 Sept. 1922, p. 1.
187. CM, Queen's Rooms Cinema Syndicate, Ltd, Minutes, Meetings of Directors, 6 Nov.; 15 Nov.; 22 Nov. 1916.
188. Ibid., Meetings of Directors, 8 March; 13 June; 22 Aug. 1924.
189. SSA, 5/22/4, Glasgow Picture House, Ltd, Minutes, 9 Feb.; 7 July 1925.
190. *Bioscope*, 17 July 1924, p. 51.
191. *Kinematograph Year Book* (London, 1928).
192. SSA, 5/22/4, Glasgow Picture House, Ltd, Minutes, Meeting of Directors, 23 May 1929.
193. *Kinematograph Year Book* (London, 1923), p. 4; SKR, 30 Sept. 1922, p. 1, which advanced the motto 'Early to bed, early to rise/Don't matter a damn, if you don't advertise'.
194. SKR, 19 Nov. 1921, p. 1.
195. *Rutherglen Reformer*, 19 March 1926, p. 3, noting an appearance by 'Charlie Chaplin's Navvy Jazz Band'; *Bioscope*, 29 May 1924, p. 45.
196. SSA, 5/7/345, Palmers of Lesmahagow, Notes on Palmer's Picture House.
197. *Entertainer and SKR*, 17 May, p. 10; 15 Nov. 1919, p. 12.
198. SKR, 11 June 1921, p. 10.
199. SSA, 5/22/4, Glasgow Picture House, Ltd, Minutes, Meeting of Directors, 24 Dec. 1925.
200. SKR, 20 Nov. 1920, p. 13.
201. SKR, 22 Oct. 1921, p. 1.
202. SKR, 10 Dec., p. 1; 17 Dec. 1921, p. 1.
203. SSA, 5/7/345, Palmers of Lesmahagow, Notes on Palmer's Picture House.
204. SKR, 10 Dec. 1921, p. 1.
205. *Entertainer and SKR*, 26 July 1919, p. 8.

206. Hanson, *From Silent Screen to Multi-Screen*, pp. 41–2; Sharp, *The Picture Palace*, ch. 6.

207. SSA, 5/22/4, Glasgow Picture House Co., Ltd, Minutes, Annual General Meeting, 15 Nov. 1927.

208. *Bioscope*, 16 Oct. 1924, p. 56.

209. SSA, 5/8/68, George Green and Co., graphs of financial performance of houses.

210. SSA, 5/22/4, Glasgow Picture House Co., Ltd, Minutes, Informal Meeting of Shareholders, 24 April 1924.

211. Dumfries and Galloway Archives, Lockerbie, 1/6/8, Lockerbie Cinema Co., Ltd, Directors' Minutes, Meeting of Promoters and Prospective Shareholders, 16 April 1932.

212. SSA, 5/8/68, George Green and Co., graphs.

213. NAS, GD289/1/3, Palace Cinema, Profit and Loss Ledger, 1925–55.

214. SSA, 5/22/9, Glasgow Picture House Co., Ltd, Balance Sheet and Profit and Loss Accounts.

215. NAS, BT2/8516/33, The Dunfermline Cinema House, Ltd, Balance Sheet at 21 March 1929.

216. NAS, GD289/1/3, Palace Cinema, Profit and Loss Ledger, 1925–55.

217. CM, Aberdeen Picture Palaces, Ltd, Minutes, Meeting of Directors, 18 June 1929.

218. See above, p. 105.

219. T. Ryall, 'A British Studio System: The Associated British Picture Corporation and the Gaumont-British Picture Corporation in the 1930s', in Murphy, *British Cinema Book*, pp. 202–10; Low, *History of the British Film, 1918–1929*, pp. 39–46.

220. *Kinematograph Year Book* (London, 1928).

221. *SKR*, 27 Nov. 1920, p. 16.

222. Griffiths, 'Sounding Scottish'.

223. This point is developed in Chapter 5, pp. 188–93.

4

A Seven-day Wonder? Cinema and the Scottish Sabbath

I

The staging of cinema entertainment on Sundays proved a recurrent source of controversy for the exhibition sector across Britain over the first half of the twentieth century. If, by 1950, many areas in England had come to accept picture-going as a legitimate activity on the Sabbath, progress towards that end had proved, even here, to be protracted and uncertain.[1] At various points in the period, the law had intervened, first to restrict Sunday opening and then to facilitate the same, albeit under strict conditions. From 1932, Sabbath performances south of the border were declared legal, provided that local opinion could be shown to endorse their adoption, either through previous practice or by means of more direct expressions of support via the votes of local ratepayers. The acceptance and gradual consolidation of Sunday opening is often dated from this measure.[2] The story that centres on the Sunday Entertainments Act of 1932 offers a straightforward, uncontroversial narrative. Yet it also contains at least one glaring omission: the position in Scotland. North of the border, the Sabbath had acquired a wider significance, as it was seen to mark out Scotland's existence as a distinct and separate polity. Its strict observance, forbidding acts not associated with the worship of God, was deemed by some a 'precious national heritage' and had come to exemplify 'all our best Scottish traditions and convictions'.[3] Others, while acknowledging the wider hold of Sabbath observance on the nation as a whole, were less inclined to celebrate its influence. Writing in 1941, one resident of Broughty Ferry was drawn to ask the Home Secretary, Herbert Morrison, 'Don't you think we need something very badly to make Sunday a liveable happy day of the week?',[4] while another correspondent assured the Secretary of State for Scotland John Colville, in 1939, 'If ever I was forced to spend a "Month of Sundays" it certainly would'nt [sic] be spent in Scotland.'[5] For these and others of the same mind, the Act of 1932 offered no relief, as its coverage was limited to England and Wales. The pattern of Sabbath observance across Scotland remained distinct and, for the most part, untouched by legislative interference. While it was subject to change over the five decades covered here, that arose more from wider social and economic developments than from any alteration in the law.

This chapter is thus concerned to trace and account for the pace and pattern of any changes to Sunday practices observed in the period to 1950. In doing so, it addresses themes that extend considerably beyond the world of popular entertainment. The changing nature of Sabbath observance has often been linked to a long-run process of secularisation across society as a whole. Historians of popular religion have noted how attachment to the Church and its ideals appeared to be weakened by the growing availability of alternative, secular pursuits, so that leisure was often at the forefront of conflicts centred on the manner in which time was used on the Lord's Day.[6] By these accounts, the cinema would not be seen of itself as an agent of secularisation. Rather it formed part of a broader change in cultural expectations, whereby the patterns of behaviour that came to define everyday life were transformed.[7] If this captures developments over the long term, it leaves unclear the precise chronology of change, the point at and degree to which attitudes to the Seventh Day altered. The latter point is of particular importance, given recent attempts to revise the history of secularisation in Britain, whereby the position of organised religion remained central to official and popular culture until undermined by an interlocking sequence of social change in the 1960s.[8] If that decade lies beyond the scope of the current inquiry, the findings offered here may have relevance for evaluating the accuracy or otherwise of a depiction of change that was sudden in its nature and irreversible in its impact.

In charting developments across the earlier decades of the century in some detail, the impact of other sources of change may be addressed. Within the cinema industry itself, technological and commercial developments rendered Scottish owners and managers increasingly subject to decisions taken elsewhere, more especially Wardour Street in London, the centre of British film production, and Hollywood. At the same time, the experience of war exposed large numbers of Scots to cultures in which attitudes to the Sabbath were more relaxed, while obliging many service personnel stationed in Scotland to acquire, willingly or otherwise, a close acquaintance with Scottish observance of the Seventh Day.[9] Over time, the impact of such experiences seemed clear: they worked to challenge the idea of a Scotland rooted in the precepts of Presbyterian religion. Fears for the integrity of a nation's culture and identity were not confined to Scotland: as Peter Miskell has noted, Welsh opposition to any relaxation of Sabbatarian disciplines was informed by the belief that they embodied the Nonconformist conscience which, for some, defined ideas of Welshness.[10] In Scotland, where adherence to the Sabbath was just as if not more central to the national sense of self, the cinema was seen to pose a fundamental challenge to notions of what it was to be Scottish, through its international, often overtly secular character, and its reliance on a technology that made no allowance for local variation. In many ways, then, the cinema was crucial to Scotland's experience of and engagement with the wider economic, technological, and cultural transformations of the twentieth century. In the early decades of that century, those forces would coalesce around the controversy surrounding Sunday opening.

II

A variety of forces came together to shape the Scottish Sunday as it was early in the twentieth century. The law had sought through a series of enactments between the late sixteenth and early eighteenth centuries to secure due observance of the Seventh Day, and while the last successful prosecution under these statutes dated back to 1807, judgments late in the nineteenth century had determined their continued relevance in curtailing activities such as the opening of shops.[11] For places of entertainment, by contrast, the key measures governing operating conditions were more local in scope. Under the Burgh Police (Scotland) Act of 1892, by which magistrates gained the power to license all public shows, authorities also acquired the ability to specify hours of opening. The regulation of Sunday performances was strengthened by the later Act of 1903, which enabled authorities to introduce by-laws specifying the days of the week on which business could be conducted.[12] In larger burghs, these regulations were enforced by means of specific local Police Acts. Much depended on the ability and readiness of the local authority to take on the powers allotted them. Take-up was, it might be noted, highly uneven. So, in February 1937, the manager of the Victoria Cinema, Inverurie, challenged the right of the local magistrates to refuse him a licence to hold a series of shows on the Sabbath for charity, on the grounds that no local by-laws on Sunday entertainment had been introduced. The burgh's inspector of police confirmed the claim, noting that there was no provision in local legislation against Sunday shows, the burgh authority having failed to adopt the relevant section of the Burgh Police Act of 1903.[13] By the end of that decade, by-laws regulating places of entertainment had been introduced by some twenty-eight burgh councils across Scotland. Of these, twenty-three placed explicit restrictions on Sunday opening, although in most cases councillors retained the right to grant exceptions to the rules on closure.[14] As this suggests, the Scottish Sabbath and cinema's place in it rested not on the law alone, but on a variety of forces, from the opinions of local civic and council leaders, to the commercial calculations of figures within the industry itself as to the perceived costs and benefits of a further day's business. The interplay of these forces and their changes over time ensured that appropriate use of the Sabbath would remain an ongoing controversy for much of the period.

From the late nineteenth century, the view gained ground that strict Sabbatarianism had served to create a vacuum that could only be filled by activities inimical to the moral and physical welfare of individuals and the wider society. The drive to provide alternative, more improving pursuits on Sundays had encountered determined opposition, sufficient to block proposals to open places of rational amusement, such as Edinburgh's Botanical Gardens in 1863.[15] By 1889, however, the cause of reform had prevailed and in later years was taken further by agencies such as the Edinburgh Sunday Society, established in 1898, which sought to provide 'for the people on Sundays sacred and classical music, lectures on interesting subjects in science, literature, history, and art, and generally to promote the rational observance of the Sunday'.[16] The campaign for what the Glasgow *Evening Times* dubbed a 'Saner Sunday' enjoyed fitful success, so that in the same year that local museums in Edinburgh were allowed to open briefly on Sunday afternoons, the Sunday Society was refused permission to hold a sacred concert on Waverley Market.[17] Yet this serves to indicate that even in what many regarded as 'the metropolis of Sabbatarianism', the nature of Sundays was not fixed and immutable.[18] The cinema thus emerged into a society in which, while the notion of Sunday as a day apart was broadly accepted, the precise nature of the 'Day of Rest' continued to be keenly debated.

While Scots had access to moving pictures on Sundays from the earliest days of cinema, the shows themselves and the context within which they were mounted served to point up the particular character of the day. In Glasgow, films were incorporated into an established series of sacred concerts run from the Waterloo Rooms, appropriately enough a hall converted from earlier use as a church. Here, alongside live music, moving images were supplied by a variety of means, from Hubner's Animatograph, to Chalmers' Cinematograph, and Bendon's Bioscope. While each show included a subject with clear religious associations, such as scenes from the Oberammergau Passion Play, and adaptations of key evangelical texts, such as *Uncle Tom's Cabin*, these were often juxtaposed with footage of immediate topical interest, including in 1900 images from the war in South Africa, scenic treatments, including a trip *Down the Clyde*, or items geared explicitly to entertain, including *The American Train Robbery* and *Saved by the Wireless Telegraphy*.[19] A comparable variety was evident in a second series of sacred concerts inaugurated at the Town Hall, King's Park in Glasgow in the autumn of 1902.[20] Further east, film formed a staple of the 'rational' programme of amusements offered by the Edinburgh Sunday Society at venues including the Operetta House and the New Gaiety Theatre in Leith.[21] Alongside such fixtures in the seasonal calendar, occasional concerts were also mounted for specified charitable purposes and with the backing of the local magistracy. In February 1905, the Wellington Palace in the Gorbals opened on a Sunday evening for an entertainment intended to raise money for the Jewish Board of Guardians and Philanthropic Association, while in October 1910, the Gaiety in Aberdeen was the setting for a concert in aid of the local Life-Boat Fund.[22] In each case, as indeed in all Sunday entertainments at this date sanctioned by local justices, funds were raised by means of collections from the audience, as regulations generally prohibited the levying of a charge for entry.

If the commercial possibilities offered by such shows were negligible, several early picture-house proprietors sought to explore the potential they offered for boosting the respectability of the trade. The Sunday Night Meetings launched by J. J. Bennell at the Wellington Palace from 1908 may be seen as part of his drive to promote rational and temperate recreations among the poor of Glasgow.[23] Similarly, in the economic downturn of 1908–9, Sunday concerts were proposed to raise funds for the relief of the unemployed, investing the cinema business with a wider civic function. So, in September 1908, applications to hold such concerts were placed before Glasgow's magistrates by, among others, E. H. Bostock of the Scottish Zoo and Hippodrome, Ralph Pringle at his Picture Palace, and A. E. Pickard, proprietor of the Panopticon Music Hall.[24] The following November, Norman Macleod Allan approached the city magistrates for permission to open his premises in Argyll Street, which included coin-operated stereoscopes and phonographs, on Sundays. It was emphasised that only sacred music would be available to play. After initial doubts, the magistrates agreed, conditional on all changes to the music being submitted to the town clerk for approval.[25] Across the first decade of the century, therefore, Sunday opening was becoming an increasingly accepted feature of the entertainment culture of urban Scotland, albeit in closely regulated circumstances which sought to underscore the differences between such shows and the standard weekly fare, thereby reiterating the particular nature of the Sabbath.

The idea that the Scottish Sunday was sufficiently flexible to accommodate a range of practices was called into question, however, in the years immediately before the outbreak of the First World War, as a more determined Sabbatarian outlook, hostile to the discretion allowed cinematic entertainments on the Seventh Day, emerged. Key to this change was the Cinematograph Act of 1909. Although ostensibly a measure concerned to secure the safety of audiences in licensed premises, its provisions allowed local authorities to add conditions to the basic licence under which shows were mounted.[26] In Glasgow, a clause was inserted stipulating that 'the premises shall not be opened under the licence on Sundays'.[27] Where such additions were not made, the ability to regulate times of opening continued to derive from local Police Acts. Such was the conclusion of the courts following the prosecution of John Stewart for seeking to operate a Bioscope show in Edinburgh on Sundays early in 1910.[28] Whether based on the 1909 Act or earlier statutes, the decision whether or not to allow Sunday exhibitions rested largely with local magistrates. In September 1910, the bench in Glasgow received a deputation from the local Christian Endeavour Union, which raised concerns over the staging of sacred concerts across the city. In response, a subcommittee was appointed to look into the conditions governing such shows. This reaffirmed existing policy, which allowed concerts provided their content was deemed appropriate and that, where the intention was to raise funds, this should be for charitable or benevolent causes.[29]

Doubts had been raised the previous year as to the nature of the Sunday Night Meetings at the Wellington Palace. For the magistrates, a standard cinema programme, similar to those put on during the week, preceded by the singing of a hymn or two, did not constitute what they considered a 'sacred' occasion.[30]

Sabbatarian sentiment hardened further in the months that followed the Glasgow enquiry, a tendency driven in part by developments south of the border. Here, the view of the courts, in line with that offered in Edinburgh, had been that the 1909 Act was primarily a safety measure and so could not be used to impose additional regulations governing the right to operate on Sundays. That initial adjudication was reversed on appeal late in 1910, a verdict that had the effect, as Rachael Low has observed, of embolden-ing the Sabbatarian lobby to press the case for closure on the Seventh Day. In London, steps were taken to clarify the conditions under which Sunday entertainments could be mounted. In particular, it was emphasised that all profits should be devoted to charitable ends.[31] In Scotland, reflect-ing perhaps the underlying strength of Sabbatarian feeling, the impact of change was more far-reaching. Here, the narrow definition of the 1909 Act continued to apply, so that regulation was still exercised via locally applied by-laws. The first move specifically to prohibit moving picture shows on Sundays was made in Arbroath, where the by-laws to this end were con-firmed in November 1911.[32] Developments here heralded a tightening in regulations more generally over the months that followed. In December, Bo'ness magistrates refused to renew the seven-day licence hitherto granted to a local electric theatre, while a similar decision was made by Aberdeen justices the following February.[33] In Falkirk, claims that the shows mounted on Sundays at the local Picturedrome, comprising lantern slides and images projected by means of non-flammable film, did not require a licence under the 1909 Act, failed to overcome local pressure for change. Councillors were able to insist that no moving pictures be exhibited on Sundays regardless of the film stock being used.[34] Perhaps most tellingly, by the autumn of 1912, the Sabbatarian offensive extended to Glasgow. Here, the authorities had broadly sanctioned Sunday exhibitions provided the conditions covering content and the application of proceeds were satisfied. So, while permission was granted for a concert at the Scottish Zoo and Hippodrome in aid of the building fund of a local Catholic Church, the application by J. J. Bennell's BB Pictures to stage an entertainment for residents of the two native villages on show at the Scottish National Exhibition, who would have made up an unu-sually cosmopolitan audience of West Africans and Laplanders, was greeted less sympathetically.[35] From October 1912, the magistrates adopted an unequivocal line, whereby no cinematograph exhibition would be allowed at Sunday meetings. The series of sacred concerts at Hengler's Circus was thus only able to continue on condition that no films were shown.[36]

The scope for Sunday cinema narrowed considerably in the years from

1910, as opposition made itself felt even in areas where the practice was well established. In Dalkeith, to the south and east of Edinburgh, the granting of seven-day licences had allowed all three cinemas in the town to open regularly on Sundays. Audiences were generally healthy, one hall reporting attendances of 1,400–1,500 each week. Yet, even here, Sabbatarian feeling was gaining ground by late 1913. Along with the moral objections of local churches, opposition also came from those active in other branches of the entertainment/drink trade who were prevented by law from operating on Sundays and who protested at the unfair advantage enjoyed by cinema proprietors.[37] A potent combination of beer and clericalism pressed for a revision of local by-laws prohibiting moving picture shows on Sundays. Although other expressions of local opinion, articulated through the ballot box or petitions, indicated a sizeable constituency favourable to cinema on the Sabbath, the change was agreed by councillors and was ratified at a subsequent sitting of Edinburgh Sheriff Court.[38] As a result of pressures exerted since 1910, by the outbreak of war only one authority in Scotland was reported to be maintaining the issue of seven-day licences: that in the mining settlement of Lochgelly in Fife.[39] Elsewhere, the Sabbatarian cause had prevailed, ensuring that Sunday cinema, never the rule north of the border, was by 1914 very much the exception.

Initially at least, the outbreak of war signalled no profound change in attitudes. Continuity was most marked in Edinburgh, whose standing as the metropolis of Sabbatarianism remained largely uncontested. In September 1914, a proposal by the Edinburgh and East of Scotland branch of the Cinematograph Exhibitors' Association to hold shows at selected venues on Sundays to raise money for the War Relief Fund was unanimously vetoed by the city's magistrates, prompted in part by resolutions of protest from both the Church of Scotland and the United Free Church Presbytery.[40] Ten months later, the authorities were no more accommodating to a request from the Scottish War Savings Committee for permission to organise meetings in local picture houses to publicise the War Loan.[41] Elsewhere, justices proved rather more willing to countenance Sunday shows, provided they were for a charitable cause and specified conditions were met. In Glasgow, these included no payment for admission at the door and the requirement that the content of each programme receive prior approval. Even then, the magistrates declined to consider an approach from exhibitors to allow Sunday shows on behalf of Belgian refugees in May 1915 and flatly rejected proposals in November the same year for matinees to raise money for the Cinema Ambulance Fund. An evening performance at Hengler's Circus for the same cause was, however, allowed.[42] Perhaps against expectations, a more tolerant attitude appears to have prevailed further north. Dove Paterson was thus able to stage a sacred concert for the Belgian Relief Fund at Aberdeen's Music Hall in October 1914, while through 1915 Dundee's magistrates sanctioned Sunday performances for causes including the Red Cross and the

Polish Fund on at least five occasions.[43] Yet the extent of the challenge posed to Sabbatarian principles should not be overstated. With the final lapsing of seven-day licences in Dalkeith from April 1915, Lochgelly continued to stand out as the sole Scottish authority to sanction regular Sunday shows.[44]

A greater threat was seen to flow from legal decisions south of the border. In 1916, the ability of councils across England to use the Cinematograph Act to prevent Sunday opening was called into question by the Law Officers. Across the area controlled by the London County Council, some 150 cinemas were reported to be open on Sundays by the August of that year, leading the Glasgow paper *The Entertainer* to pose the inevitable question of whether Scotland would follow suit.[45] For one correspondent to *The Scotsman*, defence of the sanctity of the Lord's Day necessitated the forma-tion of a National and Patriotic League of Scottish Churchmen, as they would embody, through their Sabbatarian ideals, a true sense of nation-hood.[46] In the short term, however, the question put by *The Entertainer* was not put to the test by those within the trade. At a time when takings were depressed by the disruption of war and the imposition of the entertainments tax, there appeared, at least in the view of *The Bioscope*, little enthusiasm within the industry for operating an extra day.[47] In the face of continued opposition from magistrates, proposals for Sunday shows in support of National Service in the spring of 1917 secured only fitful support among exhibitors. In the end, shows were held in Greenock, Perth, and Dundee, although houses in Glasgow and Edinburgh remained closed.[48] So, although in May 1917 the Committee on Church Life and Work and Public Morals of the United Free Church expressed concern that Sabbath observance was increasingly subject to challenge, the problem was not seen to emanate from local cinemas.[49] Indeed, references to Sunday concerts in local authority records and the trade press are largely lacking for the middle years of the war. A resurgence in interest can, however, be detected during the upturn in trade that occurred in the latter stages of the conflict. The change was most marked in Aberdeen, where a series of Sunday entertainments was agreed in 1918 in aid of the Cinema Trade Benevolent Fund, the Red Cross, and the local Hospital Sunday Gala Fund. Over three weeks in April, some twelve halls opened on Sundays, raising almost £280 for charity. By June, *The Entertainer*'s correspondent was of the view that 'Sunday concerts are now practically an established institution in the Granite City.'[50]

The boom in trade immediately after the war encouraged a more general move among exhibitors to stage performances on Sundays, encouraged by the belief that a seventh day's business would not unduly depress receipts during the rest of the week. Between 1919 and 1920, the number of Sunday concerts sanctioned by magistrates in Dundee increased from four to twenty-seven, while by May of the latter year, councillors in Motherwell were expressing concern at the frequency with which such shows were being mounted locally.[51] Given this, the decision in March of the same year by the local authority in Blantyre to refuse permission for the local Picture House to hold a sacred concert in aid of local church funds seemed out of step with prevailing sentiment. For the trade press, the conclusion appeared inescapable that 'Sunday concerts with worthy ends in view have come to stay.'[52] That such a claim could be made at all is a powerful indication of the change in attitudes wrought by the war and the boom years that followed. The Sabbatarian offensive that had swept all before it, the mining districts of Fife apart, before 1914 had experienced a sharp reversal, to the extent that by the early 1920s Sunday concerts were a more common feature of life in areas of Scotland than they had been prior to the outbreak of war.

Nevertheless, *The Entertainer*'s observation also serves to point up the limitations of change. Particular conditions continued to attach to Sabbath shows and while film was once more a prominent element in programmes, the subjects offered remained of a distinct, often religious character. So, in September 1919, the concert staged at Dundee's Palladium Theatre on behalf of the local branch of the Discharged and Demobilised Sailors' and Soldiers' Federation included the 1916 production *The Treasure of Heaven*.[53] More importantly, any relaxation in Sabbatarian disciplines remained confined to parts of Scotland only. Edinburgh's cinemas remained closed to charitable entertainments on Sundays through these years. This was in spite of calls for some compromise towards the end of the war, largely to benefit troops stationed in or around the capital, who would otherwise be exposed to the full rigours of the Presbyterian Sunday. In October 1918, Professor Littlejohn, chairman of the city's Overseas Club, approached local exhibitors to press the case that one hall on Princes Street be opened each Sunday specifically for the benefit of men in uniform. The authorities declined to take action, prompted in part by protests from the Edinburgh Working Men's and Women's Christian Sabbath Society. By that point, however, the exhibitors had themselves rejected 'the Sunday opening of Cinemas for business purposes'.[54] The following May, a request on behalf of demobilised servicemen's organisations for a concert to be held at Pringle's Picture House on Elm Row was refused by local magistrates, leading the local correspondent of *The Entertainer and Scottish Kinema Record* to conclude that 'The Sunday opening idea is dead so far as Edinburgh is concerned.'[55] While understandable, the note of finality assumed here quickly proved misplaced. Over the following winter, several Edinburgh halls opened their doors on Sundays. In January 1920, the Tollcross and Princes Cinemas were the settings for evangelical church services, while in February the West End Cinema in Shandwick Place hosted a meeting of special constables.[56] The self-same correspondent who had proclaimed the doom of Sunday shows was now obliged to amend his tone, acknowledging, 'It seems now that the public have taken kindly to attending Sunday afternoon and evening demonstrations where they can have a comfortable seat in a comfortable hall.'[57] The apparent shift in attitudes perhaps encouraged local exhibitors to consider a series of concerts in the autumn in aid of the Chief Constable's Fund for Destitute Children.[58] Even in the stronghold of Sabbatarianism, then, opinion was moving, however slowly, in favour of some form of Sunday opening.

A measure of the degree to which a more relaxed attitude was gaining ground across Scotland more generally was provided early the following year, when officials of the Haig Fund proposed that special matinees be held, with proceeds going to the relief of ex-servicemen. In response, the Cinematograph Exhibitors' Association declared its preference for the holding of Sunday shows for the benefit of the Fund. Although the argument was put that the potential take from such entertainments would be higher than from any held during the week, the suspicion remained that elements within the exhibition business were seeking a precedent from which to press the case for further attacks on the Sabbath. Unsurprisingly, then, opposition to the proposed Warriors' Day concerts planned for 3 April 1921 was quick to emerge and was based on the view that not only did this represent an infringement of the Fourth Commandment, it would also add to the pressure for larger numbers to work on Sundays to satisfy a minority of determined pleasure-seekers. At a meeting organised by the Edinburgh Working Men's and Women's Christian Sabbatarian Society, a resolution opposing the choice of Sunday for Warriors' Day was moved, along with the declaration that such a development was 'not Scottish'.[59] In general, municipal authorities across Scotland broadly acquiesced in the proposed arrangements. If the agreement of magistrates in Glasgow and Aberdeen occasioned little comment, the readiness of the authorities in Edinburgh and Inverness to endorse Warriors' Day, albeit in the latter case only on a casting vote, was considered more noteworthy.[60] In the end, outright opposition was confined to a few, smaller centres, such as Blairgowrie in Perthshire, where the council proposed that performances for the Fund be held on a weekday, and Stranraer, where one cinema proprietor lodged a protest against what he considered a decision informed 'by a puritanical and arbitrary spirit, quite out of keeping with the present age'.[61] The final observation chimed in with the views of those critical of the decision to allow Warriors' Day to proceed as planned, although their perspective was that justices were acting in advance of public opinion. Ultimately, the extent to which events on and around 3 April offended against popular sensibilities is perhaps best caught via the box office, which offers the most disinterested measure of prevailing attitudes. So, queues were reported outside each of the fourteen Edinburgh cinemas open on Warriors' Day, despite the absence of any established pattern of entertainment on the Sabbath across the capital. Takings varied between £15 at the Easter Road Picturedrome, a small house by the early 1920s, at which prices of 3d to 9d applied during the week, and £93 15s at the Picture House on Princes Street, where prices were considerably higher at 1s to 1s 6d.[62] Popular enthusiasm for this limited exercise in Sunday opening appeared extensive. Where obstacles were encountered, they were more the result of the recalcitrance of cinema labour. In Aberdeen, operators declined to offer their services free of charge on the day in protest at the failure of exhibitors to consult them in advance of approaching the city magistrates. As a result, only two halls opened on 3 April, with takings at the Woodside Picture Palace no more than £4.[63] Warriors' Day was thus rescheduled for the final Sunday in the month and, on this occasion, with the cooperation of operators, was adjudged a success by the trade press.[64]

Expectations among critics that Warriors' Day would prove the thin end of a wedge leading to wholesale openings on Sundays were not realised in the years that followed. That said, it had served to consolidate the perceptible shift in attitudes towards Sabbath observance that had set in during the latter stages of the war. Locally, its impact was even more telling. In Glasgow, ad hoc Sunday concerts continued to receive magisterial sanction, provided they could be shown to fulfil a broadly charitable purpose.[65] From 1922, however, a more systematic approach to opening was adopted, prompted by an approach from the Lord Provost, proposing that, following the precedent set by Warriors' Day, cinemas open on one Sunday each year, with takings to be devoted to funds for the relief of the unemployed. Other beneficiaries would include the city's hospitals and the Cinematograph Trade Benevolent Fund.[66] Proceeds from what became the annual Cinema Sunday in Glasgow rose markedly over the second half of the decade, from £1,903 in 1924 to £3,482 16s 4d by 1930.[67] Beyond the central belt, the principle of Sunday opening gained increasing acceptance in the first post-war decade. In 1927, magistrates at Montrose rejected a call from local ministers to enforce the closure on the Sabbath of all halls under council control, along with all cinemas in the burgh.[68] Sunday concerts were allowed, subject to approval of all programmes. Two years later, in January 1929, The Cinema House in the Moray town of Grantown on Spey was sufficiently confident of local support to plan a Sunday showing of the Herbert Wilcox film *Dawn*. Although put on in the depths of a Scottish winter, interest in the exhibition was widespread, so that large numbers were reported to have 'travelled over the ice-bound roads from the outlying districts'. Their journeys proved abortive, however, as the town's magistrates moved to prevent the show taking place, a decision which drew sharp criticism from some quarters that children's charities, the intended recipients of the moneys raised, had lost out as a result of 'narrow, petty, personal views'.[69]

For defenders of the Sabbath, a sense that wider forces were at work to undermine established modes of observance gained ground as the decade drew to a close. In October 1929, a report by the Scottish Sabbath Protection Association noted the increased availability of secular amusements on Sundays and linked this to a change in business structures. Many of the cinemas pressing for Sunday opening were observed to belong to chains centred on London, driven by a looser metropolitan morality.[70] Similarly, in the following year, the General Assembly of the Free Church of Scotland not only expressed concern over the growth of organised excursions on Sundays, but also protested against what was seen to be 'the deliberate attempt on the part of English-controlled railway companies to thrust the Continental Sabbath upon the Highlands of Scotland'.[71] That same year, fears that a central tenet of Scottishness was being undermined by forces originating from outside the country were reinforced by developments in Edinburgh. Here, in contrast to Glasgow, the impact of Warriors' Day had been slight. The local cinema trade acquiesced in a broad rejection of Sunday concerts. Through the 1920s, then, the city's councillors were exercised less by the behaviour of film exhibitors and more by issues such as the provision of music in Princes Street Gardens. Originally proposed in 1923 as a means of providing work for unemployed musicians, concerts were opposed on the grounds that they represented the thin end of a very broad wedge, for, it was asked, if musicians were allowed to raise money by charging spectators, 'what logical objection could they have to the cinemas and theatres and the concert halls opening and charging for admission?'[72] The proposal was voted down by councillors, although the belief that opinion on such questions was far from fixed encouraged a reconsideration of the matter in 1927. On this occasion, and in the absence of any provision for charging for admission, the vote was narrowly in favour, while later in the year agreement was reached on allowing Waverley Market to be let for a series of sacred concerts.[73]

The first break with the broadly observed abstention from the exhibition of moving pictures on Sunday in Edinburgh came with the concessions made to film societies, whose screenings were confined to a closely defined membership and so could not be regarded as open to the general public.[74] In November 1930, the example of bodies such as the Edinburgh Workers' Progressive Film Society and the recently formed Edinburgh Film Guild was taken up by commercial exhibitors, who approached the city magistrates with proposals for a series of Sabbath shows for charity along lines already established in Glasgow. In response to concerns that such a move could set a precedent for a more fundamental departure from existing practices, the local CEA offered the reassurance that 'the Cinema Trade was averse to the general opening of Cinemas on Sunday'.[75] Under new regulations enabling them to grant permission for Sunday shows, the magistrates sanctioned a series of Cinema Sundays, to be held on three consecutive weeks in January and February 1931. In all, thirty-four halls would open on one Sunday each, with three-quarters of the proceeds going to the Royal Infirmary and the remaining 25 per cent to the Cinema Trade Benevolent Fund.[76] Opposition to the magistrates' decision was swift to manifest itself. The views of the ordinary citizen were voiced by, among others, Annie Pearson, who claimed to speak on behalf of the women of the Gorgie district in asserting that 'We cannot agree to have our much needed day of rest filched from us.'[77] Elsewhere, the prospect of Edinburgh adopting Sunday opening, even in this limited fashion, provoked alarm. At a meeting organised by the Inverness and North of Scotland branch of the Lord's Day Observance Society, the Rev. Alexander Boyd stressed the decision's wider ramifications: 'Edinburgh is the capital of Scotland, and leads the way, and every Scotsman is interested in what goes on in the capital city of his land.'[78]

The sense of a nation and a culture at bay as a result of the magistrates' move informed much comment. J. Carter Swain, an American temporarily resident in Edinburgh, lamented evidence of the further Americanisation of Scotland.[79] Others detected the commercial influence of Hollywood behind the exhibitors' scheme. As the local Church of Scotland Presbytery had it, a foreign plutocracy was working to ensure that 'Edinburgh was to be ruled by the standard and morals of Hollywood.'[80] Historical precedent was cited to warn of the consequences of relaxing Sabbath disciplines. Dr Norman Maclean of the Church Presbytery found parallels in the forces that had undermined Imperial Rome, while reference was made to Edinburgh's own past to illustrate the extent of the problems confronting the nation. The mobilisation of the citizenry following the defeat at Flodden held out some hope that opinion would rally in defence of the Presbyterian establishment, but, on this, Maclean was not optimistic: 'To-day is more solemn and tragic than even that. Forces over which we have little control are pauperising the nation, and loosening the fabric of our social system.'[81] That Glasgow had operated Cinema Sundays for several years, in the process generating increasing amounts for charity, was, for many, hardly a source of reassurance. Edinburgh's Free Church Presbytery rejected any attempt to compare the two cities, as Glasgow 'owing to alien elements, was not the extremely well governed city that Edinburgh [was]'.[82] The contrast between east and west was explored in equally forthright terms in a letter to *The Scotsman* by Col A. R. Munro, eastern secretary of the Lord's Day Observance Association of Scotland. Edinburgh, he proceeded, 'is pre-eminently a Scottish and a Protestant city whereas about a quarter of the inhabitants of Glasgow are really aliens'.[83] Whether informed by a sense of history or contemporary racial theory, the idea being posited was of a nationhood rooted in Presbyterianism, now obliged to confront a variety of forces, international in their reach, comprising familiar adversaries such as the Catholic Church as well as the institutions of capitalist modernity based in London and New York. Although rarely articulated, concerns over the latter were compounded by the perceived preponderance in the boardrooms of film and finance capital of Jews, a further group for whom Scottish traditions appeared to count for little.[84]

In the face of these many and varied objections, Edinburgh's first experiment in Cinema Sundays went ahead in January 1931. Programmes were intended to reflect the nature of the day, so that while comedy films were prohibited, biblical subjects featured on all the bills. Given this and a spell of wintry weather, audiences were adjudged to have been healthy, with queues reported outside most halls, so that in several cases a number of cinema-goers had to be turned away. Upwards of 1,000 were reported to have been refused admission to the Blue Halls in Lauriston Street.[85] The nature of the Sunday audiences attracted particular comment. *The Scotsman*'s correspondent was of the view that seats were mostly filled by 'the usual cinema-going public', although some managers detected the presence of a more sizeable 'rough' element. One was drawn to predict that 'we'll probably find that more damage has been done by this crowd in one night than is usually sustained in several weeks'.[86] The reception accorded biblical films confirmed such impressions, one minister reporting that this varied from indifference to downright hostility, with jeering reported in some houses.[87]

As Edinburgh audiences prepared to queue and, in some cases, boo, the legal standing of Sunday shows as a whole became subject to judicial review on both sides of the border. In December 1930, the Eastern Committee of the Lord's Day Observance Association of Scotland (LDOAS) voted to bring a prosecution against Edinburgh's magistrates on the grounds that their decision to grant permission for the opening of cinemas on the Sabbath was contrary to Scottish law.[88] At the same time, in London, a case against Sunday film exhibitions had been launched, largely at the prompting of the theatrical trade, frustrated by laws which allowed cinemas to operate seven days a week while preventing those offering live performances in theatre or music hall from doing the same. The distinction between these forms of entertainment, never absolute, had weakened further, it was argued, with the advent of talking pictures, whose narratives, initially at least, were mostly dialogue driven. The decision of the King's Bench Divisional Court, confirmed late in January 1931 by the Court of Appeal, was that Sunday shows, including those intended for charitable purposes, were illegal.[89] The implications of this verdict for Scotland were keenly debated north of the border. The original case had centred on the Sunday Observance Act of 1781, a measure which, although this was never explicitly stated, was deemed to apply to England and Wales only. The view of officials at the Scottish Home Department was that the verdict in the English courts had no bearing on matters in Scotland, and further that any legislation introduced in the light of the rulings would be equally limited in scope.[90] For Scotland, the key decision was that awaited from the Court of Session in Edinburgh.

Here, the principal points of contention lay between the LDOAS, which argued that the Edinburgh magistrates had acted against Scottish law in allowing Sunday performances, and the justices themselves, who represented that any prosecution should have been brought against those mounting the shows (the exhibitors) and that statutes on Sabbath observance were in desuetude. They were now deemed of limited relevance due to 'the change of manners and habits of the people of Scotland and [the fact that] the public opinion of Scotland does not demand their enforcement'.[91] Legal opinion, sought by the Scottish Home Department, was inclined to question the latter claim. The

Lord Advocate's Office noted that the statutes of 1661 and 1696 had been upheld as recently as 1870, indicating their continued utility in determining the right of cinemas to operate on Sundays.[92] Other authorities argued that the intention of the law was to prohibit the conduct of ordinary trade and labour on Sundays and that 'this construction, reasonably applied, is wide enough to include the carrying on of ordinary cinema business on Sunday'.[93] The powers claimed by the magistrates to allow or to prohibit Sabbath day operations could thus be seen to be *ultra vires*. The judgment delivered by Lord Mackay in June 1931 followed the logic of these arguments, but did not accept their ultimate conclusion. So, the action of the LDOAS was found to be 'incompetent and irrelevant', as the law did not allow individuals as rate-payers to sue the magistrates where no monetary interests were threatened. Equally, the argument that existing statutes had fallen into desuetude was found wanting in the absence of any evidence of prolonged practice contrary to their stated purpose. Nevertheless, while the statutes were found to make specific provision against actions such as salmon fishing, the operation of salt pans and coal mines, as well as the hiring of shearers, Mackay was unable

> even under the general category of profanation of the Sabbath to find anything which did definitely prohibit under the laws of Scotland the presentation of a moving pictorial representation to a body of the public collected within an enclosed area, and causing no disturbance to church and church-goers without its walls.[94]

Immediate responses in the press captured the enduring sense of ambiguity following the judgment. *The Evening Times* in Glasgow tellingly employed a double negative in reporting that Sunday cinema north of the border had been declared 'Not Illegal'.[95] Doubts persisted as to whether Scottish statutes on the Sabbath remained in force and until that issue was tested in court, the legal status of Sunday shows across the country would remain 'obscure'. The Scottish Home Department, the general approach of which, as one of its officials acknowledged, 'has not been to encourage the anxious seekers after knowledge',[96] showed no desire to have the matter tested legally, the effect of which would be 'to disturb the present Scottish position by new legislation'.[97] The belief was that existing local Police Acts gave magistrates sufficient powers to regulate Sunday opening in line with prevailing sentiment.[98] So, while annual Cinema Sundays continued in Glasgow, Edinburgh's justices vetoed a repeat of the 1931 experiment, a decision upheld over the following decade.[99]

Reluctance to secure a clarification of Scots law on the Sabbath owed something to concern over developments at Westminster. Here, against the expectations of the theatrical trade, which had hoped to secure uniformity of treatment with cinema exhibitors, the Labour government responded to the judgment of the Court of Appeal by introducing legislation to restore the status quo ante. Sunday performances which had been allowed prior to the ruling would be restored and could be extended where local opinion was shown to be in favour.[100] Although the bill was intended to apply to England and Wales only, its provisions gave rise to concern in Scotland. The LDOAS feared that a move to legalise Sunday cinema south of the border would prejudice the case then in progress in the Court of Session.[101] For the secretary of the Church of Scotland's Committee on Church and Nation, the worry was that the Act, although ostensibly confined to England, would be extended in short measure to Scotland.[102] One Baptist minister from Monmouthshire warned the Secretary of State, 'Labour claims to be the Party with the highest political morality, but if they legislate in support of Sunday encroachments, it will stigmatise them forever.'[103]

Unsurprisingly, then, Scottish members figured prominently in debates on the bill's progress through the Commons. The long-standing Liberal MP for Ross and Cromarty, James Ian Macpherson, argued that Scotland's exclusion from the measure offered no protection against what he termed 'rampant and ruthless commercialism', further noting that 'most of those syndicates which were behind the opening of the cinema on a Christian Sunday were not unconnected [for which presumably read were connected] with the Jewish persuasion'.[104] Another Liberal, Cecil Dudgeon, the member for Galloway, put the alternative view, pressing that opinion was shifting in favour of a 'brighter Sunday' among both Scots and visitors to Scotland. The latter, he claimed, 'started on Monday and finished on Saturday, because they said, it was extremely difficult to find anything to do on a Sunday afternoon and evening'.[105] The active part taken by Scottish members in seeking to shape a measure that dealt with England and Wales only drew protests, to the extent that backbenchers, not formally identified, gave voice to the cry 'Home Rule for England'.[106] In the end, this early manifestation of what later generations would come to know as the 'West Lothian Question' had few lasting implications, save for the aforementioned member for Galloway, whose speech and vote in favour of the bill drew criticism from the Presbytery of Stranraer and Kirkcudbright. Dudgeon's attempts to defend his stance found little favour, the Presbytery minutes recording with swift finality, 'Letter received; writer not thanked.'[107] Perhaps sensing a growing estrangement from local opinion, Dudgeon resigned the Liberal Whip to stand in 1931 as a candidate for Mosley's New Party.[108] A Scottish majority of twenty-three against the Sunday Entertainments Bill on Second Reading was more than balanced by a sizeable vote in favour from members representing London (seventy-one for, five against) and English borough constituencies (ninety-seven for, forty-one against).[109] The fall of the Labour government in the autumn of 1931 ensured that the measure did not pass into law. Initially at least, the national government considered the matter to be too controversial to be addressed at a time of economic crisis, and so while statutory provision was made to enable Sunday operations to continue where they already applied, broader legislation was delayed until the following year.[110] Scottish opposition persisted, despite reassurances that the bill's provisions would be confined to south of the border. The Free Church minister at Kingussie warned the Secretary of State, Archibald Sinclair, that moves to tamper with observance of the Sabbath which 'has been accompanied by inestimable blessings on the part of all classes in all past ages', would 'undoubtedly conduce to severance and slavery, desolation and destruction'.[111] The first bill in 1932 foundered at the Committee stage, but the decision to make a second bill that year a government measure ensured it a comparatively unproblematic passage through Parliament, so that, in sharp contrast to 1931, most Scottish members were absent from the bill's Second and Third Readings.[112] As finally passed, the Act allowed Sunday opening where it was already in place and permitted its extension where expressions of opinion locally, via popular votes, were favourable.[113] In England, as in Scotland, the progress or otherwise of Sunday opening would be decided at the local level.

For one Church of Scotland minister, Edinburgh's brief flirtation with Cinema Sundays offered clear signs that by 1931 'the mind of Scotland on Sabbath keeping has changed greatly'.[114] Developments across the decade indicated a lasting and if anything accelerating trend towards viewing Sunday as a time for recreation rather than simply of rest and reverence. For the president of the Congregational Union of Scotland, speaking in 1936, the growing range of entertainments deemed permissible on Sundays suggested that Scotland was moving inexorably to becoming 'stupidly Continental, and blatantly Pagan'.[115] Evidence to sustain this and similar arguments was found in various centres. Early in the 1930s, the holding of Cinema Sundays in Glasgow was capable of arousing determined opposition, to the extent that on two occasions the application for the annual round of charity showings was rejected. In each case, the decision was quickly reversed.[116] By 1937, however, any controversy over Cinema Sunday within the city appeared to have passed, as magistrates unanimously endorsed the latest round of openings.[117] Elsewhere, a more relaxed attitude to Sunday amusements could be discerned. In 1936, albeit in the face of some criticism, magistrates in Aberdeen agreed to allow Sunday concerts held for private profit, while unease was also expressed at permission being granted for the staging of jazz concerts at Dundee's Caird Hall, the appearance of Roy Fox and his orchestra being considered by some 'a perfect disgrace to the city'.[118] Later that same year, Peebles Council voted not only to allow Sunday play on a municipal golf course, but also to apply for a liquor licence for the clubhouse.[119] As before, however, developments in Edinburgh would provide for many the clearest pointer to the strength or otherwise of Sabbatarian sentiment. In adopting the powers to sanction Sunday concerts in December 1930, the magistrates had undertaken to apply their discretion sparingly.[120] The reality behind such promises would be revealed in the years from 1932. Having vetoed a further round of Cinema Sundays, the justices allowed a series of charitable concerts to be held on Sundays at five cinemas across the city centre, from the King's Cinema on Lothian Road to the Salon, close to the top of Leith Walk. In each case, agreement was conditional on no films being shown, the entertainments to consist of musical items only.[121] Freestanding events were, by this stage, few, although in March, an application was made for a lecture to be held by the Scottish Labour College Society at the Princes Cinema, while in November, the Tollcross Picture House hosted a series of talks on 'Modern Russia' by Mr and Mrs Arthur Woodburn.[122]

Thereafter, the changing nature of the Edinburgh Sunday is traceable through the deliberations of the city's Magistrates Committee and while the multiple nature of many permissions, covering whole seasons, makes accurate quantification of the number of concerts held elusive, the applications themselves provide some indication of the magnitude of change over time. Information is also available on the number of venues seeking to open on Sundays, as well as the range of organisations which were intended to benefit from the shows, and the varied nature of the entertainments offered. By mid decade, applications for Sunday opening were received from some eighteen cinemas, or approximately half of all picture houses, across the city. Support was extended to local causes, such as the Royal Blind Asylum and School, and the Old Folks' Outing Fund of the City of Edinburgh Band, along with political campaigns, including the National Campaign for Pensions at Sixty, the May Day Committee of Edinburgh and District Trades and Labour Council, and the Leith branch of the Scottish Socialist Party.[123] Although most entertainments were still prohibited from including film, cinema exhibitions were not unknown. A programme of educational subjects was offered at the Salon Picture House by the Edinburgh Zionist Association, while the Jan Kiepura vehicle *My Heart is Calling* played at the New Victoria in Clerk Street, to raise money for the Newspaper Press Fund.[124]

By 1938, the magistrates' conception of the sparing use of their powers over Sunday entertainments had been further stretched. That year, fifty-one applications were received for concerts to be held in cinemas or for the exhibition of films at other venues. The latter included three shows made up of cultural and educational subjects mounted at the Westfield Halls, Gorgie, by the People's Film and Theatre Guild.[125] In all, twenty separate venues applied to open on the Sabbath, some on several occasions through the year. Particularly active in this regard was the newly opened Rio Cinema in the city's Craigmillar district, at which twenty-seven Sunday entertainments were planned over the course of 1938, including a series organised by Craigmillar Labour Party for the local Children's Gala Day Fund, and one concert in May for the Niddrie Mains Unemployed Children's Outing Committee.[126] As these examples suggest, the range of organisations and causes supported by means of Sunday shows was extensive, and associations with the 'sacred', central to their function before 1914, were now increasingly tenuous, if they could be said to exist at all. The change was vividly caught by meetings held by the Edinburgh branch of the Communist Party of Great Britain at the New Palace Cinema on the High Street, and those organised by the National Secular Society and the Rationalist Press Association, Ltd at the Monseigneur News Theatre at the west end of Princes Street.[127] Cinema shows were also more common, as the charity exhibitions at the New Victoria were now supplemented by screenings such as those at the Salon Picture House on Elm Row, intended for the city's Italian community, which involved films celebrating the achievements of the Mussolini regime.[128] Towards the end of the year, shows were proposed and permitted at the four houses run by the Gaumont-British Picture Corporation, the New Victoria, the New Picture House, the Rutland, and the St Andrew Square Picture House, on behalf of the Save the Children Fund, and at the Associated British Cinema's Regal Cinema, in aid of local unemployed clubs.[129] All this was in addition to the autumn and winter screenings mounted by the Edinburgh Film Guild.[130]

Sabbatarians protested at the progressive encroachment on the particular character of the Lord's Day. The growth in Sunday concerts was noted by the Edinburgh Presbytery which complained in 1935 of one cinema which had opened on twenty-seven consecutive Sundays, and inspired a deputation to Glasgow's magistrates in April 1939, comprising the LDOAS, the Social Problems Committee of the Presbytery of Glasgow, the Glasgow Christian Council, the Scottish Reformation Society, and the Glasgow City Mission. Despite its breadth, no action resulted.[131] In Dundee, concern was recorded over the failure of the Police Committee, unlike authorities elsewhere, to stipulate a minimum proportion of takings to be devoted to charitable ends.[132] Expressions of opposition, whether directed at the general principle of Sunday entertainments or to particular features of individual shows, as with the protest against a poster used to advertise a concert at the Broadway Cinema in Edinburgh in January 1938, did little to alter the drift towards a more varied diet of Sunday amusements.[133] In November 1938, the LDOAS pressed Edinburgh's magistrates for a change in the hours at which Sunday concerts would be allowed, so as to prevent them commencing before 8 p.m., thereby precluding any overlap with the times of divine service. The authorities, however, declined to take action.[134] Altogether more effective in checking the growth in Sunday shows was a decision by the exhibitors themselves. In May 1939, the Edinburgh and East of Scotland branch of the CEA voted that no cinema should open on Sunday for a film show, including those intended for charity. Furthermore, each hall would be confined to three Sunday concerts a year. Commercial calculations informed the decision, the Association noting that 'The Sunday cinema shows and concerts represented a drain on the money available among members of the public for entertainment. What was spent on Sunday was not available for spending during the subsequent week.'[135] Awareness of the cost imposed on 'ordinary' business by Sunday operations was all the greater at a time, as will be seen, of largely stagnant or declining receipts.[136] Hit by the broad downturn in the economy at the end of the 1930s, many in the cinema trade came to see the Sunday concert as a self-inflicted burden. So, whereas before 1914, the Sabbatarian lobby had taken the lead in the campaign to defend the special character of the Scottish Sunday, that role was now taken up by cinema managers and proprietors, guided more by the certainties of the balance sheet than by considerations of general morality.

That attitudes among the wider population had also undergone a radical change by the last year of peace was confirmed by controversies surrounding the exhibition of films designed to boost interest and involvement in the Air Raid Protection scheme. The decision to mount these shows on Sunday evenings, the one time when the availability of cinema buildings and prospective wardens could be expected to coincide, led several recruits to the scheme in Edinburgh to resign. The local National Service Committee responded by confirming existing arrangements, arguing that 'the extremists who were likely to resign on such grounds were fewer in number than the recruits who could be gained'.[137] The choice of language was such as to draw one correspondent to *The Scotsman*, who adopted the city's own motto *Nisi Dominus Frustra* (Except the Lord in Vain) to express the view that 'We have indeed progressed amazingly when it can be said, in the capital of Scotland, that those who maintain the validity of the Fourth Commandment are "extremists".'[138] This observation encapsulated a broader change: prior to 1914, it was possible to see those advocating Sunday opening as operating outside the bounds of conventional morality, whereas by 1939, Sabbatarians themselves had become the outliers, holding a position which in urban Scotland at least seemed increasingly contrary to the prevailing public mood.

If anything, the outbreak of war in September 1939 served to widen further the controversy over Sunday opening. Once the concerns over public safety, which resulted in an order (quickly rescinded) to close all places of entertainment, had been overcome, attention turned to issues of morale, particularly among troops and those working in industries vital to the war effort and living at some distance from home. By October, the Home Office had under consideration a move towards Sabbath opening, more especially in areas where concentrations of men under arms were found. To this end, it moved to apply an Order in Council, overriding the requirement in the 1932 Sunday Entertainments Act that local electors give their backing to any change in operating hours.[139] Sabbatarians were quick to object to a measure which, in the words of the Sabbatarian Observance Committee of the Free Presbyterian Church of Scotland, involved the government and more importantly the monarch 'in a solemn act of national sin against God'.[140] The protests raised were many and varied. Beyond the profanation of the Lord's Day itself, it was seen to impose an additional day's labour on workers in the entertainment industry, and also overrode controls previously exercised at local level.[141] What is more, a decision ostensibly taken in the interests

of national unity would, it was argued, actively work to undermine commitment to the 'Common Cause', while the use of a statutory instrument
bypassing the need for Parliamentary scrutiny did not sit easily with the
claim to be fighting a war in defence of democracy and Christian values.[142]
Finally, the suspicion remained, as voiced by the Social Welfare Secretary
of the Methodist Church in Scotland, that the move to provide Sunday
amusements 'may easily prove so completely to alter our national habits as
to be found irrevocable when peace returns'.[143] North of the border, inquiries were made into conditions on the ground in advance of any legislative
intervention. An Intelligence Report on the position in Scotland early in
November noted no evidence of 'Sunday night rowdyism' in blacked-out
towns and cities, while an investigation into the morale of troops stationed
in Galashiels, Stirling, and Inverness commented on the extensive use made
of canteens and rest rooms in mitigating the worst effects of the Scottish
Sabbath.[144] In the last of these areas, local feeling against Sunday opening was
thought to be such that places of entertainment would have to be commandeered were shows to proceed. In the end, as officials at the Scottish Home
Department noted, the Order had no bearing on Scotland, involving as it
did an extension of powers under an Act which did not apply north of the
border. For the time being at least, responsibility would continue to reside
with local authorities.[145]

In the first winter of the war, the status quo as regards Sunday cinemas
remained substantially in place. While Glasgow's annual Cinema Sunday
continued to be held, a move by Edinburgh exhibitors to restore the practice, in response, it was claimed, to requests from various charities, was
turned down by the city magistrates.[146] However, even here consideration
would be given, it was noted, to requests for the staging of individual concerts. Other developments in these early months of war gave some indication
of the changes wrought in the preceding years. In the First World War, the
churches had set their faces decidedly against any relaxation of Sabbath disciplines. Yet in 1939, as the secretary of the Church of Scotland's Committee
on Church and the Nation could observe, many religious organisations were
moving to provide soldiers billeted in their local areas with entertainment
and rest facilities, mostly in the form of canteens, along with rest and recreation rooms.[147]

As the war emerged from its 'twilight' phase in the summer of 1940,
evidence of change became, if anything, more pronounced. Entertainments
specifically intended for service personnel were provided through Garrison
Theatres, established in most of the larger burghs across Scotland. That in
Edinburgh was reported by October 1940 to be 'overwhelmed' at the level
of demand.[148] Along with this, the Ministry of Information commenced in
the autumn of 1940 series of themed film shows. The first, at Edinburgh's
Synod Hall in August, was designed to encourage interest in the Empire and
included an address by officials from the Canadian High Commissioner's

Office.[149] In certain instances, local authorities also became active providers of Sunday entertainments. In October 1940, councillors in Edinburgh
agreed to hold a series of concerts on Waverley Market, site of previous
Sabbatarian controversies.[150] By the end of the year, the concerts were
reported to be drawing audiences of around 6,000, attracted by programmes
which included appearances by, among others, the American film star
Frances Day and Sarafin's Piano Accordion Band.[151] In December, the concerts were switched to Synod Hall, where a series of weekly 'Sunday Night
at Seven' concerts was inaugurated, later transferring to the nearby Usher
Hall. Here, the emphasis was on music and the opportunity afforded collective acts designed to boost morale, such as community singing. In January
1941, the principal attractions being advertised were Eric Smith, organist at
the Paramount Cinema, Glasgow, and Vic Vallely and his Accordion, who
entertained an audience mostly comprising servicemen each of whom was
allowed to bring 'one friend'; civilians were admitted to the shows, albeit for
6d extra.[152]

For all the growth in provision, Sunday opening remained a contentious
issue. Two initiatives roused the critics early in 1941. The first involved a
move by the Home Office, under prompting from the Ministry of Labour,
to extend the terms of the 1939 Order in Council to allow workers in war-
related industries greater access to Sunday entertainments. For the first time,
the Regulation extended the right to open to theatres.[153] While Scotland's
exclusion from the Order, on the grounds as in 1939 that the relevant legislation had never applied north of the border, reassured Sabbatarians, the
theatrical profession protested that the decision placed it at a disadvantage
compared with similar entertainments in England.[154] A greater challenge to
the status quo was seen to follow from the request from Scottish Command
to the Convention of Royal Burghs in January 1941, that cinemas be allowed
to open on Sunday evenings for the benefit of troops. An attempt to address
Sabbatarian concerns was made by the undertaking that performances would
not coincide with the hours of worship and that civilians would be prohibited
from attending, unless accompanying a serviceman.[155] Not all accepted the
distinction implied by the wearing of a uniform. In a letter to the Secretary of
State, Tom Johnston, the general secretary of Glasgow's YMCA, concerned
at 'the effect that the de-Christianising of Sunday will have on the rising generation', questioned the wisdom of exposing soldiers to such forces.[156] The
view of the Convention was that public opinion was more likely to favour
a partial relaxation, provided this did not extend to Civilian Defence and
munitions workers.[157] If leading figures in the Church of Scotland appeared
ready to countenance the greater provision of entertainments for men under
arms, for one minister from Broxburn, the spread of the Continental Sunday
represented a threat that was more insidious and thus more likely to succeed
than any posed by the Nazis.[158] A review of Scottish opinion more generally
found a broad tolerance for the greater provision of recreational facilities

for servicemen and the young and confirmed the increasing marginalisation of strict Sabbatarian views, so that outright opposition to Sunday entertainments was thought more likely to elicit sympathy for the cause of reform.[159]

The effect of the appeal by Scottish Command was a rather more piecemeal and partial extension of Sunday opening than had been envisaged. In March, councillors in Forfar voted to allow cinemas to operate on the Sabbath, while in the summer, halls across Falkirk gave exhibitions on behalf of the local infirmary.[160] More significantly, perhaps, exhibitors in Edinburgh once more sought to revive the idea of a Cinema Sunday, which, with the agreement of the magistrates, was held in the late summer of 1941. On this occasion, the proscription on the showing of comedy films and the requirement that religious subjects figure on all bills were waived. Indeed, the only stipulation proposed by one bailie was that the entertainment comprise 'films a fellow would easily take his mother to see'.[161] How far the programme at the city's Playhouse matched this requirement is not immediately obvious, including as it did the Columbia comedy reissue *There's Always a Woman*, with Joan Blondell and Melvyn Douglas, supported by the Buster Keaton short *Pardon My Berth Marks*.[162] Over the following winter, most additional activity centred on individual shows for charity, although not all were allowed to proceed. Magistrates in Barrhead, for example, rejected proposals for an exhibition at the Central Picture House on behalf of the National Council of Labour's 'Help for Russia' Fund, leading the show's organisers to protest against what they saw as the 'Victorian age principals [sic]' informing the decision of the bench.[163]

A more significant departure was signalled in September 1942, when the Scottish branch of the Cinematograph Exhibitors' Association agreed a general policy of Sunday opening, subject to magisterial approval. The change was proposed following an appeal from the military authorities, who called for halls to be opened in Edinburgh, Glasgow, Perth, Aberdeen, Dundee, and Inverness. The CEA pressed the case for additional facilities being made available to men in uniform as 'By the opening of cinemas it is hoped to go a long way towards clearing the streets of servicemen – who, on Sunday evenings, find they have nothing to do and nowhere to go.'[164] Before any general move to Sabbath day openings was agreed, the Scottish Home Department issued a questionnaire to chief constables across Scotland, seeking information on the range of legitimate amusements already available and the reaction anticipated from a further extension of recreational facilities.[165] The returns provide the most comprehensive summary of the extent of Sunday opening, illustrating the degree to which Sabbatarian sentiment had been challenged away from the large burghs, on which much of the debate had been centred up to this point.

In all, some forty-seven of Scotland's 600 or so cinemas were reported to be open on any one Sunday, although this did not include those functioning as Garrison Theatres or those offering Ministry of Information (MOI)

Table 4.1 *Cinemas operating on Sundays, November 1942, burghs and counties.
(Source: NAS, HH1/2648, Scottish Home Dept, Chief Constables' Reports on Sunday
Cinema Opening.)*

Burgh	No. of cinemas
Alloa	1
Arbroath	2
Edinburgh	4
Glasgow	5
Paisley	1
Stirling	1

County	No. of cinemas
Angus	4
Argyllshire	1
Ayrshire	12
Bute	1
Dumfriesshire	5
East Lothian	1
Lanarkshire	1
Midlothian	1
Orkney	1
Perth and Kinross	2
Renfrewshire	2
Ross and Cromarty	1
Selkirkshire	1

Note: No openings were reported in Aberdeen, Airdrie, Ayr, Coatbridge,
Dumbarton, Dundee, Dunfermline, Greenock, Inverness, Kirkcaldy,
Motherwell, Perth, Aberdeenshire, Banff, Berwick, Caithness, Dunbartonshire,
Fife, Inverness-shire, Kincardineshire, Kirkcudbrightshire, Moray and Nairn,
Peeblesshire, Roxburghshire, West Lothian, Wigtownshire, and Zetland.

shows.[166] Further screenings not covered in the returns included those taking
place in or near military camps. On Orkney, for example, shows limited to
service personnel were offered at Stromness and Kirkwall.[167] More generally,
responses indicated limited openings north of the central belt. In an exchange
with the National Liberal member for Inverness, Sir Murdoch Macdonald,
Tom Johnston made much of the fact that a mere four halls across the
Highlands were exhibiting films on the Sabbath.[168] Elsewhere, the majority
of screenings appear to have taken place in county areas, where alternative
provision was limited. What is more, one-third of cinemas active on each
Sunday were located in two areas: Ayrshire and Dumfriesshire. Even here,
local variations in practice remained marked. While one cinema operated

in Ardrossan, perhaps reflecting the presence of war-related industry in the form of an aviation fuel-canning factory, magistrates in the nearby resort of Saltcoats refused an application from the military authorities for a relaxation in licensing regulations.[169] Differences, rather less susceptible to ready explanation, extended to the conditions governing screenings in various localities. In Glasgow, the original decision to limit admission to service personnel was overturned on the grounds that those engaged in war work were as entitled to access to Sunday entertainments as those in uniform.[170] The term 'war work' was here interpreted rather freely, so that the Chief Constable's report indicated that civilians made up between 67 and 88 per cent of audiences at screenings in November 1942.[171] In other large burghs, conditions were laid down which made clear that concessions were being made for the benefit of troops. In Edinburgh, admission to Garrison Cinemas was limited to servicemen in uniform and members of the Women's Land Army, who in each case could be accompanied by no more than one civilian each.[172] Overall, continued local discretion over matters of urban governance produced a patchwork of regulations on Sunday opening which extended through the war. Across Dumfriesshire, where five cinemas showed films on the Sabbath in November 1942, those in Dumfries and Kirkconnel placed no restrictions on entry as regards service personnel and civilians. By contrast, the latter were denied admission at Thornhill, while no one under the age of sixteen was allowed to attend the cinema at Gretna.[173]

In terms of reactions locally to change, hostility to any relaxation in Sabbatarian disciplines was detected in Highland and eastern Border counties. The Chief Constable of Inverness-shire remarked that

> The observance of the Sunday as a day of rest and holiness has always been an outstanding feature of Highland life, and there is generally a strong feeling of opposition to the disruption of this way of life by the holding of concerts and the opening of cinemas on that day.[174]

Even in these areas, however, greater tolerance was detected towards the presentation of films to troops. In Ross and Cromarty, the opening of the cinema at Strathpeffer for service personnel aroused little opposition.[175] More generally, where religious groups sought to register a protest against any relaxation of Sabbath disciplines, such views were increasingly seen as swimming against the tide of wider opinion. For the Chief Constable of Glasgow, 'as far as the great majority of the public is concerned it would appear that the latter is quite indifferent as to whether or not permission is granted to open places of entertainment on Sunday'.[176] While that city's capacity to reflect Scottish feeling as a whole was doubted by some, further instances suggest that such a way of thinking was increasingly representative of the whole. In Galashiels, the Sabbatarian position was most forcefully stated by a local Baptist minister, although the Deputy Chief Constable of Selkirkshire was inclined to discount its broader significance, arguing that 'anything he says will not carry much weight in the town except with the "ultra guid"'.[177] A sense that the Church no longer spoke for Scotland appeared to become more deeply rooted as the war progressed, so that one bailie in Montrose, in expressing his frustration at the opposition voiced by local churches to the opening of cinemas for civilians on Sundays, presented as a departure a view which previous generations would have regarded as axiomatic: 'To him it seemed that the Church was wanting to dictate to people in Montrose as to what was right and what was wrong.'[178]

The pattern of opening set in November 1942 appears to have applied for the remainder of the conflict. Across Edinburgh, houses opened one Sunday in four on a rota basis.[179] The programmes offered, while different from those which played through the week, continued to comprise standard Hollywood fare, albeit films seldom less than two years beyond their original release date. Box-office data suggest that this consistent diet of recent American product played well with a largely service audience. Attendance figures for the Playhouse over the final weeks of the war suggest that at no time was the auditorium less than 97 per cent full for Garrison Sundays.[180] The Chief Constable's observation in 1942 that 'all seating accommodation is invariably occupied' continued to hold good for the duration of the conflict.[181]

The manifest popularity of Garrison Cinema shows and the like served to confirm Sabbatarian fears that concessions made in the particular conditions of wartime would become a source of 'persistent evil and danger'.[182] In a move designed to mitigate the threat to the nature of the Scottish Sunday, the LDOAS petitioned all responsible authorities in March 1945 to rescind all permissions for Sabbath entertainments.[183] Across Scotland, the call went largely unheeded, so that although in areas such as Montrose and Arbroath, Sunday openings ceased with the onset of peace, elsewhere wartime arrangements were maintained.[184] At Forfar and Dumfries, performances on the Sabbath persisted in the face of criticism from local Presbyteries, while in Edinburgh, Garrison Cinema screenings continued through the first postwar winter and were only ended in April 1946 on the initiative of local exhibitors.[185] So, rather than the restoration of pre-war 'normality', sought by the LDOAS, the tendency was for the relaxation in Sabbath disciplines to be maintained or, in places, to be taken further. Concern that the withdrawal of Sunday amusements would leave people little if any choice in seeking to fill their evenings led councillors in Perth and Stirling to press the case for cinemas to open seven days a week. Justifying Stirling's decision to sanction Sunday opening over the winter months of 1946–7, one councillor observed that 'If the cinemas are open, they will keep people off the streets and from hanging about closes on Sunday nights.' Such was the prevailing view on the issue when the council debated the matter, that a motion to take no action received no seconder.[186]

The way to full commercial operations on Sundays now appeared open and, in the following winter, other authorities followed Stirling's example. In January 1948, Greenock magistrates voted to allow cinemas to open on a rota basis, a decision subsequently confirmed, despite the opposition of local churches and representatives of cinema staff.[187] The trade press anticipated that the move would have repercussions for practice across Scotland. Two months later, Glasgow announced its own Sunday rota, by which five cinemas across the city, two in the centre and three in suburban districts, would be allowed to open on each Sunday. *The Glasgow Herald* needed no persuading as to the importance of this development, declaring it to be 'a milestone in the social history of Glasgow'.[188] While *The Herald* saw little of merit in picture-house entertainments of themselves, it was persuaded as to their wider social utility, alleviating as they were seen to do levels of domestic overcrowding and reducing any threat of disorder arising from idleness. Given this, the conclusion was that 'The Glasgow experiment is both realistic and in tune with the times.'[189] How far events elsewhere were coloured by developments in the west was not at first clear. A year earlier, Edinburgh's Trades and Labour Council had pressed the case for extending Sunday shows beyond the annual screening for charity.[190] The magistrates chose to take no action, although not before various organisations representing local Protestantism in its many and varied guises, from the Presbytery of Edinburgh, to the Loyal Orange Institute, and the Masonic order, had registered their protests.[191] For all this, greater weight in shaping the eventual outcome appears to have been given to opinion within the cinema trade itself. On receiving the Trades Council's original application, the magistrates requested the town clerk to seek the views of the CEA and members of the National Association of Theatrical and Kine Employees (NATKE). While the exhibitors failed to reach a final decision on the issue, the local branch of NATKE declared its unanimous opposition to any extension of opening hours, and it appears to have been this, rather than the moral objection of Church-related bodies, which persuaded the city justices to block any move to Sunday opening in the capital.[192]

Elsewhere, the Church's importance to a debate in which it had played a central role in previous decades was also called into question. In November 1947, councillors in Lochmaben, Dumfriesshire, agreed to grant a licence allowing Sunday shows at the local cinema, The Barras, having previously turned down a similar application. Within the council, debate centred on the timing of any show to ensure against any clash with the hours of divine worship. The local minister, however, disclaimed any interest in the matter, arguing that 'the church ought to be left out of it [on the grounds that] [i]t was quite able to look after itself'.[193] If, in other parts of Scotland, the Church did become embroiled in the controversy, this was not always in a manner of its own choosing. In June 1948, a prosecution was brought in Montrose Police Court against the proprietor of a local hall for staging a public cinema show for which an admission charge had been levied on one Sunday the previous November. The premises, a local church hall, were, so the prosecution alleged, not licensed for entertainments. The proprietor charged with this contravention of local licensing regulations was a Church of Scotland minister. While initially successful, the case was overturned on appeal, as the minister was able to show that he had sought and had been granted permission to put on cinema shows on Sundays.[194] At the very least, then, the case reflected the increasingly equivocal stance assumed by the Church in the late 1940s and the continued importance of local variations in practice and outlook.

Even before the adoption of commercial Sunday opening, the Church in Glasgow had come to acknowledge that a straightforwardly oppositional stance to Sabbath entertainments was no longer practicable. In the first winter after the war, churches within the city had launched an 'Open Doors' campaign, designed to provide local youth with meeting places more attractive and activities more inspiring than those offered by cinema and street corner.[195] Reactions to the initiative were mixed. While attendances indicated that support among the intended audience was strong, opinion within the Church itself was more sceptical. Some questioned the spiritual nature of the entertainment offered, with particular doubt expressed about the rendition offered by Sir Harry Lauder at the first 'Open Doors' meeting of 'I Belong to Glasgow'. Otherwise, ministers from suburban parishes bemoaned the loss of congregations encouraged, they argued, by a policy designed to attract the young to the city centre. One minister complained that attendances at his afternoon Bible class had fallen by half on the first of the 'Open Doors' Sundays.[196]

If the Church appeared increasingly incapable of providing a consistent voice on Sabbatarian issues, the ability of local authorities to exercise a clear judgment on such points of controversy also appeared open to question. Although they retained the ultimate legal responsibility for determining what did and what did not constitute acceptable Sunday amusements, elected representatives displayed a greater readiness from the later 1940s to consult local opinion before decisions were finalised. So, when Lochmaben councillors rejected the application by The Barras Cinema to open on Sundays, they then agreed to a poll of local electors on the matter. The subsequent vote of ratepayers of 348 to 133 in favour of Sabbath screenings proved sufficient to justify a reversal of the original decision.[197] In subsequent years, public opinion would be further tested. In 1949, electors in Loanhead in Midlothian voted almost 2:1 in favour of Sunday openings, on a turnout of just over 50 per cent.[198] By contrast, a plebiscite in Dunoon over whether to permit Sunday openings through the season resulted in a majority against, an outcome which stiffened the resolve of local representatives to resist such an innovation.[199] Although limited in extent and variable in their outcome, such exercises in local opinion represented a significant departure. No longer were Sabbath practices to be influenced solely or even largely by groups seeking to represent a conventional Presbyterian-based morality. Rather, the views of 'ordinary' Scots, who had long shown a more relaxed attitude to questions of Sabbath observance than had either Church leaders or elected representatives, would be of increasing importance in determining the future of the Scottish Sunday.

III

By mid century, then, cinema as a seven-day operation was firmly established across large parts of Britain. It was most notable in England's larger towns and cities, with over 90 per cent of county boroughs and almost three-quarters of all other boroughs permitting regular screenings on Sundays.[200] North of the border, change to 1950 was more incremental and piecemeal. The commercial exhibition of moving pictures remained confined to a few large centres. More generally, there was no certainty that the concessions made in the exceptional conditions of wartime would be maintained. To that extent, the Scottish Sabbath remained distinctive. Yet the degree to which it acted as a defining part of Scottish nationhood appeared increasingly open to question. The Sabbatarian cause, which had appeared a dynamic force for change before 1914, was by 1950 squarely on the defensive and facing fundamental erosion on most fronts. So, while magistrates in Edinburgh had set their face against the commercial exhibition of film on Sundays, sanction was given to cinema's use in series of charity concerts, screenings across the autumn and winter by various organisations, including the Edinburgh Film Guild, the Ministry of Information, the Local Department of Health, and the Edinburgh Scientific Film Society, as well as Sunday shows associated with the newly established Documentary Film Festival. All this was in addition to the annual Cinema Sunday, the acceptance of which was in marked contrast to the controversy provoked by a similar move as recently as 1931; so much for the 'metropolis of Sabbatarianism'.[201] In other areas, just as if not more renowned for their steadfast adherence to strict Sunday disciplines, doubts as to the efficacy of such a stance were also being voiced. In 1947, councillors in Inverness debated the need to provide Sunday entertainments locally if visitors were to continue to be drawn to the area.[202] Contemporaries needed no persuading that the changes being witnessed in the years to 1950 were radical and profound. Many were also clear that these developments heralded wider consequences. *The Glasgow Herald* saw in the adoption of commercial opening early in 1948 evidence of a fundamentally changed attitude towards religion.[203] The extent of any alteration should not, perhaps, be overstated. For all the protests that relaxations of Sabbatarian disciplines marked Scotland's descent into paganism, Sunday shows were at best a partial and secondary measure of secularisation. At no point did cinema-going actively preclude attendance at divine worship. Indeed, shows were, more often than not, specifically timed so as to accommodate both practices. Yet the spread of seven-day leisure may be seen as symptomatic of a society in which the influence of organised religion and the ideas which it endeavoured to promote were less pervasive and were increasingly limited to specific aspects of everyday life. For many, the worship of God was now slotted in amidst a growing range of secular amusements.

As this suggests, Scotland's engagement with the 'modern', as exemplified by the cinema in the early twentieth century, was far from straightforward. It was the outcome of an interplay of several forces, religious, civic, commercial, and popular, whose precise balance would vary by locality and over time. Received certainties on issues such as Sunday opening were most obviously subject to revision during the two wars, although the impact of change would extend into the peacetime years that followed. Reports during the Second World War and local plebiscites thereafter caught a public mood often sharply at variance with the views expressed by Church and civic leaders, one that appeared more outward looking and altogether less constrained by adherence to a particular religious outlook. So, although Presbyterian concerns continued to inform public debate over the period, Scots in general were accepting and supportive of a cultural form shaped by forces originating beyond the confines of the nation. Over time, the extended debate over Sunday opening served to bring into sharper focus the tastes and preferences of cinema-goers themselves, on which the fortunes of the industry as a whole rested. The audience was a continued source of concern for businessmen as well as moralists throughout the period, and it is to the nature of picture-going in the years leading up to the Second World War, when the nature of the product to which they were exposed became a matter of official concern, that the next chapter turns.

NOTES

1. NAS, HH1/2647, Scottish Home Dept, Opening of Places of Entertainment. Reports, Representations, etc., House of Commons Debates, 10 May 1949.
2. Low, *History of the British Film, 1929–1939*, p. 60; Hanson, *From Silent Screen to Multi-Screen*, p. 36.
3. NAS, HH1/ 2634, Scottish Home Dept, Sunday Observance. Representations and Enquiries, 14 Jan. 1941, Francis Bridson, Convener of Committee on Public Questions, and John Dickson, member of Scottish Churches' Council to Rt. Hon. Ernest Brown; HH1/2632, Scottish Home Dept, Sunday Entertainments. Representations and Enquiries, 28 Oct. 1939, J. R. S. Wilson, The Manse, Lomond Road, Trinity, Edinburgh, to Brown.
4. NAS, HH1/2635, Scottish Home Dept, Sunday Observance. Representations and Enquiries, 20 Feb. 1941, M. Halley, Broughty Ferry, to Morrison.
5. NAS, HH1/2632, n.d., 'An Ear of the World' to Colville.
6. H. McLeod, *Class and Religion in the Late Victorian City* (London, 1974), ch. 8; id., *Religion and Society in England, 1850–1914* (Basingstoke, 1996); C. G. Brown, *Religion and Society in Twentieth-Century Britain* (Harlow, 2006), chs 1 and 2.

7. C. M. M. Macdonald, *Whaur Extremes Meet: Scotland's Twentieth Century* (Edinburgh, 2009), pp. 273–4; C. G. Brown, 'Spectacle, Restraint and the Sabbath Wars: The "Everyday" Scottish Sunday', in L. Abrams and C. G. Brown (eds), *A History of Everyday Life in Twentieth-Century Scotland* (Edinburgh, 2010), pp. 153–80.

8. Brown, *Death of Christian Britain*, chs 7 and 8.

9. For example, NAS, HH1/2644, Scottish Home Dept, Sunday Observance, Press Cuttings, cutting from *Scotsman*, 28 Feb. 1941, letter from a 'Soldier', who noted the attempt by the churches to deprive him and his colleagues of entertainment on the one day available to them.

10. Miskell, *Social History*, pp. 173–81.

11. NAS, HH1/2618, Scottish Home Dept, Sunday Observance Act (1780) Amendment (No. 2) Bill, 1931, Representations, n.d., Legal Position as Stated by Sheriff Wark, KC, and Mr Philip, Advocate; HH1/2622, Sabbath Day Observance, Sunday Performance (Regulation) Bill, 1931, Note by Lord Advocate re Statutes anent Sunday Observance, 3 March 1931.

12. NAS, HH1/2643, Scottish Home Dept, Cinema Openings, 1939–41, Home Policy Committee, Sunday Opening of Cinemas, 29 Nov. 1939; Sunday Closing in Regard to Places of Entertainment.

13. NAS, HH1/2632, Scottish Home Dept, Sunday Entertainments, Representations and Enquiries, 9 Feb. 1937, A. F. Young, Manager, Victoria Cinema, Inverurie, to President of Board of Trade; 24 Feb. 1937, John Jeffery to Young.

14. NAS, HH1/2643, n.d., Sunday Closing of Theatres and Cinemas.

15. J. Wigley, *The Rise and Fall of the Victorian Sunday* (Manchester, 1980), pp. 200–1.

16. *Scotsman*, 6 April 1898, p. 11.

17. *ET*, 20 March, p. 4; 8 April 1901, p. 2; *Scotsman*, 23 Feb., p. 8; 27 Feb., p. 9; 4 March 1901, p. 5.

18. *ET*, 30 Nov. 1901, p. 2.

19. *ET*, 16 Feb., p. 8; 12 March, p. 6; 8 Oct. 1900, p. 8; 13 Sept., p. 8; 25 Oct. 1901, p. 8; 5 Sept. 1902, p. 8; 30 Jan., p. 8; 14 Sept. 1903, p. 8; 9 Oct., p. 8; 16 Oct. 1905, p. 8; 5 Feb. 1906, p. 8; 16 May 1908, p. 6; 16 Jan., p. 6; 8 May 1909, p. 6.

20. *ET*, 15 Sept., p. 8; 20 Dec. 1902, p. 6.

21. *Scotsman*, 29 March, p. 6; 13 Dec. 1909, p. 6; *Bioscope*, 23 Nov. 1911, p. 577.

22. *ET*, 27 Feb. 1905, p. 8; *Bioscope*, 6 Oct. 1910, p. 11.

23. GCA, Minutes of Corporation of Glasgow, April–Nov. 1911, Magistrates Committee, 18 May 1911; SSA, 5/7/135, *The Story of B.B. Pictures* (n.d.), p. 3.

24. GCA, Minutes of Corporation of Glasgow, May–Nov. 1908, Magistrates Committee, 17, 24 Sept. 1908.

25. GCA, Minutes of Corporation of Glasgow, Nov. 1908–April 1909, Magistrates Committee, 19 Nov.; 17 Dec.; 29 Dec. 1908.

26. Low, *History of the British Film, 1906–1914*, pp. 61–2; Williams, 'Cinematograph Act', pp. 341–50.

27. GCA, MP41/106, Memorandum by the Town Clerk on the Cinematograph

Act, 1909, and relative regulations made by the Secretary of State for Scotland on 10th March 1910, p. 2.

28. See Chapter 2, pp. 59–60.
29. GCA, Minutes of Corporation of Glasgow, April–Nov. 1910, Magistrates Committee, 8, 22 Sept. 1910.
30. *ET*, 10 May 1909, p. 6.
31. Low, *History of the British Film, 1906–1914*, pp. 62–6; Williams, 'Cinematograph Act'.
32. *Bioscope*, 9 Nov. 1911, p. 397.
33. *Bioscope*, 28 Dec. 1911, p. 895; 15 Feb. 1912, p. 459.
34. *Bioscope*, 9 May 1912, p. 411.
35. GCA, Minutes of Corporation of Glasgow, April–Nov. 1911, Magistrates Committee, 18 May 1911; April–Nov. 1910, Magistrates Committee, 8 Sept. 1910.
36. *Bioscope*, 31 Oct. 1912, p. 341; GCA, Minutes of Corporation of Glasgow, April–Nov. 1912, Magistrates Committee, 4 Oct. 1912.
37. *Bioscope*, 9 Oct. 1913, p. 129.
38. *Bioscope*, 9 April, pp. 193, 195; 14 May 1914, p. 559.
39. *Bioscope*, 21 May 1914, p. 867.
40. *Scotsman*, 26 Sept., p. 9; 30 Sept. 1914, p. 10; *Bioscope*, 10 Sept., p. 936; 1 Oct. 1914, p. 11; ECA, SL119/2/6, Edinburgh Corporation, Magistrates Committee Minutes, 25 Sept.; 2 Nov. 1914.
41. ECA, SL119/2/6, 22 July 1915.
42. *Entertainer*, 1 May, p. 7; 8 May, p. 5; 6 Nov. 1915, p. 6; *Bioscope*, 29 April, p. 453; 6 May, p. 553; 13 May, p. 669; 27 May, p. 885; 11 Nov. 1915, p. 701.
43. *Bioscope*, 29 Oct. 1914, pp. 396–7; DCA, Dundee Town Council Minutes, 4 Nov. 1914–8 Nov. 1915, Police and Lighting Committee, 9 March; 11 May 1915; 5 Nov. 1915–6 Nov. 1916, Police and Lighting Committee, 14 Dec. 1915.
44. *Bioscope*, 29 April 1915, p. 453.
45. *Entertainer*, 12 Aug. 1916, p. 6; Low, *History of the British Film, 1914–1918*, pp. 105–6.
46. *Scotsman*, 2 Nov. 1916, p. 6.
47. *Bioscope*, 1 March 1917, p. 963.
48. *Bioscope*, 5 April 1917, p. 79.
49. *Scotsman*, 15 May 1917, p. 7.
50. *Entertainer*, 6 April, p. 10; 13 April, p. 12; 20 April, p. 11; 15 June, p. 14; 22 June, p. 10; 29 June 1918, p. 10.
51. DCA, Dundee Town Council Minutes, 8 Nov. 1918–3 Nov. 1919; 5 Nov. 1919–1 Nov. 1920; *Entertainer and SKR*, 15 May 1920, p. 8.
52. *Entertainer and SKR*, 27 March 1920, p. 10.
53. *Entertainer and SKR*, 6 Sept. 1919, p. 11.
54. ECA, SL119/1/2, Edinburgh Corporation, Magistrates Committee Meeting Book, Feb. 1910–July 1920, 24 Oct.; 22 Nov. 1918; SSA, 5/11/17, Edinburgh and East of Scotland CEA Minutes, Meetings at Princes Cinema, 8 Oct.; 25 Oct.; 19 Nov. 1918.

55. ECA, SL119/1/2, 27 May 1919; *Entertainer and SKR*, 5 June 1919, p. 9.
56. *Entertainer and SKR*, 10 Jan., p. 11; 14 Feb. 1920, p. 11.
57. *Entertainer and SKR*, 20 March 1920, p. 11.
58. SSA, 5/11/17, CEA Minutes, Meeting at Princes Cinema, 23 Nov. 1920.
59. *Scotsman*, 23 Feb., p. 8; 28 Feb., p. 9; 3 March, p. 8; 25 March 1921, p. 4.
60. *Entertainer and SKR*, 5 March, p. 3; 12 March, p. 10; 26 March 1921, p. 9; *Scotsman*, 22 March 1921, p. 4.
61. *Scotsman*, 19 March 1921, p. 9; *SKR*, 2 April 1921, p. 1.
62. *Scotsman*, 4 April 1921, p. 6; *Kinematograph Year Book* (London, 1921).
63. *SKR*, 26 March, p. 9; 9 April 1921, p. 13.
64. *SKR*, 16 April, p. 14; 7 May 1921, p. 9.
65. *Scotsman*, 9 Dec. 1922, p. 7.
66. *Scotsman*, 29 Nov. 1930, p. 10, reporting the CEA's application to Edinburgh's magistrates, in which Glasgow's experience was cited in support.
67. *Scotsman*, 24 May 1924, p. 9; 19 May 1930, p. 9.
68. *Scotsman*, 23 Jan. 1927, p. 9.
69. See Chapter 2, p. 67, for the background to the controversy over *Dawn*; *Scotsman*, 9 Jan. 1929, p. 7.
70. *Scotsman*, 23 Oct. 1929, p. 14.
71. NAS, HH1/2615, Scottish Home Dept, Sabbath Day Observance, Resolutions, 26 May 1930, Resolution of General Assembly of Free Church of Scotland.
72. *Scotsman*, 4 May 1923, p. 7.
73. *Scotsman*, 7 Jan., p. 11; 2 Dec. 1927, p. 6.
74. See Chapter 2, pp. 67–8.
75. ECA, SL119/3/1, Edinburgh Corporation Minutes, Magistrates Committee, 16 May 1930–16 Oct. 1931, 28 Nov. 1930; *Scotsman*, 29 Nov. 1930, p. 10.
76. ECA, SL119/3/1, General Purposes Committee, 19 Dec. 1930; *Scotsman*, 1 Dec. 1930, p. 13.
77. *Scotsman*, 2 Dec. 1930, p. 7; see also, ECA, SL119/3/1, 23 Dec. 1930; 20 Jan. 1931.
78. *Scotsman*, 21 Jan. 1931, p. 6.
79. *Scotsman*, 4 Dec. 1930, p. 7.
80. *Scotsman*, 3 Dec. 1930, p. 8.
81. *Scotsman*, 9 Dec. 1930, p. 9.
82. *Scotsman*, 10 Dec. 1930, p. 8.
83. *Scotsman*, 13 Dec. 1930, p. 9.
84. See the views expressed by one Edinburgh professional during a later phase of the Sunday controversy, NAS, HH1/2632, Scottish Home Dept, Sunday Entertainments, Representations and Enquiries, 25 Oct. 1939, Dr James White to Col Colville, MP, in which legislation nationally to allow Sunday opening was seen as 'a most undistinguished surrender to a class (mostly Jewish financiers) who are whining because their vested interests are being affected by the "Black Out"'.
85. ECA, SL119/3/1, 20 Feb. 1931. In all, Cinema Sundays were said to have raised £1,199 2s 7d; *Scotsman*, 26 Jan. 1931, p. 9.

86. *Scotsman*, 19 Jan., p. 9; 26 Jan., p. 9; 2 Feb. 1931, p. 9.
87. *Scotsman*, 26 Jan., p. 9; 2 Feb. 1931, p. 9.
88. *Scotsman*, 27 Dec. 1930, p. 9.
89. NAS, HH1/2616, Scottish Home Dept, Miscellaneous Files, Sabbath Day Observance, Press Cuttings, etc., 28 Jan. 1931, cutting from *Daily Herald*; 11 Dec. 1930, extract, H of C Debates, Places of Amusement (Sunday Performances); *Scotsman*, 24 Jan., p. 14; 28 Jan. 1931, p. 11.
90. NAS, HH1/2617, Scottish Home Dept, Sabbath Day Observance, Sunday Observance Act (1780) Amendment (No. 2) Bill, 1931, 5 Feb. 1931, Minute, Mr Fairgrieve.
91. NAS, HH1/2619, Scottish Home Dept, Sabbath Day Observance, Resolutions, 18 March 1931, cutting *Glasgow Herald*; *Scotsman*, 18 March 1931, p. 9.
92. NAS, HH1/2622, Scottish Home Dept, Sabbath Day Observance, Sunday Performance (Regulation) Bill, 1931, 3 March 1931, Note by Lord Advocate re Statutes anent Sunday Observance, which concluded 'that the Courts of Scotland would decide that the opening of cinemas and theatres on Sundays is in breach of the Statute law of Scotland'.
93. NAS, HH1/2618, Scottish Home Dept, Sunday Observance Act (1780) Amendment (No. 2) Bill, 1931, Representations, n.d., pamphlet, *Guard Your Sunday*, issued by the Lord's Day Observance Association of Scotland, Legal Position as Stated by Sheriff Wark, KC, and Mr Philip, Advocate, n.p.
94. NAS, HH1/2625, Scottish Home Dept, Sunday Performances (Temporary Regulation) Act, Parliamentary Procedures, n.d., Note; *Scotsman*, 20 June 1931, p. 14.
95. *ET*, 19 June 1931, p. 1.
96. NAS, HH1/2632, Scottish Home Dept, Sunday Entertainments, Representations and Enquiries, 11 Dec. 1934, Minute, Mr Fairgrieve.
97. NAS, HH1/2626, Scottish Home Dept, Sunday Performances (Regulation) Bill, 1932, Parliamentary Procedures, 15 Dec. 1931, Note for Secretary of State as to the Scottish position re Sunday Performance Bill.
98. NAS, HH1/2626, 20 April 1932, Scottish Office Note on Sunday Performance (Regulation) Bill.
99. ECA, SL119/3/2, Edinburgh Corporation Minutes, Magistrates Committee, 1931–2, 6 Jan. 1932.
100. *Scotsman*, 11 April 1931, p. 13; *ET*, 10 April 1931, p. 5; NAS, HH1/2617, 21 Geo. 5.
101. NAS, HH1/2618, 19 Feb. 1931, Major A. R. Munro, secretary of Lord's Day Observance Association of Scotland, to Secretary of State.
102. NAS, HH1/2618, 14 March 1931, Secretary, Church of Scotland Committee on Church and the Nation to Secretary of State.
103. NAS, HH1/2618, 14 March 1931, Huw Edwards, Baptist Minister, Raglan, Monmouths., to Secretary of State.
104. *Scotsman*, 21 April 1931, p. 10.
105. *Scotsman*, 21 April 1931, p. 10.
106. *Scotsman*, 21 April 1931, p. 9.

107. *Scotsman*, 25 April 1931, p. 15.
108. F. W. S. Craig (ed.), *British Parliamentary Election Results, 1918–49*, 3rd edn (London, 1983), p. 626.
109. *Scotsman*, 22 April 1931, p. 10.
110. *Scotsman*, 2 Sept., p. 9; 15 Sept., p. 7; 30 Sept., p. 12; 8 Oct. 1931, p. 11.
111. NAS, HH1/2627, Scottish Home Dept, Sunday Performances (Regulation) Bill, 1932, Representations, 7 April 1932, A. Mackay, Free Church Manse, to Rt. Hon. Sir Archibald Sinclair.
112. *Scotsman*, 20 Feb., p. 17; 14 April, p. 9; 15 April, p. 11; 19 April, p. 10; 21 April, p. 11; 6 May, p. 13; 7 May, p. 17; 11 May, p. 10; 12 May, p. 8; 24 May, p. 11; 28 May, p. 11; 30 May, p. 8; 27 June, p. 8; 30 June 1932, p. 10; NAS, HH1/2626, 13 April 1932, H of C Debates, Second Reading of Sunday Performance (Regulation) Bill; HH1/2628, Scottish Home Dept, Sunday Entertainment Bill, 1932, 27 May 1932, H of C Debates
113. *Scotsman*, 12 May 1932, p. 8; and 17 Oct. 1932, p. 8, for an early example of the Act in action, in Croydon.
114. *Scotsman*, 9 Feb. 1931, p. 11.
115. *Scotsman*, 28 April 1936, p. 8.
116. *Scotsman*, 18 Nov., p. 9; 23 Nov. 1931, p. 6; 21 Dec. 1932, p. 13; 15 Feb. 1933, p. 8.
117. *Scotsman*, 15 Sept. 1937, p. 7.
118. *Scotsman*, 8 April, p. 16; 3 Sept. 1936, pp. 6, 8.
119. *Scotsman*, 13 Oct. 1936, p. 8.
120. ECA, SL119/3/1, 28 Nov. 1930; *Scotsman*, 1 Dec. 1930, p. 13.
121. ECA, SL119/3/2, 3 Feb.; 2 March 1932.
122. ECA, SL119/3/2, 2 March; 28 Sept. 1932,
123. ECA, SL119/3/5, Edinburgh Corporation Minutes, Magistrates Committee, 1934–5, 9 Jan.; 6 Feb.; 3 April 1935.
124. ECA, SL119/3/5, 6 Feb.; 6 March 1935.
125. ECA, SL119/3/8, Edinburgh Corporation Minutes, Magistrates Committee, Session 1937–8, 26 Oct. 1938.
126. ECA, SL119/3/8, 2 March; 4 May 1938.
127. ECA, SL119/3/8, 2 March; 28 Sept. 1938.
128. ECA, SL119/3/8, 6 July 1938; SL119/3/9, Edinburgh Corporation Minutes, Magistrates Committee, Session 1938–9, 30 Nov. 1938.
129. ECA, SL119/3/9, 30 Nov. 1938.
130. ECA, SL119/3/8, 28 Sept. 1938.
131. *Scotsman*, 6 Nov. 1935, p. 8; 5 April 1939, p. 17.
132. *Scotsman*, 13 Dec. 1938, p. 12, minima varied from 90 per cent in Glasgow, 33.33 per cent in Edinburgh, and 45 per cent in Aberdeen. Earlier that year, there had been a move to raise the minimum in Edinburgh to 50 per cent, ECA, SL119/3/8, 2 Feb. 1938.
133. ECA, SL119/3/8, 5 Jan. 1938.
134. ECA, SL119/3/9, 30 Nov. 1938.
135. *Scotsman*, 13 May 1939, p. 18.

136. See Chapter 5, pp. 188–90.

137. *Scotsman*, 10 May 1939, p. 16.

138. *Scotsman*, 11 May 1939, p. 13.

139. Dickinson and Street, *Cinema and State*, p. 103; *Scotsman*, 25 Oct. 1939, p. 7.

140. NAS, HH1/2633, Scottish Home Dept, Sunday Entertainments, Representations and Enquiries, n.d., John Colquhoun, Convener, Sabbatarian Observance Committee, Free Church of Scotland to Secretary of State.

141. NAS, HH1/2633, 22 Nov. 1939, Principal Clerk of General Assembly of the Church of Scotland to Secretary of State; HH1/2632, Scottish Home Dept, Sunday Entertainments, Representations and Enquiries, 10 Nov. 1939, J. M. Munro, Clerk, Church of Scotland Presbytery of Linlithgow and Falkirk to n.k.; 28 Oct. 1939, J. R. S. Wilson, The Manse, Lomond Road, Trinity, Edinburgh, to Rt. Hon. Ernest Brown; HH1/2642, Scottish Home Dept, Notice for Question for Thursday 16th November 1939, 1 Nov. 1939, George Macnab, Moderator, D. J. Moir-Porteous, Senior Clerk, R. J. Mackay, Junior Clerk, Church of Scotland Presbytery of Greenock to Robert Gibson.

142. NAS, HH1/2632, 26 Oct. 1939, J. W. Scott, Secretary of Lord's Day Observance Association of Scotland, Western Committee, Paisley, to Secretary of State; HH1/2633, 29 Nov. 1939, Peter Lord, Secretary, Coatbridge Churches' Council, to Colville; 13 Dec. 1939, A. D. Cameron, Church Manse, Bonarbridge, to Walter Elliot.

143. NAS, HH1/2632, 30 Oct. 1939, J. Brazier Green, Social Welfare Secretary, Methodist Church in Scotland, to Colville.

144. NAS, HH1/2643, 8 Nov. 1939, C. H. Band to N. F. McNicoll, Intelligence Department, Special Inquiry into the Opening of Cinemas on Sundays for Troops and Munitions Workers.

145. NAS, HH1/2633, 22 Dec. 1939, Minute; HH1/2634, Minute; HH1/2642, Scottish Home Dept, Notice for Question for Thursday 16th Nov. 1939, Note of suggested reply.

146. *Scotsman*, 5 Feb., p. 3; 29 Feb. 1940, p. 5; ECA, SL119/3/10, Edinburgh Corporation Committee Minutes, Magistrates, Session 1939–40, 31 Jan.; 22 Feb.; 6 March 1940.

147. *Scotsman*, 28 Nov. 1939, p. 12; NAS, HH1/2632, 27 Oct. 1939, R. Mackintosh, Hon. Sec., Church of Scotland Committee on Church and the Nation, to Secretary of State.

148. *Scotsman*, 11 June, p. 3; 2 Oct., p. 5; 4 Oct. 1940, p. 3.

149. *Scotsman*, 3 Aug. 1940, p. 6.

150. *Scotsman*, 11 Oct. 1940, p. 3.

151. *Scotsman*, 25 Nov., p. 3; 29 Nov., p. 3; 5 Dec. 1940, p. 10.

152. Scotsman, 21 Dec. 1940, p. 5.

153. NAS, HH1/2634, 20 Jan. 1941, C. C. Cunningham to R. Milne, Scottish Home Dept.

154. *Scotsman*, 21 Feb., p. 6; 24 Feb. 1941, p. 6.

155. NAS, HH1/2634, n.d., Note for Deputation from Church of Scotland Committee on Church and Nation; 5 Feb. 1941, War Cabinet, Sunday Opening

of Cinemas and Theatres, Memorandum by Secretary of State for Scotland; 5 Jan. 1941, Major C. H. Callender, h.q., Scottish Command to Secretary, Convention of Royal Burghs.

156. NAS, HH1/2635, 20 March 1941, Brian N. Gandon, General Secretary, Glasgow YMCA to Johnston.

157. NAS, HH1/2634, n.d., Note for Deputation for Church of Scotland Committee on Church and Nation.

158. *Scotsman*, 26 Feb. 1941, p. 9.

159. NAS, HH1/2647, 31 March 1941, Confidential Note on Sunday Opening of Theatres etc. in Scotland. Intelligence 54.

160. NAS, HH1/2644, cutting from *Courier and Advertiser*, 20 March 1941; *Scotsman*, 21 March, p. 6; 6 June 1941, p. 3.

161. ECA, SL119/3/11, Edinburgh Corporation Committee Minutes, Magistrates, Session 1940–1, 5 March 1941; NAS, HH1/2644, cutting from *Edinburgh Evening Dispatch*, 3 April 1941; cutting from *Daily Express*, 4 April 1941.

162. NAS, GD289/2/4, Playhouse Cinema, Running Book, 11 Oct. 1940–30 Jan. 1943, Cinema Sunday, 24 Aug. 1941.

163. NAS, HH1/2635, 2 Feb., James Thornley, Gallery Street, Paisley, National Council of Labour 'Help for Russia' Fund to Town Clerk, Barrhead; 12 Feb., Town Clerk to Thornley; 3 March, Thornley to Johnston; 5 March 1942, R. H. Law, Scottish Office to W. Park, Scottish Home Dept, confirming that authority resided locally and not with the Secretary of State.

164. *Scotsman*, 18 Sept. 1942, p. 3; NAS, HH1/2643, cutting *Edinburgh Evening Dispatch*, 17 Sept. 1942; HH1/2647, Minute, 18 Sept. 1942.

165. NAS, HH1/2647, 17 Nov. 1942, Fairgrieve to Chief Constables.

166. NAS, HH1/2647, 25 Nov. 1942, Opening of Cinemas on Sundays in Scotland; *Scotsman*, 1 Oct. 1942, pp. 3, 9, letter of A. S. Albin, chair of Edinburgh branch of CEA.

167. NAS, HH1/2648, Scottish Home Dept, Chief Constables' Reports on Sunday Cinema Opening, 20 Nov. 1942, Chief Constable, Orkney Constabulary, Kirkwall, to Fairgrieve.

168. NAS, HH1/2647, 18 Jan. 1943, Thomas Johnston to Sir Murdoch Macdonald.

169. NAS, HH1/2648, 18 Nov. 1942, Chief Constable of Ayrshire to Fairgrieve.

170. *Scotsman*, 2 Oct., p. 3; 13 Oct., p. 3; 14 Oct., p. 3; 15 Oct., p. 3; 20 Oct. 1942, p. 3.

171. NAS, HH1/2648, 18 Nov. 1942, P. I. Sillitoe, Chief Constable, City of Glasgow Police to Fairgrieve.

172. NAS, HH1/2647, cutting from *Scotsman*, 16 Oct. 1942; HH1/2648, 19 Nov. 1942, Chief Constable, City of Edinburgh Police to Fairgrieve.

173. NAS, HH1/2648, 20 Nov. 1942, Superintendent and Deputy Chief Constable, Dumfries County Police to Fairgrieve.

174. NAS, HH1/2648, 19 Nov. 1942, Chief Constable, Inverness-shire Constabulary to Fairgrieve.

175. NAS, HH1/2648, 18 Nov. 1942, Chief Constable, Ross and Cromarty Constabulary, Dingwall to Fairgrieve.

176. NAS, HH1/2648, 18 Nov. 1942, Sillitoe to Fairgrieve.

177. NAS, HH1/2648, 18 Nov. 1942, Superintendent and Deputy Chief Constable, Selkirkshire Constabulary to Fairgrieve.

178. NAS, HH1/2644, cutting from *Dundee Courier*, 7 May 1943.

179. ECA, SL119/3/12, Edinburgh Corporation Committee Minutes, Magistrates, Session 1941–2, 9, 15 Oct. 1942.

180. NAS, GD289/2/5, Playhouse Cinema, Running Book, 1 Feb. 1943–1 May 1948.

181. NAS, HH1/2648, 19 Nov. 1942, Chief Constable, City of Edinburgh Police to Fairgrieve.

182. *Scotsman*, 23 May 1944, p. 3, observation by the President of Edinburgh YMCA at the Annual Assemblies' Rally in Defence of the Sabbath; see also 25 May 1943, p. 6.

183. NAS, HH1/2635, 30 March 1945, General Secretary of LDOAS to Johnston.

184. NAS, HH1/2635, cutting from *Glasgow Herald*, 16 April 1945; *Scotsman*, 7 Nov. 1945, p. 3.

185. NAS, GD289/2/5, Playhouse Cinema, Running Book, 1943–8, 31 March 1946; GD289/2/18, Palace Cinema, Running Book, 1943–8, 7 April 1946; HH1/2647, cutting from *Glasgow Herald*, 3 June 1948.

186. NAS, HH1/2647, cutting from *Edinburgh Evening Dispatch*, 20 Aug. 1946; SSA, 2/1/2, Federation of Scottish Film Societies, Minutes of Council, Meeting at Waverley Hotel, London, 7 Sept. 1946, at which it was noted that Stirling was 'the first town to have Sunday opening in Scotland'.

187. *Scotsman*, 16 Jan., p. 3; 16 Jan., p. 3; 17 Jan., p. 3; 11 Feb., p. 3; 20 Feb. 1948, p. 3.

188. NAS, HH1/2647, cutting from *Glasgow Herald*, 31 March 1948; *Scotsman*, 4 Feb., p. 3; 18 Feb. 1948, p. 3.

189. NAS, HH1/2647, cutting from *Glasgow Herald*, 31 March 1948.

190. NAS, HH1/2647, cutting from *Edinburgh Evening Dispatch*, 27 March 1947; *Scotsman*, 27 March 1947; ECA, SL119/3/17, Edinburgh Corporation Committee Minutes, Magistrates, 2 April 1947.

191. ECA, SL119/3/17, 30 April 1947.

192. NAS, HH1/2647, cutting from *Scotsman*, 3 April 1947; ECA, SL119/3/17, 30 April 1947; *Scotsman*, 1 May 1947, p. 5.

193. *Scotsman*, 10 Nov., p. 3; 6 Dec. 1947, p. 3.

194. *Scotsman*, 24 June 1948, p. 3.

195. *Scotsman*, 5 Nov. 1945, p. 3.

196. *Scotsman*, 7 Nov., p. 3; 12 Nov. 1948, p. 3, reporting that 500 were turned away from the show at the Ca'dano Restaurant.

197. *Scotsman*, 5 Dec., p. 3; 6 Dec. 1947, p. 3.

198. NAS, HH1/2647, cutting from *Edinburgh Evening Dispatch*, 21 Jan. 1949; *Scotsman*, 19 March 1949; Town Clerk, Burgh of Loanhead to Secretary, Scottish Home Dept, 19 Feb. 1949; Secretary to Town Clerk, 2 March 1949.

199. *Scotsman*, 15 March 1950, p. 5.

200. NAS, HH1/2647, H of C Debates, 10 May 1949.

201. ECA, SL119/3/18–20, Edinburgh Corporation Committee Minutes, Magistrates, 1948–50.

202. *Scotsman*, 26 April 1947, p. 3; the local Film Society was also allowed to hold performances on Sundays from 1946, a right denied it before 1939, see Chapter 6, p. 231.
203. NAS, HH1/2647, cutting from *Glasgow Herald*, 31 March 1948.

5

An Essential Social Habit: Cinema-going in the Early Sound Era, c. 1927–39

I

Several features mark out the years from the late 1920s as a distinct phase in cinema history. The period opened with the most radical technological innovation to affect the industry since its late-nineteenth-century origins; the advent of pictures with synchronised sound.[1] It was a development whose potential ramifications were thought to be extensive, taking in not only the aural experience of cinema-goers, but extending to the structure of the exhibition business itself. The coming of sound worked, it has been argued, to consolidate the position of large theatre combines, already growing through the 1920s, and the importance of the centrally sited picture palace over smaller, less well-appointed venues.[2] It also made additional demands of the cinema audience, the appreciation of mainly dialogue-driven narratives requiring the application of a wider range of senses and enjoining what, for some, was an unusual and unwelcome quiet to the auditorium.[3] Alongside sound, exhibitors were also confronted by an altered legislative context, in which they were obliged to devote specified portions of screen time to productions of British origin. Initiated in 1927, the same year that the release of *The Jazz Singer* in the USA alerted audiences to the potential of synchronised sound, quota regulations applied with varying degrees of severity for the remainder of the period covered by this book.[4] Their impact is reflected most obviously through the changing fortunes of the production sector in Britain. For Rachael Low, the Act of 1927 did much to discredit the British film in the eyes of native cinema-goers, as it encouraged the proliferation of hastily and cheaply mounted productions, some of which, so legend has it, were deemed only fit for screening early in the morning to cleaning staff.[5] Others have discerned a more positive outcome for this early exercise in State protection, as products of British origin are seen to have had a marked appeal at the box office. Nevertheless, debate continues as to whether popularity was confined to films whose production values and budgets matched the best coming out of Hollywood, and which emerged in greater number from the mid 1930s, or whether material culturally derided as quota fodder in fact secured a sizeable following, particularly among picture-goers in the English provinces, providing the basis for a popular, commercially viable native cinema.[6]

As this suggests, interpretations of developments in the 1930s rest to a substantial degree on perceptions of the audience, and it is in this period that the study of cinema-going is transformed from a branch of the alchemist's art, deriving conclusions from diverse material of often indirect relevance, to a fit subject for the statistician. From the mid 1930s, returns from the payment of entertainments tax provide a continuous series charting change in the size of the national (UK) audience for film.[7] While such figures form the basis for more robust generalisations concerning the extent of the cinema-going habit, they leave unresolved more detailed questions concerning audience behaviour and preferences. On the latter, those within the trade gained regular insights into patrons' views through returns at the box office. Some sought to supplement the information thus provided through more direct and detailed surveys, such as the questionnaires devised by Sydney Bernstein and periodically distributed to customers at his Granada chain of theatres, or by means of local exploitation campaigns, such as that mounted by Sydney Friedman of the King's Theatre, Greenock, in 1929, in which patrons were invited to declare their preferences and offer a critical evaluation of their favourite film in return for a prize of £5.[8] As the period progressed, insights into such questions were gathered from beyond the industry itself, as cinema's importance as an aspect of the new mass entertainment culture gained increasing recognition. As part of its drive to extend understanding of popular patterns of belief and behaviour, Mass-Observation was a regular visitor to the cinema in the years from 1937, its efforts supplemented by other investigators as cinema-going reached a new peak in numerical terms.

These surveys generated important findings, which have provided the basis for enduring generalisations concerning audience behaviour and attitudes in this period. Mass-Observation's enquiries, particularly that undertaken in 'Worktown' (Bolton) in 1937, discovered a marked preference among cinema-goers for American over British films, a tendency most pronounced among patrons of halls in the poorer areas of the town. A fracturing of taste according to class was thus detected, with working-class picture-goers most receptive to the products of Hollywood studios, and, at the same time, least tolerant of perceived shortcomings in British subjects.[9] Subsequent research, often drawing on another kind of source material or adopting an alternative methodological approach, has sought to test such depictions, while offering new perspectives of its own. A more detailed understanding of film preferences among particular audiences has been attempted through the analysis of surviving box-office data for individual cinemas. While the isolated and fragmentary nature of such material discourages attempts to extrapolate from the trends indicated, such studies, encompassing halls in London and Portsmouth, have served to point up enduring geographical differences in taste.[10] In the absence of a widespread and accessible body of box-office data, a more indirect approach to the question of film preferences has been attempted through the study of booking practices at both a national and local level. The readiness of managements to book particular features, to the extent that choice could be exercised, and the potential returns generated from screenings at various venues provide the basis for John Sedgwick's reconstruction of audience taste in the mid 1930s. The result has been to call into question one of the key conclusions offered by the Mass-Observation survey, the superior appeal of American films, but has also served to confirm the existence of regional variations in taste, in this case captured by a comparison of two English towns, one in the industrial north (Bolton once more) and the other a popular resort on the south coast (Brighton).[11] If Sedgwick's work has done much to identify the popularity of larger-budget British productions, the investigation by Steve Chibnall into the reception of cheaper home-produced features suggests a distinctive outlook among provincial audiences. The thrust of this work is thus to confirm growing doubts as to the existence of anything approximating to a coherent and unified national audience for film.[12]

Scotland's place within this picture of regional and social diversity has not, as yet, been subject to systematic investigation. Yet the survival north of the border of a sizeable body of business data, albeit one subject to a degree of geographical and chronological clustering, offers the potential for a detailed evaluation of the principal issues surrounding the cinema-going experience in the early sound era. Records relating to some thirty-five cinemas have been utilised, extending from Stranraer and Galashiels in the south to Aberdeen in the north. While coverage is inevitably uneven, the material enables us to look beyond the aggregated coverage provided by the tax returns to reconstruct cinema-goers' behaviour at various levels, extending in some cases to daily attendance patterns. The prospect thus held out of reconstructing in close detail a key recreational pursuit of the period is undoubtedly alluring, but the results generated also have shortcomings. The figures convey levels of attendance, takings, and profit generated by particular features, but say little of the quality of patrons' response and are frustratingly mute on the potential for varying experiences within the audience, particularly those arising from age and gender differences. Nevertheless, any problems with the figures should not be overdone. A comparison between cinemas facilitates an exploration of fractures in taste along the lines of geography and, in certain cases, class. In addition, by reconstructing patterns of attendance over time, a central feature of cinema-going in this period may be evaluated, the degree to which it was driven by force of habit or was informed at all times by the exercise of choice. The factors determining the decision whether or not to enter the cinema ranged from the attraction of particular programmes, the availability of alternative amusements, and the state of the weather, ever a consideration thus far north. To that extent, quantification can offer insights into more qualitative aspects of cinema-going through the period.

This is not, however, to downplay the potential contribution of other forms of evidence. Insights into the manner in which cinema-goers responded to the films they witnessed have been sought through the recollections, gathered through written and oral testimony, of those who attended picture houses in the early days of sound. Yet, while such approaches help to clarify the manner in which picture-going is remembered, utilising particular tropes of memory, the patina accruing over the intervening decades almost inevitably precludes precise recall of immediate responses to particular films.[13] With that in mind, this chapter seeks to draw on two guides to contemporary reception of early sound films: the growing body of journalistic discussion of cinema in the local press, which became more systematic and reflective from the 1930s, and surviving diaries of picture-goers. The latter, although few in number, provide some measure of reception unmediated by time and serve to locate cinema-going more firmly within the fabric of everyday life.

In the chapter that follows, these perspectives are applied first in considering the impact of sound film, both for cinema-goers and for the exhibition sector more generally. Attention then turns to patterns of cinema-going over varying spans of time as a way into evaluating the issue of film preferences, as expressed through box-office returns and rationalised, as far as that was possible, by press or diary entry. In the process, an attempt is made to identify contours of taste and to consider the degree to which there may be said to have existed a distinctive, national audience for film across Scotland.

II

The rise of the 'talkies' north of the border, as elsewhere, was rapid and profound. Late in 1928, the Playhouse in Edinburgh was heralded as the first theatre north of the Tweed to have a complete sound system installed, a move which marked the abandonment of plans to operate as a cine-variety hall, combining film with live entertainment, in favour of functioning as a dedicated cinema.[14] At the other end of Princes Street, the wiring of Synod Hall for sound in July 1929 signalled the end of the hall's career as a provider of varied entertainments. As a result, the appearance of Poole's Myriorama the previous Christmas proved to be its last at that venue.[15] From the later months of 1929, the transition from silence to sound accelerated. The 1930 edition of *Kinematograph Year Book* recorded sound installations at fifty-six of Scotland's 605 cinemas, while further change was anticipated by the re-equipment of over seventy houses which, through the good offices of John Maxwell, were part of the Associated British Cinemas chain.[16] If the output of sound films at this point allowed few cinemas to function as talkie-only houses, so that silents figured on bills at the Edinburgh Playhouse when it finally opened in August 1929, this proved a passing phase.[17] A survey of exhibitors in the east of Scotland early in 1930 found that sixty-nine halls planned to continue functioning as silent cinemas, a potential level of demand which it was acknowledged would not suffice to justify the continued production of such films in any volume. As Louis Dickson of the Bo'ness Hippodrome remarked at the exhibitors' meeting at which the returns were discussed, 'It looked as if the silent halls were not going to have much to look forward to.'[18] The prescience of this view became clear the following year when the Hamilton Picture House Co., Ltd opted for voluntary liquidation 'owing to the dearth of silent pictures of the type that appealed to their clientele'. With choice limited to the kind of 'wild and woolly' western subjects, which in the opinion of one of the company's directors 'would bore our patrons stiff', and with the cost of hiring sound films considered 'altogether prohibitive', the decision to close rather than re-equip the house seemed inescapable.[19] More generally, market pressures drove cinemas relentlessly in the direction of sound.

Yet the talkies' triumph was achieved in the face of considerable critical scepticism as to their artistic merit and popular appeal. Into the last weeks of 1928, senior figures in the British film industry, including Basil Dean of Gainsborough Pictures, continued to see sound as an occasional supplement to the mature art form that was silent cinema.[20] It was a view endorsed by local writers on film, including the correspondent of the *Evening Times* in Glasgow, 'Kinoman', for whom the future of sound lay in 'the provision of "turns" as interludes, effects in presentation, and (conceded with reluctance) the occasional introduction of the human voice'.[21] Its wider application was considered a backward step artistically and technically for the industry, as the requirements of dialogue confined production to interior settings. The spatial and imaginative freedoms encouraged by silent film were being lost, so that for 'Kinoman', 'The spoken word has set up a barrier in Filmdom'.[22]

For all the criticisms levelled against the talkie, audience reaction to the coming of sound was, at first sight at least, altogether more positive. Certainly, the debut of talking pictures in Glasgow in January 1929 occasioned notable expressions of enthusiasm from picture-goers, the audience at the Coliseum breaking into spontaneous applause at the screening of *The Singing Fool*, with Al Jolson.[23] For one local patron, whose views come down to us via her diaries, the response was equally favourable. Kitty McGinniss, who attended one show of *The Singing Fool* two days after her twenty-first birthday, adjudged it a splendid picture, the only note of disappointment caused by its failure to induce her friend, who was also in attendance, to cry.[24] At the end of the month, 'Kinoman' canvassed readers' opinions on the sound film, and while some, such as one correspondent signing him- or herself 'Silent Art', expressed concern that talkies would discourage the creative camera work that distinguished the best silent subjects, others, including a reader from Clydebank, were of the view that sound added a new realism to screen characterisations, now conveyed through the voice and not through gesture alone.[25]

That the latter expressed a sentiment that was more widely shared became apparent over time, as prevailing opinion was forcibly reflected through box-office returns. Halls making the transition to sound reaped an immediate bounty, as audiences responded to the promise of novelty. At Synod Hall, where the talkie era was launched in July 1929 with a Fox double bill comprising *Speakeasy*, a drama starring Lola Lane, and a comedy support, *The Diplomats*, featuring former vaudeville performer Bobby Clark, profits jumped by some 37 per cent, an achievement all the more impressive given both the high and consistent levels of profitability achieved here as elsewhere in the late silent period, and the higher cost of renting sound films.[26] By contrast, where screens remained silent, the fall-off in business was rapid and pronounced. As has been seen, Edinburgh's Palace Cinema operated almost invariably in the black through the later silent years. In 1928, profits were recorded in all fifty-two weeks and if, on occasion, the surplus was minor, twice falling below £10, in most weeks (over thirty in all) it exceeded £100.[27] Takings continued to be healthy well into the following year, averaging £463.34p across the first thirty-two weeks of 1929, less than £8 down on the figure for the whole of 1928 (expressed as decimals where averages calculated).[28] From that point, the Palace found itself competing not only against established businesses re-equipped for sound, but also new cinemas built to exploit the talkies, such as the nearby Playhouse, owned by the same company, which opened its doors in mid August. The balance sheet recorded a marked downturn in trade. In the final twenty weeks of 1929, weekly receipts fell by almost a quarter, averaging £350.40p.[29] The squeeze in profits was even more pronounced. Whereas, in the first thirty-two weeks of the year, an average surplus of £80.91p had been recorded, the business experiencing a loss in just four weeks, in two of which a local flu epidemic had worked to depress attendances, in the last four and a half months, losses were recorded on eight occasions, reducing the average profit margin to a mere £7.25p.[30] Conditions worsened further in 1930. In the final phase of the hall's career as a silent cinema, comprising the first forty weeks of the year, takings at an average of £278.05p a week were down by 41 per cent on the 1928 level. Losses were returned in twenty-five weeks, while in one more the hall did no more than break even. Where profits were earned, the returns were meagre, exceeding £50 on only three occasions.[31] The descent into loss proved lasting, despite significant savings achieved in the cost of hiring films, as silent subjects increasingly became a drug on the market. In 1928–9, the average cost of each programme varied between £90.86p and £104.36p. By 1930, this had fallen to an average of £53.15p, encompassing a low point in one week of £16. Even this failed to avert a loss, the combination of a German film, *Their Son*, released at home under the rather more promising title *Sensation im Wintergarten*, and a British support feature, *The Love Story of Aliette Brunton*, generating only £190 at the box office, thus ensuring a deficit of £68 on the week.[32] The economics of the business, reflecting in large degree shifts in popular sentiment, now worked inexorably against the silent film.

Yet the evidence of Kitty McGinniss' diaries suggests that acceptance of the talkie was neither immediate nor unequivocal. The advent of sound did little to alter the frequency of her visits to the cinema, the forty-seven attendances recorded in 1929 matching the average for three of the preceding years.[33] In the early weeks of the year, she continued to attend screenings of silent films and broadly approved of what she saw, the rather tepid verdict passed on Frank Borzage's *Street Angel* as 'Not Bad' contrasting with more favourable judgements, such as that offered for John Ford's *Four Sons* ('very good').[34] In later months, talkies figured more prominently in her choice of pictures and, here again, her comments were broadly favourable, Hitchcock's *Blackmail*, *The Broadway Melody*, and Fox's *Movietone Follies of 1929* all securing the grading 'A1'.[35] Yet, significantly, it was only with the Vitaphone musical *Broadway Babies*, seen at the New Savoy at the end of November, that she felt able to confide, 'Liking talkies better now.'[36] Her readiness to continue patronising sound pictures, even when doubtful of their merits, is testimony to how decisively audience opinion had shifted against the silent film. By the second half of 1929, few exhibitors needed persuading that sound represented the future. For those who continued to hold out, the prospect, as the examples of the Palace and the Hamilton Picture House demonstrated, was bleak.

The changing technological and legislative context of the period had further consequences for the exhibition sector. Previous chapters have noted an increasing tendency, particularly after the First World War, to centralise film-booking arrangements and to consolidate the ownership of cinemas into circuits of increasing size and complexity.[37] That trend was given renewed impetus by quota legislation, which created conditions conducive to the emergence of vertically integrated concerns on lines similar to those active in the USA.[38] Both the Gaumont-British Picture Corporation and the Associated British Picture Corporation were active in the late 1920s in seeking to acquire theatrical interests in Scotland. At different points in 1928–9, the Aberdeen Picture Palaces, Ltd was in negotiations with the Ostrer brothers, owners of the Denman Picture Houses, Ltd, a subsidiary of Gaumont, and John Maxwell of ABC, for the sale of the whole or part of the business.[39] At the same time, the Regent Picture House in Glasgow, formerly the Cinema House, was subject to an approach by the London-based British Foreign and Colonial Corporation, Ltd, which the board seemed more than happy to entertain.[40] The process continued into the following decade, so that in 1936, Singletons, with several halls in and around Glasgow, sold their interests in United Cinemas, Ltd and Vogue Cinemas, Ltd to Odeon Theatres, Ltd of Birmingham.[41] The growing incursion of English capital into the exhibition business north of the border gave rise, as earlier chapters have noted, to expressions of concern as to its potential cultural implications, with various aspects of Scottish life, some of which such as Sabbath observance helped to define a sense of nationhood, exposed to threat.[42] Yet the challenge to Scotland's economic and cultural autonomy should not be overstated. The approaches made to the Aberdeen Picture Palaces, Ltd by Denman and ABC both came to nothing. In each case, the value to be placed on the business proved the sticking point.[43] At the same time, the readiness of the Regent's directors to sell provoked legal action by shareholders opposed to any such move. By the summer of 1928, the London syndicate had withdrawn from the agreement and the existing board had sold its shares to the complainants, resulting in the appointment of a new set of directors.[44] This now sought an alternative way forward for the Regent as an independent concern, functioning as 'a second run house, or at any rate a second rate house with cheap features'. The hall thus became part of the booking circuit being built up by Alexander B. King.[45]

For all the alarm expressed at the increased influence of English values and capital on key aspects of Scottish life, the presence of the leading southern circuits among exhibition outlets north of the border was, when viewed in the aggregate, limited at best. Between them, the ABPC, Gaumont, and Odeon circuits controlled eighty-four or 14.1 per cent of the 597 venues active across Scotland in 1937. Reflecting its roots in Maxwell's Scottish Cinemas and Variety Theatres, Ltd, ABPC had much the largest presence with forty-nine houses. By comparison, the circuit overseen by King stood at fifty-five.[46] Into the early sound era, then, if the trend was to seek economies of scale through the pooling of managerial or booking arrangements, control for the most part continued to reside within Scotland. Not untypical of such arrangements was the Lockerbie Cinema Co., Ltd, established in 1932, which booked films through Green's of Glasgow, the company which also supplied the house's manager.[47] Similarly, the Stranraer Picture House, Ltd drew on the experience of the Maguire family, long active in the management of two Edinburgh halls, the Palace and the Playhouse.[48] It might also be noted that, in common with earlier waves of cinema development, companies launched in the 1930s endeavoured to exploit local sources of capital. So, of seventy applications for shares in the Stranraer house in 1931, only two came from beyond Scotland, one from a London salesman and the other from a manufacturer based in Lisburn, Northern Ireland.[49] A comparable distribution was evident at Stornoway on the isle of Lewis, where in 1933 the local Playhouse, Ltd was floated on what some might regard as the rather optimistic belief 'that there is a widespread demand in Stornoway for a modern and well-equipped picture house'.[50] Of seventy-four share allocations made by the company between 1933 and 1938, twenty-three were to local residents and only one went beyond the national boundary, to a teacher in Hereford.[51] Although subject, like so much of British industry in this period, to corporate forms of organisation, the cinema trade north of the border retained a distinctively Scottish character into the early sound era.

The promise of sustained profitability held out by the favourable trading context in the wake of the Quota Act of 1927 had been the principal factor tempting the major British circuits to acquire halls in Scotland. As has been seen, many cinemas which had struggled financially in the early 1920s were operating with secure and stable margins as the decade approached its close.[52] While understandable, expectations that such conditions would be maintained were not borne out in practice. Rewiring for sound offered an immediate boost to receipts, sufficient that graphs charting the financial performance of houses run by Green's had to be recalibrated to reflect the growth in business.[53] In 1930, the inauguration of sound at the Palace in Edinburgh with the Fox comedy musical *Sunny Side Up*, starring Janet Gaynor and Charles Farrell, generated takings in excess of £500 over the week for the first time since August 1929.[54] Beyond the short term, however, returns were much less certain. The consistent profitability of the late silent era was not sustained with the coming of sound, so that for the Palace the 1930s proved to be a decade in which the balance sheet recorded low and fluctuating margins. The highest annual profit achieved in the period, £2,603 in 1935–6, was below returns in the later 1920s, and in three further years in the 1930s the concern slipped into the red.[55] While the Palace's new status as a second-run house to the more prestigious Playhouse undoubtedly contributed to this modest performance, it fails by itself fully to account for it. Elsewhere, the early sound years were also distinguished by profit levels that were, in comparison with other periods, low. At the Playhouse in Edinburgh, access to first-run features generated sufficient business to ensure against losses, but in four years to 1939 net margins were barely half those recorded in the cinema's first two years of operations and, in the final pre-war year, fell below £1,000.[56] Away from the capital, a broadly comparable pattern applied. Across the Forth, profits at the Dunfermline Cinema House, Ltd, contracted markedly from 1931, falling to less than half their late-silent equivalents, although here takings recovered strongly from 1936.[57] Margins were also squeezed further north, in Aberdeen, so that while all houses run by the local Picture Palaces, Ltd continued to operate in the black, balances were mostly well down on the levels achieved in the later 1920s. Taking 1927–8, the last full year in which the silent film held undisputed sway over the affections of cinema-goers across the city, as the standard, profits at the Star Picture Palace shrank between a quarter and a third to the mid point of the following decade. At other houses, the decline was even more pronounced, so that at the Globe and the Playhouse, returns declined to below 40 per cent of their pre-talkie levels.

Shareholders, whose expectations had been considerably pared down since the 'Klondyke' phase of the early post-war years, now found that even modest rates of return on their investments could not be guaranteed. At the Playhouse, Galashiels (1920), Ltd, conditions were considered so unfavourable that directors were unable to recommend the payment of any dividend in the years prior to the hall's sale to ABPC in 1936.[58] Further west, the first year of operations for the Stranraer Picture House had generated

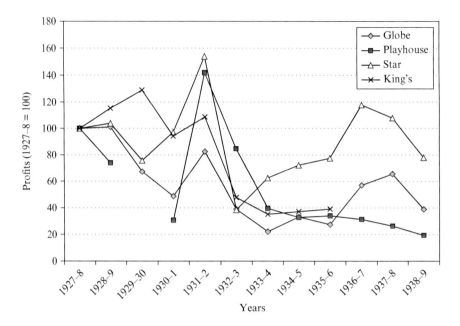

Figure 5.1   *Aberdeen Picture Palaces, Ltd, profits, 1927–39. (Source: Cinema Museum, Aberdeen Picture Palaces, Ltd, Accounts.)*

results which the board adjudged to be 'fairly satisfactory', the operating profit of £1,314 7s 5d sufficing to justify payment of a 5 per cent dividend. Yet returns later in the decade failed to match this result, so that shareholders at the firm's annual general meetings in both 1934 and 1935 demanded explanations for what were seen to be unsatisfactory trading performances.[59] Across much of Scotland, then, the 'Age of the Dream Palace', was a period of limited profitability and considerable investor unease.

Responses to expressions of concern over the deteriorating state of company balance sheets tended at times to stress particular, often highly localised circumstances. In accounting for a considerably reduced surplus following the Stranraer Picture House, Ltd's third year of business to July 1934, directors pointed to the impact of 'the exceptionally fine weather conditions', although they acknowledged 'the continued depression in trade generally'.[60] The following year, as profits plunged further to £106 18s 5d, much was made of the house's location, as the fall-off in business 'had been pretty general in Cinemas situated in agricultural areas'. In this instance, however, local conditions also offered salvation in the anticipated siting of an RAF base for 700 men close by.[61] Local peculiarities aside, a number of generic explanations were offered for the trends observed. The most immediate concerned returns at the box office. Although aggregate statistics, based on tax returns, suggested growth of 10 per cent in the national audience from mid decade, such figures omit the more economically volatile years prior to that date, and take no account of local variations within the period covered.[62] The records of individual businesses available for all or significant parts of the decade suggest that at the micro level, the experience was of takings that were at best stagnant and which more often showed a clear decline. At four halls owned by the Aberdeen Picture Palaces, Ltd that had operated in the silent era, drawings net of taxation were broadly down on their pre-talkie levels. At the Star, the fall bottomed out in 1933–4 at 83.4 per cent of the figure for 1927–8. This was, however, modest compared with the Globe, the Playhouse, and the King's, where the equivalent figures showed declines of between 31 and 38 per cent. From that point, any upturn was modest, and only at the Star did takings briefly exceed those achieved in the late silent period.

Returns from halls belonging to the nearby Donald's circuit convey a similar impression. Although figures are more sporadic, with a continuous series only available from 1934–5, these still suggest that drawings at mid decade were substantially down on those of 1930–1. At both the Grand Central Picture House and the Cinema House, falls of over a quarter were recorded over the five years, a trend that continued over the final years leading up to the outbreak of war.[63] Extending the geographical coverage beyond the north-east does nothing to challenge the pattern presented

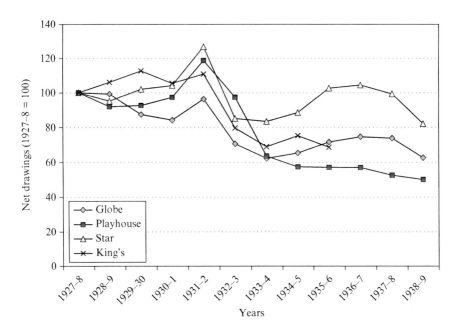

Figure 5.2 *Aberdeen Picture Palaces, Ltd, net drawings, 1927–39. (Source: Cinema Museum, Aberdeen Picture Palaces, Ltd, Accounts.)*

thus far. Over the quinquennium from 1930, receipts at Glasgow's Regent Cinema fell by almost 20 per cent, slipping by a further 10 per cent in the years to 1938.[64]

For contemporaries, explanations for trends such as these were clear. Two related developments received particular attention. The first was the marked economic downturn of the early 1930s, but to this was added a further factor of significance for an industry heavily reliant on an audience whose discretionary spending power was limited: an increase in the rate of entertainments tax in the emergency Budget of 1931, resulting in the first upward revision in seat prices since the start of the 1920s.[65] With higher rates applying to all seats priced 3d and over, A. B. King was drawn to predict before the annual meeting of the Scottish CEA in January 1932 that 'If that tax was not abolished, many of the working-class cinemas would go out of existence.'[66] With businesses unable or unwilling themselves to take on the extra cost imposed by higher rates of duty, the burden was, almost invariably, passed on to consumers in the form of higher prices. Directors of the Aberdeen Picture Palaces, Ltd calculated that the hike in tax rates would reduce business at the concern's east-end houses by £20 a week, transforming a modest operating profit into a loss. Admission prices were consequently raised, with the result that while profits continued to be earned, 'very much decreased returns from these houses' were reported.[67] In the circumstances, upkeep of the physical fabric became more difficult, so that in March 1933, it was reported that paint was peeling off the ceiling of the Globe and falling onto patrons below.[68] The higher prices being charged for such unpromising conditions were increasingly seen as unjustified commercially. With audiences rarely exceeding one-third of the capacity of each hall, the board moved to reduce the cost of admission, with the first concession made for children. The significant increase in attendances that resulted encouraged further reductions in prices, but, although audiences grew further, the requirement that the firm itself absorb a greater proportion of the tax burden mitigated any gain in profits.[69]

In most cases, higher prices continued to apply until 1935, when in the Budget of that year, reflecting the broad improvement in government finances as economic recovery took hold, the rate of duty was reduced.[70] At halls where profits had been squeezed to that point, there was some reluctance to pass the reduction on to customers. Many, like the Stranraer Picture House, Ltd, were driven to do so, as the secretary explained, 'not by desire, but from necessity', as the only other exhibitor in the town, the Kinema, had already moved to reduce its prices.[71] Across the decade, then, price changes offered firms little relief from financial difficulty. Unless matched by competitors, any upward revision in prices, unmatched by an improvement in facilities, would result in a loss of custom. So, the only change in the cost of admission in the period covered by this chapter came through the variations in tax rates. Competition between houses continued to be driven more by product than by price, a practice that had important implications for another part of the balance sheet.

If, through the early 1930s, the CEA in Scotland remained convinced that the burden of entertainments tax represented the trade's 'real bugbear', it remained difficult to disentangle its effects completely from those wrought by changes in the wider economy.[72] The increase in duty formed part of emergency measures introduced in September 1931 designed to plug a growing gap in government finances, as tax revenues fell and transfer payments to the growing army of unemployed rose.[73] The ability of regular cinema-goers to bear the cost of higher seat prices in a recession was doubted, so that a small number of concerns, including the Playhouse in Edinburgh, opted to maintain existing charges on most seats, absorbing the increased tax burden themselves.[74] Significantly, there is little evidence that this concession did much to boost business. At the Playhouse, attendances fell by almost 20 per cent in the years to 1932–3, and although they then recovered, in line with movements in the economic cycle to peak in 1937–8, the figure of 1,352,110 was still 7.5 per cent down on the hall's first year of operations in 1929–30.[75] The contrast was even more pronounced at the Palace on Princes Street, where takings were by 1932–3 over 30 per cent down on the pre-talkie peak of 1927–8. Recovery from that point was modest, and the most productive year, both in terms of receipts and admissions across the 1930s, in 1935–6, was still 25 per cent shy of the hall's best year as a silent picture palace.[76] Further north and east, at the Aberdeen Picture Palaces, Ltd's new centrally located cinema, the Capitol, which opened in 1933, weekly attendances peaked at a point before the remission in entertainments tax came into force, before stabilising towards the end of the decade at a level some 10 per cent lower.[77]

The suggestion from all this is that changes in the rate of taxation, although clearly a problem for the industry, were not of themselves decisive in shaping the fortunes of the exhibition sector through the early sound era. That broader economic circumstances had, on balance, a more important bearing on movements in the balance sheet is suggested by the experience of halls in the heavy industrial areas of west-central Scotland. Here, whatever stimulus to business may have been offered by the reduction in tax in 1935 was exceeded by increased levels of industrial activity more generally, first as a consequence of the upturn in the wider economy and then through increased rearmament expenditure.[78] The Picture House in the industrial town of Wishaw near Motherwell thus recorded a 33.1 per cent increase in weekly takings between 1934 and 1938, considerably in excess of any national upturn in business.[79] Even this was dwarfed by growth achieved at the Picture House's sister hall, the newly refurbished Wellington Palace in Glasgow's Gorbals district. Here, average monthly receipts of £349 in 1934 had risen three years later to just over £883, an increase in excess of 250 per cent.[80] Where local conditions allowed, then, box-office returns were capable of considerable buoyancy. Nevertheless, the evidence across much of Scotland suggests that drawings and attendances remained at best flat over the decade as a whole and failed to respond to any stimulus provided by the reduction in taxation. Such trends gave point to claims that the industry was labouring under excess capacity. Reports to the Scottish CEA as early as 1932 had identified Edinburgh as being 'over-cinemad'.[81]

Before considering the implications such patterns might have for an understanding of cinema-going in the early sound era, attention must also be given to developments on the expenditure side of the balance sheet. Along with declining income levels, exhibitors identified an increase in costs, directly attributable to the coming of sound, as a factor compounding their difficulties. So, in explaining a fall in net profits from £521 7s 3d to £41 0s 5d between 1929 and 1930, the directors of the Playhouse in Galashiels made much of 'the exorbitant charges exerted by the Film Renters for the hire of Talking Films'.[82] The point was reiterated in reports to shareholders over each of the next four years, suggesting its importance for the industry as a whole.[83] In the silent era, cinemas acquired films mostly through payment of a flat fee, so that any bounty from the greater popularity of a particular feature accrued to the exhibitor. With the advent of sound, however, the hire of principal features was increasingly conducted on a percentage basis, with the proportion of receipts payable to the distributor rising as takings increased. For example, in June 1935, the Playhouse acquired the Warner thriller *Bordertown*, with Paul Muni and Bette Davis, on terms which reserved 33.33 per cent for the distributor on drawings up to £1,200, rising to 40 per cent on the next £300, and to 50 per cent when receipts exceeded £1,500.[84] The impact on hall finances could be profound. At the Palace in Edinburgh, the flat-rate system limited the weekly outlay on film hire to between £57 and £122 in 1928. With payments linked to a percentage of the box office, fluctuations became more marked, so that in 1936 the variation was between £41 and £279. Profit margins were thus narrower, averaging £48 8s in the latter year compared with £115 14s in the former, and were altogether less predictable.[85]

For films expected to generate high levels of interest, a single percentage figure applied, regardless of amounts taken on the door. In October 1935, for example, the Playhouse in Edinburgh acquired the MGM adaptation of Dickens' *David Copperfield*, starring Freddie Bartholomew, Basil Rathbone, and W. C. Fields, at a flat 50 per cent. In the one week the film played, some 35,024 picture-goers were drawn to the hall, an audience some 45 per cent above the weekly average for the year as a whole. Although the cost of hire, at £864, was more than double the sum usually paid to distributors, the profit on the week of £185 exceeded the average figure by 55 per cent.[86] Provided expectations of higher than usual returns were realised, therefore, it paid cinemas to hire expensive star vehicles. A further calculation informed booking decisions. In 1932, another MGM spectacular, *Grand Hotel*, which

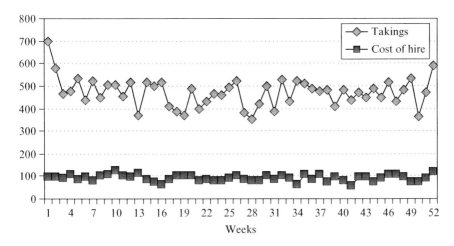

Figure 5.3 *Palace Cinema, takings and cost of film hire, 1928. (Source: NAS, GD289/1/3, Palace Cinema, Profit and Loss Ledger, weeks ending 7 Jan.–29 Dec. 1928.)*

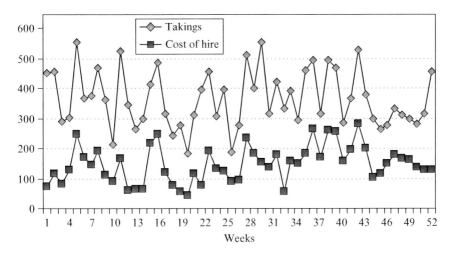

Figure 5.4 *Palace Cinema, weekly takings and cost of film hire, 1936. (Source: NAS, GD289/1/3, Palace Cinema, Profit and Loss Ledger, weeks ending 4 Jan. 1936– 2 Jan. 1937.)*

boasted among its cast Greta Garbo, John Barrymore, and Joan Crawford, was offered to the Aberdeen Picture Palaces, Ltd for its new cinema, the Capitol. The terms were 50 per cent over two weeks and were agreed by directors, in part as it was calculated to have the effect of securing the firm's standing with MGM, ensuring access to future productions.[87] A year later, the manager was able to report the booking of a sizeable proportion of MGM's output for the company's halls.[88] The arrangement endured to the end of the decade and beyond, so that in June 1940, the firm was offered exclusive rights in Aberdeen to *Gone With the Wind*. The terms reflected the film's anticipated box-office potential, even in the uncertain times of war, as the distributor sought a 70 per cent share of takings over four weeks, with a minimum guarantee of £1,928. Although without precedent, the company agreed to the conditions with little hesitation, reflecting the value which attached to securing the most attractive product.[89]

In summary, then, while the coming of sound held out the prospect of continued or even enhanced levels of profitability to cinema exhibitors, the effects over its first decade proved, in practice, more mixed. In the early 1930s in particular, the industry found itself burdened with significantly increased costs, as a consequence of the installation of sound equipment, the escalation in booking fees, and the imposition of higher rates of tax on admissions, all this at a time when spending power for the bulk of picture-goers was depleted due to the wider economic downturn. The early sound years were thus a time of considerable difficulty for many businesses. Yet the relief which might have been anticipated from the lifting of some of the industry's burdens from mid decade proved elusive. If the remission in the rate of entertainments tax and the completion of payments for the hall's Western Electric Sound System offered some alleviation to the Stranraer Picture House's balance sheet from 1935, the upturn in business proved comparatively modest.[90] Away from the industrial areas of west-central Scotland, attendances continued to disappoint in the years leading up to the outbreak of war. The optimistic impression conveyed by aggregate trends concealed a more fitful and altogether less predictable reality at the level of the individual business. Here, importance continued to attach to securing programmes likely to attract patrons. Directors at Glasgow's Regent Cinema were clear as to the kind of films that appealed to an audience drawn sub-stantially from the city's southern suburbs. Among the 'sure draws' were subjects featuring Laurel and Hardy, Wheeler and Woolsey, and Norma Shearer, while little was expected of the Buck Jones vehicle *White Eagle*, as 'Western pictures had not been a success in recent years' at the theatre.[91] In an uncertain decade, the need to pay close attention to the preferences of local film-goers remained paramount.

III

The shifting financial fortunes of the exhibition business also offer some important preliminary generalisations on the nature of cinema-going in the early sound era. So, the variable income levels recorded by Scottish picture houses indicate the degree to which attendance was determined by broader economic forces. While this may seem axiomatic, given the limited means of most movie-goers, it rather goes against the prevailing sense of a literature which has emphasised the absence of financial obstacles to regular attendance. Contemporary investigations, for example, found that the young were able to continue the picture-going habit even when unemployed.[92] A comparative lack of household responsibilities may have helped to maintain the practice among such groups. For others, however, the barriers proved more difficult to overcome. The discretionary spending of women often proved the first item in the household budget to be sacrificed when finances deteriorated, so it is entirely plausible that the growing feminisation of the cinema audience over time should have rendered the industry more vulnerable to the effects of an economic downturn.[93] The importance which managements attached to securing what they judged to be the most appropriate schedule of pictures also suggests that the decision over whether or not to go to the pictures and, if to go, which house to attend, were determined in large part by the programme on offer, more especially at a time when cinemas competed more on product than on price.

Both points call into question the idea of cinema-going practices shaped overwhelmingly by force of habit and routine. Investigations into audience trends and preferences found that while attendance levels were high, the bulk of adult cinema-goers exercised some discretion over their choice of pleasures. The force of habit, where it existed, appeared most deeply rooted among the young, so that the child audience attracted particular attention for its supposed inability to discriminate between films.[94] Among adults, the readiness to differentiate between programmes appeared more pronounced, giving point to the importance which continued to be given to the principles of exploitation and showmanship in picture-house management. Campaigns, for the most part, drew on practices familiar to previous generations of patrons. The continued appeal of the local topical was exploited by many, including Alf Averne, manager of the Lockerbie Cinema Co., Ltd and a former cameraman at Green's, who filmed three subjects in October 1934, drawing the praise of the company directors.[95] Elsewhere, the importance of front-of-house shows for early exhibitors was recalled in foyer displays designed to puff the latest attraction. At the Ritz in Edinburgh's Stockbridge district, James Nairn emphasised the importance of 'motion and reality' in publicity material and to that end, in November 1933, constructed a model airport with planes moving across the scene by means of a continuous band attached to a bicycle wheel, all of which went to publicise the showing of the Warner–First National production *Central Airport* at a total cost of 8s.[96] Some weeks earlier, his efforts for the Douglas Fairbanks vehicle Mr. *Robinson Crusoe* had involved the erection of a suitably exotic landscape, populated with 'six love birds, canaries, tortoises, and three lizards'. The birds were reported to have attracted particular interest 'as they flew about and perched on the cut outs of Douglas Fairbanks and Maria Alba'.[97]

Beyond the economy, other factors shaping audience behaviour were identified by contemporaries. In his presentation to the Royal Statistical Society, reviewing the state of the exhibition business in 1934, Simon

Rowson of the CEA pointed to the significance of seasonal variations in demand for cinema tickets. Figures for the yield of entertainments tax indicated a fall of one-third in attendances between January and June, as longer daylight hours and the wider availability of outdoor amusements blunted enthusiasm for the cinema.[98] In surveying the forces at work to determine levels of attendance, Rowson gave pride of place to the weather, a point reiterated by the CEA more generally, which in the mid 1930s observed that 'the most formidable antagonist of the exhibitor was the summer sun'.[99] A passing familiarity with the Scottish climate might induce a degree of scepticism as to the extent of any challenge posed. Nevertheless, business records indicate a tendency for trade to slacken as daylight hours increased. At the hall provisionally identified as the Paragon in Glasgow, takings between January and June 1914 fell by some 17 per cent.[100] A dip over the summer months was built into expectations elsewhere. As has been seen, companies endeavoured to secure economies so as to mitigate the effects of depressed receipts. At the Public Hall in Uphall, West Lothian, rentals on the building were halved between early April and late August.[101] The impact of efforts at retrenchment varied: among Green's houses, by the later 1920s, margins could be severely squeezed at the height of summer. By that point, smaller, older Picturedromes, such as that at Bridgeton, were unable to offset the fall in business and lapsed consistently into the red.[102]

Seasonal variations continued to feature into the early sound era. At Edinburgh's Playhouse, monthly takings averaged out over the hall's first ten years of operations followed a pattern similar to that described by Rowson, reaching a low point in June, approximately one-third down on levels at the start of the year.[103] For most Scottish exhibitors, New Year week represented a peak in terms of profitability, as audiences deprived of both daylight and many alternative attractions flocked to cinemas with little regard for what was being shown. For the Playhouse, for example, 1930 opened with the early MGM talkie *Excess Baggage*, first released in 1928. Neither the audience (41,778), nor the takings (£2,236) were the highest achieved by the house that year, but the low cost of hire (£238, compared with an average over the year of £465 a week) contributed to a profit of £1,343, almost double that recorded in the next most profitable week.[104] Individual cinemagoers' attendance patterns also observed seasonal trends. For example, Kitty McGinniss, whose diaries indicate that she visited the cinema between forty and sixty-three times a year between the ages of sixteen and twenty-seven, was most likely to attend at the height of winter in December (thirty-eight visits) and January (thirty-seven). Her attendances tailed off markedly from March, reaching a low point in July, with a mere nine visits over six years.[105]

If New Year week was a point when cinema-going may be said to have been habitual, the summer offered exhibitors altogether less certain returns. Heatwave conditions, while rare, were capable of confounding even the most inventive attempts at exploitation. As Scotland, in common with the rest of

Britain, sweltered in the early days of July 1934, her cinemas emptied, so that at the Playhouse an apparently promising programme headed by the Warner comedy musical *Fashions of 1934*, with William Powell and Bette Davis, attracted an audience of 9,750, by some distance the lowest of the year. The takings of £452 produced a loss of £288 on the week.[106] Along Princes Street, at the Palace, another musical, *Going Hollywood* with Bing Crosby and Marion Davies, fared no better. An attendance of 3,126 meant that the house returned a loss on the week of £113.[107] Fortunately for exhibitors, and as generations of Scots can attest, such conditions were rare and a more detailed examination of the factors at work to generate seasonal variations suggests that the weather was not alone in shaping audience behaviour.

It might be observed that changes across the year were far from uniform. Cinemas located in or close to Scotland's coastal resorts tended, against the pattern described thus far, to experience a spike in attendance at points during the summer. So, at Green's Playhouse in Ayr, business in the mid 1930s was some 23 per cent higher in August than in January.[108] To a degree then, cinema-going did not cease during the summer months; rather, it was subject to relocation, as Scots took the habit with them on their holidays. Of itself, this merely serves to identify an alternative seasonal pattern, but one still overridingly subject to forces outwith the industry. Yet, as Rowson acknowledged in his submission to the Royal Statistical Society, the picture was more complex than the basic monthly shifts suggest. In particular, film booking practices often took account of seasonal differences, so that potentially attractive subjects were less likely to be marketed during the summer months, but would be brought forward later in the year. Equally, exhibitors rarely took on expensive product at a time when audiences were expected to drift downwards.[109] Renting and release cycles thus synchronised with changes in the weather, making it difficult to isolate the impact of either. In this regard, the experience of second-run and smaller houses is instructive, as these often observed a rather different booking pattern from the first-run halls that provide the basis for Rowson's observations. Here, access to prestige productions was delayed until they had exhausted their first-run potential.[110] A rather different sequence of attendance may thus be observed. At the Palace, which in the 1930s often acted as a second-run house to the Playhouse, films appeared between a month and six weeks after their initial outing in Edinburgh. So, while some fall-off in business was evident over the first half of the year, this was rather less marked than at first-run houses.[111] Equally, at the Wishaw Picture House, in the mid to later part of the decade, the low point in terms of takings was reached in May, a modest upswing following over the summer.[112] While this does not dispose of the notion of a cinema-going cycle influenced by the climate, it does suggest that the pattern owed at least as much, if not on occasion more, to film booking practices.

The point is confirmed if attendance trends are considered across the rather shorter span of the week. Here, it must be acknowledged, the basis

Table 5.1 Seasonal variations in attendance, 1930s. (Source: S. Rowson, 'A Statistical Survey of the Cinema Industry in Great Britain in 1934', Journal of the Royal Statistical Society, 99 (1936), p. 74; NAS, GD289/1/1, Playhouse Cinema, Profit and Loss Ledger; GD289/1/3, Palace Cinema, Profit and Loss Ledger; GCA, TD273/3, Wishaw Picture Palace, Ltd, Cash Book; SSA, 5/8/49–51, Green Family Collection, Cash Books; Cinema Museum, Capitol Cinema, Aberdeen, Takings Books.)

Month	Rowson	Playhouse	Palace	Wishaw 1	Wishaw 2	Ayr	Capitol
Jan.	100	100	100	100	100	100	100
Feb.	85.3	94.1	92.5	84.5	96.1	77	74.8
March	84.9	87.7	90.6	88.4	89.7	85.6	78.2
April	97.2	89.1	92	73.5	83.2	81.1	81.25
May	77.5	88.7	83.9	64.2	75	77.2	81.2
June	63.3	67.6	81.8	78.8	80.8	84	72.2
July	67	74.5	91.1	78	88.6	116	86.5
Aug.	81.6	96.1	100.8	82.2	99.1	123	89.7
Sept.	95.9	93.4	121	86.3	100.1	101	92.8
Oct.	94.9	98.7	113.9	95	93.4	84.7	73.8
Nov.	83.5	91.6	91	82.5	94.9	85.3	74.9
Dec.	89	86.2	91.5	79.7	91.6	81.4	84

Note: Wishaw 1 and 2 refer to programmes playing in the first and second half of the week respectively.

for robust generalisation is rather less substantial, as returns of sufficient detail are available for only three cinemas: the 'Paragon' and the Wishaw Picture House, both of which record takings by the day, and the Capitol in Aberdeen, for which we have daily figures on attendance from its opening in 1933 through to the outbreak of war. As John Fairweather had advised promoters of the cinema company in Lockerbie, the Saturday audience was crucial to commercial success.[113] At the first two houses under study here, that day generated between 25 per cent and 33 per cent of the week's business.[114] In terms of attendance, its importance was slightly less pronounced, accounting for 24 per cent of admissions at the Capitol.[115] The difference is largely attributable to the practice of charging more for Saturday screenings: at both the Palace and the Playhouse in Edinburgh, Saturday prices were the same as those for evening shows during the week.[116] As a means of further exploiting the Saturday trade, a larger number of screenings were scheduled through the day than was the norm earlier in the week: Wishaw thus ran three shows rather than the usual two.[117] The importance which managements came to attach to maximising business on this one day reflected the belief that the weekend audience was qualitatively as well as quantitatively distinct. So, in terms of both takings and attendances, Saturday was the most predictable day of the week. At Wishaw, receipts on that day fell within 10 per cent of the weekly mean on twenty-five of the fifty-two weeks the house was open for business in 1935. Three years later, when the Picture House closed for a month for refurbishment, the figure was twenty-nine out of forty-eight weeks. On Mondays, the next most remunerative day, marking the start of the week and the commencement of a new programme, the numbers were eleven and fifteen respectively.[118] Habitual cinema-going appeared more pronounced on Saturday than on any other day of the week, justifying the observation offered by the trade paper *Scottish Cinema* in 1919 that 'the Saturday night crowds are the back-bone of the business'.[119] Perhaps predictably, Saturday was one of the days Kitty McGinniss most often chose to attend the cinema, although its importance for her declined in later years, as picture-going became linked to courting and attending the cinema an experience increasingly shared with her fiancé, on his afternoons off work on Tuesdays.[120]

For all this, cinema-goers through the rest of the week could not be ignored. On average, three-quarters of all admissions and two-thirds of takings were generated between Mondays and Fridays, when habitual attendance was much less evident.[121] At such times, it may be anticipated, the impact of the programme could prove especially powerful. Such is suggested by the pattern across two consecutive weeks at the Wishaw Picture House, in May 1937. Taking each week as a whole, receipts varied by just 1s. Yet across the week, the pattern of business as disclosed by the box office showed significant variations. Almost invariably, the Picture House ran two programmes each week, changing subjects on Mondays and Thursdays. In the first week, the Paramount comedy *Along Came Love*, with Irene Hervey and Charles Starrett, generated £40 16s between Monday and Wednesday, while the programme for the second half, comprising the Universal crime drama *Parole!*, supported by the Buck Jones western *The Boss Rider of Gun Creek*, reaped over £111. In the following week, the balance between the two programmes was more even, lower returns for Thursday's programme, made up of the Paramount drama *Straight from the Shoulder* (£91 8s), being balanced by the higher receipts generated by another Paramount comedy *Three Married Men*, this time supported by the Hopalong Cassidy adventure *Heart of the West*.[122]

Whether viewed across the year or over the more concentrated span of a week, cinema-going was an activity overwhelmingly subject to the exercise of choice, with the comparative attraction of particular programmes the most important determinant of behaviour. Attention is thus directed to the nature of film preferences, as revealed through the observations of contemporaries, both critics and picture-house patrons, and surviving box-office data.

In so doing, a key perception both at the time and in subsequent treatments of the decade is addressed: the popularity or absence thereof among audiences of films originating from Britain. The effect of the boost to native output provided by the Quota Act of 1927 was being debated as early as September 1930. In a series of exchanges in the correspondence columns of the Glasgow *Evening Times*, opinions were aired that would subsequently assume the force of orthodoxy. For most, there was little question that British films were unable to match the attractions offered by Hollywood. Particularly forthright was 'Lex', whose view that 'British films are the worst in the world' was backed up by the observation that 'When a third-rate American film is shown it means standing-room only, and when a first-class British film is shown there are sure to be plenty of seats everywhere.'[123]

For 'The Yank', any attempt to make the cinema the kind of 'All British' entertainment provided over the airwaves by the BBC would only result in the closure of half of all picture houses.[124] The diary entries of other cinema-goers confirm that such opinions were not isolated. Kitty McGinniss could on occasion be critical of early talkies: the MGM comedy *The Idle Rich* was thus adjudged to be 'not very good'; the Warner drama *Second Choice* was considered 'nothing special'; and the Weiss Brothers' mystery *Unmasked* was dismissed as a 'dud talkie'.[125] Nevertheless, her special ire was reserved for the BIP comedy musical *Elstree Calling*, which she characterised as 'Purely British' and a 'Sad show'.[126] For another Glasgow picture-goer, Bette Robertson, only two of the films seen in 1937 merited the adjective 'awful'; both were British, the Claude Hulbert drama *Hail and Farewell* and the Arthur Tracy vehicle *The Street Singer*.[127] Given this, there appeared particular point to the observation of the *Evening Times*' cinema correspondent 'Kinoman', that publicity to the effect that 'This is a British Picture' often took on the character of a threat rather than a boast.[128]

For Scots, the phrase seemed to carry additional menace, so that audiences north of the border were seen to be especially resistant to the output of British studios. The managing director of the Park Cinema, Dennistoun, reported that the exhibition of British productions tended to depress takings by between 40 per cent and 100 per cent, so that 'Time after time in Glasgow, British pictures have had to be taken off after the first day.'[129] In explaining such rejection, opinion within the trade made much of the cultivated accents affected by most stage-trained British actors and the comparative lack of action in scenarios. 'Kinoman' perceived a broader failing, with films 'filled with nothing else but English scenery and English traditions. And Scots folk', he proceeded, 'don't give two hoots for either.' Scenes which, across most of the country offered a visual shorthand for 'Britishness', but which only served to alienate Scottish cinema-goers, included 'repeated views of the Thames, the Embankment, Piccadilly, the Changing of the Guard, 'Ampstead 'Eath, Hyde Park Corner, and "John Peel" being sung in a pub'.[130]

If the critical perspective predominated, it did not go unanswered. Writing to the *Evening Times* in September 1930, 'Justice' found British films which offered visual smoothness and vocal clarity to be infinitely preferable to 'the distasteful American monkey-like stuff'.[131] Box-office returns indicate that, even north of the border, such views were not wholly unrepresentative. In November 1932, the manager of Edinburgh's New Victoria Cinema, part of the Gaumont-British circuit, reported that the hall's best weeks coincided with the showing of British films and proceeded to declare, 'I am proud to show them, and I know our patrons prefer them.' Also in Edinburgh, at the Ritz in Stockbridge, the manager James Nairn noted that upwards of 30 per cent of programmes comprised British titles, well in excess of the minimum requirement laid down by quota legislation. Both remarks were offered towards the start of a British Film Week, marked in fifty cinemas across the capital and eastern Scotland more generally.[132] It was a venture thought to reflect the growing number and popularity of British-produced subjects, indicating the progress achieved under the 1927 Act. For Forsyth Hardy of *The Scotsman*, British output showed an increasing ability to use original scenarios to reflect the realities of modern life, an achievement exemplified for him by the Gainsborough musical *Love on Wheels*, with Jack Hulbert and Leonora Corbett, whose story centred on two key aspects of inter-war society: the omnibus and the department store.[133] For all Hardy's determined advocacy, however, the popular response was more muted. When the film played at Edinburgh's Palace Cinema in late February 1933, with the Tim McCoy western *Daring Danger* in support, the takings of £180 were barely half the weekly average for the house across the year as a whole, so that losses over the week exceeded £100.[134]

The most sustained and systematic test of the many and varied opinions circulating as to the preferences of cinema-goers was, as this suggests, provided at the box office. If the survival of such material is sparse, particularly compared with the number of businesses known to have gathered such data, the evidence it is capable of yielding must still be judged of value. For Scotland, detailed information on the performance of individual programmes is available for a small number of halls, all of which functioned independently of the major theatrical chains, Gaumont-British and ABPC. This is important for two reasons: not only does it reflect the nature of the great majority of halls across Scotland, it also offers additional insights into the comparative standing of British films. Lacking the ready access to the output of the production arms of the two combines, Gainsborough for Gaumont-British, and BIP for ABPC, independent exhibitors were forced onto the open market in the search for appropriate product that qualified for quota and so were all the more vulnerable to feeling the draught of audience displeasure when cinema-goers found themselves exposed to substandard titles. Such at least was the view of two representatives of the leading combines, J. J. Bennell of Gaumont-British and David Stewart of ABPC, when interviewed by the *Evening Times* in November 1932.[135] The degree to which such expectations were met may be assessed via surviving business data.

That information is not, it should be stressed, used here in its raw state. As John Sedgwick's work on exhibition patterns acknowledges, capacities varied markedly, so that mere numbers of cinema-goers have little to tell us about comparative levels of popularity.[136] So, while an attendance of 17,733 achieved in one week in April 1934 represented an unparalleled return for the 800-seater Palace Cinema in Edinburgh, it would have proved the ninth lowest figure that year at the Playhouse, with its capacity of 3,048.[137] Equally, as has been seen, audiences were likely to vary markedly over the year, so while a sizeable attendance in New Year week represented, for most halls, the usual state of things, a healthy return at the height of summer was scarcely to be anticipated. To eliminate as far as possible the distortions produced by periods of exceptionally high or low demand and to render cinemas of varying sizes broadly comparable, monthly means of attendances or takings were calculated for each house. Where available, admission figures were preferred as the most reliable measure of the volume of business. However, across the 1930s, changes in the rate of entertainments tax aside, seat prices were broadly stable. What is more, in most cases, figures relate to the period following the reduction in rates or to houses where tax changes were not fully applied. Given that, drawings may be thought to provide a reasonable proxy for levels of attendance. Finally, where programme changes were made during the week, averages were calculated for the relevant span of days. In each case, the figures generated by a particular programme were expressed as a percentage of the mean. Popularity was thus indicated by the degree to which average behaviour altered in a manner favourable or adverse to the films being shown.

Applying this method to the question of the popularity of British films reveals attitudes often at variance with those expected. At the Edinburgh Playhouse, British-produced features topped the bill in seventy-two weeks between August 1929, the hall's opening, and the outbreak of war. In thirty-five of these, the programme scored in excess of the monthly mean, while in thirty-seven it fell below.[138] Divergence from the mean was, in some cases, marked. So, British titles featured in both the most and least popular programmes with Playhouse picture-goers over the decade. The first comprised the London film drama *The Scarlet Pimpernel*, starring Leslie Howard, a consistent favourite with local audiences, and Merle Oberon, which achieved an attendance of 48,754 in one week in August 1935, some 80 per cent above the relevant mean.[139] The other end of the scale was represented by the British Lion comedy *I've Got a Horse*, featuring Yorkshire comedian Sandy Powell, whose audience of 11,223 in 1939 was more than 60 per cent shy of the January average.[140] In overall terms, weeks in which British films were the principal attraction returned a mean score of 100.04, suggesting that features of indigenous studios at least held their own against the Hollywood product, with larger-budget, prestigious productions performing particularly well compared with the relevant monthly mean: *The Private Life of Henry VIII* (+56 per cent in March 1934); *Sanders of the River* (+43 per cent in November 1935); *Victoria the Great* (+40.7 per cent in February 1938); and *Pygmalion* (+65.2 per cent in February 1939).[141] A broadly similar pattern could be observed at the Playhouse's second-run house the Palace, although the picture here is altered by the lower figures generated by return visits. So, in March 1939, *Pygmalion* generated takings 110.1 per cent in excess of the relevant mean, whereas by August and its fifth week at the Palace that year, admissions had fallen to some 21.1 per cent below 'normal'.[142] Here, British films topped the bill in 109 weeks across the 1930s, scoring above their respective means on thirty-eight occasions, but falling short on seventy-one. Nevertheless, the overall score of 96.4 indicates that where films failed to match expected levels of popularity, the shortfall was rarely significant, so that few approached the worst performance registered by a British film, that achieved by the Stanley Lupino comedy *Sleepless Nights*, for which receipts in June 1933 were barely half the hall's average.[143] Here again, large-budget releases did well: *The Private Life of Henry VIII* (+71.6 per cent in March 1934); *The Scarlet Pimpernel* (+60.7 per cent in September 1935); and *Escape Me Never* (+59.2 per cent in November 1935).[144] Some programmes seem to have benefited from favourable scheduling. Its screening in New Year week 1935 may go some way to account for the score of +99.3 per cent achieved by the B&D Sydney Howard comedy *Girls Please!*[145] While support for British films was far from invariable, the evidence for two leading Edinburgh houses suggests that a programme's national origins rarely exercised a decisive influence over audience behaviour. British productions were judged on their merits and were not often found wanting.

If anything, the returns from the Palace indicate a growing tolerance of

British films as the decade progressed, a sequence consistent with the argument advanced by Linda Wood that greater investment in a quality product, encouraged by the first taste of international success enjoyed by a British talkie (Korda's *The Private Life of Henry VIII*), garnered higher receipts at the box office.[146] So, whereas in the calendar year 1933, thirteen British films achieved an average popularity score at the Palace of 0.75 (25 per cent below the mean), with only the comedy musical *Tell Me Tonight* and the Gracie Fields vehicle *This Week of Grace* exceeding expected levels of popularity, two years later eleven programmes headed by British titles attracted audiences 18.2 per cent above the average overall. This marked upswing in performance considerably outpaced the increase in takings more generally, which was barely 2 per cent over the three years. The success of large-budget titles in the latter year has already been noted, so that over the twelve months only *The Private Life of Don Juan* and the comedy musical featuring the American singing star Sophie Tucker, *Gay Love*, whose title may be presumed to have carried rather less ambiguity for contemporary audiences, fell well short of expectations.[147]

For all that, the suspicion must remain that the socially mixed audiences likely to be drawn to cinemas located in the centre of a city often suspected of being in Scotland but not wholly of Scotland hardly provides the most robust test of generalisations concerning the standing of the British film. More telling in this regard may be the experience of the Wishaw Picture House, located in the heavy industrial heartland of west-central Scotland. Here, if the findings of Mass-Observation that working-class picture-goers were more hostile to the efforts of British studios are accurate, we might expect to encounter resistance to the screening of British titles. Between April 1934 and February 1939, the period covered by available documentation, British films played on seventy-four occasions, topping the bill on sixty-six. In terms of popularity, thirty-one programmes scored above the monthly mean, while forty-three fell below, producing an overall score of 98.2.[148] As elsewhere, the average conceals a wide divergence in performance, two films securing less than half the usual takings for the time of year: the Warner comedy *Her Imaginary Lover*, with Laura La Plante, which played in the second half of the week in mid June 1934, and from the same studio the Douglas Fairbanks Jr comedy *Man of the Moment*, with which the house commenced business in the final week of May 1936.[149] By contrast, on a few occasions the mean was easily exceeded. Successful films included the George Formby comedy *Keep Fit* (+52.5 per cent in April 1938) and the British Lion comedy musical *Melody and Romance*, with a juvenile Hughie Green in the lead role (+89.7 per cent in New Year week 1939).[150] Significantly, few of the large-budget features which attracted Edinburgh cinema-goers figured on the Picture House's programmes and those that did failed to prosper: for example, the screen adaptation of H. G. Wells' *Things to Come* drew an audience over 25 per cent down on the mean in its three days in Wishaw in December 1936.[151] Rather more successful were a variety of British-produced musicals, which, while they accounted for just over one-third of all British films shown at the Picture House, made up over half those with above-average takings. The style of film comprehended by the term 'musical' varied markedly, from revues based around popular radio stars, such as *On the Air* (+61.9 per cent in New Year week 1936), to vehicles for stars such as Gracie Fields, whose *Queen of Hearts* attracted takings 62.3 per cent in excess of the mean in November 1936, and films self-consciously mimicking the style and content of Hollywood productions, including *Limelight*, with street singer Arthur Tracy and Anna Neagle (+40.3 per cent in October 1936), and the early efforts of child star Binkie Stewart, Kilmarnock-born but heralded as 'England's Answer to Shirley Temple' in studio copy, whose *Rose of Tralee* gained drawings 53 per cent above the mean in October 1937.[152]

The Wishaw returns suggest that, even among a predominantly working-class audience, British films were capable of prospering. Yet here, as in Edinburgh, patrons were selective as to which programmes they chose to attend, their decision determined more by the genre of a film and the stars it showcased than by questions of national origin. Such observations apply with equal force to the one cinema away from the central belt for which a comprehensive series of returns exists, the Capitol in Aberdeen, which opened its doors towards the end of January 1933. Over the years to September 1939, British films figured on ninety programmes, for thirty-five of which they provided the first feature.[153] As their predominantly supporting role suggests, the Capitol rarely acquired productions from the larger studios of Gainsborough, BIP, or London. Nevertheless, their few appearances were often successful, *The Private Life of Henry VIII* attracting an audience some 60 per cent above the mean for March 1934.[154] Here, as at Wishaw, the greatest success was enjoyed by musicals, accounting for just over half of all British films with popularity scores above the mean. The most successful of these was the Argyle British production *My Irish Molly*, in which Binkie Stewart appeared along with the 'Lancashire Caruso' Tom Burke, drawing an audience of 23,230, 37 per cent above the mean for July 1939.[155] Significantly, although support or 'B' pictures figured prominently on the Capitol's bills, there is no evidence of the taste for cheap quickie fare detected in England by Steve Chibnall. If British first features secured an average popularity score of 93 (7 per cent below the mean), comfortably the weakest overall performance among the houses surveyed here, 'B' pictures fared even worse, securing an average audience some 14 per cent below the mean.[156]

Scottish picture-goers, so the box-office returns indicate, rarely took kindly to the standard productions of many British studios in the 1930s. Comedy subjects, often adjudged the most characteristic and consistently successful of British genres, and which accounted on a broad definition for over one-third of the industry's total output across the decade, did not always travel well.[157] At the Capitol, of thirty-seven British films which fell short of the mean by 20 per cent or more, fourteen, by far the largest single category, were comedies.[158] Sandy Powell, it emerges, was not the only English comedian to die on Scottish screens. Max Miller's appearances on celluloid north of the border seldom attracted large audiences. His 1936 horse-racing comedy *Educated Evans* secured only 62 per cent of the monthly mean at Wishaw in April 1937, while picture-goers at Green's cinemas in Bathgate and Ayr were no more taken with his earlier feature *Get Off My Foot* (scores of 78.1 and 79.3 respectively in June and July 1936).[159] Somewhat against expectations, the 'Cheekie Chappie's' greatest success appears to have come at Edinburgh's Playhouse in May 1939, when *Everything Happens to Me* secured an audience 17 per cent above the average. However, given that it formed the second half of a double bill, supporting James Cagney and Pat O'Brien in *Angels with Dirty Faces*, this should not perhaps be taken as evidence of a growing taste among Scots for Miller's particular brand of 'knowingness'.[160] Other comedians ranking below average for the most part included Ernest Lotinga, Stanley Lupino, Will Hay, and Flanagan and Allen. Even the two Lancashire stars, George Formby and Gracie Fields, often presented as the biggest British box-office draws in this period, did not enjoy unqualified success.[161] While Wishaw's endorsement of Formby's *Keep Fit* has been noted, his previous effort for Associated Talking Pictures, *Keep Your Seats Please*, failed to win over audiences at the Capitol, where attendances in 1937 were barely two-thirds of the mean for January.[162] Fields enjoyed success in both Edinburgh and Wishaw with *Queen of Hearts*, the second most popular film at the Picture House in 1936, behind only Fred Astaire and Ginger Rogers in *Top Hat*.[163] That said, her appearance in *Sing as We Go* at Green's Picturedrome in the Gorbals in April 1935 generated receipts considerably below the average (73.1), indicating some resistance to its tale of stoical good humour in the face of economic adversity, culminating in scenes of mill hands returning to work uplifted in spirit and united in song beneath union flags.[164] The only comedians to match and to some degree outshine Fields and Formby were husband and wife team Arthur Lucan and Kitty McShane, whose film careers as the Irish washerwoman Old Mother Riley and her daughter commenced towards the end of the decade. Their first starring vehicle, *Old Mother Riley*, garnered takings over 35 per cent above the average for Wishaw's Picture House in September 1938, while in New Year week 1939, the follow-up, *Old Mother Riley in Paris*, became only the second British comedy topping the bill at the Capitol to attract an audience higher than the mean (+37 per cent).[165]

The fortunes of comedy subjects, like British films more generally, varied markedly across Scotland. It is thus difficult to discern, even from the limited returns available to us, anything approaching a nationally uniform audience for film. Taste remained highly diversified along social and geographical lines. In assessing the effectiveness of British productions in the industry's most prolific decade, the variety of features, in terms of subject matter and budget, emerges as a source of commercial strength, however critically derided the body of work as a whole may have been. Most British genres secured an audience among the myriad taste communities that made up the cinema-going population.

Evidence of a fundamental divergence in preferences within Scotland is provided by the varied fortunes of another, decidedly non-British, genre, the western. For much of the decade, the typical western comprised low-budget, 'B' movie fodder, unpromising material to put before city-centre audiences.[166] So, in five years to September 1939, only sixteen films which could be broadly categorised as westerns played at the Edinburgh Playhouse, topping the bill on a mere six occasions.[167] At the Capitol, westerns made more frequent appearances, figuring on twenty-three bills. Here again, however, they rarely played as first features, providing the principal attraction in only nine weeks.[168] In terms of popularity, programmes with western subjects performed close to the average, with higher than normal returns for the most part achieved by productions in which the presence of particular stars may have acted as a more powerful attraction than the western subject matter. Both the Laurel and Hardy comedy *Way Out West*, and *The Girl of the Golden West*, a musical vehicle for Jeanette MacDonald and Nelson Eddy, drew attendances considerably in excess of their respective means, scoring respectively +22 per cent and +73 per cent, and +40.2 per cent and +66.9 per cent at Edinburgh and Aberdeen.[169] By contrast, at Wishaw, the 'B' western became a staple attraction, figuring in seventy programmes over four years. The frequency of screenings reflected their popularity with local audiences, as in fifty-one cases the monthly mean was exceeded.[170] Significantly, such films tended to be scheduled early in the week, when attendances were particularly volatile. Takings figures for the Picture House indicate that their appearances worked for the most part to moderate fluctuations in income. So, in the first six months of 1938, westerns played at Wishaw in fourteen out of twenty-three weeks. With the exception of one programme, in which a Hopalong Cassidy subject played in support of *Bulldog Drummond Comes Back*, which generated receipts 84 per cent in excess of the mean, western programmes returned scores between 7 per cent below and 40 per cent above the average. When viewed in the round, western weeks drew takings 28 per cent above expectations. In other weeks, not only were variations in popularity more marked, ranging from 35 per cent below to 59 per cent above the mean, but the overall performance was also lower at 15 per cent above the average for 1934–9. The presence of a western on the Picture House's bills thus worked to enhance the hall's attraction for local audiences, helping to boost the share of total income generated in the first half of each week from a long-run average of 40 per cent to nearer 45 per cent in 1938.[171]

If Wishaw can be regarded as a more class-specific audience, given its likely catchment area, then such figures also provide clear evidence of a fragmenting of taste along lines of socio-economic status. If anything, this suggests that cinema-goers did not discard their wider identities in the foyer, but took them with them into the auditorium, where they worked to inform film preferences through the period. Given this, the response of Scottish audiences to films with Scottish settings and subject matter acquires an additional significance. It is important to keep in mind that such subjects rarely originated from within Scotland. Financial barriers, raised further by the cost of producing sound films, worked to limit local output to mostly short, documentary features, which in the absence of quota regulations for such subjects rarely figured on the bills of commercial picture houses.[172] Most representations of Scotland likely to be encountered on the screen thus originated from studios in London or Hollywood. The result was, in the view of many critics, often unfortunate and occasionally offensive. 'Kinoman' of the *Evening Times* gave voice to a recurrent lament at presentations of Scottish character, dress, and traditions which frequently assumed the character of a burlesque. A complaint was thus entered against John Ford's 1929 production, *King of the Khyber Rifles*, in which it was considered that fidelity in the matter of costume had not extended to the depiction of character.[173] A decade later, reviews of the Twentieth-Century Fox picture *Stanley and Livingstone* also catalogued several inaccuracies, including the praise offered of Livingstone by Spencer Tracy's Stanley as 'A man who has restored my faith in England', and a scene in which Cedric Hardwicke's Livingstone was depicted leading natives in the singing of 'Onward Christian Soldiers' 'to a tune he could not possibly have known'.[174] Particular ire was, however, reserved for another Ford film, the 1936 RKO production of Maxwell Anderson's Broadway success, *Mary of Scotland*, with Katharine Hepburn in the role of the unfortunate Queen of Scots. If critics were divided over the picture's cinematic worth, they were in no doubt as to the level of factual accuracy to be found therein. 'Kinoman' wrote for many in declaring the film 'as untruthful a document as was ever published', while Forsyth Hardy declared it a 'Headache for Historians'. Objections centred on dialogue that was deemed less than authentic (Mary taking leave of her courtiers by declaring 'I'm through'; and Bothwell's inquiry of his rival, 'Well, Darnley still hanging around, eh?'), an evening at Holyrood spent listening to a performance of 'Loch Lomond', and a historically inaccurate but cinematically inevitable encounter between Hepburn's Mary and Florence Eldridge's Elizabeth I.[175]

British studios were, it was noted, no less culpable in offering distorted representations of Scotland's past and present. 'Kinoman' recalled an early example, centred on the same episode in the nation's history, Ideal's 1923 production, *The Loves of Mary, Queen of Scots*, in which Fay Compton, sister of Compton Mackenzie, playing the doomed Queen, was shown incarcerated at Fotheringay. Despite this, she was still capable of calling forth images of her homeland, including, in a prodigious feat of imagination, the Wallace Monument at Stirling.[176] In the following decade, Forsyth Hardy, film critic of *The Scotsman*, would enter a protest against John Laurie's portrayal of a misanthropic crofter in Hitchcock's *The Thirty-Nine Steps*, while towards the end of the decade, concern came to centre on the latest vehicle for musical comedy star Gracie Fields.[177] *Shipyard Sally*, produced by Twentieth-Century Fox in 1939 and set on Clydeside, revisited themes first touched upon in *Sing As We Go* five years earlier. Then, Gracie had, almost single-handedly, saved the Lancashire cotton industry. Now, her powers of economic regeneration were focused on the shipbuilding industry of the Clyde, in a film that was, in many respects, *Sing As We Go* with rivets. The film occasioned unease, even while still in production, following a description in pre-publicity of a scene set in what was intended to be a 'typical' Glasgow pub on the evening of the launch of the *Queen Mary*. Among those present were 'One hundred and fifty extras, varying from bedraggled Clydeside workers to Scots pipers attired in full ceremonial regalia'.[178] Responding to criticism of what many considered a resort to crude stereotype, the producers acknowledged artistic licence in the inclusion of the pipers and disclaimed any intention of impugning either the sobriety or the sartorial standards of the workforce. They went on to insist that the film constituted 'the finest tribute ever paid to Scotland', a view with which 'Kinoman' perhaps unsurprisingly took issue. For him, a film in which the fortunes of a major industry were played out in broad comedy set largely in the drawing rooms of London could only be regarded as 'farcical nonsense'.[179]

If critics often adopted a hard-faced attitude to depictions of the nation on the screen, audience responses were more varied. In some cases, the critical perspective received endorsement. Forewarned of the excesses of *Mary of Scotland*, and perhaps conscious of Katharine Hepburn's reputation as 'box-office poison', cinema-goers at the Edinburgh Playhouse in January 1937 were decidedly lukewarm about the film, ensuring a loss over the week of £173, a return which sufficed to dissuade the company from proceeding with a later showing at the Palace.[180] In other respects, the two audiences, critical and popular, diverged markedly. In May 1930, the documentary *Drifters*, lauded by Forsyth Hardy as 'the one outstanding Scottish film', topped the bill at the Playhouse, with the Paramount comedy *Fashions in Love* in support. The attendance of 14,510 represented only 58 per cent of the monthly mean.[181] Another Grierson essay on the fishing industry, *Granton Trawler*, did rather better when it was shown at Edinburgh's Ritz Cinema in 1933. The large numbers thought to have been drawn from the communities of Granton and Newhaven indicated the popularity of a subject of immediate relevance, but also suggested that the screening in this case was more in the nature of a local topical.[182] Aside from such cases of immediate and particular appeal, audiences exercised the same discretion over Scottish subjects as they applied to films more generally. The 1937 adaptation of James Bridie's *Storm in a Teacup* drew below average attendances at both the Playhouse (−12.7 per cent) and the Palace (−6.4 per cent).[183] Rather more successful was

René Clair's ironic take on the tartan myth in *The Ghost Goes West*, which drew an audience higher than the monthly mean on its first outing at the Palace in September 1936 (+8.4 per cent).[184] However, by some distance the most successful 'Scottish' film of the decade was the Laurel and Hardy (or, as *Film Weekly* had them, 'MacLaurel and MacHardy') comedy *Bonnie Scotland*. Trading on the kind of representation of Scotland that, in more weighty fare, usually attracted critical derision, the film secured above-average audiences in Glasgow at Green's Bedford (+57.6 per cent) and Tollcross (+22 per cent) cinemas and scored popular successes both in small-town Scotland (+42 per cent at the Wishaw Picture House) and city-centre houses in the east (+52 per cent at the Edinburgh Playhouse, +64.9 per cent at the Palace, and +74.9 per cent at the Capitol).[185] In a case such as this, where stars and story so obviously cohered, the authenticity of the setting counted for little. Yet, *Bonnie Scotland* apart, evidence for a national audience for cinema, predisposed to favour Scottish subjects is less than compelling. Rather, this survey confirms that cinema-goers remained sharply divided, box-office returns exposing fractures along the lines of class, region and, if children's tastes are also considered, age. They also hint at the religious/ethnic differences underlying Scottish society through the period. The unusual popularity of Irish-themed musicals with Binkie Stewart and the early Old Mother Riley comedies have been noted. What is more, *Mary of Scotland* appeared for three days in February 1937 at Green's Picturedrome in the Gorbals and, in marked contrast to its rejection by Scottish picture-goers elsewhere, secured takings marginally above the mean (+5.9 per cent).[186] How far this reflected greater sympathy with the film's subject matter cannot be known, but at the very least it is consistent with an interpretation that recognises the film audience as an independent body, capable of exercising discretion in pursuit of its pleasures. Cinema-going was a habit driven less by routine than by the ability to discriminate and to select subjects that 'spoke', both literally and figuratively, to individual interests and tastes.

IV

For all its capacity outwardly to communicate prosperity, whether through the ostentation of its buildings or through the buoyancy of aggregate attendance figures, the cinema industry of the 1930s emerges as subject to considerable uncertainty. This was a consequence of technological, legislative, and commercial developments. The coming of sound marked a departure at several levels. The readiness with which audiences turned their backs on the mature art form that was silent film imposed significant additional costs on exhibitors, obliged to re-equip their theatres and to pay more for the product that sustained them. While expenses rose, incomes were reduced as economic recession depressed the purchasing power of many cinema-goers just as seat prices increased with the imposition of higher rates of entertainments tax. The outcome for many businesses was a marked and sustained squeeze in profit margins. The possibility of throwing off these financial constraints was hampered throughout by the absence of the kind of collusive pricing practices evident in other branches of industry in this period, and the impact of exclusive booking arrangements which ensured that the product, comprising the cinema programme and the setting within which it was viewed, rather than the cost of admission remained the basis on which houses competed.[187]

The work of exhibitors was complicated further by the legal requirement to show a proportion of footage of British origin. For halls unconnected with the major production, distribution, and theatrical chains, the quest for appropriate product was often far from straightforward. Yet box-office data indicate that overall businesses north of the border did not suffer adversely from the requirements of the Quota Act. The conventional wisdom that British films were unpalatable to Scottish cinema-goers finds little validation in the available business evidence. So, if the quota complicated, it did not fundamentally compromise the quest for commercial success. The growing rehabilitation of British production in the 1930s which can be traced through recent writings, is thus confirmed by the view from Scotland. Nevertheless, the key to success remained the diversity of output, possible at a point of peak production of feature films.[188] The appeal of British titles varied according to the particular audience, so that if large-budget features went down well with picture-goers at city-centre dream palaces such as the Playhouse in Edinburgh, elsewhere, specific genres, especially the musical, proved attractive. Successful managers were required to be sensitive to variations in taste by programme and over time, explaining to a large degree the diligence with which preferences were recorded via the box office.

The characteristics of cinema-going identified in previous chapters is confirmed here: an activity shaped less by force of habit and more by the regular exercise of choice over which programme to attend or, at times of acute financial difficulty, whether to attend at all. Features of the mass audience discerned by contemporary cultural critics, in particular its passivity and pliability, would not have been recognised by most exhibitors.[189] The cinema-goers they encountered were attracted to films that resonated with them. Previous chapters have noted the appeal of features dealing with matters of sexual health and it may be worth noting, before bringing down the curtain on the 1930s, that the most popular film of the decade, adopting the methodology outlined above, was *Damaged Lives*, the low-budget 'treatment' of the problem of VD that played for three weeks at the Palace in April 1934. Above-average audiences were in attendance each week, but additional matinee performances in the first week ensured receipts for those six days that were 168.9 per cent above the monthly mean.[190] As this example illustrates, audiences did not come fully formed to most picture shows. Rather, they were constructed through a combination of advance publicity, word of mouth, and appropriate exploitation. The cinema-going public comprised a multitude of shifting taste communities, whose preferences were charted with a fidelity unmatched by contemporary consumer industries.

This diversity in taste communities extended beyond those considered in this chapter. Film was encountered in settings other than the conventional picture palace. As has been seen, documentary footage of Scotland, *Drifters* apart, did not figure on regular commercial programmes. If it was seen at all, it was through shows mounted by organisations keen to explore film's artistic potential rather than its commercial possibilities. A rounded appreciation of Scotland's engagement with the moving image takes us beyond the confines of conventional cinema into a world in which film became a vehicle for cultural enlightenment and civic education, and which reached new heights around mid century.

NOTES

1. D. Crafton, *The Talkies: American Cinema's Transition to Sound* (Berkeley and Los Angeles, 1999); S. Eyman, *The Speed of Sound: Hollywood and the Talkie Revolution, 1926–30* (Baltimore, 1997); D. Gomery, 'The Coming of Sound: Technological Change in the American Film Industry', in T. Balio (ed.), *The American Film Industry* (Madison, 1985), pp. 229–51.

2. Hanson, *From Silent Screen to Multi-Screen*, pp. 59–65; Hiley, 'Let's Go to the Pictures', pp. 41–2; Ryall, 'A British Studio System', pp. 202–4; M. Jancovich and L. Faire, *The Place of the Audience: Cultural Geographies of Film Consumption* (London, 2003), part three.

3. G. Bachman, 'Still in the Dark: Silent Film Audiences', *Film History*, 9 (1997), pp. 23–48.

4. Dickinson and Street, *Cinema and State*; S. Street, *British Cinema in Documents* (London, 2000), ch. 2.

5. Low, *History of the British Film, 1929–1939*, p. 45; J. Richards, *The Age of the Dream Palace: Cinema and Society in Britain, 1930–1939* (London, 1984), pp. 30–2; L. Napper, *British Cinema and Middlebrow Culture in the Interwar Years* (Exeter, 2009), ch. 1.

6. J. Sedgwick, *Popular Filmgoing in 1930s Britain: A Choice of Pleasures* (Exeter, 2000), ch. 4; L. Wood, 'Low-budget British Films in the 1930s', in Murphy, *British Cinema Book*, pp. 211–19; Chibnall, *Quota Quickies*, ch. 7.

7. S. Rowson, 'A Statistical Survey of the Cinema Industry in Great Britain in 1934', *Journal of the Royal Statistical Society*, 99 (1936), pp. 68–9; Browning and Sorrell, 'Cinemas and Cinema-Going', p. 134; the consolidated series may be followed on the BFI's Screenonline website, http://www.screenonline.org.uk/film/facts/fact1.html (accessed 25 November 2011).

8. Street, *British Cinema in Documents*, pp. 125–32; R. James, *Popular Culture and Working-class Taste in Britain, 1930–1939: A Round of Cheap Diversions?* (Manchester, 2010), pp. 85–93; *KW*, 11 July 1929, p. 46.

9. J. Richards and D. Sheridan (eds), *Mass-Observation at the Movies* (London, 1987), pp. 21–136; James, *Popular Culture*, pp. 93–103.

10. The most detailed study is Harper, 'Lower Middle-Class Taste-Community', pp. 565–87.

11. Sedgwick, *Popular Filmgoing*, ch. 6; id., 'Cinema-going Preferences', pp. 1–35.

12. Chibnall, *Quota Quickies*; see also James, *Popular Culture*, chs 6–8.

13. A. Kuhn, 'Cinema-going in Britain in the 1930s: Report of a Questionnaire Survey', *Historical Journal of Film, Radio and Television*, 19 (1999), pp. 531–43; id., *An Everyday Magic: Cinema and Cultural Memory* (London, 2002).

14. *Scotsman*, 10 Aug. 1929, p. 9; *ET*, 8 Nov. 1928, p. 3; B. Thomas, *The Last Picture Shows. Edinburgh: Ninety Years of Cinema Entertainment in Scotland's Capital City* (Edinburgh, 1984), p. 50.

15. SSA, 5/4/15, Poole Family, Diary of Attendances, Synod Hall, Edinburgh, 24 and 31 Dec. 1928.

16. *Kinematograph Year Book* (London, 1930); *ET*, 9 April 1929, p. 3.

17. NAS, GD289/1/1, Playhouse Cinema, Profit and Loss Ledger, 17 Aug.–28 Dec. 1929.

18. *KW*, 5 June 1930, p. 39.

19. *ET*, 10 July 1931, p. 11.

20. *ET*, 6 Nov. 1928, p. 4.

21. *ET*, 7 Sept. 1928, p. 3.

22. *ET*, 3 Oct. 1929, p. 3.

23. *ET*, 3 Jan., p. 3; 5 Jan., p. 7; 24 Jan., p. 3; 23 May 1929, p. 3, for 'Kinoman's lament on the popularity of talking pictures'.

24. C. McGinniss, Diary, 24 Jan. 1929. From collection in possession of Mrs Rita Connelly. I am very grateful to Mrs Connelly for allowing me unrestricted access to her mother's diaries.

25. *ET*, 24 Jan. 1929, p. 3.

26. SSA, 5/4/15, Poole Family, Diary of Attendances, 29 July–5 Aug. 1929, week commencing 29 July 1929.

27. NAS, GD289/1/3, Palace Cinema, Profit and Loss Ledger, weeks ending 7 Jan.–29 Dec. 1928.

28. NAS, GD289/1/3, weeks ending 5 Jan.–10 Aug. 1929.

29. NAS, GD289/1/3, weeks ending 17 Aug.–28 Dec. 1929.

30. NAS, GD289/1/3, weeks ending 5 Jan.–28 Dec. 1929

31. NAS, GD289/1/3, weeks ending 4 Jan.–4 Oct. 1930.

32. NAS, GD289/1/3, week ending 30 Aug. 1930

33. Calculated from C. McGinniss, Diaries, 1925; 1927; 1928; 1929.

34. C. McGinniss, Diary, 29 Jan.; 5 Feb.; 4 March 1929.

35. C. McGinniss, Diary, 24 Oct.; 18 Nov.; 28 Nov. 1929.

36. C. McGinniss, Diary, 30 Nov. 1929.

37. See Chapter 3, pp. 122–3, 127.

38. Ryall, 'A British Studio System', pp. 202–10; Low, *History of the British Film, 1918–1929*, p. 43; Hanson, *From Silent Screen to Multi-Screen*, pp. 58–65; D. Gomery, *The Hollywood Studio System: A History* (London, 2005), part 1; R. Maltby, *Hollywood Cinema*, 2nd edn (Oxford, 2003), pp. 130–41; T. Balio,

Grand Design: Hollywood as a Modern Business Enterprise, 1930–1939 (Berkeley and Los Angeles, 1993), ch. 4.

39. CM, Aberdeen Picture Palaces, Ltd, Minutes, Meetings of Directors, 16 March; 16 April 1928; 30 Jan.; 27 March; 23 July; 6 Sept.; 27 Sept. 1929; 14 Feb. 1930.

40. SSA, 5/22/4, Glasgow Picture House Co., Ltd, Minutes, Meetings of Directors, 28 Jan.; 25 Feb. 1928.

41. NAS, BT2/18488/10, Vogue Cinemas, Ltd, Special Resolution, 21 Oct. 1936; BT2/16911/34, United Cinemas, Ltd, Special Resolution, 21 Oct. 1936.

42. See Chapter 4, pp. 148, 150.

43. CM, Aberdeen Picture Palaces, Ltd, Minutes, Meetings of Directors, 16 April 1928; 14 Feb. 1930.

44. SSA, 5/22/4, Glasgow Picture House Co., Ltd, Minute Book, 17 March 1924–7 Jan. 1930, General Meeting of Shareholders, 25 Feb.; Meetings of Directors, 10 March; 25 May; 26 June; 13 July; Extraordinary General Meeting of Shareholders, 16 Nov. 1928.

45. SSA, 5/22/4, Meeting of Directors, 28 Jan. 1928; 22 May 1929.

46. *Kinematograph Year Book* (London, 1938); ET, 22 Nov. 1928, p. 7, for early comment on Maxwell's propensity to acquire Scottish houses.

47. Dumfries and Galloway Archives, Lockerbie Town Hall, 1/6/8, Lockerbie Cinema Co., Ltd, Directors' Minute Book, April 1932–Aug. 1938, Meetings of Directors, 29 April; 16 May; 30 May 1932; 10 Feb.; 2 Aug. 1933.

48. SSA, 5/25/4, Stranraer Picture House, Ltd, Minute Book, 1931–60, Meetings of Directors, 17 Oct. 1932; 14 Jan. 1936.

49. SSA, 5/25/4, Meeting of Directors, Applications for Shares, Applications for Debenture Stock, 1 April 1931.

50. NAS, BT2/17497/12, Stornoway Playhouse, Ltd, Prospectus, 10 Nov. 1933.

51. NAS, BT2/17497/13, 15, 24, Allotments of Shares, 1 Dec. 1933; 17–30 Jan. 1934; 8 Aug. 1938.

52. See Chapter 3, pp. 126–7.

53. SSA, 5/8/68, George Green and Co., graphs.

54. NAS, GD289/1/3, Palace Cinema, Profit and Loss Ledger, week ending 15 Nov. 1930.

55. NAS, GD289/1/3, Net Profits: 1927–8, £6,084; Losses Recorded in 1930–1, £420; 1932–3, £435; 1938–9, £217.

56. NAS, GD2891/1/, Playhouse Cinema, Profit and Loss Ledger, Net Profits: 1929–30, £12,134; 1930–1, £10,520; 1932–3, £5,085; 1936–7, £4,289; 1937–8, £4,746; 1938–9, £853.

57. NAS, BT2/8516/33, 35–41, 43–4, Balance Sheets at 21 March 1929; 21 March 1931; 21 March 1932; 21 March 1933; 21 March 1934; 21 March 1935; 21 March 1936; 21 March 1937; 21 March 1938; 21 March 1939.

58. NAS, BT2/11407/43–47, Annual Returns, 31 Dec. 1931; 30 Dec. 1932; 5 Jan. 1934; 3 Jan. 1935; 10 Jan. 1936.

59. SSA, 5/25/3, Stranraer Picture House, Ltd, Shareholders' Minute Book, 1931–60, Minutes of Second AGM, 6 July 1933; Minutes of Third AGM, 7 Aug. 1934; Minutes of Fourth AGM, 27 Aug. 1935.

60. SSA, 5/25/3, Minutes of Third AGM, 7 Aug. 1934.
61. SSA, 5/25/3, Minutes of Fourth AGM, 27 Aug. 1935.
62. Browning and Sorrell, 'Cinemas and Cinema-Going', p. 134; http://www. screenonline.org.uk/film/facts/fact1.html (accessed 25 November 2011), the figures suggest growth from 903 million in 1933 to 990 million by 1939.
63. CM, James F. Donald (Aberdeen Cinemas), Ltd, Accounts.
64. SSA, 5/22/9, Glasgow Picture House, Ltd, Balance Sheets and Profit and Loss Accounts, 31 May 1930–28 May 1938 (1930, £25,338 3s 10d; 1935, £19,360 18s 5d; 1938, £18,585 17s 6d).
65. *Scotsman*, 4 Sept., p. 4; 11 Sept. 1931, p. 9.
66. *Scotsman*, 28 Jan. 1932, p. 7.
67. CM, Aberdeen Picture Palaces, Ltd, Minute Book, 1930–4, Meetings of Directors, 25 Sept.; 9 Oct. 1931; 8 Dec. 1932.
68. Ibid., Meeting of Directors, 13 March 1933.
69. Ibid., Meetings of Directors, 13 Oct.; 6 Nov.; 18 Nov. 1933; 4 Jan. 1934.
70. *Scotsman*, 16 April 1935, pp. 11, 16.
71. SSA, 5/25/3, Stranraer Picture House, Ltd, Shareholders' Minute Book, 1931–60, Minutes of Fourth AGM, 27 Aug. 1935.
72. *Scotsman*, 28 Jan. 1932, p. 7.
73. R. Middleton, 'The Constant Employment Budget Balance and British Budgetary Policy, 1929–39', *Economic History Review*, 2nd ser., XXXIV (1981), pp. 266–86; Eichengreen, 'British Economy between the Wars', pp. 330–7; R. Skidelsky, *Politicians and the Slump: The Labour Government of 1929–1931* (London, 1967), pp. 287–9.
74. SSA, 5/14/13, James S. Nairn Collection, Volume of Press Cuttings, cutting from *KW*, 10 Dec. 1931; *Cine Times*, 5 Dec. 1931.
75. NAS, GD289/1/1, Playhouse Cinema, Profit and Loss Ledger, 1929–38.
76. NAS, GD289/1/3, Palace Cinema, Profit and Loss Ledger, 1927–38.
77. CM, Capitol Cinema, Aberdeen, Takings Books, 1933–9 (1934, aggregate attendance of 891,955 over fifty-two weeks; 1938, 808,094 over fifty-two weeks).
78. Dewey, *War and Progress*, ch. 13; M. Thomas, 'Rearmament and Economic Recovery in the late 1930s', *Economic History Review*, 2nd ser., XXXVI (1983), pp. 552–73.
79. GCA, TD273/3, The Wishaw Picture Palace, Ltd, Cash Book, April 1934–Feb. 1939.
80. GCA, TD273/1, Wellington Picture Palace (1933), Ltd, Ledger No. 1.
81. *Scotsman*, 28 Jan. 1932, p. 7.
82. NAS, BT2/11407/42, The Playhouse, Galashiels (1920), Ltd, Summary of Share Capital, 1 Jan. 1931.
83. NAS, BT2/11407/43–6, Annual returns, 31 Dec. 1931–3 Jan. 1935.
84. NAS, GD289/1/1, Playhouse Cinema, Profit and Loss Ledger, week ending 22 June 1935.
85. NAS, GD289/1/3, Palace Cinema, Profit and Loss Ledger, 1928 and 1936.
86. NAS, GD289/1/1, Playhouse Cinema, Profit and Loss Ledger, week ending 19 Oct. 1935.

87. CM, Aberdeen Picture Palaces, Ltd, Minute Book, 1930–4, Meeting of Directors, 3 Nov. 1932.
88. Ibid., Meeting of Directors, 4 Jan. 1934.
89. CM, Aberdeen Picture Palaces, Ltd, Minute Book, 1934–44, Meeting of Directors, 14 June 1940.
90. SSA, 5/25/9, The Stranraer Picture House, Ltd, Annual Accounts. House receipts in the year to 21 April 1935 totalled £6,896 18s 9d, compared with £7,648 16s 5d for the year to 21 April 1939.
91. SSA, 5/22/5, The Glasgow Picture House Co., Ltd, Minute Book, 1930–6, Meetings of Directors, 3 Feb.; 21 Feb. 1933.
92. Richards, *Age of the Dream Palace*, pp. 13–14; A. Davies, *Leisure, Gender and Poverty: Working-class Culture in Salford and Manchester, 1900–1939* (Buckingham, 1992), p. 45; E. W. Bakke, *The Unemployed Man: A Social Study* (London, 1933), pp. 178–83, 262–3.
93. Griffiths, *Lancashire Working Classes*, p. 240; see Chapter 3, pp. 101, 117, 128.
94. See Chapter 2, p. 73.
95. Dumfries and Galloway Archives, Lockerbie Cinema Co., Ltd, Directors' Minute Book, 1932–8, Meeting of Directors, 31 Oct. 1934.
96. SSA, 5/14/13, Nairn Collection, cutting from *KW*, 9 Nov. 1933; 5/14/17, Volume of Correspondence, 31 Oct. 1933, W. A. Stewart, Director of Scottish Cinema and Variety Theatres, Ltd, to Nairn.
97. SSA, 5/14/13, Nairn Collection, cutting from *KW*, 29 July 1933; still of display.
98. Rowson, 'A Statistical Survey', p. 74.
99. SSA, 5/11/14, Cinematograph Exhibitors' Association, unidentified cutting, 'Cinema in the Depression'.
100. SSA, 5/26/112, Singleton Collection, Notebook, Weekly Accounts, Aug. 1913–Aug. 1914.
101. West Lothian Local History Library, Blackburn, Uphall Public Hall and Cinema, Cash Book, 1923–7.
102. SSA, 5/8/68, George Green and Co., Graphs, Sheet for 1927–8, covering Tollcross, Rutherglen, Bridgeton.
103. NAS, GD289/1/1, Playhouse Cinema, Profit and Loss Ledger, 1929–39.
104. NAS, GD289/1/1, week ending 4 Jan. 1930.
105. C. McGinniss, Diaries, 1925; 1927–30; 1933; 1935; 1937.
106. NAS, GD289/1/1, week ending 7 July 1934.
107. GD289/1/3, Palace Cinema, Profit and Loss Ledger, week ending 7 July 1934.
108. SSA, 5/8/49–51, Green Family Collection, General Cash Books, Jan. 1935–March 1937.
109. Rowson, 'A Statistical Survey', pp. 72–3.
110. Sedgwick, *Popular Filmgoing*, pp. 56–61, describes the system of cascading, as films made the transition from first-run to second-run and lower houses.
111. NAS, GD289/1/3, Palace Cinema, Profit and Loss Ledger.
112. GCA, TD273/3, Wishaw Picture Palace, Ltd, Cash Book, 1934–9.
113. See Chapter 3, pp. 125–6.

114. SSA, 5/26/112, Singleton Collection, Notebook, Weekly Accounts, Aug. 1913– Aug. 1914; GCA, TD273/3, Wishaw Picture Palace, Ltd, Cash Book.

115. CM, Capitol Cinema, Takings Books, 4 Feb. 1933–28 Aug. 1939.

116. NAS, GD289/2/1, Playhouse Cinema, Running Book, 1929–32; GD289/2/14, Palace Cinema, Running Book, 1929–32.

117. *Wishaw Herald*, 7 Jan. 1935, p. 6.

118. GCA, TD273/3, Wishaw Picture Palace, Ltd, Cash Book.

119. *Scottish Cinema*, 24 Nov. 1919, p. 7.

120. C. McGinniss, Diaries, 1925; 1927–30; 1933; 1935; 1937.

121. Calculated from GCA, TD273/3, Wishaw Picture Palace, Ltd, Cash Book; CM, Capitol Cinema, Takings Books, 1933–9.

122. GCA, TD273/3, Wishaw Picture Palace, Ltd, Cash Book, weeks ending 1 and 8 May 1937; *Wishaw Herald*, 22 April, p. 8; 29 April 1937, p. 8.

123. *ET*, 12 Sept. 1930, p. 6.

124. *ET*, 15 Sept. 1930, p. 4.

125. C. McGinniss, Diary, 15 Feb.; 24 May; 26 June 1930.

126. C. McGinniss, Diary, 13 May 1930.

127. SSA, 5/7/273, Bette Robertson Diary, weeks beginning 18 April; 12 Dec. 1937.

128. *ET*, 10 Nov. 1932, p. 3.

129. *ET*, 3 Nov. 1932, p. 3.

130. *ET*, 27 Oct. 1932, p. 3.

131. *ET*, 16 Sept. 1930, p. 4.

132. SSA, 5/14/13, Nairn Collection, cutting from *Evening Dispatch*, 30 Nov. 1932.

133. *Scotsman*, 29 Nov. 1932, p. 6.

134. NAS, GD289/1/3, Palace Cinema, Profit and Loss Ledger, week ending 25 Feb. 1933.

135. *ET*, 17 Nov. 1932, p. 3.

136. Sedgwick, *Popular Filmgoing*, p. 70; id., 'Cinema-Going Preferences', p. 4.

137. NAS, GD289/1/3, Palace Cinema, Profit and Loss Ledger, week ending 21 April 1934; GD289/1/1, Playhouse Cinema, Profit and Loss Ledger, weeks ending 6 Jan.–29 Dec. 1934.

138. NAS, GD289/1/1, Playhouse Cinema, Profit and Loss Ledger, weeks ending 17 Aug. 1929–2 Sept. 1939.

139. NAS, GD289/1/1, week ending 17 Aug. 1935.

140. NAS, GD289/1/1, week ending 14 Jan. 1939.

141. NAS, GD289/1/1, weeks ending 10 March 1934; 16 Nov. 1935; 12 Feb. 1938; 4 Feb. 1939.

142. NAS, GD289/1/3, Palace Cinema, Profit and Loss Ledger, weeks ending 4 March; 11 March; 18 March; 12 Aug.; 19 Aug. 1939.

143. NAS, GD289/1/3, week ending 3 June 1933.

144. NAS, GD289/1/3, weeks ending 10 March 1934; 21 Sept.; 23 Nov. 1935.

145. NAS, GD289/1/3, week ending 5 Jan. 1935.

146. Wood, 'Low-budget British Films', p. 213.

147. NAS, GD289/1/3, Palace Cinema, Profit and Loss Ledger, weeks ending 7 Jan.–30 Dec. 1933; 5 Jan.–28 Dec. 1935.

148. GCA, TD273/3, Wishaw Picture Palace, Ltd, Cash Book; *Wishaw Herald*, 1934–9.

149. GCA, TD273/3, Wishaw Picture Palace, Ltd, Cash Book, weeks ending 16 June 1934; 30 May 1936; *Wishaw Herald*, 7 June 1934, p. 6; 21 May 1936, p. 8.

150. GCA, TD273/3, Wishaw Picture Palace, Ltd, Cash Book, weeks ending 9 April 1938; 7 Jan. 1939; *Wishaw Herald*, 31 March, p. 8; 29 Dec. 1938, p. 8.

151. GCA, TD273/3, Wishaw Picture Palace, Ltd, Cash Book, week ending 19 Dec. 1936; *Wishaw Herald*, 10 Dec. 1936, p. 8.

152. GCA, TD273/3, Wishaw Picture Palace, Ltd, Cash Book, weeks ending 4 Jan.; 17 Oct.; 14 Nov. 1936; 23 Oct. 1937; *Wishaw Herald*, 26 Dec. 1935, p. 6; 8 Oct., p. 8; 5 Nov. 1936, p. 8; 14 Oct. 1937, p. 8.

153. CM, Capitol Cinema, Aberdeen, Takings Books, weeks beginning 30 Jan. 1933–28 Aug. 1939.

154. CM, Capitol Cinema, Takings Book, week beginning 26 March 1934.

155. CM, Capitol Cinema, Takings Book, week beginning 17 July 1939.

156. Chibnall, *Quota Quickies*, ch. 7; CM, Capitol Cinema, Takings Books, 1933–9.

157. S. C. Shafer, *British Popular Films, 1929–1939: The Cinema of Reassurance* (London, 1997), pp. 22–4, 45; D. Sutton, *A Chorus of Raspberries; British Film Comedy, 1929–39* (Exeter, 2000); Chibnall, *Quota Quickies*, pp. 95–8.

158. CM, Capitol Cinema, Aberdeen, Takings Books, 1933–9.

159. GCA, TD273/3, Wishaw Picture Palace, Ltd, Cash Book, 5–7 April 1937; *Wishaw Herald*, 1 April 1937, p. 8; SSA, 5/8/51, Green Family Collection, Cash Book, April 1936–March 1937, Bathgate, 16–18 July 1936; Ayr, 18–20 June 1936.

160. NAS, GD289/1/1, Playhouse Cinema, Profit and Loss Ledger, week ending 27 May 1939.

161. Richards, *Age of the Dream Palace*, pp. 160–3.

162. CM, Capitol Cinema, Takings Book, week beginning 11 Jan. 1937.

163. GCA, TD273/3, Wishaw Picture Palace, Ltd, Cash Book, 9–12 Nov.; 27 April–2 May 1936; *Wishaw Herald*, 23 April, p. 8; 5 Nov. 1936, p. 8.

164. A. Higson, *Waving the Flag: Constructing a National Cinema in Britain* (Oxford, 1995), pp. 142–75; SSA, 5/8/50, Green Family Collection, Cash Book, Gorbals, 15–17 April 1935.

165. GCA, TD273/3, Wishaw Picture Palace, Ltd, Cash Book, 19–21 Sept. 1938; *Wishaw Herald*, 15 Sept. 1938, p. 8; CM, Capitol Cinema, Takings Book, week beginning 2 Jan. 1939.

166. P. Stanfield, *Hollywood, Westerns and the 1930s: The Lost Trail* (Exeter, 2001).

167. NAS, GD289/1/1, Playhouse Cinema, Profit and Loss Ledger, 1934–9.

168. CM, Capitol Cinema, Takings Books, 1933–9.

169. NAS, GD289/1/1, weeks ending 5 Feb.; 20 Aug. 1938; CM, Capitol Cinema, Takings Books, weeks beginning 3 Jan.; 3 Oct. 1938.

170. GCA, TD273/3, Wishaw Picture Palace, Ltd, Cash Book, 1934–9.

171. GCA, TD 273/3, Wishaw Picture Palace, Ltd, Cash Book, weeks ending 8 Jan.–4 June 1938; *Wishaw Herald*, 30 Dec. 1937–26 May 1938, p. 8.

172. Dickinson and Street, *Cinema and State*, pp. 65–6; *ET*, 21 Oct. 1937, p. 2, reporting Grierson's threat to withdraw from documentary production.
173. *ET*, 25 July 1929, p. 3.
174. *ET*, 24 Aug. 1939, p. 9.
175. *ET*, 13 Aug., p. 2; 27 Aug. 1936, p. 2; ; *Courier and Advertiser*, 31 Aug., p. 6; 10 Dec. 1936, p. 5; *Scotsman*, 28 Sept., p. 14; 12 Jan. 1937, p. 13; *World Film News*, 1(6) (Sept. 1936), p. 7; Hardy, *Scotland in Film*, p. 24.
176. *ET*, 19 Oct. 1933, p. 2.
177. *Scotsman*, 5 Nov. 1935, p. 15.
178. *ET*, 6 April, p. 9; 20 April, p. 9; 27 July 1939, p. 9.
179. *ET*, 27 July 1939, p. 9.
180. NAS, GD289/1/1, Playhouse Cinema, Profit and Loss Ledger, week ending 16 Jan. 1937; GD289/1/3, Palace Cinema, Profit and Loss Ledger, week ending 13 Feb. 1937, when *Mary's* place was taken by the 1935 Ginger Rogers comedy *In Person*.
181. *Scotsman*, 5 Nov. 1935, p. 15; NAS, GD289/1/1, Playhouse Cinema, Profit and Loss Ledger, week ending 31 May 1930.
182. SSA, 5/14/13, Nairn Collection, cutting from *KW*, 28 Sept. 1933; *Daily Record*, 16 Sept. 1933; unidentified cutting, p. 29; on local topicals in Scotland, see McBain, 'Mitchell and Kenyon's Legacy in Scotland', pp. 113–21.
183. NAS, GD289/1/1, Playhouse Cinema, Profit and Loss Ledger, week ending 22 Jan. 1938; GD289/1/3, Palace Cinema, Profit and Loss Ledger, week ending 22 Jan. 1938.
184. NAS, GD289/1/3, Palace Cinema, Profit and Loss Ledger, week ending 5 Sept. 1936.
185. *Film Weekly*, 28 June 1935, p. 15; SSA, 5/8/50–1, Green's Cash Books, week ending 11 Jan. 1936 (Bedford); 1–3 June 1936 (Tollcross); GCA, TD273/3, Wishaw Picture Palace, Ltd, Cash Book, 4–6 Jan. 1937; *Wishaw Herald*, 31 Dec. 1936, p. 8; NAS, GD289/1/1, Playhouse Cinema, Profit and Loss Ledger, week ending 11 Jan. 1936; GD289/1/13, Palace Cinema, Profit and Loss Ledger, week ending 14 March 1936; CM, Capitol Cinema, Takings Books, week beginning 30 Dec. 1935.
186. SSA, 5/8/51, Green's Cash Book, Gorbals, 18–20 Feb. 1937; *ET*, 18 Feb. 1937, p. 6.
187. On collusive practices, see for example S. Bowden and D. M. Higgins, 'Short-Time Working and Price Maintenance: Collusive Tendencies in the Cotton-Spinning Industry, 1919–1939', *Economic History Review*, 2nd ser., LI (1998), pp. 319–43.
188. The output of features peaked in 1936 at 192. Longer-term trends are outlined at http://www.screenonline.org.uk/film/facts/fact2.html (accessed 26 November 2011).
189. See Introduction, p. 5 and Chapter 5, pp. 192–3.
190. NAS, GD289/1/3, Palace Cinema, Profit and Loss Ledger, week ending 21 April 1934; GD289/2/15, Palace Cinema, Running Book, 16–21 April 1934; *The Evening Dispatch* (Edinburgh), 17 April, p. 1; 19 April, p. 1; 21 April 1934, p. 1.

6

Beyond the Dream Palace: The Role of Non-commercial Cinema in Scotland

I

In the final two decades covered by this study, at a time when cinema's mass appeal reached new heights, an alternative approach to film and its place in society enjoyed growing influence. Here, film's worth was measured, not in terms of box-office returns, but with regard to the wider political and cultural significance of both its subject matter and the techniques deployed to convey it. Drawing on the example of The Film Society in London, organisations emerged from the later 1920s which aimed to develop an appreciation of film as an important cultural artefact. Across the 1930s and then into the 1940s, a network of societies was established and came to flourish across Scotland, their work coordinated by a national federation that had no equivalent to the south. By 1950, that body's own publication, *Film Forum*, was reporting on the activities of thirty-three film societies across the country, with a combined membership of around 14,000. Such numbers were seen to provide convincing evidence that 'there [was] rapidly developing a mature and adult audience eager to support films of artistic merit'.[1] Yet the importance of the societies extended beyond the exhibition of subjects deemed unsuitable for commercial exploitation. In larger centres in particular, they were also active in educative work, mounting performances specifically designed for and aimed at children, and offering courses that aimed to enhance an appreciation of advanced cinematic techniques and their practitioners.[2] In Edinburgh, the ambitions of the local society, the Film Guild, went further, as it began the period by promoting the publication of one of the first periodicals outside London to adopt a critical approach to evaluation of the moving image, *Cinema Quarterly*, and ended it by overseeing the development of an annual Festival of Documentary Film, a remit reflecting an aesthetic preference for actuality footage and the importance of such productions to Scotland's film culture more generally.[3]

Alongside the film societies, another approach sought to explore the wider utilisation of the moving image in classroom and pulpit. The educative potential of film, long recognised, was pursued through projects designed to integrate the moving picture into the everyday curriculum. For churches also, an awareness that congregations were increasingly receptive to messages conveyed by visual means encouraged a belief in film's capacity to amplify the force of God's word. While the products of conventional cinema were viewed for the most part with profound distaste, both teachers and ministers would come to see film as a potentially powerful ally in furthering their work. By the later 1930s, organisations were active in both areas that aspired to operate at a national (Scottish) level. Both the Scottish Educational Film Association and the Scottish Churches' Film Guild sought to harness film's potential, hitherto latent, to reach out to a new, more visually literate audience.[4] The following decade, in areas still innocent of the kind of mass, commercialised recreational culture exemplified by the picture palace, film acquired an even broader significance, as one of the key building blocks in the construction of a viable civil society. The work of the Highlands and Islands Film Guild, a further example of Scotland's non-commercial engagement with the moving image, was not simply to purvey much-needed entertainment, but also to act as a vehicle by which a viable sense of community could develop among remote areas of dispersed population.[5]

Even prior to this, at the start of the 1940s, the opinion was being voiced by, among others, the Scottish Film Council, that 'In Scotland far more than in England the film now plays an ever increasing and useful part in the life of the community.'[6] The aim of this chapter is not to subject the first part of this claim to extended scrutiny, although occasional comparisons with developments south of the border may help to convey a sense of the degree to which it was informed by more than mere hubris. Rather, the intention is to examine the role of film in the world beyond the conventional cinema circuits. As well as outlining the work of the various organisations, a necessary task given the absence of systematic studies of the non-metropolitan film society movement in the period, it also seeks to evaluate their contribution in practice.[7] Throughout, attempts to promote the wider function of film encountered political, economic, and cultural obstacles, which would operate to determine both the pace and pattern of development over time.

II

It is perhaps in the non-commercial application of film that a distinctive Scottish experience appears most pronounced. That outcome could not have been predicted, however, when the first film society north of the border, in Glasgow, was inaugurated late in 1929.[8] As with similar organisations that followed, the Glasgow Society, established so one account had it as the result of a chance encounter atop a tram between two film enthusiasts, D. Paterson Walker and Stanley Russell, encountered several obstacles to its effective operation. The selection and hire of films to fill a season's programmes proved a major challenge given a lack of information as to available titles and the reluctance of conventional distributors to handle subjects of doubtful commercial worth. In addressing both, assistance was sought from the only comparable body to pre-date the Glasgow Society, the Film Society in London.[9] Active since 1925, the latter was the earliest organised manifestation of a growing propensity to see film as an artistic medium. As set out in its first programme, the London society aspired to

> show a group of films which are in some degree interesting and which represent the work which has been done, or is being done experimentally in various parts of the world. It is in the nature of such films that they are (it is said) commercially unsuitable for this country; and that is why they have become the especial province of the Film Society.[10]

As Forsyth Hardy later reflected, the regular production of Society programmes provided an important guide for enthusiasts elsewhere as to the range of films available for hire.[11] What is more, the London body also assisted societies north of the border by enabling them to circumvent established channels of distribution and so secure prints of appropriate titles. The Glasgow Society was thus able to screen, at its first meeting in November 1929, Robert Wiene's 1920 expressionist classic *The Cabinet of Dr. Caligari*.[12] Other problems were addressed more locally. The exhibition of films from 35 mm prints necessitated the use of licensed premises, the availability of which during the week was uncertain. With Sunday the only day on which licensed theatres were not in use, society meetings had threatened to run up against prevailing Sabbatarian sentiment. In the case of Glasgow, at least, both issues were readily overcome: local magistrates proved amenable to private screenings on Sundays, the initial Society subscription of two guineas removing any suspicion that shows might be 'public' in character, while premises were secured through the hire for early meetings of the small, private theatre of First National-Pathé, Ltd.[13]

Although efforts were made to secure Eisenstein's *Battleship Potemkin* for a Society show, the aims of the organisation more generally were broadly in line with those of the London body. 'Kinoman' of the *Evening Times* was thus able to reassure readers that 'Their only purpose is to show artistic films that were not available in the ordinary commercial cinema.'[14] To modesty of ambition was added moderate growth initially. Some fifty local worthies had expressed an interest in the formation of a society when discussions commenced late in 1928.[15] After three years of operations, membership stood at 200, shows having transferred to the 600-seater Gem Cinema on the Great Western Road.[16] Growth was constrained by differences over the adoption of sound, many committee members adhering to the view that cinema was an essentially visual medium, whose character would be compromised by the intrusion of a soundtrack.[17] From that point, however, a deliberate move to expand membership was launched. Subscriptions had already been reduced to 26s and were now more than halved again to 12s a year.[18] With the move to larger accommodation, first at the King's on Sauchiehall Street and then at Cranston's on Renfield Street, growth was such that, by 1936,

World Film News could claim Glasgow as having 'perhaps the largest British Society'.[19] The note of qualification had been removed the following year, by which point membership had reached 1,000.[20] Along with the growth in enrolments, Society activities were also extended, so that by the late 1930s, two performances were mounted on Sundays during the season, and regular talks were delivered by figures prominent in the industry, while in 1936 a repertory season of significant recent productions was inaugurated.[21] By that point, expansion had come to reflect growth in the society movement more generally across Scotland.

Before turning to consider that pattern, the emergence of an alternative, more overtly political strand of non-commercial cinema must be considered. Three months after the Glasgow Film Society made its bow, in February 1930, the Edinburgh Workers' Progressive Film Society held the first of what was intended to be a series of monthly shows, at the Oddfellows' Hall in Forrest Road.[22] The opening programme and those that followed gave deliberate prominence to the products of Soviet cinema, valued alike for the progressive values informing them and for demonstrating, through advanced editing techniques, the highest achievements in cinematic art. An equivalent Glasgow organisation emerged later in the year and both societies affiliated to a British-wide Federation of Workers' Film Societies, a body which assisted in the distribution of appropriate subjects.[23] The Edinburgh Society's dealings with the local magistracy with regard to the exhibition of politically contentious material has already been documented.[24] While objections were raised against certain titles, in particular Pudovkin's *Storm over Asia*, the authorities' attention centred more on the conditions governing admission to the shows, to ensure their 'private' nature. This was all the more important given the need, from the second meeting on, to schedule screenings on Sundays, a day on which few if any cinematic exhibitions had hitherto been allowed in the capital. At that second gathering, held at Pringle's Atmospheric Theatre, some 400 gathered to see films on the triumphs of the Five Year Plan, and the comedy *The Girl With the Hat Box*, whose six reels, in the opinion of one critic, went to show that 'Humour has never been a strong characteristic of the Russian temperament.'[25] An attempt by the orchestra at the end of the programme to play the national anthem was drowned out by 'laughter and booing' from members of the audience, who then proceeded to sing the 'Internationale', the strains of which would conclude meetings of the Society over the next two years.[26] Reviewing progress in anticipation of a third season over the winter of 1931–2, officials could point to an enrolment of 278, greater it might be noted than the figure achieved to that date by the Glasgow Film Society.[27]

Yet indications are that plans for a third season remained in prospect only. Reports in the mainstream press on Society meetings cease in the summer of 1931 and, at about the same time, it is thought that the Glasgow Workers' Film Society ceased operations also.[28] The brief efflorescence experienced by both set the pattern for the remainder of the decade. Organisations concerned to explore film's political as well as artistic potential emerged sporadically through the 1930s. Most were based in Glasgow and, in most cases, their careers appear to have been brief. So, the West of Scotland Workers' Film Society was launched in 1934, with the aim of exhibiting titles 'dealing with culture and art, which are not generally shown in the commercial theatre'. Yet a political perspective was also admitted: 'With the advent of Fascism with its inherent danger to the masses it will be appreciated that a Workers' Film Society can do much to neutralise the reactionary element peculiar to certain leading newspapers and several commercially shown films.'[29] The context did nothing to ensure lasting growth, however, and, despite early reports of success, the Society's existence appears to have proved as fleeting as those of its predecessors, a fact which Douglas Allen, surveying the decade as a whole, attributes to a largely hostile licensing system.[30] The conditions attending 'private' shows had long proved an obstacle to the effective functioning of such societies, the tendency to seek to open meetings to non-members attracting particular attention. Yet the extent to which this can, of itself, account for the failure of most societies may be doubted. The regulations governing 'private' shows applied to all societies, whether political in intent or not, so that the problems confounding workers' organisations more probably reflect the difficulties encountered in generating sufficient support via subscriptions alone. At 10s a year, membership of the West of Scotland Society cost much the same as did that of the Glasgow Film Society.[31] Indeed, the Edinburgh Workers' Progressive Film Society had found its membership roll was subject to marked fluctuations over its two-year span.[32] A further and perhaps more telling obstacle may have been gaining access to appropriate material, a problem compounded by the passing of a central distribution agency as the Federation of Workers' Film Societies lapsed.[33] Even the presence of experienced figures from the cinema trade, such as George Singleton and James Welsh on the Advisory Council of the West of Scotland Society did not work fully to overcome such problems.[34] Finally, the appeal of Soviet films to more than a dedicated minority of politically inspired cineastes cannot be assumed. Members of the Glasgow Film Society during its second season were reported to find the Russian films included in the programmes 'depressing', while the audience at the Edinburgh Workers' Progressive Film Society show in June 1930, when faced by the non-appearance of the promised main feature *The End of St. Petersburg* rejected calls that they march in a body to the rail depot to demand access to the print, preferring instead to listen to the music provided by the orchestra.[35]

Workers' film societies enjoyed greater success in the more propitious circumstances that obtained after the Second World War. Yet organisations such as the Glasgow Trades Council Film Society, established in 1946 to provide educational films for local trade unionists, also prospered by diluting their political character. The Trades Council Society thus juxtaposed documentary subjects with older commercial features, in which any political message was wholly secondary. Programmes included the 1935 MGM production *Mutiny on the Bounty*, and the 1937 Deanna Durbin vehicle *One Hundred Men and a Girl*, which admittedly explored the plight of unemployed orchestral musicians.[36] In 1948, the Society's character was further amended by its affiliation to the Federation of Scottish Film Societies, which, while it gave access to a well-developed distribution system, also (through the Federation's Code of Practice) required the disavowal of any political intent.[37] Overall, then, the workers' film societies proved a recurrent, if muted, counterpoint to the development of the society movement as a whole.

Here, with the exception of an organisation briefly active in Dundee at the start of the decade, progress was, if initially modest, at least measured and secure.[38] In October 1930, plans for a body that would 'bring together those interested in the development of film art and . . . arrange for the exhibition of films not generally shown in the ordinary commercial picture house' and would be run on explicitly non-political lines, were announced in Edinburgh.[39] The Film Guild, so called to differentiate it from the still-active Workers' Society, aimed, in Forsyth Hardy's words, to create a 'cultured and intelligent cinema public'.[40] The belief was, as the Guild's secretary Norman Wilson explained, that given the chance cinema-goers would welcome alternatives to Hollywood and 'its weeping daddies, its hot mammas, and its crazy babies'.[41] The initial intention, in contrast to practices in Glasgow and elsewhere, was to incorporate films of 'outstanding interest and importance' in the standard programme of a conventional cinema, the Princes, which would effectively become the first repertory picture house in Scotland.[42] Returns soon indicated that Edinburgh was not ready for such a radical departure, so that by February of the following year, an approach was made to the city magistrates for permission to hold a private performance in March at the Salon Picture House. As in Glasgow, the first programme included *The Cabinet of Dr. Caligari*, on this occasion supported by an early production by the Empire Marketing Board, *Conquest*.[43] Further shows continued at the Salon, including one of the Japanese film *Jújiro* or *Crossways*, before in October 1931 the Guild transferred its activities to the Caley Picture House on Lothian Road.[44]

In seeking to nurture an intelligent and discerning audience for cinema, the Guild's activities extended well beyond the standard season of Sunday screenings. Additional shows were occasionally mounted to give prominence to producers of particular interest locally. In April 1932, an exhibition was organised at the YMCA Hall of Jenny Brown's *A Crofter's Life in Shetland*, while two years later a week was set aside for the screening of Brown's *The Rugged Island*. Such was the demand that further shows were put on at short notice for the following week.[45] In addition, members could attend talks by figures in the trade, including Victor Saville, and luminaries of the documentary movement, such as Basil Wright and Cavalcanti.[46] Other sessions sought to explore the broader significance of the moving image, so that in February 1931 Compton Mackenzie became the Guild's first guest speaker on the subject of 'Nationality and the Film', during which he declared that one of his first measures if appointed Minister of Fine Arts in an independent Scotland would be to ban all American films for two years.[47] At times, the Guild also undertook a wider public role, organising in January 1932 an exhibition of film stills at the premises of the Edinburgh Photographic Society, while the following year a further show was mounted in conjunction with the local branch of the Scottish USSR Society, on Russian cinema, comprising stills, posters, and related publications. While the propagandistic purpose of Soviet productions was acknowledged, this was explained in part by cinema's ability as a visual medium to reach out to communities populated, as the exhibition catalogue somewhat superciliously observed, 'mainly by peasants of simple intelligence'. In so doing, it was noted, directors had made major advances in the construction of narratives, so that 'the system of montage, or the cutting and assembling of the pieces of celluloid which go to make the completed film has had an incalculable influence on film technique'.[48] If nothing else, this went some way towards justifying claims by exhibition organisers that its purpose was entirely non-political.

A more practical engagement with developments in production methods was encouraged by plans, announced at the Guild's first general meeting, to produce a film on Edinburgh, a subject worthy it was thought of a 'city symphony' on the lines of Ruttmann's essay on Berlin.[49] To that end, a competition was launched in April 1931 with a prize of £10 offered by Guild President and editor of *The Modern Scot*, J. H. Whyte, for the best scenario. Following adjudication by John Grierson, the money was shared between the authors of two treatments, one of which sought to contrast the city's 'sinister medievalism, . . . with its calm classicism', while the other, by an undergraduate studying history at the University, was considered rather too close to Ruttmann's original.[50] Despite Grierson's doubts, production went ahead, overseen by local cinema manager and Guild Committee member, J. S. Nairn, and, after being shown at a Guild performance in November 1932, would achieve wider circulation through the efforts of the Scottish Travel Association.[51]

As this necessarily brief survey suggests, the Guild's educative work assumed varied forms. Young cinema-goers were encouraged to develop an intelligent appreciation of film through the provision of special matinee programmes at Nairn's Ritz Cinema during the winter of 1932–3. The first show included the British Instructional documentary on Africa, *Stampede*, leavened to some degree by the Disney Silly Symphony, *Mother Goose Melodies*.[52] Among more seasoned cineastes, film appreciation was encouraged by the publication of *Cinema Quarterly*, the first Scottish journal to cast a critical eye on the cinematic art. Although nominally independent, the *Quarterly* was edited by Guild Secretary, Norman Wilson, whose opening editorial as 'Spectator' amounted to a restatement of the Guild's aims.[53] The range of its efforts means that the Guild's impact cannot be measured by membership enrolments alone. Nevertheless, on this narrowest of gauges, growth must be judged steady, if unspectacular. By the end of the third season, Wilson reported a membership of around 300, which three years later had increased to 550, and by the end of the last pre-war season stood at 822.[54]

As the decade progressed, the film society movement spread well beyond the twin poles of the central belt. An organisation in Aberdeen, under consideration since 1929, was fully active by the later months of 1934 and claimed, by 1936, the second largest enrolment in Scotland at 750.[55] By that date, activity had resumed in Dundee, although now in conjunction with like-minded enthusiasts in St Andrews. Screenings took place on Sundays in both centres, those in Dundee being mounted in the afternoons at the King's Theatre, before the films were transferred by ferry to St Andrews to be shown in the evening at the New Picture House.[56] This arrangement sustained a membership of just over 300 by early 1937, a level of support which, it was noted, was insufficient to maintain solvency. By the end of the year, however, a marked improvement in the Society's finances was reported.[57] Further west, and through encouragement offered by members of the Glasgow Society, a body was established to serve Ayrshire from 1936. Shows were mounted on Sundays at Prestwick, to which it was hoped to attract cineastes from across the county.[58] Elsewhere, continued opposition to recreational activity on the Sabbath posed obstacles to the effective func- tioning of societies. Prevented from exhibiting at a local picture house, the Stirlingshire Society was obliged to exhibit at the Regent in Bannockburn.[59] To the north, the difficulties were even more profound. In 1936, a Society was formed in Inverness, with the backing of the editor of the city's *Courier* newspaper, which aimed 'to stimulate an interest in intellectual cinema throughout the North of Scotland'.[60] Such aspirations were complicated, however, by the problems encountered in securing licensed premises for shows. Attempts to use the city's Little Theatre came to nothing, as the owner insisted that the Society bear the cost of installing projection and sound equipment. With enrolments below 100, the decision was taken to suspend operations part way through the second season.[61] Similar problems attended the formation of the Lochaber Society in 1937. With Sunday shows rendered impossible through the strength of local feeling, and few licensed venues available, the Society's first meeting was held in Fort William Town Hall. It was a less than promising opening, with the effectiveness of the main film, *The Life of Louis Pasteur*, somewhat compromised by being projected at the wrong speed.[62] Thereafter, shows switched to the Playhouse in Fort William, although programmes had to be scheduled to meet the demands of normal commercial screenings. Meetings were therefore held between 5 and 8 p.m. on Wednesdays at the Playhouse, with parallel meetings organised for Kinlochleven, some 20 miles distant.[63] Unlike its counterpart in Inverness, the Lochaber Society, guided by its secretary, Robert MacEwan, son of SNP leader Alexander MacEwan and himself a member of the party's ruling council, continued to function with a membership of some 150 up to the outbreak of war.[64] Engagement with film as an art was also sustained by societies in Lanarkshire, Dunfermline and West Fife, and Caithness.[65] In the case of the latter, a body primarily devoted to the production of films on local subjects, winter evenings were set aside for the screening of films of interest in its club rooms, located in a disused laundry. In what had become almost a tradition of the movement, the film selected to inaugurate this phase of the Society's work was *The Cabinet of Dr. Caligari*, shown on this occasion from a 16 mm print.[66]

If, as Norman Wilson argued, society developments were largely driven by the efforts of local enthusiasts, they were also influenced, from late 1934, by a central governing body, the Federation of Scottish Film Societies.[67] With membership open to those bodies 'existing chiefly for the propagation of an interest in the artistic and critical value of the film', implicitly excluding organisations with more overtly political leanings, the Federation was formed to promote the development of the movement through the provision of information and by facilitating the cooperative renting of films, ensuring a ready supply of appropriate titles at a cost most would find bearable.[68] Initially, the intention was to work as part of a British-wide organisation. In September 1932, representatives of both the Glasgow Film Society and the Edinburgh Film Guild had attended a conference in Welwyn, at which the formation of a Federation of Film Societies covering Britain as a whole was under consideration.[69] The failure of this and a second conference at Leicester in 1936 persuaded the Scottish Federation to go its own way. In explaining the decision, one correspondent to *World Film News* struck an especially critical note: 'the Scottish societies are thoroughly disgusted with the chaos existing in the south'.[70] Particular frustration was vented at what was seen to be the obstructive attitude of the Film Society in London. Having long relied on that body for information and film booking facilities, the Federation moved in August 1936 to appoint its own London agent.[71] More by accident than design, therefore, the society movement north of the border acquired a peculiarly Scottish character. This idea was consolidated in the final months of peace by the publication of a journal devoted to the Federation and its affiliates: *Film Forum*.[72]

The Federation was not the first body which aimed to develop a distinctively 'Scottish' approach to the moving image. In 1933, following publication of the report by the Commission on Educational and Cultural Films, *The Film in National Life*, the British Film Institute was established to foster links between the cinema trade and 'all who are interested in the artistic, educational, and cultural possibilities of the film'.[73] Scottish opinion was broadly supportive of the move, endorsing the creation of a National (i.e., British) Film Institute at a conference held in Glasgow in December 1932.[74] With the BFI in being and in the absence of any equivalent body north of the border, Scottish organisations actively supported the London initiative. Glasgow's Education Committee, long exercised by the issue of cinema's moral impact on the young, became a corporate member of the Institute, while the Educational Institute of Scotland was represented on the BFI's Advisory Council.[75] As the Institute sought to extend its work via a network of local agencies, the question of the relationship with any representative Scottish body became a point of contention. A complicating factor concerned the arrangements whereby the BFI was funded from the proceeds of shows sanctioned under the Sunday Entertainments Act of 1932, a measure which, as has been seen, did not apply in Scotland.[76] A further problem arose from an acute difference of opinion between the Glasgow Film Society and the Edinburgh Film Guild over the constitutional status of any Scottish body, some arguing that it be wholly separate from the BFI. The latter approach was rejected as unworkable for the various publicly funded bodies likely to be represented in a Scottish organisation and was also vigorously opposed by representatives of the Carnegie UK Trust. An initial meeting in Edinburgh in May 1934, chaired by John Buchan, agreed that 'The Scottish body would have to be in no sense subordinate to the Institute', but set aside calls for full independence.[77] A classic 'Unionist-Nationalist' solution resulted, whereby the Scottish Film Council would be 'an integral part of the British Film Institute but with a status superior to that of the provincial Branches in England'.[78] The Council's chair was offered to Col J. M. Mitchell of the Carnegie UK Trust, as someone associated with neither the cinema trade nor the educational interest and who had no involvement in 'the clash of opinion between the East and the West of Scotland'.[79]

As formally constituted in September 1934, the Scottish Film Council would devote the bulk of its energies to developing film's role in education, a theme which engaged two of the four 'panels' active in the 1930s. Alongside that explicitly concerned with education, the Social Science Panel was concerned to draw up lists of films suitable for children's matinees, as well as shows put on by youth organisations.[80] The Council's other efforts centred on the encouragement of amateur cinematography and measures supportive of the work of film societies in nurturing an informed and critically literate audience.[81] The Entertainment Panel, under the chairmanship of Forsyth Hardy, sought to generate support for productions of unusual merit which failed to 'obtain appreciation from the ordinary cinema-going public'.[82] To this end, a list of commercially screened films would be published in newspapers, with readers invited to indicate which they found most satisfying. In addition, panel members, who included Jack Brown, 'Kinoman' of the *Evening Times*, would recommend titles which it was felt picture-goers 'should endeavour to see'.[83] As published in the Council's *Monthly Bulletin* from November 1935, the list comprised a critically approved corpus of American and British features available via the commercial screen. The first group included *Becky Sharp*, Hollywood's take on Thackeray's *Vanity Fair*, with Miriam Hopkins and Frances Dee, recommended as the first major Technicolor production, and Hitchcock's *The Thirty-Nine Steps*, whose 'ungenerous and unconvincing' depiction of a crofter was set against the presentation of a political meeting which was found to be 'natural and convincing'.[84] Another 'Scottish' subject to feature was *The Ghost Goes West* in February 1936. Here, although an element of caricature was to be observed, this was not felt to be informed by malice, so that 'After so many films misrepresenting Scotland, it is a pleasure to have one in which the Scot does not appear as a compound of toper and miser.'[85] No such ambiguity marked the recommendation afforded Michael Powell's *The Edge of the World* in October 1937, while praise was also forthcoming for the production of *As You Like It*, with Laurence Olivier and Elisabeth Bergner, adjudged 'the most satisfactory Shakespeare adaptation yet made', and *Tudor Rose*, a dramatisation of the life of Lady Jane Grey with Nova Pilbeam, in which historical inaccuracies were, in contrast to those found in *Mary of Scotland*, deemed to have dramatic justification.[86] A diverse range of Hollywood fare received commendation, from Frank Capra's *Mr. Deeds Goes to Town*, seen as 'one of the events of the film year' in 1936, to the Technicolor exploits of Errol Flynn in *The Adventures of Robin Hood*, considered 'A film for the young of all ages'.[87] Quite what impact the efforts of the Entertainment Panel had is impossible to quantify. The circulation of the Council's *Monthly Bulletin*, put at 7,800 early in 1937, provides a base estimate of those with access to the listings.[88] Beyond that, their impact must be weighed against that afforded by other modes of publicity and cinema-goers' continued reliance on recommendations gathered by word of mouth.

Another, more tangible consequence of growth in the film society movement was the inauguration in 1939 of Scotland's first repertory cinema, the Cosmo in Glasgow. Projected by George Singleton, who the previous year had divested himself of exhibition sites across the central belt, the Cosmo was planned as a venue for the showing of 'foreign and outstanding films exclusively' and was inspired in part, so press reports had it, by 'the great popularity of the West of Scotland Film Societies'.[89] Singleton himself, as has been noted, was an active supporter of the workers' film society movement and, in running the Cosmo, endeavoured to draw upon the experience garnered by the Glasgow Film Society, advice on film bookings being provided by the Society's chairman, Charles Oakley. If the Cosmo's opening reflected the growing influence of moves to promote the cultural appreciation of film, it also posed a challenge to that movement, as its programmes threatened to replicate those offered at Society meetings. In a similar vein, the decision of the Poole family to operate the Cameo Cinema in Edinburgh as a venue for the exhibition of foreign-language features from the late 1940s necessitated a change of approach by the local Film Guild, involving a shift towards the selection of films not otherwise available for public screenings.[90] More generally, the development of repertory and foreign-language cinema was not so extensive as to pose a major challenge to the societies. For all that, the movement encountered other, more insistent complications from the later 1930s.

The first involved changes in quota legislation, as the Cinematograph Films Act of 1927 came up for renewal. In particular, the Act passed in 1938 altered conditions for the screening of short, documentary subjects, staples of film society programmes, making them eligible for quota for the first time and so encouraging their take-up by commercial exhibitors.[91] So, the films produced under the auspices of the Scottish Development Council for showing at the Glasgow Empire Exhibition of 1938 were acquired by MGM and ABPC for wider distribution and, by the end of 1942, had secured close on 4,000 bookings at cinemas across England, as well as just over 1,000 at venues across Scotland. In all, in that time, they were seen by an estimated 24.5 million cinema-goers.[92] As short subjects secured wider exposure, their availability for society shows was markedly reduced.[93] Such problems were further compounded by the outbreak of war from September 1939. Initial concern that the cost of rentals would become prohibitive as income from subscriptions fell soon gave way to more fundamental anxieties about the supply of film itself.[94] With many distributors departing London at the height of the Blitz, the Scottish Federation's agent anticipated growing difficulties securing the necessary product.[95] By September 1941, with the Federation's booking agent in London, Fairfax-Jones, in the forces, Scottish societies were obliged to book films through the BFI.[96] As access to film became more problematic, societies opted for themed programmes, reflecting the output of particular nations. In the second winter of the war, the Edinburgh Film Guild mounted evenings of Dutch and Polish films.[97] The problem here was that subjects were not always supplied with subtitles, necessitating recourse to an older mode of presentation. So, the Ayrshire Society's showing of the Soviet film *The Little Humpbacked Horse*, towards the end of 1943, was accompanied by a commentary provided by a woman of Russian descent resident in the district.[98]

Increasing reliance on the Soviet Union as the most reliable source of non-English material exposed societies in places to increasing critical scrutiny. Magistrates in Kilmarnock thus blocked performances by the Ayrshire Society in 1942, following objections by the chief constable to the proposed showing of two Russian films.[99] Elsewhere, the attitude of local licensing authorities was a leading factor behind the decision to suspend activities during the conflict. Magistrates in St Andrews and Dunfermline moved to block the staging of Sunday shows once war broke out.[100] In Glasgow and Lochaber, the escalating cost of film proved a more telling constraint, the

Glasgow Society's decision to suspend operations eased somewhat by the alternative outlet for cultural film offered by the Cosmo.[101] Through the war, then, society activity came to centre on Edinburgh, Dundee, Aberdeen, and Ayrshire, and although all recorded reduced enrolments in early wartime seasons, growth thereafter was marked, with attendances further boosted by the decision to open performances to members of the armed forces stationed locally. The Edinburgh Film Guild's membership of 470 in December 1939 had more than doubled three years later, while 200–300 tickets were regularly set aside for men under arms.[102] Such was the level of demand that the Guild's usual afternoon performances were supplemented from 1942 by evening screenings.[103] By the war's end, the Guild's membership had been closed at 2,092, while limited accommodation had obliged the Dundee Society to take a similar decision as enrolments approached 1,000.[104] The final months of the war also saw the revival of the Glasgow Society, with meetings now held at the Cosmo. Here, as elsewhere, membership rose to levels that obliged officials to refuse new subscriptions.[105] Measured purely in quantitative terms, the society movement was flourishing as never before, but doubts as to how far growth served to weaken the commitment to cultural uplift soon began to circulate. By the spring of 1944, concerns were being voiced in Dundee 'that there was always possible the danger of the Society developing into a mere purveyor of Sunday entertainment'.[106] Developments after 1945 did nothing to quell such fears.

First impressions suggest that the film society movement across Scotland experienced vigorous growth in the post-war years. Following Glasgow's example, organisations at Dunfermline, Lochaber, and Inverness resumed operations with the return to peace, and were now supplemented by bodies which extended the movement's geographical reach considerably.[107] In the first two winters after the war, societies were reported to be active in Perth (membership 550) and Kirkwall, where the film section of the local Arts Club organised screenings of, among other titles, *Henry V* and *A Night at the Opera*.[108] By the end of the decade, these had been joined by organisations at Lanarkshire, Dumfries, Galashiels, and Shetland, where enthusiasts made use of the installation at the local Garrison Theatre.[109] The Galashiels Society, admitted to the Federation in December 1948, introduced the movement to the eastern border counties. With membership open to all over the age of sixteen, the Society declared its aim to be

> to encourage the study and advancement of Film Art by holding exhibitions of films illustrating or contributing to film development, by arranging lectures and discussions on relevant film subjects and by acquiring a collection of films, film literature and film stills.[110]

With meetings centred on the local Pavilion Theatre, the Society drew support from a population dispersed across several towns, from Hawick in the south to Kelso in the east. Within two years, it reported enrolments in excess of 350. Echoing patterns of attendance at commercial cinemas, over half its members were female, with unmarried women forming the largest single group of subscribers at 28.3 per cent of the whole.[111] This remains one of the few insights afforded into the following generated by socie-ties, a subject on which the written record is, more often than not, mute. For all that, the breadth of appeal indicated here invites some attempt at explanation.

Circumstances from 1945 were peculiarly propitious for the movement's prospects. The increasing availability of non-flammable 16 mm film widened the potential scope for screenings, as societies were no longer obliged to operate from licensed premises, the terms of most licences covering flam-mable 35 mm stock only. The Federation thus saw in substandard film the opportunity to extend cultural interest in film to areas as yet untouched by organisation. The first such body to affiliate to the Federation was based at the University of Edinburgh. With audiences augmented by students from Heriot-Watt and the College of Art, the Society claimed a membership of some 170 by 1949.[112] More significant, perhaps, in extending the movement's social and geographical reach was the Film Appreciation Group on Lewis, active from 1946, whose first season included such Society standards as *Potemkin*, *Metropolis*, and *The Cabinet of Dr. Caligari*. In its third full season, a membership of fifty-two witnessed eight performances in the school canteen of the Nicolson Institute, and attended six discussion meetings, at which films shown at the Playhouse in Stornoway were considered.[113] By the end of the decade, 16 mm societies also flourished in Greenock, Dumbarton, Dumfries, Shotts, and Wishaw, while the Edinburgh University Society had been joined by organisations based at the University in Glasgow and George Watson's College in Edinburgh.[114]

Broader cultural changes also worked in the societies' favour. As has been seen, before 1939 the strength of Sabbatarian feeling obliged enthusiasts in Inverness to hold meetings during the week. By the time activity resumed after the war, constraints on Sunday meetings had been lifted and only where commercial screenings were allowed on the Sabbath, as at Greenock from 1948, were societies encouraged to mount performances on weekdays.[115] For the most part, however, the absence of commercial openings and the lack of alternative Sunday amusements during the lengthy Scottish autumn and winter afforded societies the space to flourish. This was not, however, a development welcomed by all. Concern that buoyant membership rolls con-cealed developments inimical to the societies' prime purpose surfaced in the pages of the Federation's own publication, *Film Forum*, in 1949. For 'D. H.' of Dundee, interest in film as an art form was limited to a small minority of members. Most, it was argued, 'are simply people who want a pleasant way of spending a Sunday afternoon or evening "at the pictures"'.[116] The point was taken up later the same year by J. Middleton of the Glasgow Society, who pressed the need for a more concerted attempt to encourage film appreciation among new members, in particular. For him, 'The film society seems to have become obsessed with the idea of numbers rather than quality nowadays and I think that greater attention to its educational function would be more in keeping with its principles.'[117] The apparent health of the movement belied what for some was a fundamental departure from its original aims.

If the evidence invites scepticism as to the impact of attempts to encourage a more reflective and intellectual engagement with the moving image, more measurable progress appeared to be made in developing a wider social purpose for film. In two areas in particular, education and religion, both crucial to Scotland's sense of self, practitioners showed increasing awareness of the capacity of moving pictures to communicate with a population increasingly attuned to visual modes of representation. More often than not, the power of film was viewed warily. Teachers and clerics have figured thus far in this work as critics of commercial cinema and advocates of closer regulation, particularly of shows directed at the young.[118] Nevertheless, as inquiries such as that conducted in Edinburgh in 1933 discovered, hostility within the teaching profession was leavened to a degree by a belief that film could also act to broaden perspectives and to stimulate new areas of interest. It occasions no surprise, then, that attempts to harness films more directly in educational work were evident through the silent era. These usually assumed one of two forms: the first involved screenings of approved films at local cinemas. In 1919–20, for example, Gracie's Banking Cinema in Annan ran a series of educational shows for schoolchildren in the immediate area.[119] More often, these took the form of one-off exhibitions, as with the matinees organised in Aberdeen in February 1921 to enable local children to witness a film on the Prince of Wales.[120] As an alternative, cinema equipment could be introduced into the classroom, so that film became an additional teaching resource, capable of being incorporated into lessons. Prior to 1914, such developments were rare and isolated. Few initiatives were attempted during the Great War, although in 1917, Motherwell School Board financed the layout of a cinematograph theatre for the teaching of geography and the sciences at the local high school.[121] More concerted moves to exploit the educative potential of celluloid were evident following the Armistice. A portable projector capable of being used in the schoolroom was demonstrated to interested teachers by the manager of Leith's Gaiety Theatre early in 1920.[122] Subsequent to that, educational authorities in Fife and Renfrewshire encouraged experiments in the use of the cinematograph, in the belief, as expressed in advance of its introduction into schools in East Wemyss, that it would help to relieve 'the monotony of being taught'.[123]

For pupils here as elsewhere, relief was not immediate, as a lack of equipment allied to a limited supply of suitable films delayed wider implementation. It would be the 1930s before a more sustained adoption of film in education became evident. In the face of renewed concerns over the films which children were likely to encounter in commercial cinemas, attention turned once more to the provision of performances geared more explicitly to the needs of the young, which would at the same time fulfil more openly film's educational function. John Grierson, director of the Empire Marketing Board Film Unit, touched on both issues in addressing an early meeting of the Edinburgh Film Guild in October 1931. The problem of the supply of appropriate subjects had, so Grierson argued, been substantially addressed, but difficulties remained in coordinating and communicating the needs of educationalists.[124] That work would be addressed by organisations established by interested groups of teachers across the central belt. In April 1933, teachers in Edinburgh established the Scottish Educational Sight and Sound Association, the title indicating a broader interest in the use of the gramophone in the classroom.[125] At the end of the year, the Association was complemented by the formation of a similar organisation in the west, the Scottish Educational Cinema Society, whose avowed aim was 'the creation of a body of opinion favourable to the furtherance of educational cinematography within the schools of Scotland'.[126] Both organisations affiliated to the Scottish Film Council on its formation in 1934 and, one year later, came together to constitute a single national body, the Scottish Educational Film Association.[127] From that point, the movement extended rapidly beyond its initial twin centres, so that by October 1936 a branch of the Association had been established in Ayrshire and others were being contemplated at Aberdeen, Dundee, Dumfries, and Inverness. By 1938, membership of the Association stood at close on 5,000, equivalent to some 18 per cent of the teaching profession across Scotland.[128] Growth thereafter was more modest, as the outbreak of war obliged many branches to suspend operations. Most resumed activity in the years from 1945 and the Association's operations were further extended into rural areas, with branches established in 1948–9 in Shetland, Angus, and East Lothian.[129]

Activity centred on two areas in particular. Building on the initial efforts of bodies such as the Edinburgh Film Guild, both the Educational Sight and Sound Association and the Educational Cinema Society organised matinees specifically structured with the needs, as they were perceived, of children in mind. In the east, shows commenced in October 1934 at the Capitol in Leith, at which 2,000 local schoolchildren were treated to a programme mounted in cooperation with Edinburgh Education Committee and the Gaumont-British Picture Corporation, the cinema's owners, which comprised studies of the River Thames and life in Malay. The same programme was then offered at other Gaumont houses across the city.[130] At the same time, further west, the Society promoted material of similar character at four cinemas across Glasgow and suburbs, while in April 1934 Grierson presented a programme of Empire Marketing Board films, including his own *Drifters* and *Granton Trawler*.[131] With the growth in the movement later in the decade, the areas covered by matinee provision widened. By March 1937, in the west of

Scotland, shows were being organised in Paisley, Greenock, Ayr, Saltcoats, and Kilmarnock, as well as Glasgow.[132] Early in 1939, children in the latter city were able to watch a matinee entirely comprising foreign-language films.[133]

The outbreak of war later that year posed new challenges for the educational film movement, as evacuation dispersed large numbers of urban schoolchildren, long used to regular access to the cinema, to areas where provision was more limited. To ease the transition to new surroundings and so discourage a drift back to danger areas, a network of travelling film shows was instituted, recalling cinema's early roots in itinerancy. With circuits so organised to ensure that each centre was visited at least once a week, exhibitions were staged in the kind of settings familiar to earlier generations of filmgoers, from village halls to schoolrooms, although the provision of shows in private homes represented something of a departure.[134] Funded by grants from the Ministry of Information and overseen by A. B. King in his role as Film Officer of Scotland, the scheme was sustained by individual teachers who drove across large areas of Scotland each supplied with a 16 mm projector and six reels of silent film, two of comedies, and four of an instructional character.[135] In all, prior to the conclusion of the scheme in January 1940, some 1,484 shows had been offered to 217,549 people.[136] Many had been introduced to a form of entertainment of which they hitherto had had little experience and such was the perceived value of the scheme that, after its termination, travelling shows were maintained for the duration of the conflict by the Ministry of Information.[137]

Other developments worked to narrow the scope of the educational film movement's activities. The formation of scientific film societies, the first in Aberdeen in 1939, followed a year later by Glasgow, provided a further regular outlet for instructional programmes.[138] By the middle of the war, the idea had been taken up in Edinburgh, encouraged by the local Film Guild. Here, a series of monthly performances ran at the Dominion Cinema in suburban Morningside, each programme comprising up to eight items, covering subjects from natural history to more practical science, including in December 1946, *First Principles of the Petrol Engine* and, in February 1947, *Old Wives' Tales: Health and Hygiene*.[139] By the end of the war, some six scientific film societies were active across Scotland.[140] At the same time, the commercial cinema sought to respond to the criticisms raised over its approach to the child audience. The Scottish Educational Film Association noted the rise of the Mickey Mouse Clubs, linked to the Odeon circuit, whose activities in geographical terms overlapped with areas previously served by matinees overseen by the Association. Here, entertainment was now explicitly associated with uplift and the encouragement, through songs, mottoes, and the wider paraphernalia of club organisation, of a sense of civic responsibility.[141] By the 1940s, then, the ideas informing the educational film movement's provision of matinee performances were being promoted by the cinema trade itself.

In early 1945, some thirteen clubs were reported to be active across Scotland, introducing some 10,000 children to the Odeon circuit's ideas on good citizenship and the healthy functioning of democracy.[142] If such work inevitably narrowed the scope for educational matinees, it did not eliminate them entirely. A performance of children's films was given prominence in the Documentary Film Festival held in Edinburgh in the later 1940s. In 1948, the chairman of the city's Education Committee was present at the Rutland Cinema to introduce a programme which included films from Britain and Canada.[143] A similar performance was mounted the following year, when members of the Education Committee were present to take particular note of children's reactions to what was screened.[144] Finally, in 1950, a series of educational matinees was held at Edinburgh's Gateway Theatre, under the auspices of the Scottish Educational Film Association in conjunction with the Educational Institute of Scotland. Unusually, the shows were staged during the week, on Friday afternoons, in the belief that this would be less likely to divert children from the kind of outdoor activities available on Saturday mornings. It would also, it was hoped, go some way to addressing what J. B. Frizzell, the city's Director of Education, referred to as 'the great emptiness and loneliness, and even ugliness' in the lives of contemporary adolescents.[145]

Such initiatives aside, the focus of the educational film movement came to centre increasingly on the second strand of its endeavours: the role of film within the classroom. Until the 1930s, progress largely reflected occasional and intermittent interest in the use of visual aids to complement teaching. Following the inauguration of a cinema classroom at a school in the Gorbals in 1931, Glasgow's Education Committee had voted for funds to equip five schools with projectors.[146] More sustained development awaited the emergence of organisations explicitly concerned to promote the educational use of film. By 1937, the number of projectors available across all Scottish schools stood at 200 and within twelve months this had increased to 350.[147] Several key constraints remained. Reporting on behalf of the Educational Panel of the Scottish Film Council in October 1936, Frizzell noted continued problems over the supply of films suitable for use in the classroom. To that point, recourse had been had to private film libraries, including those of the Empire Marketing Board and also the collections of Kodak and Ensign in London.[148] As a means of addressing issues of supply, the creation of a library of educational films that could be hired out to schools was under consideration from early 1936. This was to be supplemented by a reviewing system, whereby all films would be subject to assessment by two groups of teachers, whose evaluations would be published by the Scottish Film Council and the *Educational Film Review*.[149] Some forty viewing groups were active by early 1937, increasing to seventy a year later.[150] Their efforts were furthered by the consolidation of library provision from 1939, with the formation of the Scottish Central Film Library, assisted by a grant of

£5,000 from the Carnegie UK Trust.[151] Although primarily concerned to supply films for use in schools, the Library was also used by other groups keen to explore the educational potential of the moving image, including youth organisations and churches. In terms of titles hired out, growth was marked despite the wider context of war, peaking in 1942–3 at 41,872, before falling back as the supply of relevant subjects decreased and problems over the physical maintenance of projectors limited numbers of screenings.[152] So, the number of projectors in Scottish schools, which had stood at 700 in 1942, was down to 550 by 1944.[153] Demand thereafter remained buoyant, so that the Library reported increased activity across the later 1940s, hiring out subjects to a variety of organisations, including youth welfare agencies and clubs. In terms of the overall circulation of educational films, as well as the means taken to ensure their suitability for use by teachers, Scotland appeared a leader in international terms: the Central Film Library was noted to be the largest such collection in Europe.[154]

In other respects, however, the record was more mixed. As early as 1935, it was noted that access to the films of many leading producers of educational subjects was limited by the lack of access to sound. Most projectors in Scottish schools allowed for the screening of silent films only. Indeed, only fifty sound projectors were in use across the country by 1941.[155] The preference for silent film was, in part, a pragmatic response to the relative cost of projection equipment, the additional expenses accompanying sound installations limiting their adoption. In addition, however, silent projection was deemed more effective in the classroom setting, as it was less likely to interfere with the exposition of the lesson. The Scottish Film Council's report on educational film, published in 1940, thus displayed what *Sight and Sound*'s reviewer considered a 'heavy bias' in favour of the silent film, an attitude found to be at variance with that prevailing across England, where sound projection was utilised more extensively.[156] The effectiveness of each approach was subject to more extended evaluation early in the war, when an experiment into various modes of presentation was undertaken in two schools in Fife. The findings, reported in April 1942, indicated that the silent film accompanied by commentary from the teacher was the most effective means of communicating the desired information. Sound projection and the use of silent film with no commentary were considered of equal but lesser merit.[157] Suspicions as to the value of sound were informed in part by enduring 'differences of dialect and vocabulary which are met with from district to district'.[158] Thereafter, shortage of materials precluded extensive re-equipment and made even the maintenance of existing installations problematic, so that the silent film remained the default mode for instruction where film was employed, into the post-war era. Further inquiries into the relative merits of silence and sound were undertaken shortly after the war, with a move to sound projection at secondary level being recommended.[159]

Aside from such narrow technical considerations, the value of film in supporting the teaching of subjects such as geography and natural history had long been recognised. In the immediate post-war years, however, the moving image was assigned a central role in a scheme overseen by Glasgow Education Committee to promote a sense of civic responsibility among the young. To that end, rather than utilising existing footage, a series of twelve films was commissioned from local producers, including Thames and Clyde in Glasgow, and Campbell Harper in Edinburgh. The films were to be shown at secondary schools across the city, in addition to some eighteen corporation-run youth clubs in the area.[160] Film was thus assigned a central role in the shaping of early post-war Scottish society.

At the same time that educationists sought to integrate the moving image into their work, so Scotland's churches came to re-evaluate their relationship with film. For some time attuned to regarding the cinema with suspicion due to its apparent moral impact, individual churches had occasionally sought to develop more constructive ties with the industry, using picture houses for services so as to reach out to a more diverse congregation.[161] At Christmas 1934, for example, the Evangelism Committee of the Glasgow Presbytery arranged for meetings at the Regal Cinema to be addressed on consecutive nights by the Moderator of the General Assembly of the Church of Scotland and the Episcopal Bishop of Glasgow and Galloway.[162] Over time, the potential for mounting special exhibitions of films which promoted the churches' wider work was explored. In 1935, the Presbytery in Paisley pressed for local cinemas to be allowed to open on Sundays for the showing of a programme of films dealing with the Church's work overseas, and the holding of related mission services.[163] Such efforts remained, for the most part, local and piece-meal in character, with the supply of suitable titles a constraint on wider effort. The latter problem was addressed from 1936 through the formation of a central coordinating body, the Scottish Churches' Film Guild, born out of a conviction, expressed by the Rev. A. H. Dunnett, Joint Secretary of the Church of Scotland's Home Mission Society, 'that there was a place for the film in the works of the Church'.[164] To promote the Guild's work, and as a prelude to its launch, a performance of films considered suitable for exhibition by church organisations was staged during that year's General Assembly at the Monseigneur News Theatre in Edinburgh. Along with films dealing with mission work, the programme included productions of the GPO and British Commercial Gas Association Film Units, *Night Mail* and *Housing Problems*, a selection indicative of the wide view the Guild would take of its remit.[165]

In its early months, priority was given to selecting and making available subjects appropriate for church gatherings, and the organisation of exhibitions to demonstrate the potential film had both to further the work of religious agencies and to offer an alternative to what one minister dubbed the 'thinly-veiled pornography' that made up the fare of much commercial cinema.[166] To this end, the Guild sponsored the production of a film depicting the life of a country minister. Shot in the Drymen district and produced by Glasgow's Meteor Film Society, *Minister's Monday* made use of substandard 16 mm film, making it eligible for exhibition at non-licensed venues.[167] More generally, the Guild, which by 1938 comprised five branches, in Glasgow, Edinburgh, Ayr, Aberdeen, and Kirkcaldy, sought to develop a library of subjects that could be made available to churches.[168] One of the most popular in its third year of operations was another amateur production from Scotland, *Hope Springs Eternal*, a film which addressed the dangers both personal and social wrought by the football pools. Such was the demand for screenings that the Guild's copy had been 'mutilated'.[169] Through its affiliation to the Scottish Film Council, on which it formed part of the Social Services Panel, the Guild gained access to a wider body of material, primarily through the Scottish Central Film Library.[170] Even so, the supply of religious subjects remained sufficiently uncertain to act as a constraint on the Guild's work. So, while some branches were active in the provision of shows for troops on Sundays, organisation more generally appears to have atrophied in the early years of the war. By 1943, inactivity had become the norm, so that the Scottish Film Council could note at its September meeting that the Guild as a whole 'has tended to become somewhat moribund'.[171]

Sufficient importance attached to the Guild's work, however, to ensure that it was not allowed fully to lapse. A matter of weeks after its atrophied state had been noted, it was revived as the Scottish Religious Film Society.[172] This nominally new organisation announced its intention of continuing the work of its predecessor, offering advice on the availability of suitable films and establishing a Viewing Panel to recommend titles appropriate for screening by religious bodies. To assist the Society's work, a separate library specifically concerned with religious subjects was created as the war ended. Finally, to ensure that all shows mounted under its auspices were of the appropriate quality, the Society organised training courses in cinema projection for its younger members.[173] While it remains difficult to offer a precise evaluation of the wider impact of such work, one, admittedly narrow, measure suggests that by the end of the period, the Society had put the 'moribund' state of the war years long behind it. So, the number of films distributed by the Society increased markedly over the later 1940s, rising from 1,318 in 1947 to 4,157 by 1950.[174] Exhibitions were mounted in a variety of venues and to diverse audiences, so that religious films were made available to workers on the hydro-electric scheme that seemed set fair to transform life across the Highlands in the post-war years.[175]

As this suggests, film was seen to have a crucial role to play in addressing the problems associated with Scotland's more remote regions. A long-term trend towards depopulation was thought likely to be quickened by imbalances in the provision of popular entertainments. Before 1939, the comparative absence of amusements north of the Highland line was judged a powerful disincentive for people moving into let alone remaining in the area. Speaking at the Caledonian dinner of the Scottish group of the Forum Club in 1936, Sir Donald Cameron of Lochiel noted ruefully, 'If they asked a woman to go and live in a glen the first thing she would ask was "Where's the nearest cinema?"'[176] The problem was compounded by the experience of the war years, as those who had left for war service had been exposed to a wider range of amusements and so found the limited pleasures awaiting them on their return even more irksome. Yet those who had remained had also gained greater acquaintance with the cinema through the provision of mobile shows by, among other bodies, the Ministry of Information.[177] A population thus emerged from the conflict with higher expectations regarding recreational opportunities than was likely to be met by existing levels of provision. With only an estimated thirty commercial cinemas active across Highland districts in 1945, the potential for a continued entertainment deficit was clear and was only likely to worsen as Ministry of Information operations were wound down.[178] To address this problem, the Scottish Agricultural Organisation Society proposed the creation of mobile film units capable of serving large parts of the Highlands and Islands through regular circuits of shows. The conviction was expressed that 'for the moment mobile cinema units would do more to remove the feeling of isolation and neglect in isolated communities than the thought of electricity, which was something for the future'.[179]

The costs attending commercial exhibition and the lack of materials for building precluded the development of a network of fixed cinema sites. It was emphasised that the mobile units, a minimum of seven of which was considered essential if all districts were to be served effectively, would operate on a non-profit-making basis, thereby ensuring also that shows were not subject to payment of entertainments tax.[180] Programmes were to last approximately 2.25 hours and would comprise fourteen reels, made up of a feature, a news magazine (preferred to the standard cinema newsreel), a cartoon, and a documentary. A longer programme was deemed impracticable 'In view of the quality of the seating accommodation in most Highland halls', suggesting that there may have been point to the occasional charge that locals were somewhat thin-skinned.[181] Each programme was intended to combine entertainment with education, the latter function confirmed by regular screenings for schools and youth organisations across the region.[182] Funding for the body constituted in July 1946 as the Highlands and Islands Film Guild came in part from the Carnegie UK Trust, which provided full backing for two of the circuits, based on Shetland, and Ross and Cromarty. The remaining costs were met out of grants from local education authorities, with services also provided by the Scottish Information Office, which in 1946 acquired control of the equipment formerly operated by the Ministry of Information.[183] In all, four further circuits were inaugurated in 1946, centred on Caithness and Sutherland, Inverness-shire, Argyll, and Lewis and Harris.[184] In addition, the Guild also staged shows for workers on the hydro-electric project. One unit served those employed at Loch Sloy, while also providing exhibitions for the neighbouring village of Arrochar, while the camps at Glen Affric and Fannich formed part of a further circuit funded by the Hydro Board.[185]

The shows which commenced early in 1947 employed 16 mm film, with titles drawn from existing commercial libraries, principally those of Gaumont-British, Wigmore Films, Ltd, the substandard arm of Columbia Pictures, and MGM. In addition, the Guild was affiliated to the BFI, giving it access to the Scottish Central Film Library, an important source of actuality footage.[186] Films were selected by a committee, combining commercial, cultural, and technical interests. Its chair was R. Wotherspoon of Caledonian Associated Cinemas, a combine which operated some twenty-seven sites across Scotland in the later 1940s, assisted by film critic Forsyth Hardy, the writer Neil Gunn, and a Mr Wannop, who acted as Technical Agricultural Adviser.[187] In making its choices, the Committee sought to plunder the back catalogues of Gaumont-British and other studios, extending back into the 1930s. Throughout, the aim was 'to influence film taste upwards in the Highlands and Islands', and to that end films dealing with aspects of British history, from *The Private Life of Henry VIII*, through *The Young Mr. Pitt*, to *Victoria the Great*, were acquired, alongside subjects that dealt more directly with life on the geographical and material margin, such as *Man of Aran*, and *The Edge of the World*.[188] Even given the inclusion of educational titles to accompany all features, it was felt that the Guild's 'very careful' exercise of choice in the acquisition of films offered a clear safeguard against suspicions of vulgarity.[189] The first show mounted by the Guild in April 1947 was to an audience of schoolchildren in Hillswick on Shetland. The programme, repeated that evening for the benefit of local adults, comprised documentary, educational, travel, and religious subjects, with cartoons offering some light relief. Prior to the first performance, the audience was addressed by the Guild's organising secretary, Neil Weir, who was also Highland Officer of the Scottish Agricultural Organisation Society, who referred to the Guild as 'the citizen's cinema', a description which pointed up the particular relationship which that organisation sought to foster with its patrons.[190]

This was an issue which, over time, would greatly exercise Guild officials. Initially, it was acknowledged, the link between the Guild and those attending its shows was little different from that which applied in the ordinary commercial cinema. The 'cash nexus' encompassed all, with audience involvement limited to the payment of the agreed admission charges of 1s 6d for adults and 6d for children.[191] While that arrangement posed few problems for urban Scotland, the implications for work in more remote rural areas were more worrying, given the perception voiced at Guild meetings that 'the level of civic sense in most Highland communities was very low'.[192] The Guild's educational purpose thus went considerably beyond merely the cultivation of a cinematic aesthetic. Film would play a role, it was hoped, in developing an effective civil society across northern and western parts of Scotland, a development that would also work 'to keep young people in the areas'.[193] There was also in this, it must be noted, a narrower financial calculation, given that the grant from the Scottish Information Office to meet the operating costs of four of the circuits was finite.[194] The Guild's success thus rested on local communities agreeing to meet the costs of mounting shows. In the process, a broader moral purpose would be served. As Guild officials acknowledged early in 1948, 'The practice of self-help and cooperative organisation – thus begun through an amenity which is much desired – might spread to other aspects of rural community living.'[195] The first moves in this direction involved allowing circuits some choice over what films were screened. The first year of work by the Guild had already indicated marked variations in taste across districts, so devolving authority to Circuit Committees would help to accommodate such differences. It was recognised that, on occasion, preference would be extended to films of little cultural or educational value, the Tarzan series being singled out as an example of such, but the showing of such titles could be accepted 'as long as they are healthy and moral'.[196] If circuits were, in practice, rather large units around which to construct a sense of civic responsibility, this end would be furthered by encouraging individual settlements to acquire and run projection equipment, a move that would also have the effect of widening the areas covered by mobile units.[197] In the end, it was hoped, communities would assume responsibility for operating expenses, leaving the cost of administration to be met out of central funds from the Scottish Education Department. Continued support from the latter was, however, made conditional on 'the development of informal further education and . . . the question of community responsibility was an important feature of this'.[198]

Local initiatives, such as the purchase of projection equipment by supporters in Ardross, near Invergordon, were welcomed as evidence of progress in this direction.[199] Importance also attached to the formation in 1949 of a local committee covering Lewis and Harris, which it was hoped would provide a model for future development elsewhere, while the following year across Sutherland, it was proposed that local film clubs be established to encourage further interest in the Guild and its work.[200] Evidence more generally, however, suggests that engagement was fitful and patchy in nature. By September 1950, the decision had been taken to end shows on Tiree, as attendances were limited and support from the local Education Authority proved unforthcoming. A petition from residents at Scarinish persuaded the Guild to maintain performances there for an experimental period.[201] Elsewhere, increasing competition was encountered from itinerant exhibitors operating commercially. The presence of two such concerns at Ullapool in June 1950 created problems for the Guild, given that the town generated a quarter of the revenue from the circuit of which it formed a part. Here, as at Kinloch Laggan, where a similar challenge was faced, the decision was taken to continue shows while local support remained evident.[202]

Overall, in the year to December 1950, the Guild mounted some 2,078 shows, attended by over 135,000 locals. If such figures suggested to officials that 'The high standard of films shown is creating a good taste for films', the degree to which the movement could work to foster wider social change remained to be determined as the decade drew to a close.[203]

III

The work of the Guild across the Highlands and Islands confirms that by 1950 few areas of Scotland or of Scottish life remained untouched by film and its attendant cultures. At a time when commercial cinema-going, in numerical terms at least, reached new heights, the potential contribution of the moving image to the wider development of contemporary society was being meaningfully explored, to the extent that in certain areas it was seen to constitute one of the main building blocks of an effective sense of community. Such was the acceptance of film's central place in post-war culture that it occasioned little surprise when film was added to the range of activities comprehended by the proposed Festival of Music and Drama planned for Edinburgh in 1947.[204] The organisation of what became the first International Festival of Documentary Films fell to the Edinburgh Film Guild, which offered daily screenings at its newly acquired theatre in Hill Street, while the principal performances were held over two Sundays at the city's largest cinema, the Playhouse.[205] In terms of scale, the Festival expanded rapidly, the programme of seventy films in 1947 growing to one of over 150 within two years. At the same time, its remit was widened to encompass 'Realist, Documentary, and Experimental' films, enabling the 1950 gathering to open with the dramatisation of Eric Williams' book on life in a prisoner of war camp, *The Wooden Horse*.[206] The diversity of the programme, including as it did performances devoted to educational and scientific film, was testimony to the breath of Scotland's engagement with moving pictures beyond the world of mainstream cinema.

In the present state of the evidence, it remains difficult to assign a precise social and cultural importance to film. Quantitative measures are available to indicate the extent of growth in the film society movement, the take-up of titles from the Scottish Central Film Library, or attendances at performances mounted by the Highlands and Islands Film Guild. Against that, alternative indicators of the depth and quality of popular engagement remain elusive and in many cases there is justification for some scepticism as to the meaning to be ascribed to mere numbers, given the constraints on alternative amusements imposed by a powerful combination of austerity and Presbyterian morality. For the most part, therefore, this chapter has had to content itself with describing the growing social use of film, offering only occasional reflections on the wider implications of the trends outlined. Yet even a preliminary survey such as this has served to indicate the degree to which film touched aspects of life that were central to Scotland's sense of nationhood, in particular its educational and religious institutions. Film must be judged a central component of early twentieth-century Scottish society in more ways than one. Nor has this discussion exhausted that theme, as the country's involvement in developing representations of itself to both itself and the outside world through the production of films has, as yet, only been touched on in passing. A final chapter will investigate that far from negligible aspect of Scotland's cinematic history. Before that, however, the focus returns to film's role in mass culture, as the fortunes of the exhibition sector and its relationship with audiences during a second period of total war and the transition to peace are considered.

NOTES

1. *Film Forum*, 5(6) (March 1950), p. 2; see Appendix 3.
2. *Scotsman*, 1 Oct., p. 7; 7 Oct. 1931, p. 13, for the early plans of the Film Guild in Edinburgh.
3. *Cinema Quarterly*, 1(1) (Autumn 1932); *Documentary 47* (Edinburgh, 1947).
4. J. B. Barclay, *The Film in Scottish Schools* (Edinburgh, 1992), p. 5; *Scotsman*, 22 May 1936, p. 13; NAS, GD291/92/1, British Film Institute, Scotland, Scottish Film Council, *Monthly Bulletin*, 2(8) (Oct. 1936), p. 3, for the formation of the Scottish Churches' Film Guild.
5. NAS, ED30/2, Highlands and Islands Film Guild, Minutes of Meetings, Meeting of Financial Sub-Committee, 10 Nov. 1949.
6. SSA, 1/1/251, Scottish Film Council, Minutes, 1939–44, Eighth AGM, 29 Oct. 1941; also reported in *Scotsman*, 1 Nov. 1941, p. 3, where the remark is attributed to Oliver Bell, Director of the BFI.
7. Much of the writing on film societies continues to centre on the London body, J. Samson, 'The Film Society, 1925–1939', in Barr, *All Our Yesterdays*, pp. 306–13; J. Sexton, *Alternative Film Culture in Inter-War Britain* (Exeter, 2008).
8. Although the formation of a society had been under consideration since late the previous year, *ET*, 20 Dec., p. 3; 27 Dec. 1928, p. 3.
9. Such is the account provided by Walker himself, *Cinema Quarterly*, 1(2), pp. 119–20; SSA, 3/2/1, Film Societies Collection, cutting from *Scotsman*, 11 Feb. 1980, Forsyth Hardy on 'Film Guild's Fifty Years'.
10. *The Film Society. Programme. The First Performance at 2.30 P. M., on Sunday, October 25th, 1925*, n.p.
11. SSA, 3/2/6, Film Societies Collection, H. Forsyth Hardy, 'When "The Blue Angel" became respectable'.
12. *Cinema Quarterly*, 1(2), pp. 119–20.
13. *ET*, 21 Nov. 1929, p. 1; NAS, GD281/92/1, British Film Institute, Scotland, Scottish Film Council, *Monthly Bulletin*, No. 5 (Feb. 1936).
14. *ET*, 21 Nov. 1929, p. 1.
15. *ET*, 20 Dec. 1928, p. 3.
16. *Cinema Quarterly*, 1(2), pp. 120–1.

17. SSA, 3/2/4, Film Societies Collection, C. Oakley, 'How it began in Glasgow', from *Film*, Oct./Nov. 1975, Special Edition to Celebrate Fifty Years of Film Societies.

18. *Cinema Quarterly*, 1(2), p. 121.

19. *Cinema Quarterly*, 2(1) (Autumn 1933), p. 54; *World Film News and Television Progress*, 1(1) (April 1936), p. 20.

20. *World Film News*, 2(2) (May 1937), p. 43.

21. NAS, GD281/92/1, British Film Institute, Scotland. Scottish Film Council, *Monthly Bulletin*, 2(8) (Oct. 1936), p. 10; *World Film News*, 2(2) (May 1937), p. 43.

22. *Scotsman*, 13 Feb. 1930, p. 7.

23. Hogenkamp, *Deadly Parallels*, pp. 52–3, 60; Jones, *British Labour Movement*, pp. 168–9.

24. See Chapter 2, p. 68.

25. *Scotsman*, 17 March 1930, p. 11.

26. *Scotsman*, 17 March 1930, p. 11; 1 June 1931, p. 7.

27. *Workers' Cinema*, Nov. 1931, p. 4.

28. Hogenkamp, *Deadly Parallels*, p. 64.

29. *ET*, 13 Sept. 1934, p. 2; SSA, 3/2/2, Film Societies Collection, West of Scotland Workers' Film Society, printed broadsheet, n.d.; *Cinema Quarterly*, 3(1) (Autumn 1934), p. 57; see also *ET*, 10 Nov. 1932, p. 3, for the first meeting of the Scottish USSR Film Society.

30. *ET*, 15 Nov. 1934, p. 2, reporting the Society's fourth meeting; D. Allen, 'Workers' Films: Scotland's Hidden Film Culture', in McArthur (ed.), *Scotch Reels*, p. 94; Hogenkamp, *Deadly Parallels*, p. 65.

31. SSA, 3/2/2, Film Societies Collection, West of Scotland Workers' Film Society, printed broadsheet, n.d.

32. *Workers' Cinema*, Nov. 1931, p. 4.

33. Jones, *British Labour Movement*, p. 172.

34. SSA, 3/2/2, Film Societies Collection, West of Scotland Workers' Film Society, printed broadsheet; *ET*, 13 Sept. 1934, p. 2.

35. *Cinema Quarterly*, 1(2), p. 120; *Scotsman*, 23 June 1930, p. 11.

36. SSA, 3/2/15, Film Societies Collection, cutting from *Film Forum*, 7(2) (Nov. 1951).

37. SSA, 2/1/2, Federation of Scottish Film Societies, Minutes of Council, 1946–50, Meeting of Executive Committee, 6 Dec. 1946, at which the Society's application for affiliation was refused, due to the political nature of its bulletin; Meeting at Peebles Hotel Hydro [sic], 8 May 1948; Meeting at Central Hotel, Glasgow, 18 Sept. 1948, at which affiliation was agreed on a trial basis; on the Federation's rules, see Border Archives, Hawick, D/78/1/2, Galashiels Film Society, Federation of Scottish Film Societies, Code of Practice.

38. *Film Forum*, 3(2) (Winter 1948), p. 6, on the early organisation in Dundee.

39. *Scotsman*, 3 Oct. 1930, p. 12.

40. *Scotsman*, 14 Sept. 1932, p. 9; SSA, 3/2/1, Film Societies Collection, cutting from *Scotsman*, 11 Feb. 1980, Forsyth Hardy on 'Film Guilds'.

41. *Scotsman*, 28 Oct. 1930, p. 10.
42. SSA, 3/2/6, Film Societies Collection, H. Forsyth Hardy, 'When "The Blue Angel" became respectable'; 3/2/4, Hardy, 'How it Began in Edinburgh', *Film*, Oct./Nov. 1975, Special Edition to Celebrate Fifty Years of Film Societies, p. 11; *Scotsman*, 28 Oct. 1930, p. 10.
43. *Scotsman*, 16 March 1931, p. 12; ECA, SL119/3/1, Edinburgh Corporation, Committee Minutes, Magistrates, 1930–1, General Purposes Committee, 16 Feb. 1931.
44. *Scotsman*, 4 May, p. 13; 19 Oct. 1931, p. 7.
45. *Scotsman*, 2 April 1932, p. 15; 10 March, p. 1; 24 March 1934, p. 1.
46. *Scotsman*, 29 Dec. 1932, p. 6 (Wright); 17 Oct. 1933, p. 11 (Saville); 12 Feb. 1938, p. 19 (Cavalcanti).
47. *Scotsman*, 4 Feb. 1931, p. 12.
48. *Scotsman*, 19 Jan. 1932, p. 11; 21 Feb., p. 12; 22 Feb. 1933, p. 8; SSA, 3/4/3, Edinburgh Film Guild, Catalogue of USSR Cinema Exhibition, 21–27 Feb. 1933, p. 3.
49. *Scotsman*, 28 Oct. 1930, p. 10.
50. *Scotsman*, 13 April, p. 7; 21 Sept. 1931, p. 7.
51. SSA, 5/14/13, Nairn Collection, cuttings from *Evening Dispatch*, 21 Sept. 1931; unidentified cutting, p. 12; *Daily Record*, n.d.; *Scotsman*, 15 Nov. 1932, p. 6; 5 Jan., p. 6; 20 May 1933, p. 14.
52. *Scotsman*, 28 Nov. 1932, p. 7.
53. *Cinema Quarterly*, 1(1), pp. 3–6.
54. *Scotsman*, 20 May 1933, p. 14; 7 May 1936, p. 10; 31 May 1939, p. 10.
55. *Film Forum*, 3(1) (Autumn 1947), p. 7; *World Film News and Television Progress*, 1(1) (April 1936), p. 20; SSA, 2/1/1, Federation of Scottish Film Societies, Minutes of Council, 1934–45, 15 Dec. 1934.
56. *Film Forum*, 3(2) (Winter 1947), p. 6; *World Film News and Television Progress*, 1(1) (April 1936), p. 20.
57. SSA, 2/1/1, Federation of Scottish Film Societies, Minutes of Council, 1934–45, Meeting at Station Hotel, Perth, 24 April; Meeting at Golden Lion Hotel, Stirling, 11 Dec. 1937.
58. NAS, GD281/92/1, British Film Institute, Scotland, Scottish Film Council, Monthly Bulletin, No. 5 (Feb. 1936); SSA, 2/1/1, Federation of Scottish Film Societies, Minutes of Council, 4 April 1936
59. SSA, 2/1/1, Meeting at Monseigneur News Theatre, Edinburgh, 19 Sept.; Meeting at St Vincent St, Glasgow, 21 Nov. 1936.
60. *World Film News and Television Progress*, 1(1) (April 1936), p. 20.
61. *World Film News*, 2(3) (June 1937), p. 39; SSA, 2/1/1, Meeting at Station Hotel, Perth, 24 April; Meeting at Dunblane Hydro, 19 June 1937.
62. *Film Forum*, 4(4) (March 1949), p. 3. This is the title given in the source, which probably refers to the 1937 biopic *The Story of Louis Pasteur*, directed by William Dieterle and starring Paul Muni.
63. SSA, 2/1/1, Meeting at Golden Lion Hotel, Stirling, 11 Dec. 1937; *Film Forum*, 4(4), (March 1949), p. 3.

64. *Film Forum*, 3(1) (Autumn 1947), p. 7; SSA, 2/1/1, Meeting at St Enoch Hotel, Glasgow, 12 Feb. 1938.

65. SSA, 2/1/1, Meeting at Golden Lion Hotel, Stirling, 11 Dec. 1937; Meeting at Palace Hotel, Aberdeen, 12 Nov. 1938; *World Film News*, 1(6) (Sept. 1936), p. 40.

66. *World Film News*, 2(1) (April 1937), p. 43.

67. *World Film News*, 1(5) (Aug. 1936), p. 43, for Wilson's reflections on how to found a film society.

68. SSA, 2/1/1, Minutes of Meeting, 15 Dec. 1934.

69. *Scotsman*, 13 Sept. 1932, p. 6.

70. *World Film News*, 1(6) (Sept. 1936), p. 43; SSA, 2/1/1, Meeting at Monseigneur News Theatre, Edinburgh, 22 Aug. 1936.

71. *World Film News*, 1(6) (Sept. 1936), p. 40; NAS, GD281/92/1, British Film Institute, Scotland, Scottish Film Council, *Monthly Bulletin*, 2(8) (Oct. 1936), p. 10.

72. SSA, 2/1/1, Meeting at Dunblane Hydro, 22 April 1939

73. Sexton, *Alternative Film Culture*, p. 32; *The Film in National Life: being the Report of an Enquiry conducted by the Commission on Educational and Cultural Films into the Service which the Cinematograph may render to Education and Social Progress* (London, 1932); NAS, GD281/92/1, pamphlet, *The British Film Institute: Its Aims and Objectives*, p. 3.

74. NAS, GD281/92/1, 1 June 1934, 'The Cinematograph in Scotland' (Notes for Meeting on 4 June 1934).

75. *Scotsman*, 5 Dec., p. 6; 11 Dec. 1933, p. 11; NAS, GD281/92/1, n.d., British Film Institute, Memorandum for Scotland; 1 June 1934, 'The Cinematograph in Scotland'.

76. See Chapter 4, pp. 138, 152–4; NAS, GD281/92/1, *The British Film Institute: Its Aims and Objectives*, p. 3.

77. NAS, GD281/92/1, 3 May 1934, Note of Meeting held in Edinburgh on Wednesday, 2 May, to discuss the formation of a Scottish Council of the BFI; 26 May 1934, Col. J. M. Mitchell to R. M. Allardyce, Director of Education, Glasgow, stating the Carnegie UK Trust's opposition to independence.

78. For Unionist-Nationalism, see G. Morton, *Unionist Nationalism: Governing Urban Scotland, 1830–1860* (East Linton, 1999), ch. 8; NAS, GD281/92/1, 1 June 1934, 'The Cinematograph in Scotland'.

79. NAS, GD281/92/1, 4 Sept. 1934, Col. Mitchell to Rt. Hon. The Earl of Elgin; 7 Sept. 1934, Mitchell to C. A. Oakley.

80. SSA, 1/1/250, Scottish Film Council, Minutes, Meeting of Council, 20 Dec. 1934; NAS, GD281/92/1, Scottish Film Council, Leaflet No. 1, pp. 3–5.

81. SSA, 1/1/250, Meetings of Council, 20 Dec. 1934; 25 May 1935.

82. SSA, 1/1/250, Meeting of Council, 10 Nov. 1934.

83. NAS, GD281/92/1, Scottish Film Council, Leaflet No. 1; *Monthly Bulletin*, No. 2 (Nov. 1935); SSA, 1/1/250, Meetings of Council, 25 May; 6 Dec. 1935.

84. NAS, GD281/92/1, Scottish Film Council, *Monthly Bulletin*, No. 2 (Nov. 1935).

85. NAS, GD281/92/1, Scottish Film Council, *Monthly Bulletin*, No. 5 (Feb. 1936).

86. NAS, GD281/92/1, Scottish Film Council, *Monthly Bulletin*, 2(8) (Oct. 1936), pp. 8–9; 2(9) (Nov. 1936), p. 5; 3(14) (Oct. 1937), p. 7.

87. NAS, GD281/92/1, Scottish Film Council, *Monthly Bulletin*, 2(8) (Oct. 1936), pp. 8–9; 4(18) (Nov. 1938), pp. 6–7.

88. SSA, 1/1/250, 16th Meeting of Council, 5 Feb. 1937.

89. *ET*, 30 March 1938, p. 1; 9 March, p. 9; 6 April 1939, p. 9.

90. SSA, 2/1/2, Federation of Scottish Film Societies, Minutes of Council, 1946–50, Meeting at Charing Cross Hotel, London, 26 May 1949.

91. Dickinson and Street, *Cinema and State*, p. 93.

92. NAS, DD10/141, Scottish Home Dept, Cinematograph Acts, Films of Scotland Committee, 16 Jan. 1942, Appendix to Minute; 21 Jan. 1943, A. B. King to Steven Bilsland.

93. SSA, 2/1/1, Meeting at St Enoch Hotel, Glasgow, 27 April 1940, in which it was noted that film supply posed fewer problems for features than for shorts.

94. SSA, 2/1/1, Meetings at St Enoch Hotel, Glasgow, 7 Oct. 1939; 27 April 1940.

95. SSA, 2/1/1, Meeting at Monseigneur News Theatre, Edinburgh, 14 Dec. 1940; *Scotsman*, 11 Oct. 1940, p. 7.

96. SSA, 2/1/1, Meeting at Royal British Hotel, Dundee, 13 Sept. 1941.

97. *Scotsman*, 19 Nov. 1940, p. 7; 7 March 1941, p. 4.

98. SSA, 2/1/1, Meeting at North British Station Hotel, Edinburgh, 11 Dec. 1943. This is the title given in the source, which probably refers to the 1941 film *The Humpbacked Horse*, directed by Aleksander Rou.

99. SSA, 2/1/1, Meeting at Central Hotel, Glasgow, 12 Sept. 1942.

100. *Film Forum*, 3(2) (Winter 1948), p. 6; SSA, 2/1/1, Meetings at St Enoch Hotel, Glasgow, 7 Oct. 1939; 27 April 1940.

101. SSA, 2/1/1, Meetings at St Enoch Hotel, Glasgow, 7 Oct. 1939; 27 April 1940; Meeting at Monseigneur News Theatre, Edinburgh, 2 Dec. 1939.

102. SSA, 2/1/1, Meeting at Monseigneur News Theatre, 2 Dec. 1939; Meeting at North British Station Hotel, 12 Dec. 1942; *Scotsman*, 22 June 1943, p. 6.

103. *Scotsman*, 6 Oct. 1942, p. 3; ECA, SL119/3/12, Edinburgh Corporation Committee Minutes, Magistrates, Session 1941–2, 22 July 1942.

104. SSA, 2/1/1, Meeting at Imperial Hotel, Aberdeen, 29 April 1944; Meeting at North British Hotel, 16 Dec. 1944.

105. SSA, 3/1/39, Film Society of Glasgow, Minute Book, 1944–9, General Meeting, 29 Oct. 1944; SSA, 2/1/1, Meeting at North British Hotel, 16 Dec. 1944.

106. SSA, 2/1/1, Meeting at Imperial Hotel, Aberdeen, 29 April 1944.

107. SSA, 2/1/2, Meeting at North British Station Hotel, 29 Jan. 1946; Meeting at Waverley Hotel, London, 7 Sept. 1946; *Film Forum*, 4(1) (Autumn 1948), p. 6; 5(1) (Oct. 1949), p. 3.

108. *Film Forum*, 2(2) (Oct. 1946), p. 2; SSA, 2/1/2, Meeting at North British Station Hotel, 29 Jan. 1946.

109. SSA, 2/1/2, Meeting at Waverley Hotel, London, 7 Sept. 1946; Meeting at Central Hotel, Glasgow, 18 Sept. 1948; Meeting at Film House, 18 Dec. 1948; Meeting at Central Hotel, Glasgow, 1 Oct. 1949.

110. Borders Archive, Hawick, D/78/1/1, Galashiels Film Society, Constitution and Rules, cl. 2.
111. Border Archive, D/78/2/3, Galashiels Film Society, Membership Book; GD/78/2/4/2, Abstract of Receipts and Payments for year ended 29 April 1950; SSA, 2/1/2, Meeting at Northern Hotel, Kittybrewster, Aberdeen, 7 Jan. 1950.
112. SSA, 2/1/2, Meeting at St Margaret's Hotel, Dunfermline, 26 April 1947; Meeting at Charing Cross Hotel, London, 26 May 1949.
113. SSA, 2/1/2, Meeting at Waverley Hotel, London, 7 Sept. 1946; Meeting at Peebles Hotel Hydro [sic], 8 May 1948; *Film Forum*, 2(2) (Oct. 1946), p. 10; 3(1) (Autumn 1947), p. 2; 4(3) (Feb. 1949), p. 1.
114. *Film Forum*, 5(2) (Nov. 1949), p. 7; 5(5) (Feb. 1950), p. 3; 6(1) (Oct. 1950), p. 2; SSA, 2/1/2, Meeting at Charing Cross Hotel, London, 26 May 1949; Meeting at Northern Hotel, Kittybrewster, 7 Jan. 1950.
115. *Film Forum*, 4(1) (Autumn 1948), p. 6; 5(4) (Jan. 1950), p. 2; SSA, 2/1/2, Meeting at North British Station Hotel, 14 Dec. 1946.
116. *Film Forum*, 4(2) (Jan. 1949), p. 8.
117. *Film Forum*, 5(2) (Nov. 1949), p. 2.
118. See Chapter 2, pp. 74, 77, 81.
119. *Entertainer and SKR*, 20 March 1920, p. 1.
120. *SKR*, 5 Feb. 1921, p. 13.
121. *Entertainer*, 22 Dec. 1917, p. 13.
122. *Entertainer and SKR*, 13 March 1920, p. 1.
123. *SKR*, 14 May, p. 3; 21 May 1921, p. 1.
124. *Scotsman*, 16 Oct. 1931, p. 8.
125. *Scotsman*, 24 April 1933, p. 10; Barclay, *The Film in Scottish Schools*, p. 4.
126. SSA, 1/5/1, Scottish Educational Cinema Society, Minute Book, 2 Dec. 1933, Meeting of Delegates of branches of Society.
127. NAS, GD281/92/1, British Film Institute, Scotland, 8 June 1934, Minute of Meeting of those Interested in Formation of a Film Institute in Scotland; *Scotsman*, 17 June 1935, p. 7; SSA, 1/5/1, Scottish Educational Cinema Society, Minute Book, Executive Committee Meetings, 23 Aug.; 25 Oct. 1934.
128. SSA, GD281/92/1, Scottish Film Council, *Monthly Bulletin*, 2(8) (Oct. 1936), p. 3; 4(17) (Oct. 1938), p. 7.
129. SSA, 1/1/252, Scottish Film Council, Minutes, 1944–50, 61st Meeting, 22 Jan. 1948; 62nd Meeting, 20 May 1948; 68th Meeting, 17 May 1949.
130. *Scotsman*, 22 Oct. 1934, p. 7.
131. SSA, 1/5/1, Scottish Educational Cinema Society, Minute Book, Executive Committee Meetings, 3 Jan.; 12 Jan.; National Council Meeting, 25 April 1934.
132. NAS, GD281/92/1, British Film Institute, Scotland, Scottish Film Council, *Monthly Bulletin*, 2(13) (March 1937), p. 4.
133. NAS, GD281/92/1, Scottish Film Council, *Monthly Bulletin*, 4(20) (Jan. 1939), p. 8.
134. SSA, 1/1/251, Scottish Film Council, Minutes, 1939–44, 32nd Meeting, 20 Oct. 1939; 1/1/108, Volume of Press Cuttings, *Times*, 9 Oct. 1939.
135. SSA, 1/1/108, *Sunday Chronicle*, 8 Oct. 1939; *Times*, 5 Feb. 1940; 1/1/251, 33rd

Council Meeting, 20 Dec. 1939; 1/5/2, Scottish Educational Film Association, Minutes, Meeting of Council, 4 Nov. 1939.

136. SSA, 1/1/108, *Times*, 5 Feb. 1940; 1/1/251, 34th Council Meeting, 4 April 1940.

137. SSA, 1/1/251, 35th Council Meeting, 20 Sept. 1940; 1/1/252, Minutes, 1944–50, Minutes of 11th AGM, 13 Dec. 1944; 1/5/2, Meeting of Council, 12 Dec. 1942; The Arts Enquiry, *The Factual Film* (Oxford, 1947), p. 77.

138. *Scotsman*, 11 Oct. 1940, p. 7; SSA, 1/1/251, 36th Council Meeting, 30 Oct. 1940.

139. *Scotsman*, 30 Sept. 1943, p. 4; SSA, 1/1/251, 44th Meeting of Council, 23 Sept. 1943; 3/2/10, Film Societies Collection, Edinburgh Scientific Film Society, Printed Programmes, Third Season, Third Exhibition, 8 Dec. 1946; Fifth Exhibition, 16 Feb. 1947.

140. SSA, 1/1/252, 12th AGM, 19 Sept. 1945.

141. SSA, 1/5/2, Meeting of Council, 12 June 1943; Staples, *All Pals Together*, ch. 6.

142. *Scotsman*, 16 Feb. 1945, p. 3.

143. *Scotsman*, 6 Sept. 1948, p. 4; *Documentary 48* (Edinburgh, 1948).

144. *Scotsman*, 10 Sept. 1949, p. 6.

145. *Scotsman*, 28 Feb. 1950, p. 4.

146. NAS, GD281/92/1, British Film Institute, Scotland, Scottish Film Council, *Monthly Bulletin*, No. 3 (Dec. 1935); E. Lebas, 'Sadness and Gladness: The Films of Glasgow Corporation, 1922–1938', *Film Studies*, 6 (Summer 2005), p. 42.

147. NAS, GD281/92/1, *Monthly Bulletin*, 4(17) (Oct. 1938), p. 5.

148. SSA, 1/1/250, Scottish Film Council, Minutes, 14th Meeting, of Council, 10 Oct. 1936; Barclay, *The Film in Scottish Schools*, pp. 6–7.

149. SSA, 1/1/250, 10th Meeting of Council, 7 Feb.; 12th Meeting of Council, 5 June 1936.

150. SSA, 1/1/250, 16th Meeting of Council, 5 Feb. 1937; 24th Meeting of Council, 25 March 1938.

151. Barclay, *The Film in Scottish Schools*, p. 9; NAS, GD281/92/1, Scottish Film Council, *Monthly Bulletin*, 4(18) (Nov. 1938), p. 9.

152. SSA, 1/1/251, Scottish Film Council, Minutes, 36th Meeting of Council, 30 Oct. 1940; 1/1/252, Minutes of 11th AGM, 13 Dec. 1944; 49th Meeting of Council, 20 Sept. 1945.

153. SSA, 1/1/252, 53rd Meeting of Council, 12 Sept. 1946.

154. SSA, 1/1/252, 69th Meeting of Council, 8 Dec. 1950; Barclay, *The Film in Scottish Schools*, p. 9.

155. SSA, 1/1/250, 9th Meeting of Council, 6 Dec. 1935; Barclay, *The Film in Scottish Schools*, p. 16.

156. *Sight and Sound*, 9(36) (Winter 1940–1), pp. 68–9.

157. SSA, 1/1/251, 39th Meeting of Council, 30 April 1942.

158. SSA, 1/1/251, Minutes of 10th AGM, 23 Sept. 1943.

159. Barclay, *The Film in Scottish Schools*, pp. 21, 23.

160. *Scotsman*, 6 May 1947, p. 3; SSA, 1/1/252, Minutes of 13th AGM, 12 Sept. 1946; E. Lebas, 'Glasgow's Progress: The Films of Glasgow Corporation, 1938–1978', *Film Studies*, 10 (Spring 2007), pp. 41–5.

161. See Chapter 4, p. 146; *Scotsman*, 8 March 1939, p. 16, on the 'Recall to Religion' campaign in Glasgow, which centred on services held in nine cinemas.
162. *Scotsman*, 26 Dec. 1934, p. 10.
163. *Scotsman*, 2 Oct. 1935, p. 8.
164. *Scotsman*, 19 March 1936, p. 7.
165. *Scotsman*, 9 April, p. 9; 16 May 1936, p. 20.
166. *Scotsman*, 3 Sept. 1936, p. 6, reporting an address by Rev. J. Strathearn McNab of Ayr.
167. *Scotsman*, 18 Feb. 1938, p. 15.
168. NAS, GD281/92/1, *Monthly Bulletin*, 4(17) (Oct. 1938), p. 7; *Scotsman*, 20 May 1939, p. 12.
169. *Scotsman*, 24 May, p. 1; 26 May 1939, p. 7.
170. SSA, 1/1/250, 11th Meeting of Council, 3 April 1936.
171. *Scotsman*, 21 Nov. 1940, p. 4; SSA, 1/1/251, 37th Meeting of Council, 8 July 1941; 44th Meeting of Council, 23 Sept. 1943.
172. SSA, 1/1/252, Minutes of 11th AGM, 13 Dec. 1944.
173. SSA, 1/1/252, 48th Meeting of Council, 19 March 1945; 49th Meeting of Council, 20 Sept. 1945.
174. *Film Forum*, 6(1) (Oct. 1950), p. 12; *Scotsman*, 11 May 1950, p. 5.
175. *Film Forum*, 6(1) (Oct. 1950), p. 12; on the problems of the Highlands and the role of the Hydro scheme in addressing them, see H. Quigley, *A Plan for the Highlands: Proposals for a Highland Development Board* (London, 1936); North of Scotland Hydro-Electric Board, *Highland Water Power* (Edinburgh, n.d.); P. L. Payne, *The Hydro* (Aberdeen, 1988); E. A. Cameron, *Impaled Upon a Thistle: Scotland since 1880* (Edinburgh, 2010), p. 190.
176. *Scotsman*, 28 Nov. 1936, p. 14.
177. NAS, ED30/2, Highlands and Islands Film Guild, Minutes of Meetings, Memorandum, Scottish Agricultural Organisation Society, Ltd, p. 1.
178. NAS, ED30/2, Memorandum, p. 1.
179. NAS, ED30/2, Memorandum; Report of Discussions at Conference in Inverness, 30 May 1946; SSA, 3/2/13, Film Societies Collection, 'Novel Mobile Cinema Scheme for the Highlands', cutting from *Cinema and Theatre Construction*, 13 (Dec. 1946), p. 17.
180. NAS, ED30/2, Report of Discussions, p. 3.
181. NAS, ED30/2, Memorandum, Appendix B.
182. NAS, ED30/2, Memorandum, p. 2; Report of Discussions, 30 May 1946, p. 2; *Scotsman*, 11 Oct. 1946, p. 7.
183. NAS, ED30/2, Report of Discussions, p. 3; Report on Activity by the Scottish Agricultural Organisation Society since the Conference, 13 July 1946, pp. 1, 3.
184. NAS, ED30/2, Council Meeting, Inverness, 26 July 1946.
185. NAS, ED30/2, Hon. Sec. to Guild members, 12 Sept. 1946; Report of Activities since Executive Committee Meeting on 29 Jan. 1947; Meeting in Inverness, 24 June 1947.
186. NAS, ED30/2, Report on Activities since Conference, 13 July 1946.
187. NAS, ED30/2, Executive Committee Meeting, 26 July 1946.

188. NAS, ED30/2, Council Meeting, Inverness, 29 July 1948; Executive Committee Meeting, 28 Oct. 1947.

189. NAS, ED30/2, Meeting of Film Production Sub-committee, 17 June 1949.

190. *Scotsman*, 26 April 1947, p. 3.

191. NAS, ED30/2, Proposed Reconstruction of the Financial Basis of the Guild, 'no feeling of community responsibility is likely to develop so long as no other link is established between public and promoters than the individual box-office transaction'; Council Meeting, Inverness, 26 July 1946.

192. NAS, ED30/2, Council Meeting, Inverness, 29 July 1948, p. 3.

193. NAS, ED30/2, Report on Reactions to Community Responsibility Proposals; SSA, 3/2/13, 'Novel Mobile Cinema Scheme', p. 17

194. NAS, ED30/2, Proposed Reconstruction of the Financial Basis of the Guild, p. 1.

195. NAS, ED30/2, Proposed Reconstruction, p. 3.

196. NAS, ED30/2, Development Officer's Report, Oct. 1947.

197. NAS, ED30/2, Meeting of Council, 28 April 1949.

198. NAS, ED30/2, Meeting of Financial Sub-committee, 10 Nov. 1949; SSA, 3/2/12, Film Societies Collection, cutting from Hugh Ross, *The Highlands and Islands Film Guild – A Rural Service* (1958), p. 30.

199. NAS, ED30/2, Scottish Education Dept to Secretary, Highland and Islands Film Guild, 25 Nov. 1949

200. NAS, ED30/2, Meetings of Financial Sub-committee, 28 June 1949, pp. 1–2; 4 Oct. 1950, p. 1.

201. *Scotsman*, 7 Sept. 1950, p. 5; NAS, ED 30/2, Meeting of Council, 11 May, p. 1; Meetings of Financial Sub-committee, 4 Oct., p. 2; 14 Nov. 1950, p. 1.

202. NAS, ED30/2, Meetings of Financial Sub-committee, 5 June; 11 July 1950, p. 1.

203. NAS, ED30/2, Use of Guild's Services in Schools; Report of Secretary for period April to Dec. 1950; the attendance figure is based on average attendances per show of thirty-nine adults and twenty-six children.

204. A. Bartie, 'Culture in the Everyday: Art and Society', in Abrams and Brown, *History of Everyday Life in Twentieth-Century Scotland*, pp. 212–3; F. Hardy, *Slightly Mad and Full of Dangers: The Story of Edinburgh Film Festival* (Edinburgh, 1992).

205. *Scotsman*, 9 Jan., p. 4; 11 Aug. 1947, p. 5; *Documentary 47*, Programme of Performances, insert.

206. *Scotsman*, 17 Oct. 1947, p. 4; 4 Aug. 1949, p. 8; 10 Aug. 1950, p. 4.

7

To the Summit and Beyond: Cinema-going in the 1940s

I

The period during and immediately after the Second World War marked a high point for cinema in Scotland, in more ways than one. The numbers attending picture houses reached unprecedented levels and if attendances showed a tendency to decline as mid century approached, they remained comfortably above those seen in pre-war decades.[1] Not only that, film was a significant presence in diverse areas of Scottish life, as a variety of agencies from government downwards used the moving image and the cinema to promote their ideas. In the late 1940s, the vision of the New Jerusalem was being projected via celluloid, courtesy of the Central Office of Information, the latest incarnation of a documentary trend that extended back through the Crown and GPO to the Empire Marketing Board Film Units.[2] The suggestion was that as film approached its jubilee, the mistrust which had characterised its early career was giving way to acceptance and support. Certainly, the Second World War, despite its greater scale and more profound impact on everyday patterns of living, generated little of that sense of crisis for the cinema that had marked the years of the Great War.[3] Any doubts entertained over whether the industry could still continue to function centred on questions of physical rather than moral safety, as the wisdom of allowing large numbers to congregate in areas vulnerable to air attack was debated. That matter was quickly resolved in a manner favourable to the trade and which recognised cinema's role in maintaining civilian and troop morale. Instead of moves to restrict access, pressure was mounted, as has been noted, to extend operations to seven days a week.[4] Not only this, but the economic context, which had proved so troubling to the trade in the midst of the First World War, worked to bolster optimism. Although prices rose at a rate and to a degree unseen since the previous conflict, aggregate figures record a relentless rise in the national (UK) audience to reach a peak of 1,635 million in 1946.[5] The intention here is not to challenge fundamentally the depiction of a largely benign and prosperous decade, but rather to seek a balanced appreciation of the industry's fortunes as it approached and surmounted its peak of popularity. Areas of doubt and controversy continued to emerge. An earlier chapter has noted the concerns which circulated over the impact of children's attendance through the decade, despite the reassuring presence of Methodism's own movie mogul, J. Arthur Rank.[6] Other problems, some with longer-term importance, would emerge in a period when operating profits went largely to boost the national exchequer and when financial and material constraints would hinder the industry's ability to respond to change in the post-war years. The seeds of cinema's subsequent decline can, to a degree, be traced to developments at the height of its popularity.

The contrast with earlier periods extends beyond the fortunes of the exhibition sector. British film production rarely approached the volume of output achieved in the 1930s and indeed in the later stages of the war had fallen back to levels not seen since the period of crisis that had preceded the Quota Act of 1927.[7] Yet while down in quantitative terms, production appeared, according to most authorities, to advance in terms of quality. Such was the view of Ritson Bennell, Divisional Superintendent of the Gaumont-British Picture Corporation in Scotland, speaking at a lunch in September 1944 to mark the press preview of Powell and Pressburger's *A Canterbury Tale*.[8] If the origins of this shift could be traced to the 1938 revision of quota regulations, which gave greater emphasis to support for bigger-budget productions at the expense of cheaper quickies, its logic was fully worked out in the unusual conditions of wartime, as production was pared back and resources often devoted to films concerned to promote an approved version of 'Britishness'.[9] In support of his claim for the enhanced status of the home industry, Bennell cited titles which have come to form part of a critical canon of worthy and culturally meaningful British productions, including *49th Parallel, In Which We Serve, The First of the Few, The Life and Death of Colonel Blimp*, and *The Way Ahead*.[10] Taken together, it is argued, such films offered an integrated vision of the nation based around a narrative of solidarity in the face of external threat. The diverse, almost fragmentary output of the pre-war years gave way to a range of productions that was narrower in scope, but which offered a more coherent vision of the national interest.[11] The basis for the greater cultural traction of film in this period was being laid, as the projection of Britishness on the screen was amplified by a post-war agenda of social and political change. The Attlee administrations, with their emphasis on uniformity of provision across both welfare services and the major utilities, gave the new Socialist Commonwealth a relentlessly 'British' character.[12] For the film industry, these were also years in which the quota became, for a time, an instrument in ongoing trade negotiations with the USA, the result being a short-lived increase in quota requirements that served to expose audiences to British productions to a much greater degree than previously. The final years of the decade thus assume a particular interest for this study, particularly as the social and cultural implications of the developments outlined here have still to be explored in detail. Popular responses to officially sanctioned versions of Britishness conveyed by means of the cinema screen remain, as yet, obscure. Nevertheless, it might be noted, the few local studies so far undertaken raise doubts as to the extent to which existing 'taste communities' were transformed by the experience of war and the coming of the New Jerusalem.[13] In the case of Scotland, further evaluation of the appeal or otherwise of British films seems especially pertinent given the ambiguities which marked responses before the war and the apparent contrast with growing political support for the Unionist cause reflected in post-war elections.[14] In essence, then, this chapter offers reflections on Scotland's engagement with a very British model of modernity.

II

Whatever its implications in the longer term, the impact of war on the cinema industry appeared, at the outset at least, wholly unfavourable. In some areas, the effects were felt in advance of any formal declaration of hostilities. The Stranraer Picture House was obliged to close its doors for business on Saturday, 2 September 1939, the building having been commandeered for the receipt of evacuated children. The hall would eventually receive compensation for the income foregone.[15] Of wider concern was the government order, issued on the outbreak of war, requiring the closure of all places of public entertainment so as to reduce the danger of loss of life through air raids. The immediate future for cinema was thus rendered uncertain, as staff at halls across Glasgow were issued with unemployment insurance books, in anticipation of them claiming benefit. At some houses, only key staff, including the manager, operator, and chief cashier, were to be retained. At the Regent, it was decided that 'with the exception of one of the chief operators, as many of the staff as were willing to remain in the employment of the Company should be retained for a fortnight'.[16] The stay of execution would prove prescient, as the order was swiftly revoked in recognition of recreation's key role in maintaining civilian morale. Cinemas in Aberdeen thus reopened on the first Saturday of the war, while by the following week activity had been resumed across eastern Scotland, including Edinburgh.[17]

For a time, however, trading conditions remained unpropitious. Lighting restrictions limited hours of business, so that Edinburgh's Palace Cinema closed at 10 p.m. through October, while at Lockerbie, the final show ended at 9.45.[18] It also had the effect of discouraging travel, particularly into town and city centres. For most houses, then, business during the first winter of the war was down, often considerably, even on the less than buoyant levels of the years immediately preceding. At Aberdeen's Capitol, audiences across the final months of 1939 were 13 per cent down on the equivalent figure for 1938.[19] At Edinburgh's Playhouse, the fall of 15.67 per cent was broadly comparable, but the contrast with pre-war levels was most marked at the Palace, where average weekly admissions of 4,922 were over 25 per cent down on the same period a year earlier.[20] The effect on company accounts was profound. The Playhouse returned losses in six of the final fifteen weeks of 1939, so that the average weekly profit over that same period amounted to only £49.37p. [21] At the Palace, the balance sheet remained stubbornly in the red for all but three weeks.[22] At houses elsewhere, the available evidence also points to a fall-off in business. At the Torry Picture House, near Aberdeen, receipts net of entertainments tax in the year to January 1940 were the lowest recorded since the mid 1920s.[23] Early in 1940, Poole's Entertainments, Ltd reported profits only half of those of the year before, a decline substantially attributable to what were described as difficult trading conditions in wartime.[24] For many, business remained depressed through 1940, as the uncertainties of the Twilight War gave way to the repeated threat of attack from the air. If the Palace and Playhouse are representative, audiences in central Edinburgh persisted at below their pre-war levels through the first twelve months of the war. At the Palace, admissions across the first eight months of 1940 were almost 20 per cent down on the equivalent period the year before, with only the 'social problem' film *Marriage Forbidden* securing an audience well in excess of the long-run average for the house at 13,222, or almost 37 per cent above the mean figure for the duration of the war.[25] Further west, as attacks on industrial areas intensified, enthusiasm for the cinema was seen, quite understandably, to waver. The picture house located in the Glasgow suburb of Uddingston reported a 25 per cent fall in business in November 1940 compared with the same month a year earlier, a decline considered to be 'mainly due to the black-out and air raid warnings'.[26]

Problems in this phase of the war were not confined to the income side of the ledger. The supply of product gave rise to much uncertainty, as British production was scaled back and the nation's ability to continue funding the acquisition of a sufficient volume of American features was far from clear.[27] One response, which had the additional virtue of expressing loyalty to a gallant ally, was the exhibition of films from countries other than the USA. In the early months of the war, three French productions were screened at the Edinburgh Playhouse, although the modest response, with audiences one-third down on the house's wartime average, ensured that the experiment was not repeated in 1940.[28] With few realistic alternatives to continued reliance on the American product, competition for film hire remained intense. Costs at most cinemas were thus subject to upward pressure as box-office returns declined. Increases were particularly felt on the two largest items of expenditure for most businesses, the price of film bookings and the cost of labour. Wage increases in the form of war bonuses were paid to all staff, as the failure to hold down prices in the first year of the war generated demands for enhanced pay levels to match the inflated cost of living. The CEA agreed an advance of 7.5 per cent on basic wages from May 1940, the first of a series of increases that would see the annual wage bill at Glasgow's Regent Cinema rise by 75 per cent over the remainder of the war.[29] At Aberdeen's Capitol, the increase was a more modest but still sizeable 42.8 per cent.[30] Expenditure on film hire also rose markedly, to the extent that at the Stranraer Picture House the proportion of takings absorbed by the cost of rentals increased from 33.6 per cent in 1941–2 to a peak wartime figure of just over 38 per cent in 1943–4.[31] Without a significant growth in income, company balances were likely to come under severe pressure. In the first year of the war, in particular, the prospect of such relief appeared remote, so that the largely stable drawings enjoyed by the Stranraer Picture House could not avert a halving in profits in the year to April 1940, the surplus of £516 7s 6d compared with one of £934 14s a year earlier.[32]

By the autumn of 1940, the uncertainties created by wartime trading conditions threatened to be compounded by changes in the tax regime. As in the First World War, government looked to exploit the taste for amusements in order to boost its revenues. Entertainments duty was thus revised upwards in October 1940, with further increases following in the Budgets of 1942 and 1943. By then, the cost of cinema-going had increased markedly. At Edinburgh's Palace, prices rose by between 40 per cent for a box seat to 100 per cent for children in the stalls.[33] More generally, the charge for admission was some 75–80 per cent higher by the middle years of the war, with tax now accounting for between 39 per cent and 42 per cent of the cost of a ticket.[34] In previous decades, rises of a magnitude considerably below this had precipitated or exacerbated a downturn in business. Indications are, however, that in the unusual conditions of wartime, the impact of the substantial price hike on this occasion was altogether different. From the second year of the war, most houses recorded a sizeable upturn in receipts, only partly attributable to the rise in prices. At the Stranraer Picture House, takings which in the final full pre-war year to April 1939 had totalled £7,648 16s 5d, had risen by 1943–4 to £26,448 – 3d, an increase of 345.8 per cent.[35] Nor was this unusual. Over a comparable period, income at the Regent Cinema in Glasgow also showed a threefold rise, from £18,585 17s 6d to £54,390 13s 11½d.[36] As this indicates, the escalation in ticket prices did not act, as previous experience may have suggested was likely, to discourage cinema-going; rather, it coincided with a surge in attendances. This varied in extent, so that weekly audiences at Aberdeen's Capitol were, by 1944, some 17.7 per cent up on the pre-war average.[37] At Edinburgh's Playhouse, growth in business was of the order of 27.3 per cent between 1940 and the peak wartime year of 1943, while over the same period at the Palace, admissions rose from a weekly average of 6,086 to one of 11,076, an increase of 82 per cent.[38]

Wider conditions helped to determine this benign outcome for the trade. In contrast to the First World War, the application by government of demand management techniques through a combination of rationing and price controls helped to contain inflationary pressures. The retail price index had doubled over the course of the Great War, whereas over nearly six years from 1939 the increase was limited to 30 per cent.[39] At the same time, restrictions on the supply of consumer goods more generally limited opportunities for expenditure, so that effective demand was concentrated on a narrower range of goods and services. With the supply of film secured first by agreement with the USA and then by America's formal entry into the war, cinema-going was not an activity subject to the ration, so that a visit to the picture house remained one of the few unrestricted pleasures available.[40] As initial unease over black-out conditions abated, a greater readiness to venture out of doors in the evening boosted potential attendances, and the means to do so was now enhanced. If, for two decades, cinema had operated within a context of persistently high unemployment, the needs of a wartime economy ensured that, by 1942–3, that problem had been reduced to one of statistical insignificance.[41] A combination of full-time working and full employment enabled growing numbers of people to meet the higher costs attending one of the few distractions to which access remained unfettered. The impact is reflected in the diaries of Eileen Crowford, an Edinburgh typist, aged twenty-six when the war broke out, who listed cinema-going among her 'favourite occupations', behind only 'Reading'. The twenty-seven visits to the cinema she recorded in 1939 were dwarfed by the forty-nine attendances noted in 1942.[42]

The enthusiasm of picture-goers such as Ms Crowford restored the exhibition industry to a condition of financial security not experienced since the late silent era. Indeed, in several respects, it appeared that the 'Klondyke' days of the immediate post-First World War period had returned. Business decisions were re-evaluated in the light of altered circumstances. In October 1941, the management of the Lockerbie Cinema Co., Ltd reported that takings were so buoyant on Monday and Saturday evenings that the practice of allowing children in at the start of the week at half price could be discontinued.[43] That this was a decision driven more by the desire to exclude potentially unruly elements that might deter adult cinema-goers than by the drive for ever greater surpluses is suggested by other policies adopted at the time. The quest for product most likely to maintain attendances was allowed to proceed with less regard for its likely cost. In January 1942, the Lockerbie directors presented Green's with a list of titles it was considered desirable to hire, observing that 'an argument to the effect that a deal was uneconomic did not carry much weight in view of the fact that profits were not a material consideration'.[44] The cinema-going habit was now so firmly entrenched that a margin comfortably in excess of operating costs could be anticipated. Houses now almost invariably traded week in and week out in the black and, where balances had been squeezed by falling receipts early in the war, a sizeable surplus was now the norm. At Stranraer, annual profits exceeded £1,500 over the last two years of the war, while at Edinburgh's Palace, net profits per year rose almost tenfold, from an average across the 1930s of £895.80p to one of £8,521.80p for the four year to 1945.[45] The impact was strikingly reflected in the hall's weekly returns. Across 1940, losses were recorded in nineteen weeks, with a final lapse into the red occurring early in September, just before the first hike in entertainments tax. Thereafter, to the end of the war in Europe, only one programme failed to generate a profit, a loss of £35 being recorded in the week commencing 17 March 1941 on a double bill comprising the MGM comedy *The Golden Fleecing* with Lew Ayres, and the Republic comedy musical *Grand Ole Opry*. This week apart, for the first time since its conversion to sound, the Palace became a consistently profit-making concern.[46]

Elsewhere, company accounts record the relentless accumulation of surpluses. In the five years to January 1944, annual profits at the Capitol in Aberdeen rose from £7,974 13s 4d to £18,646 11s 2d, while a comparable growth in margins was recorded at nearby houses run by Donald's Cinemas. Between 1941 and 1944, the Grand Central Picture House increased profits more than fourfold, from £1,252 7s 5d to £5,170 1s 3d.[47] Similarly, at Edinburgh's Playhouse, profits net of entertainments tax rose to over £25,000 by the fifth year of war, to August 1944.[48] Yet if such figures suggest times of bounty for exhibitors, the reality was somewhat different and casts doubt on any return to a 'Klondyke' period for the industry. As the war progressed, firms were obliged to set aside a growing proportion of their incomes to pay excess profits duty. Introduced in 1939 at a rate of 60 per cent, this increased to 100 per cent as the military situation worsened in 1940.[49] So, while film hire remained the largest single item of expenditure for houses such as the Regent in Glasgow, rising to £20,629 6s out of receipts totalling £54,390 13s 11½d in the year to May 1944, the company's tax reserve represented by some margin the next largest outlay at £15,500.[50] At Stranraer, income tax and excess profits duty were often the largest item on the expenditure side, so that overall profit levels remained comparatively modest for the duration of the conflict. That such a large proportion of exhibitors' income was diverted to national coffers gave further weight to the disavowal of profit as a key feature of business strategy by the Lockerbie directors.

A further problem constraining normal commercial practices centred on the ability to utilise any profits generated. Over the course of the war, high levels of attendance and a greater propensity to operate seven days a week ensured that cinema space was more intensively exploited than had been the case in earlier periods. Depreciation of fixed and movable assets, from projection equipment and seating to the uniforms adorning members of staff, accelerated, requiring higher rates of renewal. However, broader material shortages made programmes of replacement and refurbishment difficult to implement. The Uddingston Picture House was not alone in seeking an overhaul of its projection apparatus in 1942, while a year later the replacement of much of the existing seating was under consideration. The lack of men and materials ruled out the installation of new seating and so the purchase of second-hand replacements was considered for a time. When these were found to be less than satisfactory, the decision was taken simply to re-cover existing seats.[51] At Lockerbie, restrictions on the use of paper persuaded the local

Table 7.1 *Stranraer Picture House, income and expenditure, 1941–5. (Source: SSA, 5/28/9, The Stranraer Picture House, Ltd, Annual Accounts.)*

Year	Receipts (£)	Expenditure (£)	Tax (£)
1940–1	12,642 – 2d	n.k.	n.k.
1941–2	22,375 19s 1d	21,958 17s 7d	9,055 – 4d
1942–3	25,718 5s 9d	24,727 4s 5d	10,021 16s
1943–4	26,448 – 3d	25,105 10s 11d	9,578 3s 6d
1944–5	23,100 14s 4d	21,568 19s 8d	8,447 6s

Cinema Co. to dispense with posters and to adopt an alternative means of publicising programmes, having them written on blackboards which would be placed in shops across the town.[52] By the end of the war, many halls were in advanced states of disrepair. At Uddingston, a loan of £5,000 went to fund vital refurbishments. Yet even though the money was forthcoming, a further barrier existed in the need to secure a licence from the Ministry of Labour to allow the repairs to proceed.[53] The same problems confronted management at the Regent in Glasgow, which early in 1946 sought a licence to allow the expenditure of £28 on repairs to the Renfield Street canopy, now considered in a dangerous state.[54] Equally, refurbishment of the inside of the Lockerbie Cinema was complicated by the lack of materials. Existing resources were thus put to creative use, so that new uniforms for the front of house staff at Lockerbie were fashioned out of reconditioned American army tunics.[55]

The contrast with the period following the Great War was marked. Then, high levels of profitability had encouraged a building boom that some Labour politicians had seen as an undue diversion from important housing programmes. In a more centrally controlled economy from 1945, no comparable misallocation of resources would be countenanced. The needs of housing now won out over those of the cinema trade, so that Scotland, like the rest of Britain, went into the post-war years with an exhibition infrastructure little altered from that put in place in the first decade of sound. Changes were confined, for the most part, to straightforward shifts in ownership, as profit was used to acquire existing plant rather than for the construction of a new generation of picture houses. So, the Stornoway Playhouse, after experiencing its most profitable year to January 1942, was sold to J. B. Milne of Dundee, while towards the end of the war, the Mecca Cinema, Ltd became part of George Singleton's moves to extend his interests in and around Glasgow.[56] The trend across the 1940s was thus to consolidate ownership of the exhibition sector within Scotland, rather than seeing further acquisitions by circuits based beyond the nation's boundaries. Editions of the *Kinematograph Year Book* published towards the end of the decade found that the proportion of halls run by the major English combines ABPC, Gaumont-British, and Odeon remained stuck where it had been in the later

1930s at around 14 per cent, or 87 out of 618. By contrast, the number of small and medium-sized circuits within Scotland had grown, so that the well-established Green's stable of fourteen houses was now joined by circuits run by Milne of Dundee (eleven) and George Palmer in Glasgow (fourteen). The most influential figure north of the border remained Alex B. King, whose interests now extended to over eighty cinemas across the country.[57] Changes in ownership did not work fundamentally to undermine the importance of the small independent exhibitor, who retained an unusually large presence in the industry north of the border through to the century's mid point.

Although obliged to adapt to the prevailing culture of 'Make Do and Mend', the cinema trade in Scotland was able to maintain profitability at historically high levels into the post-war period. Continued controls on consumer expenditure, combined with a political commitment to full employment, ensured that the conditions under which the industry had thrived in wartime were not quickly dismantled, as demand continued to be directed down well-worn channels.[58] So, while there was a decline in overall levels of cinema-going from the peak of 1946, the fall was modest and audience numbers even into the early 1950s remained above the pre-war peak.[59] Adjusting the focus to a more micro level indicates a degree of local variation from the aggregate picture. In Edinburgh, attendances at both the Palace and Playhouse cinemas fell by over 20 per cent in the five years following the end of the war, with takings tracking a comparable decline.[60] Further west, at Wishaw, the decline in receipts was less marked, representing a fall of just over 15 per cent between 1946 and 1949, while to the north-east at Aberdeen's Capitol Cinema, the loss of income to the end of 1949 was nearer 10 per cent.[61] All indications are that, across Scotland, trade while depressed remained at a level comfortably in excess of that which applied before 1939. Even after allowing for the payment of entertainments tax at the augmented rates that had operated since early in the war, takings at halls across Scotland were markedly higher than their 1930s equivalents. At the Torry Picture House, near Aberdeen, receipts of £11,894 10s 10d in the year to the end of January 1951 were more than twice the level of the late 1930s.[62] Unsurprisingly, then, the decline in admissions was not of the order likely to precipitate a return to the financial travails of the previous decade. Profit margins, if down on their wartime and immediate post-war peaks, were maintained at a level that would have passed for prosperity in the early sound era. Returning to the Torry Picture House, a profit of £3,327 6s 11d in 1950–1 compared favourably, even allowing for inflation, with a peak figure before the war of £1,519 in 1931–2.[63] The lifting of excess profits duty at the end of the war provided some cushion against the impact of any fall in receipts. At the Dunfermline Cinema House, despite a sustained decline in income, profits rose from a wartime average of £2,135.42p per year to £3,404.92p over the later 1940s, in the process reaching levels not recorded since the boom of the months immediately following the Great War.[64] In few places, perhaps, were the implications of the benign economic climate more apparent than at the Palace in Edinburgh. A hall that had acquired an unwelcome familiarity with trading in the red following its rewiring for sound, the Palace's finances had been transformed during the latter stages of the war, to the extent that no losses were recorded for any week after the early part of 1941. Consistent profitability was not wholly maintained into the post-war period, but losses, recorded in sixteen weeks over five years from 1946, remained very much the exception. A surplus across the year in 1950 of £4,308 indicated more than anything the stable and secure financial state of the exhibition sector around mid century.[65]

The comforting message conveyed by the balance sheet did not, however, extend to all aspects of the business. Britain's 'financial Dunkirk' of 1945, following the prompt termination of Lend-Lease arrangements by the USA, necessitated both an export drive to restore currency reserves, and attempts to stem an undue drain in dollar holdings.[66] The cinema trade's long-established reliance on imports from the United States ensured it a prominent place in policy debates across the later 1940s. In 1947, as the impending convertibility of currencies heightened concern over the state of the nation's finances, the government moved to impose a duty of 75 per cent on the value of film imports into the UK. When Hollywood responded with a boycott of exports to Britain, trade in film was suspended, a position only ended in March 1948 when the British government agreed to remove the duty, in return for new controls over the amount of money American distributors could repatriate from their earnings from screenings in Britain.[67] While the dispute remained unresolved, the government sought to bolster British production through new quota regulations, alongside measures to ensure the widest possible distribution of home-produced features. Following the agreement with the USA, the quota became an alternative vehicle for protecting British interests, with the result that, from the summer of 1948, 45 per cent of first features shown were to be British.[68] This move, embodied in the Cinematograph Films Act of 1948, dismayed exhibitors, concerned over the likely availability of qualifying product, and gave rise to particular comment in Scotland, where folk memories of deep-rooted local antipathy to the output of British studios were revived. Calls were made for Scotland to be more fully represented on the National Film Production Council and, further, for the creation of a separate Scottish committee as the best guarantee against the screening of what were described as 'totally unsuitable films' north of the border.[69] In the Parliamentary debate on the Cinematograph Films Bill, the Conservative member for Perth, Col Gomme-Duncan, sought to illustrate the basis for such concerns. Citing a film which purported to depict the Black Watch on the eve of the Great War, he described a scene in which men gathered in a mess 'which looked like a cross between the Albert Hall and a Lyons Corner House', before proceeding to voice a long-familiar lament: 'Never has my Scottish soul been so rent as it was when watching some of my country's ancestors and the representation of what they were supposed to have done according to English or American producers.'[70] As before, objections extended beyond depictions of Scotland and the Scots by outsiders to the very nature of the British product itself. This, as Lt Cdr Clark-Hutchison, Conservative member for Edinburgh West asserted, often failed to resonate with Scottish audiences. Indeed, as he remarked during the debate on the Committee stage of the 1948 bill, 'He was advised that relatively few British films enjoyed a good run in Scotland because the majority of them, however good they might be, had an English background and they did not appeal to the majority of Scottish people.'[71]

A similar point was made in comparable language the following year, when an amendment to quota regulations was under discussion. In a debate in the House of Lords, the Earl of Rosebery emphasised, perhaps in exaggerated terms, the importance of the cinema to his fellow countrymen, claiming that 'In Scotland, the only method of entertainment was really the films.' Given this, it was considered wholly unreasonable that Scots should have forced upon them films 'made in England for England'. Two titles were cited in support of this point: *The Bad Lord Byron*, a drama starring Dennis Price and Mai Zetterling, and the romantic comedy *Warning to Wantons*, with Harold Warrender and Anne Vernon.[72] To cultural barriers were added economic difficulties, as the many small, independent exhibitors still active in Scotland found themselves obliged to compete for unpopular product to satisfy the requirements of legislation that appeared, at best, ill-advised.

The reiteration of familiar folk wisdom on the film preferences of Scots did not go unchallenged. Responding to the objections raised by Clark-Hutchison, John Belcher, Parliamentary Secretary to the Board of Trade, indicated that available box-office figures did not support the idea that British films were rejected as the products of an alien culture.[73] Such competing claims provide some justification for revisiting the debate over audience tastes that had surfaced in the wake of the earliest quota legislation. Before proceeding to that, however, some reflections may be offered on the nature of cinema-going more generally across the decade and the degree to which this marked a departure from pre-war patterns. Before 1939, seasonal variations in the propensity to attend cinema shows, driven by a combination of weather and the release schedules of major distributors, had been marked.[74] Perhaps reflecting the comparative absence of alternative spending opportunities, audiences during the war were rather more consistent across the year.

At both the Edinburgh Playhouse and the Capitol in Aberdeen, January no longer stood out as the peak month for attendances. Not only was the mean for that month exceeded on several occasions across the year, the fall-off in business at the height of summer was also much less pronounced. Indeed, during the war, July emerged as one of the high points in the annual cycle. Here, it may be presumed, the absence of large-scale movement during the holiday season, encouraged by the 'Holidays at Home' campaign,

Table 7.2 *Seasonal variations in attendance, 1939–45. (Source: NAS, GD289/1/1, Playhouse Cinema, Profit and Loss Ledger; GD289/1/3, Palace Cinema, Profit and Loss Ledger; Cinema Museum, Capitol Cinema, Aberdeen, Takings Books.)*

Month	Playhouse	Palace	Capitol
Jan.	100	100	100
Feb.	102.9	97.4	92.4
March	100.6	106.2	100.9
April	114.3	106.6	104.5
May	107.2	96.4	105.3
June	94.8	92.3	96.1
July	112	106.6	107.8
Aug.	105.5	116.3	106.2
Sept.	98.5	97.4	107.2
Oct.	98.7	91.6	104.3
Nov.	86.9	91.6	90.8
Dec.	100.1	96.6	98.3

worked to maintain levels of consumer spending locally.[75] So, at both the Palace and the Playhouse, at the height of the war in 1942 and 1943, the summer months witnessed the highest attendances. In each case, the same film was involved. The largest audiences in 1942 were for the MGM musical *Babes on Broadway*, starring Mickey Rooney and Judy Garland, which played in mid July at the Playhouse and featured a month later at the Palace. The following year, the garland went to Warner's *Yankee Doodle Dandy*, which again played a month apart at the two houses, in June and July respectively.[76] As this suggests, the summer was no longer a fallow period for releases, but rather became the point at which distributors sought to market their most attractive product. By contrast, the winter months, when previously exhibitors had anticipated higher levels of business, now marked, if anything, a lull in cinema-going, as black-out conditions discouraged the more casual picture-goer. It is perhaps telling that November, with no holidays and shorter daylight hours, now marked the low point for admissions across the year.

After 1945, at the Playhouse and Palace at least, a partial reversion to pre-war patterns of attendance was discernible. New Year week once more emerged as one of the key episodes in the exhibitor's calendar, generating the largest audience at the Playhouse in both 1947 (headed by the Paramount musical comedy *Blue Skies*, with Bing Crosby and Fred Astaire) and 1948 (the Paramount comedy musical *Variety Girl*, with Mary Hatcher and Olga San Juan).[77] Yet the maintenance of economic controls also ensured some carry over from wartime, so that shifts in the audience across the year remained less marked than in the 1930s. Whereas in the latter decade, variations

Table 7.3 *Seasonal variations in attendance, 1945–50. (Source: NAS, GD289/1/1, Playhouse Cinema, Profit and Loss Ledger; GD289/1/3, Palace Cinema, Profit and Loss Ledger.)*

Month	Playhouse	Palace
Jan.	100	100
Feb.	91.6	88.5
March	98.1	93.9
April	100.1	99.5
May	95.9	89.5
June	88.4	89
July	97	98.9
Aug.	97.5	100.8
Sept.	100.3	106.7
Oct.	91.7	97
Nov.	85	79.2
Dec.	93.7	82.1

between the highest and lowest mean figures at the Playhouse approached 33 per cent, the span in the post-war period was rather narrower at 15 per cent.

The suggestion following from this is that as popular cinema-going reached its statistical peak, the greater frequency of attendance meant that the practice acquired a more habitual character. Yet a more detailed breakdown of the figures qualifies such a ready conclusion and suggests a degree of continuity with pre-war patterns. By most measures, it must be admitted, variations in admissions became less pronounced in the 1940s. If attendance is considered in terms of the degree to which it diverged from the expected, as indicated by the monthly mean, then differences in popularity between programmes at the Capitol were marked in the mid 1930s. In 1935–6, this varied between 52.2 (or 47.8 per cent below the mean) to 194.9. By the war's middle years, 1942–3, the gap between the extremes was marginally down at 54 to 172.4. Away from the extremes, however, there was a greater clustering around the mean. In the mid 1930s, just over 44 per cent of programmes (46 out of 105) secured scores within 10 per cent of their respective means. During the war, this rose to 52 per cent (54 out of 104).[78] A similar trend could be observed at the Edinburgh Playhouse, where the proportion of programmes falling close to the mean (10 per cent or less out) rose from 38.1 per cent in 1935–6 (40 out of 105 weeks) to 54.3 per cent in 1942–3 (57 out of 105), before falling in the post-war period to 48.6 per cent in 1947–8 (51 out of 105).[79] From this it may be observed that, even at the height of the war, while weekly fluctuations were less obvious, they had by no means been eliminated. At the Wishaw Picture House, for which daily takings figures are available for the immediate post-war period, the early part of the week continued to generate markedly varied returns in a manner reminiscent of the 1930s. Monday takings across 1947 and 1948 thus fell within 10 per cent of the monthly mean on 28 out of a possible 101 occasions (the house was closed on two weeks in each year), a figure broadly in line with those for before 1939.[80] The suggestion is then that, for all the evidence of more stable levels of cinema-going in the 1940s, the fate of individual programmes continued to be susceptible to shifts in sentiment among prospective picture-goers. Audiences continued to exercise choice even within a narrower range of available pleasures, so that best commercial practice continued to rest on a close appreciation of popular preferences, and it is to these, as expressed via the box office, that attention now turns.

In seeking to measure the comparative popularity of British films, the method adopted for the 1930s, whereby a programme's appeal was expressed in terms of variations from a monthly mean, was again utilised. However, the particular conditions of the war and the period immediately following required some refinement in approach. Fluctuations in the aggregate audience were much greater than the 10 per cent growth witnessed between 1933 and 1939. Between the latter year and the peak in 1946, attendances nationally rose by over 65 per cent, before falling back by just under 15 per cent by the end of the decade.[81] When it is also considered that the quota regime under which exhibitors operated changed markedly in this period, particularly with the tightening in requirements in 1948, there is a real danger that straightforward measures of popularity may be unduly influenced by the point in time that a film played, with higher scores all round in the middle of the decade distorting judgements as to comparative appeal. To allow for such variations, the average popularity score achieved by all films was calculated on an annual basis for each cinema. This was then compared with the popularity achieved by programmes in which British productions were the principal attraction, along with those in which all films qualifying for quota played, whether as first feature or support.

The pattern at both the Playhouse and the Palace is one of broad congruence between the popularity of all programmes and those including British titles across most of the war years.

The popularity scores of British first features increased significantly between 1940 and 1943, broadly in step with more general trends. Variations in performance between 'British' programmes and those overall were most apparent at the beginning and end of the conflict. British films scored better than average in the first weeks of the war, but also showed a more marked decline in support from 1944. Early success was based on the appeal of two films: *The Spy in Black*, an espionage thriller set during the Great War, and the more overtly propagandistic *The Lion Has Wings*. Both attracted audiences in excess of the monthly mean calculated over the period of the European war (+8.1 per cent and +14.1 per cent respectively), a considerable achievement at a time when cinema-going was depressed by the

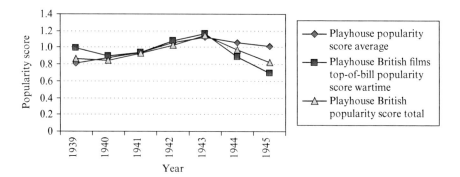

Figure 7.1   *Popularity scores of all programmes and programmes featuring British films at Playhouse, 1939–45. (Source: NAS, GD289/1/1, Playhouse Cinema, Profit and Loss Ledger.)*

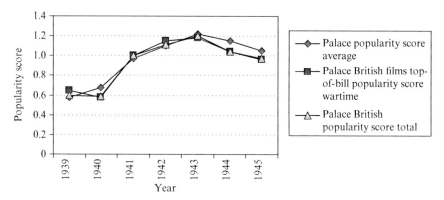

Figure 7.2   *Popularity scores of all programmes and programmes featuring British films at Palace, 1939–45. (Source: NAS, GD289/1/3, Palace Cinema, Profit and Loss Ledger.)*

uncertainties following the outbreak of hostilities.[82] Thereafter, audiences at the Playhouse seemed particularly responsive to films dealing with the war, so that such subjects scored highest among British films in each year from 1940 to 1943, the highest scores being achieved by, respectively, *Contraband* (+3 per cent in July 1940), *Pimpernel Smith* (+41 per cent in November 1941), *49th Parallel* (+51 per cent in January 1942), and *The Life and Death of Colonel Blimp* (+44 per cent in August 1943).[83] As the list suggests, the attraction of war features did not necessarily rest on dramatic realism. The absorption of the documentary aesthetic into mainstream film-making, so often presented as a major gain for British production, does not seem to have excited significant popular approval. So, treatments which drew on documentary methods attracted levels of support that were respectable but, in comparative terms, must be judged less than spectacular. In September 1941, Harry Watt's *Target for Tonight*, playing in support of the First National drama *East of the*

River, drew an audience 6 per cent above the mean, while in June 1944 attendances for *Tunisian Victory* fell 10 per cent short of the mean, when it was shown alongside the re-release of MGM's *Captains Courageous*.[84] Further west, Ealing's *San Demetrio London* generated the lowest takings of any film shown at the Regent in Glasgow over the summer of 1943.[85]

The use of film in wartime to project images of a nation drawing together in the face of shared adversity drew a variable response from Scottish cinema-goers. The spy thriller *An Englishman's Home* struggled when released north of the border in more ways than one, popular sentiment requiring an adjustment in the title to the rather less felicitous *A Britisher's Home*. Its first appearance at the Playhouse in March 1940 drew an audience broadly in line with popularity levels overall at 11 per cent below the wartime mean. One month later, however, its screening at the Palace resulted in a distinctly below-par score of 51 (or 49 per cent below the mean).[86] Picture-goers were equally unreceptive towards *This England*, repackaged as *Our Heritage*, the appearances of which in Edinburgh and Aberdeen secured audiences that fell short of the mean by between 11 per cent and 32 per cent.[87] Rather more successful were two altogether more whimsical essays in Britishness, making much of a perceived national propensity for eccentricity, *The Demi-Paradise* (+5.7 per cent) and *Tawny Pipit* (+7.9 per cent), the only British films to secure above-average audiences at the Playhouse in 1944.[88] By contrast, the more sober realism of *The Shipbuilders*, John Baxter's updated version of the George Blake novel, drew a muted response from patrons at the Playhouse (−23 per cent). It enjoyed rather more success on resurfacing at the Palace, although a popularity score of +6 per cent achieved in the first of its two weeks was still below the overall average for the year.[89]

At the Capitol, as before the war, British films performed rather less well than elsewhere, failing by some margin to match average popularity scores across both 1941 and 1943.

Greater success was recorded in 1940 (for which only one month's figures survive) and 1942, and in each case a war subject worked to boost audiences. In January 1940, *The Lion Has Wings* repeated the success enjoyed in Edinburgh with an attendance 18 per cent above the mean, while in December 1942 Noel Coward's one excursion into naval heroics, captured in *In Which We Serve*, secured the highest popularity score of any British film at the Capitol, with an audience 72 per cent above the average.[90] The comparative success of British films in both years may also be traced to the enduring appeal of another, familiar genre. As had been the case before 1939, further outings for Arthur Lucan as Old Mother Riley proved a popular draw at the Capitol. *Old Mother Riley, MP* was, by some distance, the most popular film shown in the early weeks of 1940, attracting an attendance 50 per cent above the mean, while *Old Mother Riley's Circus*, even though it enjoyed slightly less success in May 1942, with an audience 17 per cent higher than 'normal', still exceeded the overall average popularity scores secured by programmes at

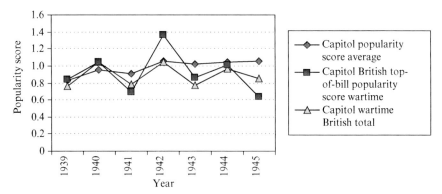

Figure 7.3 *Popularity scores of all programmes and 'British' programmes at the Capitol Cinema, Aberdeen, 1939–45. (Source: CM, Capitol Cinema, Takings Books.)*

the Capitol that year.[91] It might also be noted that *Old Mother Riley's Ghosts*, which appeared as a support in July 1941 to the RKO comedy romance *Play Girl*, was the only British film that year to feature in a programme whose popularity was above average both for the year and across the period of the war as a whole (+25.9 per cent).[92] Other comedies which worked to lift the performance of British films in 1942 were the George Formby vehicles *South American George* and *Much Too Shy* (scores of +23 per cent and +34 per cent respectively).[93] Established British stars thus remained reliable box-office draws through the war. Those apart, however, the Capitol's patrons, as had been the case in the 1930s, showed limited enthusiasm for British comedy titles. Excluding the examples already cited, such films featured on twelve programmes over the war years, in eight of which they fulfilled a support-ing role. On average, audiences for these weeks fell short of the average by some 22 per cent.[94] A similar pattern obtained at the Playhouse, where most programmes with British comedies as the second feature returned audiences below the wartime mean. Of the films to secure attendances above 'normal', two were reissues of George Formby titles first released earlier in the war: *Turned Out Nice Again* in October 1944 (+5 per cent) and *Spare a Copper* in April 1945 (+7 per cent).[95] If the performance of comedies overall points to continuity either side of 1939, the fortunes of another genre capture the inci-dence of change. Musicals, which through the 1930s had worked to boost the popularity of the British product with Capitol audiences, featured infre-quently on the hall's bills during the war and, when they did, drew a tepid response. In all, three musicals played at the Capitol: the Vera Lynn vehicle *Rhythm Serenade* in September 1943; Butcher's Films' *Variety Jubilee* in December 1944; and the Ealing production of *Champagne Charlie*, directed by Cavalcanti and starring Tommy Trinder, in January 1945. All recorded audiences between 25 per cent and 37 per cent below the wartime average.[96]

In summary, greater critical acceptance of British films during wartime signalled no fundamental departure in attitudes among ordinary cinema-goers. Where particular genres or stars had prospered before 1939, success mostly continued into the early 1940s. In war as in peace, a preference for larger-budget productions alongside comedies with favoured performers remained apparent.

From 1945 to the end of the decade, while British titles shared broadly in the decline in popularity of films more generally, the shifts in support were if anything more pronounced. In the first months following VE Day, a number of British productions played at the Playhouse and the Palace in Edinburgh, securing attendances well above those seen across the year and the period as a whole to 1950. If *The Way to the Stars*, with scores of +40 per cent at the Playhouse and +53 per cent at the Palace in November and December 1945, reflected the continued appeal of war themes, films combining fantasy and romance also proved attractive: David Lean's *Blithe Spirit* drew audiences respectively 48 per cent and 28 per cent above the mean in the first post-war autumn, while Powell and Pressburger's *I Know Where I'm Going* enjoyed even greater success at +51 per cent and +35 per cent the following spring. Comfortably eclipsing these and securing unparalleled levels of popularity in the four weeks it played in Edinburgh in February and March 1946 was *The Seventh Veil*, in which the 'treatment' of psycho-analysis was rendered attractive by the brooding saturnine presence of James Mason, the star also of the most popular film of 1947, the thriller *Odd Man Out*.[97] Even at this peak of the cinema-going cycle, success was not assured. In May 1946, the drama *They Knew Mr. Knight*, with Mervyn Johns and Nora Swinburne, proved an unequivocal failure at the Playhouse with an audience 41 per cent below the mean.[98] As the period progressed, the balance between box-office hits and misses moved in favour of the latter, as the presence of a British film proved a drag rather than a boost to popularity. In 1948, British films topped the bill at the Playhouse in sixteen out of fifty-three weeks. Only two films secured attendances above the post-war average: the Gainsborough fantasy comedy *Miranda*, with Googie Withers and Glynis Johns, and the altogether more hard-edged *Good-Time Girl*, with Jean Kent, each coming in 27 per cent above the relevant mean. Of the remainder, twelve fell below the average popularity score for the year, with the Apollo Production *Corridor of Mirrors* marking a low point of 53 per cent below the mean.[99]

Such findings provide statistical support for the claims made by Parliamentarians that the increased quota had forced exhibitors to book a larger number of inappropriate and unpopular British titles. The defence offered by the Board of Trade, while accurate in questioning claims for a long-standing and deeply felt antipathy to British films in Scotland, failed to reflect the impact of the higher quota and the inability of British production to meet the greater demands placed upon it. In this context, a brief comparison may be offered with an earlier period in which quota legislation had imposed escalating demands on production capacity. In 1935, at which point the exhibitors' quota stood at 15 per cent, British films featured in eighteen of the fifty-two programmes offered at the Playhouse. As might be anticipated, their popularity varied markedly, from an attendance 42 per cent below the mean secured by the Laura La Plante romance *The Church Mouse*, the support for Dolores del Rio in *Madame DuBarry*, to the score of over 80 per cent in excess of the mean for *The Scarlet Pimpernel*. The overall figure of 98, a mere 2 per cent below the average, compares more than favourably with one of 82.8 achieved by the sixteen programmes incorporating British titles that played in 1948.[100] Whether seen in terms of the post-war period as a whole or across the year itself, this performance must be adjudged distinctly below par, and casts doubt on the commercial effectiveness of British production and in particular on its ability to function at the kind of volume and at the level of support achieved in the 1930s, perceived as a less than successful decade artistically. For all the greater critical acceptance of British titles, evidence of a significant change in popular attitudes to the domestic product remains less than compelling, although it must be acknowledged that the evidential base for such conclusions is thinner than for earlier periods. The problem is compounded by the decision of the Wishaw Picture House, the one non-Edinburgh hall for which full returns have been located for the immediate post-war era, to rebrand itself towards the end of the decade as a cinema specialising in the showing of 'B' movies and serials. As a result, the proportion of British films screened fell to a bare minimum, accounting for only three of 184 films shown across 1950.[101]

Nevertheless, the accounts for earlier years, when British titles figured rather more prominently on picture house bills, are of value both in broadening the basis for an assessment of the comparative popularity of the home product and in establishing the degree to which the experience of the war years and beyond encouraged the emergence of a more uniform taste community across Scotland. It is perhaps telling in this context that the subjects which enjoyed success in Edinburgh also played well in Wishaw. In 1946, *The Seventh Veil* and *I Know Where I'm Going* were the top attractions in both east and west, while the picture-goers of Wishaw were no more enthusiastic about *They Knew Mr. Knight* than the patrons of the Playhouse (popularity scores of 56 per cent and 58.9 per cent respectively).[102] Thereafter, the performance of British films weakened considerably, with only *Odd Man Out* and Powell and Pressburger's *Black Narcissus* attracting attendances greater than the mean out of fifteen bills that qualified for quota.[103] As at the Capitol, the boost to receipts previously anticipated from the showing of musicals no longer applied. In March 1947, the appearance of Wesley Ruggles' *London Town*, with Sid Field and Greta Gynt, resulted in takings 14 per cent below the mean.[104] In other respects, however, the preferences which helped to define Wishaw as a distinct taste community remained in evidence beyond 1945. Picture house patrons appear to have retained their love of western features. So, whereas such films, broadly defined, appeared on twenty-one

Table 7.4 *Popularity scores, Wishaw Picture House. (Source:* GCA, TD723/4, *The Wishaw Picture Palace, Ltd, Cash Book, Nov. 1945–April 1953; The Wishaw Press and Advertiser, 1946–8.)*

Year	Average popularity score	British films	Westerns
1946	107.3	108.9	107.8
1947	92.4	77.2	99.35
1948	99.2	92.8	109.7

or 13.4 per cent of programmes at the Playhouse between 1946 and 1948, their visits to Wishaw were more frequent at just under a third of potential programmes.[105] What is more, their appearances more often than not generated larger attendances than when non-western or, more particularly, British programmes played.

Nor was their impact confined, as previously, to the first half of the week, suggesting a greater readiness to schedule them for larger weekend audiences. In 1949–50, serials were often screened in the second half of the week, providing further evidence of an enduring fracturing in popular tastes in the later 1940s.[106]

The diversity which marked the Scottish audience in the 1930s remained in evidence as mid century approached and was one of the factors informing the decision of the Highlands and Islands Film Guild to encourage the formation of local selection committees, which would ensure that programmes were tailored to a specific set of preferences. In October 1947, the Guild's Development Officer reflected on fractures in film taste across the area:

> *The Overlanders* although popular in Caithness had an indifferent reception further west. Conversely, *I Know Where I'm Going* broke records in the west, but caused no commotion at all in Shetland where the first choice would seem to be outdoor and sea dramas (*San Demetrio London* and *Captains Courageous*).[107]

A preference for the familiar or the locally meaningful was noted by others. The experience of one operator on the Guild's mobile units led to the conclusion that, 'give them a good story, preferably a Scottish background, but at least related in some way to their own way of life and their own knowledge of literature, and they are happy'.[108] Booking arrangements also captured an important contrast in tastes compared with urban picture-goers. Reports early in 1949 noted indifference to films such as *Blithe Spirit* and *Odd Man Out*, which had prospered in the central belt, and discovered instead a preference for outdoor subjects such as *Lassie Come Home*, and the Randolph Scott western *When the Daltons Rode*.[109] Few titles appeared capable of transcending geographical differences, although the widespread popularity of *Whisky Galore!* across all areas served by the Guild was noted in 1950.[110] For the most part, however, the audience appears to have remained an agglomeration of disparate taste communities, whose changing preferences acted to challenge and occasionally confound business expectations.

III

That cinema should, outwardly at least, have prospered in a decade of war and austerity occasions little surprise. An era of full employment, in which alternative outlets for consumer spending were severely constrained, provided precisely the conditions required to fuel a boom in cinema-going. Profit margins registered the restoration of financial health, so that dividends, while rarely aspiring to the heights achieved immediately after the First World War, were consistent and sizeable. Conventional measures of prosperity nevertheless cannot entirely conceal underlying challenges facing the industry through this period. Profits benefited stockholders and could be used to acquire more lucrative product, but was rarely used to maintain, let alone improve, the physical infrastructure. As rates of depreciation quickened with more intensive use, the fabric of most cinemas underwent deterioration to some degree. Luxury had not as yet given way to dilapidation, but the process was under way as cinema approached its jubilee. If film's place in Scottish society appeared more assured, its role in promoting civic consciousness being recognised across both rural and urban areas, concerns as to its moral impact continued to circulate. The deliberations of the Wheare Committee towards the end of the decade revealed enduring doubts over the efficacy of Scotland's take on censorship, which the reported presence of children of school age at screenings in Edinburgh of the British crime and social problem film *Good-Time Girl* did little to assuage.[111]

The most consistent challenge facing the industry, however, continued to be posed by cinema-goers themselves. Higher levels of attendance and the absence of alternative amusements did little to alter the nature of picture-going, in that patrons continued to exercise preferences in a manner liable to generate marked fluctuations at the box office. Indications are, although it must be admitted that the basis for such observations remains frustratingly slight, that tastes were not transformed by either the experience of war or by the heightened critical reputation of British films. War subjects performed well at the height of the conflict, although their attraction owed as much, if not more, to the presence of particular stars and a sizeable budget as it did to subject matter alone. Otherwise, genres and performers who had commanded an audience before 1939 continued, for the most part, to do so thereafter. Aberdeen, or at least patrons of the Capitol, remained loyal to the films of Arthur Lucan, while Wishaw picture-goers continued to thrill to the exploits of William Boyd as Hopalong Cassidy, and his like. The impact of British films rested, as before, on the particular appeal of a title, so that the claims of deep-rooted hostility to native productions were overdone. At the same time, attempts to increase the number of British films to which cinema-goers were exposed through tighter quota requirements encountered clear consumer resistance. In the process, the commercial effectiveness of the production industry, especially when compared with its performance in the 1930s, is brought into question.

Taking the output of British and American studios, considerations of national origin rarely appeared to exercise a decisive impact on audience behaviour. A film's attractions lay elsewhere, a point which also informed popular responses to titles which addressed Scottish themes, so that critical preoccupation with the accuracy of historical fact or cultural detail seems not to have been shared by most picture house patrons. This leaves open the question of the reception of productions originating from within Scotland. Although not numerous, they were, in terms of approach, diverse and could be encountered in many and varied settings, as a previous chapter has indicated. The pattern assumed by Scottish film production, the constraints and opportunities to which it was subject, and its variable record of success provide the basis for a further, and final chapter.

NOTES

1. In 1950, attendances across the UK stood at 1,395.8 million, compared with the pre-war peak of 990 million, http://www.screenonline.org.uk/film/facts/fact1. html (accessed 25 October 2011).
2. P. Russell and J. P. Taylor (eds), *Shadows of Progress: Documentary Film in Post-War Britain* (Basingstoke, 2010), part one; The Arts Enquiry, *The Factual Film*, chs I and II. Similar work was also being undertaken locally, see Lebas, 'Glasgow's Progress', pp. 34–53.
3. See Chapter 3, pp. 103–8.
4. See Chapter 4, pp. 157–63.
5. http://www.screenonline.org.uk/film/facts/fact1.html (accessed 22 November 2011); Browning and Sorrell, 'Cinemas and Cinema-Going', p. 134.
6. See Chapter 2, pp. 84–5; *Scotsman*, 21 April 1947, p. 7, for an advertisement for Rank's film clubs, which sought to reassure the parents of 'Bobby' that 'at the Gaumont or Odeon Cinema Club, he sees more and more of the right films, especially made for him. Teacher may be on the committee with Bobby himself (he's captain of the club's football team, too). And mother, doing the Saturday shopping, knows he's safe and happy.'
7. In 1944 and 1945, production of features numbered thirty-five and thirty-nine respectively, compared with thirty-three in 1925–6, the British industry's pre-quota nadir, http://www.screenonline.org.uk/film/facts/facts2.html (accessed 22 November 2011).
8. *Scotsman*, 20 Sept. 1944, p. 3.
9. Dickinson and Street, *Cinema and State*, pp. 97–100; Murphy, *Realism and Tinsel*, pp. 29–33.
10. *Scotsman*, 20 Sept. 1944, p. 3; A. Aldgate and J. Richards, *Britain Can Take It: The British Cinema in the Second World War* (Edinburgh, 1994).

11. R. Murphy, 'The Heart of Britain: British Cinema at War', in id., *British Cinema Book*, pp. 223–31; id., *British Cinema and the Second World War*, ch. 3; Richards, *Films and British National Identity*, ch. 4; id., 'National Identity in British Wartime Films' and P. Stead, 'The People as Stars: Feature Films as National Expression', in P. M. Taylor (ed.), *Britain and the Cinema in the Second World War* (Basingstoke, 1988), pp. 42–61, 62–83.

12. M. Chick, *Industrial Policy in Britain, 1945–1951: Economic Planning, Nationalisation and the Labour Governments* (Cambridge, 1998), ch. 4; J. Tomlinson, 'Managing the Economy, Managing the People', in F. Carnevali and J.-M. Strange (eds), *Twentieth-Century Britain: Economic, Cultural and Social Change* (Harlow, 2007), pp. 233–46.

13. J. Poole, 'British Cinema Attendance in Wartime: Audience Preference at the Majestic, Macclesfield, 1939–46', *Historical Journal of Film, Radio and Television*, 7 (1987), pp. 15–34; S. Harper, 'Fragmentation and Crisis: 1940s Admissions Figures at the Regent Cinema, Portsmouth, UK', *Historical Journal of Film, Radio and Television*, 26 (2006), pp. 361–94.

14. Cameron, *Impaled Upon a Thistle*, pp. 263–79.

15. SSA, 5/25/4, The Stranraer Picture House, Ltd, Minute Book, No. 1, 1 April 1931–5 Sept. 1960, Meetings of Directors, 30 Nov. 1939; 4 June 1940.

16. SSA, 5/22/6, The Glasgow Picture House, Ltd, Minute Book No. 5, 7 July 1936–5 April 1949, Meeting of Directors, 4 Sept. 1939.

17. CM, Capitol Cinema, Aberdeen, Takings Book, 1939–40, week beginning 4 Sept. 1939; NAS, GD289/1/1, Playhouse Cinema, Profit and Loss Ledger, week ending 16 Sept. 1939; GD289/1/3, Palace Cinema, Profit and Loss Ledger, week ending 16 Sept. 1939.

18. NAS, GD289/1/3, week ending, 4 Nov. 1939; Dumfries and Galloway Archives, 1/6/9, Lockerbie Cinema Co., Ltd, Directors' Minute Book No. 2, 30 Sept. 1938–30 June 1950, Meeting of Directors, 11 Sept. 1939.

19. CM, Capitol, Aberdeen, Takings Books, 1938–40.

20. NAS, GD289/1/1; GD289/1/3, figures for Sept.–Dec. 1938 and 1939.

21. NAS, GD289/1/1, weeks ending 9 Sept.–30 Dec. 1939.

22. NAS, GD289/1/3, weeks ending 9 Sept.–30 Dec. 1939.

23. CM, Torry Cinemas, Ltd, Accounts, receipts of £4,529 4s 11d were the lowest since the year to April 1925.

24. SSA, 5/7/11, Poole's Entertainments, Ltd, Minute Book, 25 Jan. 1938–23 Feb. 1967, Annual Meetings of Company, 10 March 1939; 14 March 1940.

25. NAS, GD289/1/3, week ending 9 March 1940; the wartime average here and in the pages that follow was calculated over the duration of the European war, from September 1939 to May 1945.

26. SSA, 5/7/254, Uddingston Picture House, Co., Ltd, Minute Book, 14 Oct. 1940–5 Dec. 1958, Meeting of Directors, 17 Dec. 1940.

27. Dickinson and Street, *Cinema and State*, pp. 120–9.

28. *Scotsman*, 31 Oct. 1939, p. 9; NAS, GD289/1/1, Playhouse Cinema Profit and Loss Ledger, weeks ending 30 Sept. (*Katia*); 11 Nov. (*Alerte en Méditerranée*); 25 Nov. 1939 (*Les Gens du Voyage*).

29. SSA, 5/22/6, Glasgow Picture House, Ltd, Minute Book No. 5, Meeting of Directors, 3 June 1940; 5/22/9, Balance Sheets and Profit and Loss Accounts, the wage bill rose from £3,741 15s in the year to 1 June 1940 to £6,545 7s 10d in the year to 2 June 1945.

30. CM, Aberdeen Picture Palaces, Ltd, Accounts, increase from £3,829 5s 10d in the year to 31 Jan. 1940 to £5,580 10s 5d in the year to 31 Jan. 1945.

31. SSA, 5/25/9, Stranraer Picture House, Ltd, Accounts, year to 21 April 1942; year to 21 April 1944.

32. SSA, 5/25/3, Stranraer Picture House, Ltd, Shareholders' Minute Book No. 1, 18 June 1931–5 Sept. 1960, Minute of Eighth Ordinary General Meeting, 4 Aug. 1939; Ninth Ordinary General Meeting, 1 July 1940.

33. NAS, GD289/2/17–18, Palace Cinema, Running Books, 16 Oct. 1939–1 May 1948; SSA, 5/25/4, Stranraer Picture House, Ltd, Minute Book No. 1, Meetings of Directors, 5 Nov. 1940; 16 Sept. 1942; 25 Aug. 1943.

34. NAS, GD289/1/1, Playhouse Cinema, Running Book, 1 Feb. 1943–1 May 1948.

35. SSA, 5/25/9, Stranraer Picture House, Ltd, Annual Accounts.

36. SSA, 5/22/8, Glasgow Picture House, Ltd, Balance Sheets and Profit and Loss Accounts, at 28 May 1938 and 27 May 1944.

37. CM, Capitol Cinema, Takings Books.

38. NAS, GD289/1/1, Playhouse Cinema, Profit and Loss Ledger; GD289/1/3, Palace Cinema, Profit and Loss Ledger.

39. Dewey, *War and Progress*, p. 287; P. Howlett, 'The Wartime Economy, 1939–45', in R. Floud and P. Johnson (eds), *The Cambridge Economic History of Modern Britain. Volume III. Structural Change and Growth, 1939–2000* (Cambridge, 2004), pp. 12–15.

40. Dickinson and Street, *Cinema and State*, pp. 128–9.

41. Howlett, 'Wartime Economy', pp. 5–6; S. Pollard, *The Development of the British Economy, Third Edition, 1914–1980* (London, 1983), p. 228.

42. National Museum of Scotland, Scottish Life Archive, Eileen Crowford Collection, Diaries, 1937–50. I am grateful to John Burnett of the NMS for bringing this collection to my attention.

43. Dumfries and Galloway Archives, 1/6/9, Lockerbie Cinema Co., Directors' Minute Book No. 2, Meeting of Directors, 27 Oct. 1940.

44. Dumfries and Galloway Archives, 1/6/9, Meeting of Directors, 30 Jan. 1942.

45. SSA, 5/25/9, Stranraer Picture House, Ltd, Annual Accounts; NAS, GD289/1/3, Palace Cinema, Profit and Loss Ledger.

46. NAS, GD289/1/3, Palace Cinema, Profit and Loss Ledger.

47. CM, Aberdeen Picture Palaces, Ltd, Accounts; James F. Donald (Aberdeen Cinemas), Ltd, Accounts.

48. NAS, GD289/1/1, Playhouse Cinema, Profit and Loss Ledger.

49. Dewey, *War and Progress*, p. 285.

50. SSA, 5/22/9, Glasgow Picture House, Ltd, Balance Sheets and Profit and Loss Ledgers.

51. SSA, 5/7/254, Uddingston Picture House Co., Ltd, Minute Book, Meetings of Directors, 7 April; 11 Aug.; 9 Sept. 1942; 4 May 1943.

52. Dumfries and Galloway Archives, 1/6/9, Lockerbie Cinema Co., Ltd, Directors' Minute Book, No. 2, Meeting of Directors, 27 March 1942.

53. SSA, 5/7/254, Uddingston Picture House Co., Ltd, Minute Book, Extraordinary General Meeting of Shareholders, 5 Oct. 1944.

54. SSA, 5/22/6, Glasgow Picture House, Ltd, Minute Book No. 5, Meeting of Directors, 6 Feb. 1946.

55. Dumfries and Galloway Archives, 1/6/9, Lockerbie Cinema Co., Ltd, Minute Book, Meetings of Directors, 28 Sept. 1945; 22 Feb.; 26 April; 27 Sept. 1946.

56. NAS, BT2/17497/29–30, Stornoway Playhouse, Ltd, Directors' Report and Statement of Accounts for year to 28 Jan. 1942; Resolution of Extraordinary General Meeting, 29 July 1942; BT2/17243/33, Mecca Cinema, Ltd, Declaration of Solvency, 29 June 1945.

57. *Kinematograph Year Book* (London, 1948).

58. I. Zweiniger-Bargielowska, *Austerity in Britain: Rationing, Controls and Consumption, 1939–1955* (Oxford, 2000), pp. 45–59.

59. Browning and Sorrell, 'Cinemas and Cinema-going', p. 134.

60. NAS, GD289/1/1, Playhouse Cinema, Profit and Loss Ledger, 1945–50; GD289/1/3, Palace Cinema, Profit and Loss Ledger, 1945–50.

61. GCA, TD723/4, The Wishaw Picture Palace, Ltd, Cash Book, Nov. 1945–April 1953; CM, Aberdeen Picture Palaces, Ltd, Accounts.

62. CM, Torry Picture House, Ltd, Accounts.

63. CM, Torry Picture House, Ltd, Accounts.

64. NAS, BT2/8516/45–7, 49–50, 52–57, 60, The Dunfermline Cinema House, Ltd, Annual Returns, 1939–50.

65. NAS, GD289/1/3, Palace Cinema, Profit and Loss Ledger.

66. A. Cairncross, *Years of Recovery: British Economic Policy, 1945–51* (London, 1985), ch. 1; C. R. Schenk, 'Austerity and Boom', in Johnson, *Twentieth-Century Britain*, pp. 300–19.

67. Dickinson and Street, *Cinema and State*, pp. 184–95; N. Pronay, 'The Film Industry', in H. Mercer, N. Rollings, and J. D. Tomlinson (eds), *Labour Governments and Private Industry: The Experience of 1945–1951* (Edinburgh, 1992), pp. 222–5.

68. Dickinson and Street, *Cinema and State*, pp. 195–8.

69. *Scotsman*, 14 Feb., p. 5; 30 June 1948, p. 3

70. *Scotsman*, 22 Jan. 1948, p. 4.

71. *Scotsman*, 5 Feb. 1948, p. 5.

72. *Scotsman*, 1 April 1949, p. 6.

73. *Scotsman*, 5 Feb. 1948, p. 5.

74. See Chapter 5, pp. 193–6.

75. C. Sladen, 'Holidays at Home in the Second World War', *Journal of Contemporary History*, 37 (2002), pp. 67–89; A. Calder, *The People's War: Britain, 1939–45* (London, 1969), p. 366.

76. NAS, GD289/1/1, Playhouse Cinema, Profit and Loss Ledger, weeks beginning 13 July 1942; 14 June 1943; GD289/1/3, Palace Cinema, Profit and Loss Ledger, weeks beginning 10,17 Aug. 1942; 5, 12, 19 July 1943.

77. NAS, GD289/1/1, Playhouse Cinema, Profit and Loss Ledger, weeks beginning 30 Dec. 1946; 29 Dec. 1947.
78. CM, Capitol Cinema, Takings Books, 1935–6; 1942–3.
79. NAS, GD289/1/1, Playhouse Cinema, Profit and Loss Ledger, 1935–6; 1942–3; 1947–8.
80. GCA, TD723/4, The Wishaw Picture Palace, Ltd, Cash Book, Nov. 1945–April 1953; for the 1930s, see Chapter 5, p. 197.
81. Browning and Sorrell, 'Cinemas and Cinema-going', p. 134.
82. NAS, GD289/1/1, Playhouse Cinema, Profit and Loss Ledger, weeks ending, 21 Oct.; 9 Dec. 1939; Richards and Sheridan, *Mass-Observation*, pp. 299–330 for reaction to *The Lion Has Wings*.
83. NAS, GD289/1/1, week ending 27 July 1940; weeks beginning 17 Nov. 1941; 12 Jan. 1942; 23 Aug. 1943.
84. NAS, GD289/1/1, weeks beginning 8 Sept. 1941; 5 June 1944.
85. SSA, 5/22/6, Glasgow Picture House, Ltd, Minute Book No. 5, loose sheet insert at Meeting of Directors, 12 April 1940.
86. NAS, GD289/1/1, Playhouse Cinema, Profit and Loss Ledger, week ending 23 March 1940; GD289/1/3, Palace Cinema, Profit and Loss Ledger, week ending 13 April 1940.
87. NAS, GD289/1/1, week beginning 2 June 1941; CM, Capitol Cinema, Takings Book, week beginning 12 May 1941.
88. NAS, GD289/1/1, weeks beginning 10 April; 18 Sept. 1944.
89. NAS, GD289/1/1, week beginning 12 June 1944; GD289/1/3, week beginning 10 July 1944.
90. CM, Capitol Cinema, Takings Books, weeks beginning 8 Jan. 1940; 21 Dec. 1942.
91. CM, Capitol Cinema, Takings Books, weeks beginning 1 Jan. 1940; 4 May 1942.
92. CM, Capitol Cinema, Takings Book, week beginning 21 July 1941.
93. CM, Capitol Cinema, Takings Book, weeks beginning 23 March; 3 Aug. 1942.
94. CM, Capitol Cinema, Takings Books, 1939–45.
95. NAS, GD289/1/1, Playhouse Cinema, Profit and Loss Ledger, weeks beginning 16 Oct. 1944; 23 April 1945.
96. CM, Capitol Cinema, Takings Books, weeks beginning 20 Sept. 1943; 4 Dec. 1944; 22 Jan. 1945.
97. NAS, GD289/1/1, Playhouse Cinema, Profit and Loss Ledger, weeks beginning 13 Aug.; 19 Nov. 1945; 25 Feb.; 18 March 1946; 12 May 1947; GD289/1/3, Palace Cinema, Profit and Loss Ledger, weeks beginning 24 Sept.; 24 Dec. 1945; 22 April; 6 May 1946; 16 June 1947.
98. NAS, GD289/1/1, Playhouse Cinema, Profit and Loss Ledger, week beginning 6 May 1946.
99. NAS, GD289/1/1, weeks beginning 26 July; 9, 16 Aug. 1948.
100. NAS, GD289/1/1, 1935 and 1948.
101. *The Wishaw Press and Advertiser* (hereafter *WP*), 1950.
102. GCA, TD723/4, The Wishaw Picture Palace, Ltd, Cash Book, 18–23 March; 29

April–4 May; 3–5 June 1946; *WP*, 15 March, p. 12; 26 April, p. 8; 31 May 1946, p. 8.

103. GCA, TD723/4, 1946–8; *WP*, 1946–8.

104. GCA, TD723/4, 17–22 March 1947; *WP*, 14 March 1947, p. 8.

105. NAS, GD289/1/1/, Playhouse Cinema, Profit and Loss Ledger, 1946–8; *WP*, 1946–8.

106. *WP*, 1949–50.

107. NAS, ED30/2, Highlands and Islands Film Guild, Minutes of Meetings, Development Officer's Report on Activities since Oct. 1947.

108. SSA, 3/2/14, Film Societies Collection, cutting from *The Mini Cinema* (March 1951), T. S. Morris, 'The Edge of the World', *The Mini Cinema* (March 1951), p. 10.

109. NAS, ED30/2, Meeting of Council, 21 Dec. 1948.

110. D. L. Peacock, 'Highland Cinema', *The Countryman*, XLIV, 2 (Winter 1951), pp. 257–60.

111. NAS, CO1/4/200, Committee on Children and the Cinema, Ninth Meeting of Committee held in St Andrew's House, Edinburgh, 30 Sept.–1 Oct. 1948, p. 5.

8

A Flickering Image: Scottish Film Production

I

Previous chapters have disclosed a pattern of cinema-going driven by the appeal of the immediate and the local, juxtaposed against footage that was often transnational in scope. The local topical worked alongside actuality and fictional images derived from occasionally unfamiliar cultures to cement cinema's place in popular esteem. Often, however, an authentic and distinctively Scottish perspective appeared to be lacking, as Scots seemed slow to embrace the potential of celluloid to present themselves to each other or to the citizens of other nations. Reviewing progress to a point immediately after the Second World War, the Scottish Film Council felt bound to observe 'Production is Scotland's weak point.'[1] While investment had resulted in the proliferation of sites for the exhibition of the moving image, facilities for their production remained, in comparison with the position elsewhere, underdeveloped. The failing was particularly evident in the field of commercial fictional film-making, so that in the wake of the Great War, at a time when Scottish production was small-scale and of questionable quality, films from other nations secured an extensive distribution within Scotland. In November 1920, the Irish Film Co.'s *In the Days of St Patrick* was screened at several venues across west-central Scotland, including St Mungo's Hall in Glasgow, the latest in a series of screenings for films of Irish origin.[2] The apparent failure of a nation of inveterate picture-goers to generate a body of work reflective of film's popularity merits investigation, and draws attention to the institutional and technical constraints that worked to direct creativity to areas other than the fiction feature. For all the shortcomings of Scottish attempts at commercial film-making, developments in related fields appeared more promising, ensuring if nothing else that this book does not end on an extended note of diminuendo.[3]

The documentary constituted a form which from its earliest days was seen to bear a strong Scottish imprint, largely due to the commanding presence of John Grierson. From a Scottish perspective, the work inaugurated by Grierson at the Empire Marketing Board in the late 1920s would lead a decade later to the series of films produced for the Glasgow Empire Exhibition, which taken together were held to constitute an unusually rounded and coherent view of a nation on celluloid. The Scottish voice, mute in the mainstream feature, is seen in several accounts to have sung forth in the 'creative interpretation of everyday life'.[4] Such a view should not, however, go unchallenged. Although sponsored by the Scottish Development Council and with Grierson as presiding genius, most of the original seven Films of Scotland productions were, as at least one contemporary observed, the creations of companies based outwith Scotland and so offer at best a limited insight into Scotland's film-making capacity towards the end of the interwar period.[5] The concern of this chapter is with images produced within Scotland, providing a corrective to a literature often preoccupied with representations imposed by external agencies based in England and the USA.[6] How Scots sought to speak to each other via the moving picture has much to tell us about a national sense of self and Scottish engagement with the modern in the early twentieth century. It also requires us to view such efforts, as far as is possible given the minimal survival rate of most of the films discussed here, in the round, supplementing formally constructed documentary footage with the local topicals and newsreels that figured on most cinema programmes, and the work, particularly from the later 1920s, of amateur film-makers, whose efforts were coordinated by a network of cine clubs and societies, and the amateur film festivals, which gave their efforts wider prominence.[7] In the process, areas of activity are disclosed over which the long shadow so often cast by Grierson looms less large. For all the importance that attaches to his ideas on the nature of the documentary and the role of film-making generally, Grierson's involvement with developments north of the border was often indirect and intermittent. A broader approach thus serves to place his contribution in a more realistic perspective.

The chapter that follows traces Scottish essays in film production from the earliest topical to ambitious post-war plans to develop a studio facility for large-scale commercial film-making in the eastern Highlands. While, as in the case of the latter venture, the concern is often to chart a substantial gap between aspiration and achievement, this must be set alongside occasional success in fictional production and more sustained achievement among amateurs and in the making of short documentary subjects. How far this amounted to an integrated overview of the nation on film rather than a random collection of flickering images remains to be determined.

II

Locally produced footage, depicting scenes of immediate relevance to audiences, had been one of the earliest and most effective ways in which cinema sought to build an enduring popular following. Exhibitors active in the 1890s spiced their programmes through the inclusion of films that presented incidents and figures familiar to potential patrons.[8] That practice, offering the enticing prospect of seeing yourself as others saw you, was maintained through subsequent decades, so that local scenes remained an important aspect of cinema's commercial appeal into the 1940s. Such footage offered images of immediate topicality, as with film of the unemployed demonstration in Glasgow's George Square and that of the 'Ruins at Hampden Park' in the wake of the riot following the Scottish Cup Final replay between Celtic and Rangers, when frustration at the refusal to schedule extra time in case of a draw led fans to attack the turnstiles. Both featured, in September 1908 and April 1909 respectively, at the Panopticon, whose proprietor, A. E. Pickard, ever sensitive to points of attraction, also arranged for the recording of recurring public events that helped set the rhythm underlying urban life in this period.[9] Pickard's operator was thus active in June 1908 in filming the annual Glasgow Police Sports.[10] Six years later, the screening by the local Picture House of a topical depicting a bowling-green garden party was considered 'quite an event out Cathcart way'.[11] Events in the wider world were also capable of being viewed through a local lens. With the outbreak of war in 1914, scenes of local troops departing for action, last deployed during the conflict in South Africa, were revived as vehicles of popular patriotism. In January 1915, for example, Green's Film Service captured the Glasgow Highlanders en route to the train south.[12]

In the early days at least, few Scottish exhibitors appear to have moved beyond the commissioning of such short, occasional subjects. Material at the Panopticon was acquired through the American Bioscope.[13] Few businesses at this point were of a size to encourage diversification. There were, however, exceptions, such as BB Pictures, Ltd, which appears to have been the earliest concern north of the border to extend its activities into film hire and production. In quick succession early in 1911, BB's Production Department was reported to be active filming a football international at Ibrox Park, the opening of the Scottish Exhibition of Natural History, Art and Industry in Glasgow's Kelvingrove Park, and the aftermath of the fire at Edinburgh's Empire Theatre, including the funeral of its most prominent victim, the Great Lafayette.[14] By the following year, *The Bioscope* was reporting a more concerted move into production, extending beyond the fitful recording of local events to take on the construction of specially composed subjects, both actualities in the form of local scenics and fictional narratives. Both forms would appear to be represented in the titles produced for exhibition at Ayr's Picture Palace in August 1912, *Tam O' Shanter's Ride* and *Land of Burns*.[15] This is all the more telling, as BB Pictures had no direct interest in the venue and so would appear to have been receiving commissions from other businesses. In many respects, this represented BB at its peak. After 1911, resources were squeezed to the extent that the company recorded a sizeable loss in the final pre-war year.[16] Continued difficulties during the war, compounded by a shortage of manpower, signalled a scaling back of activity, so that in September 1917, the firm ceased distributing film, while a month later its production plant at the Wellington Palace was acquired by Green's, a firm which had followed a similar trajectory to BB Pictures, and which was by then well launched on a career as a vertically integrated concern covering production and distribution as well as the exhibition of moving pictures.[17]

By some distance the most ambitious incursion into the film-making business in Scotland before the Great War was the result of efforts not of existing exhibition interests, but of a newly established concern. Barely six months after its formal inception, United Films, Ltd of Glasgow was reported to be preparing a film version of *Rob Roy*, a project which involved location work at Aberfoyle. The production was overseen by the one shareholder in the company with experience of the cinema trade, Arthur Vivian, who mounted regular film screenings at St George's Theatre, Paisley; it also featured prominent actor-manager John Clyde in the lead role.[18] Released early in October 1911, the film had the distinction at 2,500 ft, of being the first three-reel production in Britain; the contemporaneous Gaumont production of the same subject came in at a more standard 995 ft.[19] The principal attraction of the United treatment, amplified in accompanying publicity material, was its potential to appeal to national sentiment. At an early screening, *The Bioscope*'s correspondent assured readers that 'the film bristles with excitement, and thrills everyone' and would, it was thought, meet with the approval of all Scots.[20] United's own publicity declared it to be 'a great ambitious work that will stir the heart of every Scotchman throughout the world' and went on to make much of its national associations as 'The Scottish Drama, produced by Scottish Actors on Scottish ground by the Scottish Firm'.[21] Its status was reinforced by an initial screening attended by the Lord Provost and magistrates of Glasgow, prior to playing for a week before what *The Bioscope* described as large audiences at the Picture House on Sauchiehall Street. That apart, one of its few other outings appears to have been at Vivian's own theatre in Paisley, where the techniques of exploitation were employed to maximise support. During the run, the house staff were arrayed in full Highland costume, while each performance was punctuated by the playing of appropriate airs on the pipes.[22]

Not for the last time, the promise held out by the publicity attending a release proved in practice to be unrealised. Soon after its much-trumpeted debut, *Rob Roy* disappeared from the scene, with *The Bioscope* noting only one further screening, at the Burgh Hall, Pollokshaws.[23] The United Films, Ltd continued to trade for just over three months after the film's release, before the decision was taken late in January 1912 to wind the company up voluntarily due to the weight of liabilities incurred.[24] In the current state of the evidence, it is difficult not to conclude that the production was unable to secure sufficient bookings to enable costs to be recovered. A complicating factor was the almost simultaneous appearance of the Gaumont treatment, which, as accompanying advertising copy emphasised, was 'Taken in the MacGregor Country on the actual spots in Perthshire & Argyllshire'.[25] This was to be the first of several titles produced by Gaumont with Scottish associations. The same month that the company's version of *Rob Roy* was released saw the appearance of *Gems of Scottish Scenery*, followed early the following year by the 900 ft coloured drama *Mary, Queen of Scots*.[26] The vogue for such subjects extended across the Atlantic, so that a third version of *Rob Roy*, produced by Eclair American, was available in Britain from July 1914, and drew praise for the accuracy of its presentation.[27] Given this concerted burst of film-making, a bespoke, modestly budgeted Scottish production almost inevitably struggled for attention. If the film's precise fate remains uncertain, it may be significant that in March 1916, a version of *Rob Roy* failed to secure a purchaser at a sale in Glasgow. Although offered with full exhibition rights across the British Isles, the film attracted only one bid, which, at £10, failed to meet the reserve.[28]

The only other documented Scottish excursion into fiction film-making before the war was on an altogether less ambitious scale. In the summer of 1914, *Mairi, the Romance of a Highland Maiden* played at the Central Hall, Inverness. Production was overseen by a local photographer, Andrew Paterson, who two years earlier had acquired a film camera from Gaumont. With a cast of eight, substantially comprising local amateurs, the production made much of the local setting, being shot along the Moray coast. The experience would appear to have persuaded Paterson that his future did not lie in film as, shortly afterwards, the camera was returned to Gaumont.[29] Unlike most of the footage discussed here, however, *Mairi* survived and four decades later was incorporated into a programme of the Inverness Film Society, in which it featured alongside Jean Renoir's *The Golden Coach* and *Return to Glennascaul*, with Orson Welles.[30]

At least until the outbreak of war, production in Scotland progressed fitfully, with activity for the most part isolated and short-lived. Attempts at more organised provision, where evident, endeavoured to exploit a perspective on Scotland that had gained popularity over the previous century: that of the tourist.[31] Scenics, which built on the appeal of the landscape, had featured in cinema programmes from the earliest days of the medium. Released in 1910, *A Holiday in the Highlands* by the Barker Motion Photography, Ltd included within its 565 ft the kind of stereoscopic effects popularised by commercial photographers.[32] Four years later, a more systematic approach to the filming of scenics was projected by Scotia Films, Ltd of Edinburgh, which announced plans to film throughout Scotland.[33] If wartime conditions did not offer the most propitious circumstances in which to launch such a venture, the idea was taken up by the Scottish Artistic Film Producing Co., which in early 1915 announced plans to supplement its first production, *The Crests of Scottish Regiments*, with two scenics: *Loch Lomond in Early Spring*, which it was claimed would be 'Tinted and Toned' and would run to 430 ft, and *Round Lanark and the Falls of Clyde*.[34] The latter is known to have played at the Hillhead Picture Salon in Glasgow, which later the same year exhibited another Scottish Artistic scenic, on *Grantown on Spey*.[35] Further information on both companies is sparse and neither figures in the Register of Dissolved Companies, suggesting that their grandiloquent titles described operations that were essentially small-scale and individualistic in character. Certainly, Scottish Artistic is known to have ceased operations when one of its members was recruited by another production concern.[36] As the example of BB Pictures suggests, significant departures in the production of moving pictures were not to be anticipated at the height of the war. No sooner had *The Bioscope* announced plans for a new production company based in Inverness, whose output would encompass dramas, comedies, and scenics, than word went out that the scheme was on hold, as it was reported that conscription had worked to deplete the area of the necessary acting talent.[37]

This was not the first such pointer to production activity during wartime in the trade press. In October 1915, *The Bioscope* reported that a series of comedies along with a version of *Annie Laurie* were under consideration.[38] While the latter came to nothing, early the following year, Green's were said to be in the process of completing *His Highness*, the latest of some dozen Club Comedies, which to date were reported to have enjoyed some success. One of Green's staff, a Mr Verne, presumably Alf Averne who has already featured in these pages in his future role as a cinema manager in Lockerbie, was behind the camera, while direction was undertaken by an American, Mr Foote.[39] At this point, plans were in train for the development of an outdoor studio, but would appear to have come to nothing, as the problems which afflicted production plans in Inverness also had an impact further south. By the last year of the war, Green's production efforts, even after the acquisition of BB's plant, lay wholly in the field of actuality. The company had continued to produce individual topicals during the war, as in March 1916 with footage of the visit to Glasgow of Florence Turner, 'The Vitagraph Girl'.[40] By October the following year, such subjects were being packaged together in a regular Scottish Topical. This mostly constituted familiar cinematic fare, so that the programme for November 1917 included a Church parade with a detachment of Gordon Highlanders, and film of Glasgow's new Lord Provost.[41] As business generally revived in the final year of the war, enhanced demand justified the more frequent release of what was now billed as *Scottish Moving Picture News*. By August 1918, *The Entertainer* was noting that this service was available 'in every town and village of importance in Scotland'. Three months later, production shifted from a weekly to a twice-weekly basis.[42]

Conditions within the trade more generally and a succession of dramatic and eminently filmable events ensured that the production of topical footage continued to flourish. The loss of over 200 lives when HMS *Iolaire* foundered off Stornoway provided the basis for a special edition of the *News*. As Green's publicity confidently asserted, there would be considerable demand for scenes which married the drama of the immediate with views of broader anthropological interest: 'They'll all want to see – The Stornoway

Disaster. The wrecked troopship *Iolaire* and Scenes of remote life on the Island.'[43] In quick succession, attention turned to 'Glasgow's Riots. Wild Scenes in George Square. Military Called Out and Troops in Possession of City's Public Buildings.' Potential exhibitors were assured that 'It Stands to Reason that your Patrons will be more interested in viewing above than they would be in viewing a picture of Riots in England or on the Continent.'[44] If the appeal of the local remained marked, this did not inhibit Green's from expanding their operations to exploit more effectually the boom conditions of the post-war years. In May 1919, the firm's topical was renamed the *British Moving Picture News*, reflecting a broader remit that endured until the downturn in business in 1921 signalled a renewed narrowing in focus. The title thus reverted to *Scottish Moving Picture News* from August of that year.[45] All indications are that the decline in cinema-going in the early 1920s was of such an order that Green's opted to concentrate their efforts on the exhibition business, ending what had been to date the most sustained exercise in topical production north of the border.[46]

As well as a regular news service, conditions after the war also encouraged a revival in attempts to produce fictional film. Although undeniably modest in global or even British terms, this was, in the absence of an effective film-making capacity prior to 1914, of considerable local significance. On this occasion, the impetus came not from exhibitors but from businesses concerned to exploit the growing appeal of film stardom. A number of self-styled cinema colleges were active across the central belt during 1919, offering opportunities for prospective artistes lured by the possibility of widespread fame and considerable wealth. In October 1919, the college in central Edinburgh invited applications from those with no previous acting experience, making much of the potential levels of reward held out by existing star salaries: 'Mary Pickford earns £4,000 per week. Charlie Chaplin earns £250,000 per year. What do you earn?'[47] Here, as was the case more generally, at the end of the course, the prospect was held out of appearing on screen. Initially, the intention appears to have been to enable students to evaluate their own performances, to which end the proprietors of the Edinburgh college were reported early in 1919 to have made a film on the promenade at Portobello.[48] More ambitious plans were outlined by the A1 Cinema College in Glasgow, which proclaimed itself to be 'tutor of Vera Burns, Phylis Lea [sic] and other film stars'.[49] Here, it might be thought, the concept of stardom was being employed rather loosely, given that, so far as is known, Ms Lea's only credit was in a production overseen by one of the A1's proprietors, Max Leder, a Swiss national, resident at this point in Whitecraigs near Glasgow.[50] Working alongside Thomas Keir Murray, who was said to have worked in the USA with Bronco Billy Anderson and who appears in subsequent documentation as a 'Film Actor', Leder was being credited in September 1919 with the discovery of a young Glasgow woman set to become 'a Scottish Mary Pickford'.[51] It seems likely that this was a reference to Elizabeth (Nan) Wilkie of Pollokshields, formerly employed at the Public Baths in Alloa, who enrolled at the A1 in September and who was adjudged on completion of the course to be 'an excellent Artiste, most natural in her movements and actions, and . . . specially qualified for Light Drama'.[52] This sufficed to justify the offer of a leading part in an A1 production being planned for what *Scottish Cinema* described as the first open-air studio in Scotland, at Spiers Bridge, Thornliebank, the site of the former Queen Mary Tea Rooms and leased from the Paisley and District Tramway Co.[53]

The resulting production, heralded somewhat inaccurately by *Kinematograph Weekly* as 'The first all-Scottish film', was the five-reel romance *The Harp King*.[54] With a scenario written by J. C. Barker, who also handled the film's distribution, *The Harp King* was trade shown at the central Cinema House in November 1919. Responses tended towards the charitable, *The Scottish Kinema Record* remarking on the need to take account of the circumstances surrounding the production, with the cast made up of students for whom this was their first appearance before the camera, but made note of the slender, disconnected narrative and occasionally 'stagey' acting, while adjudging Leder's camerawork to be variable.[55] Publicity in the trade press sought to appeal to local patriotism, emphasising the national character of a film 'Written in Scotland. Played in Scotland. Filmed in Scotland.'[56] Even then, the programme for its first appearance at the Cinema House acknowledged that it did not constitute 'exactly what one would call a typically Scottish story'. Its virtues were seen to lie rather in setting and mood, so that 'the surrounding scenery (which includes excellent views of Bearsden and Rouken Glen), the Highland dances, and the harvest scenes, all impart the real Scottish atmosphere'.[57] Such strengths aside, it was the reservations voiced in the trade press which anticipated the film's subsequent reception. After playing at the Cinema House for three days during December, its appearances thereafter were few and far between, although it was reported to be enjoying good business at small houses in January 1920, with large attendances reported at the Electric Theatre, Dalmellington, near Ayr.[58]

The impact of *The Harp King* extended beyond the box office. It provided the basis for the incorporation of the Ace Film Producing Co., Ltd in February 1920, which numbered Leder and Murray among its directors. If the intention behind the company was to trade on *The Harp King*'s success, such hopes were quickly disappointed. Within four months, Leder and Murray had resigned from the board and control had passed to Arthur Reid, a Glasgow property agent.[59] A more lasting consequence of what the Cinema House termed 'The First All-Glasgow Production' was the studio facility at Rouken Glen, subsequently made available for the productions of other companies, and the marriage of the film's two stars, both graduates of the A1 College, Nan Wilkie and David Watt.[60] If *The Harp King* represented their one outing on celluloid, for Leder it was merely the latest in a string of such ventures. One year later, he figured as producer of the Glasgow comedy *The Referee's Eye*, described less than promisingly in advance copy as 'A most laughable story of a Football, a Pudding, and an Amateur Detective'. Distributed, like *The Harp King*, by J. C. Barker, the film flickered even more briefly across the pages of the trade press, before disappearing from view, its only impact being to taint the reputation of Scottish productions that followed.[61] In some areas, the reception of another comedy *Football Daft* was said to have been coloured by the showing of a film 'of the same class of a very poor kind'.[62] It seems reasonable to assume that this cinematic upas tree was *The Referee's Eye*.

While in this case confusion arose in part from the similar subject matter, a further complicating factor may have been Leder's involvement in both films. In the late summer of 1921, another concern claiming to groom aspirants for acting stardom, the Broadway Stage and Cinema Productions, Ltd, commenced work on its own film. As one of the Broadway's directors later recalled, in the absence of anyone with the requisite experience, 'We had employed a man Leader [*sic*] as a prospective producer, but from what we had seen of his results, he was no use to us.'[63] Undaunted by such assessments and the underwhelming critical and popular response accorded *The Harp King* and *The Referee's Eye*, Leder remained active in the production of films employing local talent, so that in May 1922 the completion of three 'Delightful, Refined, All-Scottish Comedies' was announced. They comprised two two-reelers, *His Last Bachelor Night* and *Blasted Ambitions*, and the one-reel *Keep to the Left*. Among those enjoying their first taste of film stardom was Winifred Adam, a pupil at a school in Rutherglen, whose appearance as Queen of the Fairies at a local pageant led to her casting as a fairy in *His Last Bachelor Night*, considered by *The Weekly News* in Dundee to be 'a fine comedy, which promises to have a successful run'.[64] The trade show of two of the films at Cranston's Picture House in Glasgow generated a rather different assessment. *The Bioscope*'s correspondent had been obliged to delegate attending the show to his assistant. As he subsequently reported it, he could be considered to have escaped lightly, as 'I think I had sometimes used vitriol instead of ink myself, but my assistant must have secured an even more biting fluid, for his opinions of the pictures are unprintable. I had better leave it at that.'[65]

In spite of this less than flattering copy, the screening was used as the basis for launching another company, the Arc Film Producing, Ltd, with Leder joined on the board by another self-ascribed film producer, John Forbes McEwan.[66] Although the intention to inflict another production had been declared in advance of the trade show, the Arc's career proved as brief and unprofitable as those of its predecessors, the film careers of Winifred Adam and the two cinema artistes who acquired shares in the company ending almost as soon as they had begun.[67]

Altogether more successful, commercially if not artistically, was the effort of the Broadway company noted earlier, which resulted in the release towards the end of 1921 of *Football Daft*. The factors shaping the production of what was heralded, in rather modest terms, as 'The Best All-Scottish Comedy Yet Produced' can be reconstructed in a detail that for most of the films under discussion here is impracticable, the consequence of a dispute over copyright between scenario writer James Howie Milligan and the Broadway Company, which went before the courts in December 1922. The Broadway had been formed in November 1919 to provide training for those seeking work in the cinema industry.[68] In August 1921, Milligan proposed that students gain practical experience of their chosen profession by appearing in the company's own film. This would be based on a music hall sketch written by Milligan, entitled 'Two-Nothing', and assessment of students for their suitability for screen roles commenced with the involvement, as has been seen, of Max Leder. Among those tested by Leder was James Beirne of Glasgow, who had recently completed a course of study at the Broadway at a cost of ten guineas, a burden compounded by adoption of the screen pseudonym 'Bulmer Mewless', a compelling argument it might be thought against seeing one's name up in lights.[69] Dissatisfaction with Leder's methods led the company to look elsewhere for a possible producer. The person eventually selected was Victor Weston Rowe, then resident in London, who had been active in film production for some eighteen years. Rowe recalled that he considered 'Two-Nothing' to be 'very very poor' and wholly unsuitable for film treatment due to dependence on dialogue to carry the plot. In all, he considered, there was enough material for some 250 ft, well short of the 2,200 ft required for a two-reel subject. Not only that, the company's existing facilities at West Nile Street, Glasgow, were considered inadequate, so that production switched to Rouken Glen, made available through the good offices of Arthur Reid of the Ace Producing Co.[70] On arriving in Glasgow, Rowe set about devising a workable scenario for the film, the dispute over copyright turning on the degree to which the end result was Rowe's work or how far its true author remained Milligan, confined to bed during the crucial period recovering from the effects of extensive dental surgery.[71] The narrow domestic setting of the original sketch was transformed on screen, with filming carried out at Rouken Glen and along Sauchiehall Street. Camera work was overseen by 'Alfred Avern[e]', loaned to the Broadway by the Bendon Trading Company.[72] With production costs of £1,001 15s 2d, *Football Daft* was trade shown in December 1921. *The Scottish Kinema Record* reported a largely favourable reaction and offered its own verdict, declaring the film to be 'a very presentable picture, and [one which] reflects credit on all concerned'.[73] The views of some of the latter were rather less complimentary. In court, Rowe expressed antipathy towards the end product:

> Q. Did you express to the photographer dissatisfaction with the film which had been produced?

A. When I saw it, yes, I did; I did not like it at all.
Q. What was wrong with it?
A. Everything was wrong with it; I did not care for it at all.[74]

Averne substantially endorsed this verdict, despite what he acknowledged to be the film's success at the box office: 'Q. So both Mr Rowe and you were wrong? A. We were wrong; either that or the people in the theatre were.'[75] Precise figures for the financial performance of *Football Daft* are lacking. However, after playing in January 1922 at the Cinema House and Grand Central Picture House in Glasgow, the film remained in circulation for some months after the trade show.[76] At the end of April 1922, Milligan secured the rights to all the scenarios written for the Broadway. Yet the film continued to be marketed by the Broadway, the company disputing Milligan's claim to authorship and so precipitating the action for breach of copyright.[77] In support of his claim, Milligan cited the various bookings secured for *Football Daft* from the start of May. In the three weeks that followed, it played at seventeen cinemas across Scotland, covering an area from Inverness to Campbeltown (see Table 8.1, p. 290).

In contrast to the Scottish productions that had preceded it, *Football Daft* remained a marketable property five months after its first commercial screening. Perhaps significantly, what can, with justification, be seen as Scotland's first cinematic hit involved a narrative rooted not in a romantic lost past but in the contemporary reality of city streets and football grounds.

Buoyant returns from the box office encouraged plans for a series of related productions. *The Scottish Kinema Record* indicated plans for further entries in what promised to become a series of films: *Racing Daft* and *Picture Daft* were both reported to be under consideration in May 1922, while Milligan suggested that the full set of subjects would amount to six. He was to provide the scenarios for each at a salary of £10 a week plus 20 per cent of the profits.[78] Within two months, however, all agreements were terminated, as the Broadway withdrew from its involvement in the tuition of artistes and divested itself of the West Nile Street studios. Retrenchment was a consequence, so Milligan argued, of a lack of capital, suggesting that even extensive showings across Scotland would not suffice to enable even a modest production to show a reasonable rate of return. In the end, then, *Football Daft* gave rise to no sequels.[79]

Another approach to film-making, which offered a more familiar representation of Scotland, also continued to flourish in the immediate post-war years. In July 1921, the Square Film Co. announced plans to produce a seven-part scenic on *The Clyde, from its Source to the Sea*. Released in December, the film was reported to have secured a large number of bookings, bolstering the opinion of *The Scottish Kinema Record* that it would 'gladden the heart of all true Scots at home and abroad'.[80] While such claims are not susceptible to statistical or other forms of verification, the conviction expressed in the

Table 8.1   *Screenings of* Football Daft, *1–22 May 1922. (Source: NAS,
CS46/1923/7/28, Court of Session, James H. Milligan and The Broadway Cinema
Productions, Ltd, Closed record in Suspension and Interdict, 26 Oct. 1922, p. 7.)*

Date	Cinema
1 May	Kirkcaldy Picture Palace
1 May	Victoria Hall, Kilsyth
1 May	Empire Theatre, Kilbirnie
1 May	La Scala, Inverness
4 May	The Railway Institute, Inverurie
4 May	La Scala, Helensburgh
4 May	Picture House, Campbeltown
8 May	Empire Theatre, Shotts
11 May	Cinema House, Edinburgh
11 May	Crieff Cinema, Crieff
11 May	Picture House, Stirling
11 May	Picture House, Old Cumnock
13 May	Picture House, Darvel
15 May	Picture House, Renfrew
15 May	Cinema House, Burntisland
15 May	Gothenburg Hall, Cardenden
22 May	Picture House, Troon

Square's publicity accompanying the film that 'Everyone Loves Scottish
Scenery' worked to inspire the next wave of production around the middle
of the decade.[81] This centred on the efforts of Maurice Sandground, whose
previous work during and immediately after the war had included the
production of comedies for the Gaiety Film Co. in Croydon.[82] In 1923,
Sandground developed *Bonnie Scotland Calls You*, which illustrated familiar
songs and stories through film and music. Although interiors were shot in
what was described as a 'poky little attic' in Jamaica Street, Sandground
also sought to use authentic locations 'from the quiet and peaceful haunts
of Burns to the rugged and majestic grandeur of the Highlands'. After a
prologue based around a sketch 'A Nicht with Burns', the film proceeded
to depict the stories and lyrics surrounding Jeannie Deans, Auld Robin
Gray, Tam O' Shanter, Caller Herrin', and Annie Laurie, ending with a
presentation of the Bonnie Banks of Loch Lomond. All were accompanied
by four solo voices and a 'highly trained Choir'.[83] The initial response to
what *The Bulletin* in Glasgow described as 'A pictorial record of Scottish
beauty spots' was favourable. In three weeks at the Lyric Theatre early in
1924, Glasgow cinema-goers were said to have delivered their verdict that
'Scotland Can Make Pictures'.[84] From there, the production proceeded
to Edinburgh's Synod Hall, where it generated enough interest to justify a

return visit in May. By then, *Bonnie Scotland Calls You* was being trumpeted as 'The National Film'.[85] Its stay, extended over a month, reflected continued popular support, augmented on this occasion by the addition of scenes of topical interest, including the opening of the General Assembly and the Royal Infirmary Pageant.[86] The film thus succeeded by being firmly located within a well-established exhibition tradition, with scenic attractions allied to items of immediate appeal.

Following the success of this first production, which late in 1924 was being prepared for a tour of Canada and the USA, Sandground moved to explore other Scottish subjects, utilising local performing talent in the process.[87] His plans resulted in two films, released in 1926–7, *The Life of Robert Burns* and *Glimpses from the Life of Sir Walter Scott*. Both subjects were illustrated through episodes from their works rendered on film and backed by appropriate music, performed in the case of the Burns film by the All-Scottish Picture Quartette and Choir. The latter's appearance at Glasgow's Coliseum was reported to have enjoyed such success that its production costs were more than recouped by the run. It then proceeded, as *Bonnie Scotland Calls You* had before it, to Synod Hall where, with the support of four soloists, a choir of twelve, a piper, and an augmented orchestra, it generated one of the highest returns of any film in the first half of 1927.[88] By contrast, the treatment of Scott, although adjudged by *The Scotsman* 'an excellent and educative production' with representations of episodes from *Rob Roy* and *Lady of the Lake*, was altogether less successful, its showing at Synod Hall early in April 1927 producing the hall's lowest earnings of the year.[89] In an attempt to render the Scott footage more marketable, selected sequences were re-edited into a combined treatment covering the lives of both authors, entitled *The Immortals of Bonnie Scotland*, a production which was reputed to have secured extensive bookings across Canada.[90]

Production credit on the Burns and Scott footage, in its varied forms, was claimed by the Scottish Film Academy, a title which suggests that the example of the earlier cinema colleges was still being followed. The films themselves were handled by Burns-Scott Films, Ltd, a company incorporated in September 1926, on whose board Sandground sat alongside Malcolm M. Irvine, also a director of Double Arc Electric Welders, Ltd and Phoenix Electrical Co., Ltd.[91] The failure of the Scott film appears to have persuaded Sandground to transfer his interests elsewhere. By 1928, he had moved to Wardour Street, while his production ambitions now centred on Ireland and a Hibernian variant of *Bonnie Scotland Calls You*. *Come Back to Erin* was planned to have a scenario comprising 'a group of romances with settings in the better known beauty spots of Ireland'.[92] The assets of Burns-Scott Films were transferred to Scottish Films Productions (1928), Ltd, a concern headed by Irvine and based at the old Burns-Scott studio at India Street, Glasgow. Almost immediately, the company's existing plans for a series of silent films faced a challenge with the onset of synchronised sound. Drawing on his engineering background, Irvine responded by developing his own sound system, the Albion Truphonic, which was also marketed to local cinemas.[93] In April 1930, the Regent agreed to install the company's equipment to act as a standby sound system.[94] Progress was such that when 'Kinoman' of the *Evening Times* visited the India Street premises in November 1931, he encountered a business with extensive ambitions in the field of talkie production. These included a series of one-reel films illustrating popular songs, to be collectively marketed as 'Gems of Vaudeville'. In addition, a sequence of short comedies was in progress, beginning with a one-reel farce *The Scottish Italians*. 'Kinoman' also reported plans for an adaptation of a dialect play, T. M. Watson's *Diplomacy and the Draughtsman*, set in a Govan tenement, while the company's most ambitious project inhabited more familiar territory, in terms of subject matter, in what was projected as an eight-reel version of *Jeannie Deans*.[95] One month later, the India Street studio was once more the subject of a visit from the *Evening Times*. On this occasion, it was reported that work on three of the planned sequence of twelve films had been completed, while the premises were undergoing expansion to allow for the production of feature-length talkies. The spirit of optimism at this point in the company's history was further communicated by Irvine's somewhat improbable claim that the Scottish climate favoured film-making more than did the weather in California, the softer light being considered more conducive to good pictorial results.[96] Early the following year and inspired by the success of Mickey Mouse, ambitions extended to the production of a cartoon series, featuring the first animated Scottish star 'Jock', to be drawn by Kirkcaldy artist Andrew Kirk. Live action subjects were also in course of production, including *The Neighbour's Gramophone*, set in a council house, and *Diplomacy*, the studio's first 'Talkie', the press showing of which was marred by the use of a rough cutter's copy.[97]

Not for the first time, plans which impressed with the breadth of their ambition yielded few if any practical results. So far as is known, 'Jock' remained on the drawing board, alongside most of the company's early aspirations. Balance sheets for the two years to March 1934 revealed the business trading in the red, with little evidence of the kind of production roster promised in the first talkie years. Expenditure over 1933–4 of only £2 2s on scenario writing suggests a limited investment in creative effort.[98] A change in approach, away from fictional film-making, was signalled two years later, when Irvine was joined on the board by Stanley L. Russell. A founder member of the Glasgow Film Society, Russell had been active in amateur production through the Meteor Film Society in the same city. A study of the economic conditions facing commercial producers served to convince him, as he explained to 'Kinoman' in August 1937, that the fiction film represented too great a risk for a venture of the limited resources of the India Street concern. In the absence of the kind of wealthy backer who helped to underwrite production south of the border, and given both the high costs of distribution, and the limited opportunity for the exhibition of shorts due to the absence of quota support and the prevalence of the double feature at commercial cinemas, the prudent course was held to be the production of films in response to specific commissions. In 1937, the company's efforts centred on three projects: *New Senses* for the Ear, Nose and Throat Hospital; *Glasgow Festival of Fellowship* for the City Corporation; and *Sam the Assassin*, one of a series of productions for the Necessitous Children's Holiday Camp Fund. However understandable, the limitations inherent in such an approach were noted by 'Kinoman': 'although the company had made films, none of them had been seen publicly in Scotland. Was that', he proceeded, 'not just as good as saying that the films were non-existent?'[99] One way of addressing the problems arising from anonymity, explored that year, was the creation of a Scottish news magazine, along the lines of *The March of Time*. Two specimen reels were assembled under the less assertive title *Things That Happen*, covering the work of Glasgow's fire brigade, the creation of a Scottish Coronation coiffure ('An item of feminine interest'), the funeral of R. B. Cunninghame Graham, 'Grand Parents!' (showing 'The amazing number of old people in Scotland'), and footage of the Loch Ness Monster ('We have actually filmed the giant creature').[100]

Activity at India Street intensified the following year, with the Empire Exhibition in Glasgow, for which a number of films were produced with the backing of industrial sponsors, including among others Beardmore's, Colville's, and the Clyde Navigation Trust.[101] In addition, the company was commissioned to provide an entry for the series overseen by the Films of Scotland Committee, *Sport in Scotland*, as well as the 1939 production *Dundee*, made at the behest of the local Chamber of Commerce.[102]

As this suggests, the commissioning of titles for specific ends offered the most productive outlet for Scottish film-making talent through the 1930s and succeeding decades. The demand for educational subjects for classroom screenings, for example, engaged the energies of Ronnie Jay, whose first experience of exhibiting films had been gained at the age of twelve. In 1931, Jay was responsible for the installation of projection equipment at a school in the Gorbals.[103] He went on to demonstrate films for the Scottish Educational Cinema Society and to assist in the production of footage in support of the corporation's Necessitous Children's Holiday Camp Fund. The earliest release linked to this endeavour, *Sunny Days*, became Scotland's first sound picture after undergoing post-production dubbing at Elstree.[104] Other concerns active in the production of educational subjects were Campbell Harper Productions, which developed from a photographer's business in Edinburgh, and Elder-Dalrymple Productions of Ayr.[105] The foundations of a small but viable production base were thus being laid through the growth of non-theatrical cinema.

The outbreak of war in September 1939 would pose a serious challenge to this business model. Private sponsorship all but dried up, a consequence of restrictions on the production of advertising films and the impact of excess profits duty on those likely to proffer commissions. The growth in demand from schools was also checked, as the lack of new equipment ensured that few if any additional installations were carried out. An increasing dependence on government commissions created further problems for Scottish producers, as most films required official approval before they could be screened more widely and this could only be granted by heads of department, most of whom were based in London. Although Scottish Films Productions (1928), Ltd was able to secure commissions from the Ministry of Information, including a film record of Clydebank following the Blitz of March 1941, and a study of the school for evacuee children in Galloway, *Cally House*, even these came at a price, as the MOI insisted on the use of a sound system other than the Albion Truphonic. The existing installation at India Street was thus dismantled, so that all footage shot in Scotland had to be sent south for dubbing. Writing in 1942, Russell considered it 'a tragic commentary on the state of affairs when a country the size of Scotland has no method of recording her voice except by recourse to London'.[106] The production of a number of films with Scottish settings or subject matter was thus entrusted to established documentary makers in England. Paul Rotha, for example, was responsible for *Power for the Highlands*, *Highland Doctor*, and *Children of the City*, based on work with young offenders in Dundee. Rotha himself explained this development to the *Glasgow Herald* in 1944, referring to the absence of a facility 'of adequate professional standards' in Scotland.[107] The difficulties facing existing concerns were such that Scottish Films Productions merged with an English company to form Kay's Scottish Pictures, Ltd.[108]

Russell, for one, remained convinced of the importance both in the immediate context of war and for Scotland's long-term future of an independent film-making capability being maintained north of the border. As he expressed it in a letter to the *Herald* which gave rise to Rotha's observations, 'It is essential that a fully equipped film producing company should be operating in Scotland, if Scotland, more than in the past, is to revive her individuality, and not become merely a "region".'[109] To that end, he had, a year earlier, left Scottish Films Productions to establish an independent concern in conjunction with Jack Robertson, a fellow founder member of the Glasgow Film Society. Russell Productions, Ltd, later to become Thames and Clyde Film Co., Ltd, would maintain an emphasis on sponsored film, even though initial plans announced to the press hinted at work on a fictional treatment dealing with life on Arran.[110] Some seven films, all actualities, were produced in the company's first year and, in the immediate post-war period, the business would benefit from commissions from agencies such as Glasgow Corporation. As Thames and Clyde, the company contributed significantly to the programme of films on civic education projected by the corporation in 1947.[111]

The key role accorded film in the articulation of political ideals at both national and municipal level, along with renewed demand for educational subjects, benefited other producers also. Along with Thames and Clyde, established film-makers Elder-Dalrymple, Kay's Scottish, and Campbell Harper came together in June 1948 to form the Scottish Film Producers' Association, Ltd to promote work in actualities.[112] Within months, however, Kay's Scottish premises in India Street were put up for sale, ending a varied and variable career for the studio extending back to Sandground's early essays in picturesque romanticism.[113] Despite that, the survival of the three remaining concerns indicated that, even in the seemingly unpromising conditions of the 1940s, a secure and viable production base could exist, geared primarily to the needs of non-commercial cinema.

As has been noted, prior to his involvement in the India Street business, Russell had been active in amateur film-making, a reminder that the companies considered here were but part of a broader creative movement across Scotland in the years either side of the Second World War. The Meteor Film Producing Society, of which Russell was a leading light, was founded in 1932 and is often held to mark the beginnings of an organised amateur movement north of the border.[114] Yet it had been anticipated some years earlier by the rather more grandly titled Scottish Amateur Cinematographers' Association. Formed in 1928, this met weekly in a hall in Pollokshields, where films were produced and then exhibited. Late in 1929, when the Association came to the attention of 'Kinoman', it was said to have in preparation a city symphony of Glasgow, along the lines of Ruttmann's *Berlin*, along with an adaptation of *The Laird o' Cockspur*, part of which was to be shot at Rouken Glen, the setting for an earlier generation of Scottish films.[115] Consistent with many of those efforts, the Association passed quickly from the record, so that Glasgow would have to wait until 1934–5 to be rendered on film, when Charles Oakley of the local Film Society produced *Brigton Cross*, colourfully described by 'Kinoman' as 'a symphony of the Umbrella, the tramcars, the types, the cats, and the lums [sic] of Maxtonland'.[116] The Meteor's ambitions from 1932 were more modest than those projected by the Association. At least, such is suggested by the films it submitted to Scotland's first Amateur Film Festival in 1933. Out of five films selected for exhibition at Glasgow's Athenaeum Theatre by adjudicator Victor Saville, three were the work of the Meteor, which also organised the festival: *All on a Summer's Day*, 'an impression of a city typist's holiday'; *Nadia*, an account of 'what happened when a gipsy girl broke into society'; and *Hair*, simply described as 'an imaginative tale'. The remaining submissions included *Edinburgh*, the Edinburgh Film Guild's attempt to capture Edinburgh on film, and *The Masked Rider*, 'a tale of desperate doings in the wildest, woolliest West' by the Damyamount Picture Club. While Forsyth Hardy expressed disappointment in the pages of *The Scotsman* that many of the films slavishly copied commercial production techniques, *Edinburgh* and *All on a Summer's Day* were thought to indicate the potential of amateur film-making to reach out to subjects overlooked by mainstream production. It was, he believed, through the non-fiction film that the amateur could most likely achieve what appeared beyond the capacity of commercial companies: to express 'the spirit of Scotland on the screen in peculiarly national films'.[117]

For the second festival, held at Glasgow's Lyric Theatre the following year, submissions were received from a wider range of organisations. The award for best film, and the Victor Saville Cup, went to *Seven Till Five*, a production of the Glasgow School of Art Kinecraft Society, which depicted a day in the life of the college and which provided early evidence of the creative talents of director Norman McLaren and Stewart McAllister.[118] The 1934 festival would be the last to be organised by the Meteor Society. From 1935, responsibility passed to the Scottish Film Council and its Amateur Cinematography Panel, though continuity was assured through the presence, as head of the Panel, of Stanley Russell.[119] The third festival, held in January 1936, attracted thirty entries, including films from English societies. In his adjudication that year, John Grierson welcomed what he saw as a greater readiness to engage with wider social issues, rather than merely seeking to entertain, a trend exemplified by *Preparatory Class*, produced by the Uddingston Grammar School Amateur Film Society. McLaren's latest entry, *Colour Cocktail*, was also singled out for praise, although Grierson's tribute was not unqualified, as he judged the film to be 'enormously brilliant, but also enormously shallow'.[120] Equally notable was McLaren's contribution the following year, *Hell Unlimited*, an anti-war polemic, which Forsyth Hardy considered 'a graphic if slightly hysterical piece of work'.[121] For all this, Hardy's preference remained the 'non-story' film as the most productive field for amateur effort. It was, nevertheless, a view with which society members themselves were inclined to differ. As Ian S. Ross argued, in a response to Hardy, if a key aim of the movement was to encourage participation in film-making, that was best achieved through fictional narratives which required a larger and more varied input.[122] The continuation of the fiction class at festivals through the later 1930s suggests that Ross' opinion had wider support.

A narrower focus on the 'non-story' film was evident at the first Edinburgh Amateur Film Festival, held in November 1938, in which alongside categories covering actuality and treatments of Edinburgh, awards were offered for subjects suitable for Church purposes, promoted by the Scottish Churches' Film Guild. Here, competition was confined to film-makers in and around Edinburgh, taking in Fife, the Lothians, and eastern Border counties.[123] A second festival was planned for the following year and was to include an award for Scottish films, sponsored by the Saltire Society, but fell victim to world events that autumn.[124] By contrast, the annual competitions overseen by the Film Council continued to be held. That in April 1940 attracted fifty-three submissions, twenty-three from Scotland, with the award in the 'Scottish' class going to *Handba' at Kirkwall*, a work of the Craft Society of Edinburgh.[125] Viewed in terms of numbers, entries held up in 1941, possibly assisted by the addition of a category for films intended for use in the classroom. On this occasion, the 'Scottish' prize went to *Deer Stalking in Wartime*, a film by J. B. McDonald of Fraserburgh, while the two principal awards went to film-makers based in Surrey.[126] By 1942, wartime restrictions worked to limit the scope of amateur production and that year's festival largely comprised a retrospective of previous winners, with their relative merits decided by an audience vote.[127]

This heralded a suspension in festival competition until 1948, by which point amateur cinematography had revived to such a degree that the number of entrants, at sixty-seven, was the highest of any year other than 1938, when the scope of the event had been widened to allow it to form part of the Empire Exhibition of that year.[128] Existing classes were restored, with Firth Films of Ayr triumphing in the non-fiction and colour categories.[129] At the same time, a meeting of interested parties was held in Glasgow to build on the renewed impetus the festival gave to amateur film-making. Some twenty organisations were represented at the gathering, at which the formation of a Scottish Association of Amateur Cinematographers was discussed.[130] With a remit to coordinate and promote the efforts of amateur film-makers across the country, among the first initiatives of the Association was a day school held in Edinburgh in April 1950, at which Alan Harper of Campbell Harper explained the working of film soundtracks.[131] Later that same year, the Association held its first film festival, to run alongside that organised by the Film Council, at which twenty-two entries were received, the first prize going to I. G. McLeod of Cambuslang for a film on the Viking invasion of Scotland.[132] Across two decades, then, amateur film-making made up an important aspect of Scottish output, one in which the filmic imagination was given free rein across a variety of formats, both fiction and non-fiction, a sharp contrast to the constraints imposed by sponsorship or the priorities of an officially approved documentary agenda.

This latter strand of production, often presented as Britain's most distinctive and characteristic contribution to the cinematic art, carried throughout a strong Scottish imprint, reflecting the organisational and intellectual influence exerted by John Grierson. The particular forces shaping Grierson's conception of the documentary, his own coinage to describe the latest incarnation of the actuality or interest film, have been extensively rehearsed in the literature.[133] For the purposes of this study, it is his thinking on the place of Scotland within the documentary movement that merits particular attention. While Scotland was rarely explicitly the subject of films produced by either the Empire Marketing Board or the GPO Film Units, Grierson made much of his efforts 'to turn London money to patriotic uses', through productions such as *Drifters, Granton Trawler, O'er Hill and Dale* (directed in 1932 by Basil Wright and shot on land owned by the Minister of Agriculture, Walter

Elliot), and *Night Mail*.[134] If such films ensured Scotland a place in the cinematic representation of Britain, they also worked to still her own screen voice. It was a problem that Grierson acknowledged in December 1936 in an address to the newly formed Stirlingshire Film Society when, looking ahead to the 1938 Exhibition, he remarked on a telling gap: while most parts of the Empire would celebrate their progress by, among other means, film, Scotland would be mute. A solution was seen to lie in the production of a prestigious feature by one of the leading British combines: London, BIP, or Gaumont-British, and a suite of some dozen documentaries, in which 'the industry and the life of the country are recorded'.[135] The decline in British feature production in the months that followed his pronouncement ensured that the first part of Grierson's programme, at least, remained stillborn. Funding was, however, forthcoming for a slate of documentaries, with contributions from the British Council, the Commissioner for the Special Areas, and most significantly in terms of amount the industrialist John A. Mactaggart.[136] In February 1938, the Scottish Development Council in consultation with Elliot, now Secretary of State, appointed a Films of Scotland Committee which, even with the presence of leading figures from the industry, such as Alex B. King and C. A. Oakley, was it was later acknowledged markedly under the influence of Grierson. Initially, a programme of six films was planned, comprising a general survey of the nation, the New Generation, Developments in Agriculture, the Scottish Fisheries, Scottish Sports, and Planning in Scotland. In the end, planning gave way to a study of industries old and new, in *Wealth of a Nation*, while a treatment on fitness, reflecting acute contemporary concern at the physical health of the nation in the later 1930s, was added.[137]

The status of these films, at least for the purposes of this study, is ambiguous. Although undoubtedly of Scotland in terms of their subject matter and offering, as Grierson expressed it in a presentation to members of the Dundee Chamber of Commerce, a 'thorough picture of Scotland', 'a sensible picture of Scotland', and 'a democratic picture of Scotland', only one was made in Scotland: *Sport in Scotland*, the work of Scottish Films Productions (1928), Ltd and considered by officials to be 'the weakest of the seven'.[138] While Irvine recognised the problems with the film, he ascribed these to 'Mr John Grierson', who had delayed production by demanding extensive revisions to the script.[139] Equally, while the films are often discussed in terms of the 1938 Exhibition, their appearance was delayed, so that by the start of August, three months into the Exhibition's brief existence, only one, on *Sea Food*, had been completed and shown. The remainder were due for completion by September, the Exhibition's penultimate month.[140] More representative of local efforts was the extensive range of sponsored films on industrial processes which featured in the Beardmore-Colville Pavilion at Bellahouston, as well as the programmes of screenings at the Social Service Cinema, in the Scottish Pavilion. This involved titles touching on many aspects of Scottish social life, from education and child welfare to public health, and housing and town planning.[141] For all Paul Rotha's enthusiastic advocacy of the efforts of the Films of Scotland Committee, arguing that 'for the first time in the history of the cinema, films have been used to present a complete picture of a country to the world', the Scottish cinematic presence at Bellahouston was most effectively represented by a range of productions sponsored by other agencies.[142]

The initial seven Films of Scotland Committee titles would assume more significance once the Exhibition site was cleared. So, early in 1939, they acquired a degree of notoriety as the subject of a short-lived but intensive controversy over their wider distribution. In a talk to the Edinburgh Film Guild, Grierson made reference to a decision taken by a committee of the British Council to refuse the films a screening at the British Pavilion at the New York World Fair. This, along with the failure to appoint a Scottish representative to the committee, demonstrated to Grierson that 'our national identity has been ignored, and our right to express ourselves in our own Scottish way has been denied'. Comments attributed to the Committee chairman, Philip Guedalla, that the record of Scottish achievements offered by the films was not 'large enough or important enough to include in Britain's official picture', merely served to fan the flames of Grierson's ire.[143] The resulting controversy called forth a statement of clarification in the Commons by the Secretary of the Department of Overseas Trade, who noted that while the films were not considered suitable, due to their subject matter, for general dissemination by the British Council, at least two had been accepted for exhibition in New York.[144] This, and a letter from the chairman of the Films of Scotland Committee, Gilbert Archer, in which the constructive relationship that existed with the Films Committee of the British Council was reaffirmed, served to temper the wider controversy. Although reluctant to concede on all points, Grierson recognised that his initial claims had been overstated.[145]

In the longer term, the productions of 1938–9 benefited from the change in quota regulations which encouraged the wider take-up of short subjects by mainstream exhibitors. The titles overseen by the Films of Scotland Committee thus enjoyed a renewed life through their distribution by MGM and ABPC, gaining in the process a wider circulation than earlier waves of Scottish production had enjoyed.[146] *The Face of Scotland* arrived at the Playhouse in Edinburgh in the first week of September 1939, only for its screening to be blocked by the outbreak of war. It would, however, feature on bills at the Palace in October, following an earlier appearance by *They Made the Land*, while Playhouse audiences would see another Committee production, *The Children's Story*, late in the first month of war.[147] As well as the films themselves, the creation of a body explicitly concerned to commission the production of Scottish subjects gave institutional underpinning to the claim made by Grierson in April 1938 that 'The foundations of a Scottish cinema have been laid.'[148] That said, events from 1939 severely limited activity. With the commencement of war, responsibility for actuality production came to centre on the Ministry of Information and, where subjects were intended for wider markets, the British Council. The possibility of the Films of Scotland Committee undertaking work for government departments north of the border was raised early in 1942. However, such a move was discountenanced; as a privately funded body, the Committee was considered an inappropriate vehicle for the manufacture of official propaganda; this should be the responsibility of agencies financed out of general taxation.[149] The very future of the Committee was being debated at this point, its initial three-year remit having expired in 1941.[150] Significantly, it would appear that the option to cease operations was never seriously considered. The Committee provided the one means available to project a distinctive Scottish interest via the screen and so attention turned to attempting to define a role for it in wartime. Proposals were advanced early in 1943 for the production of a regular Scottish Film Magazine, capable of promoting the nation overseas. In the end, it was concluded that the field of activity left open was, as a consequence of MOI involvement in production north of the border, too narrow to merit renewed activity in wartime.[151] The expectation remained, however, that as government retreated from production after the war, the Committee would take on a new importance in sustaining Scotland's cinematic voice. In the short term, the main issue was the use of the money raised by the commercial screening of the original eight titles, estimated in 1944 at £888.[152] The decisions here were entrusted to three trustees: Gilbert Archer, former chairman of the Committee; A. B. King, Scottish Films Officer of the MOI; and Steven Bilsland, a banker, who candidly confessed to the Secretary of State in September 1943, 'I am a bad adviser on anything to do with films, because, although I should not like to say so to our mutual friend A. B. King, I never enter a cinema if I can avoid it.'[153] As the trustees' work largely involved seeking safe investments for outstanding funds, Bilsland's aesthetic preferences did not become a point of controversy.[154]

After 1945, the Attlee government's continued use of film to make the case for welfare reform and extensions to public ownership raised renewed questions as to the role of the Films of Scotland Committee, to the extent that its revival as a working unit was considered unlikely by 1949.[155] The original distribution agreements had lapsed in 1945 and although attempts were made to extend the screen life of *Dundee* as demand for British-produced shorts was boosted by the Hollywood boycott in 1947, the resolution of the dispute greatly reduced the film's attractions as a commercial property.[156] Even so, a sum of close on £1,000 remained, to go towards, even if not capable of fully funding, a further production. In the early 1950s, consideration would be given to the part-financing of a film marking the fifth centenary of the University of Glasgow, a production on the impact of Marshall Aid in Scotland, in conjunction with the Economic Co-operation Administration in the USA, and a subject designed to boost tourism in Scotland. The latter, pursued in discussions with both Messrs MacBrayne ferries and the British European Airways Corporation, foundered on the levels of funding partners would commit to a project that would be comparatively slow in generating additional revenues.[157] In the end, the £1,000 went to Campbell Harper for the production of a film on afforestation. Work on what might be regarded as the much-delayed ninth Films of Scotland production was reported to be complete by November 1953. By then, with government involvement in film-making being scaled back by the new Conservative administration, plans were under way for the formal revival of the Committee and so the Campbell Harper film was held back pending that development.[158]

The importance which continued to attach to the articulation of Scottish interests and experiences via the cinema screen, and which survived a prolonged lull in activity during and immediately after the war, represents the most enduring legacy of the original 1938 initiative. If emphasis came increasingly to be placed on modestly budgeted subjects that were privately sponsored or officially commissioned, experience suggested that that was the most realistic way forward for Scottish producers. That conclusion was forcefully reiterated by the fortunes attending an altogether more ambitious attempt to boost film-making north of the border in the years after 1945. At a time when the Trustees of the Films of Scotland Committee remained content to allow the State to shape Scotland's cinematic representation, plans were advanced to develop what amounted to a 'Scottish Hollywood'. The idea appears to have originated, in this latest incarnation at least, in essays written by a T. G. Wolk, described in the press as a 'Russian expert', in which the importance of film in expressing and promoting the outlook and energies of a modern society were set out. This could be most effectually realised, so Wolk argued, through the creation of a National Film Studio, the output of which would encourage a national audience for film and would help to boost visitor numbers to Scotland. At the same time, wider benefits would flow from the need to develop ancillary industries to meet the studio's technical needs, and from the study of film production in local educational institutions.[159] Discussions with interested parties were held in the autumn of 1945, resulting in the appointment of a governing council, on which representatives of local government, including the Lord Provosts of Edinburgh and Dundee, sat alongside figures drawn from a variety of agencies, including the Scottish Agricultural Organisation Society, the Scottish Religious Film Society, the Iona Trust, the Scottish Co-operative Wholesale Society (SCWS), and individuals prominent in Scottish cultural life, such as Naomi Mitchison, and Sir Hugh Roberton.[160] The ideas guiding their work were summarised in a leaflet entitled *Scotland on the Screen*, in which the shortcomings of existing representations of Scotland, devised in London and California, were rehearsed. These would be addressed, it was argued, through the supply of films of Scottish scenery and beauty spots, films of historic places and incidents accurately and brilliantly made, and films that show also Scotland as she lives today, her sports and pastimes, her people's lives and hopes and plans, and the way they are solving post-war problems.[161]

If this agenda appeared little different from that of contemporary documentaries produced by the COI, the ambitions underlying the scheme extended beyond the films themselves. By locating activities in the north, the aim was to 'bring a secondary prosperity particularly to the Highlands'. The studio would work alongside the hydro-electric scheme to bring about an economic transformation in the area, creating demand for skilled labour to service the industry's needs.[162] In a submission to the Board of Trade the following year, an initial workforce of 100 was anticipated, which would expand as the scale of operations increased. With the construction also of developing and printing laboratories, opportunities would be created for a technically proficient labour force. The gain to the area would, it was hoped, be immediate and permanent, resulting in the foundation of 'a new and healthy industrial town'.[163] Summarising this aspect of the Studio's plans, its managing director, Joseph Macleod, noted that 'a film industry centred on the Highlands would soon attract round it other light industries of a precision character which Highlanders, whose fingers and eyes are naturally deft and sure, could man without losing their independence or their haims [sic]'.[164] The favoured location for this work was the area around Inverness. Not only was this held to have climatic advantages compared to sites further west, but the local technical college offered the kind of practical training that would benefit the Studio's endeavours. In addition, the local accent was considered advantageous 'from an artistic and-general-purpose angle'.[165] The hope was that an aerodrome surplus to post-war requirements could be acquired at a reasonable rental to accommodate the Studio. Plans for Dalcross aerodrome, with good rail links and with villages close by, were, however, disappointed when the Air Ministry declared its intention of retaining use of the site.[166]

The disappointment over Dalcross would not be the last to be endured by the venture, despite securing a prominent figure as managing director. Macleod had acquired national renown as a news presenter for the BBC during the war. Hopes that his involvement would assist in enabling the Studio to raise the necessary capital were, however, to be disappointed. While the overall cost of the scheme was put at £500,000, the aim initially was to raise £100,000, using the earnings from productions to generate the remainder.[167] The starting sum would be raised not by inviting the purchase of stock with the prospect of dividend earnings as the lure, but by a method which its promoters claimed represented in 'a realistic manner . . . the transition from Capitalism to Socialism'.[168] This involved soliciting support via three forms of financial assistance: donations; loans of at least £10 with interest payable, on request, at up to 2.5 per cent; and annual subscriptions, entitling those making payments to membership of an Association of Friends.[169] The result would be, or so its supporters argued, 'a public corporation owned and managed by Scots', an outcome in keeping with the political preferences of both Wolk and Macleod, described respectively in distinctly uncomplimentary terms in the pages of *Light and Liberty* as 'a Russian Jew' and 'a Marxist and a devotee of Stalin'.[170] Contributions were invited from resident Scots and an estimated sixteen million fellow nationals living outwith her boundaries. A circular letter made the case for 'the setting up of full scale studios and other facilities which will allow an independent Scottish film industry to grow'.[171]

The response to this appeal was less than encouraging. Correspondents, while sympathetic to the scheme's broader aims, professed an inability to render more practical help, pointing to incomes squeezed by an increased tax burden and the decline in the value of capital assets. In one case, doubts were expressed as to the aesthetic sensibilities of those promoting the Studio. This followed Macleod's praise, in a speech in Edinburgh, of *I Know Where I'm Going*. George Bett, for one, was not encouraged: 'I have seen the film and some of it was appalling.'[172] Opinion was not uniformly hostile. The SCWS welcomed the move to augment existing production facilities, arguing that

> By supporting and making use of the studios, the S.C.W.S. would be helping Scotland to recreate a new spirit of enterprise and a revival of cultural activity which will have enormous benefit to the *whole* country, including of course co-operators. (Emphasis in original)[173]

To this end, a loan of £2,000 at 1 per cent was agreed. It proved, however, the largest single contribution to a loan account which, by the end of the year, stood at £5,868, a further £1,500 having been provided by Co-operative Societies in Greenock, Lanark, and Dunfermline. Donations were even less forthcoming, totalling £561 8s by January 1947. Here, the largest contribution was the £100 received from the Glasgow Orpheus Choir, but more representative of the kind of sums raised were the payments of two guineas and three guineas respectively by the South Shields Caledonian Society and the Kilmarnock Burns Club.[174] Otherwise, resident and diasporic Scots spoke with a single, impecunious voice.

Along with the problem of reduced means, the business model on which the venture was based, which held out little hope of a financial return, with profits going to developing the Studio infrastructure, was considered, as one correspondent observed, 'not attractive as an investment'.[175] In response to the sluggish accumulation of funds, a temporary increase in the rate payable on funds loaned to the business to 5 per cent was proposed.[176] Predictably, it did little to quicken the capital flow, so that in July 1946, an appeal was made to the government seeking credit facilities of up to £600,000. A detailed estimate of the likely returns on various types of production was included, to demonstrate some familiarity with the economic realities of the business. One estimate had it that a first feature would have to be shown in 2,709 cinemas before it would be able to cover its costs, while for second features, booked on a flat-rate basis, the number of halls needed to break even rose to 15,000.[177] While such figures added authority to the Studio's case, they also served, when contrasted with the company's existing attempts at production, to point up the minimal likelihood of success. The Studio's first essay in production, described in accompanying publicity as 'powerful and unforgettable', was a treatment on the theme of road safety, entitled, with what one can only presume was a complete absence of irony, *Somebody Wasn't Thinking*.[178] Planned for 3,000 ft, a length that would ensure qualification for quota, the film featured Abe Barker, later to appear in more celebrated 'Scottish' productions such as the Disney versions of *Rob Roy* and *Kidnapped*, Mary Walton of Glasgow's Unity Players, and Gordon Jackson, on loan from Ealing Studios.[179] It proved to be both the first and the last project of the Scottish National Film Studios. The judgement at a press showing at the Cosmo in Glasgow, at which 'everybody was aghast at how bad it was' appeared representative of broader opinion.[180] The major circuits declined to book the film, leaving Macleod with the choice of editing it down to a potentially more marketable twenty minutes, 'or to go for quota as it is, in the hope that it is not seen' (emphasis in original).[181] With the footage considered in its current state 'unsaleable' and likely to yield little more than a few hundred pounds in bookings, the certainty of substantial losses made the decision to wind the business up in January 1947 unanswerable.

Surveying the wreckage, the company chairman Hugh Roberton was clear where the responsibility lay: 'It is really a failure of our fellow Scotsmen; they lacked faith and failed to give the enterprise sufficient backing.'[182] For others, the problems lay closer to home, in the backgrounds of those promoting the venture. Macleod's presumed pro-Soviet sympathies were thought to have alienated many, while H. Russell Ferguson of the Scottish Religious Film Society revealed the limits of Christian charity in condemning 'Jabber-Wolk', whose 'way of doing business is not regarded as quite above board'.[183] Viewed in context, however, the brief and inglorious career of the Scottish National Film Studios stands as, more than anything, a warning against the consequences of hubris. At a time when Scottish producers, more generally, had adjusted to a world in which budget limitations were balanced by the security promised by repeated sponsorship and regular commissions, talk of a Scottish Hollywood was, as journalists such as Harold Stewart of the *Daily Record* remarked, at best imprudent.[184] It set to one side the lessons of the previous four decades, the problems long encountered in securing the necessary capital and in achieving the quality of production that would enable the efforts of Scottish film-makers to stand up against better-resourced English and American competition. The kinds of film envisaged by the Studio, including a fictional study of coalmining to evoke sympathy for the toilers underground, and biographical features on Scots heroes such as Wallace and Bruce, would eventually be made, but not, tellingly, by companies based in Scotland.[185] In a revealing commentary on contemporary realities, a letter to *The Scotsman* in October 1951, signed by James Robertson Justice, Eric Linklater, Compton Mackenzie, and Moray McLaren, pointed to the welcome emergence of a successful 'Scottish' film, whose 'author and director were Scots; Scottish actors predominated; and, perhaps most important of all, its scene setting and story were genuinely of this country – the real thing'. In this case, 'the real thing' was *Whisky Galore!*, the production, as the correspondents acknowledged, of an English studio.[186] As this example attests, wider economic and institutional realities continued to make the small-scale actuality film the most practicable form for home-based production part way through cinema's sixth decade.

III

If the obvious gap between aspiration and reality renders the story of the Scottish National Film Studios an exercise in bathos, the temptation to extend that treatment to Scottish film production as a whole, while understandable, should be resisted. By the early 1950s, Scotland's film-makers had secured a niche in the production of actuality footage, based on a business plan which provided the financial certainties required to sustain output at a steady and predictable level. It was an approach which sufficed to support the efforts of a small group of producers either side of the central belt. For fictional subjects, the record was more variable. Here, capital requirements and uncertainties of return had long precluded all but modestly budgeted scenarios that struggled to secure screen space in the face of better-resourced and more technically proficient competition. At times, it may be useful to remind ourselves, the larger industry to the south struggled in the face of similar pressures, until it found relief in official measures of protection from the later 1920s. As was the case in England before the emergence of the large vertical combines, the progress of production efforts was halting. For all that, however, the pattern of success is telling, as one of the few Scottish films which refused to tread the well-worn path of initial optimism, tempered by critical disdain, leading to commercial oblivion, was rooted in a popular culture familiar to most Scots, drawing on the realities of tenement dwelling leavened by the mass amusements of football and the music hall. *Football Daft* stands as a reminder that the images of Scotland shaped by Scots themselves often diverged from what are seen in the literature as the dominant tropes of tartanry and the kailyard tradition. Scots engaged with the modernity of film not merely through the technology but also through their choice of subject matter, which often spoke to matters of immediate concern. If the desire to address Scots both within and beyond the national boundary required that, on occasion, familiar material be plundered, the evidence suggests that this did not always resonate with audiences. In the 1920s, comparable treatments of the lives of Burns and Scott generated markedly different levels of enthusiasm, while the popularity of a work such as Sandground's *Bonnie Scotland Calls You* appeared to derive from its capacity to marry the attractions of the scenic with the immediacy of the local topical, a combination that prolonged its circulation through the first half of 1924. The failure attending the ambitions of Wolk and Macleod in the 1940s should not obscure the fact that, to an increasing degree over the preceding decades, Scottish producers had come to calibrate their product to the requirements of their local market, constructing in the process a small but viable national cinema.

Yet given the preoccupation of preceding chapters with the theme of audience preferences, it is impossible not to enter a note of qualification here. If Scotland's most enduring achievement lay in the area of documentary film-making, it must be acknowledged that, initially at least, access to these efforts was limited, with screenings in the 1930s confined to selected and selective audiences of film society members and schoolchildren. Only from the late 1930s and the change in quota regulations would such footage begin to feature consistently on commercial bills. Here, they became subject to the shifting preferences of most cinema-goers. Earlier chapters have established that local audiences were not unduly exercised by the opportunity, or lack thereof, to view Scottish scenes, so that there is little evidence that concern among political and cultural commentators that the nation's integrity was being challenged by its apparent failure to acquire an effective cinematic voice was widely shared. The fortune of documentaries dealing with aspects of Scottish life acquires, in this context, an additional significance, regardless of their point of origin. The appearance of productions of the Films of Scotland Committee at cinemas in Edinburgh in the autumn of 1939 has been noted. Their box-office performance is telling, as, even at a time of depressed attendances, the ability of programmes including *The Face of Scotland* and *They Made the Land* to secure barely half the wartime average attendance for October must be judged disappointing. *The Children's Story* enjoyed marginally more success at the Playhouse, but still came in almost 25 per cent below the mean.[187] If the performance of documentary footage improved thereafter, this reflected more than anything the improvement in business over the course of the war and the impact of the principal features for which they acted as support. That the Turner Film Co.'s *Border Weave* could enjoy an audience 50 per cent above the mean on its appearance at the Palace in April 1943 owed most, it would appear, to the main feature on the programme that week, the MGM musical *For Me and My Gal*.[188] That documentaries exercised a minimal influence over audience behaviour is indicated by the fortunes of *The Future of Scotland*, number eighteen in *The Modern Age*, produced by Sergei Nolbandov. At the end of August 1948, it appeared at the Playhouse alongside the Italian drama *To Live in Peace*.

The score of 49 per cent below the mean contrasted with one of 11 per cent above the average three weeks later, when it figured as support for the popular British feature *Miranda* at the Palace.[189] If nothing else, this serves as a stark reminder that the production of Scottish material both by and for Scots represented but a fraction of a wider global industry the products of which had long been embraced by cinema-goers, whose enthusiasm never tended towards the uncritical. The efforts of local producers were throughout subject to criteria applied to films more generally and found themselves judged accordingly.

NOTES

1. See Chapter 1, pp. 26–9; SSA, 1/1/252, Scottish Film Council, Minutes, 1944–50, 12th Meeting of Council, 19 Sept. 1945.
2. D. Condon, *Early Irish Cinema, 1895–1921* (Dublin and Portland, OR, 2008), ch. 5; K. Rockett, L. Gibbons, and J. Hill, *Cinema and Ireland* (Syracuse, NY, 1988), ch. 1; *SKR*, 6 Nov. 1920, p. 13 (the title and production company are as given in the source, which probably refer to the General Film Company of Ireland's *In the Days of Saint Patrick*); an earlier series of screenings was noted in SSA, Green's Film Service File, cutting from *KW*, 13 May 1920.
3. N. Wilson, *Presenting Scotland: A Film Survey* (Edinburgh, 1945), pp. 10–11.
4. A. Blaikie, *The Scots Imagination and Modern Memory* (Edinburgh, 2010), ch. 3; for work on Grierson and the documentary movement, see Introduction, p. 14; the 1938 films now have a dedicated DVD release, *Scotland Calling: At the Empire Exhibition, 1938* (Panamint Cinema, West Lothian, 2008).
5. NAS, DD10/141, Scottish Home Dept, Cinematograph Acts, Films of Scotland Committee, 26 Jan. 1939, Malcolm M. Irvine, Managing Director of Scottish Films Productions (1928), Ltd to Colville, complaining that the Committee was working to deny Scotland a film-making capacity and calling for 'a fair deal for film production in Scotland'.
6. McArthur, 'Scotland and Cinema', pp. 40–69; id., *The Cinema Image of Scotland* (London, 1986); id., Brigadoon, Braveheart *and the Scots: Distortions of Scotland in Hollywood Cinema* (London, 2003).
7. *Film History*, 15(2) (2003), edition on Small-Gauge and Amateur Film; 19(4) (2007), edition on Nontheatrical Film.
8. See Chapter 1, pp. 26–8.
9. *ET*, 19 Sept. 1908, p. 8; 19 April 1909, p. 8; B. Murray, *The Old Firm: Sectarianism, Sport and Society in Scotland* (Edinburgh, 1984), pp. 168–9.
10. *ET*, 29 June 1908, p. 8.
11. *Bioscope*, 25 June 1914, p. 1313.
12. *Bioscope*, 28 Jan. 1915, p. 331; see also 3 Dec. 1914, p. 1017, for a show at the Central Picture House, Inverness; for the Boer War, see Chapter 1, p. 28.
13. *ET*, 9 March 1908, p. 8.
14. *Bioscope*, 9 March, p. 41; 11 May, p. 287; 18 May 1911, p. 305.
15. *Bioscope*, 8 Aug. 1912, p. 413; the productions were recalled by C. A. Oakley

four decades later, SSA, 4/5/33, Film Productions, Miscellaneous, cutting from *Evening Citizen*, n.d.

16. NAS, BT2/7670/31, The BB Pictures, Ltd, Balance Sheet at 26 Sept. 1914 (loss of £6,963 14s).

17. *Entertainer*, 15 Sept., p. 7; 27 Oct. 1917, p. 7; McBain, 'Mitchell and Kenyon's Legacy in Scotland', pp. 114–15.

18. NAS, BT2/7704/7, The United Films, Ltd, Return of Allotments, 28 Nov.–27 Dec. 1910; *Bioscope*, 8 June, p. 467; 14 Sept. 1911, p. 534; 9 Jan. 1913, p. 193, for an example of Vivian's flare for showmanship in which he offered a banquet for the twelve oldest patrons attending the house during New Year week. In addition and perhaps showing awareness of the potential for embarrassment thus created, the person with what were adjudged to be the worst dentures would be awarded a wholly new set of teeth, valued at ten guineas.

19. Cloy and McBain, *Scotland in Silent Cinema*, p. 7; *Bioscope*, 5 Oct. 1911, pp. 10, 51.

20. *Bioscope*, 24 Aug. 1911, p. 307.

21. *Bioscope*, 14 Sept., pp. 534–5; 21 Sept. 1911, Supplement, p. xxii.

22. *Bioscope*, 19 Oct. 1911, pp. 155, 157.

23. *Bioscope*, 26 Oct. 1911, p. 233.

24. NAS, BT2/7704/15, The United Films, Ltd, 29 Jan. 1912, Extraordinary General Meeting of Members.

25. *Bioscope*, 31 Aug. 1911, p. 454.

26. *Bioscope*, 14 Sept., p. 579; 16 Nov., Supplement, pp. ix, xi; 23 Nov. 1911, p. 585.

27. *Biosope*, 2 July 1914, p. 30.

28. *Bioscope*, 30 March 1916, p. 1443.

29. SSA, 4/3/1, Andrew Paterson, Inverness, Booklet for show at Central Hall Picture House; 4/3/3, cutting from *Sunday Standard*, 9 Jan. 1983; *Bioscope*, 2 July 1914, p. 33, noting the showing of *Mairi*.

30. SSA, 4/3/1, 29 Sept. 1954, Inverness Film Society to Hector Paterson, Inverness.

31. A. J. Durie, *Scotland for the Holidays: Tourism in Scotland, c.1780–1939* (East Linton, 2003); T. C. Smout, 'Tours in the Scottish Highlands from the Eighteenth to the Nineteenth Centuries', *Northern Scotland*, 5 (1983), pp. 99–121.

32. *Bioscope*, 27 Oct. 1910, p. 99; Durie, *Scotland for the Holidays*, pp. 135–40; R. J. Morris, *Scotland 1907: The Many Scotlands of Valentine and Sons. Photographers* (Edinburgh, 2007), pp. 3–9.

33. *Entertainer*, 18 July 1914, p. 4.

34. *Bioscope*, 6 May 1915, p. 555; *Entertainer*, 30 Jan., p. 5; 1 May 1915, p. 6.

35. *Entertainer*, 31 July, p. 5; 30 Oct. 1915, p. 9.

36. Cloy and McBain, *Scotland in Silent Cinema*, p. 11.

37. *Bioscope*, 13 July, p. 165; 20 July 1916, p. 250.

38. *Bioscope*, 21 Oct. 1915, p. 325.

39. *Bioscope*, 10 Feb. 1916, p. 645; see Chapter 5, p. 193.

40. *Entertainer*, 18 March 1916, pp. 8, 9.

41. *Entertainer*, 6 Oct., p. 13; 17 Nov. 1917, p. 13.

42. *Entertainer*, 3 Aug., p. 7; 16 Nov. 1918, p. 14.

43. *Entertainer*, 18 Jan. 1919, p. 7.

44. *Entertainer*, 8 Feb. 1919, p. 14.

45. *Entertainer and SKR*, 10 May 1919, p. 5; *SKR*, 13 Aug. 1921, p. 3.

46. SSA, Green's Film Service File, 'The Lost British Newsreel: Scottish/British Moving Picture News', n.p.

47. *Scotsman*, 4 Oct. 1919, p. 3.

48. *Entertainer and SKR*, 19 April 1919, p. 7.

49. *Scotsman*, 20 June 1919, p. 1.

50. Phyllis Lea's 'career' is summarised at http://www.imdb.com/name/nm0494778/ (accessed 26 November 2011); Leder's place of residence is indicated in NAS, BT2/11004/7, Ace Film Producing Co., Ltd, Particulars respecting Directors, 25 Feb. 1920.

51. *Entertainer and SKR*, 16 Aug. 1919, p. 5; *Scottish Cinema*, 22 Sept. 1919, p. 18 for the Pickford analogy; NAS, BT2/11004/8, Return of Allotments, 22 March–8 April 1920.

52. SSA, 4/5/101, Film Productions, Miscellaneous, 15 Nov. 1919, Nan Wilkie, certificate of proficiency; cutting from *Sunday Mail*, 26 Oct. 1919.

53. *Scottish Cinema*, 20 Oct. 1919, p. 23; SSA, 4/5/33, Film Productions, Miscellaneous, File on History of Rouken Glen Studios, Notes, n.d.

54. SSA, 4/5/33, cutting from *KW*, 25 Dec. 1919.

55. *Entertainer and SKR*, 8 Nov., p. 2; 22 Nov. 1919, p. 9; see also *Scottish Cinema*, 24 Nov. 1919, p. 24.

56. SSA, 4/5/33, cutting from *Scottish Cinema*, 10 Nov. 1919.

57. SSA, 4/5/101, Cinema House, Programme, Monday, 22 Dec.–Wednesday, 24 Dec. 1919.

58. *Entertainer and SKR*, 24 Jan. 1920, p. 9.

59. NAS, BT2/11004/7, 9, Ace Film Producing Co., Ltd, Register of Directors, 25 Feb.; 15 April 1920.

60. SSA, 4/5/101, Cinema House, Programme; note of conversation with Mr Watt, son of David Watt and Nan Wilkie.

61. *SKR*, 13 Nov., p. 13; 20 Nov. 1920, p. 5.

62. NAS, CS46/1923/7/28, Court of Session, James H. Milligan and The Broadway Cinema Productions, Ltd, evidence of James Minn Kissett, p. 80.

63. NAS, CS46/1923/7/28, evidence of Robert Duncan Laurie, p. 65.

64. *SKR*, 13 May 1922, p. 4; *Bioscope*, 8 June 1922, p. 65; *The Weekly News*, 3 June 1922, p. 2.

65. *Bioscope*, 29 June 1922, p. 79.

66. NAS, BT2/12268/6, Arc Film Producing, Ltd, Particulars re Directors, 17 June 1922.

67. *SKR*, 3 June 1922, p. 10, the production was to have been called *Blinds and Blushes*; NAS, BT2/12268/7, Return of Allotments, 18 Aug. 1922, the two artistes taking out shares in the Arc were both Glaswegian residents with the improbable names of Bulmer Lawless and Clemente Francini.

68. NAS, CS46/1923/7/28, Complainer's Proof, 7 Dec. 1922, p. 2.

69. NAS, CS46/1923/7/28, Complainer's Proof, p. 3; evidence of James Beirne, pp. 38–9.
70. NAS, CS46/1923/7/28, evidence of Victor Weston Rowe, pp. 43–4, 49; evidence of Robert Wilson Muirhead, pp. 63–4.
71. NAS, CS46/1923/7/28, Complainer's Proof, p. 4, where it was noted that 'The sub-titles of this scenario were in the Glasgow vernacular which was a language Mr Rowe could not understand.'
72. NAS, CS46/1923/7/28, evidence of Alfred Avern [sic], p. 34.
73. *SKR*, 3 Dec. 1921, p. 5; NAS, CS46/1923/7/28, evidence of Muirhead, p. 62.
74. NAS, CS46/1923/7/28, evidence of Rowe, p. 59.
75. NAS, CS46/1923/7/28, evidence of Avern, p. 36.
76. *SKR*, 14 Jan., p. 7; 21 Jan. 1922, p. 15.
77. NAS, CS46/1923/7/28, Complainer's proof, pp. 7–8.
78. *SKR*, 13 May 1922, p. 5; NAS, CS46/1923/7/28, Complainer's proof, p. 6.
79. NAS, CS46/1923/7/28, Complainer's proof, p. 7.
80. *SKR*, 23 July, p. 5; 26 Nov. 1921, p. 5.
81. *SKR*, 10 Dec. 1921, p. 2.
82. An incomplete filmography of Sandground's work is available at http://ftvdb. bfi.org.uk/sift/individual/24032?view=credit (accessed 28 November 2011).
83. *Scotsman*, 14 Jan. 1924, p. 8; *ET*, 2 Aug. 1933, p. 7, recalling the film's shooting schedule.
84. *Scotsman*, 16 Jan., p. 6; 17 Jan. 1924, p. 9; 'Kinoman' later recalled the film's success, despite its critical reception by many exhibitors: 'the Scots paid their money and enjoyed the appeal of photographed glen and loch, which, perhaps, they had never seen, nor ever would see, with their own eyes', *ET*, 27 Oct. 1932, p. 3.
85. *Scotsman*, 14 May 1924, p. 1.
86. *Scotsman*, 27 May 1924, p. 9.
87. *Scotsman*, 6 May, p. 10; 14 May 1924, p. 1, for an appeal for local acting talent.
88. *Scotsman*, 1 Feb. 1927, p. 9; SSA, 5/4/15, Poole Family, Diary of Attendances, Synod Hall, 31 Jan. 1927; 4/1/12, Scottish Films Productions (1928), Ltd, Memorandum regarding the financial position of Scottish Films Productions (1928), Limited, p. 1.
89. *Scotsman*, 16 Dec. 1926, p. 7; 6 April 1927, p. 2; SSA, 5/4/15, 4 April 1927.
90. SSA, 4/1/29, Scottish Films Productions (1928), Ltd, 'Remarks on the Production of British Films', n.d., p. 3.
91. Cloy and McBain, *Scotland in Silent Cinema*, p. 10; NAS, BT2/14314/3, 6, Burns-Scott Films, Ltd, Articles of Association, 20 Sept. 1926; Particulars re Directors, 20 Sept. 1926; the company would appear to have been an outgrowth of the earlier Glasgow Film Studios, Ltd, BT2/13492.
92. NAS, BT2/14314/9, Summary of Share Capital, 31 Dec. 1928; SSA, 4/1/29, 'Remarks', p. 5.
93. SSA, 4/1/1, Scottish Films Productions (1928), Ltd, Memorandum and Articles of Association, 13 Aug. 1928; 4/1/29, 'Remarks', pp. 2–3; 4/1/8, Scottish Films Productions (1928), Ltd, cutting from *Glasgow Herald*, 1936.

94. SSA, 5/22/5, Glasgow Picture House, Ltd, Minute Book No. 4, Meeting of Directors, 8 April 1930.

95. *ET*, 11 Nov. 1931, p. 6; SSA, 4/1/42, Scottish Films Productions (1928), Ltd, cutting from *Christian Science Monitor*, 5 Dec. 1931, p. 6.

96. *ET*, 4 Dec. 1931, p. 6.

97. *ET*, 11 Feb., p. 3; 17 March, p. 3; 21 April 1932, p. 3.

98. SSA, 4/1/3–4, Scottish Films Productions (1928), Ltd, Balance Sheets at 31 March 1934; 31 March 1935.

99. *ET*, 5 Aug. 1937, p. 2; SSA, 4/1/7, Scottish Films Productions (1928), Ltd, cutting from *Evening Times*, 27 May 1936.

100. SSA, 4/1/6, Scottish Films Productions (1928), 'Policy' n.d., pp. 3–4.

101. SSA, 4/1/12, Memorandum, pp. 2–3; 4/1/18, List of Films Directed by Stanley L. Russell for Scottish Films, n.d.; 4/1/26, Minute of Agreement between Scottish Films Productions (1928), Ltd, and Trustees of the Clyde Navigation, n.d.

102. SSA, 4/1/17, Scottish Films Productions (1928), Ltd, List of Films Produced, 1934–9; 4/1/12, Memorandum, pp. 2–3.

103. SSA, 4/22/2, Ronnie Jay Collection, cutting from *Scottish Educational Journal*, 21 Aug. 1931; http://ssa.nls.uk/biography.cfm?bid=10020 (accessed 28 November 2011) for a biography of Jay.

104. SSA, 4/22/2, cutting from *Sunday Mail*, Feb. 1931.

105. SSA, 4/10/4, Campbell Harper Films, Notes on conversation with Mrs Anne Harper, June 1984; 4/4/1, Scottish National Film Studios, Ltd, pamphlet, *ED Films, Elder- Dalrymple Productions, Ltd, 178 St Vincent St, Glasgow*.

106. Wilson, *Presenting Scotland*, pp. 21–2; *Films of Scotland* (Edinburgh, 1947), p. 3; SSA, 4/1/13, Scottish Films Productions (1928), Ltd, Memorandum and Proposed Schedule of Productions of Scottish Films Productions (1928), Ltd, 26 India St, Glasgow, C2, p. 2; 4/1/18, List of Films directed by Russell.

107. Wilson, *Presenting Scotland*, pp. 21–36; SSA, 4/12/15, Russell Productions, Ltd/ Thames and Clyde Films Co., Ltd, cutting from *Glasgow Herald*, 29 Feb. 1944.

108. SSA, 4/1/15, Scottish Films Productions (1928), Ltd, cutting from *Daily Mail*, Nov. 1948.

109. SSA, 4/1/14, Scottish Films Productions (1928), Ltd, cutting from *Glasgow Herald*, 15 Feb. 1944.

110. SSA, 4/12/2, Russell Productions, Ltd, Information for the Press, 1943; 4/12/4, booklet, *Thames and Clyde Film Co., Ltd, Producers of Motion Pictures*.

111. SSA, 4/12/18, cutting from *Scotsman*, 6 May 1947; 4/12/17, cutting from *Evening Times*, c. Dec. 1947; Lebas, 'Glasgow's Progress', pp. 41–5.

112. SSA, 4/2/1, Scottish Film Producers' Association, Ltd, Memorandum and Articles of Association; 4/2/2, press cuttings.

113. SSA, 4/1/15, cutting from *Daily Mail*, Nov. 1948.

114. NAS, GD281/92/1, British Film Institute, Scotland, Scottish Film Council, *Monthly Bulletin*, No. 4, Jan. 1936, I. S. Ross, 'Amateur Films in Scotland'.

115. *ET*, 28 Nov. 1929, p. 3.

116. *ET*, 13 Dec. 1934, p. 2.

117. SSA, 4/19/31, Forsyth Hardy Papers, Notes and Cuttings on Scottish Amateur Film Festival, 1933; *Scotsman*, 16 Oct. 1933, p. 13; *ET*, 16 Oct. 1933, p. 8.
118. *Scotsman*, 10 Dec. 1934, p. 10.
119. NAS, GD281/92/1, Scottish Film Council, Leaflet No. 1, p. 5; *Monthly Bulletin* No. 2, Nov. 1935; SSA, 1/1/250, Scottish Film Council, Minute of 5th Meeting, 12 March; 6th Meeting, 25 May 1935.
120. *Scotsman*, 20 Jan. 1936, p. 6.
121. *Scotsman*, 23 Feb. 1937, p. 15.
122. SSA, 4/19/31, letter of Ian S. Ross to unnamed publication, 2 March 1937.
123. SSA, 3/5/9, Edinburgh Cine Club, First Edinburgh Amateur Film Festival, Nov. 1938; cutting from *Edinburgh Evening News*, 28 Nov. 1938.
124. SSA, 3/5/9, Programme for Second Edinburgh Amateur Film Festival, planned for 25 Nov. 1939; *Scotsman*, 9 Sept. 1939, p. 7.
125. *Scotsman*, 3 April 1940, p. 7.
126. *Scotsman*, 17 April, p. 4; 21 April 1941, p. 3.
127. SSA, 1/1/251, Scottish Film Council, Minutes, 1939–44, Minute of 39th Council Meeting, 30 April 1942.
128. SSA, 1/1/250, Minute of 25th Council Meeting, 12 May 1938.
129. SSA, 1/1/252, Scottish Film Council, Minutes, 1944–50, Minute of 62nd Council Meeting, 20 May 1948; *Scotsman*, 26 April 1948, p. 5.
130. *Scotsman*, 26 April 1948, p. 5.
131. *Scotsman*, 1 May 1950, p. 5.
132. *Scotsman*, 27 Nov. 1950, p. 3.
133. See above, n.4.
134. *Scotsman*, 5 April 1938, p. 15; 8 Jan. 1934, p. 7, for an early showing of *O'er Hill and Dale* by the Edinburgh Film Guild.
135. *Scotsman*, 9 Dec. 1936, p. 14; *Courier and Advertiser* (Dundee), 9 Dec. 1936, p. 6.
136. *Scotsman*, 1 Dec. 1937, p. 11; NAS, HH36/138, Scottish Office, Empire Exhibition (Sc) 1938, Cinema Theatre, Production of Films, Minute by Rose on Scottish Films, 2 Nov. 1937.
137. *Scotsman*, 8 Feb., p. 9; 15 Feb., p. 13; 2 March 1938, p. 8; NAS, GD281/92/1, Scottish Film Council, *Film Bulletin*, 4(18) (Nov. 1938), pp. 3–4.
138. NAS, DD10/141, Scottish Home Dept, Cinematograph Acts. Films of Scotland Committee, 31 Jan. 1939, note by Johnson; *Scotsman*, 28 Oct. 1938, p. 6, for Grierson's view; N. Wilson, 'Scotland and the Cinema', *The New Alliance*, 1(1) (Autumn 1939), p. 81.
139. NAS, DD10/141, Irvine to Colville, 26 Jan. 1939.
140. *Scotsman*, 2 Aug. 1938, p. 13.
141. SSA, 1/1/124, Scottish Film Council, Empire Exhibition, Social Service Cinema, Scottish Pavilion (North); *SMT Magazine and Scottish Country Life*, XX(5) (May 1938), p. 104.
142. *Scotsman*, 8 Nov. 1938, p. 13, for Rotha's views.
143. *Scotsman*, 20 Feb. 1939, p. 9.
144. *Scotsman*, 24 Feb. 1939, p. 7.

145. *Scotsman*, 4 March, p. 17; 2 March 1939, p. 13, for Grierson's tactical withdrawal.
146. NAS, DD10/141, 27 May 1943, W. Kirkwood to J. Anderson, Scottish Home Dept.
147. NAS, GD289/2/3–4, Playhouse Cinema, Running Books, 6 April 1936–30 Jan. 1943, weeks ending 9 and 23 Sept. 1939; GD289/2/16–17, Palace Cinema, Running Books, 6 April 1936–30 Jan. 1943, weeks ending 20, 27 Oct. 1939.
148. *Scotsman*, 5 April 1938, p. 15.
149. NAS, DD10/141, note by Milne, 21 Feb. 1942; Minute of Meeting, Under Secretary of State with Mr Milne and Mr Ballantine, 8 Jan. 1943.
150. NAS, DD10/141, HPA, meeting with Sir Gilbert Archer, 23 Dec. 1942.
151. NAS, DD10/141, Minute of Meeting, 8 Jan.; HPA to Milne, 14 Jan. 1943.
152. NAS, DD10/141, A. B. King to Sir Steven Bilsland, 21 Jan. 1943; W. Kirkwood to A. B. King, 29 March 1944.
153. NAS, DD10/141, Deed of Trust, 15 Dec. 1943; Steven Bilsland to Johnston, 20 Sept. 1943.
154. NAS, DD10/141, Milne to King, 7 April 1944.
155. NAS, DD10/141, Minute, Johnson to Anderson, 14 Feb. 1949; see also Sir Gilbert Archer to J. E. de Watterville, Scottish Home Dept, 5 Jan. 1948.
156. NAS, DD10/141, IA to Thomson, 5 July 1943; L. F. Baker, Director and Secretary, Associated British Film Distributors, Ltd, to Trustees, Films of Scotland Committee, 4 Dec. 1947; HH to Ballantine, 11 May 1948.
157. NAS, DD10/141, Ian W. Nicholson, Publicity Convener, Students' Fifth Centenary Committee, University of Glasgow to Hector McNeil, Secretary of State, 1 May 1950; Ballantine to Secretary, Scottish Home Dept, 27 July 1950; Anderson, submission to Secretary of State, 23 Sept. 1950; n.k. to H. Macdonald, Scottish Advisory Council on Civil Aviation, 20 Jan. 1951; H. R. Macdonald to R. W. Williamson, Scottish Home Dept, 18 April 1951.
158. NAS, DD10/141, Ballantine to Permanent Under Secretary of State, 25 April 1951; Minute Sheet, 16 Nov. 1953.
159. D. Bruce, 'Hollywood Comes to the Highlands', in Dick, *From Limelight to Satellite*, pp. 71–82; SSA, 4/4/1, Scottish National Film Studios, Ltd, Note on Scottish National Film Studios, 18 Dec. 1945.
160. SSA, 4/4/1, *Scotland on the Screen*.
161. Ibid., p. 5.
162. Ibid., pp. 5–7.
163. SSA, 4/4/5, Scottish National Film Studios, Ltd, Cuttings and Correspondence, 1945–7, Memorandum on Scottish National Film Studios, Ltd, for submission to H.M. Board of Trade, prior to a discussion between the Board and a deputation, July 1946; 4/4/1, letter from Macleod, n.d.
164. SSA, 4/4/13, Scottish National Film Studios, Ltd, J. Macleod, 'A Film Industry for Scotland', in J. A. A. Porteous (ed.), *Today and Tomorrow: A Review of Practical Constructiveness* (Glasgow, n.d.), p. 37.
165. SSA, 4/4/1, Press Release, Notice on Scottish National Film Studios, Ltd, 2 April 1946; 4/4/5, Memorandum, July 1946, p. 6.

166. SSA, 4/4/1, T. P. Burns to Roberton, 6 Feb. 1946; 4/4/3, Press Cuttings, cutting from *Daily Record*, 5 April 1946.
167. SSA, 4/4/5, Memorandum, July 1946, p. 25, for an estimate of total costs; 4/4/1, report of Open Meeting, 12 Jan. 1946, where Macleod referred to the aim of raising £100,000.
168. SSA, 4/4/5, Memorandum, p. 20.
169. SSA, 4/4/1, *Scotland on the Screen*, p. 11.
170. SSA, 4/4/1, letter to editor of *The Scots Independent*, 13 May 1946; cutting from *Light and Liberty*, 3(1) (May 1946), p. 4.
171. SSA, 4/4/1, *Scotland on the Screen*, p. 6; circular letter, R. H. S. Roberton, temporary secretary, n.d.
172. SSA, 4/4/2, George Bett to Roberton, 15 April 1946; see also Elspeth Brown of Hexham to Roberton, 25 Jan. [1946]; J. and W. Henderson, Ltd, Building Trades' Merchants to Roberton, 16 April 1946.
173. SSA, 4/4/1, Research Dept of SCWS, Report on the Scottish National Film Studios, 10 Nov. 1945, p. 2.
174. SSA, 4/4/1, Lists of Loans and Donations; Statement of Financial Position, 16 Jan. 1947.
175. SSA, 4/4/1, Scott H. Hume to Roberton, 2 June 1946.
176. SSA, 4/4/1, Minute of Meeting, 31 May 1946.
177. SSA, 4/4/5, Memorandum, pp. 14–15; 24.
178. SSA, 4/4/1, *Scotland on the Screen*.
179. SSA, 4/10/5, Campbell Harper Films, Notes on Conversation with Bill Fulton and William J. Maclean; 4/4/7, Credits for Film, n.d.; on Abe Barker, see http://www.imdb.com/name/nm0054811 (accessed 29 November 2011).
180. SSA, 4/10/5, Notes on Conversation with Bill Fulton and William J. Maclean.
181. SSA, 4/4/1, Draft Minute, Notes of Meeting, 16 Jan. 1947.
182. SSA, 4/4/1, Meeting of Finance Sub-committee, 16 Jan. 1947.
183. SSA, 4/4/6, Correspondence, 30 April 1946, H. Russell Ferguson to Macleod; 4/4/1, 18 April 1946, Duncan Maurie to Roberton.
184. SSA, 4/4/3, Press Cuttings, *Daily Record*, 6 April 1946, although he did proceed that, were a solid foundation to be laid, 'one day the world will be talking of Hollywood as the American Ecclefechan or the Tillietudlem of the West'.
185. SSA, 4/4/5, Cuttings and Correspondence, 1945–7, Schedule of Films in Contemplation, n.d.; the Studio's agenda would be met through productions such as *The Brave Don't Cry* (1952) and *Braveheart* (1995).
186. NAS, DD10/141, cutting from *Scotsman*, 13 Oct. 1951.
187. NAS, GD289/1/1, Playhouse Cinema, Profit and Loss Ledger; GD289/2/3, Running Book, week ending 23 Sept. 1939; GD289/1/3, Palace Cinema, Profit and Loss Ledger; GD289/2/17, Running Book, weeks ending 21 and 28 Oct. 1939.
188. NAS, GD289/1/3, Palace Cinema, Profit and Loss Ledger; GD289/2/18, Running Book, week commencing 12 April 1943.
189. NAS, GD289/1/1, Playhouse Cinema, Profit and Loss Ledger; GD289/2/5, Running Book, week commencing 30 Aug. 1948; GD289/1/3, Palace Cinema, Profit and Loss Ledger; GD289/2/18, Running Book, week commencing 20 Sept. 1948.

Conclusion

By 1950, cinema seemingly occupied a secure and central place in the recreational culture of Scots. Yet its rise to such a position had, in practice, been far from assured and straightforward. Certainly, the moving image had proved itself capable, by insinuating itself into existing entertainment settings, from the fairground to the variety theatre, of acquiring a large popular following within a few years of its public debut. This, however, proved a less than reliable guide to its subsequent prospects. To succeed in the decades of political and economic uncertainty that marked the early twentieth century, the cinema would be obliged to confront a variety of challenges. As a recreational pursuit whose most loyal constituency was formed by those groups, primarily the young and the poor, considered most susceptible to forces which worked to challenge conventional moral standards, the cinema was an obvious candidate for calls for enhanced regulation, covering both access to and the content of what was shown. Pressure for change recurred through the period, gaining renewed impetus at times of acute anxiety over levels of juvenile delinquency or the perceived impact of early talking pictures. To the alarm of many, the regulatory regime that would apply north of the border appeared altogether looser than that which applied elsewhere and continued to be shaped by local patterns of governance established in the previous century.

At various points, the impact of national agencies would be felt, as central government saw in the cinema a ready means of boosting revenues during periods of national emergency. For an industry that had long defined its role as a purveyor of cheap entertainment, the imposition of taxation posed a significant challenge to normal commercial operations, coinciding as it did with periods of inflated living costs or reduced work opportunities. The years of the First World War and the early 1930s would prove especially difficult for exhibitors across Scotland. A further complicating factor was the requirement to devote screen time to productions emanating from British studios. Yet if many were insistent that the quota obliged cinemas to acquire films whose only function appeared to be to reduce takings by alienating potential patrons, box-office evidence suggests that the effect of various measures from 1927 was broadly neutral, as British production proved sufficiently extensive and diverse to satisfy the varied preferences of audiences across

Scotland. While this serves further to rehabilitate the British film industry of the 1930s, it also calls into question the commercial effectiveness of that same industry in the following decade, despite an output that, although smaller, appeared more coherent and was certainly more critically lauded. The high tide of Britishness in the 1940s did not appear to incorporate Scottish picture-goers.

Much the most insistent challenge faced by cinema managers over the period was posed by changes in the wider economy. With the bulk of its audience drawn from those whose discretionary spending power was limited, the moving picture business remained vulnerable to swings in the economic cycle, so that in the major downturns of the early 1920s and early 1930s, the fall in activity was faithfully reflected in reduced admissions. If anything, the cinema's exposure to such fluctuations was all the greater given the prevailing gender balance among picture-goers. Female expenditure on non-essentials was frequently the first victim of domestic efforts at retrenchment. In the absence of a long-run series of aggregated audience statistics, the impact of all this on the industry must be inferred from changes in company accounts. These suggest that, for all the outward projection of confidence through the construction of larger, more elaborate structures within which to project moving pictures, there were few points when the exhibition sector was free of financial worries. So, if recovery from the recession of the early 1920s was pronounced, margins then remained depressed through much of the 1930s. Away from the west-central belt, where receipts recovered strongly with the onset of rearmament, growth in the audience during the final pre-war years did not suffice to compensate for a rise in operating costs, the structure of the industry precluding the kind of collusion over prices observed in other parts of the economy. The 1930s thus emerges as a paradoxical decade, in which, while cinema-going reached new heights in terms of both numbers and the luxurious surroundings within which film was consumed, the exhibition sector experienced the most prolonged period of low profitability in its history to date. If the outbreak of war and the limited availability of alternative amusements offered relief of sorts, it also created new problems, as opportunities to improve facilities by reinvesting the surpluses consistently earned across the decade remained constrained by the rigours of physical planning. The cinema industry thus entered its second fifty years with an ageing infrastructure which would struggle to adjust to the changes of post-war society.

At all points, the effects of wider economic developments were filtered through the audience. In terms of their overall profile, Scottish cinema-goers did not differ markedly from their counterparts across the rest of Britain. Attendance showed a comparable tendency to tail off as age increased, with children the most loyal followers of the moving picture. The low cost of admission which facilitated their support also ensured that cinema put down its strongest roots among the lower paid more generally. Scotland, with its lower than average incomes and higher than average levels of overcrowding, displayed the conditions most conducive to a flourishing mass entertainment medium. Yet it should not be thought that this pattern was invariable or inevitable. The location of the earliest picture shows, combined with a pricing structure broadly in line with that of more elevated theatrical shows, hint at an initial appeal to a diverse and respectable market. Indeed, it is only from its second decade, with the construction of dedicated picture houses and the opportunities they provided to drive prices down, that the cinema can truly be said to have engaged with the masses in any systematic fashion. Thereafter, the experiences of war would underscore perceptions of picturegoers as predominantly young and female, a profile substantially confirmed by successive investigations through the period. Such inquiries also revealed, often against expectations, a critical and selective response to the entertainments offered. Even among children, thought to constitute the most habitual and least discriminating segment of the audience, surveys found a definite set of preferences as regards both genres and stars. The readiness of filmgoers more generally to exercise choice in their selection of pleasures posed a regular challenge to cinema managers, obliging them to maintain a close check on the shifting preferences of patrons. In this, they were guided by a literature that counselled an understanding of the audience not as an undifferentiated collectivity, but as an amalgam of varied interests and tastes, to whose needs the successful manager was required to pay particular attention.

The attractions of cinema across the period were many and varied and became, if anything, more so with the emergence of an audience keen to view film as a new art form. This remained very much a minority view, even it might be thought among members of the film society movement itself, a bubble in numbers during and immediately after the Second World War generated more by an absence of alternative amusements on Sundays than by positive enthusiasm for an intellectual engagement with the moving image. Even this larger number remained dwarfed by the legions of picturegoers who flocked to mainstream picture houses through the period. Their engagement with film is often discussed in terms of escape, as film offered a release from everyday realities. The enduring popularity of larger-budget films, alongside particular genres such as the musical and certain comedies, suggests that such a view has some validity. Yet as foregoing chapters have indicated, its capacity to comprehend the whole or most of cinema-going's appeal may be doubted. The example of the old lady of Brechin who sought rest, repose, and economies in fuel consumption in her local picture house stands as a reminder that escape could assume many forms. For others, cinema often offered an amplification of rather than a release from reality. Young women looked to acquire valuable knowledge on matters of sexual health through the medium of film and were, on occasion, willing to fight for the privilege. Their male counterparts were, so the evidence suggests, more inclined to look the other way. In parts of Scotland, the cinema may have worked to enhance a sense of self-worth among those identified as an alien minority. In the face of criticisms advanced with the backing of the Presbyterian establishment, Scots of Irish descent could turn to film to offer a more positive view of their place in the contemporary world, whether through the musicals of Binkie Stewart, the comedies of Arthur Lucan, or the products of Hollywood, given prominence by Catholic exhibitors, such as the Green family. The impact of a production such as *Irish and Proud Of It*, which played at Green's houses in Glasgow early in 1937, can only be guessed at, but the firm's readiness to employ more than the basic advertising to push the title is suggestive of its perceived appeal.[1] For individual picture-goers, the cinema's function could change over time. For the teenage Kitty McGinniss, it was an experience shared, although not simultaneously, with her mother and friends, while in later years it became a space for courting.[2] Further east, Eileen Crowford found that the pictures offered an additional outlet for her political sympathies. Over the course of the Second World War, Ms Crowford would appear to have developed an allegiance to communism, which she identified as a clear favourite among contemporary political movements, with 'Advanced Socialist' a somewhat distant second. This found further expression in a list of 'Favourite Public Figures' contained in one of her later diaries, headed by 'Joseph Stalin (deceased)', 'President Kalinin (deceased)', and 'Vlashev Molotov'. The leading British figure was, perhaps unsurprisingly, Harry Pollitt of the CPGB. Away from the cinema, Ms Crowford maintained a membership of the Scottish USSR Society and if her picture-going was not consistently driven by ideology, so that in 1950, among the thirty-six visits made to the cinema during the year, was one to see Arthur Lucan as Old Mother Riley in support of the Twentieth Century Fox comedy western, *A Ticket to Tomahawk*, her ranking of films reflects rather more faithfully the impact of her political convictions. Her top film for 1945 was thus the Soviet production *Adventures in Bokhara*.[3]

Scots of many ages and persuasions, from communist to Catholic, frequented the cinema in these years. If the evidence suggests that the practice rarely worked to amend existing attitudes, its tendency rather to reaffirm and occasionally amplify them is still suggestive of a close relationship with the world beyond the auditorium. The Scotland viewed through the prism of the cinema industry was a society fully capable of adapting to and assimilating the changes associated with modernity. Scots readily mobilised their savings to fund the provision of a growing range of urban amusements, furthering in the process the transition to a consumer-based culture, of which commercialised leisure was a key building block. A network of picture houses emerged both extensively and, in some areas, in depth, in the years to 1914 by means of capital raised either directly through share purchases or indirectly by means of bank loans from Scotland's commercial middle class. In the process, Scotland's transition to the twentieth century was eased. Yet investment which was forthcoming for the building of sites for the exhibition of moving pictures proved altogether more difficult to mobilise for the production of the images themselves. Uncertainties of return and the need to secure extensive distribution for subjects if they were to recoup their costs made the production of anything beyond modestly budgeted local topicals or documentary features an unattractive proposition. Not only that, but generations of Scots, through the regularity and persistence of their attendance, expressed a broad satisfaction with the fare offered at local picture houses. If this was never accepted uncritically, its propensity to marry footage of local relevance to images drawn from cultures which, while different, became through repeated exposure familiar, heightened its attraction. The pictures provided a solid grounding in the mores of contemporary society, presenting ideals of masculinity and femininity from which young cinema-goers, preparing to encounter the challenges of the wider world, could borrow.

Scots found little that was threatening and much that was attractive in the modernity depicted on the silver screen; that it spoke in a transatlantic drawl and came, on occasion, toting a six-shooter merely added to its allure. Yet concern remained widespread that here was an alternative morality at odds with that articulated by established leaders of opinion in government and the Church. Film's often frank engagement with matters sexual, its preoccupation with the violent and the criminal ensured that powerful voices of opposition were frequently raised against it. Yet campaigns for closer regulation of content, tighter controls on access, and the observance of Sabbath closure were rarely productive of change, more especially after 1918, as Scots came to see little objectionable in gaining access even to politically contentious materials on Sundays. Scotland was still far from becoming a secular society but it was increasingly one in which Presbyterian morality exercised a progressively more narrowly circumscribed influence. For the generation coming to maturity in the wake of the First World War, cinema was a powerful solvent of established attitudes and modes of behaviour.

For many, the importance of the Sabbath extended beyond questions of morality to encompass the very nature of Scotland as a nation. Cinema sustained global networks of production and distribution that showed little regard for points of local difference. Fears of cultural effacement were real, given the propensity of the young to mimic the dress, appearance, and verbal tics of screen idols, and the growing incursion of foreign capital, extending from the film itself to the very buildings in which that film was shown. For the most part, however, concerns for Scotland's continued identity as a nation were overdone. Ownership of the exhibition sector continued to rest in Scottish hands, while systems of regulation acknowledged the distinctive character of Scottish law. In addition, local cinema-goers appeared sufficiently secure in their sense of self to embrace images and storylines fashioned elsewhere without worrying unduly, as did the more fastidious critics, over matters of factual or cultural fidelity. Audiences appeared more flattered than outraged when popular stars, such as Laurel and Hardy, paid passing regard to Scotland in their films and were broadly welcoming of productions that located Scotland within a wider cinematic vision. Acceptance of the vistas opened up by Hollywood also made for a rather tepid response among mainstream picture-goers to the largely inward-looking and self-consciously 'Scottish' agenda pursued by John Grierson and other documentary film-makers. Against that, the most consistently popular footage produced in Scotland was that of immediate local relevance, as it was this which 'spoke' most readily to an audience primarily comprising the working-class young and women, whose everyday experience was shaped in the immediate surroundings of close, street, and neighbourhood.

In some respects, however, the insights provided by box-office returns have their limitations. In the darkness of the auditorium, cinema-goers as diverse as Kitty McGinniss and Eileen Crowford could consume similar programmes without in any way compromising their wider beliefs. This reflected more than anything a conception of leisure time that was the very opposite of modern, in which its distinctive character, holding the rules that governed convention in abeyance, was celebrated.[4] Cinema, more than anything, embodied the established perception of leisure as 'the other' and was embraced on those terms by growing numbers of Scots in the years to 1950. The demands it made on its followers were, both financially and intellectually, few. At the cost of a few pennies, all it asked, temporarily, was a willing suspension of disbelief; therein lay the essence of its appeal.

NOTES

1. Macdonald, *Whaur Extremes Meet*, pp. 279–80; *ET*, 9 Jan. 1937, p. 6.
2. Kitty McGinniss, Diaries, 1925–37.
3. NMS, Scottish Life Archive, Eileen Crowford Collection, lists in Diaries for 1939 and 1942.
4. P. Borsay, *A History of Leisure: The British Experience since 1500* (Basingstoke, 2006), p. 6.

Appendix 1

Cinema Companies: Sample, 1895–1914

Source	Company name	Date registered
BT2/3015	Glasgow Real Ice Skating Palace, Ltd	Oct. 1895
BT2/3758	The Scottish Mutoscope Co., Ltd	Feb. 1898
BT2/5449	The Modern Marvel Co., Ltd	March 1899
BT2/5562	Fraser and Elrick, Ltd	March 1904
BT2/7366	West of Scotland Electric Theatres, Ltd	Dec. 1909
BT2/7369	The Govan Cross Picture Palace, Ltd	Dec. 1909
BT2/7379	The Ayr Picture Palace, Ltd	Dec. 1909
BT2/7476	The Glasgow Electric Theatres, Ltd	March 1910
BT2/7501	The Scottish Cinematograph Co., Ltd	April 1910
BT2/7555	Star Animated Picture and Vaudeville Co., Ltd	May 1910
BT2/7567	Scottish Electric Picture Palaces, Ltd	June 1910
BT2/7601	The Highland Cinematograph and Variety Co., Ltd	July 1910
BT2/7604	Paisley Road Electric Picture Palace, Ltd	July 1910
BT2/7670	The BB Pictures, Ltd	Oct. 1910
BT2/7695	The Shettleston Premier Picture Theatre Co., Ltd	Nov. 1910
BT2/7710	British-American Electric Theatres, Ltd	Nov. 1910
BT2/7981	The Aberdeen Electric Theatre Co., Ltd	Sept. 1911
SSA 5/22/3	The Glasgow Picture House, Ltd	Oct. 1911
BT2/8043	Vitagraph Electric Theatres, Ltd	Nov. 1911
BT2/8062	The Armadale Picturedrome, Ltd	Nov. 1911
BT2/8075	The Hamilton Picture House, Ltd	Dec. 1911
BT2/8154	Greenock Picture Palace Co., Ltd	Feb. 1912
BT2/8272	Maryhill Picture Theatre, Ltd	May 1912
BT2/8288	The Methil Picture Palace Co., Ltd	June 1912
BT2/8316	The Wishaw Picture Palace, Ltd	June 1912
BT2/8369	Eglinton Electreum, Ltd	Aug. 1912
BT2/8375	The Palace (Edinburgh), Ltd	Sept. 1912
BT2/8388	The Govan Central Picture House, Ltd	Sept. 1912
BT2/8421	Wishaw Cinema House, Ltd	Oct. 1912
BT2.8423	Kirkcaldy Kinema Palace, Ltd	Oct. 1912

BT2/8424	The Tollcross Cinema, Ltd	Oct. 1912
BT2/8428	The Kirkcaldy Picture House, Ltd	Nov. 1912
BT2/8439	The Dundee Princes Pictures, Ltd	Nov. 1912
BT2/8454	The Hillhead Picture House, Ltd	Nov. 1912
BT2/8468	The Motherwell Cinema House, Ltd	Dec. 1912
BT2/8515	The Portobello Picture Palace, Ltd	Jan. 1913
BT2/8516	The Dunfermline Cinema House, Ltd	Jan. 1913
CM	Aberdeen Picture Palaces, Ltd	Jan. 1913
BT2/8578	The Rothesay Electric Theatres, Ltd	March 1913
BT2/8624	The Morningside Photo Playhouse, Ltd	April 1913
BT2/8636	Scottish Picture Houses, Ltd	April 1913
BT2/8670	La Scala (Dunfermline), Ltd	May 1913
BT2/8968	Airdrie Pavilion, Ltd	Feb. 1914
BT2/9030	Central Picture House, Portobello, Ltd	March 1914
BT2/9064	The Lorne Cinema House, Ltd	March 1914
BT2/9105	The Clydebank Picture House, Ltd	April 1914
BT2/9147	The Invergordon Picture Playhouse, Ltd	June 1914
BT2/9201	The Palace (Arbroath), Ltd	July 1914
BT2/9204	The North of Scotland Cinematograph, Ltd	July 1914
BT2/9213	The Perth Cinemas, Ltd	July 1914

Appendix 2

Cinema Companies: Sample, 1914–29

Source	*Company name*	*Date registered*
BT2/9429	The Palace Kinema (Dunfermline), Ltd	June 1915
BT2/9707	Scottish Cinema and Variety Theatres, Ltd	Nov. 1916
BT2/9718	The Cinema (Dumfries), Ltd	Dec. 1916
BT2/10134	The Wellington Picture Palace, Ltd	Oct. 1918
BT2/10179	Crail Picture House, Ltd	Dec. 1918
BT2/10240	The Bo'ness Cinema, Ltd	Feb. 1919
BT2/10483	Waverley Picture House, Ltd	June 1919
BT2/10508	The Scottish Cinema Publishing Co., Ltd	July 1919
BT2/10607	The Scottish Touring Cinema Co., Ltd	Aug. 1919
BT2/10654	The Rutherglen Picture Palace, Ltd	Oct. 1919
BT2/10774	The Broadway Stage and Cinema Productions, Ltd	Nov.1919
BT2/10845	The Britannia Cinema (Dundee), Ltd	Dec. 1919
BT2/10864	Dennistoun Picture House, Ltd	Dec. 1919
BT2/10892	The Arcadia Picture House (Glasgow), Ltd	Jan. 1920
BT2/11004	Ace Film Producing Co., Ltd	Feb. 1920
BT2/11121	Kilmarnock Picture House, Ltd	April 1920
BT2/11228	The Stockbridge Picture House Co., Ltd	May 1920
BT2/11238	The Paragon Picture Theatre (Glasgow), Ltd	May 1920
BT2/11407	The Playhouse, Galashiels (1920), Ltd	Sept. 1920
BT2/11663	The St Andrew Square Picture House, Ltd	March 1921
BT2/11875	Olympia Pictures (Dunfermline), Ltd	Sept. 1921
BT2/12268	Arc Film Producing, Ltd	June 1922
BT2/12548	Empire (Cowdenbeath), Ltd	Feb. 1923
BT2/12826	Montrose Burgh Cinema Co., Ltd	Sept. 1923
BT2/13492	Glasgow Film Studios, Ltd	Jan. 1925
BT2/14314	Burns-Scott Films, Ltd	Sept. 1926

Appendix 3

Scottish Film Societies, Membership and Average Attendances, 1952–3 Season

Society	Membership	Average attendance
35 mm		
Aberdeen	1,340	1,400
Aberdeen FAG	1,080	1,200
Alloa	186	200
Angus	251	428
Broughty Ferry	382	410
Clydeside	600	700
Dumfries	300	249
Dundee	1,150	1,260
Dunfermline	460	500
Edinburgh	1,824	2,010
Galashiels	310	400
Glasgow	1,250	1,150
Inverness	280	320
North Ayrshire	340	333
Perth	299	400
Peterhead	170	200
Shetland	110	75
St Andrews	740	740
16 mm		
Dumfries	63	50
Lochaber	95	70–80
Nairn	91	60
Wishaw	60	40

Note: No returns from Ayrshire, Glasgow People's, Hawick, Kirkcaldy, Moray, Boroughmuir School, Dumbarton, Edinburgh University, Forres, Glasgow University, Greenock, Inverurie, Keith, Lewis, Loretto School, Shotts, George Watson's College.
(Source: SSA, 3/1/40, Film Society of Glasgow, Minute Book, 1949–56, Meeting of Council, 4 June 1953.)

Bibliography

PRIMARY SOURCES – PRINTED AND MANUSCRIPT

Border Archives, Hawick

Galashiels Film Society (D/78/1).

Cinema Museum, Lambeth

Aberdeen Picture Palace, Ltd
   Accounts, 1913–14; 1926–50.
   Capitol Cinema, Takings Books, 1933–46.
   Minutes, 1913–43.
   Register of Members &c.
James F. Donald (Cinemas), Ltd
   Accounts, 1929–51.
   Cinema House, Employers' Schedule E Return, 1927–8.
   Grand Central Picture House, Correspondence.
The Queen's Rooms Cinema Syndicate, Ltd
   Minute Books, 1913–29.
Torry Cinemas, Ltd
   Accounts, 1925–51.

Dumfries and Galloway Archives, Lockerbie Town Hall

Lockerbie Cinema Co., Ltd, Directors' Minute Books, 1932–50 (1/6/8–9).

Dundee City Archives

Dundee Town Council Minutes, 1909–20.
Magistrates' Committee Minutes, 1910–20.
Police and Lighting Committee Minutes, 1912–20.

Edinburgh City Archives

Edinburgh Corporation Committee Minutes, Magistrates, Sessions 1930–51
   (SL119/3/1–20).

Edinburgh Corporation, Magistrates Minutes, 1909–16 (SL119/2/6).
Edinburgh Corporation, Magistrates Committee, Scroll Minute Book, Feb. 1910–July 1920 (SL119/1/2).
Edinburgh Corporation, Magistrates Committee, Scroll Minutes, 1920–6 (SL119/1/3).
Edinburgh Corporation Magistrates Committee, Scroll Minutes, 1926–9 (SL119/1/4).

Glasgow City Archives, Mitchell Library, Glasgow

Glasgow Corporation Minutes, 1908–13.
List of Premises Licensed under the Cinematograph Act, 12 July 1913 (D-OPW61/5).
Memorandum by Town Clerk on the Cinematograph Act, 1909, and Relative Regulations made by the Secretary of State for Scotland on 10 March 1910 (MP41/106).
Rutherglen, Cinematograph Act, 1909 (RU4/2/15).
Wishaw Picture Palace and Wellington Picture Palace
    TD273/1, Wellington Picture Palace (1933), Ltd, Ledger No. 1.
    TD273/3, The Wishaw Picture Palace, Ltd, Cash Book, April 1934–Feb. 1939.
    TD723/4, The Wishaw Picture Palace, Ltd, Cash Book, Nov. 1945–April 1953

In the possession of Mrs Rita Connelly

Diaries of Ms C. McGinniss, 1925, 1927, 1928, 1929, 1930, 1933, 1935, 1937.

National Archives of Scotland, Edinburgh

Board of Trade, Register of Dissolved Companies
    BT2/3015, Glasgow Real Ice Skating Palace, Ltd.
    BT2/3758, The Scottish Mutoscope Co., Ltd.
    BT2/5449, Modern Marvel Co., Ltd.
    BT2/5562, Fraser and Elrick, Ltd.
    BT2/7366, West of Scotland Electric Theatres, Ltd.
    BT2/7369, The Govan Cross Picture Palace, Ltd.
    BT2/7379, The Ayr Picture Palace, Ltd.
    BT2/7476, The Glasgow Electric Theatres, Ltd.
    BT2/7501, The Scottish Cinematograph Co., Ltd.
    BT2/7555, Star Animated Picture and Vaudeville Co., Ltd.
    BT2/7567, Scottish Electric Picture Palaces, Ltd.
    BT2/7601, The Highland Cinematograph and Variety Co., Ltd.
    BT2/7604, Paisley Road Electric Picture Palace, Ltd.
    BT2/7670, The BB Pictures, Ltd.
    BT2/7695, The Shettleston Premier Picture Theatre Co., Ltd.
    BT2/7704, The United Films, Ltd.
    BT2/7710, British-American Electric Theatres, Ltd.
    BT2/7981, The Aberdeen Electric Theatre Co., Ltd.
    BT2/8043, Vitagraph Electric Theatres, Ltd.
    BT2/8062, The Armadale Picturedrome, Ltd.

BT2/8075, The Hamilton Picture House, Ltd.
BT2/8154, Greenock Picture Palace Co., Ltd.
BT2/8272, Maryhill Picture Theatre, Ltd.
BT2/8288, The Methil Picture Palace Co., Ltd.
BT2/8316, The Wishaw Picture Palace, Ltd.
BT2/8369, Eglinton Electreum, Ltd.
BT2/8375, The Palace (Edinburgh), Ltd.
BT2/8388, The Govan Central Picture House, Ltd.
BT2/8421, Wishaw Cinema House, Ltd.
BT2/8423, Kirkcaldy Kinema Palace, Ltd.
BT2/8424, The Tollcross Cinema, Ltd.
BT2/8428, The Kirkcaldy Picture House, Ltd.
BT2/8439, The Dundee Princes Pictures, Ltd.
BT2/8454, The Hillhead Picture House, Ltd.
BT2/8468, The Motherwell Cinema House, Ltd.
BT2/8515, The Portobello Picture Palace, Ltd.
BT2/8516, The Dunfermline Cinema House, Ltd.
BT2/8578, The Rothesay Electric Theatres, Ltd.
BT2/8624, The Morningside Photo Playhouse, Ltd.
BT2/8636, Scottish Picture Houses, Ltd.
BT2/8670, La Scala (Dunfermline), Ltd.
BT2/8968, Airdrie Pavilion, Ltd.
BT2/9030, Central Picture House, Portobello, Ltd.
BT2/9064, The Lorne Cinema House, Ltd.
BT2/9105, The Clydebank Picture House, Ltd.
BT2/9147, The Invergordon Picture Playhouse, Ltd.
BT2/9201, The Palace (Arbroath), Ltd.
BT2/9204, The North of Scotland Cinematograph, Ltd.
BT2/9213, The Perth Cinemas, Ltd.
BT2/9429, The Palace Kinema (Dunfermline), Ltd.
BT2/9707, Scottish Cinemas and Variety Theatres, Ltd.
BT2/9718, The Cinema (Dumfries), Ltd.
BT2/10134, The Wellington Picture Palace, Ltd.
BT2/10179, Crail Picture House, Ltd.
BT2/10240, The Bo'ness Cinema, Ltd.
BT2/10483, Waverley Picture House, Ltd.
BT2/10508, The Scottish Cinema Publishing Co., Ltd.
BT2/10607, The Scottish Touring Cinema Co., Ltd.
BT2/10654, The Rutherglen Picture Palace, Ltd.
BT2/10774, The Broadway Stage and Cinema Productions, Ltd.
BT2/10845, The Britannia Cinema (Dundee), Ltd.
BT2/10864, Dennistoun Picture Houses, Ltd.
BT2/10892, The Arcadia Picture House (Glasgow), Ltd.
BT2/11004, Ace Film Producing Co., Ltd.
BT2/11121, Kilmarnock Picture House, Ltd.
BT2/11228, The Stockbridge Picture House, Ltd.

BT2/11238, The Paragon Picture Theatre (Glasgow), Ltd.

BT2/11290, Waverley Picture House (1920), Ltd.

BT2/11407, The Playhouse, Galashiels (1920), Ltd.

BT2/11663, The St Andrew Square Picture House, Ltd.

BT2/11875, Olympia Pictures (Dunfermline), Ltd.

BT2/12268, Arc Film Producing, Ltd.

BT2/12548, Empire (Cowdenbeath), Ltd.

BT2/12826, Montrose Burgh Cinema Co., Ltd.

BT2/13492, Glasgow Film Studios, Ltd.

BT2/14314, Burns-Scott Films, Ltd.

BT2/16911, United Cinemas, Ltd.

BT2/17243, Mecca Cinema, Ltd.

BT2/17497, Stornoway Playhouse, Ltd.

BT2/18488, Vogue Cinemas, Ltd.

Closed Record in Causa Alexander Mathieson against J. F. Calverto (CS248/4062), First Division, Lord Kincarny Ordinary. Summons IC, Alexander Mathieson v. West Lothian Printing and Publishing Co., Ltd (CS248/4066).

Committee on Children and the Cinema, 1948 (CO1/4/200).

Court of Session, James H. Milligan and The Broadway Cinema Productions, Ltd (CS46/1923/7/28).

Highlands and Islands Film Guild Records

ED 30/2, Minutes of Meetings, 1946–59.

Letter Book of Alexander Mathieson (CS96/1483).

Letter Book of Thomas Gilbert, 1916–21 [catalogued under Glasgow Sheriff Court, Productions, Glasgow Film Services, Letter Book, 1914–17] (SC36/79/18).

Lord Advocate's Dept, Opinion of the Law Officers of the Crown and the Scottish Law Officers (AB54/95).

Messrs Fairbairn, Lightbody, and Cownie, Chartered Quantity Surveyors and Valuers, Edinburgh

GD283/6/301, Valuation Appeal of Palace Cinema, 1919.

Palace and Playhouse Cinemas, Edinburgh

GD289/1/1, Playhouse Cinema, Profit and Loss Ledger, 1929–68.

GD289/1/3, Palace Cinema, Profit and Loss Ledger, 1925–55.

GD289/2/1–5, Playhouse Cinema, Running Books, 12 Aug. 1929–1 May 1948.

GD289/2/14–18, Palace Cinema, Running Books, 2 Sept. 1929–1 May 1948.

Records of the Carnegie United Kingdom Trust

Scottish Film Council: British Film Institute (Scotland) (GD281/92).

Scottish Home Dept

DD10/141, Cinematograph Acts, Films of Scotland Committee.

HH1/1981, Cinemas, Paisley Catastrophe, Report to the Rt. Hon. The Secretary of State for Scotland on the Circumstances Attending the Loss of Life at the Glen Cinema, Paisley, on the 31st December 1929 by Major T. H. Crozier, H.M. Chief Inspector of Explosives, Dated 5 May 1930. Extended Notes of Proceedings in Paisley Cinema Disaster. Trial of Charles Dorward.

HH1/2615, Sabbath Day Observance, Resolutions.

HH1/2616, Miscellaneous Files, Sabbath Day Observance, Press Cuttings, etc.

HH1/2617, Sabbath Day Observance, Sunday Observance Act (1780) Amendment (No. 2) Bill, 1931.

HH1/2618, Sunday Observance Act (1780) Amendment (No. 2) Bill, 1931, Representations.

HH1/2619, Sabbath Day Observance, Resolutions.

HH1/2622, Sabbath Day Observance, Sunday Performance (Regulation) Bill, 1931.

HH1/2625, Sunday Performances (Temporary Regulation) Act, Parliamentary Procedures.

HH1/2626, Sunday Performances (Regulation) Bill, 1932, Parliamentary Procedures.

HH1/2627, Sunday Performances (Regulation) Bill, 1932, Representations.

HH1/2628, Sunday Entertainment Bill, 1932.

HH1/2632, Sunday Entertainments, Representations and Enquiries.

HH1/2633, Sunday Entertainments, Representations and Enquiries.

HH1/2634, Sunday Observance. Representations and Enquiries.

HH1/2635, Sunday Observance. Representations and Enquiries.

HH1/2642, Notice for Question for Thursday 16 November 1939.

HH1/2643, Cinema Openings, 1939–41.

HH1/2644, Sunday Observance, Press Cuttings.

HH1/2647, Opening of Places of Entertainment. Reports, Representations, etc.

HH1/2648, Chief Constables' Reports on Sunday Cinema Opening.

Scottish Office, Empire Exhibition (Scotland) (HH36/138).

Steel-Maitland Papers

GD193/205/36, 40, National Council of Women of Great Britain, Cinema Sectional Committee.

Trial Papers, Trial of Charles Dorward, Manager of Glen Cinema, Paisley (JC26/1930/54).

National Museum of Scotland, Scottish Life Archive

Eileen Crowford Collection, Diaries, 1937–50.

North Lanarkshire Archives, Cumbernauld

Gartcosh Public Hall, Minute Books (U129/1/1).

Scottish Screen Archive, Hillington

ABC, Sauchiehall Street (5/9).

A. B. King Collection (5/12).

Andrew Paterson, Inverness (4/3).

Campbell Harper Films (4/10).

Cinematograph Exhibitors' Association (5/11).

Edinburgh Cine Club (3/5).

Edinburgh Film Guild (3/4).

Federation of Scottish Film Societies

2/1/1–2, Minutes of Council, 1934–50.

Film Productions, Miscellaneous (4/5).
Film Societies Collection (3/2).
Film Society of Glasgow (3/1).
Forsyth Hardy Papers (4/19).
George Green, Ltd (5/8).
George Kemp Collection (5/18).
The Glasgow Picture House, Ltd (5/22).
Green's Film Service File.
Interview with Mr George Kemp (8/47).
James S. Nairn Collection (5/14).
Miscellaneous Film Material (5/7).
Poole Family Collection (5/4).
Ronnie Jay Collection (4/22).
Russell Productions, Ltd/Thames and Clyde Films Co., Ltd (4/12).
Scottish Educational Cinema Society/Scottish Educational Film Association (1/5).
Scottish Film Council
    1/1/108, Volume of Press Cuttings.
    1/1/124, Scottish Film Council, Empire Exhibition, Social Service Cinema, Scottish
        Pavilion (North).
    1/1/250–2, Minutes, 1934–50.
Scottish Film Producers' Association, Ltd (4/2).
Scottish Films Productions (1928), Ltd (4/1).
Scottish National Film Studios, Ltd (4/4).
Singleton Collection (5/26).
Stranraer Picture House, Ltd (5/25).
Walker Family Collection (5/3).

West Lothian Local History Library, Blackburn

Uphall Public Hall and Cinema, Cash Books, 1889–1927.

Official publications

Parl. Papers 1915, XXVII (7939), Report of the Departmental Committee appointed
    to Inquire into the Conditions Prevailing in the Coal-Mining Industry due to the
    War. Part I – Report.
Statutory Rules and Orders, 1910. No. 289 S.9. *Cinematograph Scotland. Regulations,
    dated March 10, 1910, Made by the Secretary for Scotland under the Cinematograph
    Act, 1909 (9 Edw. 7, c. 30).*
Statutory Rules and Orders, 1923, No. 1147/S.62. *Cinematograph, Scotland. Regulations
    Dated September 22, 1923, made by the Secretary for Scotland under the Cinematograph
    Act, 1909 (9 Edw. 7, c. 30).*

Newspapers and periodicals

Aberdeen Journal.

Aberdeen Weekly Journal.
The Bailie (Glasgow).
Bioscope.
Cinema Quarterly.
Courier and Advertiser (Dundee).
Daily Herald.
The Entertainer, Theatrical, Vaudeville, Musical, Social and Athletic (later *Scottish Kinema Record*).
Evening Citizen (Glasgow).
The Evening Dispatch (Edinburgh).
Evening Times (Glasgow).
Film Forum.
Film Weekly.
Forward (Glasgow).
Irvine Herald and Ayrshire Advertiser.
Kinematograph Weekly.
The Kirkintilloch Gazette, Lenzie and Campsie Reporter.
The Kirkintilloch Herald and Lenzie, Kilsyth, Campsie and Cumbernauld Press.
The Motion Picture News.
Rutherglen Reformer.
The Scotsman.
Scottish Cinema.
Sight and Sound.
SMT Magazine and Scottish Country Life.
The Weekly News (Dundee).
Wishaw Herald.
The Wishaw Press and Advertiser.
Workers' Cinema: Official Organ of the Federation of Workers' Film Societies.
World Film News and Television Progress.

Annual publications and works of reference

The Boys' and Girls' Cinema Clubs Annual.
The BBC Year-Book 1934 (London, 1934).
F. W. S. Craig (ed.), *British Parliamentary Election Results, 1918–49*, 3rd edn (London, 1983).
D. Gifford, *The British Film Catalogue, 1895–1970: A Guide to Entertainment Films* (Newton Abbot, 1973).
D. Gifford, *The British Film Catalogue. Volume Two: Non-Fiction Film, 1888–1994* (London, 2001).
Kinematograph Year Book, 1914–50 (London).

Contemporary works

The Arts Enquiry, *The Factual Film* (Oxford, 1947).
E. W. Bakke, *The Unemployed Man: A Social Study* (London, 1933).

J. F. Barry and E. W. Sargent, *Building Theatre Patronage. Management and Merchandising* (New York, 1927).

W. Benjamin, 'The Work of Art in the Age of Mechanical Reproduction', reprinted in G. Mast and M. Cohen (eds), *Film Theory and Criticism* (New York and Oxford, 1979), pp. 848–70.

T. A. Blake, 'The Cinematograph Comes to Scotland, 1896–1902', in *Fifty Years of Scottish Cinema* (Educational Film Bulletin, No. 23, Sept. 1946), pp. 13–14.

A. Dewar Gibb, *Scotland in Eclipse* (London, 1930).

Documentary 47 (Edinburgh, 1947).

Documentary 48 (Edinburgh, 1948).

The Film in National Life: being the Report of an Enquiry conducted by the Commission on Educational and Cultural Films into the Service which the Cinematograph may render to Education and Social Progress (London, 1932).

The Film Society. Programmes (1925–30).

Films of Scotland (Edinburgh, 1947).

R. Ford, *Children in the Cinema* (London, 1939).

B. H. Gates, 'Cinema in Aberdeen', in *Fifty Years of Scottish Cinema* (Educational Film Bulletin, No. 23, Sept. 1946), pp. 16–20.

J. Kissell, 'Cinema in the By-ways', in *Fifty Years of Scottish Cinema* (Educational Film Bulletin, No. 23, Sept. 1946), pp. 22–7.

J. Lindsay, Corporation of Glasgow, *Review of Municipal Government in Glasgow* (Glasgow and Edinburgh, n.d.).

D. M. McIntosh, *Attendance of School Children at the Cinema* (Scottish Educational Film Association, Research Publication No. 1) (Glasgow, 1945).

J. Mackie (ed.), *The Edinburgh Cinema Enquiry Being an Investigation Conducted into the Influence of the Film on School Children and Adolescents in the City* (Edinburgh, 1933).

J. P. Mayer, *Sociology of Film: Studies and Documents* (London, 1946).

T. S. Morris, 'The Edge of the World', *The Mini Cinema* (March 1951), pp. 9–10.

N. Munro, 'From Fort William', reprinted in B. D. Osborne and R. Armstrong (eds), *Erchie & Jimmy Swan* (Edinburgh, 1993), pp. 342–7.

National Council of Public Morals, *The Cinema: Its Present Position and Future Possibilities, being the Report of and Chief Evidence Taken by the Cinema Commission of Inquiry instituted by the National Council of Public Morals* (New York, [1917] 1971).

M. C. Parnaby and M. T. Woodhouse, *Children's Cinema Clubs: Report* (London, 1947).

D. L. Peacock, 'Highland Cinema', *The Countryman*, XLIV, 2 (Winter 1951), pp. 257–60.

M. Pember Reeves, *Round About a Pound a Week* (London, 1913).

H. Quigley, *A Plan for the Highlands: Proposals for a Highland Development Board* (London, 1936).

S. Rowson, 'A Statistical Survey of the Cinema Industry in Great Britain in 1934', *Journal of the Royal Statistical Society*, 99 (1936), pp. 67–118.

N. Wilson, *Presenting Scotland: A Film Survey* (Edinburgh, 1945).

N. Wilson, 'Scotland and the Cinema', *The New Alliance*, 1(1) (Autumn 1939), pp. 78–82.

SECONDARY SOURCES – BOOKS

L. Abrams and C. G. Brown (eds), *A History of Everyday Life in Twentieth-Century Scotland* (Edinburgh, 2010).

I. Aitken, *Films and Reform: John Grierson and the Documentary Film Movement* (London, 1990).

I. Aitken (ed.), *The Documentary Film Movement: An Anthology* (Edinburgh, 1998).

D. H. Aldcroft, *The British Economy between the Wars* (Oxford, 1983).

A. Aldgate and J. Richards, *Britain Can Take It: The British Cinema in the Second World War* (Edinburgh, 1994).

A. Aldgate and J. C. Robertson, *Censorship in Theatre and Cinema* (Edinburgh, 2005).

R. Altman, *Silent Film Sound* (New York and Chichester, 2004).

R. Anthony, *Herds and Hinds: Farm Labour in Lowland Scotland, 1900–1939* (East Linton, 1997).

R. Armes, *A Critical History of British Cinema* (New York, 1978).

P. Bailey, *Leisure and Class in Victorian England: Rational Recreation and the Contest for Control, 1830–1885* (London, 1978).

P. Bailey (ed.), *Music Hall: The Business of Pleasure* (Milton Keynes and Philadelphia, 1986).

T. Balio, *Grand Design: Hollywood as a Modern Business Enterprise, 1930–1939* (Berkeley and Los Angeles, 1993).

T. Balio (ed.), *The American Film Industry* (Madison, 1985).

K. Bamford, *Distorted Images: British National Identity and Film in the 1920s* (London, 1999).

J. B. Barclay, *The Film in Scottish Schools* (Edinburgh, 1992).

J. Barnes, *The Beginnings of the Cinema in England, 1894–1901*, 5 vols (Exeter, 1996).

C. Barr (ed.), *All Our Yesterdays: 90 Years of British Cinema* (London, 1986).

M. Bernstein (ed.), *Controlling Hollywood: Censorship and Regulation in the Studio Era* (London, 2000).

D. Berry, *Wales and Cinema: The First Hundred Years* (Cardiff, 1994).

A. Blaikie, *The Scots Imagination and Modern Memory* (Edinburgh, 2010).

P. Borsay, *A History of Leisure: The British Experience since 1500* (Basingstoke, 2006).

J. Bowers, *Stan Laurel and Other Stars of the Panopticon: The Story of the Britannia Music Hall* (Edinburgh, 2007).

G. Braybon, *Women Workers in the First World War* (London, 1989).

A. Briggs, *The History of Broadcasting in the United Kingdom. Volume II: The Golden Age of Wireless* (London, 1965).

C. G. Brown, *The Death of Christian Britain. Understanding Secularisation, 1800–2000* (London, 2001).

C. G. Brown, *Religion and Society in Scotland since 1707* (Edinburgh, 1997).

C. G. Brown, *Religion and Society in Twentieth-Century Britain* (Harlow, 2006).

J. Brown and A. C. Davison (eds), *The Sounds of the Silents in Britain* (Oxford, forthcoming).

R. Brown and B. Anthony, *A Victorian Film Enterprise: The History of the British Mutoscope and Biograph Company, 1897–1915* (Trowbridge, 1999).

D. Bruce, *Scotland the Movie* (Edinburgh, 1996).

F. Bruce, *Showfolk: An Oral History of a Fairground Dynasty* (Edinburgh, 2010).

J. Burnett, *Liquid Pleasures: A Social History of Drinks in Modern Britain* (London, 1999).

J. Burnett, *Riot, Revelry and Rout: Sport in Lowland Scotland before 1860* (East Linton, 2000).

A. Burton and L. Porter (eds), *The Showman, the Spectacle and the Two-Minute Silence* (Trowbridge, 2001).

R. A. Cage (ed.), *The Working Class in Glasgow, 1750–1914* (Beckenham, 1987).

A. Cairncross, *Years of Recovery: British Economic Policy, 1945–51* (London, 1985).

A. Calder, *The People's War: Britain, 1939–45* (London, 1969).

E. A. Cameron, *Impaled Upon a Thistle: Scotland since 1880* (Edinburgh, 2010).

F. Carnevali and J.-M. Strange (eds), *Twentieth-Century Britain: Economic, Cultural and Social Change* (Harlow, 2007).

M. Chanan, *The Dream That Kicks: The Prehistory and Early Years of Cinema in Britain*, 2nd edn (London, 1996).

A. Charlesworth, D. Gilbert, A. Randall, H. Southall, and C. Wrigley, *An Atlas of Industrial Protest in Britain, 1750–1990* (Basingstoke and London, 1996).

L. Charney and V. R. Schwartz (eds), *Cinema and the Invention of Modern Life* (Berkeley, Los Angeles, and London, 1995).

S. Chibnall, *Quota Quickies: The Birth of the British 'B' Film* (London, 2007).

M. Chick, *Industrial Policy in Britain, 1945–1951: Economic Planning, Nationalisation and the Labour Governments* (Cambridge, 1998).

H. Clark and E. Carnegie, *She Was Aye Workin'. Memories of Tenement Women in Edinburgh and Glasgow* (Oxford, 2003).

D. Cloy and J. McBain, *Scotland in Silent Cinema: A Commemorative Catalogue to Accompany the Scottish Reels Programme at the Pordenone Silent Film Festival, Italy, 1998* (Glasgow, 1998).

D. Condon, *Early Irish Cinema, 1895–1921* (Dublin and Portland, OR, 2008).

D. Crafton, *The Talkies: American Cinema's Transition to Sound* (Berkeley and Los Angeles, 1999).

H. Cunningham, *Children and Childhood in Western Society since 1500* (London, 1995).

J. Curran and J. Seaton, *Power Without Responsibility: The Press and Broadcasting in Britain* (London, 1985).

J. Curran and V. Porter (eds), *British Cinema History* (Totowa, NJ, 1983).

M. Daunton (ed.), *The Cambridge Urban History of Britain. Volume III: 1840–1950* (Cambridge, 2000).

A. Davies, *Leisure, Gender and Poverty: Working-class Culture in Salford and Manchester, 1900–1939* (Buckingham, 1992).

A. Davies and S. Fielding (eds), *Workers' Worlds. Culture and Communities in Manchester and Salford, 1880–1939* (Manchester, 1992).

T. M. Devine, C. H. Lee, and G. C. Peden (eds), *The Transformation of Scotland: The Economy since 1700* (Edinburgh, 2005).

P. Dewey, *War and Progress. Britain, 1914–1945* (Harlow, 1997).

E. Dick (ed.), *From Limelight to Satellite: A Scottish Film Book* (London, 1990).

M. Dickinson and S. Street, *Cinema and State: The Film Industry and the British Government, 1927–84* (London, 1985).

C. Drazin, *The Finest Years: British Cinema of the 1940s* (London, 2007).

A. J. Durie, *Scotland for the Holidays: Tourism in Scotland, c.1780–1939* (East Linton, 2003).

T. Elsaesser and A. Barker (eds), *Early Cinema: Space, Frame, Narrative* (London, 1990).

S. Eyman, *The Speed of Sound: Hollywood and the Talkie Revolution, 1926–30* (Baltimore, 1997).

R. Floud and P. Johnson (eds), *The Cambridge Economic History of Modern Britain. Volume II: Economic Maturity, 1860–1939* (Cambridge, 2004).

R. Floud and P. Johnson (eds), *The Cambridge Economic History of Modern Britain. Volume III. Structural Change and Growth, 1939–2000* (Cambridge, 2004).

R. Floud and D. McCloskey (eds), *The Economic History of Britain since 1700. Second Edition. Volume 2: 1860–1939* (Cambridge, 1994).

D. Fowler, *The First Teenagers: The Lifestyle of Young Wage-earners in Interwar Britain* (London, 1995).

K. H. Fuller, *At the Picture Show: Small-Town Audiences and the Creation of Movie Fan Culture* (Washington, DC and London, 1996).

K. H. Fuller-Seeley (ed.), *Hollywood in the Neighborhood: Historical Case Studies of Local Moviegoing* (Berkeley, 2008).

D. Gomery, *The Hollywood Studio System: A History* (London, 2005).

F. Gray (ed.), *Hove Pioneers and the Arrival of Cinema* (Brighton, 1996).

T. Griffiths, *The Lancashire Working Classes, c.1880–1930* (Oxford, 2001).

T. Griffiths and G. Morton (eds), *A History of Everyday Life in Scotland, 1800–1900* (Edinburgh, 2010).

W. Hamish Fraser and C. Lee (eds), *Aberdeen, 1800–2000: a New History* (East Linton, 2000).

W. Hamish Fraser and R. J. Morris (eds), *People and Society in Scotland. Volume II: 1830–1914* (Edinburgh, 1990).

M. Hammond, *The Big Show: British Cinema Culture in the Great War, 1914–1918* (Exeter, 2006).

S. Hanson, *From Silent Screen to Multi-Screen: A History of Cinema Exhibition in Britain since 1896* (Manchester, 2007).

C. Harding and S. Popple (eds), *In the Kingdom of Shadows: A Companion to Early Cinema* (London, 1996).

F. Hardy, *John Grierson: A Documentary Biography* (London, 1979).

F. Hardy, *Scotland in Film* (Edinburgh, 1990).

F. Hardy, *Slightly Mad and Full of Dangers: The Story of Edinburgh Film Festival* (Edinburgh, 1992).

F. Hardy (ed.), *Grierson on Documentary* (London, 1946).

J. Harris, *Private Lives, Public Spirit: Britain, 1870–1914* (Harmondsworth, 1994).

H. Hendrick, *Children, Childhood and English Society, 1880–1990* (Cambridge, 1997).

A. Higson, *Waving the Flag: Constructing a National Cinema in Britain* (Oxford, 1995).

A. Higson (ed.), *Young and Innocent? The Cinema in Britain, 1896–1930* (Exeter, 2002).

J. Hill, *Cinema and Northern Ireland: Film, Culture and Politics* (London, 2006).

E. J. Hobsbawm, *Worlds of Labour* (London, 1984).

B. Hogenkamp, *Deadly Parallels: Film and the Left in Britain, 1929–39* (London, 1986).

R. Hoggart, *A Local Habitation. Life and Times: 1918–1940* (Oxford, 1989).

R. Hoggart, *The Uses of Literacy: Aspects of Working-class Life with Special Reference to Publications and Entertainments* (London, 1957).

R. Hoggart, *The Uses of Literacy: Aspects of Working-class Life with Special Reference to Publications and Entertainments* (Harmondsworth, 1958).

S. Humphries, *Hooligans or Rebels? An Oral History of Working-class Childhood and Youth, 1889–1939* (Oxford, 1981).

R. James, *Popular Culture and Working-class Taste in Britain, 1930–1939: A Round of Cheap Diversions?* (Manchester, 2010).

M. Jancovich and L. Faire, *The Place of the Audience: Cultural Geographies of Film Consumption* (London, 2003).

P. Johnson (ed.), *Twentieth-Century Britain: Economic, Social and Cultural Change* (Harlow, 1994).

S. G. Jones, *The British Labour Movement and Film, 1918–1939* (London, 1987).

A. Kuhn, *Cinema, Censorship and Sexuality, 1909–1925* (London, 1988).

A. Kuhn, *An Everyday Magic: Cinema and Cultural Memory* (London, 2002).

C. Langhamer, *Women's Leisure in England, 1920–60* (Manchester, 2000).

R. Low, *The History of the British Film, 1906–1914* (London, 1949).

R. Low, *The History of the British Film, 1914–1918* (London, 1950).

R. Low, *The History of the British Film, 1918–1929* (London, 1971).

R. Low, *The History of the British Film, 1929–1939: Film Making in 1930s Britain* (London, 1985).

R. Low and R. Manvell, *The History of the British Film, 1896–1906* (London, 1948).

A. Lugton, *Making of Hibernian* (Edinburgh, 1995).

C. McArthur, Brigadoon, Braveheart *and the Scots: Distortions of Scotland in Hollywood Cinema* (London, 2003).

C. McArthur, *The Cinema Image of Scotland* (London, 1986).

C. McArthur (ed.), *Scotch Reels: Scotland in Cinema and Television* (London, 1982).

J. McBain, *Pictures Past: Scottish Cinemas Remembered* (Edinburgh, 1985).

C. M. M. Macdonald, *Whaur Extremes Meet: Scotland's Twentieth Century* (Edinburgh, 2009).

C. M. M. Macdonald and E. W. McFarland (eds), *Scotland and the Great War* (East Linton, 1999).

W. H. McDowell, *The History of BBC Broadcasting in Scotland, 1923–1983* (Edinburgh, 1992).

I. McGraw, *The Fairs of Dundee* (Abertay Historical Society No. 34, Dundee, 1994).

R. McKibbin, *Classes and Cultures. England, 1918–1951* (Oxford, 1998).

H. McLeod, *Class and Religion in the Late Victorian City* (London, 1974).

H. McLeod, *Religion and Society in England, 1850–1914* (Basingstoke, 1996).

G. Macnab, *J. Arthur Rank and the British Film Industry* (London, 1993).

P. Maloney, *Scotland and the Music Hall, 1850–1914* (Manchester, 2003).

R. Maltby, *Hollywood Cinema*, 2nd edn (Oxford, 2003).

R. Maltby, M. Stokes, and R. C. Allen (eds), *Going to the Movies. Hollywood and the Social Experience of Cinema* (Exeter, 2007).

A. Martin, *Going to the Pictures: Scottish Memories of Cinema* (Edinburgh, 2000).

G. Mast and M. Cohen (eds), *Film Theory and Criticism* (New York and Oxford, 1979).

T. D. Mathews, *Censored* (London, 1994).

H. Mercer, N. Rollings, and J. D. Tomlinson (eds), *Labour Governments and Private Industry: The Experience of 1945–1951* (Edinburgh, 1992).

P. Miskell, *A Social History of the Cinema in Wales, 1918–1951: Pulpits, Coal Pits and Fleapits* (Cardiff, 2006).

R. J. Morris, *Scotland 1907: The Many Scotlands of Valentine and Sons. Photographers* (Edinburgh, 2007).

G. Morton, *Unionist-Nationalism: Governing Urban Scotland, 1830–1860* (East Linton, 1999).

C. L. Mowat, *Britain between the Wars, 1918–1940* (London, 1968).

R. Murphy, *British Cinema and the Second World War* (London and New York, 2000).

R. Murphy, *Realism and Tinsel: Cinema and Society in Britain, 1939–49* (London, 1989).

R. Murphy (ed.), *The British Cinema Book*, 3rd edn (London, 2008).

B. Murray, *The Old Firm: Sectarianism, Sport and Society in Scotland* (Edinburgh, 1984).

C. Musser, *The Emergence of Cinema: The American Screen to 1907* (Berkeley, Los Angeles, and London, 1990).

L. Napper, *British Cinema and Middlebrow Culture in the Interwar Years* (Exeter, 2009).

D. M. Naulty, *Dundee Cinemas: A Personal Account* (Dundee, 2004).

North of Scotland Hydro-Electric Board, *Highland Water Power* (Edinburgh, n.d.).

A. Offer, *Property and Politics, 1870–1914: Landownership, Law, Ideology and Urban Development in England* (Cambridge, 1981).

B. D. Osborne and R. Armstrong (eds), *Erchie & Jimmy Swan* (Edinburgh, 1993).

P. L. Payne, *The Hydro* (Aberdeen, 1988).

G. Pearson, *Hooligan. A History of Respectable Fears* (London, 1983).

B. Peter, *Scotland's Cinemas* (Ramsey, Isle of Man, 2011).

S. Pollard, *The Development of the British Economy, Second Edition, 1914–1967* (London, 1969).

S. Pollard, *The Development of the British Economy, Third Edition, 1914–1980* (London, 1983).

J. Richards, *The Age of the Dream Palace: Cinema and Society in Britain, 1930–1939* (London, 1984).

J. Richards, *Films and British National Identity. From Dickens to Dad's Army* (Manchester, 1997).

J. Richards (ed.), *The Unknown 1930s: An Alternative History of the British Cinema, 1929–39* (London, 1998).

J. Richards and D. Sheridan (eds), *Mass-Observation at the Movies* (London, 1987).

R. Roberts, *The Classic Slum. Salford Life in the First Quarter of the Century* (Manchester, 1971).

J. C. Robertson, *The British Board of Film Censors: Film Censorship in Britain, 1896–1950* (London, 1985).

J. C. Robertson, *The Hidden Cinema: British Film Censorship in Action, 1913–75* (London, 1989).

K. Rockett, L. Gibbons, and J. Hill, *Cinema and Ireland* (Syracuse, NY, 1988).

R. Rodger, *Housing in Urban Britain, 1780–1914: Class, Capitalism and Construction* (Basingstoke, 1989).

R. Rodger, *The Transformation of Edinburgh: Land, Property and Trust in the Nineteenth Century* (Cambridge, 2001).

D. Ross, *The Roar of the Crowd: Following Scottish Football Down the Years* (Glendaruel, 2005).

D. Rossell, *Living Pictures: The Origins of the Movies* (Albany, 1998).

D. Russell, *Popular Music in England, 1840–1914: A Social History*, 2nd edn (Manchester, 1997).

P. Russell and J. P. Taylor (eds), *Shadows of Progress: Documentary Film in Post-War Britain* (Basingstoke, 2010).

G. R. Searle, *A New England? Peace and War, 1886–1918* (Oxford, 2004).

J. Sedgwick, *Popular Filmgoing in 1930s Britain: A Choice of Pleasures* (Exeter, 2000).

J. Sexton, *Alternative Film Culture in Inter-War Britain* (Exeter, 2008).

S. C. Shafer, *British Popular Films, 1929–1939: The Cinema of Reassurance* (London, 1997).

D. Sharp, *The Picture Palace and Other Buildings for the Movies* (London, 1969).

R. Skidelsky, *Politicians and the Slump: The Labour Government of 1929–1931* (London, 1967).

S. J. Smith, *Children, Cinema and Censorship: From Dracula to the Dead End Kids* (London, 2005).

P. Stanfield, *Hollywood, Westerns and the 1930s: The Lost Trail* (Exeter, 2001).

T. Staples, *All Pals Together: The Story of Children's Cinema* (Edinburgh, 1997).

R. D. Storch (ed.), *Popular Culture and Custom in Nineteenth-Century England* (Beckenham, 1982).

S. Street, *British Cinema in Documents* (London, 2000).

S. Street, *British National Cinema* (London, 1997).

D. Strinati, *An Introduction to Theories of Popular Culture* (London, 1995).

B. Supple, *The History of the British Coal Industry, Volume 4: 1913–1946: The Political Economy of Decline* (Oxford, 1987).

D. Sutton, *A Chorus of Raspberries: British Film Comedy, 1929–39* (Exeter, 2000).

P. Swann, *The British Documentary Film Movement, 1926–1946* (Cambridge, 1989).

P. M. Taylor (ed.), *Britain and the Cinema in the Second World War* (Basingstoke, 1988).

B. Thomas, *The Last Picture Shows. Edinburgh: Ninety Years of Cinema Entertainment in Scotland's Capital City* (Edinburgh, 1984).

F. M. L. Thompson (ed.), *The Cambridge Social History of Britain, 1750–1950*, 3 vols (Cambridge, 1990).

P. Thompson, *The Voice of the Past: Oral History*, 3rd edn (Oxford, 2000).

P. Thompson, T. Wailey, and T. Lummis, *Living the Fishing* (London, 1983).

M. Thomson, *Silver Screen in the Silver City: A History of Cinemas in Aberdeen, 1896–1987* (Aberdeen, 1988).

V. Toulmin, *Electric Edwardians: The Story of the Mitchell & Kenyon Collection* (London, 2006).

V. Toulmin, S. Popple, and P. Russell (eds), *The Lost World of Mitchell and Kenyon* (London, 2004).

W. Vamplew, *Pay Up and Play the Game: Professional Sport in Britain, 1875–1914* (Cambridge, 1988).

G. A. Waller, *Main Street Amusements. Movies and Commercial Entertainment in a Southern City, 1896–1930* (Washington, DC and London, 1995).

C. A. Whatley (ed.), *The Diary of John Sturrock, Millwright, Dundee, 1864–65* (East Linton, 1998).

J. Wigley, *The Rise and Fall of the Victorian Sunday* (Manchester, 1980).

K. Williams, *Get Me a Murder a Day! A History of Mass Communication in Britain* (London, 1998).

E. and S. Yeo (eds), *Popular Culture and Class Conflict, 1590–1914: Explorations in the History of Labour and Leisure* (Brighton, 1981).

P. Yorke, *William Haggar (1851–1925): Fairground Film-maker* (Bedlinog, 2007).

I. Zweiniger-Bargielowska, *Austerity in Britain: Rationing, Controls and Consumption, 1939–1955* (Oxford, 2000).

SECONDARY SOURCES – ARTICLES AND ESSAYS IN BOOKS

D. Allen, 'Workers' Films: Scotland's Hidden Film Culture', in C. McArthur (ed.), *Scotch Reels: Scotland in Cinema and Television* (London, 1982), pp. 93–9.

R. C. Allen, 'Race, Region, and Rusticity. Relocating U.S. Film History', in R. Maltby, M. Stokes, and R. C. Allen (eds), *Going to the Movies. Hollywood and the Social Experience of Cinema* (Exeter, 2007), pp. 25–44.

M. Anderson, 'The Social Implications of Demographic Change', in F. M. L. Thompson (ed.), *The Cambridge Social History of Britain, 1750–1950. Volume 2: People and their Environment* (Cambridge, 1990), pp. 1–70.

G. Bachman, 'Still in the Dark: Silent Film Audiences', *Film History*, 9 (1997), pp. 23–48.

P. Bailey, 'Custom, Capital and Culture in the Victorian Music Hall', in R. D. Storch (ed.), *Popular Culture and Custom in Nineteenth-Century England* (Beckenham, 1982), pp. 180–208.

G. Bakker, 'The Decline and Fall of the European Film Industry: Sunk Costs, Market Size and Market Structure, 1890–1927', *The London School of Economics and Political Science, Working Papers in Economic History*, 70/03 (Feb. 2003).

C. Barr, 'Before Blackmail: Silent British Cinema', in R. Murphy (ed.), *The British Cinema Book*, 3rd edn (London, 2008), pp. 145–54.

A. Bartie, 'Culture in the Everyday: Art and Society', in L. Abrams and C. G. Brown (eds), *A History of Everyday Life in Twentieth-Century Scotland* (Edinburgh, 2010), pp. 206–27.

S. Bowden and D. M. Higgins, 'Short-Time Working and Price Maintenance: Collusive Tendencies in the Cotton-Spinning Industry, 1919–1939', *Economic History Review*, 2nd ser., LI (1998), pp. 319–43.

S. Broadberry, 'The Emergence of Mass Unemployment: Explaining Macroeconomic Trends in Britain during the Trans-World War I Period', *Economic History Review*, 2nd ser., XLIII (1990), pp. 271–82.

C. G. Brown, 'Spectacle, Restraint and the Sabbath Wars: The "Everyday" Scottish

Sunday', in L. Abrams and C. G. Brown (eds), *A History of Everyday Life in Twentieth-Century Scotland* (Edinburgh, 2010), pp. 153–80.

R. Brown, 'New Century Pictures: Regional Enterprise in Early British Film Exhibition', in V. Toulmin, S. Popple, and P. Russell (eds), *The Lost World of Mitchell and Kenyon* (London, 2004), pp. 69–82.

H. E. Browning and A. A. Sorrell, 'Cinemas and Cinema-Going in Great Britain', *Journal of the Royal Statistical Society*, Series A (General), 117(2) (1954), pp. 133–70.

D. Bruce, 'Hollywood Comes to the Highlands', in E. Dick (ed.), *From Limelight to Satellite: A Scottish Film Book* (London, 1990), pp. 71–82.

J. Burrows, 'Penny Pleasures: Film Exhibition in London during the Nickelodeon Era, 1906–1914', *Film History*, 16 (2004), pp. 60–91.

J. Burrows, 'Penny Pleasures II: Indecency, Anarchy and Junk Film in London's "Nickelodeons", 1906–1914', *Film History*, 16 (2004), pp. 172–97.

J. Burrows and R. Brown, 'Financing the Edwardian Cinema Boom, 1909–1914', *Historical Journal of Film, Radio and Television*, 30 (2010), pp. 1–20.

J. Caughie, 'Representing Scotland: New Questions for Scottish Cinema', in E. Dick (ed.), *From Limelight to Satellite: A Scottish Film Book* (London, 1990), pp. 13–30.

L. Charney and V. R. Schwartz, 'Introduction', in id., *Cinema and the Invention of Modern Life* (Berkeley, Los Angeles, and London, 1995), pp. 1–12.

A. Davies, 'Leisure in the "Classic Slum", 1900–1939', in A. Davies and S. Fielding (eds), *Workers' Worlds. Culture and Communities in Manchester and Salford, 1880–1939* (Manchester, 1992), pp. 102–32.

J. Davis, 'Central Government and the Towns', in M. Daunton (ed.), *The Cambridge Urban History of Britain. Volume III. 1840–1950* (Cambridge, 2000), pp. 261–86.

J. Earl, 'Building the Halls', in P. Bailey (ed.), *Music Hall: The Business of Pleasure* (Milton Keynes and Philadelphia, 1986), pp. 1–32.

B. Eichengreen, 'The British Economy between the Wars', in R. Floud and P. Johnson (eds), *The Cambridge Economic History of Modern Britain. Volume II: Economic Maturity, 1860–1939* (Cambridge, 2004), pp. 314–43.

Film History, 15(2) (2003), edition on Small-Gauge and Amateur Film.

Film History, 19(4) (2007), edition on Nontheatrical Film.

I. Gazeley, 'The Cost of Living of Urban Workers in late-Victorian and Edwardian Britain', *Economic History Review*, 2nd ser., XLI (1989), pp. 207–21.

D. Gomery, 'The Coming of Sound: Technological Change in the American Film Industry', in T. Balio (ed.), *The American Film Industry* (Madison, 1985), pp. 229–51.

T. Griffiths, 'Sounding Scottish: Sound Practices and Silent Cinema in Scotland', in J. Brown and A. C. Davison (eds), *The Sounds of the Silents in Britain* (Oxford, forthcoming).

T. Griffiths, 'Work, Leisure and Time in the Nineteenth Century', in T. Griffiths and G. Morton (eds), *A History of Everyday Life in Scotland, 1800–1900* (Edinburgh, 2010), pp. 170–95.

T. Gunning, 'The Cinema of Attractions: Early Film, its Spectators and the Avant-Garde', in T. Elsaesser and A. Barker (eds), *Early Cinema: Space, Frame, Narrative* (London, 1990), pp. 56–62.

S. Harper, 'Fragmentation and Crisis: 1940s Admissions Figures at the Regent Cinema, Portsmouth, UK', *Historical Journal of Film, Radio and Television*, 26 (2006), pp. 361–94.

S. Harper, 'A Lower Middle-Class Taste-Community in the 1930s: Admissions Figures at the Regent Cinema, Portsmouth, UK', *Historical Journal of Film, Radio and Television*, 24 (2004), pp. 565–87.

A. Higson, '"Britain's Outstanding Contribution to the Film": The Documentary-Realist Tradition', in C. Barr (ed.), *All Our Yesterdays: 90 Years of British Cinema* (London, 1986), pp. 72–97.

N. Hiley, 'Let's Go to the Pictures: the British Cinema Audience in the 1920s and 1930s', *Journal of Popular British Cinema*, 2 (1999), pp. 39–53.

N. Hiley, '"No Mixed Bathing": The Creation of the British Board of Film Censors in 1913', *Journal of Popular British Cinema*, 3 (2000), pp. 5–19.

N. Hiley, '"Nothing More than a Craze": Cinema Building in Britain from 1909 to 1914', in A. Higson (ed.), *Young and Innocent? The Cinema in Britain, 1896–1930* (Exeter, 2002), pp. 111–27.

E. J. Hobsbawm, 'The Formation of British Working-class Culture', in id., *Worlds of Labour* (London, 1984), pp. 176–93.

E. J. Hobsbawm, 'The Making of the Working Class, 1870–1914', in id., *Worlds of Labour* (London, 1984), pp. 194–213.

P. Howlett, 'The Wartime Economy, 1939–45', in R. Floud and P. Johnson (eds), *The Cambridge Economic History of Modern Britain. Volume III. Structural Change and Growth, 1939–2000* (Cambridge, 2004), pp. 1–26.

P. Johnson, 'Conspicuous Consumption and Working-class Culture in late-Victorian and Edwardian Britain', *Transactions of the Royal Historical Society*, 5th ser., 38 (1988), pp. 27–42.

E. King, 'Popular Culture in Glasgow', in R. A. Cage (ed.), *The Working Class in Glasgow, 1750–1914* (Beckenham, 1987), pp. 142–87.

A. Kuhn, 'Cinema-going in Britain in the 1930s: Report of a Questionnaire Survey', *Historical Journal of Film, Radio and Television*, 19 (1999), pp. 531–43.

E. Lebas, 'Glasgow's Progress: The Films of Glasgow Corporation, 1938–1978', *Film Studies*, 10 (Spring 2007), pp. 34–53.

E. Lebas, 'Sadness and Gladness: The Films of Glasgow Corporation, 1922–1938', *Film Studies*, 6 (Summer 2005), pp. 27–45.

C. H. Lee, 'Scotland, 1860–1939: Growth and Poverty', in R. Floud and P. Johnson (eds), *The Cambridge Economic History of Modern Britain. Volume II: Economic Maturity, 1860–1939* (Cambridge, 2004), pp. 428–55.

C. H. Lee, 'The Scottish Economy in the First World War', in C. M. M. Macdonald and E. W. McFarland (eds), *Scotland and the Great War* (East Linton, 1999), pp. 11–35.

P. N. Lewis, 'Who Short Willie Park Jr? The Place of the Park v. Fernie Match in Early Scottish Film History', *Through the Green* (March 2008), pp. 40–50.

C. McArthur, 'Scotland and Cinema: The Iniquity of the Fathers', in id. (ed.), *Scotch Reels: Scotland in Cinema and Television* (London, 1982), pp. 40–69.

J. McBain, 'Green's of Glasgow: "We Want U In"', *Film Studies*, 10 (Spring 2007), pp. 54–7.

J. McBain, 'Mitchell and Kenyon's Legacy in Scotland – The Inspiration for a Forgotten Film-making Genre', in V. Toulmin, S. Popple, and P. Russell (eds), *The Lost World of Mitchell and Kenyon* (London, 2004), pp. 113–21.

L. McKernan, '"Only the Screen was Silent . . .": Memories of Children's Cinema-going in London before the First World War', *Film Studies*, 10 (Spring 2007), pp. 1–20.

M. MacKinnon, 'Living Standards, 1870–1914', in R. Floud and D. McCloskey (eds), *The Economic History of Britain since 1700. Second Edition. Volume 2: 1860–1939* (Cambridge, 1994), pp. 265–90.

R. Maltby, 'The Production Code and the Hays Office', in T. Balio, *Grand Design: Hollywood as a Modern Business Enterprise, 1930–1939* (Berkeley and Los Angeles, 1993), pp. 37–72.

I. Maver, 'Leisure and Culture: The Nineteenth Century', in W. Hamish Fraser and C. Lee (eds), *Aberdeen, 1800–2000: a New History* (East Linton, 2000), pp. 398–421.

R. Middleton, 'The Constant Employment Budget Balance and British Budgetary Policy, 1929–39', *Economic History Review*, 2nd ser., XXXIV (1981), pp. 266–86.

R. J. Morris, 'Clubs, Societies and Associations', in F. M. L. Thompson (ed.), *The Cambridge Social History of Britain, 1750–1950. Volume 3: Social Agencies and Institutions* (Cambridge, 1990), pp. 395–443.

R. J. Morris, 'Urbanisation and Scotland', in W. Hamish Fraser and R. J. Morris (eds), *People and Society in Scotland. Volume II: 1830–1914* (Edinburgh, 1990), pp. 73–102.

R. Murphy, 'The Heart of Britain: British Cinema at War', in id. (ed.), *The British Cinema Book*, 3rd edn (London, 2008), pp. 223–31.

R. Murphy, 'Under the Shadow of Hollywood', in C. Barr (ed.), *All Our Yesterdays: 90 Years of British Cinema* (London, 1986), pp. 47–71.

J. Obelkevich, 'Religion', in F. M. L. Thompson (ed.), *The Cambridge Social History of Britain, 1750–1950. Volume 3: Social Agencies and Institutions* (Cambridge, 1990), pp. 311–56.

J. Petley, 'The Lost Continent', in C. Barr (ed.), *All Our Yesterdays: 90 Years of British Cinema* (London, 1986), pp. 98–119.

J. Poole, 'British Cinema Attendance in Wartime: Audience Preference at the Majestic, Macclesfield, 1939–46', *Historical Journal of Film, Radio and Television*, 7 (1987), pp. 15–34.

V. Porter, 'Methodism versus the Marketplace: The Rank Organisation and British Cinema', in R. Murphy (ed.), *The British Cinema Book*, 3rd edn (London, 2008), pp. 267–75.

N. Pronay, 'The Film Industry', in H. Mercer, N. Rollings, and J. D. Tomlinson (eds), *Labour Governments and Private Industry: The Experience of 1945–1951* (Edinburgh, 1992), pp. 212–36.

J. Richards, 'National Identity in British Wartime Films', in P. M. Taylor (ed.), *Britain and the Cinema in the Second World War* (Basingstoke, 1988), pp. 42–61.

J. Richards and J. C. Robertson, 'British Film Censorship', in R. Murphy (ed.), *The British Cinema Book*, 3rd edn (London, 2008), pp. 67–77.

T. Ryall, 'A British Studio System: The Associated British Picture Corporation and the Gaumont-British Picture Corporation in the 1930s', in R. Murphy (ed.), *The British Cinema Book*, 3rd edn (London, 2008), pp. 202–10.

J. Samson, 'The Film Society, 1925–1939', in C. Barr (ed.), *All Our Yesterdays: 90 Years of British Cinema* (London, 1986), pp. 306–13.

L. S. Sanders, '"Indecent Incentives to Vice": Regulating Films and Audience Behaviour from the 1890s to the 1910s', in A. Higson (ed.), *Young and Innocent? The Cinema in Britain, 1896–1930* (Exeter, 2002), pp. 97–110.

C. R. Schenk, 'Austerity and Boom', in P. Johnson (ed.), *Twentieth-Century Britain: Economic, Social and Cultural Change* (Harlow, 1994), pp. 300–19.

A. Scullion, 'Geggies, Empires, Cinemas: The Scottish Experience of Early Film', *Picture House*, No. 21 (Summer 1996), pp. 13–19.

J. Sedgwick, 'Cinema-going Preferences in Britain in the 1930s', in J. Richards (ed.), *The Unknown 1930s: An Alternative History of the British Cinema, 1929–39* (London, 1998), pp. 1–35.

A. Shail, '"A Distinct Advance in Society": Early Cinema's "Proletarian Public Sphere" and Isolated Spectatorship in the UK, 1911–18', *Journal of British Cinema and Television*, 3 (2006), pp. 209–28.

B. Singer, 'Modernity, Hyperstimulus [sic], and the Rise of Popular Sensationalism', in L. Charney and V. R. Schwartz (eds), *Cinema and the Invention of Modern Life* (Berkeley, Los Angeles, and London, 1995), pp. 72–99.

C. Sladen, 'Holidays at Home in the Second World War', *Journal of Contemporary History*, 37 (2002), pp. 67–89.

T. C. Smout, 'Tours in the Scottish Highlands from the Eighteenth to the Nineteenth Centuries', *Northern Scotland*, 5 (1983), pp. 99–121.

P. Stead, 'The People as Stars: Feature Films as National Expression', in P. M. Taylor (ed.), *Britain and the Cinema in the Second World War* (Basingstoke, 1988), pp. 62–83.

P. Summerfield, 'The Effingham Arms and the Empire: Deliberate Selection in the Evolution of Music Hall in London', in E. and S. Yeo (eds), *Popular Culture and Class Conflict, 1590–1914: Explorations in the History of Labour and Leisure* (Brighton, 1981), pp. 209–40.

M. Thomas, 'Rearmament and Economic Recovery in the late 1930s', *Economic History Review*, 2nd ser., XXXVI (1983), pp. 552–73.

J. Tomlinson, 'Managing the Economy, Managing the People', in F. Carnevali and J.-M. Strange (eds), *Twentieth-Century Britain: Economic, Cultural and Social Change* (Harlow, 2007), pp. 233–46.

V. Toulmin, 'The Cinematograph at the Nottingham Goose Fair, 1896–1911', in A. Burton and L. Porter (eds), *The Showman, the Spectacle and the Two-Minute Silence* (Trowbridge, 2001), pp. 76–86.

V. Toulmin, '"Curios Things in Curios Places": Temporary Exhibition Venues in the Victorian and Edwardian Entertainment Environment', *Early Popular Visual Culture*, 4 (2006), pp. 113–37.

V. Toulmin, '"Local Films for Local People": Travelling Showmen and the Commissioning of Local Films in Great Britain, 1900–1902', *Film History*, 13 (2001), pp. 118–37.

V. Toulmin, and M. Loiperdinger, 'Is It You? Recognition, Representation and Response in Relation to the Local Film', *Film History*, 17 (2005), pp. 7–18.

P. Wardley, 'Edwardian Britain: Empire, Income and Political Discontent', in P. Johnson (ed.), *Twentieth-Century Britain: Economic, Social and Cultural Change* (Harlow, 1994), pp. 57–78.

D. R. Williams, 'The Cinematograph Act of 1909: An Introduction to the Impetus Behind the Legislation and Some Early Effects', *Film History*, 9 (1997), pp. 341–50.

L. Wood, 'Low-budget British Films in the 1930s', in R. Murphy (ed.), *The British Cinema Book*, 3rd edn (London, 2008), pp. 211–19.

J. A. Yelling, 'Land, Property and Planning', in M. Daunton (ed.), *The Cambridge Urban History of Britain. Volume III: 1840–1950* (Cambridge, 2000), pp. 467–93.

UNPUBLISHED WORKS

R. J. Morris, 'Leisure, Entertainment and the Associational Culture of British Towns, 1800–1900' (unpublished paper, delivered to the Third International Urban History Conference, Budapest, August 1996).

WEB RESOURCES AND DATABASES

British Film Institute

http://ftvdb.bfi.org.uk/searches.php
http://www.screenonline.org.uk/film/facts/fact1.html
http://www.screenonline.org.uk/film/facts/fact2.html
http://www.imdb.com/

Scottish Screen Archive

http://ssa.nls.uk/browse.cfm?sid=03.03

VISUAL SOURCES

Scotland Calling: At the Empire Exhibition, 1938 (Panamint Cinema, West Lothian, 2008).

Index